WITHDRAWN

D1563323

Chinese Magical Medicine

Chinese Magical Medicine

ARC

Asian Religions & Cultures

Edited by

Carl Bielefeldt

Bernard Faure

Michel Strickmann

EDITED BY BERNARD FAURE

Chinese Magical Medicine

Stanford University Press
Stanford, California

Stanford University Press
Stanford, California

© 2002 by the Board of Trustees of the
Leland Stanford Junior University

Printed in the United States of America

Library of Congress Cataloging-in-Publication Data
Strickmann, Michel.
Chinese magical medicine / Michel Strickmann ; edited by Bernard Faure.
p. cm.
Includes bibliographical references and index.
ISBN 0-8047-3449-6 (cloth : alk. paper)
—ISBN 0-8047-3940-4 (pbk. : alk. paper)
1. Medicine, Chinese. 2. Taoism. I. Faure, Bernard. II. Title.
R602 .S83 2002
610'.951—dc21 2001020376

⊗ This book is printed on acid-free paper.

Original printing 2002

Last figure below indicates year of this printing:
11 10 09 08 07 06 05 04 03 02

Designed by James P. Brommer
Typeset by Tseng Information Systems, Inc. in 10/14.5 Sabon

CONTENTS

ILLUSTRATIONS

FOREWORD

When Michel Strickmann died prematurely in August 1994, he left three book-length manuscripts. The only one that he had revised in its entirety before his death was "Mantras et mandarins: Le bouddhisme tantrique en Chine," published by Gallimard in 1996. An English translation (or rather, retranslation) is forthcoming from Princeton University Press. The two other manuscripts were entitled "Chinese Magical Medicine" and "Chinese Poetry and Prophecy."

I have undertaken the task of editing "Chinese Magical Medicine" for publication. Had Strickmann lived longer, he clearly would have continued to work on it, especially after the publication of *Mantras et mandarins*. Furthermore, owing to the delays in publication, some of the points first made by Strickmann have now become part of the accepted body of knowledge in the field, while other ideas have been refined or nuanced in recent scholarship. Nevertheless, no one else in the field (with the exception of Anna Seidel, another scholar and friend whose premature death is much regreted) has been able to retrieve such a broad spectrum of religious phenomena and make them accessible to the nonspecialist. Strickmann's unmistakable voice resonates in the pages of this book, and this alone justifies its publication.

Although the text of "Chinese Magical Medicine" had been revised by Strickmann, the critical apparatus (notes and bibliography) was missing. I have tried to remedy this lack with the help of several friends of the author. Ursula-Angelika Cedzich was kind enough to provide most of the annotation for the first two chapters dealing with Taoism. I would like to express my gratitude for the work she has done. I have annotated the other chapters and compiled the bibliography, though in a few cases the full reference to a work

Strickmann cited could not be found. As it now stands, the text has the limitations of a posthumous work. Needless to say, I remain solely responsible for the final editing. Fortunately, in the process of revising the manuscript, I was able to retrieve from Strickmann's papers various typed or handwritten drafts, which I have excerpted when appropriate; this material appears in the notes prefaced by "on this point, Strickmann wrote" (or words to this effect) to distinguish authorial from editorial notes. Finally, I have benefited from the publication in *Asia Major* of two articles revised by Strickmann before his death and edited by Howard Goodman, "The Seal of the Law" (1993) and "The Seal of the Jungle Woman" (1995), which correspond to large portions of Chapter 4 of "Chinese Magical Medicine."

One point needs to be addressed—that is, the fact that some ideas presented in "Chinese Magical Medicine" may overlap with those in "Mantras et mandarins." Whether Strickmann would have revised the text of "Chinese Magical Medicine" for publication with this in mind or revised the English translation of "Mantras et mandarins" remains unclear. I have decided to remain faithful to the manuscript he left and thus have not taken the liberty of deleting any sections.

Many friends and colleagues have read and commented on parts of the manuscript. I want to offer my special thanks to Kuo Li-ying, Catherine Despeux, Mieko Macé, Stephen R. Bokenkamp, David Gordon White, John Lagerwey, Howard Goodman, Stephen Teiser, Irene Lin, Hubert Durt, Fabrizio Pregadio, Jacques Emsalem, Brigitte Steinmann, Helen Tartar, Victoria Scott, Pamela MacFarland Holway, and Judith Boltz.

Finally, I would like to dedicate this work, as Michel would have done, to Leo, Marjorie, and Bonnie Strickman.

Bernard Faure
Palo Alto, California
December 2001

ABBREVIATIONS AND CONVENTIONS

CT — References to texts in the Ming *Cheng-t'ung Tao-tsang* follow the *Concordance du Tao-tsang* compiled by Kristofer M. Schipper. Paris: École Française d'Extrême-Orient, 1975.

DNBZ — *Dai Nihon bukkyō zensho*. New ed. Suzuki gakujutsu zaidan. 100 vols. Tokyo: Kōdansha, 1970–73.

HY — Harvard-Yenching Index to the Taoist Canon, *Tao-tsang tzu mu yin-te* (Combined Indices to the Authors and Titles of Books in Two Collections of Taoist Literature). Harvard-Yenching Institute Sinological Index Series, no. 25. Peking, 1935. References are to the number of a text in the canon as given on pp. 1–37, followed by the *chüan* number, the page and column. This is preferred, for the sake of clarity, to the traditional reference to the anastatic reprint of the Ming canon, done in Shanghai (and usually abbreviated TT followed by the fascicle number). For instance, certain texts of the *Chen-kao* occupy several fascicles of the Ming canon (in this case, TT 637 to 640), whereas several texts are sometimes collected in a single fascicle.

P — Pelliot Collection of Tun-huang Manuscripts. Bibliothèque Nationale, Paris.

Stein — Stein Collection of Tun-huang Manuscripts. British Library, London.

T. — Scriptures in the Chinese Buddhist canon are cited according to standard numbers in the Taishō printed edition, *Taishō shinshū daizōkyō*, edited by Takakusu Junjirō and Watanabe

Kaikyoku. Tokyo: Daizōkyōkai, 1924–35. The texts of the Buddhist canon are given by their number in the Taishō edition, followed by the volume number, the page and column.

T. Zuzō — *Taishō shinshū daizōkyō zuzōbu*, edited by Takakusu Junjirō and Watanabe Kaikyoku. 12 vols. T. 86–97. Tokyo: Taishō issaikyō kankōkai, 1924–35.

TT — References to texts in the reprint of the *Tao-tsang* of the Pai-yün Kuan, Peking. Reprint, Shanghai, 1924–26; Taipei, 1962.

ZZ — *Dai Nihon zokuzōkyō*. Kyoto: Zōkyō shoin, 1905–12. Reprint, 150 vols., Taipei: Hsin-wen-feng ch'u-pan kung-ssu, 1968–70.

Transliterations of Asian languages follow systems commonly used in the scholarly community: Wades-Giles for Chinese, revised Hepburn for Japanese. All Buddhist terms that appear in *Webster's Third New International Dictionary* are left unitalicized (e.g., saṃsāra, nirvāṇa, mantra). For a convenient listing of a hundred such words, see Roger Jackson, "Terms of Sanskrit and Pāli Origin Acceptable as English Words," *Journal of the International Association of Buddhist Studies* 5 (1982): 141–42.

Chinese Magical Medicine

1

DISEASE AND TAOIST LAW

Healing in the Taoist Tradition

Disease and its cure are a paramount focus in the earliest accounts of Taoism. A third-century historian describes the Way of the Celestial Master (T'ien-shih tao) in its original homeland in the far western province of Szechuan:

> They taught people to have wholehearted faith, and not to cheat or deceive others. If someone fell ill, he had to confess his misdeeds. . . . The priests constructed "houses of justice," [placed at regular intervals] like the post stations of the present day. Inside, they put grain and meat, and travelers might take as much as they needed. But if someone took too much, the spirits would inevitably afflict him with illness. If anyone disobeyed the rules, he was allowed three remissions; only after that was punishment applied. . . .
>
> In addition, they had "chambers of quietness," where they made sick people stay to meditate on their transgressions. . . . A priest ["director of spirits"] would pray on behalf of the sick person. The method of prayer was to write out the family name and given name of the sufferer, and words explaining that he admitted his misdeeds. Three copies of this document were to be made. One was sent up to heaven and placed on a mountaintop. One was buried in the earth, and one was sunk in water. These were called "the documents of the Three Officers."

> The family of the sick person was always made to pay out five pecks of grain for the treatment, and so the masters came to be called "Masters of the Five Pecks of Grain." Of course, this treatment really did no good at all; it was all a debauched and unauthorized deception. But ordinary people are truly stupid and deluded, and they all vied with one another in doing honor to the masters.[1]

The final disparaging remarks betray the historian's own prejudices and represent the perspective of a self-conscious outsider. These extracts are taken from the classic official account of the beginnings of Taoism, often quoted in scholarly literature and the starting point for most discussions of early Taoism.[2] If this outsider's report is to be credited, therapy was the crucial function of the religion. Even from this succinct narrative, we can draw some notion of the earliest Taoists' conception of illness and their curative methods. The presence of disease was thought to indicate some moral failing. Conversely, the faithful were kept in order by the threat of illness, which would attack them should they ever transgress the rules. Physical health was consequently a function of moral or spiritual health, and the priest was necessarily the arbiter. Should a believer fall ill, he had first to be isolated from the community in a "chamber of quietness" to ponder and repent his moral failings. Subsequently, a priest would write out a formal document, the afflicted person's confession of guilt. This was submitted in triplicate to the "Three Officers of Heaven, Earth, and Water."[3]

To put this information in clearer perspective, however—to understand its place in the subsequent history of Taoism and, ultimately, to interpret it—second- or thirdhand reports of the type just quoted are hardly adequate. We must learn something more of the Taoists' own view of their place in the world and their explanation of the genesis of Taoism. For data of this caliber, it is impossible to rely on government chronicles or the writings of officials. We must go directly to Taoist sources. In this quest, we may start at either end of the historical continuum. We may begin with the earliest original Taoist texts, preserved in the Taoist canon, or with the present-day testimony of Taoist priests still active in China, Taiwan, Hong Kong, and Chinese Southeast Asia.[4] Wherever we begin, we will find essentially the same answer to the question of Taoism's origins and functions. Contemporary ethnographic evidence supports and confirms the medieval textual evidence. Taoists ancient and modern all agree that the basic raison d'être of Taoism was to supplant the local cults with which China teemed: to replace "shamanism," "spirit possession," and "ecstatic religion." No matter which of these terms one chooses, though, such rites were the long-established means of responding to disease, disaster, and the shadowy world of the spirits. Either a god would enter the operator's body or the officiant's spirit, godlike, would travel to the land of the gods (or into the world of the dead). Whether the action was thus internalized or externalized, the outward manifestations were characterized in an oft-repeated sequence of tropes. According to Taoist descriptions (which here paralleled the government's own denunciation of unofficial local cults), the spiritist seance was wild, raucous—ecstatic in the full sense of the word. Rationality and harmony stepped out as an otherworldly, unpredictable, supramundane being stepped in. Accompanied by drumming and dancing, the ritual reached a frenzied crescendo. The gods would be coaxed and cajoled not only by wild music and lascivious dancing but also by copious animal sacrifices (there was word, even, of human sacrifice). Such was the established pattern of curative ritual in ancient China, and indeed throughout all Asia. To these practices, the early Taoists hoped to put a definitive end.[5]

The first step in the Taoists' program, as we can reconstruct it from their early medieval texts, was to unmask the so-called gods worshipped by the people. Once that had been done, it would be child's play to rebut the common claim that those deities could help—and heal—their clients. According to the Taoists, there was nothing auspicious about these false gods. In reality, they were all no more than restless and overweening spirits of the dead—ghosts at best, ghouls and demons at worst. Moreover, these spectral beings themselves caused the diseases that they claimed to cure, for illness had its principal source (as we shall soon see) in the world of the dead. The Taoists maintained that the worship of such impostor-spirits had no beneficial effect at all; worse, it usually resulted in utter disaster. According to the Taoists, votaries of ecstatic cults frequently died long before their appointed time and were often driven first to madness—a fate in keeping with the delirious frenzy of the rituals themselves.[6]

Yet even before this ghastly doom overtook them, participants in such cults would be mulcted of all their worldly goods to pay the shamans, and would sacrifice all their domestic animals to appease the ghouls' insatiable craving for blood.[7] Finally, as if all this were not enough, they could look forward to long years of torture and hard labor in the dark, subterranean demimonde of the dead. Worship of the "gods of the profane," as the Taoists called them, counted as a very serious crime against the Tao. The all-seeing spirits in the

Northern Dipper (Ursa Major) took careful note of such infractions, and the ignorant patron of shamans and unregistered exorcists would eventually have to pay a terrible penalty.[8]

The Taoists' fundamental objection, then, turned on their perception that the supposed "gods" of the people were in reality only ghosts—dead mortals wrongly deified. It therefore comes as no surprise that early Taoism showed no enthusiasm for a closely cognate phenomenon, the cult of ancestors. Here one must speak of a valiant effort, rather than a successful reform, since (like Buddhism) Taoism was soon obliged to come to terms with, and even serve, a family system too deeply rooted ever to be extirpated. For that matter, the ecstatic cults and animal sacrifice have also survived and been accommodated. Still, members of the medieval Taoist communities were enjoined to limit their offerings to dead ancestors to a single period at the end of the old year and to feast the dead with vegetarian fare exclusively.[9]

From all this it is clear that Taoism really amounted to a religious reformation in the China of late antiquity. Here the standard histories of China, which have neglected Taoist primary sources, appear to have got the story quite wrong. The chief rival of early Taoism was not Buddhism, and not the so-called Confucian state. Rather, it was the despised and neglected "nameless religion" of the people, the scores of local deities and the hundreds of practitioners who invoked and embodied them. For Taoists, the distinction between their own faith and these cults was and remains quite simply a matter of life against death: the celestial Tao against the ill-omened, unhallowed dead and everything connected with them. In opposition to the violent cults of the deified spirits of the dead, Taoists set the pure, primordial, uncreated Tao, the first principle, and its anthropomorphic transformations, the Taoist pantheon. In place of uncontrolled shamans, Taoism offered a hierarchy of carefully trained, literate priests, the Tao's own representatives on earth. Instead of ecstasy and enthusiasm, Taoists worked through meditations: a strictly prescribed and modulated system of communication with the invisible world, framed by established ritual procedures. All this is comprised within the Taoists' term for their religion and its rituals—*fa*, or "the Law." *Fa* is also used by Chinese Buddhists to render the Sanskrit word *dharma*.[10] It is perhaps the Chinese word most closely approximating our own term "religion," at least if we recall its derivation from the word for "yoke." *Fa*, then, suggests exemplary behavior or a ritual model.[11]

Turning once more to the treatment of disease, we find just how appropriate the word "law" truly is in describing Taoist concepts and practices. The public confession of sins has in itself a legal resonance. We know that in early medieval Chinese criminal law, prompt confession could lead to a diminution of sentence. But the surviving documents allow us to go well beyond mere inference in studying Taoist therapeutic practice. The Chinese envisioned both heaven and hell as vast cosmic replicas of the imperial bureaucracy.[12] Even after death, it has been said, the Chinese could conceive of no greater felicity than a career as a celestial bureaucrat. This systematic bureaucratization of the unseen world was not an adventitious evolution of so-called popular religion but, rather, the conscious, studied creation of Taoism from its very beginnings.[13] More than meditation was needed to realize this ambitious program. Such awe-inspiring empires are founded, quite literally, on paper, and the Taoist canon has preserved for us a number of highly illuminating fragments.

These texts date from the third century, the early years of the Taoist paperwork empire. They are taken from handbooks for priests—operative manuals—and provide essential inside data for a fuller comprehension of therapeutic practice. Once the patient had acknowledged his guilt, the priest had to submit a statement to the appropriate celestial office. This statement or petition named the sufferer, giving some account of the circumstances of the case and calling on the appropriate heavenly agency for assistance. Priests owned long catalogues of the so-called Twelve Hundred Officials and Generals, civil and military functionaries dealing each with a particular class of sickness or other affliction. Here are examples, from the oldest surviving version of such a text:

> For pains in the chest, with rising *ch'i* and coughing, invoke the Lord Great Pivot of the Northern Quarter, with his 120 subordinate civil and military officers. He has charge of the Mansion of the Great Balance [an astral palace, and presumably a part of the body as well] and controls the demons of coughing and rising *ch'i*; vomiting blue, yellow, red, and white; the five pestilences, virulent magical infection, and the six thirst-specters. The offerings to be made are brooms, paper, and writing-brushes.
>
> For distension of the stomach and intense pain beneath the navel, the twelve Feng-li Lords are to be invoked. They control the demons that cause the twelve sorts of malady beneath the waistband. Offerings should be of uncooked rice and grain.[14]

These are but two examples among many, and all follow the same pattern. First the physical symptoms are listed, then the name of the appropriate divine official. This is usually accompanied by a description of his retinue and an account of their functions. Finally, the appropriate offerings are indicated: "pure" offerings (as the Taoists call them), neither animal flesh nor money. Sometimes they are symbolic of the celestial official's function, but just as often the offerings are useful items—useful to the priest, that is—like the rice and grain or the frequently mentioned writing-brushes, paper, and ink, for the priest's work was in large part paperwork. He was first and foremost a scribe, and writing was his prime means of command over the spirit world. The contrast with the shaman could not be more clearly set off.

The ritual procedures themselves follow a stereotyped pattern. The priest had first to undergo purification: abstinence, ablution, and the donning of fresh vestments.[15] Only then could he enter the chamber of quietness, or chamber of purity (as it was also called). Early Taoist texts confirm the existence of these oratories, and we even have full instructions for their construction and furnishing. They were, in the first centuries of Taoism, small wooden structures with a single papered-over window on the south wall. The only furniture was a raised dais in the center of the room with a writing-table and an incense burner on it. Writing implements were also present: brush, ink-stick, inkstone and ewer for mixing ink, and paper.[16] After entering the chamber, the priest invoked Lord Lao the Most High (T'ai-shang Lao-chün), the deified Lao-tzu:

> O Lord Lao of the Spirit-Powers of the Five Directions, the Mysterious, Primordial, Most High. I am about to summon the emissaries of the Merit-Officer, the Dragon-Lord of the Left and the Tiger-Lord of the Right, the Incense-Bearing Emissary and the True Spirits of the Three Vital Breaths (*ch'i*), and cause them speedily to inform the Lord of the Tao, the Mysterious, Primordial, Most High of the Three Heavens, that I have burnt incense in the proper manner and now enter the oratory to do homage to the spirits. I beg that the true *ch'i* of the eight directions may come and enter my body, and that my request shall speedily be made known to the Monarch of Heaven.[17]

Lord Lao is himself the "Three Vital Breaths," the Mysterious, Primordial, and Most High, which constitute the Three Heavens of Taoist cosmology.[18] The Merit-Officer, Dragon-Lord, and so forth are similarly formed of *ch'i*—the vital breaths within the officiant's own body. It is by means of this little cohort of cosmonauts that the written message will be carried to the heavens.[19] After this initial announcement, the priest lights the incense burner and pronounces an invocation to the Three Masters. These three are Chang Tao-ling, the Celestial Master and alleged founder of Taoism, to whom Lord

Lao the Most High appeared in 142 C.E. to confide the mission of salvation, and Chang's son and grandson, who succeeded him in the work.[20] Then he calls on the spirits of the four quarters, starting with the east:

> I yearn for Life, I rejoice in Life, and desire that the Lords and Elders of heaven grant me prolonged survival, extended years, increased longevity. May I be chosen as one of the Elect, to endure as long as heaven and earth shall last. May my household be free from all calamities and may every kind of sickness be cured by itself. May the protective spirits attach themselves to me and may my heart be opened, my thought awakened.

Then, turning to the north, he chants:

> I desire that evil be turned into good. I desire to receive from the Single, Supreme Lord of the Great Darkness pardon and forgiveness for my faults and transgressions. May he release me from calamity and obstacle and may he keep far from me oppressive government officials. In whatever direction I go, may he cause metal and stone to open for me, flood and fire to be extinguished for me, evil men to submit to me, and dangerous demons to flee from me.

Next, the priest turns to the west and recites:

> I love the Tao and rejoice in its saints. I desire that the Celestial Master grant that I obtain all things in which I delight and success in all my undertakings. May he cause my heart to open and my mind to understand, my eyes to be clear and my ears perceptive. May every kind of sickness be eliminated and my body become light and strong.

Finally, turning to the south, the priest recites:

> I have cultivated my body and nourished my vital powers in order to reverse the years and ward off old age. I desire to receive from the Lord of the Tao and its Power his beneficent vital breaths. May they extend over all the bones of my frame so that the Tao's *ch'i* flows throughout my body. When I have experienced the Tao's benevolent grace, all illness will be driven hence. Blessings and good fortune will come in abundance, and my thoughts will dwell upon the ten thousand blessings. My Lord, please bring for me money and goods from all the four quarters, things that promote my livelihood and increase my advantages, and success in whatever I may turn to.[21]

Rather a surprise, this last wish: Although this sequence of invocations still forms the nucleus of certain Taoist rituals performed today, the final request for riches has long since been eliminated from the formulary. In its unaltered form, it seems a guarantee of authenticity, and the text just quoted may well go back to the second-century beginnings of the Taoist movement.

To summarize, then, from the east, the noblest direction (supplanted in this role, from the mid-fourth century on, by the north),[22] the officiant asks for Life. He states his request several times, in different ways, so that there can be no mistake, asking for "prolonged survival, extended years, increased longevity."

The north is a curious case, for the officiant asks from this direction that evil be changed to good. He desires forgiveness of his sins and remission of punishment, and also requires the north to deal with disease and malevolent disease-demons. For all this he addresses himself to a "Lord of the Great Darkness." The north was the dwelling place of the dead, and all these matters of evil, sins, punishment, and disease are intimately bound up with the dead and their ruler, who came to be known as the Dark Monarch and Emperor of the North.

In the west we find the Celestial Master, Chang Tao-ling himself, presiding over that region of China in which he had operated during his lifetime. It would seem, then, that after his death the founder of Taoism ascended to the western heavens to answer the prayers of his later followers. In addressing him, the priest appropriately begins by affirming that he loves the Tao and rejoices in its saints—saints among whom the Celestial Master was, of course, first and foremost. He asks from him success, heightened perception, understanding and enlightenment.

Finally, in the south the priest addresses the Lord of the Tao and its Power, who appears to be another transformation of Lao-tzu (the alleged author of the ancient *Book of the Way and Its Power*, the *Tao-te ching*).[23] From the south, the direction of heat, of the full force of *Yang*, he first requests life-giving *ch'i*, a total immersion in *Yang*. He follows this by requesting all the other good things symbolized in China by the color red, the color pertaining to the south: long life, prosperity, good fortune, and also (in this archaic version), quite shamelessly, "money and goods."

This sequence of prayers was uttered morning and evening within their incense-filled oratories by the priests of the Tao.[24] The prayers were accompanied by prescribed visualizations of the appropriately colored *ch'i* of the several directions and the deities stationed there, though none of this is specified in the primitive text we are quoting. Details of the meditations are only found in somewhat later, amplified versions.[25] The desire for health and long life runs through the entire sequence and might even be called routine. The ritual thus far is only preliminary to the central act of communication—namely, the writing out of a message that is then burnt in the flame of the incense burner. This is done when there is need for celestial intervention, especially in the case of sickness. The written memorial names the persons concerned, recounts the facts of the case, and is directed to the appropriate agency among the Twelve Hundred Officials and Generals.[26] It is carbonized, and is expedited by the little band of emissaries formed, in meditation, from the officiant's own vital breaths.[27] In one form or another, the written memorial, actualized through burning, has become an essential part of all classical Chinese ritual. In time, even the Buddhists were obliged to conform to this model.[28] Through the action of fire, the priest's writing is transmuted into a gigantic, otherworldly script bearing a command that can move the gods.[29]

The message transmitted, the priest would guide the messengers back down and reincorporate them into this body.[30] Once the heavens had been informed, they could be counted on to take action. They would send their officers and spirit-troops to deal forcefully with the demonic disease-agents. The priest's work was not yet done, though. Still seated before the incense burner, he prepared a remedy to be administered directly to the patient. Was it medicine? Only in a metaphorical sense. It was in fact yet another paper document. Taking up his writing-brush once more, the priest drew a talismanic figure in one of the scripts employed by members of the celestial hierarchy. This rarefied script was actually only an archaizing variation on ordinary Chinese writing, and so can be read and interpreted even by mortals such as we.[31] Thus we can tell that the talismans generally bear words of stern command addressed to the disease-demons that have taken possession of the patient's body.[32] Having drawn the appropriate talisman, the priest would burn it in the flame of the incense burner, collect the ashes, mix them with water, recite a spell over the potion, and give it to the patient to drink. Once more, then, Taoist doctoring proves to be a matter of meditation and paperwork, rather as if a doctor were to have you swallow the prescription itself.[33] Despite all that one reads in secondary sources on the allegedly close connection between Taoism and Chinese pharmacology, there is no doubt that, in the early years, Taoists studiously spurned the great resources of the Chinese pharmacopoeia; they had a method all their own.[34]

The early handbooks for priests do provide a very clear picture of therapeutic operations. On the whole, they tend to confirm the terse descriptions of outside observers while furnishing an abundance of detail to which only insiders could have been privy. Yet we must not forget that these manuals were all prescriptive texts. They tell priests what should be done but do not necessarily tell the historian what actually was done. At any rate, they do not tell the whole story. From these texts we learn nothing of the patient himself, his response to suffering, or his relationship to his priest. We may know all the names and functions of the occult spirit-hierarchy, as well as the procedures by which they can be contacted. Yet the most intriguing part of the therapeutic process remains to be recovered: the initial, individual diagnosis, with its inevitable social and psychological ramifications. Who is suffering, from what, and why? On these vital questions, the priests' manuals have nothing to say. But we are far from having exhausted the resources of medieval Taoist literature. The extensive collection of documents from a fourth-century Taoist household should go a long way toward satisfying our curiosity.

The Sins of the Fathers

The study of Western medieval history has recently seen a heartening resurgence of the personal and peculiar. The survival of highly individual autobiographies as well as archival materials—especially those on heretics and other nonconformists—has revealed a kaleidoscopic array of personalities and their milieux. In the case of China, official political and institutional history has tended to dominate the scene, although there has been a comparable recent trend where materials permit. Relatively few intimate dossiers from the early medieval period have been preserved. Perhaps the most circumstantial one extant is centered on a series of Taoist visions and revelations that took place between 364 and 370. The visionary, a man in his thirties named Yang Hsi, transcribed a dozen scriptures and half as many substantial hagiographies from divine originals brought to him by a group of saints (*chen-jen*, "Perfect Ones") from the newly discovered heaven of Supreme Purity (Shang-ch'ing).[35] Yang kept a record of his visions, including transcripts of the poems sung by his visitors. He also recorded their answers to his questions about the invisible world and the means of obtaining honorable rank and office there. The Perfect Ones explained that their visits were the result of Yang's great merit. He was destined, they claimed, to wed one of their number and enter into a plenitude of power once his earthly life was done.[36] Much of the information they transmitted was intended to prepare him for his future responsibilities. But they also had another end in view. Yang Hsi's patron and employer, an official in his seventies named Hsü Mi, was also destined for high office in the celestial hierarchy of Taoism.

We know of this from the surviving dossier of night-by-night transcripts that was gathered together, edited, and annotated by the great Taoist master T'ao Hung-ching (456–536).[37] Tao estimated that only a hundredth part of the originals remained. Still, there is nothing else remotely comparable before the seventh century, when the Buddhist monk Tao-hsüan (596–667) recorded his own visions, and these texts give us a unique perspective on the lives of a group of Taoist practitioners.[38] Their physical land-base was a low mountain range rising southeast of the capital (Chien-k'ang, present-day Nanking). Known as Mao Shan (Mount Mao, for the three Brothers Mao said to have ascended to heaven from that point in 98 B.C.E.), the peak gave its name to Yang Hsi's "Mao Shan revelations." It later witnessed the founding of the Mao Shan lineage of Taoism, the most powerful and influential clan of Taoist masters in medieval China. T'ao Hung-ching was the true founder of the lineage, but Yang Hsi and the two Hsüs were retroactively enrolled among its patriarchs.[39]

This subsequent publicity no doubt accounts for the preservation of a portion of the original fourth-century texts, which T'ao published in a volume entitled *Chen-kao* (Declarations of the Perfect Ones). This substantial work includes Yang's accounts of his visions and the transcripts of what his celestial visitors told or sang to him. It also contains copies of letters between Yang Hsi and his patrons, texts of prayers, confessions that they prepared, and even records of some of their dreams.[40] Yang Hsi became a full-time intermediary between the Hsü family and the invisible world. He served them as a priestly intercessor, but one with far greater privileges than ordinary Taoist masters, for he claimed to have direct access to the uppermost echelons of heavenly officialdom. We learn, too, that the members of the Hsü family were relatively recent converts to Taoism. Previously, they had patronized local non-Taoist cults.[41] This and their urbanity (for the Hsüs belonged to the old aristocracy of the region) give special poignancy to their aspirations to Taoist sainthood.[42] It is clear that most of this material was never intended for wider circulation, and its greatest value lies in its essential intimacy. In his pivotal role, Yang Hsi had to deal with all aspects of the Hsü family's life, including illness. Thus the sundry collection of documents gathered into the *Declarations of the Perfect Ones* promises to serve our inquiry very well.[43]

Yang Hsi was one of the great Chinese visionaries—one of a long line of pioneers whose efforts brought ever wider tracts of the spirit world under cultivation. Thanks to him, Taoism acquired vast regions of heaven never previously charted.[44] It also gained a clearer vision of the world of the dead, and it is this underworld that must occupy all students of the Taoist theory of disease. According to medieval Taoists, the principal pathogenic agents are "worn-out breaths" (*ku ch'i*).[45] *Ch'i* is, of course, the basis of all life, and Taoists spent much of their time attempting to absorb the living *ch'i* of the stars and planets.[46] Conversely, stale, used-up *ch'i* was the source of evil and illness. The home of such mephitic exhalations was naturally in the damp, dark realm of the dead in the far north.

This land, we are told, was known as Ultimate Yin (T'ai-yin) and the Citadel of Night.[47] There were Six Heavens or Six Palaces there (six being the number symbolic of the north, water, and the yin element).[48] Like all palaces, the six were filled with numerous officials and hangers-on. The land of the dead was also the headquarters of the Three Officers, whom we have already found mentioned in the first accounts of primitive Taoism—namely, the Officers of Heaven, Earth, and Water. In Yang Hsi's texts we learn that they are in fact the judges of the dead, the inquisitors of the shades. New arrivals must go to them for full interrogation. They consult the archives, the Registers of the Dead, for information on everything the newly dead person did during his lifetime, and mete out punishments or rewards accordingly.[49] The division of the Three Officers into Heaven, Earth, and Water was apparently related to the final dissolution of the human body into air, dust, and liquid.[50] At all events, the Water Officer seems to have been the most dreaded of the trio, and his punishments the most frightful.[51]

Within this basic framework, the world of the dead had numerous administrative personnel. There were civil and military officials of all types, ranks, and functions. It was a complete world in its own right, with (for example) a flora all its own, appropriately including the plant of forgetfulness. The ghosts had their own special writing-system, too.[52] The ruler of this teeming kingdom was the Dark Monarch, or Emperor of the North, and under him and his officials came all the lesser dead—that is, all the dead who had not been saved and ascended into the Taoist heavens.[53]

One striking fact about the officials of the dead, as listed by Yang Hsi's celestial informants, is that their names are already well known to us from other sources. Within their ranks are many legendary figures and culture-heroes of ancient China, as well as a number of rulers and military heroes of the early Chinese empire. The one feature they all shared was that they were receiving sacrificial offerings during the fourth century: In other words, they were all treated by one or another social group, outside the context of Taoism, as gods. (In traditional China, a god is someone who receives public sacrifice after death.) This is also a feature that the great lords of the land of the dead had in common with most of the "little dead," their subjects. The descendants of dead persons normally provide them with sacrifices and offerings within the private context of the family or clan. Thus it might be said that big, or public, spirits are gods, while little, private ones are ghosts. The difference is only one of degree. Both categories share a single mode of being—or nonbeing; and, of course, for the properly instructed Taoist, both are equally ill-omened and beyond the pale. Four books out of twenty—fully one-fifth of the *Declarations of the Perfect Ones*—are given over to a painstaking description of the world of the dead and its spectral denizens. This suggests the crucial importance of the subject to fourth-century Taoists, and the account constitutes a veritable pantheon of the profane, listing all known sources of danger and contagion.[54]

As we might expect, the land of the dead was not a cheerful place. It seethed with regrets and complaints, with rivalries, feuds, and intrigues. It appears, too, that the ghosts were especially given to intricate and protracted litigation. Nothing delighted their twisted, dessicated hearts more than a nice, drawn-out lawsuit. According to Yang Hsi's informants, the procedure would go more or less as follows. The minds of the dead were unquiet, tormented by memories of battles fought when they were alive and by crimes and injustices others had perpetrated against them. Above all, they were preoccupied with the minutiae of the endless chronicle of clan rivalry, warfare, and vendettas that marked Chinese society in late antiquity and the early middle ages. Thus one ghost would bring charges against another, claiming, for example, that such a one had killed one of his relatives or stolen his property.

The dead themselves had, of course, already been investigated and judged by the Three Officers. Responsibility for a crime did not begin or end with the perpetrator himself, however: In medieval China, all the members of a given patrilineage were held responsible for the misdeeds of other members of the same lineage. The extent of guilt by affiliation varied with the gravity of the offense, but for the most serious crimes, the penalty was extermination of the culprit's entire clan to the ninth degree of affinity.[55] Therefore it is not surprising that in medieval Chinese spiritual law, the living were linked to the dead in an elastic chain of mutual responsibility. The deeds of the living reflected back on their progenitors and could alter their status among the dead. Even more fearsome was the certainty that living members of a clan would be held accountable for crimes imputed to their dead ancestors. The parallel with mundane courtrooms extended to procedure, for in such trials across the barrier of death, it was licit to apply torture immediately, either to the accused or to his representative, in order to extract the necessary confession. This meant that as soon as one of your dead ancestors had been arraigned by some discontented ghost, you yourself would begin to suffer. A variety of symptoms might be interpreted as probable signs that a plaint had been filed with the judges of the dead, and that a "sepulchral lawsuit" or "plaint from beyond the tomb" (*chung-sung*), as Taoists termed them, was getting underway. You would then realize that *you* were to be the ultimate defendant, and perhaps the judicial victim.[56]

Thus when we study closely the remarkable texts preserved in the *Declarations of the Perfect Ones*, we find that the etiology of disease is far more complex than outside historians of Taoism have ever suspected. Indeed, historians appear to have drastically oversimplified a situation of considerable intricacy. In contrast to what they tell us, "pathogenic" sins or transgressions were not necessarily limited to those committed by the patient himself. If the texts in the *Declarations* are representative, such misdeeds could more frequently be traced back to one of the patient's forebears in that miasmic swamp of ill-omen, the world of the dead. Finally, to make matters even more complicated, the charge did not need to be substantiated for the living victim to suffer. As soon as the plaint had been lodged, his miseries would begin. It was the Taoist priest's task to fight the charges, dispute the allegations, and, if possible, file a countersuit against the plaintiffs. Should your family's enemies in the realm of the dead win their case against your ancestor, it would mean death for at least one member of your clan, and possibly for many more.

Yang Hsi's visitors seem to have been lavish in their communications about the Hsü family's deceased members and their adversaries. Even in the fragmentary remains of Yang's visionary log, enough survives to piece together at least part of the tale.[57] Hsü Mi was told that he had been chosen for divine instruction because of the meritorious deeds of an ancestor of his in the seventh generation (inclusive); according to the Perfect Ones, more than two centuries before, this worthy had saved 408 people from starvation during a famine.[58] He himself lived more than a hundred years as a result, but the full benefit of his altruism was reserved for Hsü Mi, his seventh-generation descendant.

This distant ancestor was said to have "planted the merit," or founded the solid stock of moral achievement, on which Hsü Mi's own spiritual gifts could blossom.[59]

Countering this beneficial influence was another, very different vein, and one of greatest peril. As we have noted, the Hsüs were fairly recent converts to Taoism. Hsü Mi's father and uncle had been the first of their line, in the 320s, to abandon the cult of local, carnivorous gods in favor of the Way of the Celestial Master.[60] Yet the Hsü family's status within the Taoist fold was not perfectly secure, for the celestials were able to adduce instances of backsliding. For example, Hsü Mi was alleged to have once sacrificed a white dog to the god of the soil.[61] It was claimed, too, that his father had not kept up the regular contributions to their family priest.[62] An exchange of correspondence in the *Declarations of the Perfect Ones* indicates that Hsü Mi himself was scandalously remiss in making the thank-offerings that were owing to four spirit-commanders who had valiantly and successfully defended the Hsüs against a demonic attack (the offerings were paper, oil, silk, and silver hairpins).[63]

The weakest strand in the Hsü family's destiny was their alliance by marriage with a family named Hua. Hsü Mi's father had married a Hua[64] and, before discovering Yang Hsi, had employed one of his Hua in-laws to communicate with the invisible world.[65] If there was still some worry about the Hsüs' prior allegiance to indigenous non-Taoist cults, there was apparently no doubt at all about the Huas' ill-omened connections. The earlier medium, named Hua Ch'iao, was a devotee of the local gods, who responded to his attentions with enthusiasm. Hua would go off in his dreams on night-long carousals with his infernal visitors, awaking from these orgies covered in vomit and reeking of wine. It was also said that the gods used him as a judge of talent, making him name living men of administrative ability for immediate employment in the realm of the dead. Thus Hua came to consider himself responsible for the deaths of a number of prominent persons. Harassed by visions and wracked with guilt, he took refuge in Taoism, applying to the Hsüs' family priest, who was able to drive off his spectral persecutors. But Hua Ch'iao's erratic nature soon broke forth again, and he began to gossip about what he was seeing and hearing.[66] The Perfect Ones impose inviolable oaths of secrecy on those whom they favor. Contravention of these vows means doom. The result was that "Hua Ch'iao was judged worthy of death. Therefore his name was long ago removed from the Registers of Life, and in the end his head and skin were transported to the Water Office."[67]

No trace of Hua Ch'iao's communications survives. Of his ill-fated anticipation of the revelations made to Yang Hsi we have only this cautionary tale, although the Hsüs were often told that, due to this unfortunate connection, there was danger to Hua offspring in their midst. Hsü Mi's second son, Hu-ya (Tiger Fang), had also married a Hua, and the Hua ancestry was a matter of some concern as he and his wife reared their infant son. On at least one occasion, the parents were advised to take their child into the family's oratory to guard him against peril. The oratory might thus serve as a refuge in times of crisis.[68] But the Hsüs were also counseled to make a forceful written defense, and the Perfect Ones supplied them with much of the necessary information, trying to stiffen the Hsüs' resistance to their spectral accusers:

> Therefore you should make every effort to submit a rejoinder to the indictment from beyond the tomb, in order to put an end to the traffic of noxious emanations. Once this has been done three times, the persecutors will skulk away. The success of such persecutions is always due to the timidity of their victims, who in their terror do not make a formal declaration of their illness. Thus their essential spirits and embryonic spirits tremble within them, causing serious ailments to develop. Nor are the effects confined to the sufferer himself [but also extend to his entire family].[69]

It is not always easy to disentangle the various constituents of these case histories. Diagnosis was evidently based quite as much on long-past events, real or imagined, as on the observation of symptoms. There was also a predictive component that was connected with what might loosely be termed the subject's astrological coordinates—in other words, his relationship to the recurrent combinations in the sexagesimal cycle by which days and years were numbered. This enabled the diagnostician to determine particular times and directions of peril. With his comprehensive knowledge of the past, the Taoist priest might thus gain certain knowledge of the future.[70] Indeed, it is the historical aspect of the texts gathered into the *Declarations of the Perfect Ones* that most impresses. The accounts received by Yang Hsi about the deeds of Hsü Mi's forebears are often vivid in the extreme, furnishing details that only an eyewitness (or a deity) might be expected to know. The most dramatic revelations of this sort concern crimes allegedly committed by Hsü Mi's father, Hsü Fu, and his paternal uncle, Hsü Ch'ao. Both had been actively involved in political and military events of the early fourth century, and though Hsü Fu lived until the age of seventy-seven, his younger brother, Ch'ao, implicated in a failed plan to assassinate the prime minister, was obliged to kill himself at the age of fifty-three, in about 323.[71] When the Perfect Ones gave Yang Hsi information about the plaints underway among the dead against the Hsü family, they had to report a number of disquieting facts about both men. According to these allegations, both had been responsible for a long series of murders and other atrocities. Victims of their cruelty were numerous among the dead. Bitter plaints had been filed against them with the Three Officers, while not a single meritorious deed could be credited to their accounts. If these charges could be substantiated, Hsü Mi's father and uncle were hardly the sort of forebears required in the ancestry of one who aspired to Taoist perfection.

Thus, not only were the Hsü family open to ceaseless pathogenic aggression, but their entire spiritual enterprise might founder as a result. The charges had to be forcefully refuted and the plaintiffs' case quashed. The Perfect Ones provided Yang Hsi with a full dossier of facts and lent him their authority to act as the Hsüs' advocate. The following extract is typical. The youngest of the three Lords Mao here addresses Yang Hsi:

> Hsü Ch'ao killed Chang Huan-chih, the Merit-Officer of Hsin-yeh Commandery. He also murdered Ch'iu Lung-ma without any reason. These men have been waiting for an opportunity and have recently filed a plaint with the Water Officer. The Water Officer has consequently compelled Hsü Tou [the deceased wife of Hsü Mi] to return to her tomb. Now they are trying to find a child of the family whose destiny is feeble. One ought to block their opposition, release [Tou] from this constraint, and stand firm before those plaintiffs. They are to come here on the anniversary of Tou's death. You, sir [= Yang Hsi], have received your official appointment and are able to annihilate all sorts of specters and apprehend every type of spirit. We should like to see you take action. We only ask that on that day you proceed to Tou's tomb and threaten Huan[-chih] and his fellows. Issue your orders to the Officer of the Left, make him select another victim for punishment, and eliminate the cause of this dispute. You are not to say anything more of this, only state that I have delegated my authority to you. I do not know if you are willing to eliminate them. It is urgent, however, that these specters be driven off.[72]

Note that there is no attempt to veil Hsü Ch'ao's crimes, nor even to adduce mitigating circumstances. What counted most was, evidently, a staunch defense, no doubt bolstered by countercharges. Yang Hsi was also informed of instances in which long-dead members of the Hsü family had suffered unjustly in their turn:

> Hsü Chien was the daughter of Tai Shih-tzu. She was killed by hereditary enemies of the family, Hsieh Shih and others. Hsieh Shih also killed the

infant she was holding, Ah-ning. Hsü Chien and her child are now in the Water Office, and their bones are floating about. At the time he was killed, [Ah-]ning was already suffering from skin eruptions on his head, and they had spread over his entire face.[73]

The innocent child's skin ailment was no doubt viewed as a further result of anti-Hsü activity on the part of the malevolent dead, thus adding to their own tally of unprovoked murders and miseries. We can see, too, that not only the living were subject to attack as a result of the machinations of the dead. The family's recent dead might also be held hostage to the accusations of long-gone antagonists. Thus Hsü Mi's late wife had reportedly been banished to the solitude of her tomb, which was to be the site of a decisive confrontation between Yang Hsi and one particular faction among the Hsü family's numerous ghostly enemies.[74]

Although Yang Hsi does not seem to have been a regular Taoist priest, his visionary powers and intimacy with the Perfect Ones of Shang-ch'ing endowed him with special abilities for serving as the Hsü family's intercessor with the invisible world. Hsü Mi, for his part, was even less a priest; as far as we know, he steadfastly resisted all celestial urging to quit his official post, abandon the capital, and retire to Mao Shan.[75] Yet we find that he, too, was empowered to take up the cause of those threatened by repercussions from the deeds of their forebears. He was to act not for members of the Hsü family but for unrelated friends and colleagues. Having learned of Yang Hsi's visions, some of Hsü Mi's associates had evidently been emboldened to make their own inquiries, through Hsü. In such cases the information that Yang Hsi received, though sometimes complex, was by and large favorable. For example, the Perfect Ones reported a legal imbroglio in the Water Office about the ailing mother of a certain Liu Tsun, who had requested a diagnosis. They declared, however, that "if Hsü Mi can come to their aid in his oratory, the entire family will be safe."[76] Other friends, the Lu family, were especially well-omened, according to Yang Hsi's informants. The grandfather of the present senior generation (like Hsü Mi's own ancestor seven generations back) had accumulated great merit, the benefits of which would extend to the seventh generation of his descendants. The Lus might therefore reasonably hope to produce their own members of the Taoist pantheon in due time. Yang Hsi's divine visitors authorized Hsü Mi to tell his friends all the encouraging news they had to report.[77]

In contrast, some of the Perfect Ones' other reports may never have been transmitted to the interested parties. Consider the following, about Hsü Mi's colleague Ch'ih Hui:

> Ch'ih Hui's father massacred several hundred innocent people and took their possessions. For this, he is receiving very heavy punishment among the dead. Those he wronged are constantly making plaints and denouncing him to the celestial officials, and Ch'ih Hui has long since been designated as correspondent [i.e., as the responsible party among the living]. According to the law, his entire family should be exterminated. Since Ch'ih Hui has performed many deeds of merit, he himself will escape with his life. Yet how can there be any security for his sons and grandsons? Ch'ih Hui will live out his natural span of years, but he is far indeed from the way of immortality.[78]

Yet the Perfect Ones were soon able to furnish greater assurances to Ch'ih Hui; he was even promised a posthumous position as supervisor in the Heaven of Great Purity (T'ai-ch'ing)—a heaven inferior to that of Supreme Purity, for which the Hsüs were destined, but still very respectable in its own right.[79] It appears that one of Ch'ih Hui's forebears and his wife had been exceedingly philanthropic during their lifetimes, and so had amassed considerable credit in the unseen world. In occult accountancy, the benefit of this accrued to Ch'ih Hui, which explained his aspiration to immortality. His ancestor's spouse had even obtained an official post herself among the immortals.[80] Thus Ch'ih Hui had a well-placed sponsor, and he was told of yet another couple among the family dead (termed their "spirits of good fortune") who were devoted to Ch'ih family interests.[81] At first, it seems, the judicial proceedings against Ch'ih Hui's late father did not implicate any living members of the family. As plaints multiplied, however, it soon became impossible for benignly disposed relations among the dead to limit the consequences to their own domain. Evidently, then, sickness had broken out among the Ch'ihs. Given the gravity and number of the charges against Ch'ih Hui's father, this was hardly surprising, but it also turned out that another ancestral couple, a certain Ch'ih Hsiung and his wife, were the family's "spirits of ill fortune." They were still engaged in hauling rocks, the punishment allotted them after death. They reportedly rejoiced in doing harm to living members of their own family and were intent on mayhem.[82]

Once again, Hsü Mi was urged to take action on behalf of these friends. A member of the Ch'ih family, referred to as Kao-ling, was apparently in critical condition. He was only a recent convert to Taoism, we are told, and his regular priest was said to be weak and ineffectual. There was, therefore, no normal channel through which the celestial powers could aid him. The youngest of the three Mao brothers declared, "Kao-ling has long been devoid of merit [i.e., has been a profane non-Taoist], and the spectral plaints are very involved and numerous. Surely Hsü Mi will be able to give him a talisman, which he should be made to consume. If he does so, he ought to be cured in a twinkling. Otherwise he will duly pay a visit to the Water Office, and that would really be a pity for him."[83] But five days later the same divinity was reporting that "the plaints from beyond the tomb have become still more numerous, and I fear they are not yet finished. For his own vainglory, [Kao-]ling once chiseled away the inscription on a memorial tablet in honor of some ancient personage. Thus he committed an act of vandalism against a denizen of the invisible world, obscuring that person's good deeds in order to put himself forward. The plaintiffs against him have many charges indeed, but this one heads the list."[84] On that discouraging note, the unfortunate Kao-ling disappears from the record.

From all these cases we can see that communication with the Taoist hierarchy in time of crisis inevitably meant learning about things in one's family background that one might well prefer not to know. To ask a Taoist priest to diagnose and treat an illness was to invite a general exhumation of all skeletons in the family closet. "Taoism" had begun as an independent state involving the all-around administration of portions of west China. Meticulous record-keeping continued as part of the priest's duties even after the theocracy had lost its autonomy and become integrated into Chinese society, spreading to other regions. Thus it was the priest's business to have full knowledge of his parishioners' family backgrounds. All births, deaths, and marriages had to be registered with him—and reported by him to the celestial hierarchy at regular assemblies thrice annually.[85] When illness occurred among the families in his care, he was particularly well equipped with socio-historical information on which to base his diagnosis and treatment. The treatment was couched in the language and carried out in the formal legalistic manner of a public official.

This much, at least, appears to have been true of Taoism as a whole in the early medieval period. For fourth-century Mao Shan adepts, the circumstances may have been more highly nuanced, and priest/patient relations somewhat more complex. In the texts gathered into the *Declarations of the Perfect Ones*, the traditional relationship of priest to patron is no doubt made more intricate by the immediacy of divine revelation and the consequent increase in both terrestrial and celestial personnel. In these texts ultimate authority is vested in the Perfect Ones, who far transcend the ordinary priest's celestial contacts. Yang Hsi was the Perfect Ones' chosen intermediary in dealing with mortals, although in cases outside the Hsü family circle, Hsü Mi served as a supplementary link in the chain, or as a buffer between the patient and Yang Hsi. Yet this elaborate chain of transmission should not be allowed to conceal the older, traditional processes at work in new forms. The crucial relationship remained that between two human beings—the patient and his consultant. The otherworldly actors were projections of the conscience of the one, the perceptions of the other. Thus diagnosis and treatment involved a collaboration between priest and patient in the reconstruction of family history. The true judgment was rendered here below by the priest, then ratified through its acceptance by the believer and his family. In attempting to make sense of this material, we must try to restore what we are told of otherworldly procedures to their authentic context in human society.

It is of great significance that living victims of the malevolent dead were actually told for whose sins they were suffering. Although the *Declarations of the Perfect Ones* represents only a limited sample, there is a striking consistency in its pattern of explanation. All the ailments of living members of the family seem to have originated in the alleged misdeeds of the immediately preceding generation, whose members were most recently dead. In the case of the Hsüs, these were the father and uncle of the senior living member of the family, Hsü Mi, who was the person making the inquiries. Similarly, illness in the Ch'ih family emanated from the slaughter said to have been perpetrated by the late father of Hsü Mi's friend Ch'ih Hui, who initiated the inquiry. Thus the man who commissioned his Taoist priest to undertake a diagnosis would learn that his family's present troubles, his own ailment, or the illness of a child or grandchild stemmed from crimes supposedly committed by his own father, or perhaps his uncle, presently among the dead.

We cannot, however, assume that the most recently deceased ancestors simply offered the most natural frame of reference, the most immediate explanation for all manner of events in the world of the living. We have already seen that the blessings and happy events that occurred in a family were also attributed to the ancestors, only to the good deeds they had performed in their lifetimes instead of to their transgressions. But in such cases, the meritorious acts were never ascribed to the most recently departed; rather, they were located far back along the patrilineage, invariably with the seventh-generation ancestor. This long-dead worthy is described as having "planted the merit" that will flower years later in the person of his distant descendant. Hsü Mi's spiritual preoccupations resulted from good works accomplished more than two hundred years earlier. Likewise, his friend Lu Na might contemplate his family's future with equanimity because his own grandfather was said to have been one of these potent merit-planters. (In the texts that remain, the Lu family appears to have been making general inquiries about their spiritual estate rather than requesting a diagnosis in time of crisis.) In this schema, it is always the seventh-generation ancestor who serves as patron of the family's good fortune. The pattern is clear: Happiness derives from good deeds carried out long before by someone whom none of the living has ever known personally. Sickness and misfortune, in contrast, are attributed to actions carried out by the most recent, most intimately familiar dead.

It is impossible to contemplate this pattern without reflecting on the nature of Chinese "filial piety." No behavior has been invested with greater importance by members of China's official class. Across the centuries, the invariable rule has been absolute obedience to one's father during his lifetime and "three years' mourning" after his death. A man's behavior was governed by a comprehensive array of restraints and taboos in relation to his father, living or dead. Despite the official portrait of the filial relationship as one in which profound gratitude inspired complete deference and respect, the outside observer can hardly avoid wondering where all the resentment has gone. Forced to suppress his own will—and no doubt all too conscious of never meeting his father's high expectations—into what corners of his psyche did the Chinese male sweep his frustration, guilt, and shame? Perhaps one day a new discipline, a "psycho-sinology," may provide the answers. Combining what we now know of family dynamics, sibling rivalries, and so forth with the minute and detailed histories that have come down to us should yield a radical revision of such classically Chinese concepts as filial piety. Couldn't the incessant promotion of filial piety in official sources in fact be the most telling indication of how very different things actually were in practice?

Our fourth-century Taoist dossier reveals much about parent-child relations and their obvious connection with disease and suffering. It is no accident that a Taoist priest had to develop the diagnosis and conduct the case: An outsider was the only one who could clearly formulate the often unspeakable charges against a victim's immediate kindred. As the representative of the impersonal Tao and a dispassionate channel of intelligence from beyond the tomb, the priest acted from a position of impregnable authority. We may wonder whether much of the priest's power, both therapeutic and social, did not derive from the skill with which he cut dangerously close to the bone in his quest for the ethical origins of misfortune. Given his special historical knowledge of the family, the priest could articulate any unspeakable thoughts his client harbored about his dead father—or at least weave a plausible tale from the facts at his disposal. Ordinarily, of course, no good son could ever admit to himself the hostility he might feel toward his father. When all the accusations were attributed to enemies in the world of the dead, however, they could be brought forward and freely discussed. In this way the legalistic intricacies of Taoist diagnosis may have created a "theater for the unspeakable."

Yet another element may have contributed to this complex of therapy and ritual. As noted earlier, one of the revolutionary measures that Taoists introduced was a strict limitation on offerings to ancestors. "The spirits do not eat or drink" was one of their key slogans.[86] According to ordinary Chinese standards, this would leave the dead without vital material support in the afterlife. Thus the burden of guilt and negligence toward their dead parents must have been especially great among members of the early Taoist community. This guilt may have been displaced by fixing the blame for their own troubles on their dead fathers and uncles, the objects of their ritual neglect.

The evidence, then, suggests that a "talking cure," a sophisticated psychotherapy, was at the heart of Taoist healing. True, the person manifesting physical symptoms may not have been identical with the direct beneficiary of the priest's analytic intervention. Yet in Chinese belief, members of a single family were in fact consubstantial, sharing bones and breath. This was clearly "family therapy" in the fullest sense of the term.[87] It would be valuable to know how its legalistic formulations compared with diagnoses produced by non-Taoist mediums or shamans of the same time and region. Since such ritual healers have left no firsthand records, we turn instead to the medical literature. We may be able to set our Taoist data in sharper focus as we attempt to track an elusive disease-entity across bibliographic frontiers.

Heredity or Contagion?

The expression used for the procedures employed by the malevolent dead was "plaint from beyond the tomb" or "sepulchral lawsuit" (*chung-sung*). This term described the origin of the pathology, but the pathology itself or its physical symptoms were designated by another term, "ghost- (or demon-)infusion" or "ghost-infestation" (*kuei-chu*).[88] The first syllable, *kuei*, denoted not only ghosts but also demons, and sometimes lesser deities as well. The second syllable, *chu*, means, literally, "a pouring-in." Scholars are familiar with this word in its more common usage as "a textual commentary"—that is, a glossatorial infusion. In nosology or disease classification, *chu* represented a class of ailments that Nathan Sivin has termed "epidemic possession."[89] The word *chu* is also homophonous with another word meaning "to stay, stand." Thus some medical texts explain *chu* as signifying a kind of "demono-stasis": The spectral pathogens visit their victim and stay on and on. However the word is glossed, the Taoist texts are describing a condition that is also treated in secular medical literature; comparison should prove enlightening.[90]

For information on fourth-century diagnostic terminology and methods of treatment, the first source to examine is Ko Hung's *Prescriptions Within Arm's Reach for Use in Emergencies* (*Chou-hou pei-chi fang*).[91] Ko Hung (283–343) is better known for his large collection of musings on ethics, customs, and occult lore, the *Pao-p'u tzu*. His medical text is particularly relevant to the study of illness in the Mao Shan circle because Ko's family had long been allied by marriage with the Hsüs. There is an additional connection: Ko's prescriptions were edited and annotated by T'ao Hung-ching, editor of the *Declarations of the Perfect Ones*. In Western writings on China, Ko Hung is usually called a Taoist, and his *Pao-p'u tzu* is often used to illustrate everything that Taoism is supposed to be about. Yet his works contain no evidence that Ko had any familiarity with the Way of the Celestial Master, the basic Taoist institution. In fact, Ko Hung was of the generation of Hsü Mi's father and uncle, and presumably shared their pre-Taoist beliefs. As we have seen, the Hsüs enrolled among the Celestial Master's followers only around 320. We do not know whether or not Ko Hung eventually followed their example, but by 320 he had already completed his most famous book. Though filled with arcane lore, Ko's writings were clearly intended for a cultivated general public. He expressly compiled his *Prescriptions* in order to place a concise account of common ailments and their treatment into the hands of all who might need them—"within arm's reach for use in emergencies."

Ko appears to have succeeded admirably. The *Prescriptions* are frequently drawn upon by later medical writers, and no doubt others made good use of its information, too. T'ao Hung-ching's editorial revision did much to promote and preserve Ko's book, though Tao is also to blame for the chief problem in using the *Prescriptions* as a historical source. Here, as in all T'ao's annotated editions, text and commentary were distinguished by ink of different colors. Later scribes soon effaced this distinction, and now it is often impossible to disentangle Ko's original text from Tao's commentary, not to mention additions made by still later writers down through the twelfth century.

The seventh section of the work offers "Prescriptions for Treating Corpse-Infestation and Ghost-Infestation."[92] According to Ko, ghost- or demon-infestation is the same as corpse-infestation, the last in a group of five types of affliction caused by five different sorts of pathogens known as "corpses" (*shih*).[93] Corpse-infestation brings along a host of accompanying demons and wraiths to cause harm. The disease undergoes a prodigious number of transformations, and comprises thirty-six or even ninety-nine varieties in all. In general, sufferers from all of these experience extreme sensations of chill and heat, pour with sweat, and are dazed and depressed. The patient does not know exactly what is afflicting him, but every part of his body is in pain and malfunctioning. This continues month after month, year after year, until his system is brought to a standstill. When he dies, the disease is passed on to someone in his family. This proceeds until the entire family has been annihilated.

The description is followed by several recipes for use in treatment. One calls for bark of mulberry root and small red beans, to be cooked and administered in a broth of mutton or venison. Another requires fifty peach kernels, macerated and administered in a decoction. Four pints of this brew, given to the patient, provokes vomiting, which should result in a cure. Otherwise the dosage is to be repeated in three days. If it fails to bring on vomiting, then the disease is not corpse-infestation. Further (and no doubt later) prescriptions using vegetable, animal, and mineral products follow.[94]

Mulberry root and peach kernels are potent anthelmintics, and their presence here underscores the basic conception of corpse-demons as having the form of worms. So although the disease is of demonic origin, the treatment is herbal or phytochemical rather than ritual. Ko's mention of thirty-six or even ninety-nine varieties, taken up by later sources, suggests that we are unlikely to find any one Western disease-entity that corresponds to such a protean array. Ko also records the *chu* disease's most terrifying aspect: After the patient's death, the demons attack each member of the family in succession until all have perished.

From Ko Hung, we proceed to Ch'ao Yüan-fang, medieval China's most systematic pathologist. Ch'ao's *On the Origins and Symptoms of Diseases* (*Chu-*

ping yüan-hou lun), completed in 610, is "the most important monograph on aetiology and symptomatology in Chinese medicine."[95] It names and describes some two thousand disorders. The description of *chu* ailments follows the section on diseases provoked by twelve different sorts of corpse-specters. In addition to a comprehensive overview of *chu* symptoms generally, Ch'ao Yüan-fang furnishes short essays on thirty-three species of the genus.

Ch'ao's basic definition of *chu* turns on the word's relation to its homophone: "When malignant *ch'i* dwells (*chu*) in a person's body, it is called infestation (*chu*)."[96] This "indwelling" suggests chronicity. He explains this as a result of systemic imbalance, depletion, or exhaustion in the patient. The malignant *ch'i* may gain entrance if the patient has been habitually immoderate in balancing his intake of hot and cold foods, or if he has suddenly come into contact with emanations from the dead or has collided with a ghost or demon (*kuei-wu*). Ch'ao mentions the reputed thirty-six and ninety-nine varieties of *chu* but notes that Ko Hung never bothered to reveal the names of most of them. Ch'ao describes an alternative nosological system of nine types of infestation: wind, cold, *ch'i*, life, chill, wine, food, water, and corpse. Wind-infestation is itself broken down into twelve subtypes. Three of these represent symptoms normally associated with the more dramatic forms of demonic possession: "If the patient loses consciousness and falls to the ground, it is called a 'fainting fit' (lit., 'wind'); if he lets down his hair and runs madly about beating people and objects, it is called a 'falling fit': if he shouts and curses, talks and laughs to himself, it is called a 'fit of madness.'"[97]

Under the separate rubric "ghost-infestation" (*kuei-chu*), Ch'ao describes a condition in which someone who is without other signs of illness is suddenly pushed or struck by a spectral being (*kuei*). At that time he may feel a sudden stabbing pain in the heart, or lose consciousness and fall to the ground. This is similar to the ailment known as "struck by evil" (*chung o*, sometimes glossed as "heart attack"). After the symptoms have been cured, the residual *ch'i* does not vanish but lingers on for a long time. It breaks out periodically and entrenches itself for a permanent stay. This goes on until the patient dies, after which it infects successive members of his family. This is why it is called "ghost-infestation."[98]

Nathan Sivin's summary of Ch'ao's data is very much to the point:

> The *chu* diseases are a broad group of chronic wasting diseases with intermittent attacks of alarming symptoms; after the victim dies, the malevolent *ch'i*

> moves on to attack someone else. From Ch'ao Yüan-fang's description of the many kinds of *chu* it is clear that no simple correspondence with a Western pathological entity can be found; some types seem to be pulmonary tuberculosis, others to be grand mal epilepsy, and others to be psychoses.[99]

The statement that the disease infects successive members of the patient's family after his death is repeated mechanically in nearly all of Ch'ao's thirty-three sketches of different sorts of *chu*. The most dramatic posthumous effects result from what he names "disaster-infestation" (*yang-chu*), in which the initial victim dies of pestilence (*i-li*).[100] The lingering evil proceeds to kill his children and grandchildren, his immediate and extended family. In this case, the pseudo-"hereditary" character of the disease seems far closer to our own understanding of contagion. But from other accounts in his *chu* series, it is quite clear that Ch'ao recognized that at least some forms of disorder susceptibility need not be a function of family relationship. For example, he describes a pair of *chu* called "living-infestation" and "dead-infestation."[101] In living-infestation, persons dwelling with the patient and perhaps caring for him are infected by the *ch'i* of his ailment while he is still alive. They thus come to resemble him, whence the name for this variety of *chu*. "Dead-infestation" arises when someone is infected in the course of visiting the house of a person who has died of *chu*. The word used here for "catching" or "becoming infected with" the disease is *jan*, which has a basic meaning "to dye" and a derived sense of "contaminate." It is clear that the sole requisite for infection in such cases was physical contact with the patient, living or dead, or his dwelling place.

Under the rubric of *chu*, Ch'ao Yüan-fang grouped together a large number of diverse ailments that had not necessarily been associated with one another by earlier authors. His rationale appears to have been their intense contagiousness, whether this was viewed as operating exclusively within a single family or as extending to outsiders. For example, in chapter 24 of his work Ch'ao describes a variety of *chu* produced by intentional poisoning, or virulent magical infection (*ku*).[102] The toxin was produced by placing the five most venomous reptiles and insects together in a vessel. The creature that emerged from this encounter was the *ku*. It was placed in the victim's food or drink, and by calculating the dosage, the sorcerer could determine the time of death at will, from within ten days to after months or years of suffering. Chapter 25 of Ch'ao's work is entirely given over to a description of *ku* magic and related matters. He anticipates all this by listing a *ku* infestation among the various species of *chu* because, in this variety of *ku* murder, the toxin goes on to infest and infect (*chu jan*) other family members after the death of its initial victim.[103]

Less prominence is given to the devastating effect on families in the writings of Sun Ssu-mo. Sun's *Important Prescriptions Worth a Thousand* [*Cash*] (*Ch'ien-chin yao-fang*), written between 650 and 659, presents an assortment of remedies for the different kinds of *chu* infestations.[104] As the work's title indicates, it focuses on the practical means of healing rather than on taxonomy and symptomology. Thus Sun is content to describe the *chu* complex with a few terse phrases culled from Ko Hung and Ch'ao Yüan-fang. He evidently intended the book to be used in conjunction with Ch'ao's *Origins and Symptoms of Diseases*, since his prescriptions are interlarded with the names of many of the disease's subtypes found in Ch'ao's work. The cures themselves are representative of Chinese polypharmacy, drawing their ingredients from mineral, animal, vegetable, and insect sources. The most impressive is a compound of forty-five different substances. Moxabustion is also recommended as a treatment.

There may be nothing particularly startling within Sun Ssu-mo's pages on *chu*, but his classification of the disease-complex as a whole does call for comment. The middle section of his book is organized according to ailments of the various internal organs, and he has placed the *chu* complex at the end of the section on lung diseases. This seems to mark a major step toward grouping the whole extravagantly varied pathology under the single rubric of tuberculosis. There are instructions, too, for observing the pathogens as one expels them. A five-ingredient herbal compound should be taken on an empty stomach. After an interval, the patient should spit onto a wall, whereupon, at the foot of the wall, the evil creatures will be seen departing, tadpole-like and toad-like, sometimes a foot or two long. Another set of instructions states that when one places one's hand on the patient's chest, the disease can be felt moving about within, like irritated, agitated insects.[105]

All this seems fairly prosaic, particularly when we consider Sun Ssu-mo's special place in the history of Chinese healing. He is not only a prominent figure in the secular medical tradition but is honored in both Buddhist and Taoist hagiography and has been credited with works on alchemy as well. In fact, there is circumstantial evidence that Sun must have been trained as a Taoist priest. Only an initiate would have known the spells and meditations he gives in the two concluding chapters of his other great work on medicine, the *Supplementary Prescriptions Worth a Thousand* [*Cash*] (*Ch'ien-chin i-fang*).

In what Sun calls a "Book of Spellbinding" (*chin-ching*; the word *chin* means, literally, "interdiction"), he presents the essentials of ritual therapy with which the healer is advised to enhance his use of drugs, moxa, and acupuncture. Control of the breath, eyes, and fingers and visualized imagery are all necessary, and Sun gives directions for their proper use. The bulk of the two spellbinding chapters, though, is taken up with incantations. Several spells are provided under each category of ailment or danger, from specific disease-entities to noxious animals or insects. The section devoted to *chu* infestation follows one on treating *ku* poisoning and is typical of the methods recommended in this magician's manual.

In the first spell, the healer vaunts his powers in verse of four syllables to the line:

From south of the heavens I have come to the north,
I have eaten three bushels of salt,
I have drunk ten thousand thousands of water,
I have crossed the Great River and measured the sea's breadth.
In my hands I grasp hills and mountains,
In my mouth I hold a hundred toxins,
In my heart I bear centipedes.
When I spit on heaven, heaven must turn.
When I spit on earth, earth sinks and opens.
When I spit on stone, it shatters and crumbles.
When I spit on fire, the flames go out.
When I spit on demons, they die at once.
When I spit on water, the abyss dries up.[106]

The spell now shifts to phrases of seven syllables as the healer names the *chu* demons of the five directions, localizes them in the patient's body, and specifies the effect that the spell pronounced by the "Master of Spirits" will have on them:

The *chu* of the eastern region is named I ("doctor"),
When it enters a person's body, it infests the heart.
When the Master of Spirits bespells the *chu*, its entire clan is annihilated.[107]

The five *chu* are named I ("doctor," east, heart), Ch'ing ("blue," south, the veins and arteries), Yao ("shake," "shaker," west, spine and waist), Tz'u ("female," north, heart and spleen), and Chih ("pheasant," center, the ten fingers). The next spell also names and localizes the five *chu* demons, but differently:

The *chu* of the eastern region is named Yang ("sheep"),
When it enters a person's body, it controls stomach and intestines.[108]
When the Master of Spirits bespells the *chu*, the *chu* at once perishes.
The *chu* of the southern region is named Kou ("dog"),
When it enters a person's body, it controls his heart and mouth,
When the Master of Spirits bespells the *chu*, it runs away at once.
The *chu* of the western region is named Chi ("chicken"),
When it enters a person's body, it controls his heart and navel,
When the Master of Spirits bespells the *chu*, it is at once confused.
The *chu* of the northern region is named Yü ("fish"),
When it enters a person's body, it rules the six agencies,[109]
When the Master of Spirits bespells the *chu*, it ceases to exist.
The *chu* of the center is named Chih ("pheasant"),
When it enters a person's body, it controls his heart's innards,
When the Master of Spirits bespells the *chu*, it dies.[110]

Only the central "pheasant" is common to both incantations. The same structure is found elsewhere in Sun Ssu-mo's "Book of Spellbinding." A spell in the section on pestilence (*wen-i*) not only follows the same prosodic pattern but even names "dog" among the pathogenic agents:

You have come from the east, your name is Kou ("dog"),
When you enter a person's body, you lodge in his heart and mouth,
When the Master of Spirits bespells you, you run away by yourself.
You have come from the south, your name is Yang ("sheep"),
When you enter a person's body, you lodge in his liver and intestines,
When the Master of Spirits bespells you, you perish by yourself.[111]

Being in possession of the demons' names was all-important, and the ritual therapist had long repertories of demonic nomenclature at his disposal. The magic of names was intimately linked with cosmology. The following spell against *chu* first names the pathogen's father, mother, and elder and younger brothers and sisters. Then it declares, "I know your family name and given names, / I possess your *kung* and *shang*. / Why don't you go far away— / What can you hope for by staying on?"[112] *Kung* and *shang* are two of the five basic musical notes. Every Chinese family name was classified as rhyming with one of the five, and was thus linked with one of the five directions and its corresponding "element," or phase of change: East was associated with wood, south with fire, west with metal, north with water, and the center with earth. A family's tombs were oriented so as to harvest the elemental benefits of this system, capturing an infusion from the "phase" that nourished the family's own (as fire is fed by wood, thus south is nourished by east, etc.). Knowing an invasive demon's family name, the healer could turn the same system to his advantage by using it aggressively (as fire is overcome by water, so south is overcome by north).

Several more incantations follow. I only quote one, for the characteristic vainglory of the therapeutic champion:

I am the child of Mount T'ai,[113]
I have now been sent here by Mount T'ai.
My mouth is like the Gate of Heaven,
So wide it cannot be propped open.

When I spit, it is like a deadly drug,
My breath is like the autumn frost.
He who stands against me dies,
He who encounters me perishes.
O demons of the five infestations,
Speedily come out, speedily depart!
You may not skulk and linger!
Quick, quick, as the Statutes and Ordinances command![114]

In his medical writings, the seventh-century Sun Ssu-mo was able to encompass the full spectrum of Chinese healing techniques, from drugs and needles to spells, spittle, and irate glares. This was not in itself unusual, and many other medical authors exhibit similar breadth. The special features in Sun's case are the consistently Taoist character of all his ritual material and his systematic mode of presentation. The next great literary monument of Chinese medicine, Wang T'ao's *Secret Essentials from the Outer Tribunal* (*Wai-t'ai pi-yao*), also promotes ritual methods, but the specific hallmarks of the Taoist initiate are absent.

The preface of Wang's large compendium is dated from 752, a hundred years after Sun Ssu-mo's two books. In the interval, a certain Su Yu had written a treatise on corpse-vector disease (*ch'uan-shih*; lit., "corpses transmitting [pathogenes]"), a variant of *chu*-infestation, and Wang T'ao reproduces substantial extracts from this to open his section on *chu* infestations. According to Su Yu, corpse-vector starts in the kidneys, passing successively to heart, lungs, liver, and spleen. He meticulously describes the symptoms of each stage of its progress and notes a few regional variations in terminology, among them "rotating infestation," "lingering debility" (?), "withering of the lungs," "bone-steaming," "concealed connection," and "extreme exhaustion." Su Yu advises treatment by polypharmacy and moxabustion.[115]

Su Yu's work (which has not otherwise been preserved) seems to have been distinguished by clarity and cool logic. Yet he was not Wang T'ao's only source of information on the treatment of corpse-vector or *chu* infestation. Shortly after these extracts, Wang (who held an official administrative position) quotes from the work of another official, one Ts'ui Chih-t'i.[116] Ts'ui lived in the seventh century and compiled a substantial collection of prescriptions. Though it has not survived as an independent entity, this was one of Wang T'ao's favorite sources; he cites it no less than 165 times.[117] Although other extracts from his collection reveal the typical concern with drugs, moxa, and acupuncture, in this treatment for the subtype of corpse-vector or *chu* known as "concealed connection" (*fu-lien*), we find Ts'ui Chih-t'i perched squarely in the broad path of Chinese exorcistic ritual:

> First find an unopened gourd and bury it in the earth. Select a "day of opening" in the first decade of the month, and open it. Boil and stuff it with three spoonfuls of congee made with fat. Further, cut out paper money and take it to a freshly made tomb. Have the sick child sit with his back to the tomb, facing the road back home. With the paper money and a new cord, go around the tomb and the patient so that they are completely encircled. Take a small quantity of additional paper money and offer it, outside the circle, to the General of the Five Ways. Have the patient hold the gourd in one hand, while with the other he uses a sword to make a hole in the ground. Then have him set the gourd in the hole and sit on it. Have a healthy person strike two locks together behind the patient's back. Recite this spell:
>
> Concealed connection, concealed connection be loosed!
> Concealed connection, concealed connection, if you are not loosed,
> I will loose you with this sword and locks.
>
> Then recite this spell:
>
> Living men possess what is on the earth,
> Dead ghosts possess what is beneath the earth.
> Living men and dead ghosts have each their different paths.
>
> When the spells have been pronounced, have the healthy person cast both locks behind the patient. They must be held back to back when throwing

them; if this was not done, have him pick them up and cast them again. When this has been accomplished, all should return home without looking back.

Once again select a "day of opening." Have the patient sit in a covered carriage outside the city wall. He should be facing the wall. With ashes and three pints of water, make a triple circle around him. Also [with the ashes and water?] make seven unturned cakes. Offer them to the General of the Five Ways, and recite this spell:

Gate of Heaven, open!
Door of Earth, shut!
Living men and dead ghosts
Have each their different paths.
On this day of fivefold opening,
Release him and return home!

When this spell has been pronounced, let everyone go back home without turning their heads around. This procedure is extremely good.[118]

In this operation, the right day had first to be selected from the calendar and various accessories prepared. The gourd was needed as an edible offering to the disease-demons, but one to be used in a special way. For (if I have read the passage correctly) the patient was to sit on the congee-filled gourd. Presumably this would attract the demons out through the victim's anus. The stuffed gourd served both as bait and demon-trap. Many an exorcist in Chinese legend captures and keeps demons in a gourd container.[119]

Paper money was also required—an early indication (in the seventh century) of the use of ghost-money to buy off spectral afflictors.[120] At exactly the same time, in the *Collected Dhāraṇī Sūtras* of 653–54, laymen were being directed to make offerings of paper money to members of the Buddhist pantheon. In Ts'ui Chih-t'i's exorcistic ritual, the site of the transaction was a newly made tomb—that of the restless ghost deemed responsible for the trouble, or simply a place where channels to the world of the dead were most likely to be open and accessible? The text does not specify. Finally, the General of the Five Ways, who commands the armies of the dead, is mentioned and paid off. He is also named in incantations found in Sun Ssu-mo's "Book of Spellbinding," as well as in Buddhist ritual texts of the period.[121]

Here there is no mention of medicaments; the operation is strictly a matter of bribery and coercion. With the spells, swords, and locks to threaten the intrusive demons, we might be in the atelier of any ordinary Chinese exorcist, rather than in the pages of one of China's most respected medical treatises. Reputable officials though they were, then, both the seventh-century Ts'ui Chih-t'i and the eighth-century Wang T'ao fully accepted exorcistic protocol. We find the usual conventions of payment and *force majeure* extending beyond the boundaries of the visible. In Ts'ui's ritual there is nothing particularly "Taoist"; in contrast to the spells provided by Sun Ssu-mo, its idiom is simply common Chinese.

If such "secular" authors were ready enough to commend and carry out therapeutic rituals, what had professed ritualists been doing about the *chu* diseases, corpse-vector, and the like all this time? In fact, the most elaborate description of corpse-vector symptomology is found in a Taoist ritual text, the *Great Rites of the Jade Hall* (*Yü-t'ang ta-fa*, HY 220). This work, compiled about 1158, is a characteristic product of what has been called "the Taoist renaissance of the twelfth century."[122]

Taoism had flourished both at court and in the provinces from the beginning of the twelfth century, and enjoyed the full support and active participation of the Emperor Hui-tsung (r. 1101–25). New celestial revelations were infusing fresh life into the medieval liturgical heritage. As the monarch's officials prepared to print the *editio princeps* of the Taoist canon (1117–19), many local ritual traditions were written down for the first time. Among them was one called the *True Rites of the Heart of Heaven* (*T'ien-hsin cheng-fa*).[123] Its priests were medical missionaries who went throughout South China, bearing their healing rituals directly into the homes of Chinese and non-Chinese alike. In common with certain other Taoist masters of the time, these men were fundamentalists. They eschewed the complexities of ordinary Taoist liturgy and claimed to return to the original practices of the second-century Way of the Celestial Master. They attempted to restore the written talisman to its early primacy as the sole "drug" in Taoist therapy. In their system, even the most challenging exorcistic tasks could all be accomplished by using three basic talismans. These particular talismans appear to have been their own invention—hardly surprising, since ritual innovation was commonly presented as a restoration of primordial practices that had subsequently been distorted or forgotten.[124]

The *Great Rites of the Jade Hall* are a local variation on the *True Rites of the Heart of Heaven*. The story of their discovery brings us back, fittingly, to Mao Shan. Writing in 1158, Lu Shih-chung tells how in 1120 he had been guided by a marvelous light to a point on the summit of Mao Shan. Digging there, he found the text of these *Rites of the Jade Hall*, which ever after formed the core of his Taoist practice.[125] The tale seems allegorical; the section on meditation in Lu's work is mainly derived from the astral meditations revealed to Yang Hsi some eight hundred years earlier. These procedures were in fact the "peak" of Mao Shan ritual. Lu's account was thus entirely appropriate, and had the advantage of linking his public healing as well as his private meditation to the most prestigious shrine of Taoism. Whether as a result of this synthesis or simply owing to his forceful personality, Lu Shih-chung enjoyed great success. We have several contemporary descriptions of Lu at work performing exorcisms, invoking rain, and even raising the dead.[126]

Since we have found that sober medical treatises are permeated with ritual, we should not be shocked by the extreme rationality that marks the *Great Rites of the Jade Hall*. We read there that corpse-malady (*shih-chai*) or corpse-exhaustion (*shih-lao*) is transmitted by nine worms. It can also be caused by physical exhaustion and depletion. Its symptoms are exceedingly complex and differ according to how the ailment was contracted (*jan-hsi*). A room or foodstuffs can gradually infect one with it, as can clothing and breath, or air (*ch'i*).[127]

Instructions follow for treating three specific sorts of contagion: from buildings, clothing, and foodstuffs.[128] Abandoned houses and chambers, for example, may retain the *ch'i* of the disease for years after being completely deserted. Sealed in, there is no way for the malignant *ch'i* to escape. Thus the first person to open such a house receives the full brunt of the poison; horripilation and chills along the spine are the immediate symptoms, followed by coughing up blood, emaciation, alternating fever and chills, and dreams of falling.

In the case of transmission by clothing, the victim may have shared a bed with someone suffering from the disease or have become infected and developed the ailment through using such a person's clothing. After the original patient's death, the clothing, bedclothes, bed, and utensils that he used are all still impregnated with his corrupt *ch'i*, and a *ku* toxin lodges in them. Frugal persons sometimes keep such objects, and poor people may indeed find it difficult to replace them with new ones. Thus the way is prepared for horrible disaster.[129]

Infection through food comes from sharing food or medicine with a corpse-disease patient. Here the consequences need not be so dire because the patient is still alive and is thus the one playing host to most of the pathogens. Evidently our author, too, believed that the worms would only be liberated to wreak further mayhem at the death of their initial victim. This, of course, explains why the disease is normally described as picking off family members one by one. Someone infected by such contaminated food should be made to inhale and swallow the smoke from burning thirty-six talismans.[130] For infection from a building, talismans are to be burnt, their ashes administered in water to the victim, and another set of special talismans buried in the courtyard. For infection by clothing, the contaminated garments are to be fumigated with talismanic smoke, then cast away into an ever-flowing stream.[131] Throughout, of course, there are the usual spells and talismans.

Lu Shih-chung proceeds to describe the pathogenic worms that are responsible for corpse-disease. There are nine different sorts, of which six undergo a series of six metamorphoses. The worms can either be produced when one's viscera encounter some toxic substance or they can be transmitted through infection (*hsi-jan*) by one's family members. Lu then tells of the worms' periodic cycle through their victim's body. They are exceptionally methodical in their deadly progress, advancing to devour and withdrawing into a drugged sleep of satiation at regular intervals. Knowledge of their habits and whereabouts permits the healer to attack them with drugs or talismans when the dormant worms will offer the least resistance.[132] Although all of chapter 23 is taken up with this disease and its treatment, so great was the menace, so complex the pathology that Lu resumes his description in the middle of the next chapter, delving deeply into the worm's itineraries and giving an exact account of their shapes and colors. He also provides another, more elaborate series of talismans.

In the initial stage of their development, the larvae resemble infants with long hair, demons, or toads and have no fixed size. As the disease advances, they come to look like three-inch strands of twisted silk, lizards, centipedes, or shrimp. And so it continues, through six stages or metamorphoses, as the pathogens take on an array of insect or animal forms or the shapes of inanimate objects. By the time the sixth stage is reached, we find the worms appearing as double-stranded horsetails (said to represent the male and the female worms), as turtles, or as something resembling overcooked noodles. Some may have the form of birds, and when the birds' wings and feet are present, they are able to transmit the infestation (*chu*) over a distance of a thousand leagues. This infestation is what is known as "flying corpse."[133]

This text was first brought to the attention of the learned world in 1971 by

Liu Ts'un-yan, in an article on "The Taoists' Knowledge of Tuberculosis in the Twelfth Century." Liu translates in full the account of the worm's six stages of development. Though professing to find parts of the description "ludicrous," Liu is also willing to believe that twelfth-century Taoists possessed accurate knowledge of the life-cycle of tuberculosis bacilli. He suggests that we need only "disregard the apparently irrelevant or doubtful parts" of the text to recognize the substantial accuracy of the Taoist author's description, and speculates that Taoist priests may have gained their knowledge by using compound microscopes.[134]

It seems more to the point to note the entire consistency of this twelfth-century account with the earlier tradition. Both the internal and external "corpse-demons" had always been described as worms or larvae. Lu Shih-chung's description is far richer in substance than his predecessors' but not different in kind. The *chu* pathogens were "corpses" or "worms" from the beginning. There were, of course, *macroscopic* worms that yielded to anthelmintic drugs from the earliest times. And nothing could be more natural than the Kafkaesque correlation of insect metamorphosis with changes in human life and pathology. A visible manifestation of the offending "worms" sometimes formed a spectacular part of the treatment. After having the patient ingest a particular talisman, when night came on and all was still, the priest would prepare a cauldron of boiling oil. Candles were set all about, completely illuminating the room. Suddenly, we are told, living creatures will come crawling and flying. They should be seized at once and flung into the boiling oil. This was subsequently disposed of in a perpetually flowing stream—do not look back! The author rails against those secular charlatans who performed this therapeutic feat, the hunting of the vermin, as a mere trick of thaumaturgy. They would deceptively prepare creatures in advance to represent the pathogens. Yet even this experienced Taoist had to admit that the hunt produced results only one or two times out of ten, so entrenched might the larvae be.[135] Though a good deal more dramatic, this remains reminiscent of the worm-finding procedure recommended by Sun Ssu-mo in the mid-seventh century, in which the patient spat atop a wall and his toad-like or tadpole-like pathogens could be seen slithering away at the foot of the wall, as already mentioned. In either case, we are far from positing an early development of microscopy.

The most significant feature of this Taoist text is its recognition of contagion irrespective of family relationship. Corpse-disease results from contact with an infected patient or with articles imbued with his malignant emanations. Infection by a member of one's own family is only one of several possibilities, and it is clear that proximity—not shared guilt or genetic predisposition—is the cause. It is important to underscore the fading of this notion of "collective responsibility" among the Taoists, who had been most vocal on the subject of inherited doom eight hundred years before. Whether comparable advances had been made in treatment is, of course, another question.[136]

We have come a long way from fourth-century Mao Shan, and all too quickly. Eight hundred years have been crossed on the shoulders of a handful of medical authors, including one or two charismatic Taoist initiates. Our sampling of views has been hasty, yet several points now seem much clearer. It is first of all evident that no rigid barrier separated the preserve of the literary medicus or therapeutically concerned official from the world of the ritual healer. On the contrary, there seems to have been something of an alliance between Taoist masters and medical functionaries. In addition to a shared literacy they had a common cosmology, based on their implicit acceptance of a grand hierarchy extending through the visible world to both the heights and depths of the unseen. Taoist master and civil magistrate saw themselves in pivotal roles, each a fulcrum of the hierarchy's operations. Their work was parallel and complementary; on occasion, a single person might play the roles of both administrator and priest. Both accomplished their functions by virtue of a cosmic law (*fa*).

The greatest contrast we have uncovered is not between secular and spiritual healing; such a distinction may in fact be uncalled-for. Instead, the contrast appears to be a breach in Taoist tradition itself. For members of the fourth-century Hsü family, it was their own dead who furnished the chief cause for anxiety. The source of disease was firmly established in family history. But it was also intangible, even mystical, and subject to elaborate verbal qualifications and negotiations. For the twelfth-century Taoist master Lu Shih-chung, describing a similarly named disease-syndrome, all such concerns have evaporated. Instead, the perceived danger is in sharing the patient's food, and in the even greater peril of wearing his clothes or entering his room after his death. The malady is caught by a process of infection called *jan*, ("dyeing," or "contagion"). Thus this term, which had already been used in 610 by Ch'ao Yüan-fang to describe the spread of one variety of the disease, as mentioned above, could serve in 1158 to account for corpse-vector's contagious action as a whole. For Lu Shih-chung, as we have seen, any biological relationship between victims was irrelevant to explaining contagion.

Did this discovery correspond to a weakening in the power of dead ancestors to sanction social behavior? Had there perhaps been a general abatement of guilt toward dead family members in the centuries since the Hsüs had prayed and trembled at Mao Shan? An impossible question—but it may be answerable. By the end of the fourth century, Taoists had begun to develop elaborate rituals for the salvation of the dead. For Taoist masters, as for Buddhist monks, it proved infinitely more practical to rescue the legions of the dead than to wean the living from their cult. In this way the laity's concern could be safely channeled, by consecrated means, toward those ancestral preoccupations that had continued to obsess converts all along. Rituals for the dead—funerals and memorials and posthumous status-enhancements—soon came to occupy the largest part of the Taoist or Buddhist officiant's repertory. Through vastly expanded ritual media, living and dead could once more be safely summoned to a harmonious family reunion, with the Taoist priest or Buddhist monk acting as master of ceremonies. Thus were consciences salved and fresh tribute-offerings heaped at the gateways of the Law.

Although this clearly helps to explain certain marked changes in orientation over time, no such explanation can ever be complete or definitive. How can we account for the continuing consultation of spirit-mediums in cases of illness, and for the ongoing quest for causes among the unquiet dead? No doubt there is still an underlying insinuation that any "contagion" so drastic must be far more than a matter of chance. And those in closest contact with the victim, and so most likely to be infected, are still the members of his or her immediate family. Surely, in a resonant universe where every action evokes its inexorable effect, such a family's sufferings must come to pass because they all somehow deserved it. Depending on the dominant system of reference, an identical set of facts might support either a theory of quasi-impersonal contagion or one of hereditary predisposition, where "contagion" is the physical expression of collective spiritual guilt. Thus it is hard to avoid the conclusion that, in a moralistic society, contagiousness itself may be hereditary.[137]

Two Types of Karma

Sinologists have long known of a seemingly indigenous Chinese form of otherworldly retribution in which the sins of the fathers are visited upon their descendants. It is called *ch'eng-fu*, "received (or inherited) burden," and is first attested to in a large and problematic scripture, the *Book of the Great Peace*

(*T'ai-p'ing ching*). This proto-Taoist or para-Taoist work seems to have come into being during the first or second century C.E., although the text as we now have it is the result of reediting and expansion carried out in the sixth and again in the ninth centuries. One may surmise that the text's most idiosyncratic portions represent the oldest stratum. It is to this stratum that the sections describing "inherited burden" seem to belong. Yet there is no reason to believe that even the oldest portions emanate from a single author, and the work as a whole is so exasperatingly gnomic that it has so far resisted all attempts at elucidation and translation.[138]

In the text's principal treatise on "received burden," we are characteristically told that ten million words would still be too few to describe fully all the intricacies of this form of retribution. We may thus count ourselves lucky that the author proposes only a general outline. These are five types of "burden"—or rather, perhaps, five analogies to actions of the principal, hereditary human sort. For example, heaven and earth give birth to all living things, but if their creations lack virtue, they destroy them. Thus when the world is in turmoil, people do not have enough to eat, and the old and weak die of cold and starvation; local officials have not collected the harvest (or tax-grain), and the granaries and storehouses are empty. This is because the earth is injuring living creatures, and human beings "receive the burden" of it. The point here is, presumably, that the earth's destruction of crops comes about to avenge wrongs committed by some person quite distinct from the innocent multitudes who actually suffer from the failure of the harvest.

Or again, rather more intelligibly, we are invited to consider the case of a teacher who instructs his ten disciples wrongly, falsely. Each of them passes the fallacious teachings to ten more persons, thus causing a hundred people to be deluded. Each of the hundred next transmits the errors to ten victims of his own, the resultant thousand proceed to create ten thousand, and once the myriad misinformed have spread their mistruth on all sides, the entire world is in possession of the lie. Since by then it is the opinion of a vast majority, none dare contradict it and it becomes conventional wisdom. An entire population is deluded and comes to grief, all because a single man once failed to tell the truth. As the *Book of the Great Peace* puts it, "This is a catastrophe of 'received burden'; it is clear that the fault does not lie with those who come afterward. Yet future generations will not know with whom it originated so long before. Instead, they will blame people of their own time, thus compounding the misery."[139]

Another example: A man goes wailing through the marketplace, spreading a great lie, crying out that the earth is about to collapse and all will be overwhelmed by water. On going home from the market, everyone repeats this, so that ten thousand households are aware of it. Young and old tell it everywhere, and soon the entire world knows it. The world is deceived or deceiving, and the lie only gets bigger and more evil as it continues to spread. Such is the received burden of lying words.

A fourth case: In the southern mountains stands a great tree, shading an area of some hundred paces. It has a single trunk and countless branches, leaves, and fruits. Its roots are not firmly set in the earth and are damaged by a great storm of wind and rain. Up above, the millions and millions of branches, leaves, and fruits are all injured, so that they shrivel and perish. This is "received burden" among plants. The fault is clearly in the root, not the branches; can the branches then be blamed?

A fifth and final example: In the southern mountains is a poisonous miasma (*ch'i*). The mountain is unable to retain it, and in spring it is carried along on the south wind until it covers the sun and moon, the entire world is afflicted by it, and many people die. At the outset, this was simply an effluvium seeping forth from the southern mountains. How, then, does it come about that people throughout the world have received the burden and are falling ill and dying? The people of the time make it worse by saying, "Heaven is killing you because of your misdeeds." Is this not abusive? These people have committed no transgressions, yet they receive and bear this calamity. Their ethereal souls have been inculpated (by the judges of the dead), and living people blame them as well. The miasma mounts until it moves heaven itself. Yet the original fault lies with the mountain's evil emanation, which was carried by the wind and came to cause this received burden.[140]

Thus does the author of the *Book of the Great Peace* illustrate the occult, distant causes of present distress, while exonerating the unfortunate sufferers themselves. The most dramatic result of this is a radical revision of a basic Chinese axiom of social cosmology. Heaven and earth are normally supposed to respond immediately to the good or evil deeds of the ruler. His benevolence will blazon forth astrologically and be rewarded by the appearance of auspicious beasts and bumper harvests. Conversely, the sovereign's wicked behavior will evoke dread anomalies in the greater cosmos, tear society apart with dissension, and cause disasters to proliferate across the land.

Yet here we are being told that the reigning monarch is not at fault when things go wrong: "It all lies very far back and still farther back. Yet foolish people do not realize this, and so accuse the current ruler and the current people; is this not to make them suffer multiple inculpation? The world is entirely evil, and they are unable to realize this. Even if the monarch were to have the virtue of ten thousand men, what would he alone be able to do about it?"[141] A welcome message for the sovereign—who was evidently intended as the book's ideal reader—but also for the ordinary man, whose sufferings might now prove to be the result of someone else's misconduct.

The text goes on to insist that this sort of deferred retribution is the reason for all kinds of otherwise inexplicable misfortunes. Everyone wants to eat, yet sick people cannot eat and so perish. Everyone enjoys sex and wants to have children to make sacrifices to the spirits and to pray for good fortune (i.e., their parents' posthumous beatitude), yet some people are unable to have children. Everyone wants to be good and handsome, yet there are certainly vicious and ugly people. All such cases can only be explained as manifestations of "received burden." As a remedy, the author recommends "guarding the One"—that is, meditating on the single, undifferentiated unity of the primordial *ch'i*, source of all phenomena. "One is the beginning of counting. One is the origin of primordial *ch'i*."[142] Evidently, this meditation is meant to function as a beneficial, therapeutic analogue to "received burden" and its ills. If the multiple forms of evil can be traced back to a single root cause, so can the manifestations of good. One must realize cosmogony in one's own person by focusing on the single source of all phenomena.[143]

This seems, then, to be a highly generalized revision of the theory of ancestral guilt and inherited responsibility. For the living, there is to be no soul-searching, no penitence and confession, no guilt and no reproach. They are simply to get on with the utopian work of perfection, through societal reform and the most elementary type of meditation. Like many long-winded prophets and missionaries, the author of the *Book of the Great Peace* has a very simple message, and his loquacity serves the cause of radical reform. Elsewhere, the book distinguishes three degrees of duration or intensity of inherited suffering, which differ according to one's place in the social hierarchy. For monarchs, the "flow" lasts 30,000 years; for officers of state, 3,000 years; for ordinary people, 300 years. This, the author insists, is the reason that people can consistently perform good deeds and yet suffer grave misfortune. Conversely, evildoers are often seen to flourish. In both cases, it has nothing to do with the living person himself but is all a matter of his moral patrimony—the deeds of his forebears.[144]

Problems in dating and localizing the text make it difficult to decide whether or not all this represents a reaction to a specific rival system of explanation. The text's criticism of "those who blame living people" for things they cannot help does call to mind the standard view of official responsibility for calamity with which Chinese rulers and their local representatives were encumbered, however. Moreover, there is much in the procedures of penitence and confession imposed by Buddhism and early Taoism that might have sparked this exculpation of the sufferers. Yet it would be a mistake to view the *Book of the Great Peace*, as is often done, as direct testimony of some primitive, Ur-Chinese state of affairs. Like all the other documents in the case, it represents a particular crystallization of notions about ancestors. It may also reflect, in its curiously tedious manner, an authentically Chinese species of "karma" that the early Mao Shan initiates embellished differently, with their own characteristic élan.

The crux lies in your exact relation to your own forebears. Not only may you be suffering from one of your own ancestor's sins, you may also be reenacting his life: You may in fact be he. Your existence may be more fully predetermined than you ever imagined; it may not even be your own.

The *Book of the Great Peace* posits a series of five generations (inclusive), after which the most distant forebear is reborn. The five generations comprise a complete circuit, exhausting a particular emanation of *ch'i*. The fifth-generation ancestor then becomes human again, and the cycle is perpetually renewed.[145] In this system, the fifth-generation ancestor and his senior living descendant appear to stand in a special relationship. Both are somehow pivotal, at the frontiers of life and death. The senior living member is soon to die, the senior dead member is about to be reborn—or possibly already is reborn, for if (as the *Book of the Great Peace* states) eighty years marks the standard length of human life, and statutory virility is attained (as it was) at seventeen or twenty, then the lineage's oldest living father might easily have son, grandson, and great-grandson in the world he is about to leave. Upon the arrival of his own fifth-generation descendant (inclusive), he himself will depart to replenish the dark pentad whose ranks his own fifth-generation ancestor has just left to be reborn. (This cyclical rhythm is recognized in standard Chinese kinship terminology, where the word for great-great-grandson is *hsüan-sun*, "descendant of the invisible, or otherworldly, forefather").

What is the effect of all this on character and fate? It may be too much to require consistency from a book that is so often inconsistent, but we are bound to recall the statement about the span of action of "received burden." For ruling families, that span is 30,000 years; for ministerial households, 3,000 years; and for ordinary folk, 300 years. Since (at least on my reading of the evidence) the five-generation cycling of the living and dead would recur roughly every twenty years, and one would in fact be incarnating one's own ancestor in the ninth degree (inclusive), the average total span involved at any one time would be about 180 years. If we reckon generations according to the age of seventeen, which in early medieval practice commonly stood for the canonical age of twenty and attainment of male adulthood, we get a total of 153 years for the "ten" (really nine) generations involved. In that case, two sets of ten generations would more or less fill the 300-year span. But all this seems too abstract and theoretical. It is asking too much to reconcile the two statements. What matters most is clearly the five-generation turnaround, involving the identity of members of a single patrilineage at nine degrees' remove.

To escape from the *Book of the Great Peace*'s trackless desert of theory, we must return again to Mao Shan, where the Taoists have names and faces. We have seen that Hsü Mi owed his happy destiny to Hsü Ching, his ancestor in the seventh generation. Was this link also one of identity? Was the fourth-century Hsü Mi actually the second-century Hsü Ching, reborn? Nothing in the Mao Shan dossier encourages us to assume this. The documents simply underscore the polarity between the perfectly benign seventh-degree forebear and the ambivalent deeds of the generation most recently deceased, the source of so many present troubles. The Hsü family did not need to look back three hundred years for their "inherited burden." It was sitting on their doorstep.

Yet there were distant determinants far back in time that also had to be reckoned into the family's destiny. When they first began giving Yang Hsi messages for Hsü Mi, the Perfect Ones encouraged Hsü Mi to retire from court life and devote himself to the practice of Perfection at Mao Shan. They told him that they would only appear to him personally if he first abandoned profane society: "We will give our Tao to Hsü the Taoist who dwells in the mountains, not to Senior Officer Hsü who lives at court."[146] They insisted, too, that he purge himself of sexual desires, which they claimed obstructed his celestial vocation. At first Hsü Mi promised to comply, but as time went on and he showed no signs of changing his ways, the Perfect Ones told him a tale. Long before, in the reign of King Wu of the Chou dynasty (traditionally 1169–1116 B.C.E.), there lived a certain Hsieh Ch'ang-li, who had achieved immortality. His younger brother, Hsieh Lü, was preparing himself for the same goal but did not attain it. He could not repress his sexual longings, and this caused him to fail the seven trials he had to undergo to test his fitness. The flesh was weak. Still, Hsieh Lu had a very gentle disposition and was also especially fond of music. To fortify his spirits, he would sing aloud as he practiced the Tao in solitude. As a result, his inner spirits and ethereal souls were so strengthened that when he died he did not undergo dissolution.

Some time before, the immortal Hsieh Ch'ang-li had petitioned the Most High that his unsuccessful younger brother (whose corporeal constituents were presumably carrying on intact in some mountain retreat) be allowed to be reborn in the world. Specifically, he asked that Hsieh Lü be permitted to profit from the credit established with the invisible world by the benevolent Hsü Ching—namely, by being reborn as Hsü Ching's descendant Hsü Mi. It was Ch'ang-li's wish that his brother, in his new existence, should have the opportunity of eliminating the carnal obstacles that had earlier kept him from success, and so have a fresh opportunity of gaining celestial immortality.

This, then, was Hsü Mi's former life: He had been Hsieh Lu, the musical carnalist. The immortal Hsieh Ch'ang-li, now among his most ardent celestial well-wishers, had been his elder brother in that life. In that long-ago existence, too, lay the origin of Hsü Mi's present obstructive entanglements with desires of the flesh. It was all the more urgent, then, that he now strive speedily to eliminate a weakness that had once before debarred him from attaining the Tao.[147]

Here at last we have a mode of explanation that owes nothing either to the biological family or to Chinese tradition (though Hsieh Ch'ang-li's fraternal interest does provide a homely, sino-familial touch).[148] This is Indian exegesis, Buddhist karma undisguised. Hsü Mi's younger colleague and contemporary, Ch'ih Ch'ao (339–77), wrote a Buddhist catechism, "The Essentials of Religion" (*Feng-fa yao*), in which he emphasised that karmic retribution does not involve the relatives of the sinner. Being based on long-ago events quite unconnected with one's own family history, the fulfillment of karma necessarily appears paradoxical. Notorious tyrants have enjoyed long reigns, while exemplary students have died years before their prime. A father and his son, too, can have entirely different fates. Thus, Ch'ih Ch'ao insists, in Buddhism family members do not suffer for crimes committed by one of their number.[149]

It was no doubt necessary to dwell on karma's independence from biological heredity, given the Chinese context. Apart from this, though, there seems to be a curious similarity between Ch'ih Ch'ao's exposition of karma and the pronouncements on "received burden" in the *Book of the Great Peace*. Both stress their system's superficial inconsistencies: The good may suffer, the unjust may prosper. And both exonerate present-day victims, though in different ways. In the *Book of the Great Peace*, their innocence is total; the crime was committed by someone entirely other, long ago (the potential consequences of fifth-generation recycling seem not to have been factored in here). For Ch'ih Ch'ao and his fellow-Buddhist, the fault is indeed one's own and is not shared with one's family, yet it was also committed long ago, in another body and by a "self" whose identity might well be matter for debate. Moreover, precise knowledge of the fault is given to very few, if any. Thus the most general formulae of penitence and confession will suffice to purge it, and countervailing good deeds performed in the present life will then tip the balance of merit in your favor.

The sophisticated Taoists of Mao Shan were able to synthesize both systems. Like Hsü Mi, they stood at the intersection of two discrete strands of destiny, two separate "genealogies of morals." Hsü Mi embodied not only a morally charged biological ancestry but a comparably weighty pseudo-Indian "past life" as well. Their convergence had framed his present existence, and both channels of fate depended on his current course of behavior for their future outcome. This is heavy moral overdetermination indeed. Thanks to his special contacts in the heavens, Hsü Mi might interrogate history quite as fully as his own conscience, then exculpate, exonerate, shrive and salve himself, in either Indian or Chinese fashion (or a mixture of both). Despite his repeated professions of Taoist dedication, it may be that such an array of spiritual amenities is found (outside the madhouse) only among luxurious worldlings.[150]

It is not as if the two "karmas," Indian and Chinese, were ever entirely distinct in Chinese life. There were parallels not only in their displacing the crime from the present to the past but also in the methods of treatment, which involved penitence and confession. In the case of Buddhism, the Law had evolved initially to regulate the conduct of a monastic community. Two hundred fifty vows were attached to ordination. Breaking any one of them, or any one of a series of further prohibitions, called for a particular class or degree of confession. As lay Buddhism grew in importance, liturgical confession became a vital feature of the active Buddhist life in early medieval China. Its ritual status inspired penitentiary formularies for recitation that purged the worshipper of past as well as present transgressions. And if both karmas used an infinitely expansible past to explain the present, they also drew on a wealth of historical examples to enforce moral standards in the present, so as not to prejudice the future.

Amongst the Taoists, written confession had from the beginning been part of the treatment of disease, as already mentioned. Initially—at least according to outside observers—the focus was said to have been on one's own sins as the source of one's own ailments. The offense against the Tao was manifest as an offense against one's self, and earnest confession both righted the spiritual wrong and healed the physical body. This can now be viewed in relation to the denunciations, in the *Book of the Great Peace*, of those who blame living persons for their own misfortunes. Did the author have Taoists and/or Buddhists specifically in mind?

In the fourth-century Mao Shan materials, we find a slightly more evolved state of affairs. There are two formulae for confession, one connected with the Five Planets (and so with the Five Phases, constituents of all things), the other with the stars of the Northern Dipper (Ursa Major), which systematically observe and record all the misdeeds of the living. For the first, one should use the "five days of communication," which are days of assembly in heaven. Kneeling, the penitent confesses both all the faults of his ancestors to the seventh degree and his own "thousand crimes and ten thousand transgressions" ever since he came into the world. He asks that his name be removed from the Black Register of the infernal Three Officers, and that he be permitted to disport himself among the Five Planets. The second method involved bringing down the stars of the Northern Dipper one by one, each on a different day and into a different organ of the body. Of each of the seven stars, the supplicant requests that all the faults and misdeeds of himself and his forebears to the seventh degree be expunged from the record. When, in a final address, he brings down the eighth and ninth stars (which lie alongside the Dipper's handle and are usually invisible to the eyes of the profane), he alters the number of generations from seven to nine. This text gives the exact liturgical formulae to be pronounced, which are more general than specific: "faults of unkindness, disobedience," "faults of impurity," "offenses," "evil deeds."[151]

Such is the richness of the Mao Shan dossier, that, apart from such normative, prescriptive works, it contains the actual text of a confession written by Hsü Mi's youngest son, Hsü Hui. During an illness of his father and elder brother, he addressed a formal statement to the senior deity among Yang Hsi's contacts, the Lady Wei of the Southern Peak. He declares that a dream he had earlier that night revealed to him that his family's present troubles must have been caused by some fault of his own. He ponders his faults with all his strength and regrets that he has done nothing to atone for past transgressions. He is filled with shame when he recalls how many times he has pleaded for an unmerited indulgence, but now pledges with all his heart that from today he will make a new beginning and purify his heart afresh. He begs that the Lady Wei pardon both his father and elder brother and excuse them from punishment. He himself is not as diligent as they, and so pleads that retribution for the fault with which they are charged be visited upon himself, and that his father and brother be pardoned. If his divine mother has pity on them, he will ponder his faults and atone for his transgressions, and the entire family will respectfully acknowledge her favor. For the rest of their lives they will feel that on this occasion they have been born anew.[152]

This document adds a fresh element to our dossier of legal negotiations. A younger son here offers himself as hostage for the recovery of his elders, including his own father. As in the prescriptive formularies, the "confession" itself is of the most general sort. Like the liturgical confessions, it is a supplication more than a declaration of repentance. Above all, it serves as a formal means for Hsü Hui to offer himself to the vengeful powers that are afflicting his father and brother, to give his life for theirs. Once again, this conflicts sharply with the contemporary challenge to the idea of collective responsibility put forward by Ch'ih Ch'ao in his "The Essentials of Religion." But it should not be imagined that Ch'ih Ch'ao's call for individual responsibility for one's own transgressions signaled the beginning of a revolution in the diagnosis and treatment of morally determined ailments. On the contrary, such assertions "were later overwhelmed by the further development of the institution of the family. People of later times on the whole accepted the principle of joint responsibility as a matter of fact"[153]—as they apparently always had done, and continue to do in the twentieth century, when vows undertaken to secure the recovery of an ailing parent are still common.

In the event, Yang Hsi's divine informants were able to report that the outlook for father and brother was not after all so grave. The Lady of the Southern Peak declared, "Hu-ya [the elder brother] should be careful not to step on impurities again, nor to see fresh human excrement. When the spirits of the body's three divisions are terrified, they delight in killing their host."[154] Another of her colleagues, the youngest of the three Mao brothers, told Yang Hsi, "Some students of the Tao never pay proper attention to what they are doing. They bring all sorts of ailments on themselves and then place the blame on the spirits. Those who expose themselves to the wind, lie in the damp, and then blame others for the results of their own negligence are raving. How can we tell such people of the sublime mysteries?"[155] From this it transpires that Hsü Hu-ya's illness did not have a moral or "spiritual" origin but was the result of sheer carelessness on his part. This clearly placed it in a separate category, demanding an entirely different approach to treatment.

Medicinal drugs may have been entirely supplanted by confession and written documents in early Taoism. Healing without recourse to drugs remains a popular theme in hagiography. Yet in the fourth-century texts from Mao Shan, there is ample evidence that the traditional materia medica were being drawn on by the Hsü family and their Taoist friends. Acupuncture and moxabustion are also mentioned. Third- and fourth-century writings from the local, pre-Taoist occult tradition are truffled with the names of healing plants and minerals. Then came the region's Taoist evangelization. To synthesize Taoism with their inherited drug culture, it appears that the first generation of Mao Shan adepts tried to establish a distinction between ailments with a moral etiology and those caused purely by accident, negligence, or chance. Amoral afflictions that were not the result of just retribution by the celestial recordkeepers or of vengeance from the spirits of the dead were susceptible to treatment by ordinary secular medicine and pharmacology. The way was thus cleared for great Taoists like T'ao Hung-ching to become great scholars of pharmacy.

Despite the fact that medicinal drugs, too, could be assimilated into the all-inclusive Mao Shan system, the emphasis in healing was still on nonmaterial means. This is exemplified in the Mao Shan scripture that contains the largest number of drug names, the *Book of the Devil-Destroyers of Wisdom* (*Hsiao-mo chih-hui ching*, HY 1333). "Devil-destroyers," we are told, is a kenning for "drugs," and the work's first chapter consists of a long list of pharmaka, classified according to the celestial region with which they are in rapport. This inventory is furnished not for pharmacological reference but, rather, for recitation. The adept should isolate himself completely and chant the scripture straight through, three thousand times. He should not interrupt this marathon recitation. If he does so, he will be severely punished. Should he have to break off in the middle, he must start all over again from the beginning. Thus it appears that the virtue of all these healing drugs will be actualized for the benefit of him who simply steeps himself utterly in the droning evocation of their names.[156]

As we will see in the following chapters, various classes of beings and objects might be catalogued to provide matter for prophylactic recitation. Here we have drugs; elsewhere in both Taoist and Buddhist scriptures, we find lists of disease-demons, or the names of their haunts, or the names of the guardian gods who dwell within the adept's body. As they intoned the names of hundreds of Buddhas, past, present, and to come, Buddhists strained their thoughts toward infinite space and infinite time. Concentration on sound, and on the exact number of repetitions prescribed for efficacy, tended to marginalize many of the more tedious and cumbersome aspects of the religious life. Buddhist Mahāyāna scriptures had already promised that even a hardened sinner *in articulo mortis* could be saved by simply reciting the name of the Buddha Amitābha. What function of religion or ritual might not then be achieved by such methods? Though hostile forces lurk all about him, let the adept only suffuse himself with invincible sound and he will be secure.[157]

Apocalyptic Intimations

Unlike Buddhism, Taoism has not generally been noted for doctrinal subtlety or elaborate speculative constructions and was never dominated by leisured, sophisticated monks. Most of the books in the Taoist canon are ritual manuals; the practical aspect has always been central for Taoism. (Recent scholarship is finally beginning to recognize that this was also true of Buddhism, despite all its endless monkish lucubrations.) The Mao Shan dossier is unique in its frankness and fullness of detail, but it obviously rests on a basis of widely shared belief and practice. Extrapolating from the Mao Shan texts to recover something of the spirit of early medieval Taoism, we confront a limitless web of tense personal relationships, each with a corresponding series of ritual resolutions. (Even the best Hsü ancestors probably figured as demonic agents in someone else's family history.) Striking, too, in these documents, is an overwhelming sense of the immanence of evil. Prior readings in the better-known texts of medieval Chinese literature do not prepare one for this dark preoccupation with demonic forces, the tense watching and waiting that attend the first signs of illness, the urgent search for causes among the malevolent dead. It almost seems to recall the tension-fraught atmosphere of sixteenth- and seventeenth-century Europe. In their attempt to pin down the origins of disease, Taoist priests seem to have been conducting a witch-hunt into the past. Quite apart from the specific details of personal interaction in each case, this also hints at a feature of their underlying cosmology—namely, that such a tortured inquisition into family history could be justified only if those concerned were truly convinced that the world as they knew it was ultimately abandoned to the forces of evil.

This was indeed the position taken by early Taoists. In their view, the phenomenal world had been provisionally turned over to the demonic princes, powers, and dominations of the dead. The situation is described by a fifth-century Taoist master, Lu Hsiu-ching (406–77):

> In the recent past, there was great trouble and turmoil, and a falling away from earlier simplicity. The cosmic order lost its cohesion, and men became confounded with demons. The old and worn-out emanations (*ch'i*) of the Six Heavens came to claim official status and began calling themselves by high and mighty titles. These emanations made themselves into the various elemental demons (*ching*, "essential spirits") and the five types of noxious specters. They assembled the dead generals of defeated armies and dead soldiers of rebel armies, the men calling themselves "generals" and the women "ladies." They led spectral troops, marching and encamping through the heavens and over the earth. They imposed their rule by force and brought trouble into the temples of men. They demanded sacrificial offerings and led the people into confusion. Their worshippers butchered the three sorts of sacrificial beasts and expended their entire resources, pouring out their wealth and exhausting their substance. Yet they received no benefits from all this—only disaster. Those who died violently, cut off in their prime, are too many to be numbered.[158]

We are already familiar with the Six Heavens as the home of the unhallowed dead and as the repository of "worn-out breath" (*ku-ch'i*). Now, though, we find the intrusion of the demons and the dead into human affairs to be the result of a process of inexorable historical decline. Matters had not always been so. Once, closer to the beginning of things, there had been purity and simplicity. The living and the dead enjoyed their separate realms, and the boundaries between men and demons were well-defined. But as time went on, the demonic powers became unruly and burst forth from their confinement. Lu Hsiu-ching's account unmasks them as the force behind the cults favored by ordinary people. From the perspective shared by Taoism and the Chinese state, all "unofficial" worship was essentially demonic and ill-omened. Lu Hsiu-ching suggestively describes the specters as invading ancestral temples and intimidating people into slaughtering sacrificial animals for them. The martial character of all this is stressed, as well as the military background of their ghostly associates. The objects of Taoist and official criticism were chiefly hero-cults dedicated to dead warriors who, slain before their destined time, still retained vast stocks of vital force.[159] From the Taoist point of view, all such bloodthirsty cults were impure. For the state, this worship of "dead generals of defeated armies" was potentially subversive. Lu Hsiu-ching reveals the true nature of the Six Heavens, the world of the dead, as the home of lost causes.

Taoism had come into existence with the precise aim of putting an end to this parlous state of affairs. The militant demons would be driven off by armed force, and resolute legal action would soon settle the unquiet dead. But even as they outlined this program, Taoist authors also revealed the full extent of the peril. The present dangers will only intensify as time goes on, and current misery is but a foretaste of the horrors to come. The historical process now underway cannot be arrested. All the disease, bloodshed, and natural catastrophes that now afflict the world are but signs of the approaching apocalypse, and the tempo of mayhem will only accelerate until the End.

Early Taoism is shot through with apocalyptic warnings—and this was no mere obsession of nameless have-nots or of the oppressed.[160] Even the upper-class Mao Shan revelations pulse with the rhythms of apocalyptic urgency. The fundamental Mao Shan scripture was a life of the savior Li Hung (another Lao-tzu persona) entitled *Annals of the Sage of Latter Time, Lord of the Golden Gateway of Supreme Purity* (HY 442).[161] Li Hung was destined to found a new heaven and earth, and his biography includes a prophecy of the coming destruction of the world.[162] This event will be followed by the Sage's advent, and the *Annals* lays down the programmatic unfolding of events. It lists the duties and qualifications of those mortals who will be chosen to survive the cataclysm and take office in the imminent kingdom of the Elect. Even now, while waiting for all this to be realized, such persons are to study a substantial collection of celestial literature that has been designed to prepare them for their future state. The *Annals* lists the titles of several of these books—manuals of ritual and meditation.[163] Subsequently, an entire corpus of scripture was revealed to implement this prophecy.

For the first Mao Shan adepts, in the 360s, signs of the times were everywhere about them: geophysical changes, violence and strife, and, above all, the prevalence of demonically induced disease. The *Annals* foretold a major crisis, to begin around the year 384, a year of the monkey:

> In an age of birds and beasts, when the auspices of the state are hovering on extinction . . . in the year *chia-shen* (monkey), earlier and thereafter and at

> that very time, the Good shall be selected and wrong-doers destroyed. Above shall mingle pestilence and flood, while war and fire join everywhere below. All wrong-doers shall be annihilated, and the workers of evil shall perish utterly. Those who love the Tao will hide in the earth, while the Good will ascend up into the mountains. The noisome host of the afflictors will everywhere run riot and be cast into the gaping abyss. So shall the final judgment be effected. Then, in the year *jen-ch'en* (dragon, i.e., 392), on the sixth day of the third month, the Lord Sage will descend and shine forth in splendor in the presence of the multitude.[164]

It was to the ultimate descent of a great Taoist divinity that the faithful raised their eyes from the carnage all around them. Early Taoist eschatology was imbued with messianic fervor; the end of the world was at hand, and Taoists ardently looked forward to salvation in an exclusive kingdom of the saints. This explains their obsession with evil in the world in which they provisionally dwelt. The prevalence of evil was convincing proof of the decay of ordinary human society, and so fully confirmed the message of Taoist prophecy. Above all, though, it was a necessary precondition for the world's transformation into a Taoist paradise, for how else could evil be cleansed from the world if not by evil itself? The ultimate rationale behind all the intrusive demonic manifestations was simply to purge the world of evil-doers. Demons and demonically possessed humans would eventually wipe each other out, leaving the field to the Taoists. Meanwhile, the faithful had merely to sit tight and weather the firestorm of wrath, using all the sanctified means at their command.

Under such conditions, survival was evidently in large part dependent on taking due precautions. Even when all the perils emanating from a family's past had been dispelled, one's own behavior had to be carefully monitored. There was always the danger of committing some offense against morality, but inadvertent contact with impurity, too, might lead to illness. In fact, the seemingly opposite etiologies—one moral, one accidental—may actually meet and coalesce on this ground. Both may transgress the rules of purity. It is not surprising that the future Elect were provided with a short rule-book called "Prohibitions of the Immortals"; significantly, it was appended to the *Annals of the Sage of Latter Time*, in which the prophecy of doom and promise of reward were both spelled out.[165]

The *Annals* includes a very curious list of physiognomic indicators, signs which, when present on the face or body, foretell not only a person's predestination for immortality but even the exact rank he or she will occupy in the celestial hierarchy.[166] The immortals' prohibitions are organized as a decalogue, listing ten categories of negative injunctions. In contrast to all the innately auspicious body-markings, these ten undesirable modes of behavior are termed "signs of failure to achieve immortality," and the practitioner is firmly warned not to rely on a promising constellation of body-marks; he must also be attentive to behavior.[167]

The first commandment in the Mao Shan decalogue is:

> Do not delight in licentiousness. Licentiousness makes the body's ethereal souls [the three *hun*] seep out, and the luminous vital-essence (*ching*) becomes desiccated. The body's indwelling spirits are scorched, the seminal souls [the seven *p'o*] disperse, the bones become brittle and their marrow is befouled. The ethereal souls cry out in their transcendent receptacle, and their plaint is heard in the pavilions of heaven. The body's three palaces [brain, heart, genitals] dispute the mastery, and their fetal- and sprout-spirits are in sorrow and confusion. This is the first sign destructive of immortality.[168]

The list continues in this fashion, each injunction being followed by an account of the damage done to the body by infringement. The second commandment is "Do not rob by stealth, or commit deeds of violence"; the third is "Do not become drunk with wine." ("Drunkenness with wine causes the body's substance to fall into decay; its inner spirit-officials are in turmoil, the ethereal souls forget their chamber, and the spermatic souls wander in the dwellings of demons. The child-spirit flies up out of range, the throat is parched, the brain exhausted.") The fourth injunction is "Do not become defiled by impurities"; the fifth is "Do not eat the animal of your parents' destiny"; and the sixth is "Do not eat the animal of your own destiny."[169] These are the animals presiding over successive years in the twelve-year sequence (rat, ox, tiger, hare, dragon, snake, horse, sheep, monkey, cock, dog, pig); one is thus forbidden to consume flesh of the beasts ruling one's own and one's parents' natal years. In his commentary on the pharmacopoeia, T'ao Hung-ching refers to this rule and states that Taoists may only eat the flesh of deer and pheasants, the two sorts of animal which, unlike the twelve, have no affiliation with the stars.[170]

The seventh commandment runs:

> Do not eat the flesh of the six domestic beasts [horse, cow, sheep, pig, dog, chicken]. If you do, the vital breaths will be clogged and the body will become putrid, the vital essence will be turbid and the inner spirits obstructed. The brain will yellow, the teeth dry out, and the spleen will fill with dead breath. The ethereal souls will be devoid of perfection, the spermatic souls will indulge in malignant activities. Your body will be drowned in the Great Abyss, and your bones will want only to sink into the earth.

The eighth commandment is another dietary rule: "Do not eat the five sharp-flavored herbs" (i.e., onions, garlic, chives, scallions, and radish). The ninth injunction runs:

> Do not kill living creatures, including insects. If you take up arms against all living beings, their accumulated corpses and blood will form a store of resentment against you. Your deeds will be violent, your spermatic souls vicious, your ethereal souls will war among themselves. Your child-spirit will run hither and yon, your infant-like spirits will desert their posts. Your corpse will be immersed in a cauldron, boiled in water, and seared by fire.

In this case, a deed of murder directly affects the comportment of the body's denizens—and the ultimate punishments that threaten the malefactor are drawn from the stock of Buddhist purgatories.[171]

Category ten is something of a grab bag, a collection of miscellaneous prohibitions. One must not urinate while facing north, or while gazing on the Three Luminaries (sun, moon, stars), nor is it licit to face north while combing one's hair or undressing (for Taoists, north was the most honorable direction, site of the noblest stars). On the fourth day of the first month, do not kill living creatures while facing north. Do not eat fish on the ninth of the second month. On the third of the third, do not eat the inner organs of animals or the inner part of plants. On the eighth of the fourth month, do not cut plants or chop down trees. Do not look at blood on the fifth of the fifth, dig in the earth on the sixth of the sixth, think of evil things on the seventh of the seventh. Do not buy footware or things that will touch the leg on the fourth of the eighth, set up a bed on the ninth of the ninth, blame other people on the fifth of the tenth, bathe or wash your hair on the eleventh of the eleventh. "These are the major prohibitions of the people of heaven. Their infringement counts as a serious crime, to be investigated by the Three Officers."[172]

Quoting this list *in extenso* nicely sets off the text's cosmic prophecies of doom and renewal against the often rather niggling anxieties of daily life. While waiting for the end of the world, one must remember not to eat fish on the ninth day of the second month, or buy shoes on the fourth of the eighth! One inspiration for this disjointed decalogue lies in the ten basic precepts of Buddhism (not to kill, steal, be unchaste, lie, slander others, insult others, chatter, covet possessions, become angry, or doubt). But the other source is found in ancient China, in the calendrical taboos that loomed so large in the conduct of government.[173] There are traces, too, of the complex astrological determinants that ruled Chinese (and Japanese) private as well as public life all through the Middle Ages.[174] This odd mingling of legislation with calendrical taboos epitomizes the Taoist synthesis, particularly when we note that it is all expressed in the context of physical health. Punishment for disobedience is at once manifest in the malefactor's own body. And with the exception of rules two (stealing) and nine (murder), the injunctions all concern dietetics or sex.

It is well that members of the Mao Shan circle attended to morality and/or purity from time to time, because otherwise all the *Annals'* assurances of predestined success might have turned their heads. Discovery on their own bodies of any of the configurations described in the *Annals* would have promoted the loftiest expectations; and the nightly words of the Perfect Ones to Yang Hsi also assured the Hsü family that they were definitely among the Elect. Their sense of privileged immunity to worldly ailments must have been reinforced when they read the messiah Li Hung's own words to readers of the *Annals*:

> The names of all those who obtain my *Annals* are fixed in the celestial registers, being those of the highest rank, inscribed in jade on tablets of gold. And even should one who has received my *Annals* do no more than treasure them in secret, without ever accomplishing other practices, he will yet be granted "deliverance by means of a corpse" in the full light of day. If, too, having obtained this text, he should cease to pay reverence to the Tao and its virtue, desist from the practice of Perfection, and become confounded with the profane, his nature reverting and resolution failing—a person of this sort must be a feckless wastrel of the meanest abilities and not a person of fragrant ossature—yet even he, inasmuch as he has obtained my *Annals*, shall still be given office as an agent-beneath-the-earth. In that capacity he may eliminate the impurities in his system and cleanse away the corruption of his spermatic souls. Thereafter he may gradually advance by degrees, until he arrives at an awakening from the great dream.[175]
>
> Be you diligent, then, and take heed! Do not divulge these my *Annals* to miscreant corpses [i.e., the profane]! And should you pass through the apocalyptic calamities of pestilence, flood, and fire bearing these my *Annals* on your person, none of the malignant influences or fell emanations of forest or mountain will be able to assail you. All others will rejoice when they behold you, since the jade youths who accompany the text will also extend their protection to your person. Should any evil-doer accost you with wicked intent, I myself will send the powers of mountains and rivers to take his life. Do not imagine that the Tao is remote, and so wonder that its transcendent perception should accompany you. From the Great Emptiness, in Celestial Vacuity, I look upon you as closely as your eye looks upon your nose.[176]

Quite apart from its prophecies and all the meditations it recommended, the text of the *Annals* was itself a matchless talisman, a badge of identity and passport through the carnage. And the ten divine guardians ("jade youths") attendant on the text would also protect its bearer. Thus the reader was assured that mere possession of the work vouchsafed him a place in the otherworldly hierarchy, for were he not predestined to achieve this, he would never have obtained a copy of the *Annals* in the first place.[177] Also, once the adept has the *Annals* in hand, he can confidently await the revelation of the remaining scriptures of Supreme Purity, which will fully inform him on the rituals he should practice. These celestial texts are exceedingly rare and secret, "Yet should one succeed in having them transmitted to him, be he wise man or fool, he has only to practice their teaching with zealous heart to become a winged immortal."[178]

How easily this soaring, visionary euphoria carries one off from a world of troubles and trivializes the host of mundane afflictions. It was the privilege of these hyperliterate Taoist adepts to assimilate and transmute all the elements of fourth-century religious life, to reconcile opposites by appealing to supreme revealed authority. An ancestry riddled with doom yet charged with blessing; two types of karma, one domestic, one exotic; healing by forensic paperwork and healing by drugs; ardent spiritual zeal and slothful, worldly self-indulgence; assured salvation and a crotchety morality; asceticism and eroticism; court life and the mountain hermitage—at Mao Shan, old elements were fused in a new synthesis, on which Taoist healers were subsequently able to draw throughout the Middle Ages.

2

DEMONOLOGY AND EPIDEMIOLOGY

Wo keine Goetter sind, walten Gespenster.

(Where there are no gods, ghosts preside.)

NOVALIS

Buddho-Taoist Eschatology

Taoists were not the only ones in early medieval China to be convinced of the imminent collapse of society and end of the world. The Chinese Buddhist pilgrim Fa-hsien, who traveled and studied in India from 399 to 414, heard a number of tales from Indian Buddhist masters about the approaching end of the Buddha's religion (which by that time was nearing its millennium) and the decay and destruction of the world and mankind that would characterize that event. But when he started to write this information down, he was told that it had no authority in Buddhist scripture and only formed part of the oral tradition.[1] It is hardly surprising, then, that appropriate scriptural authority soon came into being in fifth-century China, for not all of the Chinese Buddhist sacred literature was translated from Indian languages. Some of the most influential scriptures in the Chinese Buddhist canon were actually written in China, and directly in Chinese—even though, in accordance with the basic criterion of authenticity for Chinese Buddhist texts, they claim to be translations from Sanskrit. Among the vast quantity of Buddhist texts in Chinese, none are more interesting or less well-studied than these so-called apocryphal scriptures. They have been neglected by scholars because they are supposedly not "authentic"; "forgeries" and "fabrications" are typical pejorative names for them in the writings of both traditional Chinese Buddhist authors and modern Western scholars.[2]

In reality, it is precisely these despised texts that have the most to tell us about what was centrally important to the Chinese Buddhists who wrote them, received them, and attempted to follow their instructions. They are like Taoist scriptures in that they represent the direct expression, in prose and verse, of Chinese hopes and fears, reflections on life and death, and wish-fulfillment through ritual. The Buddhist framework—all scriptures are presented as being the word of the Buddha himself and are localized in a suitably exotic Indian setting—is precisely analogous to the framework in which Taoist scriptures are molded, save that they are set in India rather than the remote heavens and the speaker is the Buddha instead of Lao-tzu or the Tao. Even the notion that all Buddhist texts, to be properly Buddhist, must have been translated from a foreign tongue finds its parallel in the Taoist doctrine that every Taoist scripture represents a transcription into the writing of ordinary mortals from an externally extant Ur-text concealed in the heavens and written in a secret celestial script decipherable only by rare, gifted human visionaries. In addition to their formal, structural parallels, both Taoist scriptures and Chinese Buddhist "apocrypha" allow us to come far closer to otherwise lost oral traditions and actual practice than does any other class of written source.[3]

One of these "apocryphal scriptures" (which I would prefer to designate "original Chinese Buddhist scriptures") that came into being not long after Fa-hsien's return from India, early in the fifth century, is called the *Book on the Extinction of the Law* (*Fa-mieh ching*, T. 396 and T. 2874). In it we read that, at a time after the Buddha's death, a new type of devil-monk will flourish whose real motive for joining the Buddhist community will be to destroy the Law. Such persons will violate all the Buddha's precepts, and will slander and expel from the order the bodhisattvas and saints who vainly try to maintain the true practice. Among other misdeeds, these devil-monks will allow monasteries to fall into disrepair while they themselves enter into trade on a large scale. They will sell monastic slaves, fields, and agricultural produce for their own profit, without the slightest thought for the needs of the poor and destitute. Among the new recruits for monkhood at this time will be runaway slaves and refugees from justice. The mean capacities of these unsuitable monks will bring about a wholesale curtailment of ritual and the abridgement of scripture. And when the Buddha's Law is hovering on extinction, there will suddenly be a marked increase in pious works by women while men display laxity, indifference, and contempt for monks.[4]

The final years of the Law, according to this text, will also be distinguished by certain more convulsively apocalyptic signs. Excesses of flood and drought will destroy the harvests, and rampant epidemics will leave corpses heaped all across the land. The people will suffer greatly, and provincial officials will be at their most oppressive and rapacious. Evil-doers will be as numerous as the sands of the sea, but good men will be counted by ones and twos. The cycles of day and night will shorten, and man's lifetime will become briefer—men will have white hair at forty. Men's unbridled sexual license will greatly reduce their lifespans, and few will attain the age of sixty. As man's lifetime shortens, however, woman's will lengthen, until women reach seventy, eighty, ninety, or a hundred years of age. Then great floods will rise up suddenly, when they are not expected. Yet people will obstinately refuse to recognize all these palpable signs of the times, making no effort to change their wicked ways. Thereupon all sorts of people, rich and poor alike, will be swallowed up by the waters and eaten by fishes. However, the bodhisattvas, pratyeka-buddhas, and arhats of that time—all those who are still faithful to the Buddha's commandments, that is—will not mingle with the doomed multitudes. While the wicked are being hunted down and destroyed by devils, these true believers will all go up into the mountains, the place of sanctuary. There they will receive the protection of devas (gods) and will survive in joy and contentment, their lives ever lengthening. Then the Youth of Lunar Radiance will appear in the world and reign as a Buddhist monarch for fifty-two years—one Venus cycle. At the conclusion of that period, two of the fundamental Mahāyāna sūtras, the *Śūraṃgama-samādhi* (*Shou-leng-yen san-mei ching*, T. 642) and the *Pratyutpanna-samādhi* (*Pan-chou san-mei ching*, T. 417), will disappear.[5] This will be followed by the disappearance of all twelve divisions of Buddhist scripture—their letters, we are told, will simply be obliterated, and they will cease to exist. Then the robes of all Buddhist monks will turn white, connoting their automatic laicization.[6] The fifty-two-year period during which the Buddhist monarch Lunar Radiance will reign is compared by the author of this text to the final flare-up of a lamp before its extinction. It will be followed by the total disappearance of Buddhism.[7]

This brief but graphically descriptive work survives as an independent scripture in the Chinese Buddhist canon (T. 396). It is also quoted at length in an early sixth-century Buddhist compendium (T. 2040), and we have it again in a manuscript recovered from Tun-huang (ms. Stein 2109, T. 2874). In it we find the same ethical polarization as in the Taoist texts.[8] The good people, the believers, will go up into the mountains, a safe and holy refuge. The miscreants and evil-doers, left on the plain below, will be decimated by demonically induced disease and swept away by flood. The emphasis that this Buddhist work places on the role of a great flood in destroying the wicked is entirely in line with contemporary Taoist accounts, which reveal that the imminent apocalyptic deluge will be a recurrence of the mythological flood of antiquity.[9]

It is interesting to note the author's sociological analysis of the circumstances attending the collapse of Buddhism and the end of the world—circumstances that clearly represent his view of his own time. He condemns the worldliness of monks and their multifarious commercial activities. Indeed, we know that the fifth century was a time when Chinese Buddhist institutions began to grow at an unprecedented rate. From this period on, the holdings of Buddhist foundations in land and slaves were considerable; the criticisms expressed by the scripture's author bear on the early phase of a process of expansion that was to reach its apogee in the ninth century.[10] Though we cannot be certain of the milieu in which the apocryphal sūtra came into being, we would probably not be far wrong in supposing its apocalyptic predictions to be directed against those fundraising, entrepreneurial monks who found favor with the aristocracy. It seems fair to suppose that one of the author's motivations was contempt for the official monks of his day—contempt that was perhaps tinged with envy. Authors of Taoist apocalyptic works fulminated against the devotees of popular cults; for them, the "gods" of the people were really demons, as we have seen, and the "cults of the profane" were the prime targets.[11] Buddhist monkish authors of apocalyptic eschatology were also strongly opposed to local cults and their shrines, and to the blood sacrifices that characterized ordinary Chinese ritual practice. In addition, they were stalwartly opposed to Taoist priests and their followers, viewing Taoism, too, as a particularly dangerous and seductive demonic manifestation. Yet as the text just quoted makes clear, Buddhist eschatologists often aimed their most telling thunderbolts at unworthy members of their own communion: *odium buddhologicum*.[12]

For concerned Buddhists of the fifth century, the condition of religion, the efficacy of ritual and meditation, and even time itself were all qualitatively different than they had been during the age in which the Buddha had lived. According to some accounts, a radically altered state of affairs had set in five centuries after the Buddha's death. By then, the Buddha's remaining influence had so far waned as to permit the beginning of a period of "Counterfeit Law" (*pratirūpaka-dharma*) following the "True Law" (*saddharma*) that had dominated the first five hundred years. The Counterfeit Law would itself last five hundred years; following this would come the extinction of Buddhism. There were other calculations of the duration of True and Counterfeit Laws, respectively, but through the fifth century the prophecy of a total of a thousand years' duration for Buddhism had general currency.[13] In fact, the fifth century corresponded to the very period, foretold in prophecy, that completed the millennium after the death of the Buddha. But already in the first century B.C.E.—toward the end of the first five hundred years—scriptures like the influential *Book of the Lotus of the True Law* (*Saddharmapuṇḍarīka-sūtra*) were written to provide remedies against the "final age of the five defilements." It is clear, then, that the idea of the imminent decline and collapse of the religion amid a great cacophony of demonic influences was already a significant component of Buddhism when it initially reached China in the first century C.E.[14]

Buddhist Demonology

There seems to have been general agreement, then, that demonic forces had attained enormous power in the world. For some authors, this state of affairs had been ordained to serve the higher purpose of effecting a preliminary cleansing that would purge and purify humanity in preparation for an ultimate, messianic renewal. Others viewed the social symptoms of demonic takeover as confirmatory signs that validated a long-standing prophecy of collapse into utter darkness. In either event, danger from demons was everywhere, and it was crucial to know the enemy and take suitable prophylactic measures. We begin our survey of medieval demonology with the demons imported by Buddhism from India because they are the easiest to spot in the Chinese texts (where they usually stand out at once as exotic-seeming transcriptions of Sanskrit names), and because, too, we have independent descriptions of them in Indian sources. Also, as is usual with otherworldly matters, the Indian demonology (like Indian cosmology) is much more fully and systematically described in written sources than its pre-Buddhist Chinese counterpart.[15] Once Buddhism began its millennium of direct influence on China, Chinese demonology was whipped into respectable shape, however, and a number of Indian demons even found permanent niches in Taoist ritual texts.

Among the Buddhists' demonic population were, first of all, demons per se, whose malevolent nature was recognized by most if not all Indians. But another large class of Buddhist demons were really the gods of non-Buddhist Indian tradition—widely recognized divinities like Brahmā, Viṣṇu, Śiva, and Śakra ("King of the Gods"), as well as lesser or local divine figures like Kubera and Maṇibhadra. These deities existed independently of Buddhism, had their own priesthoods and devotees (whom Buddhists stigmatized as "heretics"), and were generally viewed by Buddhist authors as perverse and ill-omened. Hence one of the primary mythological themes in Buddhist scriptures concerns the voluntary conversion (or, sometimes, forceful subjugation) of the pagan gods.[16] This is most marked in the texts of Tantric Buddhism because many of the rituals that characterize Tantrism originated outside the Buddhist fold, whether in the ultra-orthodox Brahmanical tradition of Vedic fire ritual or in the more equivocal practices that Indians of all classes (and many of the "aboriginal" peoples of India as well) share with the most magical of all the Vedas, the *Atharva*.[17] From a narrow Buddhist perspective, all these diverse elements of Indian religion and ritual were originally heterodox and demonical; at one time or another, virtually all of them were modified, mythologically and doctrinally, to become an integral part of Buddhism. One man's god may well be another's demon, as Buddhism has amply illustrated. Here, as nowhere else, we find unparalleled opportunities for the assimilation of a vast panoply of demons, gods, and ancestors into one all-encompassing system.

The figure that best corresponds to the "prince of darkness," or the Evil One, is Māra, who is in fact called the "evil one" (*pāpīyān*) in Sanskrit sources. He if anyone is entitled to the name of "Devil," and his followers, the devils, also called *māra*, are frequently cited as a cause of disease.[18] They soon became fully assimilated into the Chinese worldview, under their abbreviated Chinese transcription, *mo*. Probably the most successful among all the demonic émigrés from India, the *mo* essentially functioned in pathology as a group, rather than as individual beings with well-defined personalities and mythologies. From the fourth century on, they also came to figure prominently in Taoist scriptures as "devil-kings" (*mo-wang*), rulers of demons, and were regularly called upon in ritual.[19]

Buddhist texts abound in numerical categories and frequently allude to eight classes of supernatural beings: nāgas, rākṣasas (or yakṣas), gandharvas, asuras, garuḍas, kiṃnaras, mahoragas, and bhūtas (also called pretas).[20] The nāgas represent a mythological elaboration of the hooded cobra; they were the guardian gods of springs and subterranean treasures. They might also appear in human form, as indicated by the standard question posed to postulants in Buddhist monastic ordination ceremonies: "Are you a man or are you a nāga?" The nāgas exemplify the fusion of Indian figures with native Chinese otherworldly personnel, since the word always used for the nāgas in Chinese sources is *lung* (dragon). The entire gamut of ophidian forms and functions, from tiny snake to giant rain-dragon, and from the benign and godly to the demonic and virulent, is found in ritual texts as well as in legends and art.[21] Invocation of the dragon-kings for rain was practiced by members of all the principal lineages, Taoist as well as Buddhist, and was frequently a matter of state.[22] Moreover, the local deities were often embodied in dragon form (as in Tibet, where the Lords of the Soil, or *sa-bdag*, are nāgas), and special Taoist rituals called dragon-tablets (*lung-chien*) addressed communications to them.[23] It would be pointless to disentangle native Chinese elements in the ubiquitous dragon-cult from Indian nāga-cult contributions; from the early Middle Ages on, Indian and Chinese components harmoniously coalesced. Of particular interest to us is the role of the nāga-dragons in therapy, for the cobra possesses the deadliest venom and so is thought to hold the cure for various forms of demonic envenomation. As with the snakes of Aesculapius, the nāgas are masters of curative magic and appear in Buddhist texts as the revealers of healing rituals.[24]

Proceeding with the eight classes of supernaturals, we next come to the rākṣasas. Their Sanskrit name means, euphemistically, the "protectors." In India they were known to haunt caves and trees. They roamed about at night, often in animal form, but sometimes disguised as humans and sometimes in purely monstrous form. They belch forth fire, eat meat (including human flesh), drink milk, and disturb ritual offerings.[25] They, too, come to be mentioned in Taoist texts. In their benign role as actual protectors, the rākṣasas were supplanted in Buddhist contexts by the yakṣas (also sometimes called guḥyakas, "the hidden ones"). The cult of the yakṣas is said to have achieved special popularity in Kashmir, whence it was diffused, via Buddhism, throughout Central and East Asia. Yakṣas were found everywhere, as guardians of doorways, villages, cities, kingdoms, and entire regions.[26] The females of the species, the yakṣiṇīs, remained more unreconstructedly demonic and specialized in devouring children.

Like the yakṣas, gandharvas could function much like magicians or genies in their relations with human beings, sometimes coming to people's aid by magical means but other times using their powers to deceive them. According to certain Buddhist authors, though, gandharvas also had a special role in relation to humankind: A gandharva was thought to be necessary for every act of human procreation, functioning as "the being from a previous existence who enters the womb at the moment of conception."[27] These otherworldly creatures would thus have had a crucial though ambiguous part to play in the transmission of guilt and moral responsibility from one lifetime to the next. Gandharvas are most often identified with the carefree, elegant musicians depicted in Buddhist paintings, but we should not forget that their evident love of luxury and ease extended to *luxuria* in the western medieval sense of the term; one of the least formal styles of "marriage" (i.e., sexual union) in Indian lore was called the "gandharva marriage"—impetuous, unsanctified union with the object of desire—and it is clear that these supernatural exquisites frequently made their presence felt in the domain of sexual pathology.

The remaining figures on the eightfold list also make their appearance in China, but far less often than nāgas and yakṣas. Asuras, the traditional gigantic enemies of the Indian gods, occasionally come forward, usually as manifestations of violence on a cosmic scale, threatening the sun, the moon, and the smoothly running order of the seasons. Their role is more closely linked with apocalyptic concerns than with the perils of daily domestic life.[28] The great bird-headed garuḍas found in East Asia many older bird-spirits with which to meld, and appear to have inspired still other compound creatures (like the Japanese *tengu*, "dog of heaven").[29] The garuḍas are ancient foes of the nāgas, but like the nāgas they became patrons of secret magical arts in the esoteric ritual traditions.[30]

The kiṃnaras, sixth on the list, with horses' heads and human bodies, seem never to have become excessively active or threatening as a group in East Asia, though a horse-headed figure is conspicuous in all depictions of the tribunals of the ten judges of hell; on a more beneficial note, the Chinese and Japanese god of silkworms and sericulture resembles a horse, and Hayagrīva, a horse-headed manifestation of the Bodhisattva Avalokiteśvara, is prominent in Tantric Buddhist ritual.[31] The mahoragas ("great serpents") are yet another type of serpent-demon, giant snakes that seem to be more consistently ill-disposed toward mortals than the helpful nāgas.

The final category, bhūtas ("beings"), is a generic term for demons, or low-grade troublesome elementals.[32] But a word must be said about the variant group of such beings that concludes the list, namely, the pretas. The term "preta" (in Pāli, *peta*) is a variation on *pitara*, the "fathers" of pan-Indian belief—in other words, the spirits of dead ancestors. For Buddhists they are more particularly the spirits of the unhappy dead, requiring and deserving of regular offerings from the living but also capable of doing harm. Early Buddhist authors devoted special treatises to the pretas; the Pāli *Peta-vatthu*, or "Stories of the Departed," gives accounts of the various sorts of deeds that lead, after death, to this unhappy condition, and provides graphic descriptions of the pretas' miserable appearance and squalid, comfortless mode of existence. During the first half of the sixth century, a long and comprehensive survey of preta lore was translated into Chinese. This work undertook to answer vital questions on the subject, such as who becomes what kind of preta, why and how, and what they do then.[33] The Chinese reader learned that there are two sorts of preta—those who live in the human world (and whom one may therefore run into when taking walks at night), and those who live apart in a vast world of their own, the *preta-loka*. The same book lists thirty-six different types of preta and is said to be the most complete such inventory in Buddhist literature. There are cauldron-bodied ghosts, needle-mouthed ghosts, ghosts that eat vomited food, ghosts that eat excrement, ghosts that eat incense, ghosts that feed on human heat, and so on. Each category is described in detail, including the types of actions that cause one to be born in such a state, the horrible appearance of the ghosts, the ghastly sufferings ("sometimes as bad as the sufferings of hell") that torment them, and the dismal future lives that await them. Time and duration, too, are different among the pretas; a single day and night for them are the equivalent of five hundred years among humans. The mean lifespan of a preta would therefore equal some 1.8 million human years, making the prospect of rebirth as a preta all the more depressing. The moral is clear: Mortals are well-advised to avoid any actions that might lead to posthumous pretahood.[34]

These eight categories by no means exhaust the demonic repertory of Indian Buddhist texts. There are still other bands of marauders, such as the piśācas, eaters of raw flesh sometimes grouped with the yakṣas, sometimes with the asuras, and sometimes with the rākṣasas.[35] There are the vetālas (or cetālas), who are vampires, and the swollen, pot-shaped kumbhāṇḍas.[36] There are the dākiṇīs, also redoubtable carnivores, and the shameless, evil-smelling pūtanas, who are astonishingly yet appropriately related, etymologically and functionally, to the French *putain*.[37] The grahīs, or "snatchers" (who are female), delight in possessing and destroying children, especially newborn ones, and the mātṛkās ("little mothers," or "moms") are comparably dangerous and deadly.[38] In some cases, identifications might be made or parallels drawn between entire classes of Indian demonic beings and their supposed counterparts among the indigenous demons of East Asia. Thus, in one long inventory from the early eighth century (T. 945), we find the apasmara-demons glossed as "sheep-headed demons," the chāyās as "shadow-demons," and Revatī as the "the demoness who troubles infants"—all appropriate translations or explanations. There were also Jāṃkā ("the demon in horse's shape"), the mātṛmandā ("demons in the shape of cats"), and ālambhā-demons in serpentine form. Most telling was the identification in this text of the meat-eating dākiṇīs as fox-demons. In Tibet, dākiṇīs were translated as "sky-goers" (*mka'-'gro-ma*) and thus enjoyed an essentially beneficial celestial image. But in China and Japan, the equation between them and the native fox-demons brought the dākiṇīs squarely into the complex of sexual spirit-possession, as we will see below.

So much for the demonic masses. Yet there was always room for the gifted individual demon to transcend his class and blossom forth in scripture—and in tangible, real-life institutions—as an independent personality with a domain of his own. Such is the case, for example, of Hārītī, "the Thief." She began as a ferocious demoness given to devouring children (like so many envious female demons). But by means of a trick (hiding her own favorite child), the Buddha awakened in her a sense of compassion, converted her to Buddhism, and directed monks to set aside a portion of their own food for her at every meal so that she would not be tempted by hunger to return to her sanguinary diet.[39] The Buddha thus transformed a threatening demonic presence into a trusted guardian-spirit of Buddhism specializing in the protection of children—so much so, in fact, that Hārītī's name is widely found adorning kindergartens in Japan today. And there is Skanda, who was originally one of the "seizers" (*graha*, fem. *grahī*), astral demons who attacked children. The symptoms of Skanda-possession were trembling shoulders (*skanda* means "shoulder"). Later we find such trembling shoulders described as one sign of possession in the child-medium who incarnates Skanda in his benign Buddhist role as the diagnostician of demonically induced illness.[40] Many other similar cases can be found. Figures originally (and no doubt, marginally, still) functioning as disease-demons have by the early medieval period become homeopathic protectors against the very ailments which previously, in their old, unenlightened, pre-Buddhist days, they had themselves provoked. Thus did

Buddhism interpose a *cordon sanitaire* of converted demon-commanders between the faithful and the seething mass of threatening demons that surrounded them. Both the Indian demons and the strategy for controlling them proved highly successful on Chinese soil.[41]

China's Indigenous Demons

What, then, of the indigenous world of Chinese demons into which all these Indian figures were projected, and with which they somehow had to come to terms, through shared sovereignty in the reign of terror over mankind? Once Buddhism had begun its thousand years of potent influence on Chinese visions of the invisible world, the question of "native" Chinese elements becomes hopelessly muddled. In fact, so vast was the synthesis effected by the growing presence of Buddhist oral tradition, as well as texts, that any attempt to winnow out indigenous elements supposedly untouched by Buddhist influence may well be futile; it is the synthesis itself, in all its complexity, that becomes the natural focus of detailed investigation. It is certain, though, that the Chinese had a rich demonology of their own before the coming of Buddhism, and it was of course this basic Chinese conception of the spectral and demonic that determined which elements of the imported Indian pandemonium would be grafted successfully onto the Chinese worldview. We are hobbled in our study of this lore by a basic problem of documentation. It happens that significant extant texts written by private persons start only about the second century C.E., by which time Buddhism was well launched on its Chinese phase. Of China's earlier writings we have only fragmentary survivals, most of which were first carefully filtered through a screen of official government scrutiny. Thus, until very recently (when archaeological discoveries began to furnish us with original documents from the third and second centuries B.C.E.), we were largely dependent for our knowledge of the spirit world of pre-Buddhist China on passing references in ancient texts, as well as on what could be deduced from later authors who wrote when Indian influence had clearly begun. We know from a first-century B.C.E. bibliographical catalogue that several systematic treatises on demonology existed in the imperial library at that time; from the titles it appears that they gave detailed descriptions of demons to aid in correct identification, as well as providing methods for capturing, punishing, and conjuring them.[42] We also have the text of the *Book of Mountains and Seas* (*Shan-hai ching*), a work of uncertain date that was constructed as a kind of gazeteer of ancient China and neighboring peoples. Natural features ("mountains and seas") and their denizens are set forth as a series of concentric rings, widening outward from the author's sinocentric focus, and the "peoples" are largely monstrous theriomorphic or demoniform images of the alien and fearful.[43] Transformed animals—especially foxes, snakes, dogs, and tigers—continued to provide an ever-present demonic threat in which sexual possession was a dominant theme (as we will see in Chapter 6).

Other suggestive demonographic information is discernible in accounts of the Great Exorcism (*ta-no*). This ceremony was performed at the very end of the year at the capital and was related to other exorcistic rituals, both annual and occasional, performed in other parts of the Chinese culture-area. In the ritual a team of masked and robed human exorcists incited twelve devouring creatures to consume and destroy ten sorts of menace. There are several variant lists of the twelve devouring creatures, but basically they were associated with the twelve months and the twelve "earthly branches" of the Chinese sexagesimal system of time-, space-, and fate-calculation. The devoured creatures were "baneful things," tigers, *mei*-dragons, "inauspicious things," calamities, dreams, persons publically executed who now cling to the living, visions, giants, and virulent toxins (*ku*). Such ceremonies continued in China and Korea down to early modern times. The earliest accounts have been carefully studied by Derk Bodde (1975), and important ninth- and tenth-century manuscript documents on the performance of the annual exorcism at the provincial city of Tun-huang (Kansu) have been published by Danielle Eliasberg (1984).[44]

These various sources provide us with a populous though rather confused picture of ancient Chinese demon-lore. The data have been collected and classified by J. J. M. De Groot (1892–1910, vol. 5), Marcel Granet (1926), and Kiang Chao-yuan (1937). But material of a rather different type has now become accessible as a result of the renewed archaeological activity underway in China since the early 1970s. In 1976, a number of manuscripts written on bamboo slips were recovered from a tomb of 217 B.C.E. in Hupei. Most of the texts found buried there dealt with legal and governmental matters, but two of them were of more occult significance. The first manuscript has no title, but one of its subheadings is *chieh* ("binding," or "spellbinding"), which well describes its contents. The second manuscript bears the title "Book of Days" (*jih-shu*) and is a calendar of lucky and unlucky days. Both texts belong to the specialized literature of practical, operative demonology, of which we previously had no original examples from this early period. The "spellbinding" section contains a short introduction followed by about seventy individual entries, each describing a different type of demon attack and the measures that are to be taken against it. Some of the spectral figures it describes are related to later Buddho-Taoist categories; there are, for example, "hungry ghosts" (pretas) as well as a variety of serpentine demons that may have subsequently commingled with nāgas. As for the calendar of auspicious and inauspicious days, in China, every day is tagged with a two-character designation drawn from a sexagesimal cycle. The first character belongs to a series of ten "celestial stems"; the second comes from a series of twelve "terrestrial branches." These series combine to form sixty different permutations, and each component or cyclical sign is associated with a particular orientation or direction. Thus the implications of the sexagesimal cycle are both temporal and spatial. Prohibitions of certain activities on particular days of this cycle are founded on the mutual relationship, with each designation, of the celestial and terrestrial component, each of which is linked to one of the Five Phases, or elements (earth, wood, fire, metal, and water), in their various relationships of production and destruction, and in association with the contrastive and complementary polarities of yin and yang. Such considerations still determine the auspicious or inauspicious character of individual days in the Chinese almanac today.

Thus these valuable texts from Shui-hu-ti provide some of the earliest evidence for a system of demonology and hemerology that has continued down to modern times. They are being translated and studied by Donald Harper, who has published a preliminary description.[45] They are to be read in conjunction with another significant manuscript find, a text called *Prescriptions for Fifty-Two Ailments*, which gives some three hundred recipes for treating fifty-two sorts of illness. It was unearthed in 1972 from a Hunan tomb dated 168 B.C.E.[46] Using these new primary sources, scholars have been able to demonstrate a striking continuity in Chinese demonology and ritual healing from ancient times into the medieval period, and in some cases even down to the present day. Thanks to this work, we are now equipped to confront the properly Chinese components in medieval Chinese demonology with a good deal more clarity and confidence, and can also begin to perceive how Taoist and Buddhist authors adapted much of this ancient legacy to their own systems.[47]

We can see, then, that pre-Buddhist China was by no means lacking in wild and fantastical visions of the demonic and uncanny. What seems still to have been absent, in ancient times, was a careful ordering of the rather overwhelming data; but this impression, too, may be only a trick of perspective or a result of the accidents of textual transmission, for it is evident that ancient China did indeed possess a specialized science of demons. For that matter, the seemingly highly systematized nature of Indian Buddhist demonology is all due to the work of monkish authors who selected from and imposed hierarchy and unity on a vast phantasmagoria of disparate cults, legends, and folklore. In medieval China, Buddhist and Taoist scholars performed a comparable feat. Like the Indian demonology, Chinese conceptions of the realm of the extra-human included a wide range of beings. Moreover, as in India, human outsiders were always at risk of undergoing instant demonization. The "foreigners" who figure so picturesquely as ghouls and monsters in the *Book of Mountains and Seas* included not only the residents of politically distinct states but also the various non-Chinese people or aboriginals living in close proximity to Chinese towns and villages. Such underprivileged non-Chinese were assimilated to animals, if not to demons; the very names assigned to them in Chinese are written with classificatory elements setting them among the beasts. The speech, customs, clothing, hairstyles, and skin color of such persons, or non-persons, all differed tellingly from those of the Chinese. In this they resembled yet another class of ambiguous residents and travelers: the dead. Everything in the world of the living can also be found among the dead, only reversed, horribly distorted, uncannily parodied. The dead have their own writing-system, and can speak—but their speech is like the grunting of beasts, the twittering of birds, or, indeed, the senseless jabbering of barbarians.[48] Even within the larger Chinese cultural area, dehumanization and demonization were (and still are) a frequent means of reinforcing identity and group solidarity; medieval demonographies often listed the demons of particular regions as individual demonic entities (especially frequent are mentions of the demons of Wu and Yüeh, corresponding to the modern coastal provinces of Kiangsu and Chekiang), and we may well suspect that it was the nominally Chinese natives as much as any incorporeal spirits that the demonographers had in mind.

Though elite upper-class accounts of Chinese culture would have us believe that the only attitude ever manifested toward one's own dead was solemn respect, the evidence leads us to a quite different conclusion. The terminology itself should provoke a closer look at the scope afforded to the dead, since there is no basic terminological distinction between them and the demons. In addition to being known as *wu* ("things"), ghosts and demons alike are generically called *kuei*, and the boundaries between the two groups seem to be quite fluid. Spectral or demonic manifestations were ultimately viewed as transformations or perversions of *ch'i* ("vital breaths," or emanations). As we have seen, the entire realm of the dead was a prime source of disease and misfortune for the living, and was conceived of as being composed of old, stale, or worn-out "breaths" or vapors. Perhaps the most ubiquitous pathogenic agent was that class of evil influence known as *hsieh* ("twisted," "perverse," or "malignant" breaths). This term is understood as standing in opposition to *cheng* ("straight," upright, and true)—a frequent qualification for the pure cosmic breaths with which Taoists effect their marvels of therapy and, by extension, a term applied to Taoism and the Taoists themselves.[49] Obedient to general Chinese usage, Chinese Buddhists also used the term *cheng* in referring to their own rituals and institutions, as in their translation of *saddharma*, the "True Law" of the Buddha, as *cheng-fa*. *Hsieh* ("perverse" or "twisted") was applied polemically to unbelievers or spiritual rivals.[50] In the area of medical pathology, such "perverse breaths" or influences were always ready to invade the unwary or depleted human body and cause disease; these pathogens seem almost endowed with a will of their own, a fact that justifies translating the term as "malignant wraiths."

This identification of demonic forms with *ch'i*, or breath, obviously posits a cosmic analogy to the human body, and suggests an extension of the body and its vital animating forces into the realm of the demonic. The terminology indicates that there is no clear break in continuity between the human and the demonic—nor, for that matter, between the demonic and the divine. Though the classification and localization of good and evil, auspicious and inauspicious, is theoretically stable, and though there are heavens and hells at various more or less clearly specified locations throughout the universe, the figures that people them and that manifest themselves in the world of mortals are often curiously ambiguous. Indeed, this very ambiguity is the stimulus for an ever more ambitious science of demonology, which finds its social correlative in the great variety of therapeutic specialists to whom the Chinese have always turned, then as now.

It was only to be expected, then, that both dominant elements in the human body should prove to have equally important functions in the world of the disembodied. The two vital components in ourselves, to which Chinese give untiring attention in all discussion of psychosomatic conditions, are breath (*ch'i*) and essence (*ching*). This latter substance is moist and relatively heavy compared with the light and ethereal breath; *ching* is channeled through the bones, even as *ch'i* passes through special conduits or veins of its own. *Ching* is the sexual fluid in both men and women and, mingled with *ch'i*, it forms the fetus. Thus *ch'i* and *ching*, vital breaths and vital essence, are crucial components in the human body's economy, and both are also embodied, often fantastically, in the world of the extra-human. Just as perversions of "breaths" account for a large number of ill-omened pathological manifestations, so the "vital essences" of numerous objects in the natural world are responsible for a multitude of supernatural appearances and visitations. The *ching*, or "essential spirits," of animals, plants, stones, and stars were held responsible for many pathological phenomena that could not otherwise be explained.[51]

Thus substances and processes drawing their names and attributes from the human body and its functions were freely postulated and identified in the external world, and contributed to a humanization, or personification, of man's surroundings. These personified forces were especially handy in explaining the etiology of disease. The old stereotyped notion of "nature spirits" or "animism" has little relevance here, for the Chinese terminology suggests instead that man is externalizing his own psycho-sexual processes and imprinting them upon nature. When ill and searching for causes, he takes cognizance of these projections (as if seeing his own image in a cracked mirror) and reincorporates them, intellectually and spiritually, in the form of shock, terror, disease, and debility. Thanks to this "accident" of terminology, we are able to gain a remarkable intimation of a world inhabited by perilous beings personifying breath and semen—phantom panting, demonized gasps, spectral sighs, lurking halitosis, walking nightmares, marauding wet-dreams, galloping nocturnal emissions.

This surrealistic vision of China's world of demons may seem too bizarre at first sight to the professional student of China. Still, there is no gainsaying the reality of the notion of immanent, potentially lethal breath and semen. The highly permeable and elastic nature of the spirit world's frontiers has already been noted with respect to the hazy distinction between "ghosts" and "demons." Among the various classes of spirits, as between spirits and living beings, the internal barriers are constantly shifting according to one's point of view, and so are the moral attributes of good and evil. The word *kuei*, generic for both "ghosts" and "demons," is homophonous with another word *kuei* that means "return," and for two thousand years traditional lexicographers have drawn the obvious conclusion: A *kuei* is that which returns (*kuei*). According to this widespread traditional definition, the *kuei* is literally a revenant, a "returning" soul of the "departed." Such a ghostly being, then, comes back to the scene of its own life, or to the world of the living in general, as the ghost or spirit of a dead ancestor.[52] It may do so at particular times and seasons, when it may possibly become visible or make its presence felt in other ways; it may also expect offerings or other attention from the living. Such, at least, is the official ideal. But the *kuei* that visits you may not be one of your own; it may be someone else's ancestor, and that in itself is irregular and potentially dangerous. Moreover, as we have noted, the word *kuei* is not used exclusively for the ghosts of dead ancestors but also applies wholesale to disease- or disturbance-causing demons. And even authenticated souls of the dead need not be benign. It may be that they cannot be kept in order through a simple program of regular offerings; a more precise investigation of their identity may have to be undertaken, and more stringent methods adopted for dealing with them. Still, it might be supposed that the work of distinguishing between one's own dead and alien shades would be relatively straightforward. Surely one could assume that one's own ancestors would be well-disposed toward their descendants, whereas other people's dead might be prompted by malice or envy. Once again, the generic terminology employed suggests that such a distinction may be much too simple, for the most dubious and potentially dangerous relationships of all are with one's own deceased family.

Buddhist and Taoist authors took their stand above or beyond family relationships, and so enjoyed greater detachment in classifying and dealing with ambiguous spirit-connections. It is in the writings of medieval laymen that we can sense the shifting boundaries of domestic good and evil, the transformation of family ghosts into family ghouls. Not all afflicting demons were impersonal by any means. It is certain that some of them embodied unresolved conflicts and tensions of family life (as well as representing the ill-omened impurity and pollution associated with death). Released by death from normal constraints, these departed parents and children returned to their family homes to injure and destroy their own kindred. Toward the end of the sixth century, an author described the belief, current in his time, that the dead came back to their erstwhile homes to kill—whence the origins of a particularly terrible class of demons, "the killers" (*sha*). When they were expected, their children and grandchildren would flee the family home; they would draw apotropaic signs on the roof-tiles and write out paper talismans to keep them off, lighting a bonfire before the gate and scattering ashes in front of the doors to exorcise the family's ghosts (*kuei*) and ward off "sepulchral infestation" (*chu-lien*). This account (from Yen Chih-t'ui's late sixth-century *Family Instructions for the Yen Clan*) makes it clear that more was involved here than the ordinary precautions taken immediately after death and during the funeral ceremonies. The vengeful ghost had to be reckoned with for some time thereafter.[53] Other medieval references indicate that the ghost's visitations would take place according to a schedule based on age at time of death, day of death, the cyclical affinities of the family name (classified by rhyme with one of the five musical notes, and so with one of the five directions), and so on. Thus, though "fleeing the killers" was seemingly a regular consequence of a death in the family, it might also be practiced at a later time, in anticipation of further attacks of illness perpetuated by a restless deceased member of one's own household.[54]

A secular tale set toward the end of the eighth century describes the experience of a fearless hunter who was once benighted while crossing the capital. He sought lodging from people who were evacuating their house because, as they told him, a killer-ghost was due to arrive that very night. The stalwart was not dismayed by this prospect and asked to sleep there anyway. The family decamped, and the hunter sat up in the main hall, bow and arrows at the ready. Toward the end of the third watch, a luminous object, like a big plate, flew down out of the air through the gate in the courtyard, gleaming like fire. From his dark hiding-place the hunter shot three arrows into it, until its light dimmed and it remained motionless. He got up, went over to it, plucked out the arrows, and the object fell to the ground. He called his servant, who brought a lamp; it proved to be a lump of flesh, with eyes all around—the motion of the eyes had caused the light. "So it's really true what they say about killer-ghosts!" he exclaimed with delight. Faithful to his hunter's custom, he had his servant boil it, and it proved to be utterly delicious.[55]

From ancient times to the present day, cooking and eating troublesome demons has been a practical solution to the problem; there are directions for cooking a wolf-demon in the third-century B.C.E. demonological manuscript mentioned earlier, and a similar approach to other demonic troublemakers is recommended in an instructive collection of ghost stories published in Peking in 1962, "Stories About Not Being Afraid of Ghosts" (*Pu-p'a kuei-te ku-shih*).[56] Such was certainly not the Taoist master or Buddhist monk's own way with unruly demons, but like their methods, it forcefully asserts the triumph of culture over untamed nature, of the cooked over the raw. Yet however they are best dealt with, through formal ritual or the cooking-pot, family ghouls long continued their reign of terror in the domestic circle. Nine hundred years after Yen Chih-t'ui's account, Tai Kuan (1442–1512) noted that the diviners and occultists of his day were still predicting the time of the same spirit's return, as well as its exact dimensions, using the cyclical significance of the date of death in association with a tangled web of other temporo-spatial determinants. And the family still abandoned the house on the fated day of the ghost's arrival.[57] Concerning the more complex dynamics of family life in individual cases among such ghost-struck households, the sources are lamentably silent. Thanks to their scattered appearances in the literary record, though, we are able to identify an entire class of demons with dead and vengeful family members. "Killers" also appear frequently as demonic agents in Taoist ritual texts (and even as anti-demonic demons at the Taoist master's command), and it should be fruitful to compare them with the like-named creatures described in secular sources. We can be grateful for the survival of even this fragmentary secular evidence, which allows us to catch a chilling glimpse, once again, of the dark underside of "filial piety."[58]

More information on domestic demonology and pathology emerges when we make the logical transition from "killers" to "cadavers." Writing in the first century C.E., Wang Ch'ung noted that specialists in untoward phenomena would regularly behold three sorts of evil manifestations: flying corpses, running evils, and homunculi.[59] At the beginning of the fourth century, we find Ko Hung (283–343) eager to tell us more about these "corpses" (*shih*). There are five sorts of external corpse-demons, he writes in his *Prescriptions Within Arm's Reach for Use in Emergencies*, and the conditions they provoke are generally similar but have a number of minor distinguishing features. First are the flying corpses, which roam about a person's skin and bore through to his inner organs. Their action is manifested in intermittent stabbing pains. The next type, the "reclusive corpse," attaches itself to your bones and so enters your flesh from within. It then burrows into the veins and arteries of your blood; its symptoms break out when it beholds a funeral or hears the sound of wailing. Wind-corpses, in contrast, course exuberantly through all four limbs until you are unable to say where exactly the pain is situated. They lead to dizziness and loss of consciousness, and their outbreaks are provoked by wind and snow. The "sinking corpse" enwraps the vital organs and strikes against the heart and ribs, causing a knotting, slicing sensation there; this happens whenever it encounters cold. The fifth corpse-demon syndrome is known as corpse-infusion or corpse-infestation (*shih-chu*) and is the dire culmination of the series. The victim feels that his entire body is sunken and weighted down, his vital spirits are in confusion, he is constantly oppressed by feelings of dullness and exhaustion, and the vital breaths are shifting and changing in his body's every joint: These symptoms inevitably lead to major illness (as we saw in Chapter 1).[60]

Ko Hung observes that these external corpse-demons have a well-established means of access into the human body; they enter at the invitation of the three corpses that are regular residents of the body's interior.[61] Thus like calls to like, with catastrophic effect for the unfortunate host. Our census of pathogenic agents is therefore not limited merely to the apocalyptic demonology of society or the domestic demonology of the family circle. Pathogenic entities also reside in the human body. They share an identical terminology with the external demons and, like them, are to some extent personified and individualized. There are two sets of potentially harmful indwellers against whom the well-informed must take careful precautions. The first are the seven *p'o*, the white-souls or spermatic souls with which every mortal is equipped. They are indeed an integral, necessary team in the body's operations, complementing as they do the three *hun* (cloud-souls or ethereal souls). But unlike the hun, whose nature (though flighty and inconstant) is entirely benign and whose tendencies are all heavenward, the seven *p'o* yearn for the earth. Their strongest wish is to rejoin the damp, dank underground springs whose moist, heavy nature they share, and so they seek to undermine and rid themselves of the constraining human body they inhabit. Thus at night, while their host is sleeping (and the airborne *hun*-souls are sporting and gambling with the *hun* of other sleepers, thereby causing dreams), the *p'o* beckon to passing phantoms and disease-demons and invite them in to take possession of the sleeper's body and work toward his destruction.[62] The very names of the seven *p'o*-souls suggest their harmful function, and one early list significantly begins with a corpse: corpse-dog, hidden dung, sparrow-sex, greedy-guts, flying venom, filth-for-removal, and rot-lung.[63]

These seven villains, then, are with us all and (like the body fluids they appear to personify) are functionally necessary, being internal embodiments of potential evil that we must learn to tame and control. But the three corpse-demons (also known as the three worms) represent a specialized development of the spermatic souls' destructive propensities. Fortunately, though, these internal corpse-demons can be destroyed—a course that must be steadfastly pursued if you wish to avoid disastrous visits from their colleagues, the external corpses. There was a profusion of methods for dealing with them, but such techniques were not suited to everyone, since the inner corpses' main item of diet was grain of one sort or another. This grain-dependence was shared with the bulk of China's human population; human host and demonic guest agreed perfectly in their fondness for grain, and only by a radical change of diet could one deny the corpses' nutritional requirements, starve them out, and so free oneself from their menace.[64] Clearly then, all the pharmaco-chemical means of treatment were intended for use by committed ascetics. But we would be quite mistaken to imagine that with the inner, concealed corpse-demons we have at long last reached a level of true demonic autonomy, on which demons can operate without reference to social correlatives, for the minds of ascetics are no less socially conditioned than those of less dedicated persons, as we can demonstrate by examining certain of the symptoms listed for the benefit of those who have begun the full-scale pharmaco-chemical battle against their internal corpses.

It is the dream-symptoms of such adepts that are significant. The corpse-demons may manifest themselves in the ascetic's dreams in the guise of three men garbed in rather old-fashioned costumes. As the program of anti-corpse treatment gets underway and the drugs begin to take effect, the adept will dream that his father or mother has died, or that his wife and children have been murdered. Or else the victims will be his sisters or brothers, or a woman, or he will dream that a grave has been destroyed and the coffin has vanished, or else that he is undergoing the five types of mutilating punishment. All these are said to be indications that the corpse-demons are about to be destroyed.[65] China, too, knew the principle of antithetical dream-interpretation in which the true meaning of a dream is just the opposite of what the images would normally suggest, dream-life inverting waking-life. In this case, though, the correlation of intimate family images with a feared and hated part of oneself is not at variance with what we have already found relating demonology to family dynamics.[66]

An intense concern to regularize and stabilize those relationships, both in life and after death, is evident in Chinese sources long before Buddhism and Taoism came to take up the work. No doubt the socially imposed repression of resentment lent force and color to the elaborate demonological outbreaks. A telling example of the comprehensive effort at regularization can be found in a class of documents known both from medieval literary sources and from archaeological discoveries: the tomb-contract, as well as the related texts for settling or stabilizing a grave. Like so many other types of explicit documentation, these begin appearing in the second century C.E. (though they are no doubt based on older prototypes).[67] The contracts record the purchase of the tomb-site for the use of the newly dead person. In many of these texts, the land's seller is a divine figure (often a manifestation of the god of the soil), and if witnesses to the contract are named, they are generally also spirit-personages or divinized mortals from an earlier era. The boundaries of the site are stated in terms of sacred geography, and the purchase price is usually an exorbitant sum, often of numerological significance. Clearly, such contracts were addressed to the spirit-hierarchy of the invisible world and were intended to guarantee the tomb-dweller's security of occupancy. If such a contract was not present in a tomb, there might instead be a tomb-stabilizing statement on pottery, tile, or lead. Such statements announced the newly dead person's entry into the underworld and marked the transfer of his name from the Registers of Life to the Registers of the Dead. Like the vast sums of money mentioned in the contracts, these documents also served to exculpate the dead person from any guilt that might result from violation of underworld territoriality when the grave was dug.[68] There is little doubt that, by ensuring the tranquility of their deceased family member, the living were also taking pains to protect themselves against trouble emanating from the grave or beyond it. The tomb was their own familial nexus between the visible and invisible worlds, and it is obvious (especially from the elaborate construction of Chinese tombs, with their enclosure within enclosure and their inner and outer coffins) that the tomb's primary function was containment. It is significant that a written juridical component was included, to quell in advance the site's potential for demonic emanation.[69] As we have already seen, these preexisting legalistic and contractual relations between the two worlds were elaborately developed among the Taoists;[70] in addition to the task of rectifying a decayed and disordered cosmos, Taoist and Buddhist demonologists were taking on the even more demanding task of unraveling and reweaving the knotted skein of Chinese family life.

Taoist Technical Literature

Most of these early mortuary documents conclude with a phrase of command: "Swiftly, swiftly, in accordance with the Statutes and Ordinances!"[71] The spirits are being enjoined to act in strict conformity with the written law; they are thereby warned that any infringement will unquestionably meet with rapid condign punishment. We find the same phrase at the end of early, pre-Taoist spells for recitation and inscribed on demon-commanding talismans. It recurs with great frequency in spoken spells and written talismans employed by Taoist masters (and some Chinese Buddhist spells and talismans contain it as well).[72] Curiously enough, the earliest extant examples of written Chinese law codes were discovered in the same tomb (217 B.C.E.) that yielded our earliest-known Chinese demonography (under the heading of "Spellbinding").[73] But the Taoists may have been the first to attempt to compose full-scale codes of law for the invisible world, with explicit statutes and ordinances to regulate the behavior of demons.

Despite the basically unruly nature of the creatures to whom it is addressed, the *Demon-Statutes of Nü-ch'ing* (*Nü-ch'ing kuei-lü*, HY 789) purports to be a solemn, formal document, a code of conduct for demons enunciated by a god. It is one of the earliest in a class of Taoist works which, in the fourth and fifth centuries, takes up the burden of systematic demonology inherited from ancient traditions such as those of the *Book of Mountains and Seas* and the recently discovered third-century B.C.E. demonography headed "Spellbinding." The inspiration for this fresh census of the unseen world's dangerous denizens clearly came from the emergence of the Taoists as a new guild of specialists in overseeing the relations between spirits and men, though there is a definite continuity between older methods and new literature, and a larger, more systematic view now informed the cataloguing of otherworldly forces. The Taoists were staking their claim to dominate the field of demon-quelling.

The *Demon-Statutes of Nü-ch'ing* appears to have come into existence before the end of the fourth century. The work's title sets it clearly within the rigorously legalistic Taoist worldview. As for the enigmatic component *nü-ch'ing*, its literal meaning is "woman-blue," but it should probably be read as standing for the closely related compound, *nü-ching* ("feminine sexual essence"). *Nü-ch'ing* is also the name of a malodorous plant (*Paedaria foetida*) still found in the Chinese materia medica. According to the second-century C.E. classic pharmacopoeia (the *Shen-nung pen-ts'ao ching*), the plant controls virulent magical infections, expelling malignancies and evil influences (*ch'i*, "breaths"), killer-demons, plague, and pestilence and eliminating inauspicious beings.[74] According to one of the most important original Shang-ch'ing hagiographies, it also saves from sudden death; a triturated powder of the plant, placed in the throat of one who has suddenly died, then washed down with either water or wine, will instantly restore him to life. Here we have a paradox: Even though the demonic law code, like early Taoist theory, does not recommend the use of drugs within its firmly juridical approach to prophylaxis and treatment, it nonetheless stands under the powerful sign of a plant preeminent as a demon-dispeller. As in the Shang-ch'ing *Book of the Demon-Dispellers* itself (where "demon-dispeller" is a generic term for medicinal herbs, and where plants are named only for recitation, rather than medicinal use), the name of this highly efficacious medicinal plant and its widely acknowledged curative effects have here been transferred to a book. *Nü-ch'ing* also became the name of a demon-filled hell or purgatory.[75] In the case of the *Book of the Demon-Dispellers*, the text was intended for repeated recitation, as a lengthy spell. Here, in contrast, the evocatively named book provides a census of demons. That the name of the plant and the title of the book both evoke the apotropaic powers attributed to the female sexual organs links this branch of Chinese demonology to a universal theme in world folklore.

The text opens by telling us that at the very beginning of the world there were no evil demons. In those days, men were obedient and women were chaste, rulers acted with proper ceremony and their servants were loyal to them. Every region of the earth was free from violence and peril. Only afterward (though still far back in legendary antiquity) did all the artful, deceiving creatures come into being, creatures that had no allegiance to the great Tao. Then rebellion and killing began on every side, and pestilent influences started to appear. Tigers, wolves, and all the other beasts were given vital breaths and grew, and every variety of vermin and serpent-demons became daily more numerous. The celestial reckoning (we are reminded) goes according to periods of sixty days, and each day has one benign spirit who oversees it. But for each of these days there are a thousand demons who fly about irrepressibly. Unrestrained either by the Tao or the Celestial Masters, malign creatures pursued one another throughout the entire world, wreaking destruction on the population. The dead numbered in the thousands of millions. But (we are told) the Most High Great Tao could not bear to behold this, and so at noon on the seventh day of the seventh month in the second year (we are not told of what reign-period; but if it is the Han-an period of the Han dynasty, or 143 C.E., this would be closest to the traditional date of 142, when the Most High Lord of the Tao is supposed to have initially revealed himself to the Celestial Master Chang Tao-ling), he sent down these *Demon-Statutes* in eight scrolls, registering the demons' family names and given names and the auspicious and inauspicious practices associated with them. He directed Chang Tao-ling, the Celestial Master, to control the demons so that they would not unrestrainedly wander to east, west, south, and north:

> If hereafter there are male or female Taoists who behold my secret scripture and thereby know the names of the demons, all will be well for them, the myriad demons will not dare to attack them, and the thousand spirits will all submit and comport themselves as set forth in the Statutes. But this text must not be transmitted to unqualified persons; if you do so, disaster will reach unto the seventh generation of your descendants. Do not then find fault with the Tao or blame the Master![76]

After this stern warning to secrecy, typical of the esoteric stance of early medieval Taoist scriptures, the demon-catalogue begins at once. It starts with the up-to-heaven-towering, thousand-foot-tall High Lord of the Demons, who is named "Heaven's Successor." He is chief of the demons of the six regions and dwells at the southeast corner of T'ai Shan, the ancient mountain of the dead (in Shantung province). All the dead must first proceed to T'ai Shan, whence the chief demon goes up to heaven once a month, to consult about the punishments meted out and to submit his reports. So have matters been since high antiquity, for more than 36,000 years; and therefore, the text informs us, there are 36,000 gods, to match the 36,000 demons.[77]

Next comes the Thrice-Ancient Demon of South Village, whom ordinary people call "the Demon of the Five Ways." His family-name is Chü (Carriage), his personal name Ni (Hidden). He has charge of the Registers of Death, and the records of all the misdeeds of the living are also sent to him. This demon dwells at the northwest corner of T'ai Shan, where he also has his suite of official retainers. Whenever people are summoned by T'ai Shan (i.e., called into the realm of death), they must always go to this demon. The celestial killer-demons obey his written orders alone; they have no attachment to either heaven or earth (which confirms our impression that "the killers" emanate specifically from the world of the dead).[78]

After this we find the Headless Demon in the Clouds, or Dead General of Broken Armies, the Refractory and Evil Great Demon, who has Li as his family name and San-k'o as his personal name. He is followed by five astral demons who have charge of destroying mortals, the demons of the Five Dipper-Constellations of north, west, south, center, and east, each of whom is named.[79] And so the text proceeds. Already, from these opening passages, we can see that this infernal pandemonium differs considerably from the account of the world of the dead given in the mid-fourth-century *Declarations of the Perfect Ones* (*Chen-kao*). In that visionary description, the dead were administered by known historical figures of antiquity or the recent past. In the present work, the historical or antiquarian perspective is lacking. The evil agencies are numerous and varied, but seem devoid of character and personality in comparison with the more literary Shang-ch'ing account. In these *Demon-Statutes of Nü-ch'ing*, we are far closer to the world of monsters and freaks in the *Book of Mountains and Seas*, and to the deformed, faceless terrors that have haunted East Asian secular demonology down to modern times.[80] The Demon of Great Harmony, for example, has no body but it does have a head, which is three feet long. Its eyes measure three inches in width, its ears seven inches, its eyebrows five inches, and its mouth three inches, its nose two inches. The length of its beard is three feet, its hair, ten feet. It breathes celestial vapors, and when it exhales, clouds are formed. Should you happen to be going along and see it, its name is P'i, and if you call this out three times it will appear to you with all its demon-attendants and acknowledge your authority. But take care that you are not carrying any metal coins on your person, since the radiant emanation of metal repels demons.[81]

It seems as if the expectations of a systematic law code held out to us by the work's title are to be disappointed as the text divagates into the archaic visionary obsession of ancient demonographers. The author's apparent concern was merely to assemble a complete inventory of every type of demon, and it is essentially as a catalogue that his work must be viewed and assessed. The repertory stretches on and on, from astral demons to their terrestrial counterparts.[82] The first chapter features a full list of the sixty demons assigned each to one day of the sexagesimal cycle—so that the daily enemy may be known and named, and thereby averted. Chapter 2 lists a miscellaneous assortment: the mountain specter, the tree specter, and on through demons of stones, tigers, snakes, monkeys, foxes; of twisted trees, five sorts of puddle,[83] and on and on, past demons of male and female debauchery,[84] the five sorts of pestilence,[85] the house, eating-utensils, the toilet, well, hearth, bed, the sound of drums, the pipes of the reed-organ, ditches, drains,[86] spears, knives, armor, the thousand-year-old White Bone Demon, the hundred-year-old White Bone Demon, the fifty-year-old demon,[87] and on and on. Long though the list may seem, it is still far from exhaustive, for the text reiterates that for every living being in the world, there are a thousand million demons; we mortals are far from the gods but close, all too close, to the demons.

Like so many demonologies, the text fully participates in the chaos of its subject. Despite his disclaimers, the compiler clearly would have liked to name every one of the thousand million. Moreover, the methods put forward for avoiding or gaining control over the demon-hordes seem drearily mechanical and simpleminded; you have only to know their names, and call them out, to overawe the dull-witted demons that threaten you. Knowledge is power, but knowledge of this kind is all too easily conveyed in disjointed catalogue form. Yet this is not the whole story, for in the third chapter we begin to learn of the relationship of demon-mastery to the persistent concerns of Taoist ethics. We are presented with twenty-two rules of good behavior to be followed by all Taoists; these will substantially reduce one's susceptibility to demonic attack and make the world a less demon-ridden place in which to live. Infringement of any of these prohibitions is punished by heaven's reducing one's lifespan by a precise number of years, varying for each infraction. Forbidden are backbiting, speaking evil of others, mocking the elderly, cursing parents or spouse, transmitting the Tao to unsuitable persons, and so on. There are also some livelier prohibitions, such as: "Do not transmit the Tao to a virgin girl, and by that means enter her gate of life (that is, her vagina). This injures the spirits and offends against the vital breaths; it is highly evil and immoral, and you will die without descendants. Do not use a man as a woman; this inverts the Yin and the Yang. Heaven will subtract three hundred units from your lifespan."[88]

Thus we do indeed find "statutes" in this text, although they prove to apply to human adepts who wish to be free from demonic attacks. Can it be that the picturesque monsters were only a carnival sideshow, a come-on to attract the curious to a sermon on Taoist morality? There is certainly a tone of moral urgency running through the entire book, for at the end of the first chapter the god Lao-tzu, the Most High, admonishes his Taoist followers:

> Man is born into the world for a period of less than a hundred years, uncertain of his safety from morning until evening, with death preponderating over life and the dead far outnumbering the living. Refractory murderous demons circulate everywhere among mortals, randomly causing all manner of ailments. There are the pathogenic influences of the five types of refractory beings bringing chills and hot sensations, headache, hard spots in the stomach, retching and shortness of breath, feelings of fullness and distension of the five viscera, dazed vision, gulping and gasping, extremities palsied, so that one cannot be aware or think, and one's life hangs by a thread from morning until night.
>
> Evil demons come to obtain control over all the men and women of the

world. Your priestly officers should therefore consult my writings and discover there the names of the demons. Put into practice my lowermost talismans of Grand Sublimity with their vitalizing breaths of the Three Heavens, the vitalization of the Three, Five, Seven, and Nine, and bestow them on heaven's people. If heaven's people have died, they will be brought back to life.

Ever since the Great Commencement, I have observed how men and women have been tricked and deluded by the machinations of demons and so lacked faith in my Perfect Ones. For that reason I kept this book secret, and as a consequence countless deaths have occurred. This causes me great sorrow whenever I think of it. For this reason I am now sending down these Statutes afresh, to make known throughout the world the names of the demons, the color of their clothing, and their strong and weak points.

The Statutes bring with them the *ch'i* of True Unity (*cheng-i*, i.e., Taoism). You can thus name the relevant demons according to the various days, and none of them will dare to attack you. If, in your ignorance, however, you claim that I am without supernatural power, you will offend the Great Tao on high and incur guilt among men down below in the world of mortals. Beware of this, for you will thereby only injure yourself. In the year of the three calamities and the five evils, you will yourself observe those people who have no faith in the vital breaths of Perfection mockingly revert to consorting privily with demons.[89] Take care that you separate yourself from such as they—otherwise, on that day, how can you hope to achieve life everlasting? Ponder this carefully again and yet again; do not transgress the rules. Pay heed![90]

The god's final remarks suggest something of an internal crisis between the true believers in the message of the Tao and the half-hearted skeptical participants—perhaps a majority?—who will treacherously return to their previous demon-worship as soon as hard times come upon the community. The Taoist elect saw themselves as an embattled minority, ever facing apostasy within the ranks of nominal Taoists. At least as unsettling as the multiplicity of demonically induced disease-symptoms attacking from without was the prospect of backsliding and betrayal within the community itself. The answer to both perils was found in regulation, the reaffirmation of a clear set of ethical rules. Literature and theory may have focused on demons, but practice was inevitably directed toward human beings.

Chapter 5 of the *Demon-Statutes* culminates the urgent exhortation to steadfastness. It is a stirring evocation of the coming apocalypse, in rhyming verses of seven syllables (a didactic, mnemonic verse-form much used by early

Taoists, intended for sonorous chanting).[91] It opens dramatically and sustains a large measure of intensity through to the end:

> Mars and Venus descend in human form
> and utter wild rumors among children.[92]

In other words, these two planets, indicative (in Chinese portent-astrology) of warfare and disorder, take on the shape of children, either through incarnation or possession, and give voice to the sort of prophetic utterances from children (or child-mediums) that were regularly consulted by official diviners.[93] Nor do these planetary demons confine themselves to verbal activity:

> They hasten to take on deceptive guise and ally themselves with demons;
> they strike your throat, so that you are unable to swallow.
> They take command of all the roads and so advance still more;
> I fear that you will meet your death before the year is out.[94]

In short, these hostile planetary spirits have descended to spearhead the demonic attack against mankind. They direct the spread of pestilence and contagion along the routes of communication—a gripping portrayal of epidemic proliferation.[95] The task of choosing the Elect who are to be saved from this slaughter has been given to the directors of the Three Offices; they will select a total of eighteen thousand persons who have united themselves to the vital breaths of the Tao. This quota, the reader is told, has not yet been filled; there is still a good chance of acceptance within the *numerus clausus*, if one immediately reforms one's thought and actions.

Terror at the prospect of imminent destruction next bursts forth in an explosion of chauvinism:

> From barbarian provinces beyond the frontiers come the uncouth barbarians.
> With craning necks they hobble forward, leading the wicked people.
> They are beings spawned by mutation; their poisonous aura rises to heaven.
> Great and small, all of them enter this domain.
> With bristling hair that stands straight up, they devour human blood.
> Now they are entering our Chinese realm: What recourse do you have?
> Indescribable, the turmoil and confusion of all their foot soldiers and horsemen.[96]

The bizarre outlanders were, as noted earlier, prime candidates for demonization. Here foreign humans and foreign devils are grouped together as a homogeneous apocalyptic menace, and it is suggested, too, that these disconcerting non-Chinese do not come into being by the standard route of mammalian reproduction (born from wombs), nor that of birds and serpents (born from eggs). Instead, they are assimilated to those creatures allegedly "born by transformation" or by magic—the lower insects and some reptiles—and their toxic effluvia are envisioned as permeating the air.

Under such conditions, the vast majority of humankind will perish even before the year of final destruction arrives: Not one in a hundred will survive. In heaven, the Elect will behold their own mothers down in the carnage below, trapped there by their failure to have faith in the Tao; it is not that the Elect are unfilial—the Tao will simply not preserve the unbelievers.[97] Surely, with such a prospect as this in store, it is prudent to apply oneself to the study of the Tao. The chapter goes on to foretell the coming of the messiah, Li Hung, who will preside over the instauration of the Great Peace, in which the Elect will participate.[98] The vision concludes with fourteen more rules of behavior, of the same moral tenor as the earlier twenty-two: Do not offend the gods, indulge in licentiousness, or join in league with demons.[99] A sixth and final chapter appends new lists of demons and demon-categories.

Such are the *Demon-Statutes of Nü-ch'ing* in all their diversity. They appear to reflect both the unstable conditions of the times and the transitional character of Taoism at the end of the fourth century. Clearly there was a need and opportunity for further systematization, and additional Nü-ch'ing demon-statute texts of various sorts were soon in circulation.[100] Other Taoist books written at this time testify to the same comprehensive concerns. There are a number of works bearing the title "Law-Script of Right Unity" (*Cheng-i fa-wen*) or some derivate thereof: *Law-Script of Right Unity of the Most High* (HY 1195); *Rites for Transmission of the Outer Registers of the Most High, from the Law-Script of Right Unity* (HY 1233), and so on. In fact, in addition to the nine such texts that survive in the fifteenth-century Taoist canon, at least eighteen works with *cheng-i fa-wen* in their titles are listed as missing from the canon, including one huge "Law-Script of Right Unity" in sixty chapters.[101] It seems that all such texts purported to be parts of a comprehensive Taoist law code, purportedly elaborated by Lord Lao the Most High for the benefit of the Celestial Master and his successors. They appear to have covered all aspects of institutional organization and administrative practice. Above all, the remaining examples stress the strict delineation of the human and demonic realms and enjoin high moral standards as the essential means of enforcing this vital boundary. In certain of them, too, the apocalyptic message is conspicuous, and one fifth-century specimen, called simply *Law-Script of Right Unity of the*

Most High, boldly speaks out in praise of the destined messianic role of the then-reigning dynasty (the Liu Sung).[102] Clearly, the genre of legal code was favored by authors claiming responsible authority and fidelity to Taoist tradition, and such codes continued to be composed at least down through the twelfth century, when the important *Demon-Statutes in Transcendent Script, the Marrow of the Shang-ch'ing Heaven* (HY 461) was written, in conjunction with a fresh Taoist missionary effort in south China.[103]

3

THE LITERATURE OF SPELLS

> *Anno* 1670, not far from Cirencester, was an apparition: being demanded, whether a good spirit or a bad? Returned no answer, but disappeared with a curious perfume and most melodious twang.
>
> JOHN AUBREY, *Miscellanies* (1696)

The 'Spirit-Spells of the Abyss'

A number of other works from the early medieval period are crucial to a better appreciation of the complexities of demonology and therapeutic methods. One of the most massive Taoist books in this department is a collection in twenty chapters entitled *Spirit-Spells of the Abyss* (*Tung-yüan shen-chou ching*, HY 335).[1] Its earliest sections were written at the beginning of the fifth century, but the later parts were completed only in the tenth century, and so the work represents an extended exposition of Taoist thought on the subject. Moreover, like the *Law-Script of Right Unity* series, this material generated an entire subclass of Taoist texts. Apart from the main scriptures, there are seven other "Spirit-Spells of the Abyss" books in the Taoist canon, and we have the titles of at least seven more that are lost. The names of the first ten chapters of the twenty-chapter *Spirit-Spells* scripture reveal the preoccupation of the literature of the abyss as a whole: Conjuring Devils, Banishing Demons, Binding Demons, Killing Demons, Banning Demons, Conjuring Spooks (*hsiang*, an uncommon word), Beheading Demons, Summoning Demons, Pursuing Demons, and (once again) Killing Demons. The emphasis is no less demonologic than in the *Demon-Statutes of Nü-ch'ing* (see pp. 80–87), but in this case we are promised vigorous action rather than an immutable law code.

As in other Taoist scriptures of the fourth and fifth centuries, the format suggests the influence of Buddhist scripture. Each book opens with the Tao (in place of the Buddha) speaking to an assembled multitude of auditors; that is, the book purports to reproduce the words of the deified Lao-tzu in his cosmic role of ultimate primordial being. The overarching framework is narrative; there are "historical" reminiscences and general reflections on the state of the world, but the consistent emphasis is on prediction and warning—of the evils that will steadily and successively descend on the world, the natural catastrophes that will bring the present order to a dramatic end, and the ultimate renewal for the faithful élite, possessors of this book, in an age of Great Peace:

> The Tao said, "In the year of the snake and the year of the horse, the demon armies will flood forth and the devil-kings will afflict mankind with their toxic infestations. I am now sending forty-nine million constables to arrest the devil-kings of the Thirty-Six Heavens, to subdue them and bind them by oath. According to the oath, from now on, should any people of this land die before the appointed time, or suffer from grievous ailments, prison, or forced labor, this will all be due to the devil-kings not having kept the lesser demons from afflicting and harming the people. From this time forth, the golden mouth of the Most High decrees that should there be any devil-kings who do not place those demons under restraint, and who allow them to cause the land's people to perish without due cause, through pestilence, war, suffering, prison, or forced labor, because these devil-kings are guilty of not having controlled the lesser demons, they shall be beheaded without mercy."[2]

The devil-kings (*mo-wang*) have definitely advanced in the Taoist ranks since the Shang-ch'ing revelations of the 360s. Then, devils were simply to be feared and driven off; now, the mighty among them have been subdued and bound by covenant to control the demon hordes that they formerly led in action against mortals. A generation earlier, these Indian émigrés were simply among the enemy; now they have been subdued and turned into valuable allies, and this is a further token of Buddhist influence. The Taoist pantheon was in continuous upward expansion as new celestial regions were charted, but part of the expansion originated from below. The more exalted hierarchy rested on a broadening base of local cults, and no doubt it was this class of godling—local Chinese "gods of the profane"—that came to be tolerated as "devil-kings."

As in the Nü-ch'ing text, the recalcitrant demons and their devil-masters are to be controlled and punished by means of due legal authority. Things were not always so, however. Like the *Demon-Statutes of Nü-ch'ing*, the *Spirit-Spells of the Abyss* goes on to inform us of earlier, happier days when demonic afflictions were unknown. Unknown, too, were complex scriptures like the present text, which (we are told) have now become so necessary to subjugate the omnipresent demons:

> The Tao said, "From Fu Hsi's time [in the distant mythological past] down to the end of the Han dynasty [220 C.E.], the people were vastly happy. Most of them did not have faith in the Tao; they all simply received the influences of heaven. They knew nothing about the Tao, the Law, or the scriptures—there was no need for such things in those happy days, when everyone was naturally good and naturally healthy. During the reign of the Chin dynasty [third/fourth centuries C.E.], though, as the secular order approached its end, people lost their original purity, and a race of degenerate rulers arose to lord it over mankind. The people suffered; the rulers were oppressive, and their subjects were harried. But in time, in the region south of the Yangtse, the people of heaven began to assemble and the Tao's influence started to manifest itself."

Once again we have the tale of primitive perfection and simplicity followed by inexorable decline and decay. Scriptures, ritual, and religion are only necessary in times of degeneration, a theme we find again in Buddhist sources. The third and fourth centuries—the period immediately preceding the compilation of these *Spirit-Spells*—marked a veritable nadir of humanity, and conditions were still worsening. Yet already a nucleus of the new age had appeared in the favored region just south of the Yangtse River. There was a renewal of Taoist interest among "heaven's people," and this obviously corresponds to the great florescence of revelation and scripture-writing that occurred in that region in the second half of the fourth century. First the Shang-ch'ing revelations of 364–70 brought some fifteen new celestial scriptures into the world, together with much hagiography, poetry, and prophecy. Then, in the 390s, the Ling-pao ("transcendent jewel") revelations vouchsafed a further twenty-odd scriptures to an expectant humanity. Other authors, noting the success of these two great bodies of literature, were busily producing still more texts along the same lines, freely adapting Shang-ch'ing and Ling-pao elements; the creator of the *Spirit-Spells* is clearly one of these, with a style of his own, and he places his work within this inspired south-of-the-Yangtse tradition.[3]

Now, he informs us, as the time of celestially ordained catastrophe—the fated end of the kalpa—approaches, certain fortunate residents of this region have been able to obtain either Ling-pao or Shang-ch'ing scriptures. For those who have been so favored, it is a clear sign that merit accrued in previous lifetimes by their ancestors is flowing down to their own present selves. Yet those who either hear or behold the *Spirit-Spells of the Abyss* will be given proof of even greater felicity, for they will be able to pass through the Three Rivers (of the underworld) and the calamity of the Great Deluge. We are assured that anyone who obtains this scripture, be he emperor, king, nobleman, or high officer of state, down to the stupid common-people and even male and female slaves, will thereby have his or her name entered on the registers of the immortals and will not die a violent death. When the Most High (Lao-tzu) expounded this scripture in the Palace of Sublime Effulgence, the Great Devils of the Nine Heavens and the rākṣasa demon-maurauders, together with all their attendants to the number of eight million myriads, were all assembled there to hear the Celestial Venerable expound the Law. All clasped their hands and with one accord prostrated themselves. The Celestial Venerable then proceeded to develop his great scripture for duly registered immortals, and every one among the four classes of listeners, when he heard it, felt strange effects in his own body.[4]

To readers of Buddhist scripture, these last phrases have a familiar ring, and they illustrate the firm impression made on this class of Taoist literature by the seductive Indian narrative framework, with its penchant for hyperbole. Lao-tzu, or "the Tao," then proceeds to detail the succession of prophecies that give the work its special apocalyptic urgency. There have been mighty disasters in the past, starting with the great flood of legendary antiquity, in which "half the people died." This flood continues as a basic point of reference in medieval apocalyptic literature; it is the single greatest cosmic calamity of which ancient records tell, and the world-shattering disaster that is on the verge of occurring will be something comparably horrific—only greater still. Of the three classical apocalyptic agents of Indian cosmology (a theme taken over by the *Spirit-Spells* as well as other Taoist eschatological texts of the time)—namely, fire, water, and wind (or, in this Taoist text, as in some Buddhist ones, weapons)—water held the strongest grip on the Chinese imagination. With the native mythological precedent, and in the setting of the lower Yangtse region, the danger was only too real. Hell, too, was predominantly seen in aqueous terms, and the Three Rivers of this text (like the Water Office of early medieval Taoist works generally) was viewed as a preeminent place of punishment and hard labor for the souls of dead transgressors. But neither hell nor high water will hold any terrors for the fortunate possessors of this new addition to scripture. It will vouchsafe their deliverance though the all-engulfing waves. This text thus marks the emergence of a new and sure pathway to security and ultimate salvation among the Elect, although it also puts itself forward as the rallying point for an immediate reorganization of society in the here-and-now. The ordinary social distinctions, the conventional hierarchy of classes and honors, wealth and power are henceforth to be seen as meaningless. Humanity will clearly divide into two groups: those who have the *Spirit-Spells of the Abyss* and those who do not.

As the times continue to worsen, we are told, rulers will be unable to control their subjects, the seasons will be upset, and the harvests will not ripen. People will be so evil that fathers and sons, elder and younger brothers will plot against each other, bringing about the destruction of whole families. Brigands will roam about slaughtering people without any reason. At this time, pestilent breaths (*ch'i*) will be especially numerous; there will be ninety different sorts of ailment in the world, and they will kill the wicked. There will be (for example) red-headed killer-demons. Each of these will grasp a red staff and wander about in the world of mortals with capturing human beings as his sole concern. The symptoms of these demons' success may be watched for, and will appear within the period of a day or a month. Green breaths mean swellings (*chung-ping*); yellow breaths indicate diarrhea with foreign matter (*hsia-li*); white breaths mean Sudden Turmoil Syndrome (*huo-luan*); black breaths mean government officials. The demons take these breaths and spread them throughout the world to kill the ignorant. But for men of the Tao (*tao-shih*) and Masters of the Law (*fa-shih*) who have received this book of *Spirit-Spells*, there are ninety million myriad great gods, spontaneously generated strongmen, celestial men and jade women who all come as protectors. If you make offerings to the scripture and its spirit-attendants, every sort of ailment will vanish by itself and you will not die a violent death. Also, when mighty brigands from neighboring states come and invade your territory, read this scripture and the invaders will depart of their own accord:[5]

> The Tao said, "The Great Kings of Malignant Wraiths of the Three Heavens lead a troop of forty-eight myriads that specialize in spreading red swellings. The eighty myriad Great Kings of Malignant Wraiths of the Six Heavens lead troops of seven hundred myriads that specialize in spreading white swellings.

> The Great Kings of Malignant Wraiths of the Nine Heavens and the Great Kings of Malignant Wraiths of the Three Heavens, sixty myriads of each, lead followers to the number of thirty-nine thousand that specialize in spreading black swellings. The Great Kings of Malignant Wraiths of Thirty-Six Heavens head seventy myriads that specialize in spreading yellow swellings. The Great Kings of Malignant Wraiths of the Seven Heavens lead nine million myriads that specialize in spreading blue swellings. They attach themselves to people's bodies and inundate their four limbs; their faces turn blue, red, yellow, white, or black. They are now cold, now hot, now coming, now going. As the days drag on, they sink ever deeper into misery. The miasmas come and pain their hearts; beneath their hearts they become indurated and full. They do not wish to eat or drink. As they eat and drink less and less, they vomit up everything or else, rebel against eating, and find everything flavorless. Sometimes the curses of dead ancestors reach to living persons; when there is guilty karma of this sort, it brings about troubles with officials, imprisonment, and resentment and blame. If you wish to eliminate such afflictions, you must first receive this scripture and make offerings to the Master; only after doing this will you be able to ascend on high as an immortal."[6]

In this manner the text's "predictions" offer a remarkable medley of political events, military movements, and pathogenic demon manifestations, all occultly coordinated. The wide range of pathological phenomena is striking, as is the extension of demonic causality to include trouble with the secular authorities (who are also stigmatized as demonic afflictors in Indian Buddhist texts). One is struck by the multiple dimensions of this worldview, which structures taxonomy in a descending scale according to the diagnostic signs of differently colored "breaths," beginning with sudden death, proceeding through tumors, dysentery, and shock or confusion, and concluding with "official business"—namely, trouble with the law. Demonically induced "ailments" are social or societal in the fullest sense of those terms. Illness is not merely a family affair; it is regional, national, universal. For these Taoists, the secular government itself would seem to count as one more disagreeable pathological symptom:

> The Tao said, "O you Great Kings of Malignant Wraiths! In previous lives you accomplished no acts of merit; you did not have faith in the Great Tao; you heaped up mountains of guilt. Now you are among the malignant wraiths that specialize in spreading fevers and toxic infections among mankind. Some suffer from cold and heat in their bodies, in others the whites and blacks of their eyes are reversed, some run madly about, speaking without sense; others sing and howl, sob and wail. For some, their four limbs are sore and swollen

> and their vital breaths contend wildly within them. Ailments of these kinds fill the entire world; they may confuse people's minds, causing them to get involved in lawsuits and be cast unjustly into prison. Thus are the people bitterly afflicted. And all ailments of these sorts are the doing of you Kings of Malignant Wraiths. From this time on, you are to aid and protect those who do honor to this scripture-talisman. Do not let them suffer any evil. The place where this scripture is read is to be avoided by demon-soldiers and protected by the Good Spirits. If you do not have faith in the Great Law and so come once more to attack these Masters of the Law, you Kings of Malignant Wraiths will enter the Abyss, you Kings of Malignant Wraiths will enter the water! You Kings of Malignant Wraiths will enter the fire! You Kings of Malignant Wraiths will be decapitated ten thousand times! You Kings of Malignant Wraiths will have your heads broken into eighty pieces! Swiftly they will seize your vital essence! Swiftly they will seize your souls! Then you will not be able to attack and harm and plague and torment the good, just people of the world! Swiftly, swiftly, in accordance with the Statutes and Ordinances!"[7]

The responsibility of these demonic agents is alleged to be total. They are to blame for all misfortune, and the words of Lao-tzu the Most High guarantee that they will henceforth confine their malevolent intentions to those unfortunates who do not possess a copy of this book. Indeed, possession of the *Spirit-Spells* is both a proof of status and direct evidence of Lao-tzu's promise that the book's possessors will not be attacked by the wraith-kings and their countless demon-troops. Since owning a copy of this scripture in itself ensures immunity, "treatment" of disease becomes, for these privileged Taoists, a secondary consideration. In fact, the work renders obsolete all previous treatments for demonic assault. It informs its readers that if they simply accept the scripture and pay homage to it in their family circle, they will no longer need recourse to the traditional Taoist family registers of spirits—the lists of spirit-protectors, increasing in number as the householder advanced in seniority, with which all members of the Way of the Celestial Master (the basic Taoist organization) were successively invested. "How can this be?" the scripture asks, rhetorically. "Because this scripture has countless immortals, jade maidens, celestials, dragons, and demons who constantly protect it." They will naturally extend their protection to the scripture's reverent possessors, so that "persons who have long been ill, or who have had much misfortune and little happiness and have failed in all their undertakings, have only to accept and possess this scripture to eliminate all their great calamities."[8]

In this way the *Spirit-Spells of the Abyss* presents itself as the nucleus of a new sacred genealogy. It links its possessor to the Tao, transforming him into Lao-tzu's well-protected child; it also allies him with other owners of the scripture in a new family of the saints. The original Taoist movement of the second and third centuries appears to have had no extended scriptural literature. Its main "literature" seems to have consisted of law codes and collections of documents, as we have seen. The movement toward dramatic scriptural presentation received its greatest impetus from the creation of the Shang-ch'ing corpus and was greatly expanded in the series of Ling-pao works. These latter, even more than the Shang-ch'ing writings, clearly show that the chief models for this new literary form were Buddhist scriptures.[9]

From Buddhism came not only the form—the narrative setting outside of ordinary time, beyond the quotidian world of human concerns—but also the "cult of the book," which clearly radiated from Mahāyāna Buddhism into these early Taoist creations. In the *Lotus Sūtra*, for example, which was first translated into Chinese in full in 286, we find the book itself speaking with a similar voice. Again and again the *Lotus* tells of all the good things that lie in store, in this life and the next—present safety and protection, and eventual rebirth among the happy and sensuous gods and goddesses—for the person who receives, keeps, reads and recites, copies or causes others to copy, studies and practices the *Lotus Sūtra*. The cult of the book was central to the expansion of Mahāyāna Buddhism, and it also exerted a lasting influence on Taoism and Chinese society.[10]

The typical scripture presents itself as enshrining the words of a deity. It tells a story and is full of uplifting parables. It counsels and admonishes you, like a stern but loving parent. It tells you how to perform rites essential to the safety and salvation of your entire family. Moreover, it comes into your home accompanied by a powerful troop of otherworldly guardians. This new family member, elder, and counselor—the book—only requires due reverence and respect in order to extend to you all the privileges and security that its possession confers. In some cases, you are directed to recite it, copy it, and diffuse it widely; in others, you have only to treasure it, carry it always on your person, and keep it carefully hidden from unqualified persons. It must at all events be treated with marked attention and respect, and be kept in a special receptacle in a pure place. Swaddled and boxed (like a precious child), it must have incense-offerings burnt before it (as one would burn incense before an image—or an ancestral tablet). To become a fortune-bringing talisman for your whole family, it must be venerated in its own right. The book is a true *eidolon*, a new lares-and-penates, and such devoted bibliolatry will bind to your service not only the scripture's own divine protectors but also the demonic legions that the scripture's new authority has bound by oath under the Law. As the *Spirit-Spells of the Abyss* never wearies of repeating, its recipients are the beneficiaries of a special dispensation from the devil-kings and the Kings of Malignant Wraiths, who are solely responsible for all the ills that afflict mankind. Thus the new scriptural literature also achieves a redefinition of the nature and function of demons. As in Buddhism, the chieftains of pandemonium are conquered, converted, and bound to serve the very Law that they previously defied. They have special qualifications for controlling the millions of violent demons with which the world teems, and so the devil-kings and the Kings of Malignant Wraiths—whose visible manifestations were the leading "gods" worshipped by ordinary people—are pressed into service as bondsmen of the Law. "Set a demon to catch a demon" was basic Buddhist strategy; yet we also find it, uninfluenced by Buddhism, in the old Chinese exorcistic ceremonies at year's end. As was so often the case, Buddhist institutions and literary forms simply helped to bring forward and clarify ideas and practices that were already there, and this in part explains their success in China.[11]

Starting with the Shang-ch'ing revelations, Taoist scriptures had begun to assure their possessors that simply owning the text was sufficient protection against all possible attacks from illness- or misfortune-provoking demons. Such scriptures were stated to have been eternally extant in the heavens; they were now brought into the world ready-made for all contingencies.[12] One needed only to acquire them and believe; the rest was automatic. Present social status was irrelevant to the question of ownership, for whether or not one would come into possession of the sacred book was said to have been occultly determined long before, often by deeds committed in previous existences (whether one's own or one's ancestors'). Some scriptures go beyond social egalitarianism to a complete latitudinarianism: Even if you never practice any of the rituals or observe any of the prohibitions set forth in the text, so long as you keep it in your possession and do not allow it to be defiled, your salvation is ensured.[13]

Thus the book itself is both physician and medicine; it provides both diagnosis and cure.[14] What is more, the new scriptures reaffirm the replacement, by special Taoist written means, of secular medical treatment (though in fact, rather than abrogating the older Taoist therapeutic methods, they simply provided Taoists with an additional avenue to salvation). Yet though such scriptures were a great repository of strength to the faithful, they might become monstrous sources of disease and destruction for those who did not believe in them. We have seen that the texts in question issue stern warnings to outside detractors, as well as to Taoists who irresponsibly divulge scriptural secrets to unqualified persons. Chinese Buddhist texts could be even more vehement. The *Book of Spirit-Spells of the Eightfold Yang of Heaven and Earth* (*T'ien-ti pa-yang shen-chou ching*, T. 2897), a seventh- or eighth-century Chinese Buddhist creation, warns readers:

> Anyone who lacks faith in the True Law, who holds perverse views, and who, hearing this scripture read, slanders it, saying that it is not the word of the Buddha, will be punished in his present life; he will acquire the white pustule sickness, with foul ulcers oozing pus and blood and spreading over his entire body, which will putrefy in fetid corruption. Everyone will loathe him, and on the day of his death he will fall straight into the bottommost hell, where he will be pierced by fire from above and below. Iron staves and forks will penetrate all the apertures of his body, molten copper will be poured into his mouth, and his sinews and bones will be rent asunder. Every day and every night he will die ten thousand times and ten thousand times be brought back to life, without a moment's respite—and this will happen to him because he slandered this scripture."[15]

The monk who wrote this had no hesitation in condemning his critics to what might be leprosy during their lifetimes and unspeakable tortures after death. Evidently Buddhists, too, had a short way with dissenters. Sacred scriptures were definitely not to be trifled with; if they can protect against all harm and heal all manner of afflictions, they can also fatally infect—and the sacred book is an infallible judge of character. Its very presence radiates irresistible power, guaranteeing blessing and celestial mansions for the good, destruction and infernal torment for the wicked.

Logically, at least, scriptures of such potency naturally rendered obsolete all previous methods of therapy; if it were not for the need of transmitting the scripture and spreading its message of salvation, human agency would no doubt have been virtually excluded from Taoist ritual from that time forth. But the *Spirit-Spells of the Abyss* was obviously intended for a large and varied public, and to reach them in their hour of need, it required a special class of practitioners: "If in the world at the present time there are men or women suffering from illness or in immediate peril, the Master of the Law will take this scripture, go to their houses, and save the sufferers from disease."[16] These

"Masters of the Law" (*fa-shih*) were evidently to be the prime movers in diffusing the book of *Spirit-Spells* to those who most sorely needed it. Elsewhere the scripture speaks of Masters of the Law of the Three Caverns (*san-tung fa-shih*) who by reading the book can bring the dead back to life.[17]

Here is yet another example of a Taoist technical term and ritual function that cannot be fully understood without reference to contemporary Buddhist sources. Turning once again to the Chinese text of the *Lotus Sūtra*, we find that the expression "Master of the Law" is regularly used to translate the Sanskrit *dharma-bhāṇaka* ("preacher of the Dharma").[18] According to the *Lotus*, the transmission and explanation of this most popular of all Buddhist scriptures was assigned to a class of missionary monks who wandered up and down the land entering households, expounding the scripture, casting out demons by means of its spells (*dhāraṇī*), and confirming laymen and laywomen in its assurances of a better rebirth in some celestial abode of bliss if only they followed the scripture's instructions about reading, reciting, copying, revering it, and so on. It has been suggested that these itinerant preachers were largely responsible for the rapid spread of Mahāyāna scriptures and doctrines.[19] The references in the *Spirit-Spells of the Abyss* and other sources make it clear that comparable Masters of the Law were also instrumental in promoting Taoism in China south of the Yangtse during the fifth century—especially the Taoism of the new, Mahāyāna-style scriptures, for that is the significance of the "three caverns" (*san-tung*) prefixed to the Masters' title. The "caverns" refer to the three bodies of sacred literature in circulation among fifth-century Taoists in that region. The first and highest "cavern," that of Perfection, was reserved for the Shang-ch'ing scriptures; the second, Sublimity, for Ling-pao scriptures; and the third, Divinity, comprised the older, miscellaneous occult literature that had been produced in this spiritually intense area of China before the Shang-ch'ing revelations. This classification long outlasted any strict historical relevance; it dominates (under vastly changed conditions) even the fifteenth-century Taoist canon. The early chapters of the *Spirit-Spells of the Abyss* document a time when this codification of recently revealed literature was just beginning its career of conquest—and when the Masters of the Law were its prophets.

Though acting in the name of the Three Caverns, for immediate therapeutic purposes the Masters of the Law were obviously making use of the *Spirit-Spells of the Abyss*, a most highly idiosyncratic and obsessive book that does not appear to be linked with any one of the three categories of Taoist scripture. The first mention of "three caverns" is found in texts of the Ling-pao corpus from the 390s. But the same literature also refers to another, more obscure series of five caverns: the Primordial, the Abyss, the Void, the Numinous, and the Nil.[20] The second of these is obviously the home of our spirit-spells. Groups of threes are ranked vertically, while sets of fives are deployed horizontally, and the five subsidiary caverns appear to have been conceived of as extending across the world beneath the surface of the earth. Like China's five sacred mountains, the primary association of this pentad seems to have been with the world of the dead and demonic affairs, and the author of the *Spirit-Spells of the Abyss* appears to have been supplying a portion of the literature evoked by the Ling-pao text's list of five caverns. The demonic associations of the Abyss are made perfectly clear in the curse with which the Kings of Malignant Wraiths are threatened should they dare to break their oath to protect Taoists or let their spectral subordinates get out of hand: "If you do not have faith in the Great Law, but rather come once more to attack these Masters of the Law, you Kings of Malignant Wraiths will enter the Abyss, you Kings of Malignant Wraiths will enter the water, you Kings of Malignant Wraiths will enter the fire!" And we may recall the apocalyptic Shang-ch'ing prophecy, as well: "Then the host of afflictors will run riot and be cast into the gaping Abyss!"[21] The Abyss was clearly no garden of delights, but rather a hell that even hell-beings like the wraiths might well find highly uncomfortable.[22]

If the "Abyss" in the scripture's title is now explained, another element remains mysterious. The term "spirit-spells" seems at first sight to pose no problem; the book deals with controlling demons, and spells are an obvious means of achieving this end. But as we read through the text, it is puzzling to discover that no spells appear to be given. In fact, the warning imprecation with which the Kings of Malignant Wraiths are threatened is as close as the book comes to furnishing us with a concrete spell suitable for immediate use. Could it be that the entire text of the scripture is intended as a great spell, recitation of which will keep all demons away? Like the *Demon-Statutes of Nü-ch'ing* (which is as short on conventional "statutes" as this work is on ordinary "spells"), the *Spirit-Spells of the Abyss* is essentially a repertory of the fiends' names and numbers. Whether assimilated to a legal code or to a demonifuge incantation, such comprehensive naming and numbering was prerequisite to full control over the enemy.

Still, the subject of spells requires some consideration; it is not as if they were missing from other early Taoist scriptures. They indeed occur, and are generally couched (like the curse on the Kings of Malignant Wraiths) in highly dramatic, violent form, as strong threats or commands. Perhaps the most famous example is the spell of the star Celestial Beacon (T'ien-p'eng), first found in the Shang-ch'ing *Declarations of the Perfect Ones*:

> T'ien-p'eng, T'ien-p'eng,
> Killer-Youths of the Nine Primordials,
> Overseer of the Five Ting-Spirits,
> Northern Duke of the Lofty Ladle,
> Eight Transcendents, Seven Governors,
> The Most High—purge evil utterly! . . .
> Devour devils, consume specters,
> Toss their bodies to the wind.
> Blue of tongue, green of tooth,
> The four-eyed ancient,
> Stalwarts of heaven, celestial strongmen,
> Tower in the south, keep evil from that quarter.
> Let heaven's cavalry soar upward,
> Overawe the north with lances at the ready.
> Assign three hundred thousand infantry
> On guard about my nine-walled citadel.
> Drive corpse-specters a thousand leagues away,
> Abolish all of evil omen.
> Then should any piffling demon
> Dare to come and show himself,
> May the Heaven-Snatcher with his great axe
> strike off his head and all his other limbs,
> The Flaming Monarch crackle his blood,
> The Northern Dipper roast his bones,
> The Four Luminaries snap his skeleton,
> The Ape of Heaven wipe out his clan.
> When my spirit-sword falls a single time,
> All demons scatter in disarray![23]

This well-developed incantation assumes an entire pantheon, each member of which is fully equipped to deal with demon-aggressors in his own specialized way. It marks a notable advance in complexity over extant pre-Taoist spell-texts, but there is an obvious connection between the language of Taoist spells and the language of Chinese curses generally. The Chinese have long been famed for the richness and offensiveness of their swearing, and closer investigation of what James Matisoff has termed "psycho-ostensive expressions" is badly needed in the East Asian sphere.[24] A few selections recorded in nineteenth-century Fuchow suggest the interest of colloquial cursing for the student of Chinese demonology and society, especially in relation to Taoist spells and imprecations. "May the Five Monarchs catch you!" "May the Five Monarchs arrest you at your door!" (The "monarchs" are the plague-gods, and so this dooms your adversary to death by pestilence.)[25] "May you be fried in the cauldron of oil!" May your tongue be cut off!" (These refer to well-known punishments of hell.) "May your posterity be cut off!" "May fish be your coffin and water be your grave!" "May your body be in one place and your head in another!" "May your corpse be eaten by dogs!" "May the fire of heaven consume you!" "May demons carry you off!"[26] These are among the mildest specimens of their kind, having been collected by an American Protestant missionary. Still, it is clear that the righteous Taoist and the furious layman were to a large extent speaking the same language.

Of course, laymen might also be initiated into the mysteries of the "higher cursing" performed by ritual specialists, and interest in such matters was shared by some of the most eminent Chinese. In his commonplace book, the last emperor of the Liang dynasty (Hsiao I, 508–55; r. 552–55) informs us that his own study of spells began at the age of eight. Typically, he showed no sectarian bias in the matter. He learned to recite several important Buddhist spells under the tutelage of a monk, and went to a commandant of the palace guard for instruction in native Chinese spellbinding and the performance of the Step of Yü for curing swellings.[27] Elsewhere in his book, the emperor admiringly describes the marvels wrought by "foreign magicians" by means of their spells. They can approach a deep lake (*yüan*, "abyss") with the Step of Yü and bring a dragon up to the surface. The creature may be a hundred feet long, but when the magician recites his spell over it, it shrinks to a few inches so that he can pick it up and place it in a bottle-gourd. They always have four or five of these miniature dragons with them, and keep them supplied with water. When there is little rainfall in other countries and people send for a dragon, the magicians go to that place and sell them one; the price for one dragon is ten catties of gold. They take one of their dragons and place it in water, and it immediately raises clouds and rain.[28] In this account we discover "foreign magicians" performing the Chinese Step of Yü, and the shared concern with rain-making of the Indian nāga-cult and the Chinese cult of the dragon. We have discussed Indian Buddhist demonology and the Buddhist influence on Taoist scriptures; it should now be illuminating to examine Chinese transformations of Indian demonology and the special literature of Buddhist incantations.

Proto-Tantra and Buddhist Books of Spells

Taoist spells are usually quite intelligible to the reader, being normally written in straightforward standard Chinese. In turning to Buddhist spell-literature, however, we are approaching a thicket of Sanskrit that has traditionally been considered one of the least attractive, least rewarding areas of Buddhist studies.[29] Yet we seem to have no choice in the matter; the term "spirit-spell" (*shen-chou*) that we have encountered in Taoist texts also occurs with great frequency in Chinese Buddhist texts from the third century on. It stands there as an equivalent of the Sanskrit terms *mantra* and *dhāraṇī*. Mantras have been the basic spell-material of all Indian ritual, from Vedic times to the present day; they usually make intelligible statements and are often invocations of the gods.[30] The case of dhāraṇīs is rather more complicated. Whereas mantras are found in all forms of Indian ritual, dhāraṇīs are specific to Buddhism.[31] The etymology of the term as well as accounts of the earliest function of dhāraṇīs link them with memory, and it has been suggested that this genre of "spell" grew out of sequences of disjunct syllables, joined together as abbreviated mnemonic devices for retaining in mind large constructs of highly technical doctrinal categories.[32] Subsequently, it is said, these intrinsically meaningless scholastic devices were personified and deified. In contrast to mantras, dhāraṇīs are usually supposed to be unintelligible gibberish. Such at any rate is the usual distinction made between the two types of incantation.

In fact, when we examine early medieval Chinese Buddhist writings—translations from the Sanskrit as well as works composed directly in Chinese—we find that the supposed distinction between dhāraṇīs and mantras is a good deal less clearcut.[33] Officially, the term *dhāraṇī* is supposed to have been either translated into Chinese as *tsung-ch'ih* ("comprehensive retention," alluding to the memory-function), or else simply transliterated as *t'o-lo-ni*.[34] The Chinese term "spirit-spell" (*shen-chou*), in contrast, is said by lexicographers to apply exclusively to mantras. Not surprisingly, the documents do not obey these tidy rules. All three terms were in fact used to designate dhāraṇīs, and it is only natural that the attractive expression "spirit-spell" came to be especially widely used in texts apparently intended for a large circulation.[35]

Dhāraṇīs are found in a number of important early Mahāyāna scriptures, like the *Lotus Sūtra*—and the translator of the first complete Chinese version of the *Lotus* (286 C.E.) clearly did not subscribe to the dhāraṇīs-are-gibberish theory, since he translated all of them into lucid Chinese. But dhāraṇīs also existed in their own right, as the focal point of an extensive literature of independent dhāraṇī-sūtras.[36] The first examples were translated or transcribed into Chinese in the third century. They share the basic frame-story common to all Buddhist scripture; they, too, have their setting in India during the Buddha's lifetime and represent the Buddha's own words to the assembly of his disciples and the Indian gods. But in the case of the dhāraṇī-scriptures, the frame-stories that explain each book's origins have a very particular orientation. They all specify that these scriptures and the demon-quelling spells that they contain are intended for a time very different from the age when the Buddha first enunciated these texts. This literature describes itself as being created for the special conditions destined to obtain when the Buddha's Law and the world itself are approaching their end. Like early medieval Taoist ritual and demonological writings, the orientation of the dhāraṇī-scriptures is firmly toward apocalyptic eschatology.

A number of dhāraṇī-scriptures open with a scene like the following, taken from a fourth-century translation, the *Spirit-Spell Spoken by the Sorcerer Bhadra* (*Fo-shuo hsüan-shih Pa-t'o so-shuo shen-chou ching*, T. 1378A): The monks and nuns in the Buddha's entourage are sorely troubled by demons, disease, poisonous serpents, and robbers. A sorcerer named Bhadra approaches the Buddha and reports on the torments besetting the community. He then offers an invincible spell from his own supply. At first the Buddha vehemently declines the offer: "Nay, Bhadra," he says, "your spell will slay living beings!" (meaning, of course, all the motley crew of demons, serpents, robbers, and so on, for Buddhists are all bound by oath not to take life in any form). But the sorcerer replies that the problems now troubling the Buddhist community are nothing compared to what they will have to face when the Buddha is no longer alive in the world, during the final years of the Law, when the Buddha's religion is on the verge of extinction. Hence, in the end, the Buddha accepts the noxious spell as a means of aiding the current victims of these various afflictions, but more especially to provide his followers in times to come with a powerful means of protection against those even greater torments that the future holds in store.[37]

In the *Lotus Sūtra*, too, the dhāraṇīs are all introduced with reference to apocalyptic futurity, and it is common for them to be presented to the Buddha by figures outside the tranquil circle of respectable Buddhist deities. Those who come forward with spells for the protection of Buddhists in the times of approaching travail are usually either pagan gods or demons who have been subdued, converted, and bound by oath as protectors of the faithful: They are clearly all elder members of the same family as the devil-kings and Kings of Malignant Wraiths whom we find exercising identical functions in Taoist scriptures.[38] These features were to develop and expand within Buddhism; by the seventh century, the comprehensive system of revelation and ritual that we are accustomed to call "Tantric Buddhism" had come into being on these foundations. Tantric Buddhism had much success in China for a time, and its influence on the cultures of both Japan and Tibet was decisive (see Chapters 5 and 6). At this earlier stage, though, in the dhāraṇī-scriptures of "proto-Tantric" literature (third to sixth centuries), we can already discern a number of very close structural and strategic analogies between this form of Buddhism and Taoist thought and ritual. It is therefore scarcely surprising that there should have been a good deal of exchange, mutual influence, and even revisionism between Taoism and the Indian system as it developed in a Chinese context.

We have established the role of "apocryphal scriptures" in the work of redefining alien systems and acclimatizing them to new intellectual contexts and social conditions. It is clear, then, that the most significant evidence for the assimilation and transformation of proto-Tantric Buddhism and its demonology is likely to be found in scriptures composed in China. Dhāraṇī-scriptures share with their Taoist counterparts both an apocalyptic background and the crucial role attributed to demonic figures outside the formal pantheon. The overwhelming practical concern of both bodies of texts is the healing of ailments resulting from demonic agency. Our question now is, how do Buddhist scriptures of the period approach this problem in terms of practical therapeutic rituals—Buddhist scriptures actually written in Chinese (though purporting to be translations from Sanskrit originals), that is? If the cult of the book was India's great gift to Chinese authors, with this assurance of the high worth of their medium, how did they go about assimilating an Indian genre? What sort of ritual texts did early medieval Chinese Buddhist monks compose when they set themselves behind the mask of the Buddha and wrote as if they were writing, in Chinese, the "originals" from which they claimed that their texts derived? These monkish authors were Buddhists, and they show their unceasing consciousness of this by constant recourse to all the trappings of "authentic" Indian Buddhist scripture: the Indian proper names, a smattering of Sanskrit technical terms, and, most conspicuously in the dhāraṇī literature, the Sanskrit or pseudo-Sanskrit of the spells themselves. But when all account is taken of this, and of the Buddhist written models they had before them, the simplest answer to the question might nonetheless be that they often reacted as Taoists—as we shall see.

At first glance, the dhāraṇī books appear to offer only an impenetrable tangle of Sanskrit, but a closer look sometimes reveals a more familiar aspect, a more accustomed sound. In the *Dhāraṇī Miscellany* (*T'o-lo-ni tsa-chi*, T. 1336), a bulky Chinese anthology of dhāraṇīs compiled in the first half of the sixth century, amid all the Sanskrit spells we suddenly come upon this classic Chinese incantation against ulcers and swellings, to be recited thrice seven times:

> Seven Maidens in heaven above,
> bestow on me fine pharmaka!
> When I spit on a mountain, the mountain crumbles;
> when I spit on a stone, the stone splits apart;
> when I spit in water, the water dries up;
> when I spit in fire, the fire goes out;
> when I spit on metal, the metal cracks;
> when I spit on a tree, the tree breaks open;
> when I spit on an ulcer, the ulcer dies;
> when I spit on a swelling, the swelling vanishes.
> Great fish in the sea turn into turtles,
> thunder rises in the southwest, but its sound is not heard.
> In it is a toad that eats the heart of the moon;
> its great swellings are like mountains, its small ones like book-rolls.
> When I spit on a single swelling, all swellings die,
> when I spit on a single ulcer, all ulcers cease.
> May whatever I enchant with this spell be as I wish it![39]

This example not only illustrates the healing power of spittle (when it has been properly charged with concentrated breath) but also evokes the demon-destroying thunder and the toad that gnaws upon the moon (both staple elements of Chinese folklore). Like the moon and the toad that fattens on it, the tumors and ulcers on the patient's body can be deflated. Even as the swollen toad sucks at the heart of the swollen moon, so the spell of the seven celestial maidens draws out the poison from the swellings on the patient's body—and the newly restored moon, too, is a guarantee of success in healing.[40] The action by analogy and the epic boasting of the therapeutic champion before the fray, touting the supreme efficacy of his potent spittle—all the elements in this spell go back to ancient, pre-Taoist Chinese practice. The same rhythmical formulas were used by healers wielding therapeutic seals and talismans, and became common currency among Buddhist and Taoist specialists alike (see Chapter 4).

Another basic Chinese incantory pattern was so forceful and seductive that it, too, breached the Buddhist *cordon sanitaire* and entered Buddhist ritual. It is a litany, droning and repetitious, and takes the form of successive lines, each running "noun-noun-verb-me":

> Sun and Moon illumine me,
> Five Radiances assist me,
> Five Planets extend over me,
> Swiftly I call them, swiftly they come,
> Swiftly, swiftly, in accordance with the Statues and Ordinances!

So runs a Taoist text.[41] In the *Divine Talismans of the Seven Thousand Buddhas* (*Ch'i-ch'ien fo shen-fu ching*, T. 2904), a manuscript preserved at Tunhuang, we find this example:

> May the many Buddhas give life to me,
> the many scriptures support me,
> the luminaries shine on me,
> Yin and Yang care for me,
> the four seasons nurture me,
> the Five Elements guide me,
> the five clouds envelop me,
> the Bodhisattvas protect me,
> the six hundred cyclical signs cover me,
> the five musical notes delight me,
> the five types of weapon guard me,
> the planets and asterisms direct me,
> the five stringed instruments accompany me,
> the five fragrances perfume me,
> a golden bed receive me,
> a brocade comforter cover me,
> the immortals support me,
> jade maidens attend me,
> the green dragon precede me,
> the nobles send emissaries to bestow gifts on me,

the five families respect me,
the ten thousand families honor me,
tigers, wolves, vipers and snakes avoid me,
the five poisons and toxic envenomations avoid my person!

And a little farther along in the same text:

May the worthy cherish and respect me,
fine pharmaka may they give to me,
the divine talismans protect me,
the hundred demons avoid me,
the hundred spirits adore me,
the Gate of Heaven open for me,
the Door of Earth reject me,
the cool springs be drink for me.[42]

Of course this is a Buddhist text: Does it not mention buddhas and bodhisattvas? But the most effective reworking of the formula was to come in Taoist guise. In 1109, Lord Lao the Most High appeared in person on Mao Shan and revealed a *Marvelous Book of the Celestial Youth, Protector of Life* (*T'ai shang t'ai-ch'ing t'ien-t'ung hu-ming miao-ching*, HY 632). This short scripture consists entirely of an incantation that has a very familiar ring, opening: "May August Heaven give life to me, August Earth support me, sun and moon illumine me, stars and planets guard me." Commentaries were written on this newly revealed text, and it became widely popular.[43]

We can see, then, that even within the context of Buddhism, the exotic appeal of Sanskrit had to contend with the attractions of the intelligible and familiar. Certain basic Chinese incantatory patterns had a long life in Buddhist as well as Taoist circles. Still, the immediate challenge of Buddhism lay in its Sanskritic strangeness, and for those who did not reject the dhāraṇīs out of hand, as barbaric and demonic, there was the possibility that in their sonorities lay the language of the gods.

Among authentically Indian prototypes of specialized demonology and spellbinding, first in date and influence comes the *Book of the Peacock Spell* (*Mahāmāyūrī[vidyārājñī] sūtra*, Ch. *Fo-mu ta k'ung-ch'üeh ming-wang ching*, T. 982). The kernel-story justifying the text's existence concerns a young monk named Svāti. Bitten by a snake, he applied to the Buddha for a cure. From among the assembly stepped forward a peacock-king to offer his own venom-destroying spell. It is the now-familiar pattern. The Buddha demurred, and the well-intentioned monarch replied, predictably, that if hostile snakes and demons were numerous then, while a Buddha was still alive in the world, what would the situation be like a thousand years hence? Thus the peacock spell entered the corpus of Buddhist ritual. The work was first translated into Chinese in the third century, and subsequent translations allow us to study how the text was constantly expanded and kept up to date with the latest Tantric developments over a period of some five hundred years. As the book became steadily larger, so did its lists of spirit-protectors, until whole armies of yakṣas and nāgas are named and localized (making the work a prime source for medieval Indian religious geography).[44] The peacock image evidently exerted an attraction of its own. In India, peacocks have long been associated with sorcery and exorcism; peacocks are redoubtable enemies of snakes, and snakes stand for a wide range of pathogenic agents and vectors of poisons, whether those "poisons" are understood literally, as tangible substances, or metaphorically, as pernicious doctrines. In any case, the *Book of the Peacock Spell* served both as an inspiration and as a direct model for many medieval Chinese books of spells, and was also a principal source for the powerful *nomina barbara* that were essential to any effective manual of demon-quelling.

The 'Maṇiratna Book'

There is one short work exclusively dedicated to the detection and identification of demons: the *Maṇiratna* ("wishing-jewel") *Book* (*Fo-shuo Mo-ni lo-t'an ching*, T. 1393). It was either translated into or written directly in Chinese at the end of the fourth century. The Buddha begins it by rhetorically asking his favorite disciple, Ānanda, "How is it that the people of the world are insecure? Why is it that many of them are ill and are suffering from disease? If they experience pain on issuing from their mother's womb, if they suffer from pain in their hearts, if their heads hurt, or their eyes are clouded over, or they are unable to eat or drink, it is because devils cause all of these things." The disciples are greatly frightened, and they step forward and ask the Buddha, "Where does affliction come from? [When it departs,] whither does it go? The people are in great sorrow and unhappy about this."[45] And so the Buddha calls together his chief disciples and expounds to them the *Maṇiratna Book*. He starts by reciting the names of the Seven Buddhas, culminating with himself. The scripture had been expounded by each prior buddha in the distant past; now it was the turn of himself, the Buddha of our own epoch. He authorizes his disciples to preach this scripture throughout the ten regions of India wherever people great or small are suffering from illness. Thereupon the text opens; it consists of a long list of the names of demons, variously classified.

There are, first of all, demons within the state, demons within mountains, demons within groves, demons among grassy tombs, demons among grave-mounds, demons within grave-mounds, demons upon the earth, demons within water, demons beside water, within fire, beside fire, demons within the Northern Dipper (Ursa Major), demons in space, demons in marketplaces. This first batch, then, are clearly identified by place of residence. The list no doubt prepares the reader for an encounter with the particular demons native to the various sites. The text goes on, without a break, to name three groups based on their members' mode of existence: demons of dead persons ("ghosts" if you will, but the term *kuei* is the same for both), demons of living persons (which have no doubt left their bodies pro tem or been sent forth by sorcery, to accomplish some fell purpose), and demons of starvation ("hungry ghosts" par excellence? Those who died from starvation or those who cause it?).

Immediately after this, though, locality once more predominates. There are demons outside the way, demons within the way, demons outside the hall, demons within the hall, demons within the body, demons outside the body; and then demons of mealtimes, demons of the time when one goes to bed. Red demons, black demons, tall demons, short demons, big demons, small demons, demons one encounters, white demons, yellow demons, blue demons, demons of nightmares, demons of getting up in the morning, walking demons, flying demons, demons that interrogate peoples' ethereal and spermatic souls, and, once more, the demons of living persons, the demons of dead persons:

> The Buddha said, "At a time of anger, when swords and staves are raised, one should always recite this *Maṇiratna Book* and all the demons will be smashed and defeated." He told his monks, "If you have received this scripture and someone is wasting away with illness, you should expound the scripture to him. If his head aches, his eyes are blurred, and chills and fever assail his heart, he should always read this *Maṇiratna Book*, and the heads of all demons will break into seven pieces. If there are troubles with officials, thieves, water or fire, he should read this *Maṇiratna Book*, and the various demons will no longer be able to plague him. This scripture came forth from the mouths of all the Buddhas. Now there are two of the demons-within-the-state, one of whom is named Deep Sands (Shen-sha), the other Floating Hill (Fu-ch'iu). These two demons march boldly through the world, searching out peoples' weak points. Should your head ache, your eyes be blurred, and chills and fever assail your heart, you should at once utter the names of these

two demons, then expound the *Maṇiratna Book*, and every one of the various demons will be smashed and defeated."[46]

Deep Sands and Floating Hill evidently belong to that equivocal class of otherworldly beings, the spies or inspectors. The celestial hierarchy sends out such emissaries, suitably disguised, to observe and report on the doings of mortals; and so of course does the infernal administration. But once again, on the principle that superior demons make the best controllers of demons, they, too, can be used to serve the Buddhist's own ends. Deep Sands, in particular, was to enjoy a long and varied career throughout East Asia, founded on his helpfulness in keeping other, less refined demons away.[47]

We are now halfway through the scripture, and it would be parlous to omit any detail that might help to forearm us. If (we are told) there should appear any demons colored blue, yellow, or black, be they tall or short—any and all demons, great or small, who delight in annoying the people of the world—we should recognize them as kiṃnara and piśāca. Then there are the demons of starvation (once again), demons of covetousness and greed, of agonized suffering, of wasting sickness, of affliction with painful itching; demons of longing, demons that cause the body to waste away, demons of stumbling, of madness, of deafness, of dumbness, of groaning and moaning, of crying and wailing, of illness, of indolence, of ruin and desolation, and of jealousy. There are the Wang-liang-phantom demons, demons of the Dazzling Deluder (Mars), of Roaming Radiance (*yu-kuang*—another planet?), and of the Repressor (Saturn). There are demons of curses, demons of infection from lurking corpses, demons of infection by those who have died from leprosy, demons of infection by those who have died in officials' premises.

Here we may pause briefly to catch our breath, and note that those "infestations" or "infusions" (*chu*; another explanation glosses the word as "lingering" or "malingering") are generically related to the "demonic infestations" that we observed afflicting the Hsü family in the 360s, as a result of the litigious activity of enemy ghosts in their "lawsuits from beyond the tomb" (see pp. 14–20). Though the secular medical literature repeatedly states that such infestations come in twenty-five (or ninety-nine) varieties, in this case only three types are mentioned. They neatly demonstrate the complexities of etiology. Once again, should one here admit a clear recognition of contagion, or are the diseases involved viewed rather as resulting from heredity, with all that implies for "moral" causality? Leprosy might seem to ratify the contagion thesis, but "lurking corpses," as we have seen, is rather more ambiguous, and the third category—that of those who have died in officials' premises (presumably after wrongful imprisonment, and possibly under judicial torture)—brings us forcibly back to the world of vengeful ghosts. We can only note that the three groups are here classed together, and that their pathology is viewed as being demonic. No doubt, as already suggested in Chapter 1, contagion and heredity were seen as mutually confirmatory in these circles.

There follow demons of army camps, demons of post-stations, demons of those who died in prison, those who died in bondage, those who died by water and those who died by drowning, those who died by fire and those who died by burning, those who died away from home and have not yet been buried, those who died in the marketplace, those who died on the road, those who died of thirst, those who died of hunger, those who died of coughing, those who died of cold, those who died by a weapon, those who died by blood, those who died by rotting meat ("blood," too, may refer to poisoning by eating fresh, possibly uncooked meat), those who died by beating, those who died in a fight, those who died from being struck with a staff, those who were strangled, those who died by hanging themselves, those who died by stabbing themselves, those who died by an enemy's hand, those who died by violence. And then we have demons that cause the skin to putrefy, demons that cut off people's hair, demons that drink people's blood, demons that fly (once again), demons that ride on horseback, demons that ride in carriages, demons that go on foot (again), and "demons that encounter resentment."

We have earlier noted the fluidity of terminology between the demons and ghosts (*kuei*), on the one hand, and the gods and deified ancestors (*shen*) on the other. The *Maṇiratna Book* offers a precise terminology in the next three categories: mountain-god demons, stone-god demons, and earth-god demons. No doubt its purpose was to classify these three very widespread types of spirit, and popular recipients of offerings, with the enemies of Buddhism. There follow demons of the seaside, demons within the sea, demons of dams and bridges, demons of canals and locks, then (another repetition) demons within the way and demons outside the way. Next come demons of the western tribespeople (*hu-i*), demons of the northwestern tribespeople (*ch'iang-lu*), tree-sprite goblin-demons, insect-sprite goblin-demons, bird-or-beast-sprite goblin-demons, demons of valleys, demons within the gate, demons outside the gate, within the door, outside the door, in the well and in the hearth, in stagnant ponds, and in the toilet; demons of sorcery (*fang-tao*), demons of toxic envenomation (*ku-tao*), demons of those who fail to act deferentially as official servants and family members, demons who falsely claim rank and status not their own, and (in conclusion) all the various demons, great and small. None of them are to be allowed to annoy the faithful. The Buddha concludes, "If any demons do not obey my words, their heads will break into seven parts. If anyone has become ill, recite the names of the foregoing demons over him, and he will at once be made well. This scripture issued from the mouth of the Buddha Śākyamuni. When the various demons hear it, from that time forth they will all be destroyed, liberated, and made whole." When the Buddha had finished expounding the scripture, all the monks and nuns, laymen and laywomen, gods, dragons, demons and humans accepted this gift of the Buddha, stepped forward, paid their homage to him, and departed.[48]

This breathless catalogue, with its interminable run-on lists and its simple-minded categories and descriptions, may seem boring when read in our manner. Yet (like most of these scriptural texts) it was never meant to be "read" but rather intoned, chanted, ululated, or roared out; its power lay as much in its performance as in its contents. There are certainly signs in the text itself that the author or copyists' attention wavered at times. Yet the very compulsiveness of demonography bears witness to an obsessive concern to leave no demon unnamed, no corner of the world unexamined in which a demon might possibly lurk, no circumstance of the human condition unaccounted for that might conceivably result in a fatal demonic transformation. By reciting the entire, mind-numbing list, you can be fairly certain of lighting on at least the category of demon, if not the very individual, to which your present affliction owes its origin; and by naming the demon, everyone seems to agree, you neutralize it.

The 'Book of Consecration'

One might imagine that Buddhist practitioners would have rested reasonably secure with an inventory as meticulous as the *Maṇiratna Book*. It provided a list at least as comprehensive as the great Indian repertory of different types of pretas mentioned in Chapter 2, yet it was more convenient, in that it was well-adapted to Chinese conditions (giving demons of the western and northwestern barbarians, for example) and was in compact form, suitable for recitation. As long as demons continued to live and thrive, however, scholarly exorcists could hardly lay down their writing-brushes, and in the middle of the fifth century a reworking of the *Maṇiratna Book* was produced. For once we know the author's name; the monk Hui-chien appears to have been a specialist in expanding older works, often genuine translations, and adapting them to the conditions of his time and the needs of the community that he aimed to establish.[49] Hui-chien's version of the *Maṇiratna* forms the eighth chapter of his *Book of Consecration* (*Kuan-ting ching*, T. 1331), a large work in twelve chapters, compiled around 457. It is a most valuable source for local Chinese ritual practice at a time of ebullient synthesis, and an excellent example of the progress of proto-Tantra in early medieval China.[50]

The *Book of Consecration* is perhaps most remarkable for its many reflections of oral traditions not otherwise attested to in this period. Many practices that subsequently spread throughout East Asia are documented for the first time in this book. For example, the work's title alludes to the Tantric ritual of consecration (*abhiṣeka*).[51] A monk becomes a master (*ācārya*) qualified to perform esoteric rituals and accept disciples only after his own master has poured water on his head in this adaptation of the Indian royal consecration. The ceremony and its application to Buddhism both originate in India, and today consecration is still one of the most solemn rituals of Tantric Buddhism in Japan as well as among Tibetans (it is widely known in the West under its Tibetan name, *dbang*). But the earliest description of consecration as an actual Buddhist ritual is found in the *Book of Consecration*, written in fifth-century China. Similarly, the work's first chapter tells us that the book disappeared after the Buddha first uttered it and was destined to be discovered only a thousand years after the Buddha's death, when a wandering ascetic monk would find it hidden in a mountain cavern. This makes it the earliest Buddhist "treasure text," a genre far better known in Tibet. In the much later Tibetan tradition, a special class of lamas (*gter-ston*, "treasure-finders") went about "discovering" scriptural treasures (*gter-ma*) that had allegedly been hidden away long before, during the Buddha's lifetime, to await the foreordained moment of their revelation.[52] The *Book of Consecration* also provides the prototype for the celebrated story of Mu-lien's descent to hell to save his wicked mother (the background story justifying the great Festival of the Dead at the full moon of the seventh month),[53] the earliest Chinese text of the *Book of the Healing Buddha* (*Yao-shih liu-li-kuang ju-lai pen-yüan kung-te ching*)[54] and the first example of the type of poetic oracle by lot-drawing that is still the standard type of temple-oracle throughout East and Southeast Asia today. It is significant that the book as a whole is explicitly intended for the Last Age of the Law and seems to have been designed as a complete and self-sufficient *vade mecum* for Chinese Buddhists living at that perilous time. It contains elements drawn from many earlier texts, like the *Book of the Peacock Spell*, which it subordinates and adapts to its grand design. It should be interesting to see what a work of this sort has done with the little *Maṇiratna Book*.[55]

It is at once apparent that Hui-chien's method consisted largely in expanding upon his source. Indeed, chapter eight of the *Book of Consecration* (which bears the name "Maṇiratna Book") is about four times longer than the original text. After the standard scriptural opening, setting the scene, and the Buddha's appeal to the authority of his six predecessors, the author adds the names of eight bodhisattvas who will come to the aid of Buddhists in distress. Those in the grip of malignant spirits should call upon them, and they will cause all those pesky little devils to vanish. In addition to these powerful protectors, the Buddha names his ten great disciples, who can also be called upon in time of need by the Buddhists of future ages. The preliminary roster of guardians and helpers continues with the four great kings of the gods (one in each of the four quarters of the world), and the thirty-three gods who inhabit the Heaven of the Thirty-Three (*trāyastriṃśa*). But even then, the list of supernatural protectors rolls sonorously onward with the names of thirty-five dragon-kings, twenty-eight great spirit-generals, two spirit-generals' mothers, and three spirit-generals' daughters. More of Hui-chien's method comes to light here; the last ten names in the list of twenty-eight spirit-generals are derived from the *Maṇiratna Book*'s list of the ten regions of India! The generals, their mothers and daughters are followed by the names of an additional twenty-four demon-commanders (four of them at each of the four quarters, the zenith and the nadir).[56] These lists of champions have already taken up twice as much space as the entire text of the old *Maṇiratna Book*, but only now do we come to the inventory of the dangerous demons themselves. It opens with the two named fiends, leaders of the pack, here termed "essential-spirit goblin-demons (*ching mei kuei*), Deep Sands and Floating Hill." Then follow the various classes of demons, essentially as in the prototype text, except that those in the initial group of fifty-one are all called "goblin-demons" (*mei-kuei*), which seems to make them somewhat more colloquial, as well as qualifying the ever-ambiguous word *kuei*. Among the minor additions to the list are demons that died by overeating (preceding demons that died of hunger). Demons under the eaves of the house, demons of the four walls, and demons of choking on food are now added to the domestic pests. There are demons of gold and silver, and demons of the moment of sitting down are added to those that plague the day's activities, while striped, pink, and purple demons join the otherworldly spectrum.

Members of the next group of forty-nine demons are simply *kuei* again, and include many that the earlier work does not list.[57] In place of the demons "who interrogate peoples' ethereal and spermatic souls," we find here two distinct classes, the ethereal-soul interrogators and the beaters of spermatic souls (the activities of both groups presumably take place while the owner of the soul is asleep, during his dream-life). Then come those demons that delight in strife, those that speak loudly, laugh loudly, and play greatly, those that grasp and pummel, those that push and squeeze, those that hide in ambush at the gate of life (the reservoir of vital essence), those that gobble people's vital essence, those that drink people's blood, those that butcher human flesh, those that gnaw on human bones, those that strike peoples' bones, those that gobble people's five viscera, those that eat people's entrails, those that pluck forth people's sinews, those that shrink people's veins, those that destroy human fetuses, those that cause difficult births, those that delight in anger, those that delight in hatred, those that go along holding swords, those that go along holding sticks, those that are crooked and bent, those that go along gazing upward, those that are split at the waist, those that look backward, those that go along craning their necks, broken-marrow demons, demons whose bodies have crumbled to dust, blocked and obstructed demons, demons with down-hanging heads, demons of five blows, demons that strike the heart, demons of chills and shivers, and demons of fevers and fainting. There are demons in sand, demons among cliffs and mounds, demons who march boldly along, demons who raise their arms, head-rubbing demons, white-headed demons, red-headed demons, yellow-headed demons, headless demons, fire-belching demons, demons that delight in scorching people, and demons of the radiance of blood.

After this protracted list, our obligations to the text can be discharged by a simple summary of the remainder.[58] Next come forty-nine essential spirits of mountains (*shan-ching*), many-colored, headless, or with a variety of animal heads, in the form of serpents or of men and women, with four eyes or forty-nine eyes, crying or sighing or stumbling, fighting or spewing forth poisonous vapors in a wide spectrum of colors. There follows a motley list of *kuei* again, including those responsible for the five pestilences (*wen*) and those that have the five sorts of infestation (*chu*) in their care. Also mentioned are those demons that died falling out of bed, and a special class of those that delight in serving as district magistrates!

The list continues more or less faithful to the prototype, and this section includes ninety-eight different varieties of demon. The following, final list of forty-seven types calls them "goblin-demons" once more, and they, too, seem fairly close to their models. But Hui-chien has added new faces to the demons of the hearth; he sees demons not only within the hearth but above it and on all four sides as well. The demon of the toilet is now a "goblin-demon" of incantations in the toilet; and Hui-chien adds, as a *bonne bouche*, goblin-demons that lick peoples' heads, that dwell in the bed-curtains, the screen, the rafters, or within the chamber, and those that cause people to vomit, those that gobble excrement, those that cause homesickness(?), and those that cause evil infections.

Though the named demon-types come (in my calculation) to 198, the Buddha goes on to tell us that these demons number 60,049 in all.[59] The remainder of the chapter is devoted to strict instructions for the careful transmission of the text to qualified persons only, and to directions for its recitation. Offerings of flowers and incense should be made to the Seven Buddhas, the bodhisattvas, the arhats, and the various gods and good demons. These well-intentioned demons had all long before been sworn to an oath by the Buddha—to wit, that "in times to come, beyond the thousand-year limit, when the way of devils is flourishing and the Buddha's Law is about to disappear, and when the goblin-demons of mountains and seas and the evil devils that dwell among men are about to spew forth evil poisons and harm the four classes of the Buddha's disciples [monks and nuns, laymen and laywomen], we will roam about and protect the four classes of disciples in the villages and monasteries."[60] So far so good; here we have still another affirmation of the demons' subjugation by oath, and their undertaking to put their power at the service of the faithful. But the demons then go on to link themselves to the community of believers in a subtler way: "We will also be great patrons (*dānapati*) of monks and nuns. If anyone gives us great offerings, we will immediately bestow them on the monks, and for this reason we will protect those laypersons who support monks and nuns. We only request that the Buddha order his disciples to put aside some cakes and fruit for us at every ritual meal." The Buddha was pleased to grant the demons' request: "Thus [he declares] in the event of sickness, when you are about to read this scripture, you should perform the following rite. On a table, scatter a quantity of fine flowers, ignite several sorts of incense, light lamps, and set out assorted cakes and fruit, butter, and wild honey so that they can eat and drink. These various good spirits protect people, and if you recite this *Maṇiratna Book of Great Spirit-Spells*, you will obtain an auspicious reward."[61]

Once again, the most immediately accessible and trustworthy defenders against demons are the tame demons euphemistically designated "good spirits" (*shan shen*). By thus transforming evil into good, one can grasp the essential ambiguities of the spirit world by the horns (so to speak) and turn them to one's own advantage. But Hui-chien is not content to let the converted demons remain brutish strongmen, however well-intentioned. Instead, he craftily draws them into the mesh of socio-economic interdependence that kept Buddhist monastic institutions functioning while giving lay patrons a full return on their investment in the form of spiritual merit. The demons are put forward as model patrons, instantly turning over their entire income of cakes and fruit to the monks. Later on in his work, Hui-chien emphasizes that only the donation of all one's possessions to the monks can guarantee total felicity in one's next existence. The demons' charitable resolve anticipates this injunction, as does their undertaking to protect other, human donors. There is a certain circularity in all this, of course, but at least the prospective Buddhist demon-worshipper could be certain that his offerings to the "good spirits" would be credited to his merit-account, since they would really be indirect offerings to the monks.

Elsewhere in the *Book of Consecration*, we find numerous reflections of the hierarchically organized Chinese spirit world. We can there observe the other-worldly personnel of Buddhism carrying out their duties in a bureaucratic manner closely analogous to the one we have seen described in Taoist texts of the period. Particular disease-symptoms might even be linked to particular administrative procedures in the invisible world. The characteristic features of hebdomadal fever are thus accounted for:

> King Yama has charge of entries in the registers of those living in the world. If people do evil and commit various acts that are against the Law, if they are not filial and obedient but instead practice the five sorts of refractory behavior, if they destroy the Three Treasures and do not follow the law of sovereign and subject, or again, if there are living beings who do not maintain the precepts and do not have faith in the True Law—supposing then that someone has received the precepts but commits numerous offenses against them, then the spirits-beneath-the-earth and the watchers will submit a memoran-

> dum about them to the Five Officers. It is the Five Officers who arrange the slips in the registers, removing names from the books of death and certifying them in the books of life. It may be that a person's spirits are put under restraint, but the recording spirits have not yet decided that person's fate. When it has been determined, they submit the documents to King Yama. King Yama investigates each case and prescribes punishment in accordance with the gravity of the crime. The intense suffering from wasting yellow sickness among those in the world who agonize intensely but do not die—but now expire, now return to life—is because their punishment has not yet been determined: Their vital spirits are beings arraigned before that king. It may be in seven days, or in twice or thrice seven days, up to seven times seven days, that the registers are decided upon. Then the vital spirits are released and sent back into that person's body. Thereupon they behold their good and evil deeds, as if awakening from a dream. Should such a person be fully aware of these things, he will be able to verify his own allotment of punishment or blessings.[62]

So pervasive was the political model for spiritual health and physical well-being that bureaucratic procedure and delay might be considered a plausible explanation for the symptoms of recurrent fever. We can hardly find fault with the elaborate rosters of gods and demons when we realize the extent to which it was assumed that otherworldly denizens and their doings were fully responsible for the often puzzling manifestations of disease among mortals. Conversely, when the source of an illness actually followed the descriptions found in scripture, it served to confirm all that the scripture said about the organization of the invisible world and the best means of placating its numerous hierarchy.

Demons in the Meditation Hall

Though its first chapter is explicitly addressed to monks and its second to nuns, most of the *Book of Consecration* is directed to laymen. Hui-chien designed his work to serve a community of religious and laypersons in all circumstances of life, from Buddhist initiation through death, cremation, and rebirth in one of the ten Pure Lands of the buddhas. He recognized that the thousandth year had already passed since the death of the Buddha Śākyamuni, and that demons flourished everywhere in the world. The method best suited to such times was the demon-dispelling incantation, and long, idiosyncratic spells figure prominently throughout his book. But it is not only the specialized dhāraṇī-literature that describes demons and spells for dealing with them. Works like the *Book of Consecration* (and the Taoist *Spirit-Spells of the Abyss*) evolved in connection with missionary movements that brought ritual therapy directly into the home. Yet even within the monastery walls, demonology was of immediate concern to Buddhist professionals; if laypersons were constantly exposed to demonic attack, so were monks and nuns. Indeed, they were especially subject to assault from demons because of their dedicated anti-demonic lives.

A favorite time for demons to trouble monks and nuns was during their meditation. "Meditation sickness" was early recognized as an occupational hazard of the monastic life, and measures were taken to deal systematically with the problem. The final section of a manual on the subject written in fifth-century China, the *Secret Essentials for Treating Dhyāna Ailments* (*dhyāna*, "meditation"; Ch. *ch'an*, J. *zen*), is devoted to demonology (*Chih ch'an-ping pi-yao fa*, T. 620).[63] It opens, in good Buddhist scriptural form, with a historical precedent from the time of the Buddha himself. In those days a demon appeared with a face like a Chinese lute (*p'i-p'a*), four eyes, two mouths, its entire head shooting forth flames, beating itself under the armpits and all over the body, and chanting "Bhūtī, Bhūtī." It was like a fireball or a bolt of lightning, now arising, now disappearing, and caused great uneasiness among the onlookers. The Buddha advised his monks that, should they see this *bhūtī* (the word means "demoness") approaching while they were meditating, they were to firmly close their eyes and curse it silently, saying, "I recognize you. You are the one in Jambudvīpa [the inhabited world] that eats fire and stinks. Because of your perverse views, you delight in breaking the precepts. But as *I* am now observing the precepts, I have no fear of you at all." Then monks were to recite the preface to the precepts, whereas laypersons were to recite the Three Refuges, Five Precepts, and Eight Precepts, and the demon would immediately crawl away in defeat.[64]

The Buddha goes on to predict that a thousand years after his death demons will pose a far greater danger to monks than they do in his own lifetime. The demons that will then attack monks, nuns, laymen and laywomen when they are practicing their meditation in a tranquil place may take the form of black or red rats that scratch at the meditator's heart or tickle his feet, hands, or ears; may produce the cries of birds, the moaning of demons, or subtle whisperings; or may be fox-phantoms, some of them taking the form of brides, richly appareled, who will stroke and caress the meditator's body and speak of things contrary to the Law. Others will appear as dogs, howling incessantly, or come forth as hawks and various kinds of birds, making all manner of noises, from whispers to great shouts. Still others come to the meditator in the form of small children, in ranks of hundreds and thousands—or, it may be, by tens or fives or ones, twos, or threes—making various noises. Alternatively, the meditator may see mosquitoes, flies, gnats, lice, or serpents that may enter his ears, humming like a queen bee, or go into his eyes as if he were being pelted with sand. Some may strike against his heart and cause all sorts of other disturbances. With visitors such as these, the meditator may go mad, flee from his hermitage, and run wildly about, quite out of control.

In prescribing for these afflictions, the Buddha reveals that the demoness Bhūtī has sixty-three different names. She also has a story. Long ago, in the time of the previous buddha, Kanakamuni, there was a monk who was just on the point of achieving enlightenment, but through an evil fate he was disturbed by another monk at the very moment when he was about to attain his goal. Instead of achieving bliss, therefore, he died in a rage, vowing that he would become a demon and trouble the Buddha's disciples. This demoness lives for a kalpa, or incalculable eon, then falls into the depths of the Avīci Hell. If monks know her name and concentrate firmly on their meditation, she will not disturb them. This Bhūtī is an evil yakṣī; she is also called the Demon of Dreams. When you see her in a dream and you have a loss of vital essence, you should arise and perform an act of contrition, saying, "Bhūtī has come; because of evil karma I have encountered this evil demon that breaks the precepts and causes harm. Now I lash together my heart and bind all my passions so that they will never again be released." This demon, when it dwells in the wilds, is called the Demon of the Wilds. When it dwells between the bed and coverlet, its name is the Demon that Crawls on Its Belly. There follows a list of additional types of demons, all of which are said to belong to the sixty-three "names" of the demon. The first two names closely resemble our old friends Deep Sands and Floating Hill; the remainder are also quite reminiscent of demons listed in the *Maṇiratna Book*. There are goblins and phantoms, pus-eaters and spittle-eaters, asses' ears and tiger-heads and kittens' meows, white rats and fox-phantoms, piśācas and kumbhāṇḍas, and many more. Numerous and fearsome though they are, one has only to recite the names of the Seven Buddhas, together with a short dhāraṇī, and all will be well.

Thus the thousand-year term will be a difficult, demon-ridden era for monks as well as laymen. It is significant that the monks' worst enemy should once again prove to be one of their own number, a frustrated, demonically deformed monk. Just as members of a biological family might be tormented by a dead family member, so monks, as members of a fictive spiritual family, might be attacked by their departed fellows. Nor is it surprising that the devil-monk should focus on the most sensitive area in the monkish domestic economy—sexuality—and return to plague the monastic community with wet dreams.[65] Nocturnal emissions receive considerable attention in all Buddhist monastic codes, and in Japan the term *mara* ("devil") still designates the penis in monkish slang.[66] The tale of Bhūtī lends historical perspective to the demonization of sexuality.

4

ENSIGILLATION

A Buddho-Taoist Technique of Exorcism

A Sixth-Century Taoist Text

In his quest for the origins of printing in China, the great sinologist Paul Pelliot (1878–1945) happened upon an intriguing passage in the *History of the Sui Dynasty* (*Sui shu*). This history was written by the successors of the Sui, the T'ang, in the first quarter of the seventh century. The bibliographic section of the Sui history, listing the books in the imperial library, is an extended repertory of writings surviving in official circles at the end of the sixth century. Each division of the bibliography opens with a concise summary, a review of the achievements in each particular field during the early medieval period. Pelliot was on the lookout for textual evidence of what was later to become the standard technique of Chinese printing, in which characters are carved on wooden blocks in reverse and in relief. The passage he noted from the bibliography's description of Taoism informs us about the activities of Taoist priests: "Moreover, they make seals of wood, on which they engrave the constellations, the sun and the moon. Holding their breath, they grasp them in their hands and print [or stamp] them. Many sick persons are cured by that means."[1] Pelliot observed that this passage is somewhat ambiguous. It might refer to an impression made in clay or sand, in the presence of the patient destined for curing, of a seal carved in intaglio—a seal, that is, not requiring ink. But Pelliot believed that by that time it was far more likely that the process involved talismans actually printed using tablets similar to the official seals then in common use, on which the images or characters were carved in reverse and in relief: "In order to be efficacious, these charms had to be printed while observing the respiratory rites which played such a great role in Taoist practices; and in all likelihood, they were printed on paper."[2]

Pelliot discusses this passage in conjunction with a description furnished by the Chinese Buddhist pilgrim I-ching, who was in India from 673 to 685. Writing in 692, I-ching noted that "monks and laymen in India make *caityas* or images with earth, or impress the Buddha's image on silk or paper, and worship it with offerings wherever they go."[3] As Pelliot remarks, multiple buddha-images, scrolls of "a thousand buddhas" printed by this means in the ninth and tenth centuries, were found in Tun-huang, the Chinese gateway to Central Asia, and he was inclined to see in I-ching's account the record of a Chinese custom that had reached India: Witness not only the printing technique but above all the silk and paper, both of Chinese origin.[4] Thus we would have the Taoists first printing talismans to heal the sick, and the Buddhists then characteristically applying the technique to their own most pressing devotional need, the multiplication of buddha-images. Certainly with both these avid spiritual denominations paving the way, all would have been well prepared for the great Chinese printing ventures that began in the tenth century. And to the Taoists would go all honor as the "proto-scientific" creators of proto-printing, a role fully in keeping with the technological prowess with which Taoists have traditionally been credited.[5]

Pelliot's monograph on Chinese printing was only published in 1953, eight years after his death, although it appears to represent a draft completed as early as 1928. Since that time much has been done in the study of Taoist texts, and we should naturally expect to find material relevant to the prehistory of printing among the fifteen hundred works in the Taoist canon. There should certainly be firsthand evidence on this point in Taoist literature because the authors of the *History of the Sui* make the practice loom disproportionately large in their account of Taoism. In fact, the canon does contain a text on this subject that to all appearances dates from the Sui dynasty itself, the second half of the sixth century. It includes a lengthy section describing the use of a seal to cure disease. A careful reading permits us to correct Pelliot's translation of the crucial passage in the *Sui shu*. A shift in the punctuation radically alters the sense: "Holding [the seal] in their hands, they seal the sickness [or 'the sick person'] with it. Many are cured by that means."[6] The seal in this case is impressed neither on silk nor on paper, nor for that matter in clay or sand; instead, it is applied to the body of the patient himself.

The text's title is *Essentials of the Practice of Perfection* (*Cheng-i fa-wen hsiu-chen chih-yao*, HY 1260). The first part of this work consists of practical instructions copied from the Mao Shan revelations, from the *Declarations of the Perfect Ones*. There is, of course, nothing new in this, but these instructions presently shade off into directives on ingesting the primal breath and performing therapeutic gymnastics. Then come directives for checking the state of one's health according to the "four great ones," i.e., the Four Elements (*catur mahābhūta*) of Indian medical theory.[7] Symptoms observable on the mouth and lips are first listed, with their various indications about the predominance in the body of one or another of the elements (wind, fire, earth, and water). We are told how to rectify any imbalance in the elements through proper exhalation, in six modes: exhaling air with the syllables *ch'ui, ho, hsi, hu, hsü*, and *ssu*. Next, dream-indications of organic illness are given. If there is illness in the heart, for example, if cold, exhale *ch'ui*, if hot, exhale *hu*; the symptom consists of dreaming at night of a man dressed in red, holding a sword or staff and coming to frighten you.[8] A mirror should be set up to check on your appearance. If there is any alteration, you should withdraw to an oratory and recite the *Book of the Yellow Court*; in order to assemble your body's spirits, collect your three ethereal souls, and put your seven spermatic souls under control, you are to pace along the seven stars of the Dipper and ingest their primal breaths.[9] We are reminded that breath is absolutely vital to the preservation of the body; there has never been a living body without breath, nor breath without a living body. As for your color, your red should be like vermilion inside silk, not like ochre; your white should be like sulphur within silk gauze, not like clay; your black should be opaque like many layers of lacquer, not like earth; and your blue should be unctuous like a disk of azure jade, not like indigo.[10]

This list of symptoms and their significance is interesting in itself, and suggests that it was of some importance to Taoist masters to be able to predict their patients' chances of survival. The last and longest section of the text emphasizes that an exact knowledge of symptomology and prognosis is essential if the rites of the Tao are to succeed in saving people from illness or other afflictions. The original text gives the fullest and most immediate account we have of the ritual for treating disease with an exorcistic seal:

> If you are going to practice the cure of illness by spells, you should have the sufferer's family all perform the early morning obeisance to the Tao and purify themselves. The whole house should be quiet, and all noise and confusion should be kept away. The Taoist master then approaches the patient, burns incense, and most carefully examines the patient's state. If his physical symptoms are bad and not susceptible of cure, then the master should on his behalf visualize the spirits, circulate the breaths throughout his own body, and apply the seal three times. At noon, he should once more go and examine the patient's condition to see whether or not it has improved somewhat. If it has not yet improved, he should once more use his spell. During the night he should again examine whether there has been any alteration, and if there has not yet been any, he should once more apply his spell. The following morning at dawn [after dawn worship], he should go and examine his condition; if there has still been no change, it means that his life is finished and he cannot be cured.
>
> In curing illness, it is necessary to despise material rewards. If you act in the spirit of succor and charity, spirits will certainly assist you and the vital breaths of the Tao will definitely respond. If, however, you act in hope of gain, without concern to give help, your actions will have no efficacy; on the contrary, you yourself will be harmed by them. The talismans and spells of the rites of the Tao are for helping people in sickness and suffering. The Taoist master should frequently discourse upon the venerable scriptures in the thirty-six divisions of the Taoist canon and promote the rites of talismans and spells of the sublime saints. He should, moreover, study their profound subtleties with all his might. The instructions that follow represent the arts of talismans and spells in the secret directives of the Three and the Five of the divine transcendents of Right Unity. The Twelve Asterisms and great conjunctions of the Three and the Five reveal the instructions of the dark invisible world. The Taoists' wondrous rites of spell-recitation are numerous and complex, obscure in their diversity, and difficult for anyone to comprehend fully. But for saving lives in peril of death, there is nothing better than seals. In ancient times, Fan Li practiced this, causing mountains to crumble, rivers and seas to flow backward, spirit-powers to tremble with fear, and thunderclaps to resound.[11] With seals one can smelt metal and polish jade, restore vital breaths and bring back the ethereal souls [to reanimate corpses]; how much more easily, then, can one heal the sick by these means! But for ordinary persons in their shallow delusion, the sublime arts are difficult to master. It is for that reason that most people at the present time are unable to achieve results in these practices. This is most likely due to their not having studied the tech-

niques thoroughly, or else because their hearts are not fully focused. Li Tao-hua has said, "I do not practice this rite with the frivolous or the young."[12]

The difficult point to understand about the seal lies in the visualizations. But if you are able to perfect the breathing and understand the timing, then the visualization will be accomplished by itself and the spirits will all be fully present. If you coif and cincture yourself with the Five Spirits, and pace out the pattern of the first *I-ching* hexagram [that is, *ch'ien*, or "heaven"], rare will be those whom you cannot cure. Now we will give a terse outline of the sequence of procedures, in order to make it manifest to fellow-adepts who have not yet been able to exhaust its essential secrets.

For the sevenfold rite of the vital breaths, first one must spew forth water and eliminate impurities. In your left hand, hold a bowl filled with water, in your right, a sword. With sword and water held opposite each other, place your back to the reigning asterism of the month and face the Breaker Star. Visualize in front of you a celestial official in a vermilion robe; he is nineteen feet tall; on his head he wears a spirit-register; set in it is a nine-phoenix hat. In his mouth he takes water and sprays it out in front of him over the sick person and the room: It is brilliantly red, like the sun rising at dawn. Then, with sword and water held opposite each other, visualize the seven stars of the Dipper above your own head; the end star of the handle should be in the bowl of water. Recite [this spell]:

> I respectfully request the spirit-essences
> of the Northern Dipper's seven stars
> to descend into this water,
> so that all noxious demons
> quickly depart, ten thousand leagues away!
> If you do not leave, I will decapitate and kill you
> and consign you to the White Youth of the West.
> Speedily, as the Statutes and Ordinances command!

Spray out water in each of the five directions; then spray it on the sufferer and put the seal into operation. Stand ten feet away from the patient. You press the "supervisor" phalanx [the second segment of the fourth finger] of your left hand; your right hand holds the seal against your heart.[13] Stand facing the reigning direction.

Step One: First visualize yourself as a spirit bearing heaven on his head and stamping on the earth with his feet. A five-colored cloud of vapor covers your body.

Step Two: Over your head visualize the five planets, each in its proper place, a foot away from your head.

Step Three: In front of your face visualize on the left the sun, on the right the moon, nine inches away from your face.

Step Four: On top of your head visualize the vermilion bird, to the left the azure dragon, to the right the white tiger, beneath your feet the Eight Trigrams (of the *Book of Changes*) and the divine tortoise.[14] To the left and right are the jade youths and jade maidens who put the seal into action.

Step Five: Visualize five-colored vital breaths of Perfection, the size of strands of thread, proceeding from your five viscera, coming out of your mouth, and rising into the air to a height of eighteen feet above your head. They go three times around your head. Next visualize three little men in your liver, dressed in blue robes and blue caps, coming out and standing to your left. The three little men in your heart, dressed in red with red caps, come out and stand to your right. The three little men in your kidneys, dressed in black with black caps, come out and stand behind you. The three men in your spleen, dressed in yellow with yellow caps, come out and stand to the south. They all hold swords in their left hands and war hatchets in their right.

Next visualize above your head the seven stars of the Dipper, with the star at the end of the handle pointing at the spot where the sufferer feels pain. Then visualize the previously mentioned Perfect Official wearing the nine-phoenix hat, mounted upon red vapors of the sun. Imagine that he performs the Step of Yü with the seal in his hand, then brings it down once on the patient's heart.[15] Next he presses it once on his stomach, then once again on the place where he feels pain. Visualize the toxic vapors coming out of the patient and rushing away. When this has been done, concentrate your vision on your own body. Close off your breath and perform the Step of Yü for nine paces, bringing you to the patient. Stand there, before you apply the seal, and breathe out of your mouth on the sufferer three *hsi*, three *t'a*, and three *ch'ih* breaths. Next sound the bells of heaven six times, then strike heaven's stone-chimes six times: For summoning, use the bells; for subjugating, use the chimes.[16] Then recite this spell:

The spirit-seal of the Monarch of Heaven:
When you seal a mountain, it turns to a lake.
Seal a stone and it turns to earth.
Seal a tree, the tree withers.
Seal the earth, the earth splits.
Seal wood, the wood breaks.
Seal fire, the fire goes out.
Seal water, the water dries up.
Seal above, it penetrates below.
Seal before, it penetrates behind.
Seal the left, it penetrates the right.
Seal malignant wraiths, and wraiths perish.
Seal pain, and pain stops.

Seal sickness, sickness disperses.
Seal demons, demons flee.
It overcomes the symptoms and eliminates knotted breaths,
banishes afflictions and punishes ghost-infection.
May they all flee away of their own volition
and the True Spirits take up their abode in you.
Swiftly, swiftly, in accordance with the Statutes and Ordinances
of Lord Lao the Most High.[17]

Then bring down the seal [on the patient's body]. You must close off your breaths for a good long time; only then raise the seal and step back. Then recite:

The man or woman named so-and-so [fill in the blank], born in thus-and-such a year, month, day, and hour, in his present life is troubled by thus-and-such an ailment and has requested me, your servant, to cure it. Your servant respectfully requests the General of the Three Divisions, the General Who operates the Seal, the General Who Cures Illness, the General Who Destroys Disease-Wraiths, and the General Who Arrests Devils—requests that all of you accompany the seal and cure the illness, and save that person from the ailment in his body. Swiftly, swiftly, come out! Now, with the seal of the Yellow God's Emblem of Transcendence, I seal the heart—take it out of his heart!

Sealing his stomach, it comes out of the stomach!
Sealing the liver, it comes out of the liver!
Sealing the lungs, it comes out of the lungs!
Sealing the kidneys, it comes out of the kidneys!
Sealing the spleen, it comes out of the spleen!
Sealing the head, it comes out of the head!
Sealing the back, it comes out of the back!
Sealing the breast, it comes out of the breast!
Sealing the waist, it comes out of the waist!
Sealing the hand, it comes out of the hand!
Sealing the foot, it comes out of the foot!
Quickly come forth, quickly come forth, swiftly, swiftly,
in accordance with the Statutes and Ordinances!

Each time you apply the seal, recite this through one more time. When that has been completed, lift the seal, hold it facing the patient's heart, and recite:

Demons of the south,
demons of the north,
demons of the east,
demons of the west,

demons of the center,
demons of the earth,
demons of the spirit-demons (*shen-kuei*),
demons of the man-demons,
demons of the woman-demons,
demons of the sunken corpse-specters,
toxic ghost-infestations—
who face the seal, die!
Who meet the seal, perish!
Swiftly come forth, swiftly come forth!

Bring the seal down to rest and recite this two more times through; only then lift the seal. After sealing, have the sufferer swallow three or two talismans. [Note in text: a man consumes three talismans, a woman two.] [18]

In using spells to cure illness, always visualize the perfect breaths of the ten regions [as you recite the spells]. Before taking action, you should enjoin the sufferer not to consume the five sharp-flavored herbs for three days or flesh of the animals of the twelve asterisms [i.e., of the twelve earthly 'stems' of cyclical time-space computation]. Indeed, all shellfish, wine, and fresh meat should be avoided. Only a very small amount of dried deer meat is acceptable. Only when this has been accomplished may you apply the seal. But if the patient is unable to carry this out, then sealing will cause him harm and not do any good at all.

After using the seal, bathe it in fragrant hot water, wipe it dry with a new cloth, and place it in a box. [There follows an illustration of the face of the seal: see Figure 1.]

This seal should not be brought into a household in mourning, into one in which a woman has just given birth, or into a place where there is blood or raw flesh or milk, or filth of the six sorts of domestic beast; to none of these places may it be taken. If when asleep you should suddenly be frightened by a dream, or be unusually shaken by a sound, arise at once and call out in a loud voice: "Ye seven spirits of the house, Director of Destinies, Lord of the Hearth! How have you permitted uncouth demons to strike at a descendant of the Yellow Monarch? Apprehend them and commit them to the officer of the prison, to be punished for their crime!"

When you have said this, take the seal and hang it over the door. Return to bed, and a moment later you will hear the sound of whipping and torture.

If a person is suddenly struck by flying evil cadaver-specters, demonic hereditary infestation, chronic faintness, and pains in the heart, seal him over the heart and it will stop at once. If a person talks demon-speech incessantly, seal him according to the ritual and it will stop at once. If a person is walking along a road, or has gone into the mountains or moorlands, or is crossing a

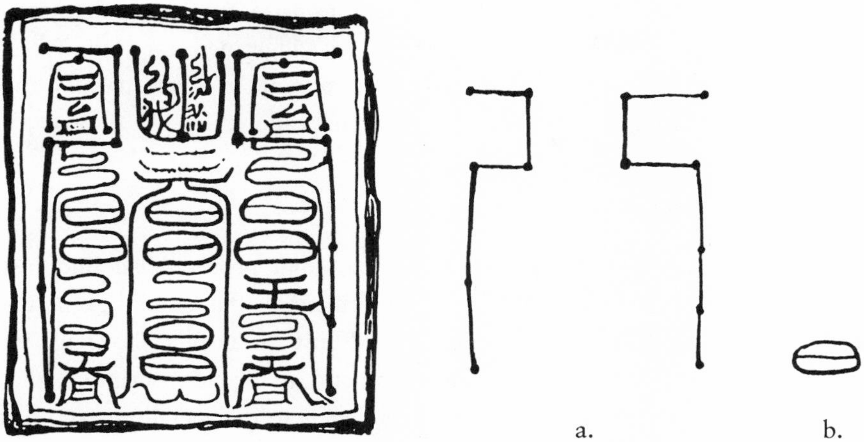

FIGURE 1 The disease-curing seal from *Essentials of the Practice of Perfection* (*Cheng-i fa-wen hsiu-chen chih-yao*, HY 1260), Six Dynasties period. This exorcistic seal illustrates the passage of the *History of the Sui Dynasty* (*Sui shu*) quoted in the text. The two inset details point out some basic elements: a schematic doublet of the Northern Dipper (Ursa Major, left detail) and numerous stylized renditions of the archaic logograph for the sun (right detail). Other elements include stylized asterisms associated with the Dipper.

> river or traversing a lake, or if he sees wolves, tigers, bears, or the like, or if such animals attack any of the six sorts of domestic beast, let him seal their tracks with the seal and tigers will run thirty leagues away; if he reverses the seal, they will come back. If, while someone is in the water, dragons, fish, turtles, crawling things, poisonous snakes, or the like attack him, make a seal-impression on clean yellow clay, throw it in the water, and the beasts will die. If male or female slaves run away, press the seal in their footprints and they will return. If a person is suddenly struck by bad vapors, or 'dies' and is unconscious, or while walking feels his limbs struck as if pierced by an awl or a knife, take the seal, close off your breaths, press it on the painful spot and on the heart, and recite: "Wraith-breaths depart, right breaths remain!"[19]

With this the text comes to an end. Here, then, we have a dramatic illustration of the extraordinary documentary value of the Taoist canon: A historical source alludes obscurely to a ritual, and a contemporary text in the long-neglected canon obligingly provides a set of instructions on precisely how it is to be performed—instructions written for initiates but still perfectly intelligible to the modern reader. This one example shows that reading only official "historical" writings can limit the historian's enterprise. Yet the search for materials cannot stop here, even when the historian's ingrained fear of the Taoist canon has been overcome. Relevant data are also found in other quarters, and the next point of inquiry should be the Buddhist canon.

A Fifth-Century Buddhist Text

It is not only the ever-present possibility of an Indian prototype—a Buddhist inspiration for some medieval Chinese phenomenon—that should excite the scholar to pursue his inquiry within the Buddhist canon but, above all, the hope of finding new reflections of Chinese practice in the many scriptures that adapt fundamentally Chinese customs and beliefs to the socially prestigious framework of Buddhism. In Chapter 3, we noted the importance of the *Book of Consecration* (*Kuan-ting ching*, T. 1331) as a repository of practice and oral tradition. Once again, it is the *Book of Consecration*, compiled in the 450s, that furnishes the most explicit account of the Taoist ritual of exorcistic "ensigillation," or impressing with a seal, but this time in a Buddhist context.

The seventh chapter of the *Book of Consecration* is given over to instructions for performing a healing ritual in which a "devil-subduing seal" is the principal implement. A literal translation of the first few pages of this text gives an impression of this Buddhist version of the procedure, in close juxtaposition with the Taoist work we have just examined. Later I identify those elements that both versions share, as well as their significant differences:

> *Devil-Subduing Seals and Great Spirit-Spells of Consecration, as Spoken by the Buddha*
>
> Thus I have heard: At one time the Buddha was dwelling in Śrāvastī, in the Jetavana hermitage, together with 1,250 persons. At that time the Celestial Venerable was in his *dhyāna*-chamber; it was just at the beginning of the Long Retreat, on the fifteenth of the month, when the stars were bright and clear. Śakra the Monarch of Heaven, the Four Great Heavenly Kings, the kings' ministers, elders among the spirits beneath the earth, and the officials and people within the realm—all had gone to visit the Buddha, each of them intending to question him on matters that puzzled them. The Celestial Venerable was silent, saying not a single word. In his *dhyāna*, the Buddha pondered, "All the numberless beings of the ten directions dwell forever in benighted ignorance, unable to realize the Perfect and True. They rejoice in performing the deeds of devils and in fabricating perversities; they are sunk in the sea of birth and death, yet who of them is aware of it? They revolve

through the Five Ways of Rebirth, and I alone know it."[20] Pondering these things in his heart, he once more closed his eyes and attached his mind to silent concentration, remaining thus for a very long time without awakening. The Monarch of Heaven had attained the Buddha's marvelous powers and hence realized what the Buddha was pondering. Therefore he rose, joined his palms, and prostrated himself before the Buddha, then withdrew to one side, snapped the fingers of his right hand to awaken him, and said, "There is something that I wish to ask."

At that the Buddha awakened and inquired of Śakra the Monarch of Heaven, "What is it that you wish to ask?" Śakra the Monarch of Heaven prostrated himself at the Buddha's feet, then knelt with palms joined and said to the Buddha: "Among the ninety-five religious rites there is still the rite of *mudrā*.[21] How is it that this practice is not included among the supreme, subtle, and triumphant rites of the Venerable of the World? I desire that the Celestial Venerable set forth an expedient means to transform my benighted ignorance, to cause my Eye of the Tao to open, so that I may be free from dangerous obstacles and the numberless diseases, may be released from the sufferings of the three worlds and mount the path to *nirvāṇa*. I wish you to expound an answer to this question."

The Buddha said to Śakra the Monarch of Heaven: "Good, good! Now listen well, and remember. I will explain to you the rite of the Great Immortal.[22] If among the four classes of the Buddha's disciples any malignant wraiths (*hsieh*) or evil demons should cause disturbance, fear, or horripilation, one should first visualize his own body as my image, with the thirty-two primary and eighty secondary marks, the color of purple gold. The body should be sixteen feet tall, with a solar radiance at the back of the neck.[23] Having visualized my body, you are next to visualize the 1,250 disciples; next, the bodhisattva-monks. When you have completed these three visualizations, visualize the great spirits of the five directions. The first is named Chan-che-ngo-ch'ia; his body is twelve feet tall, he wears a blue garment, spews forth blue vapor, and dwells in the east. The second is named Mo-ho-ch'ih-tou; he is twelve feet tall, wears a red garment, spews forth red vapor, and dwells in the south. The third is named I-tou-nieh-lou; he is twelve feet tall, wears a white garment, spews forth white vapor, and dwells in the west. The fourth is named Mo-ho-ch'ieh-ni; he is twelve feet tall, wears a black garment, spews forth black vapor, and dwells in the north. The fifth is named Wu-t'an-lou-mi; he is twelve feet tall, wears a yellow garment, spews forth yellow vapor, and dwells in the center.[24] Each of these gods of the five quarters has his own retinue; each spirit-king is accompanied by seventy thousand spirits. Thus with seventy thousand spirits in each of the five directions, there are seven times five or 350 thousand spirits, all of whom come to aid the person suffering from illness, to assist him in escaping from danger and passing through various difficulties. These spirit-kings protect human beings and keep malignant wraiths from carrying out their projects at will."

The Buddha told Śakra the Monarch of Heaven, "These are the names of the spirit-kings of the five directions. If hereafter, in the last age of the world, there is a day when the four classes of disciples are in danger, they should write the names of the spirit-kings and their retinues on a round piece of wood.[25] This is called the *mudrā* rite—such is its meaning, and you are to make it known."

Śakra the Monarch of Heaven said, "What should be the dimensions of the *mudrā* on round wood?"

The Buddha answered, "Let it be 7 inches by 0.7 inch."

"What wood is best?" asked Śakra the Monarch of Heaven.

The Buddha replied, "The best of all is gold, silver, or other precious substances. The next best is sandalwood or other fragrant woods. The *mudrā* is to be made of such materials. If anyone is suffering from illness, danger, or fear, or if malignant wraiths and demons are going to and fro, injuring people and disturbing them, they should perform the three visualizations as explained earlier, as well as visualizing the gods of the five directions with their corresponding colors and forms. All should be seen with extreme clarity as if they were present before your eyes, as when someone appears in a mirror and all sides are visible. If you succeed in realizing this without distractions but rather concentrating all your thoughts in singleness of purpose, those suffering from illness will be cured and those suffering anxiety will be reassured. Malignant wraiths and evil demons will all be driven off. If a member of one of the four classes of the Buddha's disciples wishes to employ this spirit-seal,[26] he should first bathe his body and put on a pure and fragrant garment. He should then do reverence to the entirely perfect and truly enlightened numberless buddhas of the ten directions. The way of holding the seal: It should be grasped in the right hand, while in the left you hold a seven-foot long oxtail devil-dispelling staff. On your head you should wear a red Dharmācārya spirit-cap.[27] Stand seven paces from the patient. Seal off your breath for the space of seven respirations and accomplish the visualizations. When they have been completed, raise your right foot in front of you and advance toward the patient.[28] Holding the spirit-seal, bring it to the patient's body and press it down upon his chest. If the patient is a woman, withdraw again seven paces. Stand with your thoughts concentrated as before. Visualize the five great spirits: The spirit of the blue vapor exhaling blue vapors that enter the thumb of the patient's left hand, the spirit of the red vapor exhaling red vapors that enter the big toe of the patient's left foot, the spirit of the white vapor exhaling white vapors that enter the thumb of the patient's right hand, the spirit of the black vapor exhaling black vapors that enter the big toe of the patient's right foot, and the spirit of the yellow vapor exhaling yellow vapors that enter the patient's mouth. When these spirits of the five vapors exhale their proper vapors and they enter the patient's body, the wraiths and evil vapors therein are entirely dispersed at the same moment. They go out from the patient's navel in a burst of smoke, as when a great wind breaks up the clouds and rain. If you are able carefully to control the awesome power of the spirit-seal in this manner, sickness and suffering will be cured and demon-vapors will be destroyed."

The Buddha told Śakra the Monarch of Heaven, "The spirit-kings of the five directions always respond when one visualizes their shapes and attributes. Fully dressed in coats of mail, holding bows, with arrows at their belts, they take their places in the five orientations of the seal, each according to his name. They protect the patient and keep other spirits from entering him. They drive out malignant wraiths and cause devils to scatter in disarray, so that none of them can linger on in the patient's body."

The Buddha said to Śakra the Monarch of Heaven, "By this *mudrā* all demons are crushed and annihilated, so that they are unable to act irresponsibly in opposition to the Law. If one impresses this *mudrā* on a mountain, the mountain will crumble; if on any tree, it will be overthrown. If impressed on rivers, seas, ponds, or springs, their waters will dry up. If impressed in the direction of fire or flood, they will vanish. If in any of the four quarters violent winds should arise, raising the dust before them, lift the seal toward them and they will stop. If you direct the seal toward the earth, the earth will tremble. Should brigands rise up in any quarter, only lift the seal toward them and they will at once disperse. They will no longer have any evil intentions, only kindly thoughts, and all will return to their proper bailiwick. Thus this great spirit-seal brings benefits, in whatever direction it may be pointed. If you use it to seal any of the body's diseases, all will be cured.[29] Those who possess this seal should intone incantations" [omitted here].

The Buddha went on to state, "If you seal a person's house with the names of seven gods on the *mudrā*, these gods will protect that person. They will annihilate wraiths and evils and expel demons to a distance of 400 *yojanas*—all will flee away in confusion and never dare to attack that person. Now I will describe this."

The Buddha said, "In the dwelling places of ordinary people, there are always seven protective spirits. Who are they? The spirit named To-lai-to, the spirit named Seng-ch'ia-lu, the spirit named Po-mo-ssu, the spirit named T'i-po-na, the spirit named T'an-po-lo, the spirit named Mi-shu-to, and the spirit named Ch'i-na-she.[30] When the names of these seven gods are impressed upon a person's house, devils and others with evil intent, on perceiving this

> spirit-seal, will scatter in confusion. If they do not go away but rather try to attack, their heads will break into seven pieces."
>
> The Buddha said to Śakra the Monarch of Heaven, "After my *parinirvāṇa*, these seven spirit-kings will protect the Buddha's disciples; they will drive off malignancies and evils and not allow them to abide. You should make this known to all living beings, and they will protect them in all their goings and comings. Once the spirit-kings have taken up residence in their hearts, they must not offend them. Should anyone offend the spirits, they will at once leave the person's house. If a disciple of the Buddha always observes the retreats and precepts in all purity, however, these seven spirit-kings will constantly be at his side. They will bring him good fortune and protect him, so that none of the demons of the four quarters will dare approach him. The gates of the house should be impressed with clay of a good color. The seal should be kept in a fine container covered with silk cloth. Then the gods will protect you and wicked devils will depart."[31]

The text goes on to give a version of the legend of Hārītī, who chooses this moment to come complaining to the Buddha that this ritual of sealing and spellbinding will be such a powerful safeguard that she and her demon subordinates will be effectively deprived of all nourishment and condemned to starve. The Buddha compassionately directs all Buddhists to make offerings of their leftover food to Hārītī and her demons, thus turning them into docile protectors rather than fearsome enemies. Hārītī's plea attests to the ritual's efficacy. Moreover, by appending this etiological legend explaining the Buddhist cult of Hārītī and similar demonic beings, the author of the *Book of Consecration* buttresses the authority of his ensigillation ritual by relating it to a well-established Buddhist legendary context.[32]

Despite the considerable difference in style and tone, there can be no doubt that this is essentially the same ritual we found in use among sixth-century Taoists, but in Buddhist guise. In comparing the two sets of instructions for what is actually a single type of therapeutic procedure, it becomes possible to distinguish a number of the features that set Buddhists off from Taoists in their own minds, even as they consciously assimilated Taoist practices, for despite the chronological priority of the instructions in the *Book of Consecration*, there can be little doubt that the practice described here is of an earlier Chinese origin.

The most conspicuous differences between the Buddhist and Taoist instructions, are, simply, the names. Of course, this is not a question of names alone but of what such names signify for spiritual lineage, and hence for the authentification of texts and practices. Most importantly, the shift in *nomina sacra* suggests a certain mystical obfuscation. Whereas the Taoist priest was directed to recite spells, commands, and a petition in standard literary Chinese, the Buddhist Master of the Law (whose title itself is Sanskritized as Dharmācārya) had to employ Sanskrit in Chinese phonetic transcription to invoke his divine assistants. Although such Buddhist teachers presumably received oral instruction on the significance of all these names and terms, it is difficult to imagine that the words were at all intelligible to the patient or his family. In any case, the transcriptions are often so idiosyncratic as to puzzle even the modern scholar with all the resources of Buddhist lexicography at his command. We cannot help inferring that this verbal transformation was a very important part of the process of changing Chinese rituals into potent Buddhist operations sanctioned by the authority of the Buddha. For that matter, the seal itself is rather pedantically called *mudrā*, as if the author were trying to reinforce a claim of Indian origin. But running briskly through the stages of the Taoist ritual will help us to dissect its Buddhist counterpart and identify its special features.[33]

Comparison of the texts immediately reveals how greatly written descriptions of similar rituals can differ, not only in their actual performance but also in the choice of details included in the description. In this case, despite all the elaborate nomenclature with which the Buddhist directives are festooned, the Taoist text is much more circumstantial about the practical details of the operations. There are differences in basic equipment, too: The Taoist master starts out with a sword and a bowl of water; the Buddhist retains the sword but is to equip himself with a tall "devil-dispelling staff" with an oxtail affixed to its tip—the staff of an Indian exorcist, reduced in size and gentrified as the "chowry," or fly-whisk, held by elegant gentleman and used to punctuate or emphasize points in conversation.[34] The seals themselves differ significantly, most obviously in their shape: The Taoist seal depicted in the text is of a standard square format, whereas the Buddhist seal is round. This contrast at once suggests a conscious heaven/earth antithesis on the part of the Buddhist author, for in Chinese cosmology heaven is invariably described as round, earth as square. The seal's shape may be one way in which the superiority of the Buddhist model is tacitly asserted over the claims of its Taoist counterpart.

The Taoist is directed to take up a definite astrological orientation (no mention of this for the Buddhist, but perhaps this was implicitly understood). His first visualization consists of a giant spirit-official, directly in front of him, nineteen feet tall. This prodigy prepares the way for the ritual by filling the room with brilliant red vapor. The Buddhist version also opens with a visualized giant, but a giant who is the officiant himself—self-glorified, enlarged to a height of sixteen feet, and endowed with all the distinguishing bodily marks of a buddha. The officiant's identification or union with the deity is (in my view) the prime distinguishing feature of Tantric Buddhism. Here we find this trait explicitly present in a mid-fifth-century proto-Tantric text.[35]

But though the Tantric Buddhist may take a shortcut to divinity, one must not imagine that his visualizations are any less elaborate than those of his Taoist colleagues. As the Buddha, he next mentally recreates the presence of his own 1,250 disciples, then proceeds to actualize five more giants, the guardian spirits of the five directions, each of only slightly lesser stature than himself. They fill the room with vapor of five different colors—another improvement on the monochromatic Taoist version. Moreover, each of the five is accompanied by his own retinue of seventy thousand spirits. What the Buddhist text lacks in operational precision it makes up for in sheer force of numbers. Where does this pentad come from? Looking more closely, we find them in the Taoist ritual, though featured less prominently. After reciting a long spell, the Taoist master finally brings his seal down upon the patient's body and holds his breath. When he at length raises the seal, draws breath again, and steps back from the patient, he utters a formal request, calling upon the General of the Three Divisions, the General Who Operates the Seal, the General Who Cures Illness, the General Who Destroys Disease-Wraiths, and the General Who Arrests Devils. These five spirit-commanders are asked to work together with the seal to cure the patient. It is clear that this pentad corresponds to the five externalized and gigantized spirit-kings, each accompanied by a vast spirit-army, in the Buddhist text. In comparison with the Taoist author, the Buddhist author seems to be aiming at larger-than-life effects; his conception of the ritual is virtually cinematic. Yet we can see that his version still contains many elements of a Taoist prototype, though characteristically mutated.

Absent from the Buddhist text is all mention of the central, instrumental role of the constellation of the Northern Dipper. First its handle points into the Taoist master's hand-held bowl, charging the water within; then, at a later stage of the proceedings, the handle singles out the patient himself, just before the master approaches to begin the actual sealing. From the point at which the Dipper electrifies the water, the Taoist text prescribes a number of operations omitted in the *Book of Consecration*, such as spewing the water forth, first in the five directions, then on the patient. Then, with a new astral orientation, the Taoist master holds the seal against his own heart and visualizes himself as a cosmic divinity—Lao-tzu himself. He bears heaven on his head, treads the earth under his feet, and is ringed about by the five planets, sun and moon, as well as the heraldic animal-spirits of the four points of the compass (bird, dragon, tiger, and tortoise). In a word, he is Lao-tzu in his own body: He is identical and coterminous with the Tao itself. At this point he exteriorizes his own visceral breaths, each in its characteristic color, which issue from his mouth and wind themselves thrice around his head. Three miniature officials then come forth from each of his five viscera and stand, fully armed, at the ready. The Dipper's handle is then pointed at the part of his body in which the patient feels pain. The first-visualized giant is once more mobilized on his mount of red solar vapors; he is made to approach the patient's side by means of the stylized paces of the ancient sorcerer's limping dance, the Step of Yü, and performs an initial sealing of the patient's body. Only after this mighty spirit-representative has completed an initial treatment does the Taoist master brandish his own seal and launch himself into the dance, and the therapy.

In the Buddhist text, all this, together with the phase of the proceedings represented by the spells and prayers, appears to have been compacted into the deployment of five-colored breaths from the five cosmic guardian-spirits into the patient's body through his big toes, thumbs, and mouth. This influx of powerful vapors is said instantly to drive forth the afflicting demons, who make their frantic exit through the patient's navel in a sudden burst of smoke. Indeed, the breaths of the five cosmic guardians represent virtually all the Buddhist text has to say about breath; there is none of the precision about the operator's use of *hsi, t'a*, and *ch'ih* breaths, for example, that we find in the Taoist manual. Yet it is clear from the Taoist version that the entire mystery of healing was ultimately enacted by the master through careful control of his own vital breaths, transforming and directing them to heal the patient. It seems entirely probable that the Buddhist master worked in a closely similar manner, even though the *Book of Consecration* has left this aspect to oral tradition, or to the reader's imagination.

The concluding remarks in both texts set forth the claims for their respective seal's efficacy as an all-around demonifugic tool. The hyperbolic announcement with which the Taoist instructions open is found capping the directions in the Buddhist manual; causing mountains to collapse and waters to dry up or reverse their courses are common properties of Buddhist and Taoist seals alike. The Buddhist work also specifies that a seal can be impressed in clay or plaster that is then affixed to the gates of a person's house, and that this will effectively keep away all demons. Rather than the five gods of the directions, however, this domestic seal should have the names of seven protecting divinities engraved on it. This septet of curiously named guardians does not seem to be known elsewhere in Buddhist scripture. The Taoist texts also ends by describing the variety of domestic applications to which its seal may be put. For example, if you are awakened in the middle of the night by a nightmare or some frightening sound, you can hang the seal over your door, after loudly reciting a spell. The opening words of this spell are, "Ye seven spirits of the house." With the two texts thus juxtaposed, we see that the *Book of Consecration*'s author appears to have found the inspiration for his group of seven impressively named Sanskrit guardians in the standard squadron of seven deities that normally serve as resident protectors in every Chinese household (the gods of the door, the bed-chamber, etc., under the supervision of the god of the hearth). As is so often the case, the familiar gains vastly in authority by being rendered exotic.

Despite all the information given on the subsidiary uses of these seals, there is still no mention of impressing them on paper. When not being applied directly to the patient's body, they are pressed into clay or earth, and the resultant impression serves as a phylactery bound upon the door-posts. It might seem that Pelliot's theory on the use of these seals for printing on paper must be temporarily set aside, yet we will find evidence that comparable seals were being printed on paper in Tantric Buddhist circles. First, though, we should look into some antecedents of our Buddho-Taoist seals, because the making of a depth-charge, or submarine bomb, against aquatic monsters by using an impression of the Taoist seal in clean yellow clay evokes a classic account of an offensive against water-monsters and takes the story back to the early years of the fourth century.

Prehistory and Early Development

The apotropaic use of seals was certainly well known in China more than a hundred years before the *Book of Consecration* and no doubt long before that, as well. As early as the beginning of the first century C.E., we read about seals carved on the fifth day of the fifth lunar month, and on *mao* days (held in some astrological systems to be the most unlucky days in the sixty-day cycle), and hung on the person or attached to doors to ward off evil emanations.[36] But the most detailed textual proof comes from the book *Pao-p'u tzu nei-p'ien*, written about 320 by Ko Hung (ca. 283–343). The seventeenth of its "inner chapters," on occult techniques, is specifically concerned with what the adept must do to prepare himself for entering the mountains, where ascetic practice is to be carried out. In that chapter Ko refers to the "Twelve Seals of Enclosed Primordiality" that can be impressed on all four sides of one's dwelling place. These impressions will keep away all malignant spirits.[37] The same source illustrates a complex talisman described as being the spirit-seal carried by Lord Lao (that is, Lao-tzu) for protection against the hundred demons, serpents, tigers, and wolves. It is to be incised on a piece of datewood-pith 4 inches square.[38] The mountains in which seekers after the Tao are accustomed to dwell abound with tigers and wolves, but the adept need not fear them if he, like the men of ancient times, is equipped with a seal inscribed with the Yellow God's Emblem of Transcendence.[39] The seal measures 4 inches across and its inscriptions comprises 120 characters. It is to be struck in clay, and the impressions placed on all four sides of one's dwelling at a distance of a hundred paces. Thereafter neither tigers nor wolves will dare enter those precincts. If, when walking in the mountains, one comes upon fresh tiger-tracks, impressing the seal in the direction in which they are going will cause the tiger to keep moving ahead. If the seal is reversed in the track, it will make the tiger return. Thus, even in the mountains, there is no need to fear tigers or wolves. Nor are they the only sort of menace with which the seal can cope. Should one happen upon the mountain or riverside shrines of evil, meat-eating spirits, one need only place an impression of the seal across their paths to render those spirits impotent. Ko Hung goes on to relate how a great turtle-demon in a pool of the Yangtse, responsible for numerous cases of illness in that neighborhood, was one day spotted by a Master of the Tao named Tai Ping. Tai made several hundred impressions of the seal that Ko describes, and from a boat dropped them all around the pool. After an interval an immense turtle rose to the surface of the water, and when it had been killed, all the sufferers recovered.[40]

Here again, it is the impression of the seal in clay that serves as the apotropaic agent, realizing the power of the seal itself. Such seals of the "Yellow God" are actually in existence. One example, 25 × 25 mm, bears a four-character inscription that reads, "Yellow God's Transcendent Emblem"; another, 24 × 24 mm, reads "Yellow God's Emblem of Transcendence, Seal of the Monarch of Heaven," in nine characters. Both are incised, thus giving a white inscription on a red ground when impressed in vermilion, and both have been dated to the first or second century C.E.[41] They are, to be sure, much smaller than the seal referred to by Ko Hung, and they do not bear anything like the 120-character inscription that he mentions. Since their provenance is uncertain and they were not found under controlled conditions in a precisely dated tomb, they may have been inspired by Ko Hung's account rather than representing early examples of his class of artifact. There are first- and second-century C.E. references to such seals in recently excavated texts of "tomb-quelling writs."[42] These documents, placed in graves to "stabilize" them, make it clear that the seals were issued to spirit-emissaries of the Monarch of Heaven—namely, "the Monarch of Heaven's emissary, the Yellow God," or "the Monarch of Heaven's Master of Spirits." They were to be used by them as emblems of authority and implements of power in controlling subordinate godlings and demons. By adding such seals to his own stock of implements, the medieval occultist was affirming his own identity as an official emissary of the Monarch of Heaven.[43]

Still, the use of seals in China goes back more than a thousand years before Ko Hung's book of secrets, and it is by no means impossible that earlier seals may have been used apotropaically, or in the manufacture of demonifugic amulets, as he relates. Their predominant function, though, has always been official and juridical. The oldest examples, as well as the largest and most impressive, have always been seals of state and lesser seals of office that authenticate documents and identify the bearer. The size, shape, inscriptions, and the materials from which official seals are made have always been strictly regulated by law. In the hierarchy of official seals, there have always been differences distinguishing each grade and rank in the administration, from the head of state on down. Among private persons, seals traditionally fulfilled—and still fulfill—the function of handwritten signatures in modern European society. A small seal is still carried on the person by every adult; it serves to authenticate and authorize, and functions as a man's official double, a sort of juridical second self.

The main purpose of seals was, originally, the authentication of deeds, official documents, and contracts. Thus it is understandable that most of the early surviving examples (from the Han dynasty, 206 B.C.E.–220 C.E.) should bear official titles rather than proper names, though a number of private seals, too, are extant. A cord running through an often ornamental handle served to attach the seal to one's belt. The characters, in these early examples, are most often carved in intaglio, giving a white impression when the surrounding ground is printed in red. But others are carved in relief and so print the characters in red on a white background. In time, greater variety appears in types and functions. Because a person's official seal embodied his juridical identity, different aspects of his personality could be represented by different seals—one or more for his roles as author, calligrapher, painter, collector, and so on. In addition to his routine, daily identity, a man might have other (complementary or contrasting) personae as a poet, patron, collector, Taoist or Buddhist initiate, and the like, and each of these aspects may quite normally have been represented by a special seal. There need have been nothing frivolous about this plurality of personae (any more than the multiplicity of internal souls and different spirit-factions was a matter for jest). The official character of seals and sealing—the imprinting of identity—might be in deadly earnest, as many cautionary tales about the fate of district magistrates who somehow lost their official seals all too clearly indicate: At the very least, such unfortunates were removed from office and rusticated in disgrace.[44]

Seals of Āṭavaka, the Demon-General

Sometime during the first half of the sixth century (and thus squarely between the *Book of Consecration* and the later Taoist manual), a further set of instructions for therapeutic sealing was written down in another proto-Tantric scripture, the *Dhāraṇī Book of Āṭavaka, General of the Demons* (T. 1238). The charter on which this text models itself faithfully follows the standard proto-Tantric stereotype. In the time of the Buddha, a certain monk had been despoiled by robbers, bitten by snakes, tormented by demons, and was consequently in a very sorry plight. Āṭavaka, the demon of desert places, was moved to pity by this spectacle; he betook himself to the Buddha and offered an exceedingly powerful spell for use by Buddhist monks against evil demons and wicked persons. So strong was this incantation that with it a monk could subdue the god Brahmā himself, let alone other, lesser spirits. But the Buddha, good soul, would at first have none of this; such a terrible, wicked spell might well harm living beings. Āṭavaka's response also adheres to precedent; in times to come, he says, the number and ubiquity of demonic oppressors will only increase. Indeed, we have heard all this before, so it comes as no surprise when the Buddha allows himself to be convinced by the persuasive demon, and the terrible spell is pronounced. More spells follow for specific contingencies, then directions for painting an icon of Āṭavaka and his suite of demon-officers—a painting guaranteed to strike terror into the hearts of any potential demon-assailants. This is all standard proto-Tantric fare but derives particular interest from the subsequent destiny of the demon-general Āṭavaka, who in time became the special guardian deity of the Japanese imperial house.[45] There follows an extended sequence of finger-seals, or mudrās; then at last come the diagrams of talismans and wooden seals that immediately alert us to the relevance of this text for our subject. In fact, the work proves to be of considerable interest for therapeutic ritual in general.

This section of the scripture is entitled "The Great General's Rites of Exorcism for Driving Away Demons":

> The rite is only to be undertaken after one has already achieved some success with the deity's spells; otherwise, it will not work. At dawn, the adept is to place in front of the deity's image a bowl of freshly drawn well water and an incense burner. He should then straighten his robes and sit down, his expression stern and unsmiling, his hand forming the finger-seal of great anger. Then the person suffering from demonic possession is brought in. The master should use few words and assume a stern and imperious attitude; he simply tells him, "Sit down!" and then begins to revile him furiously, as if intending to strike fear into him. He says, "How much longer do you expect the gods to be patient?" and "Quick, tie him up!" He speaks in a loud voice, and as soon as he has said this, he has his assistants tie up the patient. He then makes as if to beat him or recite spells of banishment over him. All this time he speaks very deliberately, using few words. This is the Great General's rite for driving away indwelling demons. There is no need to recite a spell, but if you want to have someone recite my spell during the proceedings, it should generally be a man of virtue and experience; otherwise, he might come to grief. What I have given here is an abridged account. There are many ways of going about it, but if I were to expound them at greater length I could speak for an entire kalpa and still not be done.[46]

The god's brevity is greatly to be regretted, since it is precisely such details that we so badly crave in our attempt to reconstruct the psychic processes which play such an important role in all forms of ritual healing. Fortunately, as we will see in Chapter 5, not all authors were equally terse in describing how to go about dealing with cases of demonic possession. We must at all events be grateful for the glimpse that this sixth-century text gives us of the master carefully preparing his dramatic scenario. The tense atmosphere of anger and

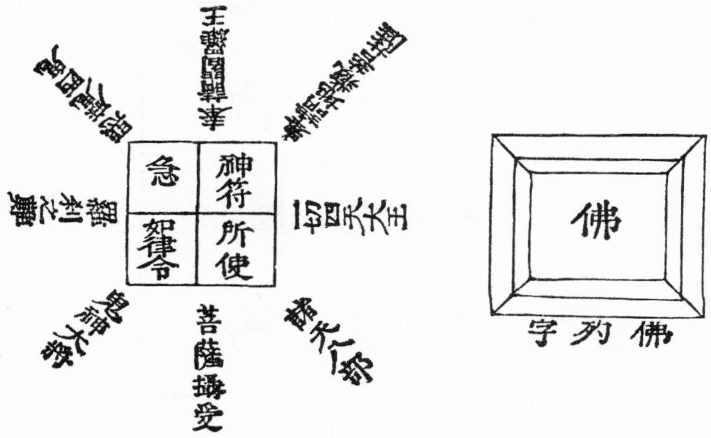

a. b.

FIGURE 2 A talisman and a spirit-seal from the *Dhāraṇī Book of Āṭavaka, General of the Demons* (*A-cha-p'o-chü kuei-shen ta-chiang shang fo t'o-lo-ni ching*, T. 1238, vol. 21: 184c), tentatively dated to the first half of the sixth century: (a) a talisman against disease-demons, showing a spell in talismanic form; and (b) a spirit-seal termed "Heart of All the Buddhas of the Past, Present, and Future" (the character "Buddha" is at its center).

denunciation is, of course, directed toward the occupying demon. Stern menace is the order of the day in this Buddhist exorcist's theater of operations, and binding, beating, and confinement are deemed entirely in place, for the patient is by no means himself but rather a hostile, recalcitrant demon that must be driven hence. A full range of variations on this approach to demonic possession was set down in writing with all explicitness by later Taoist authors, as we will see, but it is noteworthy that such procedures were already being applied in the first half of the sixth century, and in the context of Chinese Buddhism, as well. The stipulation for "a man of virtue and experience" as the spell-reciter is based on the fear that the reciter, if young and impressionable, may himself become possessed by the demon.

It is in this setting that the *Dhāraṇī Book* presents its stock of talismans and seals, beginning with a talisman against disease-demons; when worn on the person, this guarantees freedom from bad dreams, victory in battle, and permits you to "enter water without drowning, enter fire without burning" (Figure 2a). It is written in standard script, and around the periphery simply lists the spirits in whose name it operates (namely, the Bodhisattva Earth-

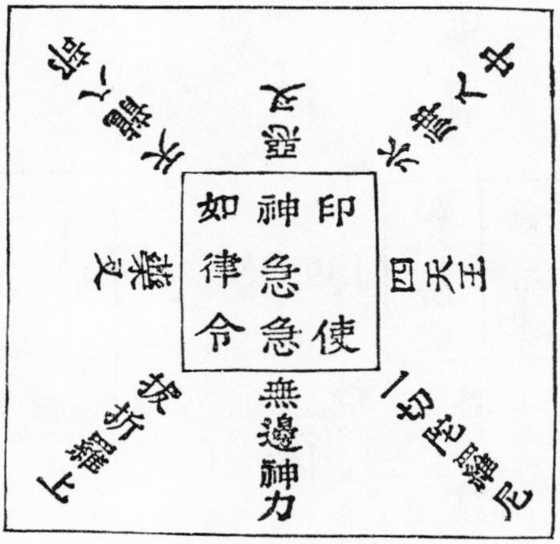

FIGURE 3 The demon-general Āṭavaka's seal, to be used in the exorcistic procedure of "summoning for interrogation" (*k'ao-chao*), and giving complete command over Āṭavaka's eight demon-armies. Like the similarly configured talisman shown in Figure 2a, this seal is from the *Dhāraṇī Book of Āṭavaka, General of the Demons* (T. 1238, vol. 21: 184c).

Matrix, i.e., the psychopomp Kṣitigarbha; the Four Celestial Kings, eight divisions of gods, and the General of the Demons). It is in fact a spell in talismanic form, and in the central square it declares, "Let those whom this spirit-talisman directs / Be swift as the Statutes and Ordinances command!" This is essentially the standard conclusion to a Taoist spell.

Immediately afterward, the Buddha presents the first spirit-seal, termed "Heart of All the Buddhas of the Past, Present, and Future," and "the seal that does away with the ailments of all living beings, eliminates obstacles, moves mountains, halts watercourses, extinguishes fire, and drains the sea" (Figure 2b). These attributes neatly compress the long list of magical properties regularly associated with miraculous seals—plucking up mountains, causing rivers to flow backward, and so on—to which we have already been exposed. The Buddha then firmly states that if one enters a place where there is illness while holding the seal, all ailments will disappear without leaving a trace behind. If you hold it and enter fire you will not be burnt, if you enter water you will not be drowned, and if you enter the mountains you need have no fear of tigers, wolves, and lions. Even if a monk has broken the rules for monks, he need only rub the seal with cow's bezoar (bezoars being concretions found in the stomachs of cows, oxen, tapirs, and certain other animals)

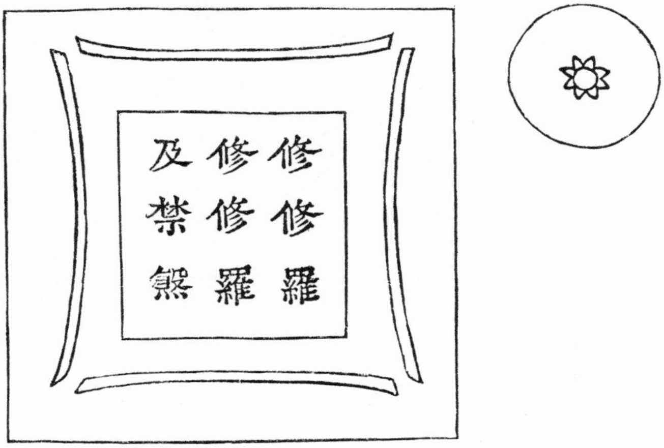

FIGURE 4 A square "lunar disk of the asuras" (left) and a small, round "golden disk" seal (right). From the *Dhāraṇī Book of Āṭavaka, General of the Demons* (T. 1238, vol. 21: 184c).

and impress it on bamboo-membrane. After he has swallowed a hundred thousand such sealed talismans, he will become a bodhisattva of the first or second stage (*bhūmi*) and all his transgressions will be obliterated.

It is then Āṭavaka's turn to present a seal, one that ensures complete command of the eight divisions of his spirit-armies, with consequent total dominion over all demons (Figure 3): "If you wish to summon for interrogation the spirit-kings of the four quarters, simply point the seal in the desired direction and recite my spell of the eight divisions twenty-one times." Much might be said about this "summoning for interrogation" (*k'ao-chao*), for it denotes an entire range of Taoist exorcistic procedures; once again, this Buddhist text provides important evidence that such practices were already in use.[47] The seal is similar in design to the preceding written talisman (see Figure 2a), but the word "seal" has been substituted for "talisman" in the central square—"This seal directs the gods swiftly, as the Statutes and Ordinances command"—and the outer list of divine personnel differs, too, including in addition to the "eight divisions of gods and dragons" a summons to the water-spirits and naming of the "limitless divine power of all *dhāraṇī*" and the *vajra*.

More seals follow, such as a small, round "golden disk" seal and a large, square "lunar disk of the asuras" (Figure 4, the asuras being the great cosmic demons that hold the sun and the moon). Next comes a seal of the "Dog of Heaven and the Leaping Snake," which is capable of subduing all poisonous

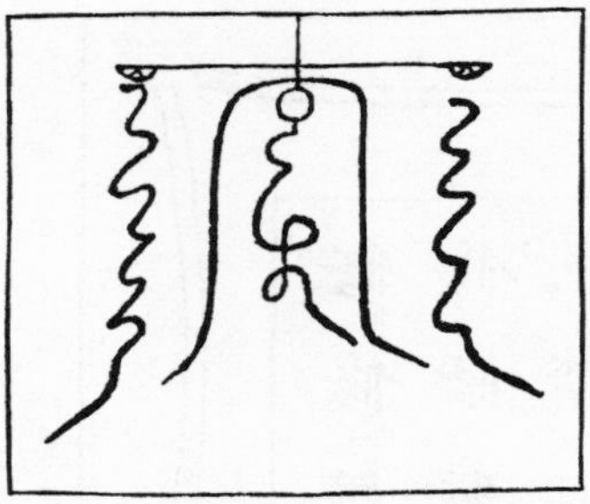

FIGURE 5 The seal named "the sword," for printing on paper as well as on the patient's body. The talisman printed with it, when swallowed, enters the patient's stomach and pierces the heart of the demon that is afflicting him. The patient's resultant unconsciousness is an indication that the seal is taking effect. From the *Dhāraṇī Book of Āṭavaka, General of the Demons* (T. 1238, vol. 21: 185a).

drugs and all disease-causing demons. Āṭavaka describes the pictorial seal as showing, above, the head of a coiling dragon, and below, the Dog of Heaven, which he tells us resembles a lion with a wide-open mouth. Unfortunately, the printed text reproduces only a blank square; the design has been lost. "Dog of Heaven" is one of the dangerous, baleful stars in Chinese astrological tradition.[48] In Japan, however, the name denotes a long-nosed, winged being that frequents the high mountains, possesses powerful occult techniques, and is noted for unbridled lechery—in all respects a ghostly double of the mountain-dwelling ascetic (*yamabushi*).[49]

After this, we are offered a "seal of flame," to be engraved in gold or copper and carried about with you. Whenever you wish to go somewhere, you simply point the seal in the desired direction, or you can imprint it on paper and swallow seven such talismans, with spectacular results. The seal is designed as a round sun-emblem, a "seal of the solar disk's samādhi-flames." In the center stands the sun's heraldic beast, the three-footed crow, resembling a phoenix and surrounded on all sides by flames.[50] Here, too, the printed version disappoints us, giving only an empty circle rather than the impressively fiery seal-emblem. Āṭavaka's next seal is named "the sword" and contains an archaic form of the character for "sword" in its center (Figure 5). It may be impressed on the patient himself, as well as on paper which is then given him to swallow, whereupon, we are told, the printed talisman enters his stomach and—swordlike—pierces the disease-demon's heart. The patient will then lose con-

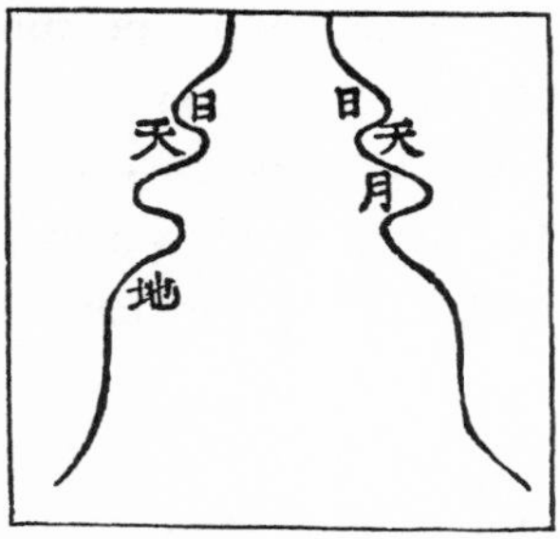

FIGURE 6 A pair of characters for "sun" and "moon" are inscribed on this seal, which is similar in shape to the "sword" seal shown in Figure 5. Below these characters on the right is the character for "moon" and, on the left, that for "earth." This appears to be a rough sketch outlining a complex iconographic seal described in the *Dhāraṇī Book of Āṭavaka* (T. 1238, vol. 21: 185a).

sciousness, which is clearly a sign of the talisman's great efficacy. Here, too, the directions for engraving are rather more elaborate than the printed illustrations (Figure 6). The top should depict the Buddha Vairocana (the Body of the Law, or Dharmakāya, and central deity of the then-nascent mature Tantric system). Above him is a canopy, on either side are flying dragons, below are lotus flowers standing in vases, and in the center the gods bound by oath to serve Buddhists standing above a great king of yakṣas; on either side of him is a dragon-king. All this should be painted on an eight-inch square piece of silk, using only cow's bezoar and no other colors. This icon is to be used in a ritual performed on a high mountaintop, beginning on the first day of the eighth month, which will assure the seal-possessor of total dominion over all gods and demons:

> If you wish to beat demons, call upon the Black King of Heaven. If you wish to overcome all poisons and dragons, call upon the golden-winged King of Birds (Garuḍa). If you wish to control serpent venom, call upon the big-bellied Kumbhāṇḍa-demon. If you wish to conquer the devils of the four quarters, call on the Celestial Devil P'o-hsün. If you wish to overcome tree-goblins, make use of the vajra-beings. If you wish to conquer diseases within the body, make use of Kuṇḍalī. If you wish to deal with robbers, call upon Saṅgha Maṇibhadra. If you wish to conquer mountain-gods, call upon King Mucilinda. For promoting life and seeking profit, invoke the Celestial King of Merit. To accompany you at all times in all your comings and goings, call upon the Fourteen Rākṣasa Kings. And for anything that has not been taken care of, call upon me, the Great General Āṭavaka![51]

After this come a series of simple healing operations, using a sword. Simply pointing the sword at the malady will often cure it; sometimes the sword is used as a lancet (or rather, as an acupuncture needle), as in cases of dysentery or diarrhea, which can be instantly cured by a sword-prick below the navel. Lacking a sword, a finger of the adept's right hand will serve just as well in all these healing functions. From here on the text becomes utterly varied, as if the author were trying to put down every useful method while ink and light still lasted. The Buddhist practitioner is to grind his teeth while reciting a spell, just like his Taoist contemporaries. The healing methods that are used focus on spells and swords, with occasional mention of drugs and embrocations. Among the kaleidoscopic variety of instructions, we find additional anticipations of later practice. For example, the Southern Dipper (Nan-tou) makes a precocious appearance in its specialized role of an aid to exorcism; you are to beat the patient—or indwelling demon—and lock him up in the prison of the Southern Dipper. Release him after seven days and he will be cured. Or again, in treating illness in someone else's household, you should first apprehend the family's hearth-god, who knows all the scuttlebut, and interrogate him. Then, with the facts in hand, you can consign the demonically possessed patient to the Lord of the Southern Dipper for a sound exorcistic thrashing. But as the author observes, "Whenever a person falls ill, if he has faith, you may treat him; if he lacks faith, even for an instant, you should not treat him, for he will be difficult to cure."

The only mention of a therapeutic seal in the final section of the *Dhāraṇī Book* is a reference to sealing a hard-to-cure patient whose condition has been caused by a heavy karmic burden carried over from previous lives, using the "transgression-destroying seal of the Bodhisattva Avalokiteśvara." There is also the passing remark that "if you wish to bind a person but cannot be bothered to use a seal, simply focus your mind intently, recite my spell, send off a spirit to bind him, and he will be bound; if you send off to have him beaten, he will be beaten, just as you wish." The text concludes with a splendid apocalyptic vision of Āṭavaka and his spirit-troops marching over the ravaged world during the dark age when the Buddha's Law has already entered its most somber phase. Wherever they pass, the mountains and rivers will split open and hordes of demons will emerge and flee in terror. Then Āṭavaka will have his dragons and other demonic followers rain down great rains, raise huge winds, and burn up all vegetation with terrible lightning bolts. All living creatures will take shelter in the cracks and crannies of the earth as Āṭavaka's armies smash the demons with their vajra-staves and pound them to dust.[52]

An interesting and significant feature of this work is that certain of its seals are intended not only for pressing on the body or directing off into space, but also for printing on paper. If the text can truly be dated to the first half of the sixth century, this makes it the earliest explicit reference to the use of seals to print paper talismans, and it thus substantiates Pelliot's very plausible suggestion. Unfortunately, though there seems to be no intrinsic improbability in this early date, the work has not survived in any continental Chinese Buddhist canon. It is known only from Japan (whither it is supposed to have been imported in the ninth century), and the printing on which the current edition is based dates only from 1753. Still, there is equally tenuous support for many medieval Chinese texts. Similar circumstances enshroud the early history of the next text to give an explicit description of seals used both on a patient's body and to print talismans for internal consumption—a text purported to date from the middle of the seventh century.

The Seal of the Jungle-Woman

The *Book of the Incantations and Dhāraṇī of the Jāṅgulī Woman* (*Ch'ang-chü-li tu-niu t'o-lo-ni chou ching*, T. 1265) is said to have been translated by a monk named Gupta, who was apparently active in China during the 650s, but (like many other Tantric and proto-Tantric ritual texts) it is extant only in a single manuscript copied in 1152 and preserved in a Japanese monastic library. The text is interesting in its own right, as an early document in the Buddhist cult of the goddess Jāṅgulī ("Jungle-Woman"), described here as an ascetic virgin of great beauty dwelling on the northern side of the Himalayas, dressed in deerskin, adorned with all sorts of poisonous snakes, and with other venomous serpents as her companions and playfellows.[53] This singular woman is said to have presented the Buddha with her powerful spell. When recited in the presence of deadly dragons or serpents, it stuns them, smashes their heads, scatters their scales, causes their fangs to fall out, rots the skin of their heads, smashes them and causes their blood to flow out, and (after all this!) binds them so that they are unable to move. If one of the Buddha's disciples simply hears Jāṅgulī's spell recited, he will be safe from snakebite for the next seven years. As is usual in such cases, the spell is specifically intended for the particularly difficult conditions under which Buddhists will have to live as the end of the world and the end of Buddhism approach. The spell is stated to be highly potent against every sort of toxic envenomation: not only the bites of snakes and scorpions but also toxic states manifesting as swellings, tumors, buboes, and wens, as well as toxicity originating in mountain springs and streams, in contact with raw gold or other poisonous pharmaka, and by various sorts of witchcraft (*ku-tu*).[54] Jāṅgulī's spell is to be recited over water, which is then swallowed by the sufferer. Such water is to be held in the mouth while the sufferer recites the spell silently seven times; then all the root-causes of the envenomation will be removed, and he will come to no harm.

The necessary ritual includes painting a detailed image of the goddess Jāṅgulī; such ritual instructions are often excellent sources for iconography, and this short text is no exception. The goddess is to be depicted in her deerskin garments.[55] Later descriptions of her in Sanskrit and Tibetan texts assign various attributes to her hands (of which she sometimes has two, but sometimes four or six): an exorcistic fly-whisk, a serpent, a cluster of snake-dispelling peacock-feathers, a sword, a poisonous flower.[56] In this medieval text, however, Jāṅgulī is given just two hands; in the right is held a poison-subduing sword, in the left is a poison-controlling wooden seal. It is clear that this goddess of the Himalayan wilderness has been incorporated into the Buddho-Taoist complex of seal therapy that we have been reconstructing.

The rest of her iconic panoply is also rather colorful. She is adorned all over her body with the intertwining bodies of serpents, wreathed into finger-rings and armlets, bracelets and anklets. In front of her is to be painted a boy dressed in blue, holding a bowl of water in one hand and an incense burner in the other. Spread out in front of her should be painted all sorts of toxic fruits and poisonous potions. All about her mountains should be painted, as well as tigers, wolves, lions, venomous dragons (i.e., cobras), vipers, and all sorts of other wicked, deadly serpents surrounding her on every side. This lively icon is to be placed within the ritual area; five bowlfuls of broth of aconite should be poured out to it in a clean place as an offering, and other poisonous plants should be burnt as an incense-offering to the goddess, whose spell is then recited seven thousand times or, more effectively, thirty thousand times, and for the highest potency, seventy thousand times.

The text then illustrates two square seals. For the first (Figure 7a) one is to use wood from a jujube tree that has been struck by lightning. The seal should be 1.7 inches square. Its use is twofold: First it should be dipped in vermilion and imprinted on the swelling itself; then it is to be printed on paper that is swallowed by the patient. The second seal (Figure 7b), slightly smaller (1.3 inches) and simpler in inscription, should be made from white sandalwood and is to be employed in the same manner. Next, five little talismans are pre-

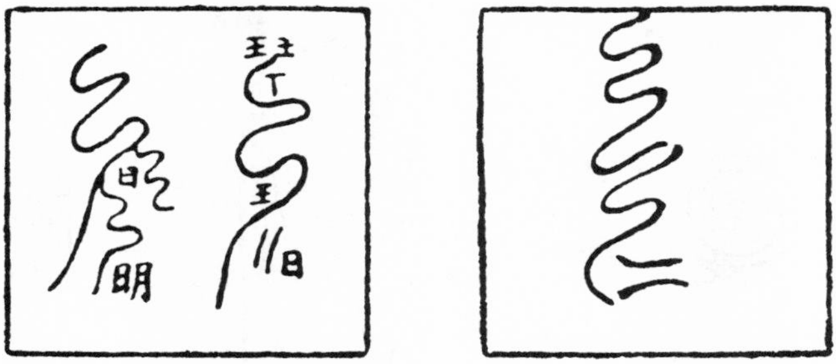

a. b.

FIGURE 7 Two square seals for use against snakebite and other toxic envenomation, from the *Book of the Incantations and Dhāraṇī of the Jāṅgulī Woman (Ch'ang-chü-li tu-nü t'o-lo-ni chou ching*, T. 1265, vol. 21: 295a), tentatively dated to the middle of the seventh century: (a) a seal to be made from the wood of a jujube tree that has been struck by lightning; and (b) a seal to be made from white sandalwood. Both are to be used in two ways: dipped in vermilion and imprinted on the swelling itself, then printed on paper that is swallowed by the patient.

sented, each suggesting a curling snake, which are to be drawn in black ink on the point of envenomation, as well as being written in vermilion on paper and then swallowed (Figure 8a). Then comes the text of a talisman that is to be written in vermilion on paper, sealed in an envelope, and carried about with one to keep off demonic influence. (The text reads "Ritual seal of Jāṅgulī; Jāṅgulī cures the hundred envenomations! Kill and bind! Enchant and bind! Apprehend, goddess! *Svāhā!*"—clearly a Chinese adaptation of the goddess's Sanskrit spell.) This, too, we are told, can be written in vermilion on paper and swallowed to remove illness and pain from the stomach, but great care must be taken not to dirty or defile the talisman. Finally, there are illustrations of a right and a left hand, on which have been carefully written which parts of which fingers relate to the treatment of which ailments (Figure 8b); hence the Tantric practitioner literally holds the cure of a wide variety of illnesses in the palm of his hand.[57]

If this text indeed dates from the middle of the seventh century, it may also rank among the earliest explicit references to printing such curative seals on paper. The talisman for internal consumption is produced by means of the same ritual implement that impresses its powerful imprint on the patient's skin. In a later version of the Jāṅgulī ritual, the *Jang-yü-li t'ung-nü ching* (T.

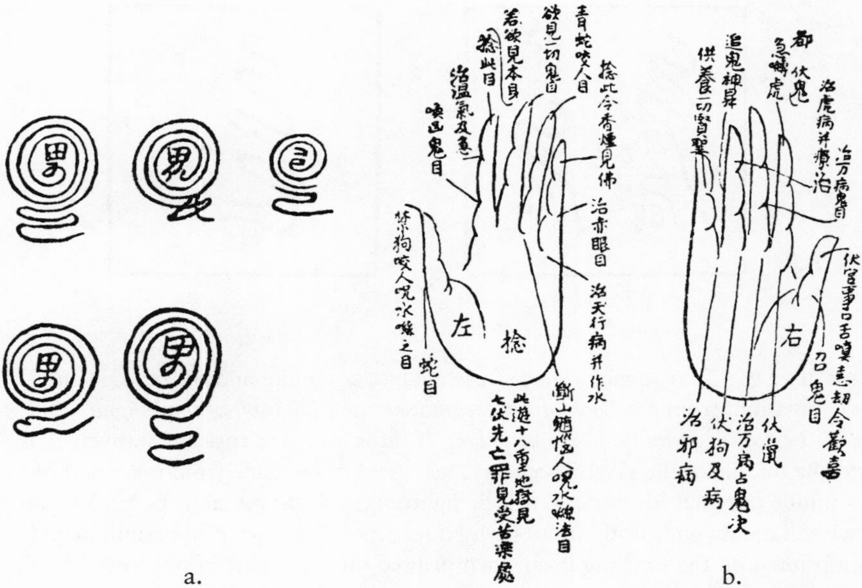

a. b.

FIGURE 8 Two additional illustrations of curative seals from the *Book of the Jāṅgulī Woman*: (a) five little talismans (T. 1265, vol. 21: 295a), each suggesting a curling snake, which are to be drawn in black ink on the point of envenomation (if Jāṅgulī's spell is recited over them seven times, they are extremely efficacious), and which can also be written in vermilion on paper and then swallowed; and (b) a left and a right hand (295b), with characters indicating the specific ailments that can be cured by pressing on various points.

1264B), which was translated or assembled by Amoghavajra in the eighth century, the "seal" concerned is the more usual sort found in Tantric Buddhist texts—namely, one formed by the officiant using his own fingers. With this hand-seal he is directed to empower his own body in five places (right and left shoulders, heart, throat, and forehead, dispersing the seal at the crown of his head). Then he is to visualize himself as the fearsome Jāṅgulī-maiden: green, like a dragon-woman, with seven heads, four arms, all the serpentine adornments, and fire streaming from every pore of his body. Visualizing himself in this way in front of the victim who has been bitten or otherwise poisoned, the priest takes a bowlful of water, enchants it with the goddess's spell, and with his right hand throws water at the victim's heart. As he does this, the toxic influence will gradually dissipate. It is interesting to note the application, under the patronage of a single Indian Tantric goddess, of two different but parallel procedures: the finger-seals, as usual hand-crafted by the priest (true "Handwerk"), and the solid wooden seal introduced in the more signified version of the ritual. Significantly, a comparable juxtaposition of finger-seals and wooden seals is found in a Taoist text of the same period. The *Red Script of the Three Registers of Divinity* (*T'ai-shang ch'ih-wen tung-shen san-lu*, HY 589), a text ascribed to T'ao Hung-ching, bears a preface dated 632, and the work as a whole reveals Tantric Buddhist influence. It concentrates on a fivefold symbolism of the planets and elements (or phases of change), and after a miscellaneous inventory of practical applications of its "seals," it lists the instruments by means of which these ends can be accomplished.[58] First come finger-seals of heaven, earth, and the Five Phases (earth, fire, metal, water, wood). They are followed by the Sanskrit spells of the elemental sages of the five directions. Then come illustrations of five seals, one for each of the Five Phases, to be carved in "wood from a jujube tree that has been frightened by a dragon." Finally, there are invocations of the gods of the five directions—Sino-Tantric constructions that include the "Great Golden Crested King of the Disk of Autonomy, of Wood and the East" and his like-named colleagues of fire, water, metal, and earth. The applications to which the two types of seals and their divine sponsors may be put are of the familiar sort; perhaps the most interesting feature of the instructions is how they nonchalantly mingle both sorts of seal. If, for example, you print the five wooden seals on five sheets of paper that you then apply to your body, form the "water" finger-seal over your shadow as cast in moonlight, and then leap ten paces, your shadow will disappear. The wooden seals can be placed in a gourd that is then taken outdoors and be-charmed under the moon; brought back in and decanted, the seals will illumine your chamber, a technique termed "supplanting the moon's light." And if pressed on the soles of your feet in the by now familiar manner, the seals will permit levitation a hundred feet into the air; the "earth" seal alone, so imprinted, will allow you to walk on water and cross rivers and streams. This text appears to be one of the earliest to give instructions on Taoist finger-seals, and it terms them simply "seals" (*yin*), rather than "secrets" or "formulae" (*chüeh*), as they came to be known in later Taoist usage. Their principles of construction are simpler than their Tantric Buddhist analogues, for they are essentially formed with a single hand; each finger is equated with one of the Five Phases—hence the pentadic orientation of this text—and the thumb serves as pointer or indicator. In Tantric Buddhism, the finger-seal applied to the body of course imprints a "seed-syllable" (*bīja-mantra*)—a single syllable evocative and emblematic of a deity—on the priest's vital points; the wooden seal, *more sinico*, makes this all perfectly concrete and tangible. A mystic gesture has been frozen into an artifact.[59]

Apart from seals made of wood and seals formed with the fingers, the other pairing found in sixth- and seventh-century scriptures aligns wooden seals with paper talismans. In view of their analogous form and function, this was only to be expected. The important point is the neat parallelism between the two techniques, for both are fully official, not to say bureaucratic. Both employ writing, the unifying cultural trait of Chinese civilization; moreover, they both make use of an archaic or archaizing "seal script" to whose secrets only officers and gentlemen, priests and administrators, scholars and commanders were privy. The written talisman was swallowed to perform its wonders deep within the body; the graven seal impressed its authority upon the body's outer surface. How appropriate, then, not only that the two techniques should have existed in tandem, as complementary aspects of treatment, but that by the middle of the seventh century, if not earlier, they should have coalesced, the wooden seals being used not only to impress the outer man but to produce the talisman that would plumb his inner depths.

Seals of Ucchuṣma, Lord of Impurities

An even more imposing conjunction of seals and talismans is found in another body of medieval Tantric Buddhist ritual literature centering on the god Ucchuṣma.[60] This figure's name may mean "garbage" or "leftovers," the remains of a meal (or offerings from the same), suggesting the god's mode of nourishment, common to an entire class of deities—namely, pagan gods converted to Buddhism and subsequently attached to the religious and lay faithful as supernatural servants. Ucchuṣma's cult was popular in the Sino-Tibetan borderland, where he was known especially under the name of Mahābāla (the Strong One), and numerous copies of his basic scripture have been recovered, in both Chinese and Tibetan, from Tun-huang.[61] Ucchuṣma is especially adept at devouring, and hence cleansing away, all impurities, and in Chinese this Ajax is called "the Vajra-Being of Impure Traces" (Hui-chi chin-kang). As one might expect, in Japan his special province has become the privy, over which he stands guard and whose contents he willingly and voraciously consumes, and so purifies. Three important texts of the Ucchuṣma cult were produced by a certain Ajitasena, who worked in the Turfan region of Chinese Central

Asia in the first half of the eighth century. The first of these (*Ta-wei-li Wu-ch'u-se-mo ming-wang ching*, T. 1227) is a longish work in three sections, much concerned with a variety of devices for summoning otherworldly beings to one's service, effecting wonders, and accomplishing miraculous cures. If, for example, you take a fresh human corpse without blemish, wash it and place it on its back with its head to the east beside a great river, at noon, and have four strong men with swords stand each on one side of it, while you take your seat on the cadaver's chest, insert realgar into its mouth, and recite the deity's spell over it, then the drug will heat up and, as all pay reverence to you, you will ascend into the heavens with a rush of smoke and brilliant light. Such matter is the daily fare of Tantric practitioners, whether Buddhist or Śaivite, but it is right in the middle of this typically Indian collection that we discover instructions for manufacturing a therapeutic seal. One is to carve it from *madhuka*-wood (*Glycyrrhiza glabra*), after a preliminary fast of three days and austerities performed in water up to one's neck. Emerging from the water, one builds a fire-altar, using *madhuka*-wood as fuel. The wooden seal is to be dipped in curds and honey and burnt—scorched, perhaps, or simply hardened in the fire—and then is ready for use: "If impressed on a mountain, the mountain crumbles; impressed on a sea, the sea dries up."[62]

Here once again are the very words of the old Chinese jingle on the efficacy of such seals, and it is thus impossible to believe that this otherwise so Indian-seeming text is as pure an export to China as might have been supposed. Like so many works even of the most extreme Tantric kind, it has signs of Chinese adaptation, if not of wholesale compilation in China. The finished seal, we are told, can be impressed on a snake that has bitten someone; the snake will then plead for mercy, and if you pardon it the victim will recover. If used to seal a person, it will bind him; if impressed on a cangue, the fettered prisoner will be released; if stamped on poisonous drugs, they can be ingested with impunity. Whatever ritual you attempt, the seal will facilitate its performance. If a wicked person approaches you, generate anger in your heart, press the seal on him, and he will either spit blood or fall unconscious. And then the seal is laid aside, as the text proceeds to tell us how grains of yellow mustard thrown seven times in the face of a person suffering from demonic bewitchment or from convulsions will cure him or her, how a tiger's claw placed seven times in the fire will guard the bearer from tigers, and so on.[63]

These claims for therapeutic sealing seem modest enough in comparison with the text's other contents, and the rite of ensigillation might appear to occupy a very limited place in Ucchuṣma's cult. But another book in the Buddhist canon, consecrated to Ucchuṣma and attributed to the same Ajitasena as translator, has fully elaborated the suggestions latent in the longer text's passing reference to seals.

This work, the *Rites of the Vajra-Being of Impure Traces for Exorcising the Hundred Weirds* (*Hui-chi chin-kang chin pai-pien-fa ching*, T. 1229), opens with what seems to be a conscious elaboration of the earlier claims for seals that can cause mountains to crumble. Ucchuṣma begins by telling the Buddha just how his male or female disciples can set about uprooting a mountain, using nothing more than three pints of white mustard seed, good quality incense, a damascened sword (to draw the boundaries of the ritual area on the ground), and a clean piece of cloth. Once the boundaries have been drawn, the incense lighted, Ucchuṣma's spell recited 1,008 times, and the mustard seeds scattered to the four quarters, up comes the mountain—and the gods who have been guarding its hidden treasures will abandon them, leaving them all to your exclusive use. Now it transpires that the ultimate purpose of the mountain-crumbling exercise has been the discovery of buried treasure. Predictably, matter-of-fact instructions for drying up the sea and causing rivers to reverse their courses follow (for the first objective, a copper dragon is thrown into the water; for the second, the image of an elephant modeled in "Parthian" incense, i.e., gum guggul). To stop the poisonous dragons that cause sudden winds, evil rains, and crackling thunder and lightning, a special finger-seal with Ucchuṣma's spell is recommended. All the world's evil demons will flock to you in clouds and reveal their true forms in response to another finger-seal or mudrā (hand-posture) and the spell—and will, moreover, renounce their wicked ways and become your willing servitors. If you wish to lay a total ban on a mountain, consecrating it to absolute quiet and sacred purposes, another finger-seal and the spell will accomplish this; stamp the mountain with it seven times, withdraw seven paces, then stamp it again seven times, and all the birds and animals will forthwith depart from their mountain home. Address your finger-seal and the spell to the air thrice seven times, and nothing will even fly over the mountain, not even a speck of dust. Or (speaking of silence!) you can make a person mute by writing his name on a piece of paper and holding it in your mouth; as long as you hold it there, he will be unable to utter a word.

Ucchuṣma goes on to state that if one wishes to recite his spell, there is no need to construct a special ritual area or altar. One need only carve a vajra (ritual thunderbolt), and inside a stūpa or a meditation chamber plaster the ground with fragrant clay and make offerings of assorted incense and flowers. When the vajra is placed in the middle of this impromptu ritual area and Ucchuṣma's spell is recited 108 times, the vajra will suddenly begin to move by itself. It may indeed turn itself into all sorts of things, but you are not to wonder at it; just go on reciting the spell until you have done so 108 times. Should the vajra rise three feet off the ground, or even five, six, seven, or up to ten feet, then the reciter should beg forgiveness for all his transgressions and state his wish. Ucchuṣma himself will then appear in his true form in the vajra, and will speedily grant whatever the officiant desires, bestowing on him a prediction that he shall attain enlightenment, as well as a promise of release from the cycle of birth and death at the end of his present incarnation. But before this rite is undertaken, the officiant must already have recited the spell a full hundred thousand times; until that has been done, the rite will not have any result.

It would appear, then, that the ornate finger-seals have here usurped the place of the cumbersome wooden seal, and that the magical implement par excellence is now the vajra, the massive thunderbolt-emblem of the Tantric master. But spectacular though this description undoubtedly is, it is all only prefatory to the second half of the text. The principal themes of seal-power have been evoked, and now it is time for the seals themselves. This Ucchuṣma scripture has the great merit of illustrating four of them (Figure 9). The first (1.8 inches) is to be enchanted with the deity's spell a thousand times and steeped in white paste incense. On the day you carve the seal, let no one observe you. If you use this seal to seal your heart, you will obtain Knowledge of the Heart, Spontaneous Knowledge, and Knowledge of Former Lives. If you hold the seal a hundred days, you will then be able to abide within all the various portals of the Great Law.

The second seal (1.2 inches) receives the god's incantation six hundred times and is to be steeped in Parthian incense. Worn on your person, it will cause everyone to love you, and will grant you total autonomy and complete freedom from every sort of pain and suffering. The third seal (1.5 inches), also enchanted by six hundred spell-recitations, is to be steeped in white paste incense. If you seal your feet with it, you will be able to fly up into space and go anywhere you wish. The fourth seal (1.8 inches) is also to be steeped in white incense but requires seven thousand spell-recitations. When that has been done, however, it will enable you to travel 3 million leagues a day without anyone seeing you.[64]

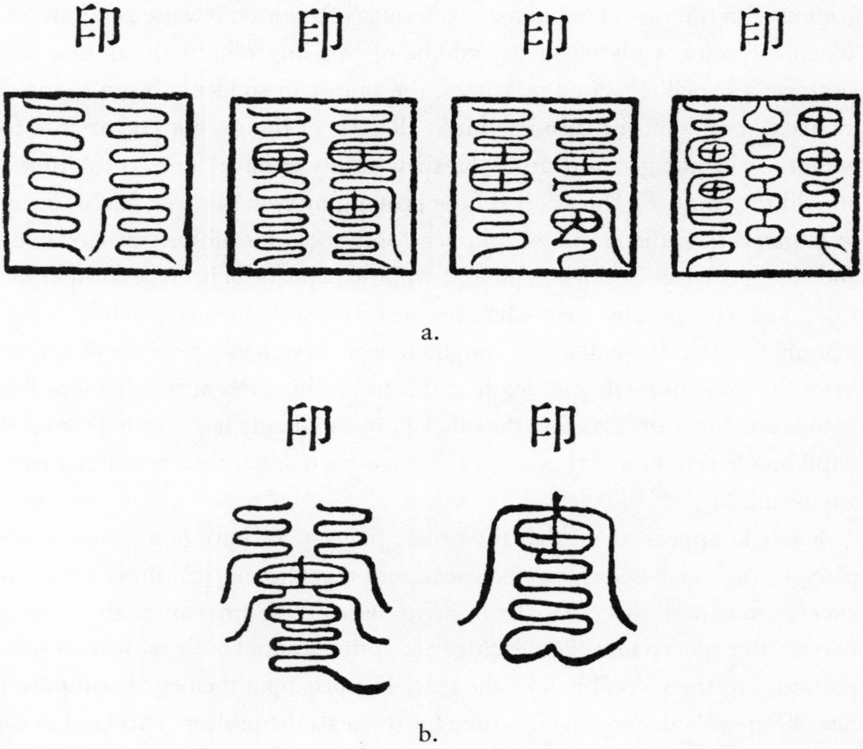

FIGURE 9 Seals and talismans from the *Rites of Ucchuṣma (the Vajra-Being of Impure Traces) for Exorcising the Hundred Weirds* (*Hui-chi chin-kang chin pai-pien-fa ching*, T. 1229, vol. 21: 160A), eighth century: (a) four seals that are to be stamped on the body or worn on the person after being enchanted with the deity Ucchuṣma's spell a specified number of times; and (b) two talismans, also entitled "seals," for writing upon the heart.

Characteristically, the four seals are followed in the text by a whole series of written talismans that comprise a section entitled "Miraculous Rites for Prolonging Life." These are to be written in vermilion on paper and swallowed, chiefly to cure a variety of complaints, although one group of seven, when swallowed regularly for seven days, will bring you all sorts of precious substances. Next come three talismans which, if written on each of your bed's four legs, guarantee you the constant watchful presence of the four great vajra-beings, on condition that you keep your bedroom spotlessly clean and undefiled. Then four more are given that operate against fire, wind, flood, and rain, respectively, when thrown (together with 108 spell-recitations) in the direction of danger (Figure 10). In this case, then, seals to be stamped on the body or otherwise brandished coexist with talismans to be written on paper and swallowed, or otherwise manipulated—and do so with the two methods being adjacent but clearly distinct. Despite the obvious close resemblance between the illustrated seal patterns and the talismans that follow them, there is no suggestion in this eighth-century source that the seals might be used to manufacture the talismans. Homology or structural similarity, and even identity of design, has not in this example led to any overlap in function.[65]

By such means, Ucchuṣma became perhaps the principal patron of therapeutic sealing and Taoist-style talismans within the context of Chinese Buddhism. Nor was his influence limited to Buddhism, or to China. In 1781, the Japanese scholar Ōe Masasuke (1728–95), who was greatly intrigued by all manifestations of Buddho-Taoist synthesis, completed a compact encyclopedia of Ucchuṣma lore. He attempted to sort out all available legendary information on the deity, and reproduced the seals and talismans from the eighth-century scripture we have just been discussing (which had been brought to Japan in the ninth century). In keeping with Ucchuṣma's specialization, Ōe also included a good deal of Chinese toilet-lore, on the proper construction and astrological orientation of toilets and the rites and customs to be observed when visiting that perilous, demon-haunted locale. He extended his interest to the stars themselves, describing and illustrating the constellation of the Celestial Cloaca (seven stars) and the Heavenly Toilet (four stars). Ever eager to document what he conceived to be the fundamental identity of purpose of the great traditions of Buddhism and Taoism, Ōe also reconstructed a comprehensive Ucchuṣma-talisman on the basis of documents on Ucchuṣma produced, he claimed, by an eleventh-century Celestial Master of Taoism. This talisman depicts the fiery god surrounded by his Sanskrit mantra below a Taoist-style inscription in an adaptation of archaic seal-script, the whole engirdled by the seven stars of the constellation of the Celestial Cloaca.[66] Even in eighteenth-century Japan, Buddho-Taoist interaction continued to flourish.

Fragments from Tun-huang

Other medieval texts suggest how widespread such practices once were among Chinese Buddhists, as well as indicating the enormous confidence of medieval practitioners in the marvelous powers of such seals. We can still sense some-

a.

b.

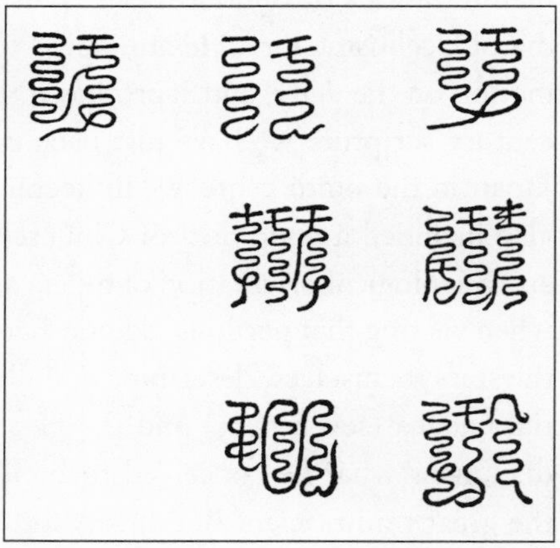

c.

FIGURE 10 A series of written talismans that comprise a section entitled "Miraculous Rites for Prolonging Life" in the *Rites of the Vajra-Being of Impure Traces* (T. 1229, vol. 21: 160a–161b). All are to be written in vermilion on paper and swallowed: (a) a group of three talismans against disease-demons and for prolonging life; (b) a set of seven talismans that cure all ailments; (c) a second heptad that prolongs life; (d) a third heptad that both cures all ailments and prolongs life; (e) a fourth heptad that brings all manner of precious treasures; (f) a group of three talismans that, written on the legs of your bed, ensure divine protection; (g) four miscellaneous talismans that serve against fire, wind, water, and rain when thrown in the direction of the trouble; and (h) a final pair of talismans that seem to be all-purpose panaceas to be swallowed by adepts and their friends.

d.

e.

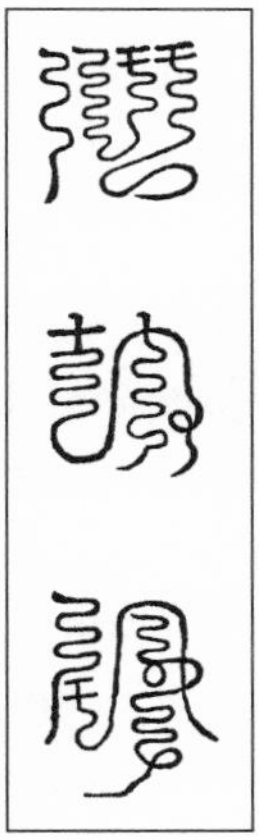

f.

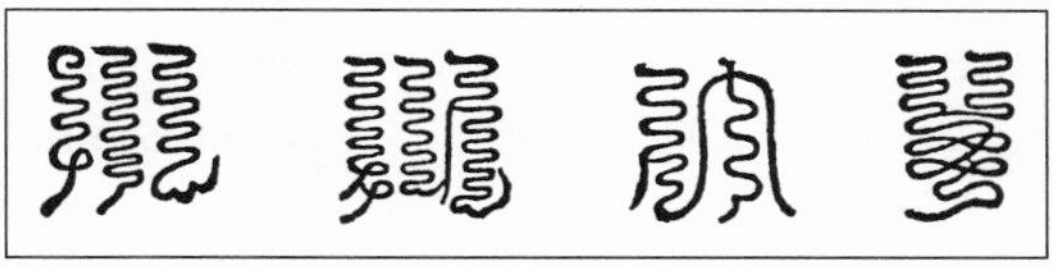

g.

h.

thing of the awe that surrounded these potent implements in a badly mutilated, untitled fragment (T. 2906) of a Chinese Buddhist scripture recovered from the Tun-huang caves at the beginning of this century.[67] The fragment opens by mentioning procedures of the airborne immortals of the Heaven of Great Purity, a recipe for going without grain-foods, a number of formulae for doing away with the body's three corpse-worm demons, and so on. Then the Supremely Venerable King Buddha of the Dragon Race (a personage otherwise unknown but suggesting Nāgārjuna, whose name is usually translated "Dragon Tree" and who is known, among his other attributes, as a patron of

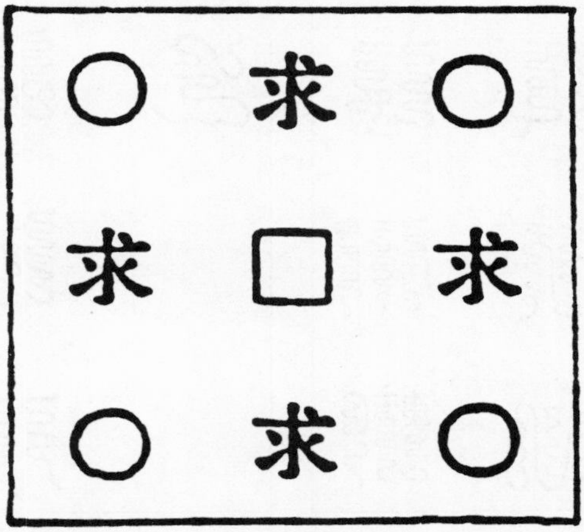

FIGURE 11 Seal carried on an untitled fragment of a Chinese Buddhist scripture recovered from the Tun-huang caves at the beginning of the twentieth century (rendering based on T. 2906, vol. 85: 145a). The character *ch'iu* ("seek" or "request") is repeated four times.

sorcerers) tells the Buddha, "There is a spirit-seal, which the more than thirty thousand buddhas earlier and later have all employed to attain supreme and perfect nirvāṇa."[68] Despite the many gaps in the text, one can still make out that this seal (Figure 11) is recommended for use by all, from advanced arhats down to quite ordinary people who are just beginning to aspire to Buddhist teaching. One should take a block of "red willow wood," 1.8 Chinese inches square. "From this you are to cut the seal and carry it at your waist . . . to have control over the thousand spirits, and understanding of the ten thousand arts":

> First you are to construct a ritual area, then go the toilet, bathe yourself, and next hold incense-water in your mouth as you carve the seal, reciting a mantra and meditating on the Supremely Venerable King Buddha of the Dragon Race; then all that you wish will speedily be accomplished. It should be kept in a leather pouch worn above the shoulder blades; do not allow it to become defiled. [. . .] Wherever you may be [. . .] sitting or lying down, nothing at all will hinder or obstruct you. Always recite my name, Namaḥ Supremely Venerable King Buddha of the Dragon Race [. . .] when you are about to carve the seal [. . .] silent and avoiding speech, incise it [. . .] make a vow, and only afterward receive the seal. On the day you are to receive the seal, I and the four classes of disciples [. . .] various spells [. . .] at dusk receive it [. . .].

After one has received the seal in the formal manner that we can glimpse through the gaps in the text, there will be three different sorts of signs, depending on the intelligence and qualifications of the recipient. Those of the highest class will wake to find beside their pillow three pills of a black "heart of wishing-jewel medicine." A recipient of lowest capacity will hear the sound of a bell in the middle of the night, while a recipient of middling capacity will immediately perceive an exotic, fragrant aroma. For persons of high intelligence in each of the three classes, these phenomena will manifest themselves instantly; but for those of middling intelligence, they will occur after three days have passed. If one should obtain the drug, one must not let outsiders have any knowledge of it but should swallow the pills down in a single gulp. Such a person then immediately becomes of the same rank as a dhāraṇī-bodhisattva. Only after having received these confirmatory signs are you to make a trial of the seal's powers in action:

> If you are going to test its powers, take seven cloves, seal them with the seal, crushing each of them with a single impression; mix them with water, swallow them, and in an instant you will obtain [. . .] knowledge. If you wish to obtain knowledge of others' hearts, take again two cloves, swallow them without water, and immediately seal your mouth with the seal three times; you will instantly gain knowledge of others' hearts, and you will know in advance what will happen on the three planes of existence [gods, men, demons]. Another method: Take any piece from a dead person's skeleton, seal it seven times with the seal, and all the evil demons in the world will come to you and offer their submission. Another method: If you wish to obtain the services of the hundred thousand myriad spirits, vajra-beings, and so on, take seven catties of bark of mulberry root, boil it until it falls apart, remove those parts that are bad, seal it with the seal, and after eating it, spit it out, and the ten thousand demons will come and offer you their submission.

Further instructions, broken off, involve sealing sand mixed with freshly drawn well water. Three pints of yellow sand, sealed and buried in the earth, will in a single day turn into gold. Seven hairs of the seal-bearer, sealed with the seal and thrown upon the ground, will turn into black earth (presumably a mineral, but which one?). A method for curing tumors or boils using snakes that have been sealed with the seal, and thereby killed (it appears), is unfortunately too mutilated to make out. Similarly, the following set of instructions for sealing human beings who wish to leave the world to achieve transcendence (i.e., die) is very lacunulose:

> Water is to be boiled; the person's face and feet are to be bathed at the midnight hour, and when he leaps up from the earth, a hundred jewelled lotus flowers take the seal. [. . .] For flying in the air, seal three pints of water a hundred times, wash your body with it, and you will at once leap up and depart. And if you conceive the overweening ambition of seeking all the ten thousand rites or techniques in the world, take an ounce of pepper, boil it in three pints of water, [. . .] seal it three times with the seal, divide it into three parts, ingest one part at dawn, one at noon, and one during the night, [. . . and there will be] signs of enlightenment. After this you will immediately attain comprehension of every one of the ten thousand techniques.

There are remarkable things in this text. For example, the red wood from which the seal is to be fashioned apparently owes its origin and color to its having sprung from the Buddha's own blood; but the text is too lacunulose to be certain on this point, or on the precise mythological circumstances of the blood-letting (apparently a battle with a wicked monk or monks?).[69] But most of the wonderful promises that were once revealed in this text must remain unknowable, for the gaps in the manuscript widen, and we seem to hear the voice of the mysterious Supremely Venerable King Buddha of the Dragon Race becoming fainter and fainter, choked and urgent, as he continues to tell the Buddha all the latent powers of his remarkable seal:

> This seal will immediately [lead one to] obtain comprehension of all the portals of limitless wisdom. [. . .] World-Honored One, this seal [. . .] the strength of one man, of three men, of a hundred men [. . .] this seal and obtain salvation [. . .] standing, sitting, or lying down, have only to focus their minds to at once achieve it. [. . .] An ounce of incense, grind it to a powder, mix with honey, heat over a fire, seal it with a seal. [. . .] Dragons and the eight divisions, great demon-kings, kings of yakṣas, kings of animals, [. . .] King of the Iron Mountain, King of the Great Iron Mountain, King of Muchen-t'o Mountain. [. . .] Whenever you wish to carry out this method, first with your big toe rub away [. . .] attach to the eye(s) [? . . .] mind, the place where you are sitting, seal it and cause it to [. . .].

As the echoes of this testimony to Chinese Buddhist enthusiasm die away in torn shreds of thousand-year-old paper, another Tun-huang manuscript fragment comes to light.[70] As usual, the text presents the words of some mythical or legendary figure to the Buddha in offering his special technique for the use of the Buddha's disciples, and in this case it is evident that the personage in question is the Bodhisattva Kuan-shih-yin, or Avalokiteśvara, himself:

[. . .] if they write my seal in silver. They may use it whenever they wish. They should impress it on their bodies and recite the wishing-jewel dhāraṇī of Avalokiteśvara 108 times.[71] One should wear clean vestments; none of the other things are necessary. One should burn clove incense, take a bowl of pure water, [. . .] then impress the seal, and he will become invisible; ten thousand persons will be unable to see him. If he enters the king's palace, he can seduce the king's women; if he enters a palace of the gods, he can seduce the divine women [. . .] obtain complete reverence; all you need do is hold fast to purity with all your heart. This seal is called "the seal that manifests all precious treasures." If anyone wishes to obtain any precious treasures, let him carve this seal in aloeswood, 1.9 inches in size. He should then recite the spell of the wishing-jewel one time through with all his heart, impress the seal on the empty air, and whatever treasures there are will all be made manifest to him. This may be made use of whenever one has need of it.

If there are those who in their successive reincarnations have been able to recite the wishing-jewel dhāraṇī spirit-spell and wish for confirmation of their spiritual accomplishment, let them write out the seal on fine copper. They must not quarrel over the price, for if they do, their seal will not reach completion. They should recite it ten thousand times and then demarcate a ritual area. For whatever wish they may have, let them take this seal and impress it on sandalwood and recite the spell over it 108 times, continuing up to twenty-one days. By then I will be manifesting my three bodies daily, and will rub the crowns of their heads and bestow a prophecy of future buddhahood on them. All that they desire they shall receive, without error.

If there are women who seek male or female children, they should write out this seal and swallow it on the eighth day of the fourth month [the birthday of the Buddha]. Then they will certainly obtain a boy or girl child, and when they grow up they will come to be in the presence of the Buddha. If anyone is seeking samādhi, he should write out the seal on the crown of his head. He should then recite the wishing-jewel spell twenty-one times and spew water into the air, and there will immediately be rays of light in all five colors, illuminating the world and all the ten regions of space. The seal impressed on the crown of his head will always give forth radiance, and this is what I meant by saying that I would "rub the crown of the head and bestow a prophecy of future buddhahood." [. . .]

Thereupon the Bodhisattva Kuan-shih-yin was elated, and told the Buddha, "If there is anyone who is seeking the samādhi of extinction [nirvāṇa], let him carve this seal on purple sandalwood. He should carry the seal to a quiet and secluded place in the mountains. There he should impress the seal on his heart, and he will at once enter samādhi—a perpetual samādhi that will last for eight great kalpas." When you finally arise from your meditation,

> you will convert all living beings and lead them to salvation. They will all become arhats of different degrees of attainment and enter the religious life. Then the entire world will become completely purified, and all defilements will be done away with [. . .].
>
> This is called "the seal that scatters flowers and fruits." If you carve the seal in sandalwood and carry it about with you, you will always have the gods and the bodhisattvas strewing splendid flowers about you, from incarnation to incarnation you will always attain samādhi, and you will always be born in the presence of a buddha [i.e., in a world where a buddha is alive]. If a person always carries my seal about with him wherever he goes, all the people in those places will also certainly attain samādhi, and will enjoy supernatural powers and roam in perfect freedom through the various buddhalands; they will all obtain the stage of non-regression, will turn the Wheel of the Law, and will always adhere to the ten good actions.

The text next provides a spell in transcribed Sanskrit. Then comes a method for treating a person suffering from illness, involving the recitation of the spell, massaging the top of the patient's head with the palm of your right hand, and more seals—but this time, seals (*mudrā*) in the more usual sense of the word in Buddhist ritual literature (i.e., hand-postures or finger-seals).[72] Unfortunately, this description, entitled "Rites for Subduing Devils," breaks off after only four lines where the remainder of the manuscript has been torn away, though not before we have been assured that this procedure will drive out the king of the demons that spread disease, as well as all *mṛta-manuṣa*—the evil spirits of the dead, or zombies, that may be afflicting the sufferer.

This intriguing fragment gives us an even wider view of the powers of such seals. There is at first a certain ambiguity in the account, for the text instructs the reader to "write" the seal in silver, for example, or on high quality copper, and under no circumstances to quibble about the expense of using such costly materials. One is also supposed to "write" the seal—presumably on paper—for swallowing by a woman who wishes to bear a child, and it should be written, too, on the crown of the head of a person who wants to achieve samādhi. One would expect the text to state that the seal should be impressed in these cases, rather than written out, and though it is certainly possible that the seal's design, which presumably closely resembled that of a written talisman (unfortunately, the text does not furnish an illustration of the seal-inscription), was in fact drawn on the paper or shaven pate in question, it might also be that the word "write" was being used, exceptionally, with the sense of "imprint" or "impress."

Even more interesting are the instructions for using the seal, carved in sandalwood this time, as a means of spiritual advancement. First, by impressing the carven seal on sandalwood, you will obtain an auspicious caress on the crown of your head and a prediction of your future attainment of buddhahood from the Bodhisattva Avalokiteśvara himself. The head so imprinted will shine forth radiantly, emitting a nimbus forevermore. The seal is also capable of bringing about an even more definitive transformation. Samādhi, or fixed attention, is the immediate aim of Buddhist meditation, the state of calm focusing in which enlightenment can be attained. But the word "samādhi" might also be used as a conventional, consecrated term for death—or, rather, as a means of putting a far higher valuation, in canonical Buddhist terms, on what appears to be death to the uninitiated. Those ascetic monks who "entered samādhi" were in reality in a profound state of concentration, enabling them to wait thousands of years until the coming of the Future Buddha Maitreya.[73] Similarly, here we are told that the sandalwood seal can be used to enter "the samādhi of extinction." When you want to withdraw definitively from this world, or when you feel that your end is near, you can carry the seal to a secluded place deep within the mountains, seat yourself with crossed legs in the lotus position—just like the monks who starved themselves into samādhi—and, turning the seal against your own breast, enter upon a span of "concentration" that will last for eight immense cosmic periods of time.[74]

How far our seals have come! Once they had been exclusively apotropaic and demonifugic, used either for stamping demon-dispelling talismans in clay or for application by ritual masters to the bodies of prostrate victims of demonic attacks. Now, similar seals can be turned toward the attainment of Buddhism's loftiest objectives. By means of a powerful seal, you can obtain a personal prediction of your future achievement of enlightenment, your own personal destiny as a buddha. Moreover, by using the potent seal on yourself, you can speedily depart from the unsatisfactory world in which you chance to be living to one where your spiritual powers are greatly enhanced and your special qualities much more fully appreciated. Having used the suicidal seal to release you from this present life, you will emerge eons hence from your chrysalis of deep meditation as a fully formed buddha, converting the multitudes and transforming the world.

The conferral of high spiritual values on techniques of proven efficacy, once these have been assimilated into the corpus of Buddhist ritual, is a familiar stage in the complex process of assimilation. It seems only natural that seals originally destined for treating the sick would have been freighted with grandiose metaphysical claims once their use had gained a firm foothold in Buddhist circles. Also, integrating Chinese seal-stamps into a complex of spiritual aspirations—and linking them closely to finger-seals as well (the same Chinese word, *yin*, designates both sorts of seal)—certainly helped the indigenous Chinese sealing process be accepted as valid Buddhist medicine by Chinese Buddhist authorities. Testimony to the success of this tactic still exists in Japanese Buddhism today, as we shall see; but first we must consider a few more pieces of medieval Chinese evidence.

Nāgārjuna's Seal Collection

Perhaps the most idiosyncratic document of the medieval fascination with seals and sealing is also supposed to have come from India. It is credited to the great Nāgārjuna, a name that may well refer to more than one personality in Indian history, and one that generally identifies a philosopher, scholiast, magician, and alchemist usually supposed to have lived in the second or third century C.E.[75] Later, in its Chinese translation as "Dragon Tree," the potent name was also used virtually independently to give authority to a wide range of occult books and techniques. We have already seen a possible Nāgārjuna reflex in the "Supremely Venerable King Buddha of the Dragon Race," a patron of therapeutic ensigillation in the fragmentary Tun-huang manuscript studied above. Another book placed under his auspices is *Nāgārjuna's Treatise on the Five Sciences* (*Lung-shu wu-ming lun*, T. 1420). This work, too, appears to survive only in a single manuscript copy, made in Japan probably in the eleventh or twelfth century and preserved there in a monastic archive.[76] The text seems to have been written in North China during the sixth century, though it situates its own origins in the time of the Indian King Aśoka (third century B.C.E.), when large numbers of "heretics"—non-Buddhists—were ordained as Buddhist monks. They inform the king that their original faith also has many excellent techniques for benefiting humanity; lest these valuable practices be lost to Buddhists, they wish to bring them into the Buddhist fold. The king assents.

These practices are, as one might expect, of the most useful and impressive sort. A human figure carved from willow wood, properly empowered with spells and buried in the courtyard of your house, will bring great riches. Medicinal pellets composed of cow's bezoar, ginger, hemp, *Scutellaria macrantha*, *Rheum officinale*, and *Glycyrrhiza*, gathered on the fifth day of the fifth month and pounded together by a young boy on the seventh of the seventh, will send demons running from the body of anyone they may have afflicted with any of a wide variety of ailments. But as we read farther, it turns out that the chief concern of the converted brahmans is with the writing of talismans—and talismans of the familiar Chinese sort. Eighteen types of talismans are listed, each for a different purpose, to be written in vermilion on silk of various colors. In addition to talismans for treating diverse maladies and for prophylactic use against disease-demons, government officials, and other robbers, this list includes talismans to aid in childbirth, others to restore harmony, as well as one guaranteed to instantly obtain high-ranking suitors for an unwed daughter who is growing perilously old.

These are followed by a series of twelve anti-demoniac talismans for curing disease, with precise instructions for their ingestion according to an exact astrological schedule; the twelve are correlated with the twelve hours (each lasting two of our hours) into which, traditionally, the East Asian day is divided. Diagnostic signs are then given to determine a patient's condition, as well as a spell to be recited over pharmaceutical preparations, which spirits would otherwise gobble up as soon as you had compounded them, drawing from them all the efficacy that should by rights go to the patient. There is also a spell against garrulousness in women and children—another impediment to spiritual progress. The text rambles on in this way, and the first of its two chapters concludes in a cacophony of Sanskrit spells. There is more coherence in the second chapter, for after a few general observations and specific instructions on the performance of ritual, it is entirely devoted to seals and talismans, all fully illustrated.

The compressed summary given here can hardly do justice to this rich source, the most elaborate single text on seals and sealing that I have found. It provides us with illustrations and instructions for using ten different engraved seals and three written talismans. It also clearly states that the patterns on most of the seals represent stars and constellations, and it is obvious that only a close acquaintance with Chinese astronomical convention could possibly guide us toward a systematic analysis of the complex, asymmetrical seal-inscriptions. As the accompanying illustrations show (Figures 12 and 13) the seals are based on linked star-diagrams, geometric patterns, Chinese characters in stylized as well as ordinary forms, and, in one case, elements of a humanoid figure. Yet the names borne by the seals evince an effort to integrate them within a Buddhist context—for example, the Crown of the Buddha's Head (Skt. Bauddhoṣṇīṣa),

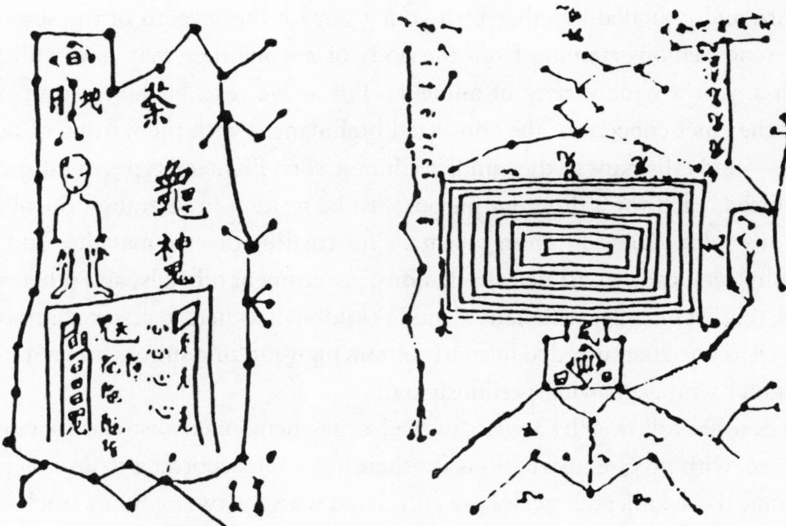

a. b.

FIGURE 12 Renderings of two seals from *Nāgārjuna's Treatise on the Five Sciences* (*Lung-shu wu-ming lun*, T. 1240, vol. 21: 962a–b), tentatively dated to the sixth century: (a) the Buddha's Crown seal, which, when properly prepared and applied, grants invisibility; and (b) an untitled seal with wide-ranging therapeutic, protective, and mischievous powers.

Bodhisattva's Mount of the Void, Like Unto the Gods, Vajra Fist, Vajra Heart, Vajra Stave, and Buddhaland.

The first seal, Buddha's Crown (Figure 12a), is to be carved from wood of a jujube-tree's root, 4 or 5 inches square.[77] It is to be reddened by rubbing with vermilion, a brief spell is to be recited over it seven hundred times, and it is to be stored in a pouch of crimson silk. If you wish to enter the dwelling of a king, great minister, or brahman householder, you are to impress the seal on the soles of both your feet and on your chest. You should then wear the seal on top of your head, and thus you will be totally invisible—neither your body nor your shadow will be seen, and you can go wherever you will, undetected. When you wish to reappear, you have only to wash your hands, face, and soles in pure water over which the charm has been recited thrice seven times, and remove the seal from your head. If you wish to cross a body of water or pass through a flood, close your eyes, seal the closed eyelids, and across you will go. If you encounter wicked persons, enchant the seal with the spell and press it

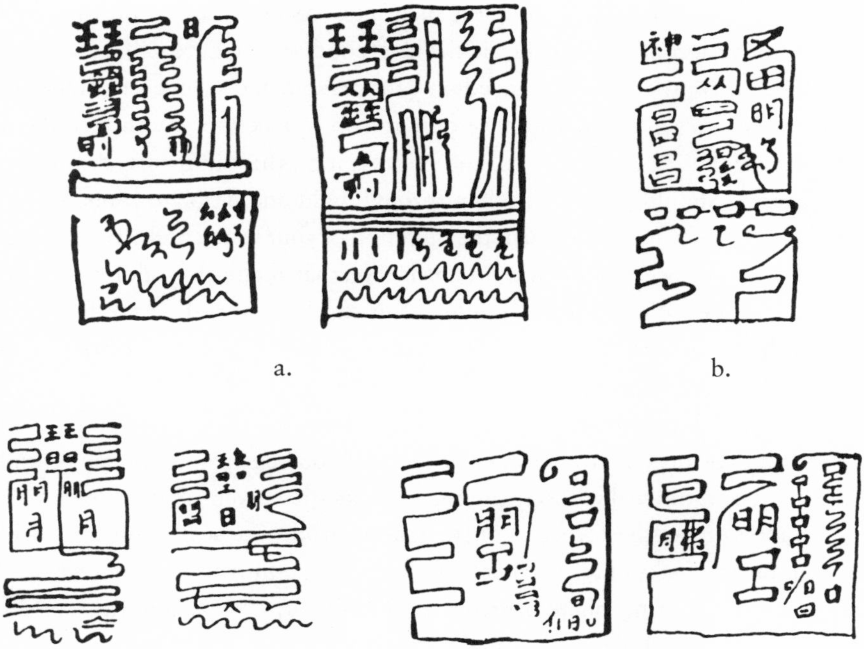

a. b.

c. d.

FIGURE 13 Additional renderings of seals from *Nāgārjuna's Treatise on the Five Sciences*: (a) two versions of the Vajra Fist seal (T. 1240, vol. 21: 965c); (b) the Vajra Heart seal (966a); (c) two versions of the Vajra Staff seal (966b); and (d) two versions of the Buddhaland seal (966c).

on your coach and you will become quite invisible to pursuers, however many they may be, and no evil person will be able to come and do you harm. Moreover, "When you perform this sealing rite, it will be extremely efficacious as long as you do not irresponsibly transmit it to unqualified persons. You may give it to those who have faith, but to those who do not, take care that you do not carelessly transmit it."[78]

The pattern remains the same for the other seals. They are all to be carved under ritual conditions from different woods of long-established apotropaic virtue: peach-tree root, white sandalwood, red jujube wood, pith of jujube wood, aloeswood. All are to be brushed with vermilion when completed and recharged with spells and vermilion before each application. The first seal appears to be specially designed for personal security and even for trickery—that is, for stealing unperceived into the homes of prominent personages—but in most of the remaining examples, such interests are founded on the more basic motivation of healing the sick. The second seal (Figure 12b, for which no name is given) should be carried on your person, and whenever you desire to cure anyone's ailment, you have only to rub it once more with vermilion, recite its spell thrice seven times, and impress it on the ailing part; the cure is guaranteed. Should you be traveling through wild and desolate country, aim the seal, properly be-charmed, in the direction of your route, and all evil beasts will scatter at once and do you no harm. For that matter, if a domestic animal should be suffering from an ailment, it can be stamped on the forehead with this white sandalwood seal and beaten with a stick of peachwood, and the illness will go away.

Typically, these therapeutic and protective concerns are followed by even more dramatic displays of the seal's prowess. If you line up ten men one behind the other, coat the seal with vermilion, recite its spell seven-times-seven times, and impress it on the forehead of the man in front, the seal impression will appear on the backs of all ten men. After this magic-mirror effect in reverse,[79] we return to an atmosphere of stealth and mischief. Once again, the worldly great are targeted. Like the Buddha's Crown, this seal enables you to enter the house of a court officer unseen, to produce there all sorts of disquieting "special effects." If you print the freshly vermilioned seal on a piece of clean paper, which you then attach secretly to a wall of the entranceway to the main hall of the house so that no one sees it, then the head of the household will behold all sorts of uncanny spectacles when on the point of falling asleep at night—yakṣas, evil horse-headed Kumbhāṇḍa-demons, and their ilk will all assemble in his house and remain there all day long. The family will everywhere seek out the best physicians to have the demons exorcised, but to no avail. Then you come upon the scene and preach the Buddha's Law to them with all the eloquence you can muster. Next secretly remove the talisman you've sequestered there, and all the family's demonic manifestations will immediately cease. The worthy householder will, of course, be entirely won over to Buddhism, and you may obtain from him any boon that you wish. Should this plan somehow miscarry, and should you be locked up, you need only point the seal at the gates and they will open for you to make your getaway. No doubt all this trickery was conceived of and enacted in a noble Buddhist cause, but it is remarkable with what brazen audacities the philosophic Nāgārjuna had come to be associated. If the perpetrator were not a card-carrying Buddhist, one might be tempted to call this witchcraft and larceny. It is at least reassuring to know that the success of this powerful seal demands not only close secrecy but strict avoidance of meat and alcohol as well.

Medical uses of seals recur frequently. In one instance, medicinal drugs are first rubbed on the painful spot before sealing. In another case a seal is used to print a paper talisman for a woman in labor to swallow; the child will be born straightaway with ease. Invisibility remains an important theme. Passing through floodwaters with eyes tightly sealed comes up again; predictably, getting out of trouble with irate, implacable kings is once more on the agenda as well. When a Buddhist finds himself being worsted in a debate with "heretics" (that is, proponents of other views), he need only clutch his seal, meditate with all his heart, recite the spell seven hundred times, and point the seal toward the heretics right in the middle of the assembly for all their plans and projects to come to naught. Point the seal at the king, and his displeasure will instantly change to delight, his thoughts soften, and you will easily win him over to your side. The seal and a damascened sword should be kept on an altar in a specially purified room on a pure mountain, hidden from human gaze. Offerings should be made to seal, sword, and the Bodhisattva Nāgārjuna day and night for forty-nine days, while maintaining a strict vegetarian diet. When so charged with reverence, the seal will be at the peak of its powers. Seal your forehead, and no one will be able to see you. Press it on the soles of your feet, and you will be able to cross an ocean as if walking on dry land. If you press it on your mouth and then expound the doctrine, you will instill faith in your listeners. If you seal your hair, your hair will grow by feet and inches. Seal your eyes, and you will clearly behold all living beings in the past and future undergoing suffering in the five modes of rebirth. Seal your heart, and you will know the exact hour and minute of death of all those now living in the world. Seal your ears, and you will understand the speech of all living creatures. Seal your chest, hands, feet, and back, and everyone who sees you will be joyful and pleased with you. Place the seal on your head, recite this spell forty-nine times, and you will immediately appear in the form of a vajra-being and may do whatever you wish.

After additional miscellaneous techniques, four more seals follow (see Figure 13): Vajra Fist, Vajra Heart, Vajra Staff, and Buddhaland; some of these names normally designate well-known finger-seals still current in Tantric Buddhist ritual. The wooden Vajra Fist seal is specially designed to deal with assailants; if a talisman is printed from it in vermilion on silk and then held in your mouth, your assailants will begin beating themselves furiously. Alternatively, a silk talisman printed from the seal can be attached to your arms, and your assailants will fall unconscious to the ground in front of you. If one of your male or female slaves has run away, stamp the seal on his or her bed, and within a day's time the slave will return with hands bound. The seal can also be impressed on a piece of paper that is then applied to the hand, or on a piece of iron, gold, or silver, and to all sorts of stone, copper, or tin: In any case, it will be imprinted as clearly as if it had been impressed in clay. Or again, if you make paper talismans with the seal and ingest them for eleven days, you will acquire the strength of a thousand or ten thousand men. The seal can also be used directly on the heart of a nonbeliever, who will be converted instantly at its touch. If you impress it on the heart of someone suffering from manic fury, the worms that caused the disease will crawl away from him that very night. If you twice seven times seal the heart of one suffering from falling frenzy (epilepsy) or madness, he will at once be cured. The seal works so well on such a variety of ailments because (the text tells us) it contains the names of all demons and spirits. It is evident, then, that embedded in the ornate script and entangled in the intricate star-charts is an entire nomenclature of the spirit world; the names of power, names that control and command, are all occultly present in the cryptic inscriptions.

For troubles in any of the five viscera, the patient is to be sealed on the heart. For deafness, blindness, dumbness, nasal occlusion, or sores and swellings on the body, the seal should be pressed in realgar ("male yellow") and applied to the patient's body twice seven times; sores so treated will clear up in less than a day. In the case of blindness or dumbness, use orpiment ("female yellow") on the seal. Mix orpiment with a pint of water and wash the patient's eyes with this mixture thrice daily until it has all been used up; blindness and dumbness will both be cured by this means. For all lesser ailments, as well as in all cases of possession or bewitchment by phantoms (*wang-liang*), you need only impress the victims directly with the seal. If a woman is undergoing difficult labor pains, give her a paper talisman imprinted with the seal to swallow, and the infant in her womb will speedily come forth holding the talisman in his hand. The seal can be used to cure persons in extremis, and also to summon spirits to ask about future events; simply print the seal on green silk, then give it to someone to attach to the top of the main gateway. The spirits wished for will immediately come to the door, and you can ask them about your fortune. Imprint the seal on water, mix the water with vermilion powder, and rinse your eyes with it, and you will be able to see things happening a thousand leagues away.

The catalogue of techniques is by no means done, but we have certainly seen enough to gain some notion of the virtually endless range of possibilities that lay open to the happy possessor of this Nāgārjuna text. It may all seem rather simpleminded and materialistic, but we should perhaps correct the impression that such arts were easily available for the asking. On the contrary, the text makes it quite clear that intense, single-minded devotion is required of the adept who wishes to fully master these kaleidoscopic techniques. Only a person of stout resolution, entirely dedicated to achieving his purpose, can compass these arts—which, we are informed, only represent a minuscule excerpt from the more than ten thousand scrolls of the complete *Treatise on the Five Sciences* composed by the Bodhisattvas Nāgārjuna and Aśvaghoṣa (or "Horse's Neigh," another famous early philosophical commentator and a good partner for Nāgārjuna, or "Dragon Tree"). The adept's propitiation of these two saints must be carried out in a carefully constructed oratory, painted green and equipped with all the necessary ritual paraphernalia—canopies and banners, an incense burner in each of the four corners, standing images of the two bodhisattvas and their divine assistants, and another incense burner before the images and one in front of the adept himself. Here, under conditions of the strictest ritual purity, the adept is to pay homage and make offerings to the bodhisattvas thrice daily for a hundred days, reciting their spells, burning incense and lamps day and night, never leaving the room, and feeding himself on the offerings only after having presented them to the deities. After he has performed these duties assiduously with the utmost devotion, the two bodhisattvas will send down a spirit-emissary who will fill the room with a red or purple radiance. This spirit will do whatever he is commanded, and it is through his agency that the adept will be able to use the seals to accomplish healing.

To treat a patient, one submits a formal petition to the two bodhisattvas, giving all the details of the case, and recites their spell. Up to twenty-one recitations may be required in a serious case, while simultaneously knotting thread of five colors.[80] Only after these preliminaries is the seal brought into action. But the practitioner must be in a state of purity, cleanliness, rectitude, chastity, quietude, and dedication before undertaking any cures. If obedient to these rules, his focused attention on the Bodhisattva Nāgārjuna may bring the bodhisattva in person, illuminating the entire world. Then the bodhisattva will grant whatever he desires: immortality, the Tao, wisdom, fame, skill, wealth, honor. The text concludes by giving two more talismans to be written out and administered internally in conjunction with the seals; finally, there are directions for ingesting various sorts of aromatics to remove all lingering impurities from the body.[81]

The power attributed to these seals may seem wildly exaggerated, and the art of sealing preposterously easy, an orgy of theater and illusion. But this text makes it clear that there was really nothing easy about the acquisition of these powers; the demands on the would-be aspirant sufficed to explain intermittent failure. Though we have no statistics about its therapeutic efficacy, it is at least certain that seal treatment of one sort or another continued to be in demand and has remained in use down to the present day. From the sources we have already examined, it is clear that by the ninth or tenth century a wide variety of prescriptive texts existed to guide the operator's mind and hand in numerous applications of therapeutic and wonder-working seals. The history of this ritual seems fairly typical of many of the ritual complexes of East Asia. First developed, it would appear, by early medieval Chinese occultists (men who were neither Buddhists nor Taoists, in the strict sense of the words), it was taken up, elaborated, and codified by Taoist priests. Indeed, by the end of the sixth century, therapeutic sealing had apparently become so conspicuous a feature in Taoist practice as to figure in an official description of the religion. Yet it had long since been incorporated into the practice of Chinese Buddhism as well. Indeed, Buddhist ritualists seem to have conferred upon such seals many of their most arcane powers, and it was in the context of Tantric Buddhism that the practice was introduced to Japan, in the ninth century if not earlier. Meanwhile, Taoist masters continued to make use of their own seals in effecting marvelous cures; each of the new movements or lineages that arose in the twelfth century had its own distinguishing seal or seals.

Later Taoists and the Japanese

Within each lineage in the burgeoning Taoism of the twelfth and thirteenth centuries, every rank in the hierarchy was at least theoretically distinguished by its own characteristic seal. As in the secular, imperial administration, there was a parallel hierarchy of Taoist insignia, and the apex of this pyramid of seals was differently identified in each major ritual lineage. A thirteenth-century compendium on Taoist ritual and institutions, the *Great Rites of Shang-ch'ing and Ling-pao* (*Shang-ch'ing ling-pao ta-fa*, HY 1211), provides a lengthy exposition of the diverse seals then current—placed, significantly, just after a discussion of the various ritual offices and functions.[82]

In addition to the seals of the more recently constituted ritual entities, we discover here a conscious link with the old tradition, for two versions of the seal of the Yellow God's Emblem of Transcendence are described and illustrated (i.e., the seal first found early in the fourth century, in the work of Ko Hung).[83] Ko's seal was supposed to have borne a 120-character inscription, yet one of the examples given in the thirteenth-century Taoist compendium has an inscription of 102 characters, the other of 107; both are the texts of incantations. Such seals were to be printed on all official ritual documents (which were mostly intended for burning); like seals in the ordinary world of workaday officialdom, they guaranteed the authenticity of the text. Thus, as we might expect, these highly official emblems and tokens were firmly established at the very center of ritual activity. In addition to the seals of various lineages that bear their names (Numinous Treasure, Jade Hall, Martial Resistance, Heart of Heaven, Three Brothers Mao, etc.), there are many other examples whose names give some notion of their occult powers: Spirit-Seal of the Sublime Maiden of the Ninefold Heavens, Whirlwind Seal for Extinguishing Thunder, and many more. Moreover, there is abundant evidence to show that a primary function of all these potent implements lay in treating the sick.

In a text like the *Script of the Inner Secrets of the Three High Lords* (*San-huang nei-pi wen*, HY 854), for example, we can observe sealing techniques at the very heart of the Taoist demonology and therapy. The work gives a circumstantial account of the different types of demons and is one of the most informative Taoist demonological repertories. The Taoist master's seal can be used to force any member of the numerous and highly variegated demon population to appear in visible form. The basic technique involves smearing the seal with vermilion and pointing it in the direction proper to the type of demon desired, calling out the creature's name, and then impressing the seal on a piece of paper. The demon will appear forthwith and can then be interrogated. With a seal in his right hand and a sword in his left, the Taoist master is fully equipped to summon, question, and intimidate whatever demon he wishes.[84] As the title indicates, this work purports to emanate from the Three High Lords of Chinese mythology, imaginary sovereigns of prehistoric times. Accordingly, it offers three distinct seals, each associated with one of the archaic triad and with a specialized sphere of efficacy. With the seal of the High Lord of Heaven, one can cause the stars to fall, the moon to wane, and the sun to be eclipsed; it also works on the wind and weather. The seal of the High Lord of Earth can cause the earth to split apart, turn plants and trees to dust and ashes, make birds fall from the sky, and kill tigers and other ferocious beasts.

It is the third seal, that of the High Lord of Man, that pertains to the human sphere and that has the special function of healing all kinds of ailments. So powerful is this seal that if you impress it upon the heart of a healthy person from behind, that person will instantly die, but if you then seal his heart from the front, he will at once be restored to life. If you wish to test the seal's efficacy by a less drastic method, you can coat it with vermilion and press it upon the heart—from the front—of a seven-year-old boy. The seal-impression will then appear on his back (once again, the magic-mirror projection effect).[85]

The same book also gives its own version of the classic Yellow God's Emblem of Transcendence, as well as another seal, that of the Ninefold Ancient Supervisor of the Immortals (Chiu-lao hsien-tu). This is a seal apparently used by a number of different Taoist lineages, and illustrations of several different designs are found. It seems to have been most closely associated with a movement that began in the ninth or tenth century but reached its full strength in the fourteenth and fifteenth: the Pure Luminous Way of Loyalty and Filial Piety. As the name indicates, this was one of many attempts to unify the major strands of Chinese tradition, this time within a Taoist framework, and therapeutic seals were an important practical component of its spiritual amalgam, which also laid great stress on the cardinal Chinese civic virtues of loyalty to the state and filial piety. Two of the seals under the authority of the Ninefold Ancient Supervisor of the Immortals serve to illustrate how diverse similarly named seals might actually be.

Thus far, we have been considering prescriptive accounts, addressed to priests and initiates, informing them of how seals should be employed. But there are a number of descriptions in existence as well, which not only prove that such techniques were actually in widespread use but also convey a surprising amount of exact socio-historical information. The best witness to the complexity of twelfth-century ritual practice in South China is the high official and distinguished scholar Hung Mai (1123–1202). For more than fifty years he worked at his great book, the *I-chien chih* (*Record of the Listener*). This collection reveals the entire range of Chinese ritual and belief as a complex living organism in which persons of all classes and conditions fully participated. Hung Mai carefully put on record hundreds of accounts of remarkable events, especially those illustrating relations with the world of the spirits—accounts that were either the fruit of his own observation or that had been reported to him by friends and relatives.[86] We learn, for example, that a younger brother (or perhaps a cousin) of Hung Mai apprenticed himself to a sorcerer for the express purpose of learning the "Nāgārjuna rituals," showing not only that early medieval practices of the sort we have been studying continued to be used for hundreds of years but that they appealed to the governing class as well.[87] Here we may mention three instances of the use of Taoist seals as instruments of healing. The first account, from 1138, describes a woman who had died but whose heart nevertheless remained warm. Noting this phenomenon, her family called in a Taoist master. He impressed his ritual seal, or "seal of the Law" (*fa-yin*), all over her body, then formally called back her departed ethereal souls (*hun*). The treatment proved successful and she was restored to life.[88]

Or again, there was the thirty-eight-year-old official physician who fell ill of a fever in 1189. His father, also a physician, felt himself too old to deal with the case and so called in a colleague. The patient's pulses were extremely feeble, and administering a pharmaceutical preparation so exacerbated his condition that he broke out in a manic frenzy, rushing and clawing about until all his fingernails were ragged and torn. Another physician was called in and, giving the patient cooling drugs, managed to restore him somewhat, so that he could eat a bit of gruel. But then the fever set in once more, and the victim called for paper and brush and—in his delirium—composed several poems, well-rhymed and cleverly written. Suddenly, he threw away the brush and turned his face to the wall, staring at it as if gazing into another country. He said he saw countless armored cavalry riders and foot soldiers battling out of control; then, trembling convulsively, he cried out: "They're taking me away in a boat and are going to beat me! I want to run away from them and come back home, but I can't move!" His father hired two strong men to hold him down, and in a while he relaxed. Then he suddenly started to chant scriptures and spells and sing bits of music; none of the verses or songs were anything that he had ever been familiar with before. Only then did those around him realize that he was possessed by a malignant spirit. They sent for a certain Master of the Law named Lung, who formally bestowed on him his seal of the Law and had him hold it in his palm while he bound it to his hand. There was an immediate improvement, and within a fortnight he was cured.[89]

The most significant feature of this account is the milieu in which it occurred: the family of a hereditary official physician. Surely the doctors' obtuseness in diagnosing the true nature of their colleague's ailment was bound up with their rationalistic, pharmaceutically based approach to healing in general. For that matter, they may have wondered (as may we) what business a professional physician, a model of rationality, had falling victim to demonic possession. But once the correct diagnosis had been established—which certainly seems to have taken the rationalists long enough, given the dramatic nature of the symptoms—they only needed to summon a qualified Taoist master and a cure was instantly forthcoming. If I understand the passage correctly, the master actually bestowed his seal of power on the patient as he would upon a disciple in a formal rite of transmission, tying the seal into the sufferer's palm and thus transforming him into an authorized official of the Tao with full control over the demons that were possessing him. Here, then, we appear to have yet another variation on the therapeutic functions of these remarkable implements. The patient, a professional healer in his own right, is not treated as the passive recipient of a healing ensigillation. Rather, he is given an enhanced identity, still as a healer but now in the Taoist tradition. In this new persona he is able to effect his own cure, and the Taoist ritual seal is the medium of this subtler technique of treatment.

The official physician was thus turned into a Taoist master in extremis, although there is also ample evidence that under less urgent circumstances Taoist initiation was sought and Taoist healing methods skillfully applied by members of the highest social echelons in the land. A final example from Hung Mai describes the therapeutic activities of a member of the imperial ruling house who practiced as a master in the Ling-pao tradition, one of the principal Taoist lineages of the day. This was a particularly delicate case involving the beautiful but dissolute wife of an official; no doubt a person of irreproachable social standing was required to treat her. In this account the wife observed a richly ornamented young lady accompanying her own maidservant into the house. As the figure neared, it suddenly transformed itself into a handsome young man in a black coat, who began flirting with the fascinated wife. She lost no time in inviting the attractive apparition to bed, and so began an intense, erotic spirit-possession that went on for months. Reproaches and admonitions were in vain, and at length the noble Taoist master was called in. He merely pressed his seal of the Law upon her chest and suddenly it was as if she had awakened from a drunken stupor. She declared that she had been just in the midst of drinking with her young man when a red-robed emissary advanced straight toward them holding a sword. Her lover made haste to withdraw while she dutifully followed the emissary back to the waking world. This kept the incubus at bay for three days, but then he returned and the Taoist master was obliged to begin more elaborate ritual operations, using a child from the family as a seer. Eventually the possessing demon was identified as the spirit of a black dog that had been buried behind the house. When its undecayed corpse was finally exhumed, dismembered with the Taoist's sword, and thrown into a river, the wife made a full recovery. Here we need only note that the cure was initiated by direct application of the master's ritual seal.

There are additional eyewitness reports of such seals in therapeutic use from more recent times. The Reverend George Mackay, a Presbyterian missionary in Taiwan from 1871 to 1895, records that in treating cases of malaria, "the Taoist priest makes charms out of peach-leaves, green bamboo, and yellow paper, which are tied around a button of the sick one's clothes, or to the cue. Sometimes a red thread is tied around the wrist, then kept there for weeks at a time. Or a stamp, like that of Lau-tsze, the founder of Tauism, is pressed on the back."[90] The Dutch scholar J. J. M. De Groot, who was in Amoy in 1877–78 and again from 1886 to 1890, observes that "the seals used to this day by the priesthood of the Taoist religion are mostly engraved with T'ai-shang Lao-kiün "Supreme Lao-kiün," the honorary name of Lao-Tszō; many bear the name or title of Chang Tao-ling [founder of Taoism and first Celestial Master]. There are, however, many other divine seals in use, each god to whom a temple is dedicated having there, like a terrestrial authority in his official mansion, a box with seals on his altar for the use of laymen and priests."[91]

Like so many other elements of Taoist and Chinese Buddhist ritual practice, therapeutic seals were adopted by non-Chinese peoples living in close proximity to the culturally and economically dominant Chinese. The assimilation of ritual was apparently viewed as a most effective means of obtaining a vital part of the power inherent in Chinese institutions. From the Chinese point of view, the spread of Chinese ritual was a means of civilizing the "tribespeople" through conversion to Taoism and Buddhism. The central role played by writing and written documents in classical Chinese ritual also meant that those in authority among the "tribes" necessarily became literate in Chinese. Indeed, the written Chinese language appears to have been considered primarily a sacerdotal medium. The Yao, for example, refugees from South China now settled in Laos and Thailand, have long been dedicated Taoists, a hierarchy of Taoist initiations having been superimposed on their own social structure.[92] Mass ordination ceremonies are still held in which all participants, regardless of age and experience, receive a formal written certificate of rank, together with a seal that reads "Order from Lord Lao the Most High for immediate execution," for use on ritual documents.[93] At the death of a fully initiated priest, his seal and certificate are burned, and thus sent before him into the heavens so that his spirit can be properly received by the celestial authorities.[94] The exorcists among the Miao people of West China were also markedly influenced by Taoist practice and had their own demon-dispelling seals. A seal figures prominently in a healing ritual performed by a Ch'uan Miao exorcist and recorded in the 1930s. The exorcist displays his seal, directing it toward the patient, then points it first at heaven, then at the earth. Next he presses it once on the patient's head, twice on his body, three times on his hand, four times on his chest, and five times on his foot. The demons thereupon make haste to abandon the body of their victim.[95]

Considering the number and variety of medieval Chinese Buddhist examples, we might expect therapeutic sealing to turn up among the rich complexities of present-day Buddhist ritual in Japan, and such is indeed the case. The most conspicuous instance comes in the ceremonies of the First Month at a number of older Buddhist temples, as well as some Shintō shrines. For example, on the third day of the new year, in the southern part of Kyoto at the Tōji (a Shingon-lineage monastery), in the course of a ceremony of purification, one priest, wearing a white mask over his nose and mouth and holding a large hexagonal seal, ceremoniously stamps the pillars of the hall. At the conclusion of the ritual, he stamps in vermilion the foreheads of the faithful and of any other onlookers who desire it. Similar rituals are carried out at the same season in the great Shingon mountain-headquarters of Kōyasan (south of Osaka), as well as in a number of the old temples of Nara (the Tōdaiji, Tōshōdaiji, etc.).

Such seals are also used to print auspicious and protective talismans for affixing to the walls of a room. Here, then, a seal is used in ways closely similar to those recommended in our medieval Chinese texts, being applied not only to the human body but also to the walls, gates, or pillars of a building. The legend carved in relief on the face of such seals is a curious one; it reads "Precious Seal of the Ox King" (*goō hōin*).[96] Before ransacking the more obscure corners of Buddhist mythology in search of this bovine monarch, we should consider a simpler solution to the ox king's identity. In Japanese, "king" and "yellow" are homophonous (*ō*). In Chinese as well, the two words are close in sound (*wang* and *huang*, respectively). In contrast to "ox king," the term "ox-yellow" presents no difficulties at all because it is the standard term for either ox bile or ox bezoar and is the literal equivalent of the Sanskrit term *gorocanā*, with the same meaning. In addition to mere homophony, the character *wang* has other qualities to recommend it, for its royal associations suggest a sovereign remedy; moreover, its mere four strokes commend it to the seal-carver, in contrast to the twelve strokes of *huang*.

The significance of these seal-inscriptions has been much discussed by Japanese scholars, and they are by no means agreed on their original meaning. The puzzling "ox king" might in fact have resulted from a misreading of some other inscription on a seal; for example, the single character for "imperial seal" (Chinese *hsi*) may have been misread as two characters, "ox" and "jade" (the latter being almost identical to "king"). In China, Niu-wang, the "Ox King," is the divine protector of cattle.[97] Or does the inscription simply designate the Buddha, who is like unto a "king of cattle," as some Japanese writers aver? Though some scholars profess to find the bezoar explanation fanciful, I am inclined to favor it as the most generally satisfactory solution. In its support, for one thing, is the shape of the seal—hexagonal, or sometimes round, and in any case approximating the roundish bezoar, whereas the vast majority of ordinary seals are square (one may recall that the seal recommended by the *Book of Consecration* was also round). Then, too, early written accounts of the great historic Japanese seals of this genre always emphasize the object's healing properties; such seals were reputed to be marvelously effective against poison and pestilence. Whatever the original sense of the inscription, there is no doubt that, early on, seals were identified metaphorically with the wonder-working bezoar.

Ox bezoars have been standard ingredients in the Chinese materia medica from ancient times. Scraped, ground up, and ingested, they were chiefly prescribed in treating children's convulsions caused by fright, as well as madness and epilepsy in adults. Their properties, then, were essentially demon-dispelling, for they were said to eliminate malignant wraiths from the body and to drive off demons. Indeed, since it was recognized that bezoars represented a pathological condition in the animals that produced them, their demonifugic action was apparently deemed to be homeopathic. Taken internally, bezoars were powerful medicine indeed, and the finest specimens commanded (and still command) a very high price. Writing around the year 500, T'ao Hung-ching observed that cow's bezoar was the most highly prized and costly of all medicines, and comparable assessments can be collected in Southeast Asia today.[98]

Another use for bezoars seems to have been peculiar to Japanese Tantric Buddhist ritual.[99] Cow's bezoar is triturated and mixed with water; this solution is be-charmed 108 times with the spell of the Bodhisattva Kannon (Avalokiteśvara) and then applied to the vagina of a woman who has reached the term of her pregnancy. It is said to assure a speedy and easy delivery.[100] This procedure was termed the "Bezoar Rite" (*goō kaji*), and it became the specialty of the abbots of a particular Shingon monastery south of Kyoto (the Daigoji). During the tenth and eleventh centuries, these specialists were often called upon to treat ladies of the imperial house and the metropolitan aristocracy when the time for giving birth drew near. But it is of course the *external* application of the bezoar, or of a bezoar surrogate or replica, that is evoked in the Japanese New Year's ceremonies, and this brings us to the threshold of a final aspect of our subject.

Parallels, Analogies, Conclusions

Bezoar, wielded by an expert, evokes a range of magical techniques and ritual operations that offer interesting typological parallels or even possible genetic relationships to our Buddho-Taoist practice of therapeutic sealing. In Central Asia, for example, among the Turks and Mongols, bezoars were manipulated by specialists to produce advantageous weather conditions: rain in time of drought, magical storms to confound one's enemies in battle, and the like. Though stones of other provenance have come to be employed in this function, it is the bezoar, a lithic substance born and nurtured in the animal realm, that is the original and still most desirable example of these yada-stones (Turkish *yada-tas*, or Mongol *jada*).[101] Power over the natural elements is also a feature of the Chinese seals.[102] For that matter, we may also note that both Central Asian Turks and Mongols made use of talismans, known among them as *vu*—which represents the Chinese word *fu*, the standard term for a written or printed talisman.[103] China's direct contact with Central Asian peoples extends over more than two millennia, and occult ritual was no less affected by this than were more mundane aspects of life and thought.

Healing through the application of a spiritually highly charged object to the body of the sufferer suggests the similar use of potent signet-rings (also emblems of identity and official status in the West). It is also clearly allied to the direct touch or other bodily contact of a person invested with comparable spiritual potency. In ancient Greece, the hands of gods and their mortal representatives were filled with healing power.[104] Later, the kings of England and France could, with a touch of their hand, cure scrofula, "the King's evil," and the laying-on of hands is still a prominent feature of faith-healing worldwide.[105] In fact, the healer's entire body may be brought into contact with that of the sick person, a technique also known from ancient Greece.[106] Carefully prescribed and modulated gestures often appear as significant elements in the composition of medicine or the implementation of cures; *ubi dolor ibi digitus*, and direct contact of the hands might be employed not only to soothe and heal surface complaints but in treating a considerable spectrum of internal ailments as well.[107] The Buddho-Taoist sealing techniques may seem fairly mechanical, simpleminded procedures until we recall the complicated details involved, as set forth in the first Buddhist instructions (in the fifth-century *Book of Consecration*) and in our initial, sixth-century Taoist example. The power of the implement is wholly related to the power of the officiating monk or priest—his control of the vital breaths within and his mastery of complex techniques of visualization. The seal is thus a concentrated tool of his own highly trained and heavily charged body. Its potency not only derives from the noble lineage to which the officiant belongs by virtue of his formal initiation but also draws strength directly from those supramundane powers for which his body serves as a conduit or transceiver. It stands to reason, then, that in the hands of a fully qualified practitioner, other objects may work upon the patient as effectively as a spirit-seal. We have already noted the considerable talismanic force that resides in sacred books, both Buddhist and Taoist. A ritual in use among priests of the Tendai Buddhist lineage in Japan today undertakes to heal all ailments of the throat by both internal and external applications. Loofah-pods (*Luffa aegyptiaca*) are wrapped ceremoniously for presentation to the sufferers, who attend a service that is usually held once a year. The packaged loofah is taken home and prepared in water, which is then drunk. But the culmination of the rites performed in the temple or shrine is the touching by the priest of the sufferer's forehead with a volume of the *Book of Perfect Wisdom* (*Mahāprajñāpāramitā-sūtra*). Traditionally the opening work in the Sino-Japanese Buddhist canon, as well as the longest, the *Perfect Wisdom* in some sense epitomizes all of Buddhist revelation. Through this direct ritual contact, the sufferer is sealed with the wisdom of all the buddhas.

Other cases of touching holy books come even closer to the notion of contact with seals. Every Japanese temple and shrine has its own characteristic seal, and many Japanese carry with them blank books in which they collect impressions of the seals of the temples they visit (*nōchō-kyō*). The more serious and systematic enthusiasts follow a recognized pilgrimage route comprising a certain number of temples that are associated administratively or according to some other divine or geographical principle. The seal-impressions that they gather thus form a studied sequence, as well as attesting to the authentic completion of the pilgrimage route. David Hall, who trained in Japan as a Tendai postulant, told me about the traditional pilgrimages included in his course of training. Old people visiting the temples to which he and his fellow-postulants went would give them alms and then ask to borrow their books of temple seal-impressions, which they pressed against those parts of their bodies that needed restorative treatment. In this instance, the impressions stood in for the seals themselves, as well as signifying the cumulative power of the holy book and the merit of the young monks' pilgrimage.

Another related corpus of practices concerns the painting, smearing, or inscribing of marks or signs on the body. Here we rejoin the estimable products of the cow, for in India *gorocanā* ("cow's yellow") designates both the bezoar and also the animal's bile, which is the preferred ingredient in the compound used to mark the forehead with the *tilaka*-mark.[108] In a Chinese Tantric manual dating from 654, one is directed to pound *gorocanā* with flowers of the "plant of longing" (*Abrus precatorius*) and smear the resulting paste on one's forehead, whereupon "all hindrances will dissolve of themselves"—including hindrances to love, no doubt.[109] Bezoar and bile were important ingredients in painting and dyeing generally in India. Marking the face with apotropaic substances is also known from early Taoist texts. According to a set of instructions in the *Declarations of the Perfect Ones* from fourth-century Mao Shan, on the first and last days of the month, as well as on two other days of the sexagesimal cycle when demonic attacks are particularly liable to occur, the adept should purify himself, fast, and sit upright in his meditation chamber in a state of perfect vigilance, without closing his eyes. He should dip a brush in vermilion and make a dot beneath his left eye; another brush dipped in realgar is used to make a yellow dot below his right nostril. Together with reciting the appropriate spell, these precautions ensure that the troublesome spermatic souls are unable to leave the body and contact potential demonic invaders; the body's three dangerous corpse-specters are also held in check.[110] It should be noted that in addition to cinnabar (vermilion), with which talismans are so often written, realgar ("male yellow") was one of the three yellow minerals frequently employed in the writing of apotropaic talismans, along with orpiment ("female yellow") and litharge or massicot ("lead yellow").[111] The application of cinnabar to the skin continued in general use down to modern times: "A curious antidote against sickness is very commonly applied by parents at Canton to their infant children on the fifth day of the fifth month. This consists in staining their foreheads and navels with cinnabar or vermilion, leaves of the sago palm and garlic bulbs being at the same time suspended over the entrance doors to prevent the intrusion of evil spirits."[112] Eyes, nostrils, and navel are crucial points of ingress and egress, and it is precisely at these apertures that the demonifugic minerals are required. But there are also more generalized applications of less rare and costly protective substances to the skin, like the marking of children's foreheads with soot from the bottom of the pots on the wood- or charcoal-fueled stoves in Japan. On a more lugubrious note, during an epidemic of plague in twelfth-century Kyoto, a Shingon monk wrote the seed syllable *Aḥ* on the foreheads of 42,300 corpses, "as a seal to the Buddha."[113]

The custom of placing colored markings on the skin to keep the body safe inevitably suggests more complex designs, whether painted on, cicatrized, or tattooed. The invaluable De Groot notes that Chinese characters of particular demonifugic power might be written by professional exorcists, medical men, or even laypersons on the chests or hearts of victims of demonic possession. The preferred medium was cinnabar or vermilion, and the most potent characters were those for "right" or "true" (*cheng*, evocative of the True Law, or True Tao), "fire" (*huo*), and "sword" (*tao*). The same authority records that talismans might also be incised or tattooed directly on the body, thus furnishing permanent protection.[114]

Much the same effect could be obtained by placing comparable signs or seals on the clothing—often a particular item of clothing expressly designed for that purpose and worn next to the skin. We have already mentioned the temple-seals that testify to one's accomplishment of a pilgrimage. Such seals might also be applied directly to the pilgrim's clothing, serving as both verification of the pilgrimage and talismanic protection.[115] Similarly, bīja-mantras, or "seed-syllables," each of which represents one deity in the Tantric Buddhist pantheon, are written or printed on the white garments still worn today by Japanese Buddhist ascetics. This deployment over the body of talismanic characters of power in Sanskrit script is a material realization of the ritual "sealing" of the body with finger-seals: A particular hand-formed mudrā can be impressed upon parts of the body, as we have seen—most often, perhaps, on the five vital loci (head, two shoulders, throat, and heart)—in this way infusing the protection of a particular deity at those spots. And the divine personnel of an entire maṇḍala can be installed over a wider area of the body using the individual seed-syllable of each deity. This procedure of *nyāsa*, the assignment of parts of the body to a series of spirit-beings, is common to all forms of Tantric practice, Buddhist and non-Buddhist alike.

For two thousand years, Chinese tradition has associated tattooing most tenaciously with the peoples on the southern fringes of the Chinese empire (it also served as a punishment among the Chinese themselves). Ancient Annam was termed "the Country of Crossed Legs" by the Chinese because of its inhabitants' resemblance to fish, an effect created by the Southeast Asian custom of tattooing the male body from the waist down with a delicate, scalelike tracery of blue designs. This custom still persists in Burma and Thailand, and Southeast Asia generally provides a rich treasury of all the forms of talismanic protection.[116] In one light, we observe the protective talisman and apotropaic medicament merging into written document; in another aspect, they become seductive ornament.

The use of Taoist and Buddhist seals for printing paper talismans intended for swallowing brings us, inevitably, to a final category of application: the use of seals to consecrate food. One of the most conspicuous and best documented examples in Christendom is furnished by the bread-stamps used either on the host intended for consecration or on loaves of bread destined for distribution to the congregation after the service. This latter usage was and remains a prominent characteristic of Eastern Orthodox liturgy.[117] The variety of traditional European bread- and cake-stamps is of course enormous, ranging from the sacred and symbolic to the fantastic and ornamental, but is (as we should expect in a living tradition) normally a harmonious blend of the two. Chinese festival cakes, too, are regularly stamped with auspicious signs and characters. Often the imprint is a simple stereotyped formula or single character promising "good fortune," "official rank," or "long life." But more specialized therapeutic applications of written or printed characters on foodstuffs are also on record from China. The all-seeing De Groot has documented the custom of feeding demonically afflicted persons cakes made of flour on which a schoolmaster or other learned individual has written characters of exorcistic power. Such a cake would often be half eaten, half thrown away by the patient, thus corresponding to the long-standing practice of bipartition in the case of contracts or other material tokens of an oath or agreement between two parties. The broken halves, rejoined and fitting perfectly together, authenticate and guarantee the contractual bond. The word *fu*, which we have been translating as "talisman," originally signified such a token or tally in two parts.[118] In the case of the half-eaten cake (as with the swallowed talismanic ashes), the binding agreement is presumably concluded with the gods.[119] In late medieval and early modern Europe, perhaps the most widely used medicinal substances to be distributed in comparable stamped or sealed form were the siliceous preparations known as *terra lemnia* and *terra sigillata*.[120] Specimens can be seen in most collections of antiquities, notably in the excellent Deutsches Apotheken-Museum at Heidelberg Castle.

There is thus nothing unusual in the use of seals to produce consecrated foodstuffs in which sacramental, medicinal, and festival virtues combine and—through ingestion—are incorporated into the human body. Indeed, this brings us back to the theme with which we began, and which has recurred throughout this study: the association in medieval China of therapeutic seals with talismans for swallowing. Inevitably, we are drawn once more to consider the evidence for the seminal role of therapeutic seals in the early history of printing.[121]

Although the details of Pelliot's interpretation of the *History of the Sui Dynasty*'s statement on Taoist seals and the treatment of disease may have been mistaken, he was certainly right to draw attention to Taoist seals as an important element in the development of printing. Nowadays, at least, the vast majority of talismans on view throughout East Asia are printed on paper and sold at temples. Appropriate printed talismans can be affixed to the walls or doorways of rooms in the house, or displayed in a shop or office (or, indeed, a car). They should be renewed annually. Traditionally printed from wooden blocks, some of them closely resemble temple-seals, and many have a temple-seal superimposed on the paper's surface. As we have seen, they represent the ultimate stage in a long process of development centered on the ritual seal of the Taoist or Buddhist master. A definite evolutionary sequence can be traced in the history of medieval Chinese ritual seals, perhaps best illustrated by the one seal whose name remains constant throughout the period of development: the Yellow God's Emblem of Transcendence. In the early fourth century, this seal was already used to manufacture solid artifacts—apotropaic talismans for installing around property boundaries or for bombarding aquatic monsters. By the thirteenth century, a seal bearing the same famous name was generally known and used on paper for printing on documents to be submitted to heaven during the performance of a ritual. This change marks the distinction between diffuse occultism and formal Taoism. But of course this change—as well as the shift to "printing" in our sense of the term—had taken place long before and can be delineated as early as the first half of the sixth century. There the same text that directs the officiant to impress his seal on the patient's body also instructs him to manufacture a talisman by printing it in vermilion on bamboo-pith or paper, and to administer it internally to the sufferer. Here we have explicit evidence to support Pelliot's hypothesis; as we might expect, it is found among the neglected ritual texts of medieval China—but among those of the Buddhists rather than the Taoists.

What we have seen of the use of seals in Buddhism and Taoism richly illustrates our long-held contention that such pervasive phenomena cannot be neatly parceled out into sectarian pigeonholes. It is fruitless to ask (as is so often done), "Is it Buddhist or Taoist?" Clearly, therapeutic ensigillation has been both "Buddhist" and "Taoist," and much more besides. In this it resembles other practices shared by China's two most prominent clans of ritual specialists. The use of official seals to control relations with the invisible world appears to have begun among early medieval occultists like Ko Hung—men who were neither Buddhist nor Taoist in the strict sense of these terms. It represents a specialized extension of an important component of secular Chinese culture: the official seal of authority. We can trace in China a special fascination with glyptic and lithic prowess that goes back to the oracle bones. Political and hieratic authority were closely bound in Chinese tradition with technological expertise in carving or incising bones, stones, or metals. Countless legends attest to this fascination—legends that may underlie any of its later manifestations in healing, religion, or governmental practice.[122]

Although the ultimate origins of the seal may be obscure, we can nevertheless speculate on who was the first to adopt ensigillation as a therapeutic technique. This honor seems to go to the Taoists, yet it must be noted that our earliest full set of instructions for performing ensigillation comes from a Buddhist source, the mid-fifth-century *Book of Consecration*. This is not an unusual case; many traits and practices associated in our minds with Taoism are in fact first documented in Buddhist scriptures—namely, in the so-called apocryphal sūtras written in China, directly in Chinese. The first Taoist book to provide a full-scale sealing ritual dates from more than a hundred years later, in the second half of the sixth century. Meanwhile, Chinese Buddhist authors had been setting down further elaborations of their own.

The seals employed by Buddhists and Taoists had an ultimate common source in standard Chinese usage; Buddhist and Taoist seals themselves might be closely similar or even identical, and they also shared a common application against demons and disease. Yet as our survey has shown, Buddhism and Taoism elaborated the complex of seal use in distinctive ways, each in accordance with its own terminology, doctrine, and ritual system. Following the standard procedure when adapting Chinese practices, Buddhist ritualists drew on the great resources of Indian tradition to absorb ensigillation into their own system. They exploited the wide range of meanings already attached to the Sanskrit word "mudrā" in a Buddhist context. Most commonly, "mudrā" meant the finger-seals that personified or commanded spirit-beings, but the same word also designated the seal that joins the two halves of a gourd-shaped alchemical curcubit—and (in later Tantric Buddhism) the female sexual partner of a Tantric adept. Buddhist scriptures also provide a rich stock of seal-metaphors comparable to the "seal of the spirit" conferred in Christian baptism, and these were also drawn on in the work of assimilation. The Taoists deftly incorporated the therapeutic seal into their own ritual matrix as an official implement, and it meshed very neatly with the operations of their own celestial bureaucracy. Yet behind each of the early texts was of course the oral tradition, the tradition of practice—of which even the best of our texts is but an imperfect reflection.

The question of origins is of considerable interest, but the patterns of assimilation are even more intriguing, for the swallowed talisman and the impressed spirit-seal actually reinforce each other and, in time, even coalesce. Once the short step had been taken from applying the seal to the patient's skin to the manufacture, by means of the seal, of the talisman that he or she would ingest, the initial distinction between the two modalities, one internal, the other external, had been bridged. Moreover, this confluence of therapeutic methods marked an even more momentous technological change: the supplanting of writing by printing. That this fusion of procedures was possible is due, I believe, to the common, overarching matrix that informed and gave meaning to both these quasi-bureaucratic operations: namely, the peculiar cause-and-effect structure of Chinese ritual, founded on the vision of cosmic Law, that governed Buddhists and Taoists alike.

5

THE GENEALOGY OF SPIRIT POSSESSION

Possession is nine points of the Law.

ENGLISH PROVERB

A "Puzzle" in Japan

Readers of the elegant literature of medieval Japan have no doubt been struck by the frequency with which spirit possession is described. It would seem that in tenth- and eleventh-century Kyoto, the court was regularly plagued by hordes of malicious demons who attacked women of distinction. Their raucous voices punctuate the refined novels and diaries written by aristocratic women of the time. Women were, indeed, the demons' principal victims (though men might also be attacked), and a wide array of maladies was laid at the demons' door.[1] The most impressive accounts of demonic activity, however, come in connection with the culmination of pregnancy, often that of empresses or imperial consorts. At such times, to counter these spirit-world forces, a group of distinguished senior monks would be called in to chant scriptures throughout the lying-in period. No doubt this precaution was frequently effective.[2] Yet the cases that stand out in the literature owe their prominence to the catastrophic demonic activities that oftentimes ensued. It was when a woman cried out in her labor pains that the demons were made manifest. And we learn of the demons' presence only through the activities of the monks, who, far from being mere scripture-readers, then became exorcists.

Thanks to their efforts in transferring the afflicting demons into the bodies of young mediums, through whom the demons could tell their stories, we come to learn the identities of the attackers. They were often jealous or vengeful spirits of the dead—whether courtiers, consorts of palace women, or rivals of the woman they afflicted (or of her family or her husband's family). But the dead were not the only demons to be feared: The attacker might also prove to be the soul of a living enemy or rival, one of whose souls had left her body without her awareness to attack someone for whom she harbored feelings of jealousy or resentment.[3]

Thus, in these accounts, social relationships are often outlined with startling clarity. As in the Taoist dossier from fourth-century Mao Shan (see pp. 11–21), we are here able to detect the mechanisms by which the ailments and afflictions of the living were attributed to particular hostile forces among the dead. But we are also given the chance to observe comparable accusations attached to living persons. The aristocratic sources may discreetly suggest that malevolent souls did their evil work without their owners' knowledge or express intent, but given the fact that there was a basic belief in such soul-attack, it seems that this was but one side of the story. Ill-disposed persons could also try to use these techniques quite consciously against their enemies. A person whose souls had been identified as the aggressors in such a case, whether consciously or unconsciously, must have felt the brunt of social opprobrium—like reputed witches and possessors of the evil eye in the West.[4]

These potent otherworldly forces manifested themselves most dramatically around the bed of an expectant mother, where all hopes, anxieties, jealousies, and ambitions were most intently focused. In one famous example, recorded in her diary by Lady Murasaki, author of the *Tale of Genji*, so numerous and powerful were the afflicting demons that even one of the elderly monks in attendance became possessed and spoke with a demon's voice. But the monks' usual procedure was to transfer the offending spirit or spirits (for there might be more than one) into the body of a special medium, usually a girl or young woman. In a typical case described in the *Pillow Book* of Sei Shōnagon (968–1025), the monk called in was suave and well-dressed, and the medium was "a heavily built girl with a splendid head of hair":

> When the girl had sat down next to the monk in front of a small three-foot screen, he turned round and handed her a thin, highly polished wand. Then with his eyes tightly shut he began to read the mystic incantations (*dhāraṇī*),

his voice coming out in staccato bursts as he uttered the sacred syllables. It was an impressive sight, and many of the ladies of the house came out from behind their screens and curtains and sat watching in a group. After a short time the medium began to tremble and fell into a trance. It was awesome indeed to see how the priest's incantations were taking effect. . . . Everyone who witnessed the scene was overcome with respect. It occurred to me how embarrassed the girl herself would feel if she were in her normal state of mind. She lay there groaning and wailing in the most terrible way, and though one realised that she was not in any pain, one could not help sympathising with her. Indeed, one of the patient's friends, feeling sorry for the girl, went up to her screen and helped to arrange her disordered clothing. Meanwhile it was announced that the patient was a little better. . . . By the hour of the Monkey (late afternoon) the monk had brought the spirit under control, and having forced it to beg for mercy, he now dismissed it. "Oh!" exclaimed the medium, "I thought I was inside the screen, and here I am on the outside. What on earth has happened?" In an access of embarrassment she hid her face in her long hair and was about to glide out of the room when the monk stopped her for a moment, and after murmuring a few incantations, said, "Well, my dear, how do you feel? You should be quite yourself by now."[5]

It is important to note that the patient, who scarcely figures in this account at all, was not likely to be suffering from "demonic possession" in our sense of the term. There is no indication that her personality was dislodged, that she spoke in voices, or that she gave any of the classic signs of being possessed. Instead, her illness had simply been diagnosed as resulting from the attentions of a demon, and in that more restricted sense a demon was in her body. The actual possession, visible and audible, was produced by a monk in a passive but willing medium; as Sei Shōnagon's account shows, it was very much a dramatic spectacle. By means of his incantations, the monk forced the demon out of the patient and into the medium's body, through which it could declare itself, make its demands, and in due course be banished. Though the same technique might of course be employed in cases of pathological spirit-possession, the dramatic possession-symptoms used to effect a diagnosis and cure were brought about in the medium by the monk. Court ladies may have been awed by the overt symptoms of demon-transfer, but the real interest for us is in the actual technique and its derivation.

Unfortunately, not much help is to be had from modern scholarship, since historians of Japanese society and literature seem not to have searched for the

relevant technical sources that might explain the procedure. The remarks of a distinguished Japanologist, the late Ivan Morris, are typical. Commenting on the description from Sei Shōnagon's *Pillow Book* just quoted, and the celebrated case of the vengeful ghost of Lady Rokujō in the *Tale of Genji*, Morris wrote,

> It will be noticed that in both these accounts the exorcists were members of the Buddhist clergy. This was normal in the period and represents one of the anomalies of Heian religious-superstitious practice. Shamanism and the idea of possession by evil spirits formed no part of Buddhist doctrine; and, if logic played any role, we should expect Shintōist priests to officiate on occasions of this kind. Such rational distinctions, however, were alien to the approach of Murasaki and her contemporaries. No more in their thinking than in the structure of their language did the idea of mutually exclusive categories prevail.[6]

These statements clearly illustrate the power of received ideas and the distorting effect of Western "logic." We are all supposed to know what Buddhist doctrine is: Was not Buddhism presented to the rationalistic nineteenth century as an enlightened, atheistic religion? Thus when we encounter any of the complex realities of Buddhist practice, we are forced to classify them as "anomalies." The problem here lies not with the eleventh-century Japanese and their supposed inability to make "rational distinctions," but with our own continuing ignorance about the actual substance of Buddhism in eleventh-century Japan and throughout medieval and modern Asia. No historian of medieval Japan who had taken the trouble to read the Chinese texts used by Japanese monks of the time could make the mistake of excluding spirit possession from the complex of orthodox Buddhist belief and practice. The ethnologist Alexander Macdonald, working in a remote corner of Buddhist Asia, did not make that mistake, for he drew attention to the intimate relationship between phenomena he had observed among Tibetans and Nepalis and certain rituals documented in medieval Chinese texts.[7]

Accounts of Japanese Buddhist exorcism through induced, voluntary spirit-possession have been studied, on the basis of medieval novels and diaries, by William McCullough (1973) and Jolanta Tubielewicz (1980), and modern survivals have been presented by Carmen Blacker (1975). We must now attempt to make clear how deeply rooted these practices were in Tantric Buddhism, for this becomes apparent as soon as we begin to examine the medieval Chinese ritual texts. It is precisely these texts that are so rich and informative and

yet so sadly neglected by historians. It may turn out, upon analysis, that the wave of demonomania that swept over the Japanese aristocracy was to a large extent iatrogenic, produced by the monkish physicians themselves. The dramatic technique of treatment by induced possession may have promoted this diagnostic propensity, vastly increasing the reported attacks by demons. Only an institution of considerable authority and prestige could have so forcefully impressed its view of the world on the upper echelons of society. If we are to understand the Japanese documents in historical perspective, it is necessary to consider the methods and materials of Tantric Buddhism.

The Tantric Revolution

Some readers may be surprised at the notion of "Tantric Buddhism" in medieval China and Japan. We are more accustomed to seeing this term in connection with India and Tibet. But Tantric Buddhist scriptures were among the numerous Indian Buddhist writings brought to China and translated into Chinese from the second through the eleventh centuries; in fact, the dated and localized Chinese translations provide the best evidence we have for the development of Buddhist Tantra during its first thousand years. The Tantric section of the current Sino-Japanese Buddhist canon contains 573 scriptures; together with the relevant hagiographical texts, they provide an unparalleled chronological sequence of primary sources for the history of this form of Buddhism in India and China. With such abundant material at our disposal, it is now possible to make certain confident statements about a phenomenon that has tantalized and titillated some scholars while repelling others.

In discussing Chinese demonology (in Chapters 2 and 3), we first encountered the Buddhist books of spells, or dhāraṇī scriptures, which are placed in an apocalyptic setting and which contain incantations suited to such demon-ridden times. I suggested that this literature may be thought of as "proto-Tantric" and observed that a full-fledged Tantric system first appears in Chinese translations at the beginning of the eighth century. It is in this system and in eighth-century texts that we find the most complete instruction for performing therapeutic, voluntary spirit-possession. But it is important to note that there is no clear break in continuity between the proto-Tantric materials and the eighth-century synthesis. As early as the beginning of the sixth century, we find many of the elements that were to comprise the mature system floating, as if in suspension, in Chinese texts. There is an essential conti-

nuity and homogeneity running through all this material: It forms a distinct tradition.

Yet it must also be stressed that there is no clear line dividing this tradition from the rest of Buddhism. Its practitioners were almost all regularly ordained monks; their esoteric Tantric initiations or consecrations simply enhanced their status and power as ritual specialists. Moreover, a number of their rituals and spells passed into common Buddhist usage. Like other monks, Tantric initiates were organized into fictive families—spiritual lineages of masters and disciples—and certain of these lineages were more highly specialized in Tantric ritual practice than in any other form of Buddhist activity. Also, since Tantric rituals held out a promise of power, both mundane and spiritual, they appealed to many persons outside the formal monastic community. Yet the Tantric materials that have come down to us as Buddhist are no less truly Buddhist for all that.

I say "the materials that have come down to us as Buddhist" because "Buddhism" was only one mode of organizing and classifying these practices. In India, closely similar texts and rites are found in use among followers of the god Śiva (Śaivites) and the god Viṣṇu (Vaiṣṇavites); in medieval times, even the Jainas had their own forms of Tantric practice. Indeed, at one time Tantric texts and rituals were known in virtually every country of South and Southeast Asia, in either Buddhist or non-Buddhist form. The chief Buddhist survivals are among the Tibetans and in Japan. In mixed Buddho-Hindu form, Tantric rituals sustain the traditional cultures of Nepal and Bali, and still pervade Indian Śaivite and Vaiṣṇavite practice. The close interrelationship of all these various "national" or ethnic traditions has been obscured by terminology. For example, it has become customary to refer to Tibetan Buddhism as Vajrayāna (the "vehicle of the vajra") or Tantric Buddhism, whereas Japanese scholars refer to their own form of practice as Mantrayāna (the "vehicle of spells") or Esoteric Buddhism. Yet they are essentially the same thing. The chief difference is that Tibet remained in direct contact with India until Buddhism waned there in the thirteenth century, while Japan remained essentially faithful to the Tantric imprinting that it had received, via China, in the ninth century. Thus the Tibetan version includes later Indian elements than are found among the Japanese. Additionally, of course, Japan and Tibet elaborated on the Indian legacy each in its own way, in synthesis with other elements; in the Japanese case, moreover, much of the material had been predigested in China. Yet for all this, both forms issue from a single, though complex, genetic stock, and

I propose to use the convenient term "Tantric Buddhism" for the entire Buddhist aspect of the phenomenon.[8]

The eighth century marked the high point of the mature Tantric system in China itself.[9] In addition to the translations made from Sanskrit, important commentaries and ritual compendia were written directly in Chinese, and a number of Chinese monks distinguished themselves in Tantric scholarship. Though many new translations of Tantric texts continued to be made in the tenth and eleventh centuries, the brilliance of the eighth-century synthesis was not surpassed. Subsequently, the Tantric presence in China came to be represented primarily by Tibetan and Mongol lamas; China's own Tantric past survived chiefly in certain rites for the dead, a few spells, some legends, and a number of Taoist adaptations. The true heirs of China's great Tantric accomplishments were the Japanese. They sent scholar-monks to China for study, who then brought back quantities of books and images to Japan. Tantric Buddhism was the form of Buddhism most in favor at the Chinese court, and was therefore naturally adopted as the official court Buddhism in ninth-century Japan. It thus assumed the dominant role among the aristocracy, a role it retains, under totally altered social conditions, at the present day. Thanks to its position at the pinnacle of Japanese society in the formative phase of Japanese cultural history, Tantric Buddhism came to influence every aspect of Japanese religious life, a process that Japanese historians refer to as the "esoterization" (*mikkyō-ka*) of Japan.

From this fact alone, the crucial interest of Japan for the scholar of medieval China should be evident. Consider: A vital movement, which has left only texts and echoes in China, is still alive and in possession of vast archives in Japan. In Japan, as in Tibet, this powerful cultural vehicle arrived early enough to have a decisive and enduring impact. Indian and Sino-Indian rituals, music, art, mythology, and scholarship were brought to Japan and survived there within this comprehensive framework. The Tantric lineages of Tendai and Shingon are the most conservative, the most highly Indian, of all the Japanese schools of Buddhism, and they long preserved the study of Sanskrit at the easternmost extreme of Asia. Like Taoism in Taiwan, Japanese Tantric Buddhism represents a living tradition in unbroken continuity and evolution from medieval times.

Though historically complex, we can now see that the phenomenon of Buddhist spirit-possession and exorcism forms part of a much greater whole. The Tantric movement that began in India swept over Asia in successive waves of great intensity from the third through the twelfth centuries. What was the nature of the movement that allowed it to predominate, and to do so on such a scale?

We have seen that Tantric Buddhism provided a flexible framework within which the most variegated local gods, cults, and practices could be assimilated within a Buddhist context. This must certainly have eased the way for Tantrism as it spread throughout Asia. But that still tells us little about its central core of belief and practice. What was truly new and crucial to its success was the fundamental basis of Tantric Buddhism. The focus of the movement was on ritual, and in the course of performing Tantric rituals, the officiant actually became the Buddha (or Śiva in Śaivite Tantra, Viṣṇu in Vaiṣṇavite Tantra). This is the common trait of all forms of Tantric practice: The practitioner propitiates a deity, with whom he then proceeds to identify himself or otherwise unite. Like other features of the developing Tantric system, this phenomenon is first explicitly documented in a Chinese text based largely on oral tradition, the mid-fifth-century *Book of Consecration*. This text instructs the healer, who is about to use his wooden seal to cure a patient, first to visualize his own body as the body of the Buddha, with the thirty-two primary and eighty secondary signs of buddhahood (see p. 133). Only then, when he has effectively turned himself into the Buddha through meditation, can he effect the miracle of healing. This is the basic premise that underlay the entire Tantric revolution and that distinguished it from the Vedic and post-Vedic phases of Indian ritual on which it freely drew. Within Tantric Buddhism itself, the "mature" system of the seventh and eighth centuries can be formally distinguished from the proto-Tantra that preceded it by the name and nature of the Buddha concerned. Whereas earlier texts prescribe identification with Śākyamuni, the historical Buddha of our present world, later scriptures derive their authority from the cosmic Buddha Vairocana. Known in Chinese and Japanese as the Great Sun, this gleaming manifestation of the "Body of the Law" (*dharmakāya*) was said to be the ever-existing primordial figure of whom all other buddhas and gods are specialized manifestations or efficient hypostases.

The Taoist master, too, assimilated himself to a celestial being in the course of carrying out his own rituals, but Tantric rites follow a different pattern. Rather than practicing bureaucratic communication by means of formal paperwork, the Tantric officiant follows the rules of Indian hospitality and enters into a host-guest relationship with his god. Having prepared and purified himself and the ritual area, he sends a carriage for the deity and then receives him as an honored guest. Water is given him to wash his feet, then more water to rinse his mouth. A seat is prepared and a meal offered, followed by music to delight the visitor.[10] Perhaps the most common way of effecting this comprehensive entertainment is through Homa, a fire ritual ultimately based on the archaic Vedic sacrificial oblation.[11] Through the action of the flames, the various components of the meal can be actualized and vitalized in the world of the gods and buddhas. But in Tantric practice (unlike Vedic), when the sacrifices and entertainment are completed, the officiant unites himself with the deity. In the fire ritual, the outward sign of this union (realized inwardly through meditation) comes when the priest joins the tips of the large and small ladles used to feed the fire. The priest himself thus becomes the base of an isosceles triangle (a triangle is the emblem of the element Fire); the deity, the fire, and the priest himself are One. In this embodied form, he is empowered to accomplish the ritual's ultimate objective.[12]

In this way, the Tantric practitioner is able to achieve transcendence in his own lifetime. Through proper ritual technology he attains immediate buddhahood, overcoming all apparent contradictions and uniting all seeming opposites; he embodies supradivine transcendence and mortal existence, nirvāṇa and saṃsāra, in his own person. It is this fusion that gives the Tantric master power over human affairs; indeed, he can work his will on the cosmos itself. When we recall the extraordinary assimilative powers that allowed Tantric Buddhism to incorporate every sort of cult and ritual, we begin to gain some notion of the comprehensive claims that characterized the movement. It is no wonder that monarchs were seduced by a program of wish-fulfillment designed to realize their most extravagant dreams; Tantric Buddhism provided the perfect spiritual correlative to imperialism.

It is easy to see how Western interpreters may feel disoriented when approaching this phenomenon—an organized religion or ritual system in which priests regularly become gods in order to effect a staggering variety of purposes, from the salvation of dead ancestors to the murder of living enemies. One solution has been to equate the process of self-apotheosis with Christian "mysticism"; C. Hooykaas has written of the Balinese Tantric priest's "way to God," expressly noting the affinity that he himself, the son of a Dutch Calvinist pastor, senses with the Balinese ritual.[13] Others have rather simplistically described the union that characterizes Tantric ritual as a form of "shamanism" or "neo-shamanism."[14] Such semantic looseness threatens to obscure all meaningful distinctions among radically different types of ritual structures and social institutions.

It is clear that the central "mystery" of Tantric Buddhism lies in an alteration or radical enhancement of identity or personality. Rimbaud's phrase "Je est un autre" might well serve as the basic credo of the Tantric master. But a crucial distinction is the systematic and predictable nature of the operations. The body and mind of the adept were trained to become worthy vehicles for the deity, yet the role of individual expression was all but excluded through strict regulation. The ritual process might best be likened to an oft-repeated, strictly controlled scientific experiment with a predictable result: A particular set of procedures with regard to initial training, material implements, verbal formulas, and psycho-physical acts will reliably produce union. This ritual assumption may have incidental features in common with Christian mysticism and Central Asian shamanism; it may, for that matter, share elements with schizophrenia, pathological spirit-possession, the mental world of the child, and certain forms of compulsive behavior in adults.[15] Yet it is scarcely identical to any of these; despite the paucity of scholarly attention it has received, Tantric Buddhism is something quite different and quite itself, as two millennia of copious written sources attest.

It is against this background that we must view the documents of voluntary Tantric Buddhist spirit-possession that we are about to consider. In the course of his ritual preparations, the controlling master himself becomes a powerful deity of the Tantric pantheon, but in a perfectly systematic manner. He is neither "ecstatic," out of the body, nor "possessed" in the ordinary sense of the term. Into the child-medium the master then conducts an otherworldly being—that is, as a deity impersonator, he coaxes or compels another, subordinate figure into the passive body of an untrained medium. This is done so that the new arrival can testify directly, and if need be publicly, thus making it known whether he is a wicked demon afflicting a patient suffering from disease or a benevolent god offering diagnosis and prognosis. The medium can incorporate a spirit from the world of the dead, or the medium's own spirit can travel to that invisible realm. In any case, the same two-tiered system of personification or (if one will) dramatic impersonation prevails: The active master, embodying a commanding buddha, dominates the passive medium, incorporating a subordinate god or demon. The drama is accomplished in these terms and in these roles, and it can be used for prophecy as well as therapy. The patient, if there is one, remains largely peripheral, an outsider in the psychomachy (as the Japanese description quoted above suggests).

'Āveśa': *Voluntary Spirit-Possession*

The first Buddhist text to give instructions for inducing spirit possession comes under the auspices of the Bodhisattva Avalokiteśvara (Ch. Kuan-yin, J. Kannon). Kuan-yin plays a large role in the *Lotus Sūtra* and became the most prominent divine patron of proto-Tantric dhāraṇī-rites. He has remained the most generally popular Buddhist deity in East Asia, in no way hampered by changing in late medieval times from a compassionate male into a compassionate female.[16] The book containing these instructions, the *Amoghapāśa-sūtra* (*Pu-k'ung chüan-so t'o-lo-ni tzu-tsai-wang chou ching*, T. 1097), was translated at the very end of the seventh or beginning of the eighth century, just when the new Tantric synthesis was about to become known in China, but still belongs to the earlier, proto-Tantric tradition. It presents an incantation recommended by Kuan-yin.[17] The powerful spell has many uses, among them healing the sick. Reciting it 108 times will cure all demonically provoked illnesses. Even a single phrase of the spell, recited clearly and forcefully, will relieve seasonal ailments and all hot illnesses. Another procedure involves reciting the spell twenty-one times over a strand of white thread, making a knot in the thread with each recitation. One then attaches the thread to the patient, who will be cured of whatever is ailing him and no longer be subject to torment by demons. Yet another procedure: If someone has already been suffering for four days from a demonic illness, first a square ritual area should be constructed of earth. Scatter various sorts of incense and flowers on it, and cause the patient to sit inside it. Then make a model of the patient in dough. Recite the spell, state the patient's name, and using a knife of damascened steel, cut the model into slices. When the patient sees this he will be terrified, and the offending demon will abandon him and never come back.

Directly following these miscellaneous therapeutic recommendations are the following instructions:

> Or again, there is this method. If it is desired to enchant a person, the spell-possessor should bathe himself and put on fresh garments. Next he should recite the spirit-spell to protect his own person. Then he is to construct a ritual area using cow dung, making it square and painting it in the appropriate colors, strewing assorted flowers, and setting out various white-colored food-offerings. Next he should take a virgin boy or girl, bathe the child, and imbue its body with fine fragrances. He should clothe it in a pure white garment and adorn it with all manner of ornaments. He should then have the

child sit cross-legged in the ritual area; he recites the spell *bandha* ("bind") and he plaits the child's hair. When he is done reciting the spell and plaiting the hair, he takes more flowers and fills the child's hands with them. In addition, he takes fine quality incense, crushes and scatters it. Then, additionally, he recites a spell over uncooked rice, which he sprinkles, together with flowers and water, within the ritual area. Next he should burn sandalwood incense and recite Kuan-yin's spirit-spell; he should recite it three times over the flowers and then cast them in the child's face. Then the child's body will begin to tremble. If you wish it to speak, pronounce another spell [given in the text] over pure water and sprinkle it in its face. As you recite the spell, be sure that your hand does not touch the child. When you have recited in this manner, the child will speak. If you ask about good or evil things in the past, future, or present, it will be able to answer all your questions. If the spell-holder wishes to send away the spirit who has lodged in the child, there is another spell given which he should recite.[18]

Plaiting the hair obviously serves the same purpose as knotting the thread in the earlier instructions—that is, to bind in the spell and charge the child with its power. The text does not specify the identity of the spirit that enters the child, nor are the spirit's answers limited to a present case of illness—it will speak of good or evil things in the past, present, or future, possibly in connection with the etiology of an illness, but perhaps more generally as well.[19] It could therefore be some helpful godling; but given the context in which these directions appear, among methods for treating victims of demonic aggression, it seems equally probable that it is the offending demon, captured by plaiting the child's hair and reduced to submission by the recitation of Kuan-yin's powerful spell.

Immediately afterward, the text proposes a method for healing a patient afflicted by a demon through direct action on the sufferer himself. After a ritual area has been prepared, flowers strewn and incense burned, the patient is seated in the middle and a spell recited over him until he begins to tremble. Then the spell-binder forms a finger-seal (*mudrā*) by pressing the fourth finger of his left hand on the middle finger and recites the Kuan-yin spell over the patient. The patient then starts to speak at once, swearing an oath: "I will release and abandon him now, and never again come back." This is obviously the voice of the possessing demon speaking through the patient's mouth, and the text goes on to state that if the patient's indwelling demon does not speak, another spell, there given, will cause the patient's body to burn with intense heat, at which the demon will certainly make his declaration and depart. Following this come instructions for freeing persons who have been possessed by yakṣas, nāgas, gods, or demons and who are manifesting symptoms of mental disorder as a result; white mustard seeds are to be empowered with the spell and thrown into a fire. We can thus see that, in this work, the use of a child-medium was only one among a number of techniques to relieve the victims of demonic attacks. It even stands in juxtaposition to a procedure for causing the demon to speak through the patient's own mouth. Such is the variety and diversity of proto-Tantric ritual.[20]

The appearance of a corpus of more highly unified Tantric texts and rituals in China is associated with the names of three great foreign masters. All enjoyed the support of the T'ang emperor Hsüan-tsang (reigned 712–55). There was, first, Śubhakarasiṃha, from Ceylon, who arrived in China in 716 and died there in 735. He worked in close collaboration with a Chinese disciple, the outstanding astronomer I-hsing (683–727); together they produced the standard translation of the system's basic scripture, the *Book of the Great Sun Buddha* (as it was also called in Chinese), or *Mahāvairocana-sūtra* (*Ta-jih ching*, T. 848), and an elaborate commentary on it as well.[21] Then there was Vajrabodhi (662–732), from Central India, who arrived in China in 719. Amoghavajra (705–74), third of the foreign masters, really belonged to a later generation. He was born in Ceylon, and accounts differ on the date and circumstances of his arrival in China, but he appears to have become a disciple of Vajrabodhi. Amoghavajra's career extended into the two reigns after that of Emperor Hsüan-tsang, and he left an enormous literary legacy. Some 167 works are attributed to him as translator, though it appears that he was really the compiler, or even the author, of most of them, for they were put together directly in Chinese either by the master himself or by some of his numerous Chinese disciples. Be that as it may, it is among the translations or adaptions made by these three important Tantric scholars, Śubhakarasiṃha, Vajrabodhi, and Amoghavajra, that we find the key instructions for using spirit-mediums.

Brief sets of directions occur in two translations made by Vajrabodhi. One of these texts is entitled *Secret Rites of the Spells of the Divine Emissary, the Immovable One (Pu-ting shih-che t'o-lo-ni pi-mi-fa*, T. 1202). This is the Tantric deity Acala, patron of many colorful rituals.[22] In the book translated by Vajrabodhi, the Immovable One's mantra is said to be a sovereign cure when recited seven to twenty-one times. One may also proceed in the following way:

> In the front of an icon of the Immovable One, cleanse the ground and burn Parthian incense (gum guggul). Then take a mirror, place it over the heart

> [presumably, the heart of the painted image], and continue reciting the spell. Have a young boy or girl look into the mirror. When you ask what they see, the child will immediately tell you all you want to know. You should then summon a dragon-spirit; once you have its name in mind, stand the young boy or girl in the purified place and recite the spell over him or her. The spirit will then enter the child's heart, and when the officiant discusses matters pertaining to past, present, or future, all questions will be answered.[23]

In this instance, the Tantric master and child-medium are carrying out the ancient technique of catoptromancy, using a mirror—a technique on which much has been written based on ancient Greek and later Arabic and European sources.[24] Here it seems that a dragon-king is summoned into the medium as the source of information. The role of the nāgas in therapy is an ancient one and continued for centuries in a Buddhist context.[25] A little later on, the Vajrabodhi text names its own favorite among the ranks of dragon-kings, Kulika, who manifests himself as a serpent twined about the sword of the Immovable One—an image still found in cultic use in present-day Japan.[26]

Another scripture translated by Vajrabodhi, the *Yogin's Book of All the Yogas of the Diamond-Pinnacle Pavilion* (*Chin-kang-feng lou-ko i-ch'ieh yü-chih ching*, T. 867), seductively promises, in rhythmic verse, that "If with spells you empower boys and girls/you can bring about *āveśa* ("possession"); /of things in the three ages and the three worlds/you can fully learn the good or evil portent." Slightly later, more information is provided:

> Take virgin boys or girls,
> Bathe them, dress them in fresh garments,
> Administer the Bodhisattva Vow,
> And place them on white flowers.
> Recite spells over them, cover their faces,
> And recite again, 1,008 times.
> Then they will directly experience it,
> Their bodies will sometimes be suspended in space.
> About all things in past, present, and future,
> They will have total, comprehensive knowledge.[27]

But that is all we are told, and after a few further observations on ritual in general, the *Yogin's Book of All the Yogas* comes to an end.

Āveśa is the standard Sanskrit word for spirit possession.[28] In Chinese texts, it usually appears in transcription: *a-wei-sha*. It is, however, sometimes translated into Chinese as "total entering" (*pien-ju*). The concept seems also to have been applied to the procedure for empowering or "animating" the ritual area and the implements and offerings within it.[29] But the most conspicuous use of the word was to designate possession rites in which a spirit was invoked into the living body of a medium. The term might also apply to procedures in which the spirit of a living person was co-opted, so to speak, into the pantheon. According to his biographer, Vajrabodhi himself made use of a ritual belonging to the same family of operations on at least one historic occasion. When the Chinese emperor's twenty-fifth daughter was at the point of death, the Tantric master is reported to have sent the souls of two girls as emissaries to Yama, the king of the dead:[30]

> Having chosen two girls seven years of age from the palace, he had their faces wrapped with red silk and had them laid on the ground. He had Niu Hsien-t'ung write an edict that was burned elsewhere, and an incantation was said over it by Vajrabodhi. The two girls recited it from memory without omitting one word. Vajrabodhi then entered into *samādhi* ("concentration"). With inconceivable force he sent the two girls to King Yama with the edict. Within the time required for a meal, King Yama ordered the princess's dead nurse Liu to accompany the princess's spirit back with the two girls. Thereupon the princess sat up, opened her eyes, and talked as usual. Having heard of this, the Emperor started for the Wai-kuan [the Taoist temple, outside the palace compound, to which the princess had been moved to die] without waiting for his guard. The princess said to him, "It is very hard to alter destiny as fixed in the other world. King Yama has sent me back to see you only for a short while." About half a day later, she died. After that, the Emperor began to have faith in Vajrabodhi.[31]

In this case, the traffic proceeds in the opposite direction, from the world of the living to the world of the dead, with the souls of the blindfolded little girls as intermediaries. Vajrabodhi dispatches them as bearers of a message from the ruler of the living to the monarch of the dead—a message which, like Taoist documents, was written out and burnt. One may assume that the message concerned the injustice of summoning the beloved princess into the halls of death before her appointed time. The princess's spirit and that of her dead nurse (perhaps speaking through one of the little girls? We are not told) do indeed return for a short time to the world of the living, but only to confirm the immutability of King Yama's summons. According to the biographer, the one to profit most from this unhappy incident was the Buddhist master: "After that, the Emperor began to have faith in Vajrabodhi."

To extend our view of what was happening in Chinese ritual therapy in those times, we must leave the Buddhist path for a moment and turn to a Taoist text. This is a short work dated 632, the *Red Script of the Three Registers of Divinity (T'ai-shang ch'ih-wen tung-shen san-lu* (HY 589), drawn on in our discussion of therapeutic seals (see pp. 155–56). After describing the use of seals to acquire invisibility and assimilate oneself to the Five Elements, the work goes on to instruct us in a curious method for using a child-medium. This section of the text is entitled "Method of the Patriarchs for Treating Night-Dreams in Which, Having Roamed to Various Regions, One's Souls Are Beguiled by Jade Maidens." The instructions that follow are so terse that it is difficult to be sure exactly what is intended. But according to my tentative unraveling of the proceedings, the Taoist master first puts to sleep the young child whom he is going to use as a medium. He may do this by hypnosis—the text does not specify. Just before doing so, he twice recites the name of the deity called "the Immovable One." Clearly this is our Buddhist friend Acala, and it is not the only sign of Tantric influence in this Taoist text. He then takes a piece of black paper, folds it in two, and has the child hold it between its teeth. Then he wraps the child's head in a piece of cotton cloth and puts it to sleep.

Next the officiant inhales twice and recites, "I send the four great spirit-generals to apprehend the jade maidens who have beguiled the souls." Then he blows his breath into the mouth of the sleeping child. At this point another person goes to sleep, or is put to sleep—and this person is evidently the patient, the object of the officiant's therapeutic concern. This is the man who has been having trouble with his souls because of the beguiling "jade maidens." Once he has been safely bedded down, the healer draws breath from the five directions and blows them over the patient's body lightly, as if blowing on a cup of tea. Then he sits down once more and recites again, "O Lord Immovable!"—his invocation of the presiding deity. He next goes to inspect the patient, then recites, "I send the four great spirit-generals to apprehend the souls that have been beguiled by the jade maidens. I call them swiftly to return!" Then he calls out the sleeper's personal name and awakens him.[32]

What we have here, I think, is the treatment for a case of pathological dreaming, whether simply a persistent tendency to debilitating erotic dreams (since the pathogenic agents are "jade maidens," beautiful celestial women who cause the dreamer to lose precious vital-essence) or, possibly, a more serious condition of soul-loss and consequent disorientation or even delirium (but again, with erotic manifestations). For the cure, it is necessary to penetrate the dreamer's world by means of an emissary: the child-medium. It is a case of setting a dreamer to catch a dream. The black paper placed between the child's teeth serves as a kind of photographic negative on which the master breathes his spell of command to Acala's four spirit-generals. The patient, meanwhile, is put back to sleep so that his departed souls can return and rejoin him in the state in which they left him. He should awaken to find himself whole once again.

The deity known as the Immovable One and the pseudo-Sanskrit spells found later in this Taoist text reveal the technique's ultimate inspiration in Tantric Buddhist practice. We should remember that our surviving texts correspond to the sparsely scattered peaks of a buried landscape; these paltry textual remnants imperfectly record selected facets of what was once a broad range of practice and oral tradition. This is the same situation we noted with respect to the early history of therapeutic seals among Buddhists and Taoists. We now have proof that the ferment of Tantric therapeutic ritual was already working in Taoism—and this demonstrates that the process of assimilation was well underway in China even before the earliest surviving Buddhist evidence for this technique had been written down.

A third Tantric text translated by Vajrabodhi, *The Medicine Buddha Contemplation Ritual* (*Yao-shih ju-lai kuan-hsing i-kuei fa*, T. 923), also mentions a messenger to the invisible world, but a divine emissary this time; though only a passing reference, it brings us close to the heart of the problem. At the conclusion of a statement of penitence and devotion, closing with the hope that all beings may benefit from the merit deriving from the ritual just accomplished, the officiant asks that "the youth Po-ssu-na," or "Po-ssu-na youth," transmit the incense-smoke bearing the officiant's request to all the buddhas of the universe.[33] This is an intriguing statement because it seems better suited to a Taoist than a Buddhist ritual context. We already know that Taoist written documents were burned in the flame of the incense burner, and that they make their way heavenward in the company of special emissaries, spirit-messengers transformed by the priest from the breaths within his own body. Here we have a Tantric Buddhist master setting up a comparable scenario. The Taoist master dispatched his communications with a little group of travelers, the Dragon-Lord of the Left and the Tiger-Lord of the Right, the Merit-Officer's emissary and the Incense-Officer. The Tantric Buddhist officiant now calls upon the youth (or youths?) Po-ssu-na to perform a similar function, carrying to the buddhas in the incense fumes the declaration of merit that will enable all living beings to profit from the ritual. Who or what is the youth Po-ssu-na?

We find the name Po-ssu-na in a text translated in 726 by Śubhakarasiṃha. This book, the *Questions of Subāhu* (*Subāhu-paripṛcchā*, Ch. *Su-po-hu t'ung-tzu ch'ing-wen ching*, T. 895), is a major Tantric scripture also known in Tibet; a second Chinese translation (*Miao-pi p'u-sa so-wen ching*, T. 896) was made at the end of the eleventh century.[34] The *Questions of Subāhu* devotes considerable space to the ways of drawing a deity down into various vehicles or abodes, typically an image or icon. When the procedures have been followed with exactness, the deity and his suite will manifest themselves to the practitioner. There will often be confirmatory signs indicating the deity's presence. The face or eyebrows of the image will move, for example, or the statue's ornaments will tremble. There may be a rain of flowers from heaven or a fragrant aroma; one may perceive a trembling of the earth, or a voice in the air saying (for example), "Now I will explain to you what you wish to know," or other such words. Or one may notice a flame, or remark that though the oil is exhausted, the lamp suddenly flares up more brightly than before. One may sense the hairs of one's own body standing on end, have a feeling of joy in one's heart, or hear celestial music. For that matter, the deity himself may appear to you in person, descending to you from out of the air. If you are so fortunate as to behold such an apparition, make offerings to it at once using incense, flowers, and fragrant consecrated water. Prostrate yourself before the deity and—with due consideration of your own stock of merit—present your request. He will surely respond favorably. Then send him off in the prescribed manner.

Instructions of this kind for animating an image are found in many other Tantric texts.[35] But the *Questions of Subāhu* also draws our attention to the possibility of using other vehicles or abodes for a deity. Immediately after recommending that a major figure of the pantheon be evoked into an image, the book devotes a section to what it calls "bringing down Po-ssu-na"—the same enigmatic word or name borne by the youthful messenger to the buddhas in Vajrabodhi's text. The young questioner, Subāhu ("Lovely Arms"), is told by Vajrayakṣa, his divine informant:

> Should the reciter of spells wish to bring down Po-ssu-na, he should summon him according to the standard ritual procedure. He may be invited to abide in a finger, a bronze mirror, clear water, a sword-blade, the flame of a lamp, or a jewel; or in a hollow statue, a child, a pearl, or a piece of flint. Into such a lodging Po-ssu-na will come if one invokes him, and he will at once explain things in the heavens or among men, as well as matters of past, present, and future; all things good and evil throughout all the three ages he will explain

> in detail. But if there is some error in the ritual, if there are too few or too many syllables in the mantra or if it is not recited correctly; if you do not have total, wholehearted faith, if you do not make the necessary offerings, or if the place is not pure or the weather not fair; or again, if the child's bodily signs are either deficient or in excess—should any of these conditions obtain, the Ssu-na will not descend.

For this procedure, one type of possible icon-abode is specified: a hollow statue that does not yet have a consecrated identity.[36] Otherwise, the recommended receptacles are all reflective or luminous substances, already embodying or seeming to embody light and life. Of course, the most fully animate of all these prospective vehicles is the child. Any one of the material objects listed may serve as the focus from which the child reads the answers, in images, about events past, present, and to come. But after directions for preparing these various material supports in which the images will appear, the focus turns to the selection, preparation, and experience of the child-medium himself. The entire section is well worth translating:

> Choose the eighth or the fourteenth or the fifteenth day of the white fortnight [i.e., when the moon is waxing, not waning]. Fast on that day, and prepare with cow dung a ritual area the size of a stretched-out ox's hide. Bathe the child, dress him in a pure white garment, and seat him in the middle. Make offerings to him with flowers and incense, then you yourself should enter the area and sit on rush-grass, facing east. If you wish the figures to show themselves in a mirror, first rub the mirror clean with ashes from a Homa fire performed by a chaste brahman, rubbing the mirror seven, eight, or up to ten times. Suspend the mirror above the maṇḍala [that is, the ritual area], have the child gaze up at it, and he will see things beyond the world of mortals. To do the same with a sword-blade, proceed as in the case of a mirror. If you want the child to see things good or evil on the surface of his fingers, first rub his fingers clean with purple ore water,[37] then apply fragrant oil, and good or evil things will immediately manifest themselves.[38] If you wish it to descend into a jewel or a pearl and be seen there, first sprinkle the jewel or pearl with pure water, concentrate fully, recite the mantra, and all forms will instantly be manifested therein. Item: If you wish a divine image to be the vehicle, make offerings with flowers and it shall manifest itself at once. The same is true of a lamp-flame. And the spirit will even come to you in your dreams to explain various things.[39]

If you follow these instructions meticulously and yet, despite all your efforts, Po-ssu-na still does not descend, you should fast for an entire day and recite the mantra of the spiritual guardians of the ritual clan to which you belong, a hundred thousand or even two hundred thousand times, in front of a stūpa or the awesome image of a deity. You should do this with intense concentration, neither moving your body nor falling asleep. "Having accomplished this, by reciting the seed-syllable *Oṃ* you could even cause the spirit to descend into a dead tree and make it speak—how much more easily into a human being!"

> If you wish it to come down into a child, select ten, eight, seven, six, five, four, three, or two children. Regarding their bodily signs: Their veins, bones, and joints should not show, they should be full-fleshed, their eyes handsome, with dark and white clearly distinguished. Their fingers must be long and slender, the soles of their feet should be flat. They should be full at all eight points without and within; all the body-marks must be present, and their hair should be dark black, so that peoples' eyes fill with delight when they behold them. Having obtained virgin boys of this sort, on the eighth, the fourteenth, or the fifteenth of the white fortnight, bathe them and dress them in fresh pure garments. Use fragrant flowers, burning lamps, powdered incense [for rubbing in the palms and applying to the lips], and burning incense, and administer to them the Eight Precepts [i.e., injunctions to fasting and abstinence]. Keep them from eating on that day and have them sit before you, within the maṇḍala. Then with fragrant flowers, burning lamps, powdered incense, burning incense, and all manner of things to eat and drink, make offerings to the deity, to the great gods who guard the eight directions, to the asuras and the host of remaining spirits, to each of them individually. Then scatter wondrous flowers on the boys' bodies and rub their bodies with incense. Next the spell-reciter takes an incense burner in his hand, does obeisance to the deity, and recites the mantras. In front of him he places [i.e., pronounces and visualizes] the seed-syllable *Hūṃ*; into it he calls the word *gṛha* ("take"); then the word *āveśa* ("possession"); next the word *kṣipra* ("quickly")—"Take possession quickly!"
>
> When the Ssu-na has descended, there are the following signs and manifestations: a look of delight in the children's eyes; ability to gaze at objects without blinking; and no evidence of inhaling or exhaling. From these signs you can tell that the Ssu-na has come down. Thereupon, immediately present consecrated water and burn incense as offerings. In your heart recite the mantra of the Supremely Victorious King of Knowledge. Then you should respectfully inquire, "What manner of god is your reverence?" If you or anyone else have any doubts about this identity, you should question him immediately. Then that spirit will speak of things past, present, and future, of profit and loss, of suffering and joy. Speedily accept and hold in memory all that he

> tells you—do not be hesitant or suspicious. When he is done answering your questions, send him away again at once. If you follow all these directions, the Ssu-na will quickly descend; if you do not, however, you will achieve no results with the ritual, and people will ridicule you.
>
> Now when the Ssu-na has descended, the boys' expressions will be radiant and joyful, their faces will be moist and gleaming. Their eyes will be wide open and the dark pupil will be lightly ringed with red. In their attitude and deportment they will act like adults. They will neither breathe in or out nor blink their eyes. Thus you will know that it is an authentic Ssu-na. If, however, some devil should descend, there are other indications. In that case their eyes are red and rounded, like those of someone glaring in anger. The pupils of their eyes do not move around, and their mouths gape open in fright. In this case, too, they neither breathe in or out nor blink their eyes. Thus you can tell that some yakṣa has descended, and you should send him away at once. If he is unwilling to depart, you should at once begin chanting auspicious verses, recite the mantra of the Impure Furious Vajra-Being (Ucchuṣma), or read out the *Great Dhāraṇī-Book Collection*. If after these readings and recitations he still will not leave, then with the mantra of the Lion Throne use consecrated water on him, or dip 108 *palāśa*-wood sticks (*Butea frondosa*) in ghee and burn them in a Homa fire, or mix sesame seeds, grains, flowers, ghee, and honey and make a hundred oblations with them in the Homa fire. At the very end, perform Homa with the mantra of Kuṇḍalī seven times or three times—and then the demon will certainly abandon the medium and go away. If the wise practitioner has understood this marvelous ritual and can carry it out in every point according to the instructions, he will attain his end without undue time or effort.[40]

The children may behold their visions in a variety of objects, but it is evidently into the child that the god himself must come and through the child's mouth that he will speak. The incarnate god is the real seer and interpreter; the child-medium is thought to see true things in the mirror, sword-blade, or oiled hand only when the proper celestial being has taken up its abode within him, and so the spirit-visitor is the active agent. Despite its close structural similarity to the methods for making statues talk, which the book presents earlier, this procedure must have given far more reliable and dramatic results. We now know a good deal more about the activities of the mysterious Po-ssu-na, or Ssu-na, as his name is sometimes abbreviated in the text (he also appears elsewhere as "the Po-god"). Yet we have still not identified him or discovered his origins.

His identity, in fact, presents us with a curious problem. The name "Po-ssu-na is obviously the transcription of a Sanskrit word, but opinions differ as to which one. Japanese scholars earlier assumed that it was *praśna* ("question"), with reference to the questions that are put to the spirit itself, and that it is perhaps a proper name. More recently, the compilers of the index to the Tantric section of the Sino-Japanese Buddhist canon have glossed the term as a transcription of a different Sanskrit word, *prasena*.[41]

The word *prasena* is something of a puzzle in itself. Boehtlingk's great Sanskrit dictionary in its 1879 revision cites an early sixth-century occurrence of the word in the *Bṛhajjātaka*, an astrological treatise by Varāhamihira. The tenth-century commentator on this work, Utpala, defines it as signifying a form of trickery or charlatanism, "eine Art Gauklerei." This is evidently an unsympathetic evaluation of techniques comparable to, or identical with, those described in our eighth-century Tantric Buddhist source; the same *prasena* is obviously meant. Yet the term's origins remain obscure. Prasena and Prasenajit ("Conqueror of Prasena") are both attested to as proper names borne by a number of rulers; the most famous Prasenajit was king of Śrāvastī in the time of the Buddha. Yet none of the authorities proposes an etymology for this well-known name. Recourse to the standard works of lexicography and consultation of several Sanskritists has taken me this far and no farther. Yet additional information is to be had, from an unexpected quarter.

The word *pra*, in Tibetan, designates a particular class of divinatory techniques and phenomena. *Pra pha-pa* ("to bring down the *pra*") means to divine by means of a charmed mirror. This is, of course, precisely what we find in the eighth-century *Questions of Subāhu*: The text speaks of bringing down Prasena and recommends prominently, among other implements, a mirror over which a spell has been pronounced. When we consult Lokesh Chandra's massive Tibetan-Sanskrit dictionary, we find the Sanskrit word *prasena* given as the equivalent for the Tibetan *pra*.[42] Thus even if the root meaning of the Sanskrit term remains tantalizingly obscure, it appears that we have at least discovered the source of the Tibetan word, as well as the origins of a spectacular form of Tibetan divination. It seems safe to assume that *pra* represents an abbreviation of *prasena*—just as *po-ssu-na*, the Chinese transcription of the Sanskrit word, was often used in shortened form, as either Ssu-na or "the Po-god."[43]

Modern accounts of Tibetan *pra*-divination are of great interest. They strikingly illustrate how the instructions contained in Buddhist ritual texts might be applied and developed in actual practice. *Pra*-consultation can be carried out in a way closely parallel to the directions given in Chinese translations. For example, when performed under the auspices of King Gesar (a legendary Tibetan epic hero, later assimilated to the Chinese god of war), a scroll depicting Gesar is suspended above a table on which various offerings are set out. On the right side of the table is a vessel filled with grain, in which a "divination arrow" has been planted, point downward. On the left side is another grain-filled vessel, on which is placed a well-polished mirror of silver or bell-metal. The mirror is covered with five pieces of silk, each of a different color. The officiating priest invokes Gesar's assistance in bringing the rite to a successful conclusion:

> Then a boy is brought into the room where the ceremony is being performed and led to the table bearing the offerings. He should be about eight years old, and should come from a better-class family; on no account must the services of the son of a butcher or a blacksmith be engaged. The boy takes his seat on a white cushion in front of the mirror. The officiating priest now removes the five covers of silk, and the boy is asked to gaze for a while into the mirror. If the divination works well, the boy will soon claim that he sees various apparitions in the mirror. He has to describe these to the priest, who derives from the account of his helpmate the answers to the questions that the divination of King Gesar should clarify. Should the boy, however, claim that he sees only the reflection of his own face, then the priest will once more implore King Gesar to grant an answer. If even the third attempt does not lead to a success, then recourse must be taken to other kinds of divination. In case it is difficult to find a suitable young subject to participate in this ceremony, the officiating priest himself will try to recognize some apparition in the mirror. The same kind of divination can be performed with a sword, in which case the various apparitions are supposed to become visible in the polished blade of the weapon.

The same authority also describes another ceremony of mirror-divination under the auspices of the goddess Vajra Jade Protectress (rDo-rje g-yu sgron-ma), varying only in its use of different offerings and accessories. The divination manuals give lists of images that may appear in the mirror, each with its meaning and auspicious or inauspicious significance.[44]

Although the use of children as seers appears to have been widespread in Tibet, the priest himself may gaze into the mirror. Some descriptions of *pra*-divination omit the child entirely, presenting the visionaries (*pra-ba*) as experienced monks. Such is the account given by Lama Chime Radha (head of the Tibetan section at the British Library). He states that the diviner focuses his attention by gazing into a small mirror of polished stone or metal. He may also employ the still waters of a lake or the clear sky itself. It is also possible for him to use his own thumb, a method that dramatically illustrates the terse reference to the use of the fingers as an alternative to a mirror in the Chinese translation of the *Questions of Subāhu*:

> The ball of the thumb (*the-bon*) can also be used for *pra* divination. It is painted red and dipped in soft wax so that it becomes covered with a film of it. All light is shut out of the room and only a single butter-lamp is left burning. The *pra-ba* holds up his thumb and to everyone present it appears to grow in size and become like a large screen. On this screen appear visions of various symbolic objects—it may be of trees, lakes, people, or other concrete forms. The visions then have to be interpreted according to the question which was asked. If the interpretation is doubtful or uncertain, the *pra-ba* asks again in his mind, and another vision appears. If he asks yet again, then letters appear on the thumb-screen. After that, the visions fade.

Like other authorities on the subject, Lama Chime Radha states that if the *pra*-method does not at first succeed, one may repeat it, seeking fresh visions, but after a third unsuccessful attempt, it is necessary to try some other method. He cites a famous example of *pra*-apparitions in a holy lake near Lhasa, which in 1935 guided the Regent of Tibet and his associates in their discovery of the present (fourteenth) Dalai Lama. He also quotes cases of successful *pra*-divination using a mirror, the ball of the thumb, and the sky from the experience of Tibetan friends and colleagues.[45]

Evidently, the child-visionary or child-medium could be left out of the procedure completely, at least in Tibet.[46] Perhaps children were eventually relegated to a secondary role as the technique came to be applied in vital decision-making processes of the Lamaist state. There can be little doubt, though, that the use of a child was basic to the original operation, and I believe it very likely that the *Questions of Subāhu* was a primary scriptural source for this form of divination, in Tibet as well as in China and Japan. It is, in any case, precisely the utilization of juveniles that we need to pursue here. After all, at least one of the Chinese texts makes it clear that this *prasena*-figure was envisioned as being a youth—the Prasena-youth who was requested to carry the officiant's message up to the buddhas in heaven. The association between a child-medium and a childlike god is, I think, no accident. It seems fully consistent with a principle that has been emerging as a fundamental modus operandi in Tantric Buddhist ritual structure: the association by nature or analogy of like elements in the divine, demonic, and mortal spheres. The better to explore this sympathetic link, we now turn to a figure of the Indian pantheon, within Buddhism as well as outside it, in whose cult such traits and propensities appear to exist in close alliance: the god Skanda.

Child-Gods and Child-Afflictors

The ensemble of temples, legends, texts, and rituals dedicated to Skanda in India is prodigious and varied. In one form or another, Skanda's cult is intensely alive throughout South India and Ceylon at the present day. His popularity is no doubt due in part to his representing an important type of god, for Skanda is a deity of many, many names. This attests to the attractiveness and adaptability of the composite Skanda-figure, since the complex nomenclature suggests that numerous other, originally independent local deities have come to be identified as Skanda's manifestations. Of course, the same could be said of all the great gods of India; both Śiva and Viṣṇu are gods "of a thousand names." Skanda, though, represents a divine category with an especially wide appeal: the young warrior-god of martial valor and childlike purity. This identity is clearly suggested in one of Skanda's most popular epithets, Kumāra ("the Youth").

In view of his present-day prominence in Hindu life, early mentions of Skanda in Buddhist texts are of great potential interest. In contrast to his phenomenal success in non-Buddhist milieux, Skanda's appearances in Buddhism seem at first to be fairly rare, and his Buddhist role soon becomes rather narrowly specialized. In fact, from the seventh century on, under a Chinese mistranscription of his name (as Wei-t'o, rather than Chien-t'o), Skanda became one of the chief guardian-gods of Chinese Buddhist monasteries, where his statue was usually found at the rear gateway. His popularity in this function is chiefly due to the role he played in a famous series of revelations. In 667, the monk Tao-hsüan, a distinguished historian of Buddhism and authority on religious law, was seventy-one. Weary and ailing, he withdrew into retreat—and then, from the second through the ninth month of that year, found himself receiving regular visionary visits from Skanda. Tao-hsüan recognized his opportunity and seized it; he posed countless questions to the deity in a heroic attempt, despite his waning powers, to resolve every lingering doubt on scriptures and ceremonies at the end of a long life of scholarship. He wrote furiously, and when he died early in the tenth month, he left a massive manuscript in ten sections that recorded the god's responses under thirty-eight hundred individual headings. Unfortunately, only a small portion of this prodigious testament has been preserved (*Tao-hsüan lü-shih kan-t'ung lu*, T. 2107). But Tao-hsüan's writings on monastic design and regulations were authoritative, and it is from this time on that we find Skanda installed as the guardian par excellence of Chinese Buddhist monasteries.[47] It is striking that Skanda should thus appear to a senior Chinese monk as a ready respondent to questions on Buddhism. Though this is not "possession" properly speaking, it nonetheless seems to confirm that Skanda's oracular role was by that time widely recognized throughout the territory of Indian cultural diffusion. And as was so often the case, "revelation" served to justify synthesis or syncretism, for Skanda is still very often found as gatekeeper in the Indian temples of his father Śiva. That guardian-gods of temple gateways have been among the most active agents of possession in East Asia may well owe much to Skanda and his cult.[48]

Skanda thus figures in Buddhism as yet another of the naturalized Indian gods who can find no worthier vocation, after having been converted to Buddhism, than mounting guard on behalf of monks. But as we have already observed in studying Buddhist demonology, the benign protective role often conceals an earlier career of crime. Such is also the case for Skanda. Other mentions of his name in Buddhist scriptures make it clear that he originally belonged to a particularly fearsome group of fifteen demon-thugs, a gang that attacked infants and young children.

In a text translated into Chinese during the first half of the sixth century, the *Book of the Dhāraṇī for Protecting Children* (*Hu chu t'ung-tzu t'o-lo-ni ching*, or simply *T'ung-tzu ching*, T. 1028A), we read that there are yakṣas and rākṣasas that delight in devouring human fetuses. They belong to the realm of the extrahuman and are powerful and difficult to control. They can cause people to be childless and kill fetuses in the womb. Also, when husband and wife are having intercourse, these demons can cause their thoughts to become distracted so that pregnancy does not occur, or can cause *kalala-arbuda*, a swelling of the womb that destroys the fetus and leaves the woman barren.[49] Or again, when a child has been born, they kill it in infancy. The Buddha names the members of this evil band of fifteen demons, and the third one is Skanda. Most of the demons have the appearance of animals, though one has the form of a rākṣasa-woman and another, the form of a married woman. Each of the others takes its own specific animal form: cow, lion, fox, monkey, horse, dog, pig, cat, crow, pheasant, owl, and snake. But in this band of miscreants, Skanda takes the form of the god Kumāra.[50]

As we have noted, Kumāra, "the Youth," is a standard epithet of Skanda throughout the literature and sets the tone for all descriptions of him. The text also describes the characteristic symptoms provoked by each of the fifteen demons, so that anxious parents can determine an attacker's identity. Among the various symptoms are rolling eyes, frequent vomiting, foaming at the mouth, clenched fists, biting the tongue, alternately screaming and laughing, and so on. Skanda's own particular sign is when the child moves both shoulders; the name Skanda itself means "shoulder" in Sanskrit (presumably abridged from an older epithet, Mahāskanda, "broad-shouldered").

It is as a child that Skanda appears once again in the list of fifteen goblins, in an expanded version of the same text translated into Chinese around the year 1000, amid a slightly altered array of animal shapes among his demonic cohort.[51] This later description also gives a heightened account of the goblins' activities, intensifying the anxiety felt by ardent couples: "No one is aware of those rākṣasas and no one is able to subdue them. Among all sentient beings who have no children or have not yet conceived, the rākṣasas are always on the lookout for an opportunity. They watch for the time when a man and woman are joined in sexual congress, then suck up the semen and vital breath so that the woman does not conceive. In this way they keep a child from being implanted and cause swellings in the womb, bringing about grave injury to that woman's womb." When, having failed to prevent conception, the demons must content themselves with killing living children, they roam about at night, terrifying babies, in search of victims. Among the various symptoms of their invasion are vomiting, foaming at the mouth, clenching the fists, choking, not drinking milk, crying out during sleep, biting the tongue, coughing, discoloration of the skin, and a fetid odor. The characteristic sign of Skanda's presence, though, is when the child shakes its head back and forth.

Skanda the demon also appears in several versions of the *Book of the Peacock Spell*, the prototypical incantation of early Tantric Buddhism. He figures in a long list of various demonic afflictors, not only in two early Chinese translations (T. 987, 988) but also in the fifth-century Sanskrit text of the Bower Manuscript, which includes a version of the *Peacock Spell*.[52] But in later, expanded versions of the *Peacock*, he appears as a protector as well as an afflictor. In a Chinese version translated in the first half of the sixth century, along with other guardians, it is Skanda's staff and the *Peacock Spell* that will drive demonic venom into the earth.[53] By this time, the basic image of Skanda the martial god had been brought over intact into a Buddhist ritual context. The spear is a constant of Skanda's Hindu iconography right down to modern times, and in Indian tradition Skanda's mount is the peacock, whose apotropaic powers are universally acknowledged—as the Buddhist *Peacock Spell* also demonstrates.[54] Even outside the monasteries, then, by the year 700 this redoubtable afflictor of children, himself a youth or child, had been enrolled among the official protectors of Buddhism, joining a motley assembly of tame gods and reformed demons.

But even after their promotion to gods, converted demons retain a measure of ambivalence, and Skanda the child-afflictor continued to live on, in both Buddhist and extra-Buddhist traditions, long after his divinity and protective qualities had been recognized. In addition to the club of fifteen goblins, he also belonged to an analogous group of twelve menacing demons with the same child-destroying tendencies. These twelve "seizers," though, are all feminine; Skandā, twelfth in the series, has undergone a change of sex. In the *Book of Rāvaṇa's Explanations of How to Cure the Ailments of Children* (*Lo-fo-nu shuo chiu-liao hsiao-erh chi-ping ching*, T. 1330), translated at the end of the tenth century, the twelve "planetary mother-demons" (the *gṛhamātṛkā*, "seizing" or "grasping mothers") are said to possess small children in order to extort offerings from their parents. Children are susceptible to them during the first twelve years of life, when they are still vulnerable and weak. The twelve planetary mother-demons roam about the world day and night, awaiting their chance to attack. When a child is sleeping, walking, or sitting, they will manifest themselves in a variety of horrific forms, terrify and disconcert the child, then gobble up its vital essence and breath, causing it to become ill and die an early death. Full of pity for such waifs, Rāvaṇa (himself a demon king, ruler of Ceylon) benevolently furnishes the reader with the particular year, month, day, hour, and minute when children are susceptible to each one of the twelve, together with a list of symptoms. He also provides the spells and describes the sacrifices by which the demonesses can be appeased and controlled, and the malady cured.[55]

In the case of the first demoness, for example, we are told that if a child shows signs of possession by a demon on the day of its birth, or during the first month or first year of its life, this means that it is possessed by the mother-demon Mātṛnandā. The victim suffers initially from chills and fever, its body becomes emaciated and dried out, its spirits are in confusion, it shivers and trembles, it cries and does not eat. The healer takes earth from both banks of a river and molds an image of the sick child. He places it inside a square ritual area (maṇḍala) facing west, together with aromatics, flowers, and white-colored food and drink (including wine and meat). Next he sets up seven banners and lights seven oil-lamps. Then he takes white mustard seeds, the dung of wild fox, the dung of kittens, Parthian incense (gum guggul), and sloughed-off snakeskin. He mixes these medicinal substances with curds from a brindled cow, making the mixture into incense pellets with which the child is to be fumigated. The child is then bathed in a decoction of leaves from five different kinds of trees. A spell is next pronounced over the offerings, and they are thrown away at midday in an easterly direction, at a place outside the town wall, as an offering to the demoness Mātṛnandā. Then the child will speedily recover.[56]

Such is the basic pattern. Mātṛnandā launches her attacks during the first day, month, or year, and each subsequent demoness is prone to attack during a subsequent day, month, and year of the child's first twelve years of life. In each case the treatment involves making an image of the victim and setting out offerings to the afflictor. The demoness is deemed to be lodging inside the child's body; therefore the offerings are placed before the image within the maṇḍala—an area completely under the spellbinder's jurisdiction. The child is next fumigated and bathed, and the offerings are cast away outside the town, away from human habitation. Such are the procedures to be followed in the event of an attack by the mother-demon Skandā during the twelfth day, month, or year of life. In this case, the chief symptom is a fixed and furious staring, as if the child wanted to attack someone, and clenching of the hands and feet. The spell-possessor should model the child's image in barley dough; the banners this time should be red, powdered cowhorn should be an ingredient of the fumigatory, and the consecrated offerings should be borne out of town at the hour of the Dog (7:00–9:00 P.M.) in an easterly direction, then carried around in all four directions before being thrown away.

This Chinese text is of special interest because it corresponds to a work still to be found in the standard Indian medical literature: *Rāvaṇa's Kumāra-tantra*, the subject of an important monograph by Jean Filliozat (1937). It forms part of a Sanskrit medical treatise composed around 1050, the *Cikitsāsaṃgraha*, and is also in circulation as a separate work in independent manuscripts as well as printed editions.[57] Though obviously the same book in all essentials, the Sanskrit and Chinese versions differ in many particulars about the names of the demonesses and the details of the offerings to be made to them. The final operation in each section of the Sanskrit text is the merit-producing meal to be offered to a brahman, a feature missing from the Chinese translation. It is evident that both versions must ultimately derive from a single Sanskrit original. The name of the twelfth demoness in the Sanskrit version is no longer Skandā but Kāmukhā ("the Face"). But this is in itself significant, for by this time Skanda's rank as a god was already so elevated that certain Indian authors refused to acknowledge his continuing role as a demon (also, one of Skanda's names is Ṣaṇmukha, 'Six-Faced"). Already in a classic treatise of secular Indian medicine, the *Suśrutasaṃhitā* (second or third century C.E.), we find a list of nine male "seizers" (*graha*) who attack children, and the first two of these are manifestations of Skanda: Skanda the Seizer and Skandāpasmāra ("Epilepsy"). The commentator Dalhaṇa declares that the seizer Skanda here mentioned is not identical with the god Skanda, who was brought up by the Pleiades (Kṛttikā) and therefore called Kārttikeya. But one wonders about these niceties of interpretation after reading, at the end of the section, the spell to be recited over the offerings: "To Agni [god of fire] and the Pleiades, *svāhā, svāhā*! Homage to Skanda, chief god of the Seizers, homage! Let my child be free from sickness, let there be no deterioration in his health, quickly!" As Filliozat remarks, despite Dalhaṇa's cautious distinction, the god invoked is Skanda, nursling of the Pleiades and chief of Śiva's demon-armies.[58]

There is certainly no doubt about Skanda's demonic nature or the seriousness of the symptoms he provokes in the pediatrics section of Vāgbhaṭa's *Aṣṭāṅgahṛdaya* (eighth century), an important secular medical treatise:

> The child attacked by Skanda will unquestionably remain crippled or else die. It may lose consciousness at any time, pull out its hair, bend its neck. It contracts its body, its mouth hangs agape, it voids feces and urine and foams at the mouth. Its eyes turn upward and its hands, eyebrows, and feet begin to dance. It bites its mother's breast or its own tongue, is completely agitated, runs a fever, stays awake, smells of pus and blood—such are the symptoms of epilepsy due to Skanda.[59]

It was as the son of Śiva and leader of the demon-armies that Skanda made his fortune. As a martial youth, defender of the righteous, he was recognized throughout India in many local and regional gods of analogous form and function. Thus he is known and worshipped today as Kārttikeya, Kumāra, Subrahmaṇya, Ṣaṇmukha, Mahāsena, Viśākha, Guha, Devasenāpati, and Murugan; he is the child of Fire and Water (Agni and the Ganges, or Śiva and

Pārvatī), cherished and brought up by the stars of the Pleiades. So widespread and influential is his cult that it is often described as a separate "religion"—the Kaumāra religion (from Kumāra, "the Youth"), one of the six "religions" of South India.[60] We have already noted the simplicity of his attributes; he bears a spear in his hand and rides a peacock (both the spear and the peacock-feather are standard instruments of exorcism). In many parts of South India, Skanda's cult is dominant; he is also the single most important god on the island of Sri Lanka, where Hindu-Buddhist interaction and conflict still continues, often violently. Though Skanda is there primarily the patron god of Tamil Hindus, he is usurping the place of the other guardian deities of Buddhism, and his cult is steadily gaining in strength, even among Buddhist Sinhalese. Other Sinhalese Buddhists take pleasure in observing how harshly the god treats his Tamil devotees, their enemies. He imposes self-torture, mutilation, and other painful ordeals in fulfillment of vows. He regularly manifests himself by taking forceful possession of his worshippers, especially during festivals at his great shrine of Kataragama. His essential character seems to be that of a dark, violent god.[61]

Thus a demonic and furious aspect remains at the core of the great patron deity, testifying to his ultimate demonic origins. It is the earlier conformation of this deified "demonality" that interests us and reveals the basic pattern, a pattern already clear in the medieval medical literature. Himself a child, he afflicted children, and did so through corporeal possession: Like called to like, and an infant demon was ideally suited for invading a child's body and taking over its personality. Skanda's presence was recognized by the wagging heads and shaking shoulders (*skanda*) of his victims. Once he had been tamed and invested with social responsibilities as commander of the gods' demon-armies, Skanda turned to philanthropic tasks, healing the same genre of afflictions that he previously had caused. His diagnosis and cure were effected through child-mediums, his incarnate representatives, whose wagging heads and shaking shoulders then betokened the god's presence.[62]

It would seem that the many-named Skanda had a role to play in the elaboration of the Tantric Buddhist *prasena*-figure. Whether or not research bears this out, his example can clearly help us understand the Buddhist analogies. Though I have not found a Prasena listed among the various demonic afflictors of children, it should by now be obvious that all the minor figures of Tantric Buddhism began their careers as demons or demonized godlings. We know that Prasena was envisioned as a youth, for Vajrabodhi's evocation of the divine messenger refers to him as such. There seems to be a logic and a satisfying structural consistency in this world of mediumship. The greater deities were, of course, duly embodied in their consecrated priests by means of a prescribed series of ritual operations. Thus empowered, the priest could act with the authority and efficacity of a buddha. Should he require information from an otherworldly figure of comparably high rank, the priest could invoke the deity into its own image, which had been consecrated and "animated" in a special ceremony when it was first placed on the altar. In this way the priest might converse with the deity, albeit in a way that was necessarily stately and reserved, in keeping both with the status of the divine figure invoked and with the rules of decorum. In cases where more immediate action was called for and no limits were to be set on interrogation, a humbler, more accessible informant was needed and a less august vehicle required. Thus in treating the ordinary crises of mundane life, the most suitable personnel were child-mediums and the child-gods that possessed them. In this scenario, the adult priest maintained and reaffirmed his authority as a buddha, bodhisattva, or king of spells (a buddha-reflex) while the child was cast in the role of an otherworldly juvenile: a mercurial, ambivalent being, part god, part demon.

We continue to find child-mediums serving as vehicles for child-gods in medieval Japan, particularly for a class of minor divinities known as *gōhō* (Chinese *hu-fa*, "protectors of the Law"). These (not always benign) youthful guardians were thought to cluster around the faithful and were especially attached to their sacred books. As we have already seen, medieval scriptures, Taoist as well as Buddhist, were all accompanied by their own complement of guardian spirits, whom Taoists called "jade youths" and "jade maidens." Upon formal transmission of a scripture, its invisible protectors were officially transferred to the text's new possessor and served him as bodyguards. Owing to the special richness of Japanese sources, many cases are on record of the activities of these guardian deities. Like Skanda, they were visualized as youthful gods with military attributes. They would often be glimpsed aiding the faithful at moments of crisis, but their usual method of communicating with those they protected was through possession, usually of a boy, a servant, or a woman.[63]

The importance of such guardian figures in East Asia was not simply imposed from above; the divine youths also evoked a powerful resonance in Chinese tradition. The youthful guardian-spirits that accompanied Taoist texts may have been inspired by their Buddhist analogues, co-promoters of the "cult of the book." But both Buddhist and Taoist guardians drew strength from an older belief in divinely inspired children: innocents whose casual words and ditties might well prove prophetic, even for great affairs of state. Serious official attention was devoted to boys' rhyming songs; who could be sure that a god did not speak through the mouths of babes? These ancient beliefs also entered the textual tradition of Buddhism and Taoism. We have already seen the *Demon-Statutes of Nü-ching* predict, as an apocalyptic sign, that the planets Mars and Venus (both associated with war) would descend into the world and utter dire prophecies through the mouths of children (see p. 86). It was the same belief that exalted the figure of the Holy Fool in medieval Buddhist and Taoist hagiography. Texts celebrated the hidden merits of young, half-witted monks who performed the vilest tasks in the monastery (cleaning latrines, for example) and babbled seeming nonsense, yet who proved in the end to be far wiser and holier than the socially eminent spiritual masters who exploited them. In such instances, the "medium" of a god-filled vessel has inverted the roles of master and simpleton; clearly, in a hierarchized monastic situation, the holy fools speak for the younger monks.[64] In the nonhierarchical conditions of modern Taiwan and Chinese Southeast Asia, however, the mediums ("oracle-youths") are mainly young men under the control of "red-head priests" (*hung-t'ou*, lay exorcists); they are likened to marionettes controlled by a puppet-master and are said not to live long.[65]

Elsewhere in Asia, vestiges of the Tantric Buddhist system are still preserved. Tibetan Buddhism is governed by incarnations, and the great bodhisattvas and saints are alive today among the Tibetan hierarchy. Within this framework, there are also institutionalized lineages of spirit possession. The professional oracle-priests of Tibetan Buddhism are known for the regularity of their possession-seizures, the exalted character of the gods that speak through them, and their onetime importance in the conduct of Tibetan state policy. They have even been studied from a neuro-psychiatric perspective. But perhaps the most celebrated example of institutionalized possession in the Buddhist world today is the living goddess of Nepal, the Kumārī, incarnate in a succession of little girls. The goddess originally manifested herself about 1750 among the Newars, the older, majority population of the Kathmandu valley. Her first incarnation was the seven-year-old daughter of a Banra family; significantly, the Banra are the married descendants of the old Tantric Buddhist Saṅgha, the former monks and nuns of Nepal. With the Gurkha invasion of 1768, which occurred during the night of the goddess's annual festival, when the citizens of Kathmandu were too fuddled to defend themselves, the Kumārī entered the larger world of state Hinduism. The military aspect of this cult of state-affirming possession is represented by the presence of soldiers in ancient, ragged uniforms at the present-day festival, alongside members of the Nepalese army in up-to-date, modern gear.[66] The Kumārī may therefore stand as a fitting emblem of the phenomenon we have been considering: ever youthful, still alive and manifest in our own time, and mingling (as the student of these matters is also obliged to do in his researches) the substance of Buddhism with other elements welling up, as it were, from the local soil. The permeability of children, their aptitude for mediumship, has been built into Buddhist therapy; it is reflected in the pantheon, and in Buddhist social institutions as well.[67]

6

TANTRISTS, FOXES, AND SHAMANS

Amoghavajra on 'Āveśa'

The largest body of literature left by any of the three great Tantric masters of eighth-century China was the work of Amoghavajra. There are variant accounts of the early life of this prodigious figure.[1] He is said to have been the son of a North Indian Brahman (though some say his family came originally from Sogdiana, in Chinese Central Asia), and was born in Ceylon in 705. At all events, by 723 Amoghavajra was at work in Lo-yang, China's Eastern Capital. He traveled to Ceylon and India during the years 741–46, then returned to the Western Capital, Ch'ang-an. Apart from short trips within China, he stayed in Ch'ang-an for the rest of his life, settling into the Ta-hsing-shan monastery in 756, where he went on with his writing and religious practice. Amoghavajra received lavish patronage from three emperors and attracted numerous Chinese disciples. He died at his Ch'ang-an monastery in 774.

The modern Sino-Japanese Buddhist canon contains 168 books credited to Amoghavajra; 167 name him as translator, and one (T. 1798) as author. His disciples, too, were responsible for a number of important translations and other works, including a great dictionary of Buddhist terms, *Sounds and Meanings of All the Scriptures* (*I-ch'ieh ching yin-i*, T. 2128), which is a cornerstone of Buddhist philology, and a collection of official documents written by Amoghavajra himself to the court (*Kuang-chih san-tsang ho-shang piao-chih chi*, T. 2120), a work of fundamental importance for Buddhist economic history. Clearly, Amoghavajra and his school made a massive contribution to Chinese Buddhism.

The most curious feature of Amoghavajra's scholarly activity concerns his 167 "translations." Properly speaking, many of these were not translations at all. Instead, they might better be called "adaptations"; essentially, he refurbished Tantric texts that had already been translated into Chinese so as to bring them into line with his own terminology and ritual practice. This becomes even more striking in those cases where texts "translated" by Amoghavajra are now known to have been written in China centuries earlier, and directly in Chinese. A substantial part of Amoghavajra's output thus comprises revisions of books already known in China, rather than new materials. Among the remainder, a good many cannot be found either in corresponding Sanskrit manuscripts or in Tibetan translations—at least not in the form in which Amoghavajra presents them. Much of what his texts tell us unquestionably goes back to Indian sources; he was clearly working fully within the Tantric Buddhist tradition, but often more as an author or compiler than as a translator in our sense of the term. This only makes his books more interesting to us, however, since they frequently record actual practice and oral tradition.

One work of this sort, codified in writing by Amoghavajra, is entitled *Instantly Efficacious Āveśa Ritual Explained by Maheśvara* (*Su-chi li-yen Mo-hsi-shou-lo t'ien shuo a-wei-she fa*, T. 1277). Maheśvara ("the Great God") is Śiva, chief of the non-Buddhist pantheon, ruler of the gods of India.[2] The text opens with a visit to Śiva by another god, Nārāyaṇa (Viṣṇu). Nārāyaṇa tells Śiva that his own mount, the great bird Garuḍa, also fulfills the role of heavenly messenger and is able to attend to all the requests that humans make of him—only Nārāyaṇa himself is unable to accomplish them quickly. Nārāyaṇa therefore asks Śiva to expound for the benefit of future generations a more expeditious procedure: the Āveśa Ritual of Swift and Instant Accomplishment.

Śiva does this willingly. The ritual can be carried out in any one of the four basic modes of Tantric ritual action: cessation of ills (*śāntika*), increase of benefits (*pauṣṭika*), subjugation of enemies (*abhicāraka*), and conciliation of friends (*vaśīkaraṇa*).[3] By this means, too, one can send messengers to and from Yama's kingdom of the dead, just as we saw Vajrabodhi doing on behalf of the emperor's daughter (see p. 208). One may thereby also come to know future auspicious and inauspicious events, success and failure; one may learn of drought and inundations, aggression by neighboring states, rebellions by wicked persons, and all manner of good and evil portents. If you wish to know the future, you should select four or five virgin girls or boys of about seven or eight years of age. Their bodies should be without blemish, and they should be perceptive and intelligent. As a preliminary, you should have them eat only vegetarian food for seven days (or if you prefer, three days). Whenever you wish to perform the ritual, you should choose an auspicious day when the moon is in the lunar mansions of either the constellation called "Demon" or the "Year Star" (Jupiter). Best of all is a day on which sweet dew has fallen ("sweet dew" was a long-standing Chinese portent of greatest auspiciousness; the term was used as an equivalent for the Sanskrit *amṛta*, the "beverage of immortality," and usually designates manna-like substances found on coniferous or other trees). Bathe the children and rub their bodies all over with incense. Dress them in pure garments and have them hold in their mouths the aromatic wood Dragon's Brain (*Dryobalanops aromatica*) and the herb *tou-k'ou* (*Alpinia globosum*, or "Chinese cardamon," still a widely used breath-purifier).

The spell-possessor sits facing west. In front of him should be a small ritual area plastered with white sandalwood incense, perhaps a yard square. Have the children stand within this area. Strew flowers and set a vessel of consecrated water before them. Take Parthian incense (gum guggul), empower it with the spell of the Great Seal (*mahāmudrā*), ignite it and fumigate the children's hands with it. Next take red flowers, empower them seven times with the spell, and place them in the children's hands. Then have them cover their eyes with their hands. The spell-possessor next forms the Great Seal: This is done by joining both palms, with fingers meeting and interlocking; the fingers of the left hand press down on those of the right, leaving the palm hollow. With this seal one empowers the five places of one's own body (the forehead, left and right shoulders, heart and throat). The practitioner then disperses this seal at the crown of his head and recites a mantra (given in the text). Next he uses the finger-seal once again, this time pressing it on the crown of the children's heads. Above their heads he visualizes a red triangular flaming Fire-emblem as he recites seven times the mantra of the Fire Sign. He then moves the seal to their hearts and visualizes the square, yellow emblem of Earth, reciting the corresponding mantra. Pressing the seal on their navels, he visualizes the Wind-emblem, round and black. At the legs, he visualizes the Garuḍa bird and chants its mantra. Then (still forming the Great Seal) he empowers the children's entire bodies by intoning the mantra of the Protective Armor (*kavaca-mantra*, to protect all participants from the force that he is about to evoke—a standard procedure).

Having done all this by way of preparation, the master turns himself into the god Maheśvara (Śiva). He has three eyes and wears on his head an ornate cap with pendants. This headgear is crowned by the image of a buddha in a crescent moon. His throat is blue and he has eighteen arms, each of which holds a different sort of implement or weapon. His robe is girded by a dragon and secured by knotting the dragon's horns. In addition, he holds a blood-smeared elephant hide (this determines the ritual area's dimensions, as did the ox-hide in the *prasena*-ritual: see pp. 211–14). In an instant the officiant should visualize his own body in this way; then, using the Great Seal and the appropriate spell, he applies protection to the 108 life-nodes on the bodies of those children. With the same seal and spell, he next empowers the offerings (flowers, incense, consecrated water, etc). Then, still using the same seal and spell, the master "knots" the worlds of all ten directions.

After all these preparations, he is at last ready to summon the spirit, called "Maheśvara's messenger." Facing the children, the master intones a special mantra seven times. The children will begin to tremble, and by this sign he knows that the Holy One has entered their bodies. When this has taken place, he is to snap his fingers and recite the mantra again. But if the looked-for manifestation does not occur, then he should recite a special mantra for harassing and compelling the messenger; this will speedily get results. He may then ask about future good and evil, and all favorable and unfavorable omens. If the messenger does not speak, or speaks too slowly, the master should form the mudrā of the Stick and threaten the spirit with that hand-posture and the corresponding mantra. Then he can ask about whatever he wishes to know. When this has been done, the Great Seal and its spell should be used to empower the consecrated water, which is then to be sprinkled three times over the children; they will at once be released.

Should you have previously recited the messenger's mantra ten thousand times, he will appear to you in person. You must then present him with consecrated water and state your wish: that you desire that the Holy One henceforth, in all places and at all times, attend to all your needs. He will then vanish and no longer be visible. When on a subsequent occasion you wish to employ him, prepare a small ritual area, place on it incense, flowers, food and drink, recite his mantra 108 times, and he will appear to you. Then you can instruct him to obtain for you the drug of long life or the precious wishing-pearl in the undersea palace of the dragons. Or you may send him to Yama's realm to prolong your term of life and increase your span of years. Or you may send him up into the heavens to obtain fine sweet dew (that is, *amṛta*, the drink of immortality), or to foreign countries to inquire about their strengths and weaknesses. He can also aid an army against its enemies; indeed, he is able to carry out every assignment. This rite is especially excellent among all the rites of Garuḍa. It is secret and hard to obtain. Therefore one ought to transmit it only after carefully selecting a proper "ritual vessel" (i.e., a worthy recipient). If conveyed to an unsuitable person it will do him harm, and afterward the ritual will not work for the transmitter either. For this reason it must be kept in the greatest secrecy and not be passed on irresponsibly. The text then presents Śiva's own Garuḍa-dhāraṇī, and informs the reader how that spell can be used to subjugate an enemy. One should paint the enemy's picture on a red banana-leaf, write his name on the figure's heart, recite the dhāraṇī 108 times, bury the image in cow dung, and the enemy will be overcome. The text concludes with several other practical instructions of this sort.

Such is the "most excellent of all Garuḍa rites." A number of other Tantric rituals were placed under the wing, so to speak, of this great bird. Amoghavajra also translated a Garuḍa book dealing largely with relief from snakebite, a text later incorporated into an influential Tantric scripture, the *Mañjuśrīmūla-kalpa*.[4] Garuḍa was known as a source of healing spells to the entire Tantric world, and Waddell reproduces a Tibetan blockprint charm displaying a full-faced Garuḍa that holds up in its beak and claws a plate, on which is inscribed a mantra against various ailments, evil spirits, and injuries.[5] But this *āveśa* procedure is actually put forward as a means of replacing Garuḍa and achieving the speed and immediacy that the cumbrous airborne messenger is unable to attain; in fact, it represents a more advanced technology. The emphasis on rapidity which even the ritual's title proclaims—"Instantly Efficious *āveśa*"—conforms to the earlier spirit-possession techniques that we studied in Chapter 5. Unlike many other ritual operations, the use of child-mediums gives immediate results. The procedure as a whole is generally like the earlier ones, with various individual touches: Instead of being blindfolded by the master, the children seal their own eyes by holding up the red flowers in their hands, and so on. But there does seem to be a change of emphasis in the possessing spirit's range of functions. The reader is told that if he recites the spell of Śiva's messenger ten thousand times, the spirit will appear to him directly, without the need for intermediaries. The use of child-mediums thus seems to be presented as a preliminary technique to promote contact and familiarity between the master and Śiva's messenger. Once the master, self-transformed into Śiva, has completed the full program of spell-recitations, the messenger will become truly his own, and he will be able to employ him for all his worldly and otherworldly needs.

Though in real life Amoghavajra seems never to have lacked for willing disciples and devoted retainers, the acquisition of otherworldly servants seems to have been of special interest to him. We find a similar emphasis in his two versions of the basic scripture on the rituals of the deity dubbed "the Immovable One" (Acala). In the translation of this work made by Vajrabodhi (*Pu-ting shih-che t'o-lo-ni pi-mi-fa*, T. 1202), there are instructions for performing *āveśa* by having the spirit of a dragon enter the child-medium. The child then describes what it beholds in a mirror suspended over Acala's heart in a painted image of that deity (see pp. 206–7). As in the earlier text, Amoghavajra's recensions call upon the great dragon-king Kulika and Acala's sword to work the wonder of possession. After describing a variety of procedures that will enable the fortunate spell-possessor to achieve a wide assortment of ends, from obtaining celestial maidens and high offices of state to annihilating his enemies, the text instructs him to paint on the wall the image of a sword with the dragon Kulika twined about it. He is then to recite Acala's spell a thousand times and visualize the seed-syllable *Aḥ* within the sword, sending forth an awe-inspiring radiance. If you cause a sick person to look at it, there will immediately be *āveśa*; he will truthfully inform you about whatever you ask him. In this case, then, the possession is induced in the patient himself, and his indwelling disease-demon is forced to speak out, compelled by the fearsome dragon and Acala's demon-dispelling sword.

The text goes on to specify that offerings of leftovers should be made regularly to Acala and set in a pure place for him. He will then faithfully serve you in every undertaking, evidently bound to your service by this sharing of scraps from your own meals, like a household retainer (as is true of other deities, like Ucchuṣma and Hārītī).[6] The text proceeds to tell of still other wonders, returning briefly to the theme of *āveśa*: "Or again, there is another method for using virgin boys or girls who are not sick to perform the *āveśa* rites, to ask about all things in the past, present, and future, and thereby to determine the proper course of action." But then this inconstant text reverts once more to the many functions that can be found for the faithful servant Acala, for the spellbinder can actually deal with him directly, without intermediaries, which is no doubt advisable in cases where he is to be employed on delicate missions, such as carrying off the consorts and handmaidens of the god Indra for your delectation. For that matter, he will even attend to your far less ambitious needs, like keeping you supplied with tooth-cleaning sticks and pure water, not to mention dealing with your cleaning and sweeping. He is truly a god-of-all-work.[7]

There is a little more detail in the second Amoghavajra text (*Ti-li san-mei-yeh pu-tung tsun wei-nu-wang shih-che nien-sung fa*, T. 1200):

> Paint the great snake Kuka [i.e., Kulika] wrapped around the sword. All around the sword, paint flames. Intone Acala's mantra over it one thousand times. If you then show it to the sick person, he will at once speak of his own accord [i.e., the possessing demon will speak, admitting his identity, etc.]. If you pronounce Acala's mantra 108 times over a sick person, he will thenceforth always be under the Holy One's protection. If you pronounce it every day over the leftovers from your meals, and set them in a pure place, the Messenger will always do whatever you wish.[8]

A bit farther on, we read, "If you recite the mantra over someone suffering from intermittent fever, it will cause him to bind himself and speak; or again, enchant a mirror with the mantra, and the Holy One will appear within it and answer whatever you ask him; or again, take a young boy (or girl), bathe him, clothe him in fresh garments, and place him inside the ritual area. Summon the Holy One to enter the area, empower the child with his mantra, and you will obtain answers to anything you ask."[9] This is followed by instructions for accomplishing the "ritual of Kiṃkara":

> At noon on the first day, place before the image of Acala various sorts of incense, flowers, and other offerings, and recite Acala's mantra 108 times without stopping; visualize that all the buddhas and bodhisattvas have come down into the ritual area and are giving you their commands. Recite and visualize in this manner for a full month. Then take sticks of aromatic wood of bitter niṃba (*Melia azedarach*) and arka-wood (*Calotropis gigantea*), smear butter on them, empower them with the mantra, and burn them in a fire. Do this from the hour of the Dog to the hour of the Rat, or even to the hour of the Tiger [7:00 to 11:00 P.M., or 3 A.M.]. Then Kiṃkara will arrive and say to the practitioner, "What is it that you want me to do?" Then give him your commands. Afterward he will always do whatever you wish and obediently provide you with everything you require: food and drink, tooth-

> cleaning sticks, pure water, and so on. He will always be at your side, and you can even send him up into the heavens to bring back celestial maidens for you.[10]

"Kiṃkara" simply means "slave"; it was the name of one of Śiva's attendants, and Kiṃkara and Ceṭaka (also meaning "slave") came to be described as the two leading figures in Acala's troop of eight boy-servants.[11] Through intense identification with Acala, the spell-possessor can evidently transfer Kiṃkara to his own service and so considerably simplify his life. Once again, the fascination of the supernatural servant is upon us. We are beguiled by the prospect of gaining as a reward for our unstinting devotion to ritual a divine personal valet, a famulus or factotum who will uncomplainingly undertake expeditions on our behalf to the heights of heaven or the bottom of the sea, and who will pander—quite literally—to our every whim. In these wonderful spirit-messengers we seem to have an anticipation of the omnicompetent Djinn of the *Thousand and One Nights* (or the Golem of Jewish folklore).[12]

Another product of Amoghavajra's atelier (*I-tzu ch'i-t'e fo-ting ching*, T. 953) offers a method designed for use by those of lesser ability and feebler gifts; it enables even the meekest, mildest practitioner to gain full control over demons, whether through a medium or directly in the body of the afflicted person. This is all done by means of the fingers, starting from a "basic seal." In this mudrā, the fingers of both hands are interlocked in a double closed fist, from which the two middle fingers project and are bent at the first joint; both thumbs also project, and the two first fingers, bent at the second joint, press against the bases of the thumbs. This "best of all seals" is the starting point. To begin operations, one stiffens both thumbs so that they are not in contact with the backs of the two first fingers: This causes *āveśa*. Moving them about causes the patient, or medium, to fall down. Striking them together forces him to speak. Intertwining them makes him dance. It is all as simple as that; through proper use of these digital semaphores, one can readily gain control over all possessing demons.[13]

In this way, indecorous physical exertion on the part of the spellbinder could be kept to a minimum. Elsewhere in the vast Amoghavajra corpus, there are also indications that *āveśa* might even be realized internally by the practitioner with considerable benefit to himself. A passage in Amoghavajra's version of the *Compendium of Truth of All the Tathāgatas* (*Sarvatathāgata-tattva-saṃgraha*, T. 865) tells the meditator that when he forms a particular mudrā and pronounces a certain hundred-syllable mantra there will be *āveśa* (possession), and he will experience a subtle and marvelous cognition. In this state he will become aware of what is in the hearts of others; he will know the past, present, and future state of all things. His mind will attain certainty in the teachings of all the buddhas, whereupon he will achieve perfect samādhi (concentration), the Portal of all Dhāraṇīs (i.e., comprehensive memory, or total recall), or whatever else he desires.[14] Thus the Tantric master may ultimately become his own medium, able to achieve the entire program single-handedly; possessed by the deity, he embodies total omniscience and the plenitude of wish-fulfillment.

Yet another book from Amoghavajra's hand, the *Pei-fang P'i-sha-men t'ien-wang sui-chün hu-fa chen-yen* (T. 1248), transports us back to the world of violent action and dramatic display. It centers on the powerful spell of Vaiśravaṇa, ruler of the north and general of the Buddha's demon-armies.[15] Amid diverse counsels, the text states that should one wish to see events in a mirror, Vaiśravaṇa's spell is to be recited over virgin boys or girls. One may ask them about things of good or evil omen; or a sick person will himself begin to speak, and can be made to state the name of the demon that is afflicting him. Once the cause of his ailment is known, if his food has been poisoned by virulent magic (*ku-tu*), then Vaiśravaṇa's spell should be recited twenty-one times over the food, and the victim will at once vomit up whatever has been poisoning him. If he has been made ill by a demon, the spell should be recited over threads of the five colors as they are plaited together, one knot per each recitation, 108 times. If the plaited cord is then attached to the crown of his head and his upper arm, all his ailments will at once be cured. If he suffers from pains in his heart, the spell should be recited over pomegranate juice, and when he drinks it he will be cured. If you wish to overcome a case of fox-goblin possession, recite the spell over thread of the five colors while having a boy plait them into a cord, one knot for each recitation, 108 times. Attach it to the patient's neck. Recite the spell once more over a poplar branch, beat the patient with it, and he will at once be cured. If he is plagued by aches and pains in the bones and joints, recite the spell over a damascened sword and exorcise (*chin*) the ailment with it; the cure will follow immediately. The text describes other lotions, potions, and compresses for a variety of complaints, but beating is once more resorted to in treating cases of recurrent fever: Twenty-one recitations of the spell over a poplar branch, then using it to administer a beating to the patient brings instant recovery. For sudden demonic possession that causes the victim to speak madly and utter wild, extravagant words, the spell is to be recited over water, which the patient then drinks. But for demonic bewitchments in general, the prescription consists of reciting Vaiśravaṇa's spell 108 times over a pomegranate branch, with which you then beat the victim soundly.[16]

Evidently the great Amoghavajra was comfortable at both ends of the Tantric spectrum; no doubt he could equally well meditate himself into an omniscient state of auto-possession and thrash his demon-infested patients when the situation required it. In the following century, drama and violence gained additional textual authorization from the translation of another large book of spells by two Indian monks, Prājña and Muniśrī, sometime between 800 and 806. This work (*Shou-hu kuo-chieh chu t'o-lo-ni ching*, T. 997) gives instructions for using children as mediums to gaze into an object and describe what they see there (as in the *Questions of Subāhu*, examined in Chapter 5). Suitable objects are a sword, a mirror, a wall, the fingers, the palm of the hand, a lamp, an image of the Buddha, water-crystal, the ritual area itself, or lapis lazuli; in any one of these you can have the medium see whatever you wish. After the usual preparation of the site, the child should be selected: either a boy or a girl, unblemished, pure, and undefiled. The child should be bathed and dressed in fresh white garments, and a special spell, provided in the text, should be chanted over it. Thereupon Vajrapāṇi, the revealer of this text, states that he will personally come and manifest himself in the body of the medium.[17] In this way, information can be obtained about the past, present, and future; doubts can be resolved and decisions made accordingly:

> If it is a case of possession by a demon of falling frenzy [that is, epilepsy, identified as a form of madness], you should take a poplar branch or a pomegranate branch and empower it seven times with the foregoing mantra. Burn Parthian incense (gum guggul) and draw that demon's image on the ground. Then have the boy take the poplar branch and beat the picture of the demon you have drawn on its breast, its back, and elsewhere. The patient will act as if his own body is being beaten—he will howl, shout, wail and weep, strike his head on the ground, and beg for mercy, saying, "From now on, I will never presume to come again!" Then the master makes the demon swear an oath: "If I should ever come here again, I vow that I and my entire family shall be annihilated with no survivors!" After the demon has sworn the oath that he will never come back, the patient will immediately return to normal. Not only will the sickness have left him, but he will be better than ever before in all respects.[18]

Although the procedures of voluntary, therapeutic spirit-possession classically involve the use of a healthy medium, such evidence suggests that these procedures might also be applied directly to the patient. This method must have been resorted to in those cases where the patient was suffering from one of the more dramatic forms of demonic affliction, especially madness or epilepsy. These ailments were generally viewed as cases of possession in the narrow, pathological sense of the term. The demon in the victim's body gave proof of its presence not only through ulcers or fever; its indwelling was displayed in the patient's irrational or violent actions, or in his illogical or unintelligible speech. Such cases demanded treatment by the firm authority of the Tantric master; if he was able to call down celestial spirits into children for diagnosis, he should succeed equally well in compelling the mean, diabolic creatures of disease to confess their identities and skulk away in confusion. In addition to his dramatic use of child-mediums, then, the master might operate directly on the patient when the force and obstreperousness of the indwelling demon dictated a direct confrontation. To better understand the context of such encounters, we should first turn from Tantric scriptures to medieval handbooks of Chinese medicine. There we may be able to learn something more about Chinese views of demonic possession and its treatment.[19]

Madness in the Medical Literature

Much information on pathological possession is given in the Chinese medical literature under the headings of "madness" or "frenzy." There is also a special category of "sexual congress with demons." But there are a number of other aberrant states that can be drawn into the category of possession as well. A good point of departure is furnished by the collection of remedies assembled by Ko Hung (283–343), the *Prescriptions Within Arm's Reach for Use in Emergencies* (*Chou-hou pei-chi fang*, HY 1295). Though in its present form this work includes the commentary of T'ao Hung-ching (456–536) as well as additions by a twelfth-century editor, its nucleus certainly goes back to the fourth century and was much drawn upon by later writers (see pp. 24–25). It includes a number of relevant entries.

For example, a comatose state is described, resembling death and no doubt leading to death if not speedily treated, termed "demon-possession sleep" (*ya-mei*, or *ya-wo mei*). The condition is due to the patient's ethereal and spermatic souls being held in duress, during their nocturnal roaming outside his body, by malevolent wraiths encountered along the way. The souls are temporarily unable to find their way back to their prostrate host. Should you discover someone in this condition, you are above all not to bring a light into his vicinity, since that would terrify his night-roving souls; they would then flee for good, and all would be lost. Thus while maintaining a reassuring darkness about him, you should employ a safe means of awakening the sleeper, and the text offers a remarkable variety of methods for doing so. Painfully biting the heel of his foot or the base of the nail of his big toe, followed by spitting in his face, will speedily bring him back to life. One may also try tickling his nose by any number of means, holding his head down a well (i.e., in darkness) while calling out his name, or putting an earthenware pot over his face (darkness again) and having someone beat on it till it breaks—all ways of awakening him. Or one may place in his mouth the ashes of a written paper talisman, mixed with water; a mirror is then to be suspended next to his ear and struck while calling out the victim's name. This treatment is said to bring the patient back to life in less than half a day.

Since here the problem concerns a loss of souls outside the body (we have considered a similar case of "pathological dreaming": see pp. 209–10), it may not seem initially to fall into the category of pathological possession. The absent souls have been captured, no doubt at some distance from the sleeping body. But one of the recommended methods of treatment clearly suggests that the souls' absence has left room for alien invaders to take over the vacant body—and the treatment prescribed is closely analogous to the ritual procedures in which we are interested:

> Place the victim on the ground, and with a sharp sword draw a circle in the earth around his head, going to the left in the case of a man, the right in that of a woman [these are standard Chinese directional correspondences]. Then with the point of the sword make an inch-deep incision in the victim's nose. Quickly hold him fast so that he does not move. He will then speak in the voice of the possessing spirit and implore mercy. Ask him, "Who are you?" "Why have you come?" [Having answered,] he will beg you to let him depart. Then with your hand rub out the circle you have made about the victim's head, a few inches above the shoulders, and let the demon go away. But you must not do so without having fully interrogated him.[20]

The show of force and the systematic interrogation are crucial, whether the demon is already lodged within the patient's body or has in fact been compelled into the body by the healer from wherever the seizure of the souls took place (thus turning the patient into his own passive medium). Nor does the healer scruple to attack the patient's body directly with his demon-dispelling sword.

We next proceed to the ailments properly styled "frenzy" or "madness"; the Chinese terms are *tien* and *k'uang* (the term *hsien* is also used for *tien* in small children). Ko Hung's collection states that in all cases of *tien*, the sufferer falls prostrate, drools, and loses consciousness. When beaten, he arises and acts as if mad (*k'uang*). If he eats his own excrement, he will be hard to cure.[21] The distinctions made by medieval diagnosticians between *tien* and *k'uang* tend to show that *tien* corresponds to an epileptic fit, or "falling frenzy" as we may call it (cf. our "falling sickness"; the Chinese word is cognate to a homophonous word meaning "falling"), whereas *k'uang* designates persons carried away by manic fits and rages. But this distinction is not always clearly maintained in the sources.[22] Mad saints and holy fools, for example, may be either *tien* or *k'uang*.[23] As for the pediatric term *hsien*, it evidently corresponds to convulsive colic. The associations of these several maladies with ideas about demonic possession also appear to vary with the circumstances. Analysis of the therapeutic procedures may bring rigor to the nosological categories.

The first prescription given by Ko Hung against falling frenzy consists of cauterization with three sticks of moxa at the shallow depression just above the penis. When the subject urinates, he will be cured. Or again, three sticks of moxa are to be burnt just above the penis, and two groups of seven along the seam beneath the testicles. Or again, three sticks on each nipple, seven in the clump of hair at the base of the big toe. The next prescription represents a different approach. Take a pint of the plant *Draba nemorosa* and pound it with three thousand pestle-strokes. Take a white dog, suspend it upside down, and beat it till the blood comes out. Take the blood, mix with the draba-powder, and form it into pellets the size of hemp seeds. Administer three of them, and the patient will recover.

The focus on the sexual organs is of potential interest; and white dogs are the preferred non-Taoist, non-Buddhist offering in China to certain classes of spirits, notably mountain-gods. Another method is to administer three pinches of the ashes of a rope used by someone to hang himself. Also suggestive are two prescriptions that make use of henbane (*Hyocyamus niger*). Three pints of henbane seeds are to be steeped in five pints of wine, then dried in the sun. They are then to be crushed and a spoonful administered to the patient thrice daily—and no more than this, otherwise it will intensify rather than diminish his seizures. Another henbane-powder for falling frenzy can be produced by steeping three pints of pulverized henbane in a pint of wine for many days. Then remove the henbane, pound it, mix it again with the juice, press out the liquid, and steam the henbane over boiling water until malleable. Mold it into pellets the size and shape of small beans and administer three per day. The patient should show perceptible twitching around the mouth or elsewhere on the face. He should have the sensation that insects are moving about in his head, and there should be redness in places on his forehead, hands, and feet. If such is the case, these are signs that he will certainly recover. If these signs do not appear, he should still continue taking the pellets until all have been consumed.[24]

In cases of madness (*k'uang*), we are told, the patient wants to run about or run away. Sometimes he exalts himself, claiming to be a god or sage. In all such cases the full range of cauterizations should be applied to achieve a permanent cure. But an important distinction is made here. If the patient, rather than exhibiting such delusions of grandeur, weeps and laments and groans, this means that he is possessed by a malignant wraith (*hsieh*) or goblin (*mei*) and not madness (*k'uang*). The sufferer should then be treated using methods appropriate for dealing with malignant demons, instead of the procedures against madness. It would therefore seem that the essential distinction being made is between mania (exaltation, delusions of grandeur, hyperactivity), which qualifies as "madness," and depressive symptoms, which are classed as demonic possession.

This rule of thumb might be useful if it were consistently applied, but once again the prescriptions reveal a good deal of ambiguity. A sudden attack of "madness" may be treated by having the patient drink, thrice daily, a spoonful of calcined toad steeped in wine. Or one may lay the victim on the ground and pour cold water over his face, continuing the whole day. Yet how, then, should we classify a sudden outbreak of "madness" such as that described in the next entry, in which the patient "speaks demon language"? He should be treated by inserting an acupuncture needle a little way into his big toe, just below the nail, which will stop the attack. Or you may quickly bind his hands with the rope that girds a rice-steamer (such ropes themselves sometimes figured as medicine) and apply seven cauteries to his left and right ribs, and to the places where the veins stand out on his hands, forearms, and head. In a short while the demon will speak, declare his name, and beg leave to depart.

First interrogate him very carefully, and only then unbind the patient's hands.[25] To treat sudden attacks of malignant demons in which the victim is delirious, strikes out at people, and curses, apply cauteries in the depression just below the nose and at the base of the nails of both big toes; use two series of seven moxa-pellets, burning without a break, and the patient will be cured.[26]

With Ko Hung's next prescription, we move into the closely related domain of sexual possession. The text addresses the problem of a woman having sexual intercourse with a malignant creature. Her symptoms are talking to herself, laughing to herself, and showing signs of depression and/or delirium. Grind up an ounce of sulphur and steep it in two ounces of pine-resin. Mix together, stirring with a tiger claw. Form the mixture into pills the size of crossbow pellets. At night, put one into a brazier and ignite it. Have the woman sit naked on the brazier and cover her completely with a coverlet, allowing only her head to protrude. Up to three pellets may be burned. An alternative treatment uses a mixture of sulphur, ginseng, the plant "wind-resister" (*Siler divaricatum*, or possibly *Peucedanum rigidum*), and anise-seeds. A pint of this potion should be stirred, strained, and a spoonful taken at dawn with freshly drawn well water. Three doses will cure the complaint.[27]

There follows a far more dramatic mode of treatment for the same ailment:

> The master goes out of the room and inserts five needles in his topknot. He then puts water in a vessel, places three strips of new red cloth over it, and sets a long sword flat across the top. When all this has been carefully arranged, he calls out the patient's name. She will try to get up and run away, but by no means allow her to do so! Next take a mouthful of water and spew it out at her, as you stare furiously at her. This should be done three times. Then wipe away the water from her face, snap your fingers three times above her forehead near the hairline, and ask, "Do you want to be cured?" She will certainly not be willing to answer. But after doing this and snapping your fingers twice seven times, she will answer. Then you should insert a needle immediately below her nose close to the inside of the nostrils. Fix one needle at the pivot of the jaw below the base of the ear. In addition, directly up from the nose, entering one inch beyond the hairline, fix a needle, and also one just above the nose. Then cross-examine her thoroughly. She will gradually be restored to consciousness, and the possession will come to an end.[28]

The element of surprise is evidently crucial in forcing the patient to emerge from her auto-erotic stupor. The acupuncture needles are to be hidden in the healer's bound-up hair, where he can rapidly pull them out and insert them at the climax of the interrogation. Ko Hung's manual is expressly directed toward nonspecialist laymen—readers without either learned medical qualifications or the ritual expertise of a qualified Taoist or Buddhist master. From this last set of instructions, we can confirm that Ko Hung was drawing on an ancient Chinese tradition of exorcism that Taoist and Buddhists also incorporated into their rituals. In studying the exorcistic rites of ensigillation used by both Buddhist monks and Taoist priests, we also found both the sword and the vessel of water; there too, the practitioner spewed forth water on the patient and in some cases used analogous techniques of interrogation. These elements can also be discovered in the recently excavated manuscripts of the second and third centuries B.C.E.; swords, water spitting, and interrogation are all employed to cast out demons. Ko Hung's fourth-century compendium presents similar basic procedures without recourse to superior otherworldly authority—that is, the sacred names which (with accompanying meditations) are the distinguishing hallmark of the Buddhist and Taoist texts.

The particular interest of Ko Hung's work is that it is both early and essentially nonsectarian. It steers a course independent of either Buddhist or Taoist specialization, but is also free of the doctrinaire self-consciousness that characterizes many later works of medical literature. For Ko Hung, pharmaceutical and ritual methods were by no means mutually exclusive. They might provide complementary modes of treatment or even coexist within a single set of procedures. Also, Ko Hung clearly states several dominant themes of secular medical tradition in the diagnosis and treatment of epilepsy, madness, and spirit possession. Some of his material is simply repeated in the relevant sections of later medical and pharmacological treatises, often updated to take subsequent developments into account. Medical authors of the following centuries have a good deal to say on all the approaches suggested by Ko Hung: pharmaceutical visions, exorcistic acupuncture and cauterization, fumigations, corporal punishment, judicial interrogation, as well as the specifically sexual etiology of certain possession-syndromes.

As an example of the incorporation of Ko Hung's material within an expanded and more closely structured framework, we quote Ch'ao Yüan-fang's systematic treatise *On the Origins and Symptoms of Diseases* (*Chu-ping yüan-hou lun*), from the early seventh century. A subtle diagnostician, Ch'ao observes that there is considerable variety in the pathology of ailments caused by malignant influences and demonic beings. Some patients' speech is confused, others scream and race wildly about. Some have the falling-frenzy madness (*tien-k'uang*) and lose consciousness, others are alternately joyous and angry, lamenting and laughing by turns. Still others exhibit signs of terror, as if someone were pursuing them. Some sing and hum and shrill, while others are unwilling to speak. Then Ch'ao puts forward what are in essence the therapeutic procedures described by Ko Hung, though he alters details and makes additions of his own:

> Put needles in your hair, enter the afflicted person's gate, take water drawn from along the crumbled bank of a stream, cover it with a three-foot length of new white cloth, place a sword across your knees, and call out to the patient to come forward. Look sternly at him, and pay close attention to his speech and appearance; his answers to you will probably be imprecise. Then take water in your mouth and spew it out at him. Do not allow the patient to rise. Next lower your head and regard him keenly once again. After spewing water at him three times, wipe his face. If the ailment is severe, he will be in a dazed state. Do not allow him to get up. Look closely at him, and if he is dazed, does not recognize anyone, and is unwilling to speak, snap your fingers in front of his forehead near the hairline and say, "Do you want to be cured?" If he is still unwilling to speak, snap your fingers twice seven times and say, "You are cured!" and as soon as he is cured [which seems here to mean "conscious," or under control], question the demon fully on the circumstances of the case.[29]

An obvious question that we have thus far skirted is by what process the identity of the afflicting demon was determined. For the first time, Ch'ao Yüan-fang presents exact instructions for identifying the agent responsible for the malady. The secret lies in the patient's pulses. Differences in rhythm and recessiveness among the six pulses enable the clinician to ascertain whether the problem lies with a malignant creature, a haunting by a ghost or some demonic agency, or a combination of effects, such as a demonic ailment on top of a malignant haunting. This is a purely secular approach, cool and rational, and it is interesting to observe that Ch'ao follows the passage on the pulses with prophylactic and therapeutic directives for such cases, taken from Taoist sources in the Shang-ch'ing tradition. The essentials of sound preventive practice lie in striking the teeth together (to ward off potential demonic invaders), employing inward vision (systematically conducting fresh vital-breaths around one's own viscera), and the use of therapeutic massage. One should also visualize a great mass of thunder and lightning, rumbling and grumbling, continuously rolling into one's stomach without ceasing, and the ailment will simply go away by itself—a primitive anticipation of the exorcistic thunder-rituals of later Taoism.

Finally, Ch'ao presents the typical symptoms of demonic bewitchment (*kuei-mei*). Anyone bewitched (*mei*) by a demonic creature (*kuei-wu*) will be sorrowful and emotional (literally, "his heart will move by itself"). Sometimes his mind will be fuddled, as if he were drunk. He speaks madly and is in a state of terror; he wails and howls, facing the wall. He has nightmares and erotic possession-dreams, and will sometimes have sexual commerce with demons and spirits. He suffers from alternating chills and fever, from fullness of stomach and shortness of breath. He is unable to eat or drink. These are the signs that someone is possessed by a demon-bewitchment.[30]

Other sources offer a clearly stated sexual etiology to explain the pernicious phenomenon of a woman caught up in an erotic liaison with a demon. This represents perhaps the most insidiously distressing of all possession-complaints, alienating the affections of a wife or mother from her family and binding her body and soul to the hostile invisible world—an auto-erotic death-in-life. A tenth-century compilation by the Japanese court physician Tanba no Yasuyori, *Prescriptions from the Heart of Medicine* (*Ishinpō*), has preserved extensive quotations from many medieval Chinese medical writings that have not otherwise survived. It is especially famous for its section on sexual techniques, filled with extracts from rare Chinese handbooks that have allowed scholars to reconstruct the bedroom arts of medieval China.[31] Comparable material is found elsewhere in the text as well. In chapter 21, on gynecology, the question of women's physical needs is addressed. A Chinese source is quoted to describe the psycho-physiological state of women in their twenties, in whom the yin-breaths are at their most vigorous. Women of that age are said to be uncontrollable in their desire for men. Their food and drink have no savor for them, their pulses race, and their bodies' overflowing vital juices pour out and wet their clothing. In the vaginas of these women are worms resembling a horse's tail, three inches long. The ones with red heads cause dizziness, those with black heads cause the juice. The way to cure this condition is by making a penis from dough, of whatever size you wish. Steep it in pure rice spirit, wrap it in cloth, insert it into the vagina, and it will draw out the worms. When you have removed them, insert it once again, and it will be as good as getting treatment by a physician. If there are a great many worms, repeat the treatment thirty times; if fewer, twenty times.

Following this comes a quotation from a book called *Secret Instructions for the Jade Chamber* (*Yü-fang pi-chüeh*), which also belongs to the genre of handbooks on sexual arcana.[32] Like other works of this type, the whole treatise is cast in the form of a dialogue between a woman learned in the arts of the bedchamber and P'eng-tsu, a legendary figure said to have lived some nine hundred years thanks to his mastery of sexual hygiene. This text describes the malady of demon-intercourse as resulting from an absence of normal yin-yang relations. Deprived of the yang-element for which she yearns, a woman's passions are made more intense, and she falls a natural prey to lecherous demons. They take on the semblance of a man and have sexual congress with her, performing the act far better than a mere man could do. When this has continued for some time, the woman becomes dazed. She strictly avoids speaking of her experiences because she enjoys them so much. Thus it can come about that she dies all alone, with no one being aware of the reason. After establishing the origins of the malady in sexual deprivation, the treatise recommends a very straightforward treatment: intercourse with a man. He should go on day and night without respite, and without having an orgasm. Even in difficult cases, the woman will be cured in this manner before seven days have passed. If the man becomes weary and is unable to carry on actively, he should simply stay deep inside her without moving.

After this rather direct approach, the same treatise counsels a fumigatory for the woman's vagina and lower body, made by burning several ounces of sulphur. Along with this treatment the patient should ingest a spoonful of powdered deer-horn every day, and she will be cured. When the possession comes to an end, one will hear the banished demon-lover sobbing as it departs.

Ko Hung suggested two henbane-powders for use against falling frenzy, or epilepsy, and the pharmaceutical approach to various sorts of spirit possession continued to be viewed with favor. The application of henbane in such cases was well established. The basic canon of materia medica, the *Shen-nung Pharmacopoeia* (*Shen-nung pen-ts'ao ching*, second century C.E.), indicates its use against toothache and as a general vermifuge. It treats numbness and stiffness, and causes people to swagger and see demons. It cures falling frenzy (*tien*), madness (*k'uang*), and wind-*hsien* (*tien*'s little brother, colic), as well as cramp and weakness of limbs. Eating much of it causes people to run madly about; ingesting it over a long period of time lightens the body, so that one can overtake a galloping horse. It improves the memory, augments bodily strength, and puts one in contact with spirits. In his critical commentary of 500 C.E., T'ao Hung-ching writes that henbane's only medical application in his day was in prescriptions against falling frenzy and madness. He takes note of the *Pharmacopoeia*'s statement that although consuming too much at one time is dangerous, it may still be taken in smaller doses over a long period with the most beneficial results. Yet he also observes that Taoist scriptures do not recommend it (and T'ao himself, in addition to being the founder of critical pharmacology in China, was also a dedicated Taoist). It was, according to T'ao, only the specialists in prescriptions and techniques who made much use of this dangerous drug; in other words, henbane fell squarely among the pragmatic secular methods of treatment.

Henbane appears again in an eighth-century prescription for dealing with demonic bewitchment (*kuei-mei*). *Iris tectorum* ("kite's head"), iron pyrite, an ounce of henbane, and an ounce of *Peucedanum japonicum* are to be pounded together and sifted. A spoonful taken in wine will cause the sufferer to see the demon that is afflicting him. Adding another ounce of peucedanum will enable him to see the demon's master, and an additional ounce will bring instant beneficial results. Both peucedanum and henbane, we are told, bring people into a dazed condition, like madness, and so must not be taken in excessive doses.[33] In this case, the deliriant properties of henbane and peucedanum are consciously exploited to promote the patient's own recognition of the spectral aggressor that is tormenting him. Though there is no reference to systematic interrogation by the attending physician, it would not be surprising if such drugs were systematically employed, even in the secular tradition, to elicit the information on the demon's identity that, all sources agree, was essential to effect a lasting cure.

Nor was henbane unknown to the ritual tradition, for that matter. We find it once more in an anonymous Chinese Tantric Buddhist text of the eighth century. The officiant is instructed to burn henbane seeds in a Homa fire of khadira-wood, together with hemp-seed (*Cannabis indica*), mandāra (*Erythrina indica*), and oil of rutabaga or kohlrabi (*Brassica oleracea*, or *Brassica rapadepressa*, Ch. *man-ching*), accompanied by the recitation of the appropriate spell. Thereupon the 840,000 devils and demons of falling frenzy (*tien*) and colic-possession (*hsien*), tiger-possession sickness, and so on will all cry out in distress and run away.[34] Here we have striking confirmation of the interlocking patterns of secular and ritual traditions of healing; henbane is brought from standard Chinese medical practice into a Tantric ritual context. Accompanying henbane are two other widely recognized psychoactive substances, seeds of *Cannibis indica* and *Erythrina indica* (of which one active principle, erythramine, causes both hyperexcitability and a curare-like paralysis).[35] Here the action of the drugs appears to be projected onto the demons without subjecting the sufferer to the additional agonies of direct treatment—unless the potent smoke from this Homa fire was to be used in fumigating a demoniac patient (which, though not expressly indicated in the text, is certainly a possibility).

Fumigation certainly continued to be a very common mode of treatment in the secular tradition, and the tenth-century Japanese collection *Ishinpō* quotes the recipe from Ko Hung's work for a fumigatory composed of pine-resin and realgar, over which a naked woman is placed to smoke out her demonic intruder. The same formula is quoted in many other standard Chinese medical works as well. In ancient China fumigation had been used for a variety of complaints; there are several prescriptions for fumigating the perineum as a treatment for hemorrhoids in the manuscripts from the second century B.C.E. excavated at Ma-wang-tui.[36] In present-day Japan, one can still see older persons using their hands to conduct the smoke from the great incense burners that stand outside the Buddhist temples to parts of their bodies in special need of protection or treatment—giving particular attention to the shoulders and groin.[37]

One of the fullest sources on anti-demoniac fumigation is the *Wai-t'ai pi-yao* (Secret Essentials from the Outer Tribunal), a large collection of medical prescriptions assembled in the middle of the eighth century by Wang T'ao. We have just quoted the henbane and peucedanum recipe against demon-bewitchment from this work. Wang T'ao also offers instructions for a fumigatory compound "guaranteed efficacious against demon-bewitchment." A tiger claw and a crab claw are to be pounded together with vermilion (cinnabar) and realgar, bound with pine-resin, and heated. The mixture is formed into pellets that are allowed to cool and harden: "Then, just at dawn, go to the dwelling place of the fox-demon and burn them. This is exceedingly efficacious. When you use it to fumigate the sorcerer, the demon will depart."[38]

We shall have more to say about fox-demons and sorcerers. First we must consider two additional fumigatories from Wang T'ao's collection, since they, too, lead in the same direction. The first, a general-purpose anti-demoniac, calls for a total of twenty-three ingredients. Some are of animal or insect origin, like musk, bezoar, and centipedes. There are minerals like realgar and cinnabar, as well as a number of herbal substances, including a subterrestrial fungus (*Pachyma cocos*), dried ginger, and ginseng. This preparation proves to be almost a universal treacle, for pounded together, mixed with honey, and formed into pellets, it can be used both as an internal medication and as a fumigatory. The pellets can also be triturated, mixed with vinegar, and applied to the skin to treat the bite of snakes and scorpions and the sting of bees. Taken internally, two pellets daily will cure symptoms of demonic bewitchment within two or three days. Phenomena such as essential-spirit demons (*ching kuei*), foxes, and the like, which throw bricks and tiles or go galloping along like a troop of mounted soldiers—all such things count as demonic bewitchments, we are told. As a fumigatory, too, the compound's applications are of the broadest. It can be employed to fumigate one's clothing and can also be used more generally in the house, for (in contrast to other noxious or foul-smelling preparations) it has no ill effects. Finally, it can even serve as a phylactery; a few of the pellets wrapped in a vermilion cloth and tied on the left shoulder will ward off tigers, poisonous snakes, essential-spirits, goblins, and similar creatures.

Intriguing though all this is, it has merely been preparatory for what must certainly be the most curious fumigatory compound of all. Designed to cure sexual intercourse with demons and spirits in dreams, as well as bewitchment by fox-goblins, it is made up of fifteen ingredients: fox-muzzle (roasted) and leopard-muzzle (roasted; seven of each), one complete roasted fox skull, realgar, castoreum (dried follicles of the beaver), branches of the plant "demon's arrow" (*Euonymus thunbergianus*), an open-air beehive (roasted), the plant *Atractylis ovata*, tiger skull-bone (roasted; an ounce of each of the foregoing), *Assafoetida ferrula* (roasted; two ounces), and hair of donkey, horse, dog, camel, and cow (four *fen* of each, burnt to ash). If it is a case of bone-steaming—a particularly dread disease—one should add an ounce of dead-man's brain-bone, roasted. Macerated and sifted, the resultant powder is mixed with pine-resin previously boiled in water. Stir until smooth, but take care not to stir it with your hand—use instead a tiger claw. Mold the preparation into pellets, with which you fumigate the victim. When you are about to fumigate, envelope her completely with coverings so that none of the smoke from the mixture seeps out. Separately pound realgar into a powder, place it on the pellets, and ignite. The timing of the fumigation should be the same as for burning incense. For best results, also burn the pellets beneath the victim's bed.[39]

In the presence of this extravagant preparation, a kind of fumigatory *olla cacciatore*, we must pause and reflect. No doubt any prescription may be broken down into its component parts and analyzed separately. But in a satisfactory analysis, it is not enough merely to assess the chemical contribution of each component to the exuberant whole. It is the genius of Chinese polypharmacy to combine ingredients that work synergistically, causing the fewest side-effects or imbalances. In the two preparations for which we have just scanned the formulae, we may safely presume that the ingredients combined, when burned, to produce an incredibly pungent smoke. Yet symbolic and chemical functions are usually closely linked. Thus it seems significant that the number and prominence of animal components in the fumigatories has been increasing as we advance. A sideways glance at some of the Indian data from the same period may again prove useful at this point. In Chapter 5, when studying the Chinese version of Rāvaṇa's pediatric treatise (*Rāvaṇa's Kumāra-tantra*; see p. 222) on demonic possession in small children, we found fox dung, kitten dung, and sloughed-off snakeskin among the ingredients in a fumigatory preparation. In other medieval Sanskrit medical treatises, there is a good deal more information on matters of this sort. Joining the various botanical ingredients for fumigatories in that literature are the skins of leopards, tigers, lions, and bears, as well as snakes. Or, in another formula, the horn, hair, and tail of a cow, snakeskin, cat excrement, plus leaves of *Azadirachta indica*, *Helleborus niger*, *Randia dumetorum*, *Solanum indicum*, *Solanum jacquinii*, he-goat hair, white mustard seeds, he-goat's urine, and so on.[40]

Here too, then, we appear to be treading on common Sino-Indian ground, and the optional "dead-man's brain-bone" in Wang T'ao's formula even has something of a Tantric ring. The animals from which the ingredients derive are fearsome, malodorous, or both—even as many of the plants are both pungent and poisonous—and the fumes of such constituents could be presumed to have a powerful demon-dispelling effect for that reason alone. But an ambivalence lurks in some of these preparations and their applications, a suspicion as insidious as the reappearing tiger claw, earlier brought in to stir Ko Hung's fourth-century brew. For animals have been turning up in the medical works not merely as sources for materia medica but in the guise of invasive pathogenic agents as well. As we have seen, Wang T'ao's fumigatory pellets of tiger claw, vermilion, realgar, and crab claw, "guaranteed effective against demon-bewitchments," are to be burned at dawn at the dwelling place of a fox-demon: "When you use it to fumigate the sorcerer, the demon will depart." In this case, both an animal and a presumably human sorcerer are somehow entangled in the etiology of pathological possession. In Chapter 5 we considered the child-persona of possessor and possessed. Now we must examine still another, this time feral face—which may prove, on closer scrutiny, to mask a human countenance.

Animal Incarnations

A constant feature of possession as involuntary, uncensored behavior is the extra-human, extra-social nature of the victim's actions. He is dehumanized, bereft of normal powers of recognition and reaction. His speech and movements alike are far distant from the societal norm, and his demonically controlled deportment often suggests that of an animal. For example, Ch'i Chung-fu, a gynecologist writing early in the thirteenth century, in addition to five sorts of falling frenzy (*tien*) classified according to their causative factors, also distinguished a further four types: cow, horse, pig, and dog frenzies, according to the sounds and movements manifested by the victim during her seizure. He records the opinion, common in his day, that people liable to suffer from falling frenzy should strictly avoid eating the flesh of any of the six types of domestic beasts; otherwise their symptoms, when the disease was upon them, would resemble those of the animals they had consumed.[41]

Animal-like behavior is also characteristic of many forms of voluntary possession throughout Asia.[42] For example, on one day every year (the day called "snake five"), a snake-god possesses his permanent medium in a North Indian village and questions are put to the embodied serpent by an interrogator on behalf of the assembled villagers.[43] Among the many well-documented trance phenomena of Bali are a series of distinctively stylized, voluntary animal-possessions: snake, pig, puppy, monkey, yellow horse, white horse, toad, and turtle. But then, in the exuberant Balinese tradition, even vegetables and what we might naively think of as "inanimate" objects (brooms, mortars for pounding rice, pot-lids) can take possession of a subject, old or young, and inspire him to mime their characteristic shape or actions. Here again, these embodiments take place at an annual festival; the "play" element is very pronounced, and the possessed dancers are treated, in their self-abasing incarnations, with marked disrespect. Such public possession, like the European Feast of Fools, provides an almost transparent purgation of the bystanders' pent-up emotions. Yet there seems to be no question about the genuineness of the dancers' trance-state.[44]

We have already seen that most of the "seizers," the *graha*-demons that threaten the lives of young children according to the Indian medical literature and Tantric Buddhist scriptures, appear in animal form: cow, lion, fox, monkey, horse, dog, pig, cat, crow, pheasant, owl, and snake.[45] But apart from these nightmare shapes, the impersonation or incarnation of animals could also be highly beneficial. "Bear-hangings" and "bird-stretchings" were part of Chinese medical gymnastics from ancient times, and are illustrated in one of the second-century B.C.E. manuscripts from Ma-wang-tui, while the characteristic movements of the heraldic beasts of the five directions (dragon, tiger, vermilion bird, tortoise, and unicorn) provided basic choreographic patterns not only for medieval medical gymnastics but for martial arts as well. We have already seen that the Taoist or Buddhist initiate about to perform the exorcistic ritual of ensigillation first musters about his head the same group of sacred animals, in faithful imitation of the theophany of Lao-tzu (see pp. 128 and 139).

Indeed, many of the gods and immortals regularly appear accompanied by specific animal companions, and members of the Buddhist pantheon have not only their characteristic "vehicle," or mount (Samantabhadra an elephant, Mañjuśrī a lion, etc.), but may also be linked with specific companion-beasts (Vaiśravaṇa, commander of the north, is associated with centipedes) or even take on animal form themselves (Mārīcī, goddess of the constellation Ursa Major, sometimes appears as a sow and is in any case accompanied by seven piglets, the constellation's seven stars).[46] Certain members of the divine menagerie even operate with a large measure of independence, like the great bird Garuḍa, messenger of the gods, enemy of nāgas, and himself a revealer of esoteric healing rituals.[47] Among China's own animals, the terrible tiger, a baneful star-demon feared both as an agent of possession and as a tangible menace in China's mountain-regions, in time became the kittenish pet of the founder of Taoism, the Celestial Master Chang Tao-ling; masters in the Ch'an Buddhist tradition are also sometimes depicted with tigers that they have subdued through the power of their meditation; and a tiger accompanies the white-bearded old man who represents the indigenous mountain-god in Korean iconography. The capering monkey Sun Wu-k'ung, anti-hero of the novel *Journey to the West* (*Hsi-yu chi*), is frequently to be seen on the Chinese stage or in festival processions; one can readily imagine his ritualized antics, like the fossilized dragon-dances of the present-day Chinese New Year's celebration, as crystallizations around an original ecstatic core. In fact there is no need for guesswork on this subject because Chinese professional mediums still regularly incarnate the formidable legendary monkey, and have even been photographed when doing so.[48]

As we might anticipate, Tantric Buddhist sources offer us tantalizing glimpses of even more intriguing mysteries of animal transformation.[49]

Among medieval Chinese texts, the most suggestive material comes in a corpus of rituals under the patronage of the Indian elephant-headed god Gaṇeśa, or Gaṇapati.[50] Gaṇeśa was Śiva's other son, the elder brother of Skanda. His major alternate name is Vināyaka ("Hindrance" or "Obstacle"); in pre-Buddhist writings, there is a class of deities so named:

> When possessed by these, a person pounds sods of earth, cuts grass, and writes on his body; and sees in dreams waters, men with shaved heads, camels, pigs, asses, etc.; and feels he is moving in the air; and when walking, sees someone pursuing him from behind. Again, when possessed by these, Princes Royal do not obtain the kingdom, though qualified to govern. Girls do not obtain bridegrooms, though possessed of the necessary qualities. Women do not get children, even if otherwise qualified. The children of other women die. A learned teacher qualified to teach does not obtain pupils, and there are many interruptions and breaks in the course of a student. Trade and agriculture are unsuccessful.[51]

Thus any persistent sign of failure in those otherwise gifted and well-suited might be interpreted as indicating possession by a *vināyaka*—the demonic or divine obstacle which explains why nothing seems to go right.[52] With what we now know of the transformation of attackers and possessors into specialized patrons and protectors, it will scarcely come as a revelation to learn that Gaṇeśa, the *vināyaka* par excellence, was soon adopted as a remover of obstacles in all Indian ritual traditions, and that offerings are still made to him in India at the beginning of almost any ritual, or at the start of any other significant undertaking.[53] This is also the case in Tantric Buddhism; and in the consecration ritual (Skt. *abhiṣeka*, Ch. *kuan-ting*, J. *kanjō*) as performed today in Japanese Shingon and Tendai Buddhist lineages, postulants must pay their respects before an image of the elephant-headed god, at a round table laden with offerings of rice wine, cakes, and fruit, before being blindfolded and led into the innermost room where the maṇḍala awaits them.

The eighth-century Chinese Tantric texts relate a tangled story. Vināyaka is described as a dual personality, in fact an elephant-headed couple locked in a close embrace. One scripture (T. 1270) accounts for this figure by relating that the god Śiva and his consort, Umā, had a total of three thousand sons who divided into two groups; the party of the left, under the chieftainship of Vināyaka, are dedicated to performing evil deeds, whereas the fifteen hundred sons on the right, whose leader is Senāyaka (described as a manifestation of the Bodhisattva Avalokiteśvara), are no less fervently devoted to the performance of good actions. The composite figure embodies their union, the gentle Senāyaka being represented in female form.[54] This is already curious, especially in its frank acknowledgment of the subsisting evil element, but still more remarkable things were to follow. A text translated by Bodhiruci in the early years of the eighth century (*Ta-shih chou-fa ching*, T. 1268) gives instructions for making the god's icon—a man and woman clasping one another—with elephants' heads and human bodies. In a series of verses, the god boasts of his powers; he possesses subtle arts by which to grant his devotees all that they desire in the world—fame, official position, treasures, beautiful women. Reciting his dhāraṇī will cure madness resulting from spirit possession as well as leprosy and all other ailments:[55]

> When persons of the highest type obtain my spell,
> I will make them kings among men;
> When those of middling type obtain it,
> I will appoint them preceptors to emperors;
> When those of the lesser sort obtain it,
> They shall have riches and honor without end.
> They shall enjoy every variety of pleasure,
> And have always sufficiency of all they desire;
> Male and female slaves shall stand in ranks before them,
> And beautiful women will overflow their courtyards.

After these promises of luxury and bliss come directives for worshipping the god, and more exact details concerning the manufacture of his icon. But at the end of this section there is a puzzling addition, relating how the text was originally translated by a brahman from Central India at the end of the sixth century, and informing us that a variant form of the image comprises one elephant's head and one pig's head.[56] This couple is actually depicted in the entourage of the thousand-armed, thousand-eyed Kuan-yin in a Tun-huang painting dated 981. Polarizing Vināyaka's sexuality, they also divide his name; on the painting they are identified as Vina, demon-father, and Yaka, demon-mother.[57] Returning to our text, more curious still are the instructions that follow, for they concern the use of two virgin girls of at least fifteen years old, and the preliminary consumption of two ounces of "drugs" to purify the body. The drugs are not identified, nor are we told what one does with the girls. The text seems badly garbled, and concludes with a warning against sleeping on one's back—if you do, the god will immediately come and press upon your chest (a classic symptom, in the West, of the nightmare), or a woman will come to have intercourse with you in your dreams; you should apparently elude her advances, arise, recite a mantra, and bathe yourself. In a colophon dated 1754, a Japanese monk noted that the text was evidently in need of restoration, being full of copyists' errors. This is all too true, yet it still permits us a glimpse into a hidden world of Buddhist sensuality.

There are also short Vināyaka texts by Vajrabodhi (T. 1270) and Amoghavajra (T. 1271), but the cult's major production was a substantial four-chapter book, translated at the end of the tenth century by Dharmabhadra (T. 1272). Here, once again, we find some of the orgiastic intimations of Bodhiruci's text. The god's icon can be used as a love-charm; buried under the gateway of a young man or young woman's house, it will cause that person to have no interest in anyone but the perpetrator. If you attach a string to the image and draw it through the marketplace, all the people in the streets will strip off their clothes, let down their hair, and dance stark naked.[58] Nor are these the only tricks you can perform with the image. If you smear it with a mixture of salt and hot mustard-seed oil, you will cause men and women to go quite mad and be entirely without restraint; to calm them down, put the salt and oil mixture in their food and drink, and they will return to normal.[59] If you make an effigy of the god with four arms and three eyes out of dead men's bones, rub it with human fat, and fumigate it in a fire of Solomon's Seal (*Polygonatum odoratum*) from the god's shrine, you will obtain the love of either a man or woman. Or envelop the image in chicken-flesh, fumigate it in the smoke of heated hemp-seed oil, and bury it in front of the loved one's gate. Then, inside the house, he (or she) will strip off his clothes, let down his hair, and go racing wildly about in all directions like a madman. Remove the image, and he will return to normal.[60] Thus whether as a love-charm, an aphrodisiac, or a delirifacient, the god's icon bore with it the power to possess people utterly, compelling them to unrestrained license and sensuality. The book's fourth and final chapter contains explicit instructions for ritual sex.[61] The erotic cult of Gaṇeśa-Vināyaka is still alive, in a non-Buddhist context, in India, and the god's image and its associations are still current in Buddhist Japan.[62]

Thus we bring to full circle the theme broached in Chapter 5: by incarnating its two extremes, the two sons of Śiva seem to represent the full spectrum of spirit possession. Skanda Kumāra, an unmarried young man, perhaps even somewhat hostile to women, stands for the possession of a youth by a youthful god. The complex of beliefs and practices centered on Skanda is essentially juvenile. A *kumāra* is a virgin youth, and the emphasis of Kumāra's cult is, fittingly, on vigorous action and clairvoyance. In contrast, Gaṇeśa-Vināyaka, an elephant-headed androgyne, promotes a complex of animal possession, more especially in its adult, erotic aspect.[63] Gaṇeśa is, appropriately, the elder son of Śiva, and his lascivious propensities are conveyed by his great phallic trunk. Like Skanda, he leads a dual life as god and demon, and also as man and woman. Between Vināyaka the uncontrolled, possessing Obstacle and Vināyaka the Remover of Obstacles, there is all the difference between a wild elephant and a tame one.

As the frame of reference shifts to the animal world, our focus of study is directed toward other forms of human activity and possession that seem to correlate with the bestial. It may be that the animal persona corresponds to a pathological state in which the victim is acted upon by irrepressible forces welling up from deep within; his animal nature is thus an involuntary pathological possession, and he truly incarnates the beast in man.[64] But even in less gripping circumstances, the animal image bears a clear message to the beholder. Whether assumed by means of true voluntary possession or simply in masquerade, the adoption of animal disguise in costume, speech, and movements offers immediate release from ordinary social constraints. This can be observed in common festival activity, and presumably underlies the cult of animals and animal-gods in complex societies generally. Even in their fragmentary (and possibly expurgated) state, the Tantric Buddhist texts of the Vināyaka cult hint at ritual situations in which suppressed desires could be fulfilled—and during which release from normal constraints might be attained through an animal deity, and perhaps even in liberating animal disguise. Given the contrast between humanity and animality, which is universally held to be the foundation-stone of civilization, it seems probable that people worship gods in animal form, employ otherworldly animals, or transform themselves into animals in order to achieve objectives well outside the ordinary social norm—possibly as a means to transcendence, but no doubt even more often to attain what are essentially asocial or even antisocial ends.

Beasts and Super-Beasts

Much of what is commonly known about cases of animal transformation in traditional China comes from its voluminous story-literature. The standard technique of Chinese authors of fictions is to set fantastic events in a dryly circumstantial historical setting. Names, places, and dates are frequently provided, in keeping with the national obsession with documentary precision. Indeed, historical authenticity is sometimes in inverse proportion to the "historical" detail provided. Students of Chinese literature are by now accustomed to this literary convention. Yet the ultimate paradox is that, once we have learned to discount these factitious historical semblances, we discover that there are collections of anecdotes which on the surface seem fabulous—collections long relegated, even by Chinese scholars, to the category of "tales of the supernatural," and hence supposed to be fiction—but which on closer scrutiny prove to be among our finest sources of historical fact. And it is also true that behind even the obvious fictions lie intimations of historical realities that find no place in official sources.

A basic story pattern concerns the detection of animals that have taken on the semblance of human beings, usually in order to work extreme mayhem and destruction. Many of the tales are constructed around a sexual nucleus; some are even invested with the dignity of etiological legends. A male dog, for example, seduces and carries off a Chinese woman; their progeny are the present-day Yao and Miao peoples, older residents of central and south China who are viewed by the Chinese settlers as only half human (as this legend makes clear). We have already seen that the spirit of a black dog-zombie, buried but not dead, was able to possess a woman sexually over a period of months, until ultimately unmasked and destroyed by a Taoist master (see pp. 182–83). The lasciviousness of monkeys is also well attested to, and Chinese womanhood has apparently often been ravished by passionate primates: "A great ape from the southern mountains / Robbed me of my beloved wife. / For fear, I dared not chase him. / I could but retire, to dwell alone." So reads one of the poems in the *I-lin*, a book of verses associated with *I-ching* hexagrams, from about 25 C.E. A collection of tales from the third or fourth century localizes a race of woman-stealing apes in the mountains of southwestern Szechuan; having impregnated their Chinese captives, the apes send them back to rear their children in human society. An entire story cycle, the *Tale of the White Ape*, grew up around this theme, which is also linked to the great novel *Hsi-yu chi* (Journey to the West).[65] Light-fingered gibbons have been known to incarnate themselves as humanoid robber-bands.[66] In addition to sex and thievery, addiction to strong drink is another failing of these monkeys, and a young woman into whom the monkey-spirit regularly entered in the 1880s was observed to guzzle quantities of liquor without exhibiting any signs of drunkenness.[67]

If dogs and monkeys appear to pose a threat to women, the zoological peril to male sexuality is even more striking. There is, for example, the much-recounted legend of the White Snake. Among the many versions of this tale, the best-known describes how a young man encounters a ravishingly beautiful widow, dressed in white, accompanied by her maid, garbed in blue. The scene is set at the Spring Festival, on the fifteenth of the first lunar month. Caught in a sudden rainstorm, the widow borrows the young man's umbrella; the next day he goes to her house to retrieve it and receives an offer of marriage from the passionate woman, "Mrs. White." He is only a poor employee in his uncle's pharmacy, and so she gives him a silver ingot, promising forty-nine more to cover all expenses. It is later determined that the ingot belongs to a set of fifty that had just been stolen from a government treasury, and the young man is arrested and banished. The woman and her servant suddenly reappear in his place of exile, and despite the young man's misgivings, they marry. All appears to be going well until one day he visits a temple festival where a Taoist master, catching sight of him, declares that he is possessed by an evil demon. The remainder of the story relates his feeble attempts to deal with the monster, and her growing violence and demands. In one version, he is instructed to spy on her when she is in the toilet—and in that place of ultimate truth, where all creatures act according to their real natures, he beholds her, to his horror, in her original form, as a great white snake with burning eyes. The exorcism is finally effected by a Buddhist monk, who directs the young man to press his alms-bowl on her head. By means of the magical bowl the snake-wife is ultimately subdued, and to restrain her permanently, the Thunder-Peak Pagoda was constructed over her—still today a prominent sight of Hangchow. The story embodies all the Chinese male's terror of voracious female sexuality. It is, indeed, such a damning catalogue of feminine cupidity, trickery, and greed that in later versions the emphasis changes radically; the dread serpent-demon is transformed into a loving, supportive wife, a classic fairy-tale "helpful animal." The villain in these later versions, need one say, has become the Taoist priest or Buddhist monk, oppressor of noble Chinese womanhood, destroyer of family life, and enemy of the people![68]

It would seem that a primal and obsessive fear of the Chinese male is of being devoured, or sucked dry. Apart from the snake, men feel gravely threatened by the tiger. Women born in the Year of the Tiger (1938, 1950, 1962, 1974, 1986, etc.) are deemed highly undesirable brides in Taiwan and Hong Kong today, and are often obliged to conceal or falsify their year of birth because prospective husbands dread their supposed rapacious, demonic propensities.[69] But easily the most commonly encountered sexual possessor in the entire East Asian menagerie of slinking shape-shifters is the fox. The *Shuo wen* (Explanation of Characters), a dictionary written about 100 C.E., states that the fox is an ill-omened beast and that demons ride upon it.[70] We now have even earlier documentation of the fox's active role in pathological possession, in two recipes in the Ma-wang-tui medical manuscript *Fifty-Two Medical Prescriptions*, found in a tomb dating from 168 B.C.E. One of the recipes presents a terse exorcistic procedure, using a spell: "Spirit of Heaven, send down the sickness-prophylactic! Spirit Maids, according to your sequence, hear the pronouncement to the spirits! A certain fox is inserted in a place where it does not belong. Desist! If you do not desist, I will cut you apart with an ax!" The healer is then directed to grasp a piece of hemp cloth and exorcistically beat the patient twice seven times.[71] The fox's propensity for possessing human victims, its ubiquity and cunning, only increased with time, until fox-shrines and fox-towers dotted the Chinese landscape. "Of all the objects worshipped in our Middle Kingdom, I believe in the Fox," as a literate Manchurian villager declared to the Reverend John MacIntyre.[72]

We have already noted that fox dung was prescribed against demon-possession in children by *Rāvaṇa's Kumāra-tantra*, and roasted fox-muzzle and skull-bone are important ingredients in the great fumigatory recommended by the eighth-century physician Wang T'ao against sexual possession and fox bewitchment (see the section on "Madness in the Medical Literature," pp. 248–50). The fox was fully recognized as a pathogenic agent in the standard medical literature, and it was also a valued contributor to the classical materia medica. Its penis enjoys chief prominence in that connection, being used to treat childlessness in women and vaginal prurience, as well as wilting of the penis and swollen testicles in young boys. Fox viscera are employed against toxic magical infection (*ku*, often glossed as witchcraft), to cure fevers, and against children's possession-colic (*hsien*) caused by fright. Fox viscera, if administered before the corpse is laid out, can even revive the newly dead. A broth of fox entrails should be given to adults who have seen a demon. Fox excrement, found on stones or amid clumps of trees or bamboo, is burned to drive off evil influences. In such ways is the devilish afflictor of mankind transformed into a benefactor; and as we might expect, the maladies for which fox-parts serve as a specific center on the sexual and demoniac.[73]

Even in present-day secular medical terminology, we usually find a similar sexual or genital orientation wherever there are significant holdovers from earlier vulpine pathology. Inguinal hernia, for example, is still called "genital fox-swelling." Contact dermatitis is termed "fox-urine pricking." Bromhidrosis (fetid perspiration) is known as "fox stench." And the suggestive term "fox-daze" (*hu-huo*) denotes a curious concatenation of effects: "a syndrome characterized by ulceration of throat, anus, and external genitals."[74]

Even as parts of the male fox can cure barren or prurient women, it is the female fox, the vixen, that is most active as an agent of erotic possession in the narrative and anecdotal literature—and her attention is, naturally, focused on men. The fox-phantom story becomes an oft-repeated, stereotyped literary genre. Narratives on the topic more and more took on the contours of exempla with a standard, formulaic pattern. They come to focus on the shy, promising young student, timidly upwardly mobile—a class that no doubt formed the chief public for this sort of literature. The fictional protagonists are mainly young gentlemen preparing for official examinations, the "examination hell" that might lead to brilliant civil-service careers. Whether owing to their midnight lucubrations, excessive rectitude, or constitutional debility, such characters are usually sexually unenterprising, not to say repressed. Their passivity proves to be their undoing: The typical young victim's hopes are fatally blasted—and his life itself destroyed—owing to his involvement with all-devouring female sexuality in vulpine form. Taking the shape of a beautiful young woman, the demonic vixen may come to him in the night, in the desolate temple to which he has retired in order to study, or she may offer him hospitality on his way to take the all-important examinations. Whatever the scenario, his seduction is speedily effected, and she proceeds to drain him of vital essence and blight his hopes for social advancement. In exceptional cases, particularly in recent times, the passionate, beguiling fox-demon assumes a more benign fairy-tale role; as in latter-day versions of the White Snake legend, she supports the young scholar, encourages him in his studies, and even makes terrible sacrifices on his behalf. But this is simply literary saccharine in the bitter brew of possession-literature. More usually, she comes into his life to distract him from the royal road to socially accredited success, drain him of his precious, never-to-be-squandered semen, and so utterly destroy him. If, as it seems, this is basically a cautionary tale, or even a test set by the gods, it is the sort of ordeal that few young men prove able to resist.[75]

In the face of this encroaching literary stereotype, it should once again prove useful and refreshing to turn aside from the beaten literary path, since the ritual texts of Tantric Buddhism offer important supplementary information on East Asian fox-phantoms. In earlier, proto-Tantric texts, a fox is a fox, as in other Chinese sources: That is to say, they are treacherous, unpredictable animals that are indeed liable to take on demonic form, but that provide serviceable ingredients for anti-demonic fumigatories. We have seen that, in the fifth century, Buddhist monks were warned against seductive demon-foxes that might come to disturb their meditations: "There will be fox-phantoms, some of them taking the form of brides, richly apparelled, who will stroke and caress the meditator's body and speak of things contrary to the Law." But with the increasing systematization of Tantric demonology, the fox gained a more highly individual identity in the catalogue of specters. The earliest indication of what was to become the fox's dominant Tantric role in East Asia occurs in a composite scripture, the *Shou-leng-yen ching* (T. 945), assembled in China on the basis of Indian materials in 705. There, among a host of other demonic beings, the name "Dākiṇī" occurs. It is glossed as referring to demons of fox-possession.[76]

Such a depiction of dākiṇīs as feral, demonic possessors may at first seem radically at variance with the associations that the word brings to mind. It is thanks to the Tibetan tradition of Tantric Buddhism that we think of dākiṇīs as sensuous celestial maidens who appear to lonely ascetics in their mountain retreats and whisper strange secrets in their ears.[77] The fourteenth-century Tibetan poet-saint Milarepa, for example, was the favored beneficiary of dākiṇī-visitors who bestowed on him their secret lore. He is usually shown as holding his right hand up to his ear in an attitude of close attention to the sayings of these beings, invisible and inaudible to most of the rest of us. This is also the usual posture of the Tibetan epic bard, depicted as hearing his songs directly from these goddesses who so closely resemble the jade maidens and other divine women of Taoist tradition.[78] The dākiṇīs have left other relics in the world of mortals, such as the black hat woven of dākiṇīs' hair, containing all the works of all the buddhas, which is the emblem of succession among the "Black Hat" Karma-pa lamas.[79] But these vignettes from later Indo-Tibetan Tantric sources develop only one side of the dākiṇī-figure to the virtual exclusion of other, earlier aspects. They do remain true to a central theme in more primitive dākiṇī lore, for they retain the notion of the dākiṇīs' sexual allure while adding their ability to impart mysterious knowledge to worthy anchorites. But the Tibetan tradition has smoothly lacquered over the demonic core in older depictions of the dākiṇīs.[80] One might say that dākiṇīs thus exemplify the change for the better that can overtake figures of Indian cult and legend after long exposure to Buddhism's refining influence. In the same way, the picture of gandharvas as dulcet celestial musicians has evolved from their earlier form of bird- or horse-headed demons, raptors of unlimited sexual appetite prone to possess their victims. As is often the case, medieval Chinese and Japanese Tantric texts preserve older and more rugged images.

We have already had occasion to note how closely cognate Chinese Tantric Buddhist materials can be with medieval Śaivite Tantra, as well as with aspects of Hindu cultic practice still found in India today. In India, the ḍākiṇīs are mentioned in one of the first epigraphic records to contain the word "Tantra" itself, dating from the first quarter of the fifth century C.E. In this inscription, found in a Central Indian village, there is a reference to the construction of a temple, called "the very terrible abode of the [divine mothers], filled full of ḍākiṇīs, . . . who stir up the very oceans with the mighty wind rising from the Tantric rites of their religion."[81] Ḍākiṇīs thus occur early on as attendants of the divine mothers, important figures in early Tantric cult.

But what of the fox, identified with ḍākiṇīs in eighth-century China? The *Purāṇas*, early medieval repositories of myth and ritual, associate various terrible forms of the Goddess (Devī) with animal manifestations. Among these, one animal—the jackal—proves most relevant to our present concerns. Wolves and jackals haunt graveyards, where a good deal of Tantric practice was supposed to take place. These vile scavengers, which tore apart and devoured corpses, were assimilated to the more horrible aspects of the cult's feminine deities (or for that matter, to the female adepts, or yoginīs, with whom the ḍākiṇīs also appear to have been identified). One name for the jackal is *śivā*, the feminine form of the noun Śiva; the *Agni-purāṇa* depicts one of the Eight Mothers, Kṣamā, as being surrounded by jackals. In the *Mārkaṇḍeya-purāṇa*, the fearsome goddess Caṇḍī is said to scream "like a hundred jackals," and one of the Sixty-Four Yoginīs, Krodhanā ("the Furious"), rides upon a jackal.[82] The *Matsya-purāṇa* describes another gruesome form of the Goddess, Śivadūtī, as having the face of a jackal (*sṛgālavadanā*).[83]

Jackals are not found in China, and the Sanskrit word *sṛgāla*, another term for jackal, was rendered by a Chinese expression meaning something like "attacker in the wilds" or "wild doglike creature" (*ye-kan*). Chinese writers describe this beast as a species of fox that comes out at night to devour human flesh. It is with this most terrible of "foxes" that the Tantric ḍākiṇīs were identified in East Asia.[84] In the painted maṇḍalas of medieval China and Japan, the ḍākiṇīs are depicted in their proper place (the southeastern corner of the great

Womb Maṇḍala, near Yama, the god of death) gnawing on human bones; they are shown in humanoid form, closely resembling the "hungry ghosts" (*preta*).

Ḍākiṇīs, jackals, and "attackers in the wilds" bring up the question of fox synonymy and metaphor. In English, for example, there is the "flying fox," a type of bat (*Pteropus elaphon*). In German, "Grösser Fuchs" and "Kleiner Fuchs" denote two butterflies; and, of course, in all European languages a "sly fox" (or "schlauer Fuchs") designates a cunning, crafty person. In the same way, we find in medieval Chinese Tantric ritual texts a "fetid fox" (*hsün hu*)—the owl (Skt. *ulūka*). This was an airborne fox-figure, active exclusively at night, like the dreaded "attacker in the wilds," or fox-vampire. Even more terrifying was an aquatic creature called the "short fox" (*tuan-hu*). This appears to have been a formidable-looking insect called the bombardier beetle, which is native to freshwater streams in central and southern China.[85] One author describes its head as closely resembling the muzzle of a fox. Another of its names was "the archer" (*she-kung*), and its attack was as swift and true as a well-aimed arrow. It is fully described in Chinese medical literature. According to Ko Hung's fourth-century handbook, *Prescriptions Within Arm's Reach for Use in Emergencies*, this dread insect dwells in mountain streams. Within its mouth is a crossbow made of bone that it shoots at people in the water or at people's shadows on the water's surface. Symptoms include an inability to speak, severe fever, and cramps in all four limbs. The victim's condition will be passable at dawn but will gravely worsen toward nightfall. In three days, blood will well forth from between his teeth, and if not promptly treated, he will die. An exact account of the initial indications of attack is given. It begins with four types of weals or swellings; at the first sign of any of these, one should at once seek treatment. On days when it is raining very heavily, the creature may even pursue people to their homes and shoot them there. Keeping pure white geese or ducks will ward off the menace, as will carrying on one's person rhinoceros horn of fine quality.[86]

Here the fox synonymy refers in the first instance to the resemblance between the creature's maul and a fox's muzzle. But it may be that the modus operandi of the two demonic afflictors was also perceived as being parallel. The "short fox" struck from a distance, through "crossbow fire," and as often as not at the victim's shadow, with full and dire effect on his material body. In a Chinese context, this seems an entirely vulpine way of proceeding; in our terms, we might call it witchcraft.

Both the Taoists and the Buddhists had long since entered the fox in their inventories of demons, and any of the methods of treatment for demonically induced ailments that we have been considering might be applied to cases of fox-possession. Sometimes ritual instructions take particular account of bewitchment by foxes. In the large and influential *Collected Dhāraṇī-Sūtras* (*T'o-lo-ni chi-ching*, T. 901) assembled by Atikūṭa in 653–54, we find fox-goblin ailments mentioned along with afflictions caused by mountain-dwelling essential-spirits, demon-goblins, and virulent toxic infection (*ku*). Against ordinary demonically induced maladies, the text recommends a potent finger-seal (called the demon-binding seal of the Buddha's Crown), to be used in conjunction with a simple spell (*Oṃ viśuddhi svāhā*: "Be pure!"). Seal and spell should first be directed twenty-one times on an unblemished, eastward-growing peach-tree branch. With this charged wand (and peachwood is both vermifuge and demonifuge in China) the patient is then to be beaten; he will at once get better. But should a fox-goblin or one of the other types of demon just mentioned be the cause, the spell should then be recited over white mustard-seeds, which are subsequently thrown in the patient's face and against his chest. He is next fumigated with Parthian incense (gum guggul) all over his body, and made to inhale and swallow the smoke as well. As for the beating with the peachwood branch: First he is to be beaten on the inside portion of the left upper arm, then on the curved part of the right inner thigh. The affliction will immediately be cured. One may also recite the spell over some ground realgar, with which the boundaries of the patient's body can be protected. He should be marked with the realgar at seven places: the crown of the head, on the forehead at the hairline, under the left and right armpits, over the heart, at the base of the neck, and between the eyebrows. The area beneath his bed should also be turned into a miniature ritual area, spread with cow dung, sprinkled and swept, and a lamp should be kept burning there throughout the night. All these measures will be conducive to a cure.[87]

Thus all the usual procedures come into play against fox-demons as well as the other familiar agents of pathological possession; as in secular medical literature, direct beatings and fumigations of the victim occupy a prominent place. But despite being grouped at times with other demons, the fox was really a special being in a category of its own. We should expect that the particular fears evoked by foxes would call forth special modes of treatment, and even a class of professional exorcists skilled in detecting and subjugating vulpine transformations. It is our good fortune that, together with other vital components of Chinese culture, the plague of foxes was brought from the mainland to Japan. It is in Japan that the most elaborate methods were developed for dealing with fox-phantoms in all their various guises.[88]

The context of these methods is still Tantric Buddhist ritual, and the practice in question is called the Ritual of the Six Syllables (*rokuji-hō*).[89] It seems first to appear in the handbooks of the Tendai lineage about the middle of the eleventh century—the very time when demonomania was reaching its height at the Heian court. Tendai authors state that the method was brought back from China by the great Tendai scholar-monk Ennin (793–864), in 847. The story goes that Ennin himself had kept the ritual strictly secret, but that it was transmitted by his disciples after his death. This claim must be weighed against the ritual's close resemblance to the Japanese Shintō purification ceremony called *misogi*; it seems very likely that the Buddhist Ritual of the Six Syllables was actually an original Japanese creation, an adaptation of Sino-Indian Tantric ritual material to an independent Japanese pattern. This would make it even more interesting than if it were simply another Indian rite acclimatized in China and then transplanted to Japan (though the "Shintō" ritual may, of course, itself prove to have an ultimate Chinese origin).

At all events, the "six syllables" are seed-syllables (*bīja-mantras*) representing six different forms of the Bodhisattva Kannon (Ch. Kuan-yin, Skt. Avalokiteśvara) and correspond to the six different modes of rebirth (gods, asuras, men, animals, pretas, hell-beings). The ritual centers on a Homa fire made in a triangular hearth. This is the hearth-shape used for the fierce subjugation mode of Tantric action (*abhicāraka*), for the conquest of demons. About the hearth are laid various weapons, usually bows and arrows, but in some versions swords as well. The Homa sacrifice is performed in six parts, each part being directed toward a different one of the six forms of Kannon. Among the substances burned in the fire of demonic subjugation are thornwood, iron filings, and various toxic plants. At the ritual's conclusion, three figures made of paper, or dolls molded in dough, should be burned in the hearth. They are (1) a "celestial fox"—the image of a predacious bird, the kite (*tobi*; *Milvus lineatus*); (2) a figurine of a woman with long, unbound hair; and (3) the image of a "terrestrial fox," which is simply a fox (Figure 14). All accounts of the ritual agree that its primary function is to combat hostile spells and enchantments. Here (as in the corresponding Shintō procedures) we have the images of the sorceress and her two agents—"foxes" celestial and terrestrial—to be incinerated and reduced to nought.[90]

The Ritual of the Six Syllables was obviously crafted to respond to a widely

FIGURE 14 An illustration of three figures, made of paper or dough, to be burned at the conclusion of the Ritual of the Six Syllables (*rokuji-hō*), a Tantric Buddhist demon-dispelling fire ritual that first appears in handbooks of the Tendai lineage in eleventh-century Japan: (a) a "celestial fox"—the image of a predacious bird; (b) a woman with long, unbound hair; and (c) a "terrestrial fox." From *Kakuzen shō*, DNBZ, vol. 46: 330.

felt need, and it enjoyed great popularity among the aristocracy in eleventh-century Japan. Monks of the other great Tantric lineage, Shingon, who were Tendai's rivals, were quick to appropriate the ritual to serve the needs of their own clientèle. It was apparently in reaction to this Shingon usurpation that Tendai specialists developed their ritual in still more elaborate form. In their new "Riverine Ritual of the Six Syllables," after seven days of uninterrupted performance on land, they moved their great fire-altar to a boat moored in a river. In the middle of the night, with the proceedings illuminated by small boats with torches surrounding the main vessel and choirs of monks intoning spells, dolls representing the witch and the witch-animals were set in the water to float away downstream. It must have been an awe-inspiring sight: the torch-lit river, the chanting, silk-robed monks, the Homa fire in the middle of the midnight waters. This elaborate ritual thus achieved its ends by combining the purifying powers of Fire and Water. Its three primary applications were said to be, first, to turn back upon their emitters evil spells and imprecations; then, as a general cure for disease; and, finally, as a specific aid in childbirth. The obvious focus of all forms of the ritual was on illness or misfortune thought to emanate from human malice—or malign witchcraft. We may gain some notion of how well-suited this ritual was to its times when we recall the conditions in eleventh-century Japan (described at the beginning of Chapter 5), when a vast array of demonic perils was perceived to emanate from the jealousy of the living, as well as the regrets or resentment of the dead.

Behind all the demonic coruscations of the fox may flicker a touch of rabies or hydrophobia, and the fox's madness, anger, or delirium is known to other traditions outside East Asia (compare the German *Fuchsteufelswut*). But as the example of the Ritual of the Six Syllables clearly shows, the image of the witch within the fox may also represent something much more concrete than the metaphorical extension of a shape-shifting animal's uncanny, imponderable ways. The question of levels of reference always remains. We have observed that the "immortals" and "bodhisattvas" in ritual texts as often as not denote human beings playing those roles in the process of preparing to assume them definitively after death. "Demons" in the same literature may often be understood as referring to evil people, just as the term "devils" in Buddhist monastic writings frequently alludes to wicked monks. Similarly, we should consider whether some of the many references to evil, demonic animals may not be thinly veiled allusions to real or imagined sorcerers or witches—either as masters of the evil animals or as malevolent human agents directly behind the animal masks.

Such an interpretation is already suggested by some of the Chinese sources we have examined, and the directions for performing the Ritual of the Six Syllables seem to make it virtually certain, at least for medieval Japan. Perhaps the most revealing data of all come from present-day Japan; paradoxically, the information that throws the clearest light on the East Asian past seems often to be found in living contexts in this most highly evolved of all East Asian countries. The material that interests us concerns the "fox-families" that are still extant in certain remote districts. These households are thought to own and feed foxes—often as many as seventy-five foxes per family—which they employ on hostile missions against other villagers. The identity of such families is known to the entire local population, and they are cruelly ostracized. Fox ownership is a form of hereditary pollution, most often transmitted in the female line. Comparable powers are attributed to families that are said to keep snakes and dogs for the same aggressive purpose, but the great majority of cases involve foxes.[91]

Carmen Blacker's excellent book, *The Catalpa Bow: A Study of Shamanistic Practices in Japan* (1975), provides the best Western-language account of this phenomenon. Dr. Blacker mentions the probable origins of these beliefs in earlier rituals, notably the "heretical" cults of Dakini or Dagini (the so-called Izuna rites, discussed below) of the Tokugawa period (seventeenth-nineteenth centuries). Yet she is reluctant to make an explicit connection between the older Buddhist or Buddhist-derived rituals and the accusations of fox sorcery among villagers in more recent times. She observes that the Izuna or Dagini rite "was a *gehō* or heretical ritual, but not necessarily an evil one,"[92] and notes that a fox or a snake may have been worshipped as a household guardian ("like a friendly watchdog or efficient mouser") without any malicious intent. This is all no doubt perfectly true. Still, in light of the ground we have been covering, it seems somewhat to undervalue the fundamentally evil role of the fox (as well as snake) in spirit possession and maladies of a sexual nature generally—a role that these creatures filled in China long before the advent of Buddhism there, and one that Tantric Buddhism has forcefully underscored. Yet Blacker's work is so comprehensive that she herself provides the further proof of the intimate linking of fox-phantoms, spirit possession, and Tantric ritual in the final chapter of her book, on exorcism. There we not only encounter the foxes once again, but also discover induced possession in use today as a therapeutic method, under the direction of a Buddhist master—thus bringing us back to the point at which we began our discussion of therapeutic spirit-possession.

The Nichiren lineage of Buddhism is particularly renowned at present for its powerful exorcistic rituals.[93] Nichiren exorcists usually employ the old method of transferring the offending demon into the body of a medium for interrogation. In one Nichiren sublineage, however, for the past hundred years or so it has been standard practice for the priest to confront the demoniac patient directly, submitting her (the victims are usually married women between the ages of twenty-five and thirty-five) to direct interrogation, without transferring the aggressive spirit to a third party. Regular exorcistic services are conducted at scheduled times. Indeed, some Nichiren temples actually function as exorcistic clinics, with the patients in residence and submitting to a rigorous, prescribed program of prayers and recitations.

The Nichiren lineage, stemming from Nichiren (1222–82), is one of several institutions born of a tendency toward segmentation and reform within the fabric of twelfth- and thirteenth-century Japanese Buddhism. Like all the new Buddhist movements of that time, it emerged from the matrix of the Tendai school, which rightly claims to be the mother of all subsequent Japanese Buddhist lineages—namely, Nichiren, Pure Land (especially in the form developed by Shinran, 1173–1262), and Zen. The special emphases taken over by Nichiren from the parent foundation were a passionate reverence for the *Lotus Sūtra* and the exorcising of demons through voluntary possession. Nichiren masters continue to be known for both these traits today—in the scholarly world, for outstanding studies of the *Lotus Sūtra* and its influence, and in the annals of practical popular Buddhism, for the casting-out of fox-phantoms. In this way Nichiren initiates perpetuate two significant aspects of medieval Buddhism in present-day Japan. These survivals must be viewed within the broader framework of which they once were part. Recitation and copying of the *Lotus Sūtra*, as we have seen, was a primary stimulus to the cult of the book in early medieval China. The *Lotus* also greatly encouraged early Buddhist eschatological fervor; devotees would make copies of the scripture that were then sealed in metal containers and buried to await the coming of the Future Buddha Maitreya (when the merit acquired through copying would be credited to the copyist's otherworldly account). In medieval Japan, such copying was often done at great ritual assemblies of monks and laypersons, and it is still carried out in the context of Tendai Buddhism today. The *Lotus Sūtra*, then, provided a central focus for the sort of Buddhism we have been studying in China's early medieval period, when incantations against demons were elaborated in ritual forms—another symptom of the pervasive eschatological anxiety. In a sense, the *Lotus* provided a systematic scriptural framework for the entire proto-Tantric phase of ritual practice. Nowadays, Nichiren Buddhism still shares a devotion to the *Lotus Sūtra* with its parent school, Tendai.

But the *āveśa* rituals, once also a practice of Tendai masters, have now chiefly devolved upon certain specialists among Nichiren's spiritual progeny. These Nichiren priests are in fact the lineal heirs of the distinguished exorcists whom we observed in action among the aristocracy of eleventh-century Kyoto. It is important to remember this, in view of the tendency of some Western authors to consider the Nichiren school as being more closely analogous to Japan's many Shintō-esque "new religions," with their focus on mediumship, rather than an authentic representative of the Buddhist tradition. Thus the Nichiren school is hardly "a sect of purely Japanese origin, . . . with no prototype or affiliations elsewhere," as Percival Lowell expressed it in introducing his own eyewitness account of possession in an eighteen-year-old female medium induced by a Nichiren master.[94] After our survey of the evidence, it is obvious that this technique of induced possession was one of the most visible features of Tantric Buddhism in earlier times, and quite possibly one of its greatest attractions as well.[95]

Tantrists, Foxes, and Shamans

The "Dakini" or "Dagini" for which this complex of modern Japanese possession-rites is named is, of course, the ḍākiṇī of older Tantric sources, identified since at least the eighth century with the fox-phantom. As we have noted, the Chinese linking of the voracious and ill-omened ḍākiṇī-demonesses with the fox was based on their Indian associations with the jackal.[96] In medieval Japan, it became customary to identify figures from the complex Indian pantheon of Tantric Buddhism with native deities (rather like the *interpretatio romana* in the world of late antiquity). Thus it was natural for this *interpretatio nipponica* to see in the supernatural fox-ḍākiṇī the original of Japan's own Inari, a god of rice cultivation often depicted in vulpine form. In this way, the ḍākiṇīs entered the world of Japanese agrarian cults and Shintō shrines while retaining all their Tantric Buddhist associations. Inari shrines are found throughout Japan and provide a natural focus for all forms of fox worship.[97] But a large number of shrines explicitly dedicated to the goddess Dakini or Dagini also survive, often in conjunction with Tendai Buddhist monasteries. In such cases, the fox-spirit is thought of as the original proprietor of the land on which the monastery was erected; after being converted to Buddhism, the fox stayed on to receive offerings and serve as the protector of the monastery and its residents. The connection between the gods and the monks is still manifest in ritual. For example, at the Spring Equinox, monks of the Shinnyodō monastery complex in eastern Kyoto file into their Dakini shrine to read from the Buddhist *Book of Perfect Wisdom* for the fox's edification. They perform other ceremonies there as well. On the altar stand images of foxes, and the main icon (a "secret buddha" only opened during rituals) depicts Dakini as a female deity mounted upon a fox. At the rear of the building is a miniature Shintō shrine, painted in characteristic vermilion; its entrance is a round foxhole.

It is not surprising that a deity of such lineage and character should have been much propitiated by sorcerers and magicians. Using well-tried means of drawing supernatural beings into their service, such persons employed the multifaceted fox-spirits to do their bidding—often, allegedly, for evil purposes. This complex of fox sorcery came to be known as the Dakini or Dagini rites, and also as Izuna rites, from the name of the mountain northwest of the city of Nagano, in Nagano prefecture, thought to be the cult's principal center.[98] It has commonly been assumed that the use of foxes in witchcraft was a Japanese development, unrecorded in China.[99] This is not correct; we need only remember the instructions of the eighth-century Wang T'ao for treating demon-bewitchment. First one was to fumigate the dwelling place of the fox-demon—the agent of possession; then the same treatment was to be applied to the person of the sorcerer, the fox's master (see pp. 248–50). Apart from all its own, independent antics, the fox was a dweller among tombs, in China as in Japan, and thus a frequent emissary of the dark, demonic powers. As the old Chinese lexicographer put it, demons rode upon foxes, and a common Dakini icon or protective talisman shows a galloping fox serving as the vehicle of a standing Tengu—the birdlike creature identified with the mountain-dwelling ascetics who were Japan's sorcerers par excellence.[100] The full range of Chinese fox lore was transmitted to Japan and elaborated there; like so many aspects of Japanese ritual and folklore, it has been deeply imbued by Tantric Buddhism.

Carmen Blacker certainly recognizes the direct relationship between the present-day Nichiren Dakini rituals and the Tantric Buddhist exorcisms of medieval times. Yet her study of Japan's "fox families," *The Catalpa Bow* (1975), is subtitled *A Study of Shamanistic Practices in Japan*, and a liberal definition of shamanism has enabled her to categorize Nichiren exorcism within a wide spectrum of traditional Japanese spiritual exercises. This seems both to weaken the potential usefulness of the term "shamanism" and to blunt or even efface the historical significance of the Buddhist contribution. The complexity of the medieval Buddhist evidence, as well as the influential position occupied by Tendai and Shingon exorcists vis-à-vis the medieval Japanese governing class, clearly suggest that Tantric Buddhist spirit-possession techniques represented something new and distinctive that definitively shaped all subsequent Japanese approaches to these matters. "Shamans" may proceed in a superficially analogous manner, but it is certain that the rituals we have been studying are an integral part of the overarching structure of Tantric practice.

To review the evidence on the various sorts of induced possession within Buddhism: We noted that Buddhism includes more than one form of "institutionalized possession." A priest and his lineal successors may be recognized as the living incarnations of a deity, or a deity may be successively embodied in a series of children—living icons, like the Kumārī of Kathmandu. But the central operative mystery of Tantric Buddhism (as well as non-Buddhist schools of Tantrism) might also be viewed as a form of "possession": the self-generation of the practitioner as a buddha or a god. Through this process of identification, union, or auto-possession, the priest is able, in his enhanced condition, to accomplish any and all of the aims posited by the system of belief, from the attainment of buddhahood ("enlightenment') to the curing of disease. Among the procedures within his grasp are a number of further, subsidiary forms of "possession": the animation of an icon by evoking a deity, in order to gain information; the animation of a doll or puppet for use in healing; and, finally, inducing possession in a living medium.[101] By this latter means, the practitioner may also obtain a divine messenger and supernatural famulus. The celestial informant may speak out directly or work through a mirror, sword-blade, or other luminous object in which the possessed child beholds the semblance of persons and events. Using a child-medium, the master can also bring back and converse with the spirits of the dead; or he may send the child's own spirit as a messenger to their kingdom. All this *va et vient* represents beneficial aspects of spirit possession, in the very broadest sense, that fall within the ordinary powers and duties of a Tantric master.

With this range of possibilities as an integral part of his ritual role, it is not to be wondered at that the same master could use his powers not merely to evoke but also to compel. He might, for example, effect the "possession" of a beloved person, the object of desire, who is technically "hooked" and drawn to the practitioner or his patron through a process of mind-altering love-magic (*ākarṣaṇa*, or *vaśīkaraṇa*).[102] He might even summon a spirit into a dead body and in this way revivify a corpse. The graveyard was a fertile source of supernatural servants, and the Amoghavajra texts include instructions for creating obedient zombies. Or again, a child-medium could be used as the lodging into which a disease-demon was forced, in order to make the afflictor speak out, identify himself, and confess his crime.

When illness is the matter at hand, there are evidently one or more demons to be dealt with. They may be said to "possess" the patient in a weak sense of the term—what some anthropologists have called "etiological possession," which seems simply to be their way of acknowledging that the ailment in question is thought to have a demonic origin. Or else the demons may manifest their presence in more vigorous and dramatic forms that better merit the designation "involuntary (or pathological) possession." As we have seen, mania, depression, or neurological conditions such as epilepsy might be identified with pathological possession of this demonstrative sort. Such victims naturally invited direct action on the part of the healer; the spirit was already manifesting its presence in obvious ways, and was sometimes vocal and articulate. Here the Tantric master might join the secular healer in a direct approach, by threatening, beating, or pricking the patient to elicit the demon's oath of good behavior and subsequent departure; alternatively, he might operate on a surrogate—an image (doll or drawing) of the patient as the demon's host and temporary home, or an image of the demon itself (once its identity, or at least its general type, had been determined). But once again, whether or not the patient was visibly "possessed," induced possession of one sort of another was a highly appropriate procedure for the Tantric master on any occasion of illness. Spirit possession and its varied analogues were as intrinsic to the exercise of his functions as were the written statement and written talisman to the healing operations of the Taoist practitioner. Tantric masters were all-around specialists in the transfer of gods, demons, and soul substance.

There were certain elaborate complexes of anti-demoniac rituals, like the Ritual of the Six Syllables' extravaganza against witchcraft (and other extended Homa-performances of the same sort), all suited to the needs and material resources of the ruling class. But most Tantric therapeutic procedures were far simpler and more accessible. Within the larger body of Tantric practice, they form a corpus of minor rites obviously designed for immediate application at times of urgent need. This is clearly expressed in the title of Amoghavajra's manual, the *Instantly Efficacious Āveśa Ritual Explained by Maheśvara*. That work's very raison d'être lies in its being a rapid method that can obtain immediate results (as discussed at the beginning of this chapter). These techniques must owe their enormous success in East Asia to a number of factors. Their originally aristocratic context is one of these, and a certain affinity with native methods must also have told in their favor. But it seems likely that they also owe a good deal of their subsequent influence to their tempo and structure—to the intrinsic swiftness of their action and their highly dramatic, often spectacular scenarios.

Most of the Tantric pomp and splendor had vanished from Chinese Buddhism well before the twentieth century (though it was maintained within China's political boundaries by Mongols and Tibetans). Yet in China, too, there is striking evidence for the influence of the *āveśa* rites. The clearest indications are found in Taoism. In Chapter 5 we noted a seventh-century Taoist text, the *Secret Rites of the Spells of the Divine Emissary* (pp. 206–7), in which a child-medium is used to issue orders to celestial commanders. The method comes under the patronage of the Immovable One, the Tantric Buddhist deity Acala. Earlier, in discussing exorcism by means of inscribed seals, it became obvious how closely interwoven many Taoist and Buddhist therapeutic techniques had become between the fifth and seventh centuries. Even before the emergence of Taoism as a distinct social entity, Chinese exorcists were occupied with summoning and interrogating disease-demons.[103] In the early medieval period, these techniques were taken over by Taoism and adapted to that system's particular objectives and worldview.

By the eighth century, Tantric Buddhist masters had attained something of a pinnacle among Chinese ritual practitioners, and it would appear that mastery of spirit-possession techniques was an important factor in their success. We have earlier seen how Vajrabodhi brought back the spirit of a dead princess by this means. The incident apparently occurred at a time when foreign monks were being threatened with expulsion from China, and after the impressive performance, "the Emperor began to have faith in Vajrabodhi" (see p. 208). In the biography of Amoghavajra's disciple, the Chinese monk Hui-kuo (746–805), we are told that a later emperor summoned Hui-kuo in 773 or 774 and asked him to show what he could do. Hui-kuo thereupon took eight boys and performed "the enchantment of summoning for interrogation." The emperor was able to obtain answers to every question that he put to the spirits, and all the answers proved to be true. From this point on, Hui-kuo's career began to prosper exceedingly.[104] The *āveśa* rites thus came first in the Tantric practitioner's repertory when immediate and dramatic proof of supernatural efficacy was required. It is significant that in this text, written in 826, the term used is "summoning for interrogation" (*k'ao-chao*), for this is the most common name for the ritual in the context of Taoism.[105]

It is scarcely surprising, then, that the characteristic methods and materials of Tantric Buddhism—the Indian mudrās, Sanskrit spells, iconography, and ritual implements—came increasingly to influence Taoist practice. It was not always a question of simple borrowing; often the Buddhist model served to inspire fresh creations within a Taoist context: new deities, spells, and rituals. There is still some uncertainty about the first appearance of this Taoist synthesis of Chinese and Indian traditions. If we can credit the dates given in an important but problematic ritual text, *Chin-so liu-chu yin* (HY 1009), it could go back as early as the seventh century, but more critical work on the sources will have to be done before we can be sure. It is in any case certain that by the twelfth century, the systematic use of therapeutic spirit-possession had become central to a number of Taoist movements throughout China, and from that time on we find the most detailed written directions for performing a wide variety of such rituals, known under the comprehensive rubric of *k'ao-chao* ("summoning for interrogation"). Whatever the earlier history of Tantric-Taoist relations, between the twelfth and fourteenth centuries there is abundant testimony to the Tantric presence within Taoist practice. This is as striking in art and iconography as in ritual action; for example, the Nepalese sculptor Anige (1243–1306) worked in Taoist temples as well as Tantric Buddhist monasteries in Peking, and though his creations have disappeared, we can still see the Taoist pantheon, painted in the suave style of the international Buddhist iconography of the time, on the walls of the Yung-lo kung, a fourteenth-century Taoist monastery complex in Shansi.

The Taoism of modern times has its roots in the twelfth and thirteenth centuries, which witnessed a virtual renaissance of Taoism. Logically, then, the greatest impact on the practice of present-day exorcists and mediums outside the Taoist hierarchy has come from these post-medieval forms of Taoism, in which Tantric influence or inspiration is highly prominent. Thus, for example, if we find today that Taoist masters in Taiwan use a bell with a three-pronged vajra handle (the *vajra-ghaṇṭā* of Tantric Buddhist ritual), we are not surprised to discover non-Taoist exorcists also employing an identical implement in their own rites. In fact, the whole triple-tiered complex of Taiwanese ritual specialists retains traces of earlier Taoist contact, long ago and on the mainland, with Tantric Buddhism. Such traces can be found among members of the Taoist priesthood, who work with ritual texts written in literary

Chinese and who form an hereditary, closed corporation with a secret oral tradition. But thanks to this Taoist model, Tantric elements can also be detected among the nonorganized exorcists, or "red-head priests" (from their red, demon-dispelling headgear), who perform relatively simple therapeutic rites in the language of the people, thereby offering aspects of Taoist healing in more accessible form. Finally come the professional spirit-mediums, who are compared to puppets—taken over by an alien spirit and under the control of a human master. In their case, the puppeteer is the vernacular exorcist, the red-head priest. He not only restrains their excesses and prevents them from harming themselves; he also interprets their communications.[106]

This brings us once again to the key question underlying this entire tradition of practice. Whatever the extent of his training and sophistication, and on whatever level of society he functions, the medium's master is necessarily an interpreter. He must elicit the required information, make sense of it, and put it to good use if his ritual is to obtain the desired result. The master's pivotal role is particularly well illustrated in modern Taiwan, for nowadays Chinese mediums express themselves as frequently in writing as in speech. This is in keeping with a long Chinese tradition of the sanctity of writing, though the earlier stages by which spirit-writing came to overtake (and even supplant) spirit-speech are still obscure. There is more than one technique for obtaining and fixing the writing of gods or spirits, but a constant feature is the presence of a sober, nonentranced observer to read out each character as the entranced medium sketches it (there may be more than one medium, and more than one reader as well; a scribe is also often employed to write down the characters as they are called out). Such methods are used not only to produce immediate responses to pressing questions and therapeutic talismans in divine script, but to produce entire scriptures as well.[107] Yet without the presence of a calm interpreter, it is doubtful that anything would come of these frenetic seances.

The same observation is obviously true for therapeutic spirit-possession in the Buddhist tradition. The dramatic focus may be fixed on the convulsed and shuddering medium, but the interpretation issues from the master. In a work written by a Japanese monk around the year 1100, there is stern warning against having recourse in the event of illness to non-Buddhist female mediums (*miko*) because such persons name any god, at random; then "the spirit considers itself at liberty to enter upon what is its own, and the illness becomes much worse."[108] The author recognized how crucial it was that the name of a spirit (or of a living person, for that matter) not be mentioned irresponsibly in the patient's presence, for fear that this would immediately deliver the patient into the power of the spirit so rashly named. Indeed, it is easy to see how uttering a name in front of an enfeebled sufferer might fix the identity of the possessing agent in the patient's mind and set off the hoped-for sequence of spirit-declarations—that is to say, the impersonation by the patient or his medium-surrogate of the supposed afflictor, at the master's suggestion. No doubt in cases of pathologic spirit-possession properly so-called, the accusation against the agent may already have been present in the victim's mind, and have needed only to be elicited in the approved form and under the proper, public circumstances. But in the many other applications of induced possession to cases of ordinary illness, one must assume that suggestion played a prominent part. Also, even when a voluntary medium was used, he or she was often chosen from among the patient's relatives, servants, or children—all very good sources of likely names. Nowhere does the role of suggestion seem more obvious than at the bedside of expectant mothers, where any symptoms of pain or discomfort might at once be interpreted as signs of activity on the part of jealous demons, living or dead. Then the monkish scripture-reciters transform themselves into exorcist-inquisitors, names are named, and the psychomachia begins (see the beginning of Chapter 5).

All the mind-revealing methods we have described have been employed, singly or in conjunction, throughout Eurasia. For example, catoptromancy—the divinatory use of a mirror to behold persons or events—is attested to in ancient Greece as early as the fifth century B.C.E. Using a chaste child as visionary, the technique is described in numerous Hellenistic papyri as well as Byzantine manuscripts. Comparable practices were known in medieval Islam and still exist throughout the Islamic world today.[109] It has been assumed that catoptromancy first reached India in the context of Islam, which would mean about the twelfth or thirteenth century. But the *Questions of Subāhu*, translated into Chinese in the first quarter of the eighth century, proves that the art was already known to the Indians in the seventh century.[110] Thus, if nothing else, the Chinese translations of Tantric ritual texts bring new data and new dates to old problems. Matters may eventually prove to be still more complex, however, for bronze mirrors were certainly being used magically and apotropaically in China long before the eighth century, though there seems to be no literary evidence indicating that catoptromancy was among their range of functions.[111]

Catoptromancy is only one among the complex of techniques centering on induced spirit-possession. All questions about ultimate origins must perhaps remain unanswered for the present. Walter Burkert has drawn attention to the potential mobility of professional diviners and has suggested that, as a class, they were agents of much cultural transmission in antiquity. Among the ideas and practices that traveled with them were, obviously, divinatory and healing techniques.[112] Thus it is quite possible to conceive of these readily transportable arts and artifacts as spreading from one culture to another even without the mediation of a major religion. Nor is the possibility of independent parallel development excluded.

There is in any case no need for us to take a stand on this complex of practices, either as radical diffusionists or as partisans of independent invention. The events that interest us took place under relatively well-documented historical conditions, and the historical conclusion that we wish to draw is a simple one. If we must recognize the universality of the various individual techniques, we should also acknowledge the uniqueness of the Tantric synthesis. Whether or not similar practices already existed in China and Japan, it is clear that once the techniques had been diffused in the context of Tantric Buddhism, this synthesis affected their subsequent use. For China, the determining influence of Tantric Buddhism is attested to by survivals in both the Taoist and the vernacular traditions of exorcism. In Japan, the evidence is both more abundant and easier to detect because the parent institutions, the Tendai and Shingon lineages of Tantric Buddhism, are still alive alongside all the diverse ritual epiphenomena that they have inspired.

It follows that present-day East Asian ritual can no longer be viewed in the same way as before. For one thing, the notion of "shamanism" (in any case a much overworked term) no longer seems to be of much relevance in East Asian studies.[113] For example, if we return to Carmen Blacker's 1975 book on "shamanistic practices in Japan," we can demonstrate that all the practices in the wide selection she describes have their sources in the comprehensive matrix of Sino-Japanese Tantric Buddhism. After studying the medieval ritual texts, it becomes obvious that virtually the entire spectrum of current Japanese ritual practice ultimately derives from Buddhist usages. Even in Japan, with its penchant for preservation, the range of rituals currently practiced in the Tantric Buddhist lineages represents a much-diminished program compared to what was once performed. Moreover, the bulk of printed and manuscript sources is vast and daunting. It is perhaps not to be wondered at, then, that even the best scholars have not always been prepared to draw the necessary historical conclusions—particularly when a full diachronic account is called for. Yet it is nonetheless surprising that among the large body of Japanese scholarship on East Asian Tantric Buddhism, there is still no study of the *āveśa* rituals and their social impact in China and Japan.

Once the confrontation of modern practice and medieval texts has taken place, however, it is no longer possible to write blithely of East Asian "shamanism" as if no systematic, learned techniques of therapeutic spirit-possession had ever existed in the region. From the viewpoint of the neurologist or psychologist, the possessed medium may be manifesting a form of age-old, transhistorical behavior (Mircea Eliade's "archaic techniques of ecstasy"), whatever the ritual trappings with which he has been invested by historical circumstance. Yet the historian is obliged to note the presence of elements derived from the dominant ritual patterns of organized "higher" religions, both in the scenario and mechanism of possession and in the theory and content of its communications. For some twelve centuries, the dominant ritual patterns in much of East Asia have been those of Tantric Buddhism and Taoism. The term "shamanism" is convenient, to be sure, but perhaps too convenient. It is certainly too slippery and imprecise to be used without qualification in complex societies like those of China and Japan, with their long written traditions (which have influenced oral tradition in many ways) and their elaborate sacerdotal guilds and hierarchies.

As a philological aside, it is worth recalling that many of the first authors to describe classical North Asian shamanism believed that the word "shaman" itself derived from the Sanskrit *śramaṇa* ("Buddhist monk"), probably through the medium of its Chinese transcription, *sha-men*.[114] This etymology has been contested but never definitively disproved. Moreover, there is considerable cultural evidence to support Shirokogorov's view that Siberian shamanism has been profoundly influenced by Tibeto-Mongol Tantric Buddhism; in its present form, shamanism is the result of Buddhist penetration into northeast Asia.[115] Data from other parts of Asia promote similar conclusions, whether with regard to Buddhism or simply to Indian ritual culture generally.

For example, among supposedly "primitive" or "aboriginal" peoples are the Bataks of Sumatra. They carry out a ceremony of recalling the soul of an ailing person—a ritual performed by a *guru* (Sanskrit for "teacher," "master") who first pronounces a *mintora* (mantra), then draws magical formulae and medical prescriptions from books called *pustaka* (Sanskrit for "book"). The therapeutic repertory of these "primitives" turns out to derive from the Indian *Āyurveda*.[116] On the mainland, we still find significant reflections of long-ago Indian influence among the Chams and the Bahnar, two peoples now surviving in the highland regions of central and southern Vietnam. The Sanskrit word *upādhyāya* ("spiritual preceptor") has become in Cham *pajau* ("priestess"). In Bahnar it has turned into *bojau* ("magician"). The *pajau* enters into a trance and communicates with various deities; she functions essentially as an oracle. The Chams' subordinate priests, who have charge of objects used in the rituals, are called *chamnei* or *samnei*—a word that also derives from the Sanskrit *śramaṇa*.

The presence of these names designating "shamanic" or priestly functions in remote regions of Asia should alert us to the probability that more than just names has reached these peoples from the complex of Indian rituals. The same can be shown for ethnic groups within the sphere of Chinese rather than Indian influence. There is nothing the least bit "primitive" about the rituals of the Yao, for example; they practice pure Taoism, adapted to their own mode of social organization.[117] I believe that it would be hard indeed to find any corner of East or Southeast Asia that has not been transformed by the power of either Indian or Chinese ritual; some regions have been exposed to both traditions. Thus the chances seem very slender that anything like pure "shamanism" should be lingering on in highly sophisticated cultures like those of China and Japan. Should we perhaps term analogous phenomena in complex cultures "secondary shamanism"? Or does the word survive in scholarly parlance simply by poetic license?

Indian and Chinese exorcisms share the trait of interrogation, and this common ground may have facilitated a merging of Buddhist and Taoist ritual styles. In both systems, the interrogator's martial stance is emphasised, yet he still questions and sentences his demonic adversary according to the dictates of the Law. Even the most highly dramatic exorcistic performances continue to respect the all-embracing juridical framework. Setting and procedures are basically legalistic, whether envisioned simply as courtroom drama or in more hallucinatory guise, as scenes from the tribunals of hell. In either case, conditions and actions are virtually identical; close cross-questioning is de rigueur, and judicial torture, too, is standard practice—sometimes directly on the body of the unfortunate person whom the demon has invaded. The demon's tale is told, his guilt is determined, and sentence meted out. In fact, the demon exorcism is a concentrated harrowing of hell, rendered visible to an astonished audience of spectators. Chinese exorcisms accommodated Tantric modes and props; Tantric exorcisms embraced the Chinese legal system, in the interests of Buddhist Law.

Clearly the intensely dramatic confrontation between Buddhist master and possessed medium has had a decisive effect on East Asian exorcistic practice, but it may also have exerted a powerful impact on the development of theater. It has been suggested that Chinese drama owes much of its impetus, and even part of its structure, to what has been called the "shamanic substrate" of Chinese religion.[118] After considering the materials on Buddhist possession-rituals, and bearing in mind the extensive Taoist corpus of procedures that they inspired, we may wonder whether the true "substrate" underlying Chinese drama may not perhaps be found in the liturgy of Tantric Buddhism. The tense dramatic encounter, the multiple levels of role-playing or personification, and the need to enact these charged scenes before witnesses, or a public—all combine to turn the exorcist's ritual area into a miniature proscenium. There is of course no single origin for all the complexities of Chinese theater, but the conventions of Buddho-Taoist liturgy have certainly played an influential part—the more so in that drama has traditionally been performed in close conjunction with liturgy. "Theatrical" role-playing and display are obviously omnipresent in Tantric and Taoist ritual, and liturgical elements are equally detectable throughout East Asian drama. It is no accident that the "demon play," essentially a prolonged and stylized exorcism, has long been a favorite theatrical genre. In studying the possession-rituals of Buddhism and Taoism, the historian of Chinese theater is certain to discover startling new evidence of the intimate links between exorcism and entertainment.

The historian of medicine, for his part, will find proof (if proof is needed) of the intrinsic theatricality of patient-healer relations. Whether drawn from fourth-century Taoists, eight-century Tantric Buddhists, or twentieth-century "vernacular" exorcists, the East Asian data simply reinforce a vision that will soon be accepted as obvious: Ancient or modern, "Eastern" or "Western," "secular" or "sacred," all healing pivots on a vital axis of ritual.

Reference Matter

NOTES

Chapter 1: Disease and Taoist Law

1. *Chen-shu San-kuo chih* 8.263, quoting the lost third-century *Tien-lüeh*. Except where otherwise noted, all translations are Strickmann's own.

2. Stein 1963 remains the most penetrating study on the origins of organized Taoism in the second century. Narrative accounts are found in Maspero 1981: 373–400. For the Movement of the Yellow Turbans, or Movement of Great Peace (T'ai-p'ing tao), which shows many similarities with the Celestial Master's organization, see H. Levy 1956. Of great importance concerning the social and historical circumstances and the worldview that gave rise to Taoism are Seidel 1970, 1978a, and 1978b. Stein 1979 explores the relationship of Taoism with contemporary popular religion.

3. All sources indicate that confession completely superseded the use of drugs in the ancient tradition of the Celestial Masters. However, the *Chen-kao* shows that Hsü Mi and his entourage made abundant use of drugs. See Strickmann 1981: 159. On the Three Officers or Offices (*san-kuan*), see the *Declarations of the Perfect Ones* (*Chen-kao*), HY 1010: 13.4a.

4. The approach from contemporary practice to the texts of the Taoist canon was taken by Kristofer M. Schipper in his pioneering studies. Based on extended fieldwork in Taiwan, Schipper's work has paved the way for the modern study of the Taoist liturgy. For a discussion of one of his first and most important—though unfortunately never published—contributions to the expansion of the field, see Welch 1969–70. Among Schipper's published works, see Schipper 1974, 1975, 1978, 1985b, 1990a, 1990b, and 1993.

5. For the rejection of popular ritual and sacrificial practice by medieval Taoism, see, for example, HY 789, 4: 1b; 5: 4b (for more on this text, see pp. 80–87); HY 1196, 1: 1b–2a; HY 1119: 1a. For a detailed description of the relationship between early medieval Taoism and popular religion, see Stein 1979.

6. See, for instance, Lu Hsiu-ching's *Lu hsien-sheng tao-men k'o-lüeh* (Abridged Code of Master Lu for the Taoist Community; HY 1119: 1a). For a full translation

of this important source on the liturgical rules of Celestial Masters Taoism, see Nickerson 1996: 347–59.

7. For a description of the ruining influence of the demonic gods of the people, see the translation of a passage from the *Abridged Code of Master Lu* (HY 1119: 1a) on p. 51; see also Nickerson 1996: 352.

8. According to the *Declarations of the Perfect Ones* (*Chen-kao*) and, in fact, most Six Dynasties Taoist texts, the spirits of inquisition whose reports bring down punishment on those worshipping the "gods of the profane" belong to the Three Officers or, more exactly, Three Offices (*san-kuan*), the institution to which, as we have already seen, the priests of the early Celestial Masters organization addressed their petitioning documents. The *Abridged Code of Master Lu*, for example, has this to say about adherents of Taoism who have fallen back into performing sacrificial offerings or other rites associated by Taoists with the vulgar religion of the people: "All fugitive and disobedient people will have their reckonings (*suan*, i.e., their predetermined lifespans) shortened and their names excised from the records [of life]. The Three Offices will secretly send out the Lords and Clerks of Summoning for Inquisition to keep watch on their households, afflict their members with inquisitorial punishments, and call disasters down upon them. . . . Thus they are made to suffer from death, disease, state officials, imprisonment, floods, fires, thieves, and bandits." The families of those who give up the Taoist religion altogether in favor of popular gods will, according to the same source, be destroyed entirely (HY 1119: 8b–9b; Nickerson 1996: 358–59). However, according to the *Declarations of the Perfect Ones*, the Three Offices are directly connected with the spirit administration located in the constellation of the Big Dipper (Pei-tou): One of the six palaces that make up the otherworldly tribunal of the Three Offices houses a Lord of the Big Dipper responsible for the affairs in the realm of the dead (Kuei-kuan Pei-tou chün), and one subdivision of this office is in charge of supervising the temples of popular gods who receive sacrifices (HY 1010: 13. 4: 3b–4a, 15: 3a–6a).

9. HY 1119: 1b and HY 1196: 1.6a limit offerings to the ancestors to five days a year; these are the so-called *la* days identified by the Taoists with the first day of the first month, the fifth of the fifth month, the seventh of the seventh month, the first of the tenth month, and the eighth of the twelfth month; see Stein 1979: 69–70. Both of the Taoist sources emphasize that "ghosts do not eat and drink," which refers particularly to meat and wine offerings. Strickmann evidently takes the expression "*la* day(s)" in the traditional sense, as referring to only one particular day in the year, namely, the twenty-third day of the twelfth month. Understood in this way, sacrifices to ancestors would be restricted to a single annual occasion.

10. On the etymology of the word *dharma*, see Benveniste 1969, 2: 101–2.

11. The interesting fact that Taoist ritual was not designated by the common Confucian term for ritual, *li*, but rather associated with legalistic terms such as *fa* or *k'o*, has first been observed and stressed by K. M. Schipper; see, for instance, Schipper 1993: 72–73. Paradoxically, in modern Chinese religion, *fa* has come to designate the magic of the Taoists' rivals, the exorcists.

12. On the bureaucratic structure of the invisible world according to fourth-

century Shang-ch'ing or Mao Shan Taoism, see Strickmann 1979: 179–80. Popular imaginations of the celestial and underworldly bureaucracies are reflected in many of the great novels of late imperial China, such as *The Journey to the West* (trans. Anthony Yu). Modern Western studies on bureaucracy in popular religion include Teiser 1993, 1994; and Shahar and Weller 1996.

13. However, as we shall see, recent research on tomb documents from the Late Warring States through the Han periods has revealed that the bureaucratization of the invisible world had its beginnings long before the emergence of organized Taoism. See in particular Seidel 1985, 1987b; and D. Harper 1994.

14. HY 421, 3:15b. The passage is found in the surviving fragment of a monumental work on Taoist practice entitled *Teng-chen yin-chüeh* (Secret Instructions for the Ascent to Perfection), compiled in the late fifth century by the renowned patriarch of the southern Chinese Taoist Mount Mao (Mao Shan) or "Supreme Purity" (Shang-ch'ing) tradition, T'ao Hung-ching (456–536). A considerable part of the material included in *chüan* 3 of T'ao Hung-ching's received text dates back to the very beginnings of organized Taoism—that is, to the tradition of the Celestial Master(s) (T'ien-shih tao) in southwest China in the second and third centuries, as described in these pages. The passage cited here comes from an ancient catalogue listing the names of twelve hundred divine "officials" to be asked for help in the healing of diseases and the aversion of other misfortunes. Each of the twelve hundred primary officials in turn commands a staff of subaltern civil and military agents, mostly 120 in number, who execute his orders. This catalogue, entitled *Manual of the Twelve Hundred Officials and Generals* (*Ch'ien-erh-pai kuan i*), was one of the most important sources for Taoist priests of early Celestial Masters Taoism. A version of this text, which was obviously put together on the basis of a variety of earlier manuscripts, has been transmitted in HY 1208, *Cheng-i fa-wen ching chang-kuan p'in*. T'ao Hung-ching compares passages from an ancient copy that had come into his possession with updated material revealed by the divine Lady Wei Hua-ts'un in the fourth century C.E. Lady Wei Hua-ts'un was revered by Mao Shan Taoists as one of the primary, immortal Perfect Ones of the Shang-ch'ing (Supreme Purity) heavens from which they derived their tradition. During her life on earth (251–334), however, Lady Wei had been a priestess of the Celestial Masters tradition. Thus her revelations to Yang Hsi (330–86?), the primary recipient of the fourth-century Mao Shan or Shang-ch'ing textual dispensation of Taoism, establish the link between this new tradition and the original (second- and third-century) Celestial Masters Taoism. For a study and translation of the section of T'ao Hung-ching's *Teng-chen yin-chüeh* dealing with Lady Wei Hua-ts'un's new revelations about Celestial Masters ritual, see Cedzich 1987.

15. HY 421, 3:7a (commentary of T'ao Hung-ching); see Cedzich 1987: 111–12.

16. For descriptions of such oratories, see HY 1010, 18: 6b–7 and HY 1119: 4b–5a; see also Cedzich 1987: 63–65.

17. HY 421, 3: 7a–b; see Cedzich 1987: 70–80 for a discussion of this invocation, which is called the "opening of the incense burner."

18. See HY 788: 12a. According to this early source, dating back to 255 B.C.E., the three breaths of the Tao constituting Lord Lao's body and the universe are called the Mysterious, the Primordial, and the Initial.

19. For an analytical discussion of the important ritual sequence in which the officiant entrusts his written message to the vital breaths, or deities, of his body exteriorized during the "opening of the incense burner," see Cedzich 1987: 88–93.

20. HY 421, 3: 8a. Here Strickmann creatively combines two versions of the ritual that are juxtaposed and compared in T'ao Hung-ching's text, neither of which actually has an invocation of the Three Masters that precedes the greetings of the divine powers in the four directions. The formulas to the four quarters quoted by Strickmann stem from an early Celestial Masters fragment dating from the second or third century. The incantation that Strickmann cites as an introit to these formulas belongs to a modified fourth-century Shang-ch'ing version of the same ritual, which first turns to the west (addressing Chang Tao-ling, his son, and his grandson), from there to the north, then to the east, and finally to the south.

21. HY 421, 3: 10–11a.

22. This can be seen in the fourth-century Shang-ch'ing adaptation of the ritual compared by T'ao Hung-ching to the older Celestial Masters source; see HY 421, 3: 8a–b, particularly the commentary.

23. The theme of the transformations of Lao-tzu, the putative author of the *Tao-te ching*, has been treated in detail by Seidel 1969.

24. See HY 421, 3: 6a, commentary, and 3: 9b.

25. Strickmann seems to allude here to practices anticipated in as early a source as the third-century *Wu-fu hsü*. See HY 388, 3: 4a–b; see also Cedzich 1987: 97–104.

26. See note 14 above.

27. See note 19 above.

28. See Schipper 1974.

29. Schipper has interpreted the burning of written memorials in Taoist rituals as "sacrifice of writings" (see, for instance, Schipper 1993: 89–91). Although it is true that the Taoists replaced the people's sacrifices to the "vulgar" gods by written communication with the invisible hierarchies (and did so quite intentionally), it is questionable whether the burning of documents can therefore be considered "sacrifices." For a discussion of this question, see Cedzich 1987: 97–104.

30. This, according to the ritual described in T'ao Hung-ching's text, is done through the rite named the "closing of the incense burner" (*fa-lu*), which is symmetrical to the "opening of the incense burner" (*fu-lu*) just described. See HY 528: 7a–b.

31. On Taoist calligraphy, see Strickmann 1981: 116–21; Ledderose 1984.

32. See Ch'en Hsiang-ch'un 1942.

33. Dr. J. J. Matignon notes that his written prescriptions were frequently rolled up and swallowed by his Chinese patients (Matignon 1936: 79). According to HY 421, 3: 12a–b, it is the memorial itself which—soaked in honey, mixed with cinnabar, and rolled into pills—is to be taken by the patient.

34. See, for instance, *Chen-kao* 7.13a9–b5; passage quoted with approbation

by T'ao Hung-ching in his preface to the *Pen-ts'ao ching* (see Okanishi 1972: 4a); see also *Ch'ung-hsiu cheng-ho ching-shih cheng-lei pei-yung pen-ts'ao*, rev. ed. Taipei, 1976: 32. For a clear rejection of traditional drug-based cures in a fifth-century work on Celestial Masters rules and liturgy, see the translation by Nickerson 1996: 352. Strickmann saw in such Taoist rejection "a paradox almost as striking as the enthusiastic use of human excrement by monastic apostles of purity," and wrote: The list of "a hundred" medicinal herbs, a clear declaration of knowledge, was to be recited by learned initiates who had vowed never to use them. Here the paradox is perhaps of the rhetorical sort, since the declaration seems conscious, somewhat perverse, and they did use them, as we know, after all. In fact, their knowledge of materia medica was an important strand in the general education and cultural heritage of these Mao Shan initiates, and it is found in the work of the greatest of them: T'ao Hung-ching (456–536), recoverer and editor of the original Mao Shan manuscripts, effective creator of the Shang-ch'ing as a distinctive school—and also the founder of the critical pharmacology in China.

35. The origins of the Shang-ch'ing tradition are described in Strickmann 1977. See also Robinet 1984, vol. 1.

36. For the Shang-ch'ing Perfect Ones' initial announcements to Yang Hsi, including Yang's first meeting with his future celestial spouse, see HY 1010, 1: 11b–18a.

37. These night-by-night transcripts are found in HY 1010, 1–4.

38. On Tao-hsüan's visions, see *Tao-hsüan lü-shih kan-t'ung lu*, T. 2107, vol. 52.

39. For the Mao Shan lineage beginning with Lady Wei Hua-ts'un, Yang Hsi, and the two Hsüs, see HY 304: 10–12.

40. These letters, prayers, confessions, and dream records are found in HY 1010, 17–18.

41. See HY 1010, 4: 10b.

42. The particular relevance of the Shang-ch'ing revelations with respect to the Hsü family's social status in south China under the Eastern Chin dynasty is discussed in Strickmann 1977.

43. For a more detailed treatment of these sources, see Strickmann 1981, especially pp. 122–69.

44. For a brief description of the hierarchy of heavenly regions according to the Shang-ch'ing tradition, see Strickmann 1979: 179–80; see also HY 167.

45. For the term "worn-out breath" in the context of Taoist healing rituals, see, for instance, HY 421, 3: 19a.

46. On the meditational absorption of the *ch'i* of the stars and planets in Shang-ch'ing Taoism, see Robinet 1993, especially chaps. 7 and 8; see also Bokenkamp 1997a: 275–372.

47. For the name T'ai-yin, one has, in abstracto, a large choice of dictionary definitions to which this term might be assigned: the Moon, Jupiter, Venus, and so on. More interesting, perhaps, is its place at the northern extreme of the earth, as a station in the travels of Lu Ao (in the *Huai nan tzu*), an aspirant to immortality.

48. There are many references in Taoist literature to Feng-tu, the city of the dead, to its six heavens or its twenty-four hells. See *Yün-chi ch'i-ch'ien*, 45.17. Ac-

cording to the *Chen-kao* (15.2a), hells (*ti-yü*, literally "earth prisons") were located in more than one place, whereas the six heavens (*liu-t'ien*) were associated with Feng-tu (ibid., 8.8b, 10.10a). Depending on the sources, Feng-tu is both the underworld, or land of the dead, and the entrance-site to the underworld.

49. A detailed description of the palaces and administration of the realm of death as revealed to Yang Hsi was included by T'ao Hung-ching in his *Chen-kao*; see HY 1010, 15–16.

50. For this hypothesis, see also Strickmann 1985: 193. Strickmann may have based his observation on HY 1010, 4: 16a–b. A confirmation of his interpretation is found, for instance, in the quotation of the *Han-shih wai-chuan* in the *T'ai-p'ing yü-lan* 883: 6a–b.

51. Indications that the Water Officer was the most feared among the Three Officers are found throughout the *Chen-kao*, but see particularly HY 1010, 7: 6a–b.

52. Probably Strickmann refers here to T'ao Hung-ching's commentary in HY 1010, 16: 7b. There T'ao reasons that Yang Hsi's information about the realm of the dead must have been based on some additional oral explanations, since the writing and language of the ghosts were too different for Yang to copy or transcribe directly either from an underworld or from underworld speech.

53. See HY 1010, 13: 3a–b and 15: 2a, commentary.

54. HY 1010, 13–16. The text lists the officials of the dead, beginning with the ranks of the so-called subterranean rulers (*ti-hsia chu-che*) on down to the lowliest clerical jobs. The former, among whom figure many immortality adepts and priests of Celestial Masters Taoism, can acquire further merit and eventually enter the ranks of true immortals. The latter positions, ironically filled by some of the most illustrious rulers and heroes of the Ch'in and Han periods, do not provide for a similar career; their holders will always remain nothing but administrators of the ghosts. Moreover, although many of the persons listed in this elaborate bureaucracy of the netherworld were undoubtedly venerated by or received sacrifices from social groups outside of Taoism, they constitute only a tiny fraction of what Strickmann calls here the "pantheon of the profane"—namely, those whose relative merit remained worthy of being rewarded with some minor office in the Taoist system. The vast majority of the figures who received sacrifices from the people of fourth-century China are not recognized in this tableau with any administrative position whatsoever. Counted as ordinary ghosts, they were controlled by the officers listed in the hierarchy but were not part of that hierarchy themselves.

55. See, for instance, Hulsewé 1955: 116.

56. We are dealing here with the ancient Chinese concept of the "inherited burden" (*ch'eng-fu*), on which see also Zürcher 1980: 136–41. Many "sepulchral lawsuits" (*chung-sung*) were recorded under the Sung, in particular with the recrudescence of Taoist practices in the twelfth and thirteenth centuries, during the so-called Taoist renaissance. See, for instance, HY 1214, *Tao-men ting-chih* (preface dated 1188), 1.27b–38b; see also Strickmann 1981: 262.

57. Most of this material is found in *chüan* 7 and 8 of the *Chen-kao* (HY 1010); see also Strickmann 1981: 122–69.

58. HY 1010, 4: 11a–b.
59. Ibid., 2: 21a.
60. Ibid., 4: 10b.
61. Ibid., 7: 11b–12a.
62. Ibid., 4: 10b.
63. Ibid., 7: 6b–7b. These thank-offerings were not thought to be actually consumed by the spirits. Rather, they served as pledges (*kuei* or *hsin*) providing a concrete measure for the merit acquired by the agents for their help in the ritual process. The kind and number of these pledges had to be detailed in the text of the petitions. Once a lawsuit had been successfully settled, that is, whenever an illness was cured or a misfortune abated after a priest's ritual intervention, a second ritual was performed, during which the merits of all spirit-helpers were announced (*yen-kung*) and converted into incremental promotions in rank. This usually happened again in written form. The concrete offerings or pledges, such as rice, grain, oil, paper, writing-brushes, and silk, were then distributed: One part went into the organization's central fund, another was donated to the poor (or to hermit-adepts of Taoist immortality arts), and the rest was given to the acting priest to support his communal work (but not his personal needs). In this way, Celestial Masters Taoism remained, on the one hand, true to its principal stipulation that gods should not eat nor priests accept pay, and maintained, on the other, a soteriological program through which spirit agents could gradually ascend in the otherworldly hierarchy. If Hsü Mi was reproached by the Perfect Ones for neglecting his obligations toward four spirit-commanders who had helped his family in a liturgical lawsuit, it was not because of the thank-offerings in themselves but because he obstructed the spirits' well-deserved promotion. For details about these thank-offerings in connection with the ritual announcement of merits, see HY 421, 3:13a, and Cedzich 1987, pp. 58–59, 97–102, and 126–27.
64. HY 1010, 20: 6a–b.
65. Ibid., 1: 5a; 12: 1b; 20: 14a.
66. Ibid., 20: 13b–14a.
67. Ibid., 7: 6a.
68. Ibid., 7: 10a.
69. Ibid., 7: 10b.
70. The *Chen-kao* does contain some evidence of the importance accorded to the prognostication of critical days, which either carried dangers for individuals on account of their birthdates or were generally considered unlucky for supplications; see, for instance, HY 1010, 7: 10a and 18: 6b. Far more material of this type, dating mostly from the fourth and fifth centuries, is found in a compilation entitled *Master Red Pine's Petition Almanac* (*Ch'ih-sung-tzu chang-li*, HY 615, 1: 19a, 2: 18a).
71. *Chen-kao*, HY 1010, 20: 6a–7b.
72. Ibid., 7: 6a–b.
73. Ibid., 7: 8b–9a.
74. See the quotation cited on p. 17 (at n. 72).
75. The frequent entreaties of the Perfect Ones directed to Hsü Mi, especially

those expressed in the form of lyrical songs by Hsü's prospective divine bride, are found in HY 1010, *chüan* 2. Among other things, the immortals there also recommend Hsü to maintain sexual abstinence. For a more detailed treatment of this topic, see Strickmann 1981: 179–208.

76. HY 1010, 8: 3b–4a.

77. Ibid., 8: 4b.

78. Ibid., 8: 5b.

79. Ibid., 8: 6a, 7a.

80. Ibid., 8: 7a.

81. Ibid., 8: 7a–b.

82. Ibid., 8: 7b.

83. Ibid., 8: 8a–b.

84. Ibid., 8: 9a.

85. For these regulations, see for instance HY 1119: 2a–4a; see also Nickerson 1996: 348–49 and 353–55.

86. HY 1119: 1b.

87. On this terminology, Strickmann wrote: I use, or abuse, the terms "psychotherapy" and "family therapy" advisedly, since the justice of Thomas Szasz's analysis is manifest. Preparing to unmask "the myth of psychotherapy," he writes, "With the development of modern psychotherapy, there arose a powerful tendency to view all previous attempts of this [interpersonal] sort through the pseudomedical spectacles of psychiatry and to relabel them as psychotherapies. Accordingly, both psychiatrists and laymen now believe that magic, religion, faith-healing, witch-doctoring, prayer, animal magnetism, electrotherapy, hypnosis, suggestion, and countless other human activities are actually different forms of psychotherapy. I consider this view objectionable" (Szasz 1978: xxiv). So do I, when the term is being used either to legitimize modern techniques in historical perspective or to relativize the practices of other cultures or historical periods. In the present instance, a one-time use, for shock value, may serve its purpose.

88. On the twenty-five kinds of ailment-demons (*chu-kuei*), see T. 1332: 559c.

89. Sivin 1968: 297. According to Ko Hung, corpse-infusions and demon-infusions include "those cases among the five varieties of corpse-attacks that are called 'corpse-infections' (*shih-chu*), as well as those in which other demons are drawn in [making them 'demon-infections,' *kuei-chu*]. In the development and action of the ailment there are thirty-six varieties, and these can [in turn] develop into a total of ninety-nine varieties. In brief, they cause people to suffer from chills or fever, loss of moisture or urine (*lin-li*), confusion and silence [the term—*huang-huang mo-mo*—means perhaps introspection, or depression]. [The persons afflicted] do not know precisely what is causing their sufferings, yet there is no part of their body which is free from pain. It can go on for months and years, gradually becoming more serious and all-encompassing, until it results in death. After death, it is once more transmitted to those about [the initial victim], and it can go on to exterminate his entire clan. If one is aware of these signs/symptoms, one ought to treat them immediately." Ko Hung then lists a number of prescriptions using herbal, mineral, and animal ingredients (*Chou-*

hou fang, 14–15). Note also Ko Hung's statement that women and small children tend to get this ailment on carriages and boats (p. 15): "The symptoms are dizziness, headaches, vomiting [i.e., modern travel-sickness, car-sickness, seasickness]. . . . Treat by making a compound of four herbs, and carrying it; or, before entering a boat, scrape off a bit of the boat, burn it, and swallow with water" (ibid.).

90. See the list of types and symptoms given in *Chu-ping yüan-hou lun* 24: 130.

91. A version of this text is contained in the Taoist canon (HY 1295), but Strickmann evidently referred to a different edition.

92. See *Chou-hou pei-chi fang*, HY 1295, 1: 17a–19a.

93. These five corpse-demons are: flying corpse; recondite/reclusive corpse; wind-corpse; sinking corpse (*chen-shih*); and corpse-infusion. On their symptoms, see *Chou-hou pei-chi fang*, 12.1. On the corpse-demons as a class, see also pp. 76–78.

94. *Chou-hou pei-chi fang*, 14–15. On Chinese materia medica, see Stuart 1924; Clarke 1925; Ishidoya 1933; Delatte 1938; Read 1936, 1941, 1987; Cooper and Sivin 1972; Li Shih-chen 1973; Li Hui-lin 1978, 1979; Perry 1980; Hu 1980; and Ulrike Unschuld 1977.

95. Sivin 1968: 311.

96. *Chu-ping yüan-hou lun* 24: 130.

97. Ibid.

98. Ibid., 24: 130–31.

99. Sivin 1968: 297.

100. *Chu-ping yüan-hou lun* 24: 133.

101. Ibid., 24: 131.

102. Ibid., 24: 132.

103. On *ku* toxin, see Feng and Skryock 1935; Paul Unschuld 1985: 46–50. On poisoning, see also Needham and Ho 1959; Obringer 1995.

104. See HY 1155.

105. *Ch'ien-chin yao-fang* 17: 320a.

106. *Ch'ien-chin i-fang* 30: 354b.

107. Ibid.

108. The word *chu*, "control," is homophonous with *chu*, "infest," "infestations."

109. The six agencies are the throat, the stomach, the large and small intestines, the gallbladder, and the bladder.

110. *Ch'ien-chin i-fang* 30: 354b.

111. Ibid., 29: 347b.

112. Ibid., 30: 355a.

113. On this sacred mountain of the east, in Shantung, which was believed to be the abode of the dead, see Chavannes 1910.

114. *Ch'ien-chin i-fang* 30: 355a.

115. *Wai-t'ai pi-yao*, vol. 1, *chüan* 13: 368, 369. The text also gives three formulas of fumigatory mixtures to use in cases of demoniac possession.

116. Ibid., vol. 1, *chüan* 13: 358, 359.

117. Okanishi 1958: 651–52.

118. *Wai-t'ai pi-yao*, vol. 1, *chüan* 13: 358b–359a.

119. On the symbolism of the gourd container in Taoism, see Stein 1990.

120. On the early use of ghost-money, see Hou 1975.

121. On the General of the Five Ways, see the recent essay by Glen Dudbridge, 1996–97.

122. See Strickmann 1975.

123. The earliest work belonging to this tradition is HY 1217, compiled and prefaced by Yüan Miao-tsung in 1116.

124. Boltz 1985.

125. HY 220, 1: 7a–8a.

126. See Strickmann 1981: 44–45; 249, n. 57; and Boltz 1987: 37; 266, n. 68.

127. HY 220, 23: 1a–2a.

128. Ibid., 23: 2a–5a, 5a–6a, and 6b–7b.

129. Ibid., 23: 5a.

130. Ibid., 23: 6b.

131. Ibid., 23: 5b.

132. Ibid., 23: 7b–8b.

133. Ibid., 24: 20a–21b.

134. Liu Ts'un-yan 1971: 300. Note that "worms" were seen very early on as pathogens, albeit hypothetically (as in Anglo-Saxon tooth-charms). Thus they are part of the long history of the medical "worm," and of the pathogen as "worm"—although this doesn't necessarily mean that these rampant disease-agents had become any more visible. There is no proof of microscopes in twelfth-century China, but the principle of an amoral, nonhereditary contagion is recognized, and even overstated (cf. HY 220: 21b: "The disease is capable of being infectious at a distance of 1,000 *li*" [Liu, p. 294]). However, to understand twelfth-century Taoists' conception of disease, we should look not only at their portrayal of diagnostic symptoms but also at their directions for treatment. In all likelihood, the worms manifest a long-standing fascination with *hua*—transformation—rather than suggesting any microscopic, systematic observation.

135. HY 220, 23: 8b.

136. On advances in treatment, Strickmann wrote: In 1173, fifteen years after Lu Shih-chung completed his *Great Rites of the Jade Hall*, a Japanese monk transcribed a short text entitled *Oral Tradition on Corpse-Vector Disease* (*Denshibyō kuden*, T. 2507). These rather disjointed jottings note symptoms as they appeared in a monastic context: demonic thoughts while meditating, feelings of lust or anger, and distractive drowsiness, in addition to feverish sensations, loss of appetite, and gradual emaciation. The ailment starts with palpitations below the left nipple; when they move to the right nipple, death is a certainty. The disease begins with a single person and is not then transmitted to others. After the sufferer dies, however, it passes to ten thousand persons. It is as when a vessel is broken and the water in it spills out in all directions.

The disease is explained by a characteristically Buddhist legend. The demon responsible for it is the yakṣa Harita, who dwelt with a family of ninety thousand demons in the Cold and Cloudy Mountains, daily devouring human vital-essence, *ch'i*, blood and flesh. One day, when Harita had left his mountain and was crossing the desert, he encountered the great god Āṭavaka, who fought and conquered him. "Even as you devour human flesh and blood, so I will devour your flesh and blood," said the god (who had long before been converted to Buddhism). Though these notes do not say as much, the implication is that Āṭavaka should be invoked in all cases of corpse-vector disease. For more on Āṭavaka as a protector and benefactor of faithful Buddhists, see pp. 143–51.

The text's principal recommendation for treatment involves burning moxa at a number of points on the patient's body, but it also advises making images of the three disease-demons, which are said to resemble the Chinese character for "six" (*liu*), and throwing them into a copper kettle of boiling oil. The three demons were particularly dangerous during the fifty-seventh day of the sexagesimal cycle (known in Japan as Kōshin), when one was supposed to stay awake all night to keep watch, while abstaining from sexual intercourse. This medieval Chinese belief long survived in Japan. Another Japanese Buddhist text, copied (or recopied) in 1171, similarly associates corpse-vector disease with the three worms and the fifty-seventh day of the cycle. The best physicians in the empire, we are told there, have proved incapable of curing this ailment, which has steadily spread everywhere and wipes out entire families. Princes, officers of state, queens, concubines, monks and nuns have all been afflicted. There are three degrees of the malady: pustules (or leprosy, *lai*), corpse-vector, and madness. Fear of infection has alienated parents and children and set husbands against wives. Moxa and herbal baths are recommended, as well as burning the demons' images in the course of performing the Tantric Buddhist oblation, Homa (T. 1221, *Ritual of the Blue-Faced Vajrayakṣa for Driving off Demons and Devils*).

137. Before examining the various conceptions of karma, it may be necessary to say a few words about Buddhist types of etiology. On this, the major work remains Demiéville 1985; see also Zysk 1991. The Buddhist encyclopedia, *Ta chih-tu lun* (T. 1509, 25: 119c) recognizes two types of ailments, one due to physical causes, the other due to karmic retribution from past lives (*karmaja*), or "force of deeds"; see also Lamotte 1949–76, 1: 494, 584–85. In the *Saddharmasmṛtyupasthāna-sūtra* (T. 721, 9: 47c), congenital illnesses in an infant are explained as residues of bad deeds that result in being sent from hell to be reborn as a fatally doomed human being. Likewise, the *Saṃyuktāgama* (T. 99: 252c, T. 100: 452b–c) distinguishes between: (1) mundane suffering caused (in the present existence) by wind, phlegm, bile, or by accidents, the seasons, etc., and (2) mental suffering or unhappiness caused by the obsessions and the passions of greed, hatred, sloth, agitation, and doubt. According to the *Catuḥsatya-śāstra* (Śāstra of the Four Truths, a treatise by Vasuvarman, T. 1647: 382c–383a), illness is of either internal or external origin, and mental illnesses are caused by illusions or wrong visions, etc. The list of 404 illnesses is usually arrived at by multiplying the 101 basic ailments by four, the number of passions. The clearest account of Buddhist etiologies and their respective treatments is found in Chih-i's *Mo-ho-chih-kuan* (T. 1911, *chüan* 8a: 106a–107c); see Demiéville 1985: 256–57. According to Chih-i, illnesses have six types

of causes: (1) an imbalance of the four elements; (2) improper diet; (3) disorders brought about by meditative practice; (4) demonic ailments (*kuei-ping*), that is, intrusion of demons in the four elements or the five viscera (this is proved by the success of exorcists when normal medicine does not work); (5) diabolic or Māra ailments (*mo-ping*), which attack the spirit (whereas *kuei* attack the body only), especially in the course of contemplation and which consist of perverse thoughts and conceptions, resulting in loss of merit accrued through contemplation; and (6) karmic retribution from previous lives or the present life (T. 1911, 46: 108a2–3, 109b). Here is how the five infractions affect the body: killing affects the eyes and liver; alcohol affects the mouth and heart; lewdness, the ears and kidneys; lies, the tongue and nose; and theft, the nose and lungs. The first and second types of illnesses can be treated by recipes and medicaments, the third one by improved, rectified Ch'an practice; the fourth and the fifth, by inspection and charms; the sixth, by inspection when internal, by contrition when external. See also Demiéville 1985: 81–89. On Chih-i's medical notions, see Yamano 1984, 1985; Andō Shun'yū 1970.

138. The best analysis of the *T'ai-p'ing ching* is Kaltenmark 1979.

139. Wang Ming 1979: 58.

140. Ibid., 58–59.

141. Ibid., 60.

142. Ibid.

143. On "guarding the One" (*shou-i*), see Andersen 1980; Kohn 1989a; Schipper 1993: 130–59; Robinet 1993: 120–38.

144. Wang Ming 1979: 22.

145. Kaltenmark 1979: 36, n. 24.

146. *Chen-kao*, HY 1010, 2: 12a.

147. Ibid., 3: 13b–14a. It was revealed to Hsü Mi that in a former life he had been a person (from another, unrelated clan) who had only just failed to achieve transcendence due to his excessive fondness for women. This was said to explain an analogous trait in Hsü Mi's own character, still an obstacle (his celestial informants told him) to his success in achieving the Tao. Thus a cultivated and spiritually ambitious Chinese in the middle of the fourth century might simultaneously recognize his essential consubstantiality with his own lineal ancestors (as well as the moral burden resulting therefrom) and also perceive himself as the product of a long series of previous lives in genetically unrelated bodies (Strickmann 1981).

148. On this point, Strickmann wrote: Hence, beyond the range of painful moral burdens derived from ancestors or one's own actions, a spectrum of "free" etiological factors was also acknowledged. Recalling Lewis's distinction between domestic/hereditary/moral cults and exotic/random/amoral cults (Lewis 1989 [1971]), we may possibly find the Chinese model, in mid-fourth century, even more complex. With the domestic ancestors, we have a fabric of responsibility and control that might seem predetermined, utterly moral, and highly fixed/stable. Yet under the ministrations of a skilled Taoist priest, the entire relationship becomes wonderfully flexible and negotiable. In one sense, the imported axis of Buddhist

karma might at first seem very exotic in its foreign origins and nature. Yet of course its entire purpose, or raison d'être, is moral suasion. It was naturally open to an infinity of adjustments, since it involved weaving a net of complete fiction back across the past—with retrospective karmic justification thus certainly constituting as much a fictional device and stimulus to the imagination as the sixteenth-century French pardon tales studied by Natalie Z. Davis (1987). But Buddhist karma was very soon acculturated in China and became quite as domestic as its Chinese ancestral counterpart, which it seems to have displaced from imaginative literature/fiction. . . . This model also suggests the very substantial difference between Buddhist karma and its Chinese pseudo-analogue because, at least in normative Buddhist texts, that purported principle of historical inevitability serves in reality as a randomizing factor: It is (we must recall) morally suasive fiction and belongs on the "exotic" rather than the domestic side of the frontier. Thus it is a massive case of "fiction in the archives" (N. Z. Davis 1987). A comparable nosological distinction was still being made in nineteenth-century India. For example, General W. H. Sleeman was informed by the head native judicial officer at Sagar that "the diseases of mankind were to be classified under three general heads: first, those suffered for sins committed in some former birth; second, those suffered for sins committed in the present birth; third, those merely accidental. 'Now,' said the old gentleman, 'it must be clear to every unprejudiced mind that the third only can be cured or checked by the physician.' Epidemics, he thought, must all be classed under the second head, and as inflicted by the Deity for some very general sin; consequently, to be removed only by prayers." Sleeman concludes by observing, "I believe that, among the great mass of the people of India, three-fourths of the diseases of individuals are attributed to evil spirits and evil eyes; and for every physician among them, there are certainly ten *exorcisers*" (Sleeman 1971 [1915]: 168).

This appears to parallel our Taoist information well enough; but it must also be recognized that, in addition to their own tangled Chinese web of familial identity and collective clan responsibility, the sophisticated Shang-ch'ing Taoists, at least, were also familiar, through Buddhism, with Indian notions of reincarnation. On comparable Indian traditions of karma, see O'Flaherty 1980. The dozen essays collected in this work provide a comprehensive view of "karma and rebirth in classical Indian traditions." Buddhist conceptions of karma describe hells and heavens filled with beings working out their individual destinies. This carefully worked-out legal system of crime and punishment became thoroughly rooted in East Asia. What happens when the destined End comes—a kalpic catastrophe of Fire or Flood, as has been foretold? Those in the hells who have paid back (*pao*) their karmic debts will be released; the others will simply be shifted to a comparable "facility" elsewhere (since the Buddhist's Indian universe is infinite, there is a plurality of worlds, and consequently no difficulty at all in making everything fit and in causing disparate-seeming systems to coincide). For a work on karma integrated, at the end, with kalpic fatality, see the *Yu-p'o-se chieh ching* (*Treatise on Upāsaka Precepts*, T. 1488, translated ca. 414–21; esp. *chüan* 7).

149. Zürcher 1959: 168–69.

150. On divine retribution for family members of the guilty party, see Yang Lien-sheng, "Hostages in Chinese History," in L. Yang 1961: 56.

151. Robinet 1984, 2: 53, 81.

152. HY 1010, 7: 12b–13a; see Strickmann 1981: 156–58.

153. L. Yang 1961: 56.

154. *Chen-kao*, HY 1010, 7: 13a–b.

155. Ibid., 7: 13b.

156. HY 1333, 1: 3a–b; see Robinet 1984, 2: 179–86.

157. On this, Strickmann wrote: Buddhist medicine, of course, had a powerful bookish, scriptural tradition of its own. Characteristically, it eschewed materia medica. However, in the second century, Mou-tzu criticizes the Buddhists, from a Taoist point of view, for using drugs while early Taoists did not. At a certain point, Buddhists seem to have adopted Indian medicine and transported it to China. A number of Chinese Buddhist scriptures represent translations of Indian medical texts; others, adaptations; still others, free embroideries. But we must note the particular Buddhist emphasis on ritual means. Indian theories, treatments, materia medica, and even surgical instruments were thoroughly ritualized. For instance, for demonically induced diseases, Chih-i, the patriarch of T'ien-t'ai, recommended insight meditation and the use of incantations but also warned that meditation, wrongly practiced, could cause illness rather than cure it. Other Buddhists, who saw all ailments as caused by demonic agencies (and this, often, as a corollary of the demoniac nature of the apocalyptic times), saw powerful ritual means as the primary mode of response.

What we term "meditation" is always found within a ritual matrix and is, in fact, the kernel of Buddhist and Taoist ritual. What is stated of meditation is true of ritual generally—namely, that it is motivated by fear of wrong, lacunulose, clumsy performance and its consequences, and made up, at least in part, of measures taken to obviate inadvertent mistakes and omissions. And Buddhism's comprehensive medical metaphor might also be ritualized—as, for example, when we find the ancient Indian optical instrument for removing cataracts, the *śalākā*, passed before the face of the Tantric Buddhist neophyte who is being inducted into the mysteries of the maṇḍala in the ritual of consecration (*abhiṣeka*), in order to remove, metaphorically, the scales of ignorance from his eyes and enable him to gaze directly on the truth of the Dharma. See Demiéville 1985: 85; Hoernle 1893–1912; Zysk 1991; Filliozat 1934; Michihata 1957: 388–406.

158. *Lu hsien-sheng tao-men k'o-lüeh*; HY 1119: 1a; see also Nickerson 1996: 352.

159. A case in point is that of Kuan Yü, who was posthumously raised to the status of the God of War, Kuan Ti. On this question, see Duara 1988.

160. On early Taoist messianism, see Seidel 1970 and 1983–85.

161. HY 442; the text has been partially translated in Strickmann 1981: 209–24; and, more recently, in Bokenkamp 1997a: 339–62.

162. On Li Hung, see Seidel 1970.

163. HY 442: 5a; 8a–b; see Strickmann 1981: 217, 222–23; Bokenkamp 1997a: 348, 353–54.

164. Ibid., 3b–4a; see Strickmann 1981: 214–15; Bokenkamp 1997a: 345–46.

165. HY 179; a translation of this text is found in Bokenkamp 1997a: 362–66; see also ibid., 280–81 and 299–302. A full discussion of all the corporeal agencies mentioned here can be found in Maspero 1971.

166. HY 442: 9b–13a; see Bokenkamp 1997a: 355–62.

167. HY 179: 1a–3b; see Bokenkamp 1997a: 362–66.

168. HY 179: 1a–b; see Bokenkamp 1997a: 362.

169. HY 179: 1b–2a; see Bokenkamp 1997a: 362–63.

170. Okanishi 1972: 105b, 106a. See also Strickmann 1978b: 473, n. 23.

171. HY 179: 2b; see Bokenkamp 1997a: 363–64.

172. HY 179: 3a–b; see Bokenkamp 1997a: 364–65. Bokenkamp (ibid., 280–81) thinks that this mixed tenth category of prohibitions was later added to the original text to bring the number of taboos to ten, on the model of the Ten Precepts in Buddhism.

173. Bodde 1975; Hulsewé 1955; Kalinowski 1986.

174. See Frank 1958.

175. HY 442: 7a; see Strickmann 1981: 220; Bokenkamp 1997a: 351–52. For "liberation by means of a corpse" (a lesser mode of attaining immortality) and "fragrant ossature" (auspicious inherited bone-structure, literal and metaphoric), see Strickmann 1979: 182–84; Robinet 1979. "Agents-beneath-the-earth" are on the lowest step of the scale of perfection, but even they will achieve celestial immortality in time, through a long series of regular official promotions; cf. Strickmann 1979: 181, n. 169.

176. HY 442: 6b–7b; see Strickmann 1981: 220–21; Bokenkamp 1997a: 351–52.

177. HY 442: 6b and 4b; see Strickmann 1981: 219, 215–16; Bokenkamp 1997a: 351, 347–48.

178. HY 442: 4b; see Strickmann 1981: 216; Bokenkamp 1997a: 347.

Chapter 2: Demonology and Epidemiology

1. See Legge 1886:109–10; and Giles 1923.

2. See Strickmann 1990. An important step has been taken in overcoming these entrenched prejudices against Buddhist apocryphal texts with *Chinese Buddhist Apocrypha*, edited by Robert E. Buswell, Jr. See in particular Buswell's Introduction and Strickmann's essay on the *Consecration Sūtra* in this volume. On the question of Buddhist apocrypha, see also Demiéville 1973b: 148–51, 153–57; and Makita 1976.

3. This has been stressed repeatedly by Strickmann; see, for instance, Strickmann 1983–85, and 1990: 77–79.

4. T. 396, 12: 1118c–1119a. The scriptural sources relative to the "Final Dharma" can be found in Lamotte 1958: 210–22; see also Strickmann 1990: 112–13, n. 32; Chappell 1980; and Nattier 1991.

5. One widespread theme was the notion that the sūtras would vanish into the earth at the extinction of the Dharma. According to the *Mahāparinirvāṇa-sūtra* (T. 375, 12: 663c), for instance, the *Nirvāṇa-sūtras* and other Mahāyāna scriptures will all disappear into the soil of Kashmir; see Demiéville, in Renou and Filliozat 1985, vol. 2, par. 2115. According to the *Mahāparinirvāṇa-sūtra* (T. 376, 12: 895a), this sūtra will be hidden in the earth of Kashmir, while all *Vaipulya-sūtras* will disappear at this time. The *Fa-mieh ching* (T. 396, 12: 1119a–b) describes the sudden deluge at the end, and the apparition of Moonlight (Yüeh-kuang); the *Fo mieh-tu hou kuan-lien tsang-sung ching* (T. 392, 12: 1114b–c) gives details on the Buddha's relics, images, and especially his alms-bowl and its eastward migration. Another widespread theory had it that the Mahāyāna scriptures, like the relics of the Buddha, would be preserved in the palace of the nāga-king, under the sea.

6. On the color of monks' robes, which must always be dark, see Lin Li-kouang 1949: 89. According to the sources quoted by Lin, wearing a white robe was imposed as a sanction for a very grave offence (like creating a schism in the Saṅgha).

7. See, for instance, T. 396, 12: 1119a–b. See also T. 145: 870b–c; T. 383: 1013b–1014c; T. 396: 1118c–1119b. On Buddhist eschatology, see the Indian cosmological texts discussed by Lin Li-kouang 1949, vol. 1: 127–46; see also Zürcher 1982a and 1982b; Nattier 1991; Michihata 1979: 172–88; Sponberg and Hardacre 1988.

8. See *Shih-chia p'u*, T. 2040, 50: 83c–84b.

9. Strickmann 1981. For the theme of the apocalyptic deluge in contemporary (fifth-century) Taoist eschatology, see, for instance, HY 442: 3b; HY 335, 1: 5a, 8a, and passim; see also Mollier 1986: 303–4. For the theme of the great flood in ancient Chinese mythology, see Kaltenmark 1985.

10. The classical work on the economics of Buddhist monasteries in medieval China is Gernet 1956, only recently translated into English (1995).

11. See Chapter 1 and later in this chapter. Another apocalyptic Taoist source attacking explicitly the "cults of the profane" is the fifth-century *Tung-yüan shen-chou ching* (HY 335), studied by Mollier 1990. See also Dzo 1984.

12. Strickmann 1990: 89, describes a reflection—or, better, an anticipation—of this critical attitude of the Buddhist establishment toward members of its own ranks in the apocryphal *Consecration Sūtra* (T. 1331).

13. For more detail, see Strickmann 1990: 87–88, and 112–13, n. 32. See also Zürcher 1982b: 18–20; and Nattier 1991.

14. On this subject, Strickmann wrote: In the sixth century, Chinese Buddhists added a third age to Buddhist history, that of the Final Law (*paścimā-dharma*). They also pushed the Buddha's own dates back some five hundred years, to the tenth century B.C.E., which not only prolonged the apocalyptic time-scale but also gave the Buddha a more venerable antiquity vis-à-vis China's own great archaic culture-heroes. Nonetheless, the apocalyptic spirit remained very much alive in Chinese Buddhism and is still vital in the sectarian movement in Taiwan and Chinese Southeast Asia, which are the direct heirs of the medieval tradition. See Tambiah 1984: 293–320; Zürcher 1982b: 8, 18–20; on the vexed question of the "dates of the Buddha," see Durt 1987.

15. The bibliography on Asian demonology is particularly rich, and we give only a few references. For South Asia, see S. Lévi 1915; Haldar 1977: 139–51, 185–88; Coomaraswamy 1928; Dumézil 1929; Vogel 1926; Filliozat 1937; Mus 1939; Lin Li-kouang 1949; Banerjea 1956. For China, see in particular Hou 1975, 1979a. See also Wolf 1974 and Jordan 1972 (for a discussion of the categories of gods, ghosts, and ancestors); Teiser 1994 (on the Ten Kings and Hell imagery); and Bush 1974 (on thunder gods). For Japan, see Peri 1917; Berthier(-Caillet) 1980 and 1981; Duquenne 1983b and 1994; Iyanaga 1983, 1985, 1994, 1996–97; and Iyanaga 1999.

16. On this process in Tantric Buddhism, see Iyanaga 1985; in Chan/Zen, see Faure 1987.

17. On this question, see Mus 1935. On Homa, the Vedic fire ritual, see Staal 1983; on versions of the Homa ritual in East Asian Buddhism, see Strickmann 1983; and Strickmann 1996: 337–68.

18. On Māra Pāpīyān, see Iyanaga 1996–97; on *māras* as a cause of disease in Buddhism, see Strickmann 1996: 125. Strickmann argues that these *māras*, like other members of the Indian pandemonium, were seen in China as exotica, that is, as rather peripheral agents without ties with the family system. Therefore, their ravages had to be treated by Buddhist rites, which were just as exotic. This distinction between the cult of peripheral spirits and that of ancestral spirits is drawn from I. M. Lewis 1989: 32–36.

19. The *mo* in the generic sense of "devils" or "demons" figure in various texts of the Shang-ch'ing tradition; see, for instance, HY 1010, 3: 10b; 6: 4a; 9: 8b, 10b; 15: 4b, 10a. In the Ling-pao tradition, the understanding of the devil-kings, or *mo-wang*, is more positive and closer to the Buddhist conception of Māra as the "tempter." Thus the *Scripture of Limitless Salvation* presents devil-kings associated with the Five Heavenly Thearchs (Emperors) and the Three Realms as divine beings with power over demonic forces that guarantee protection to those adepts who pass their trials by reciting their songs (HY 87, 2: 59b, 63b–65a, and 3: 24b–42a); see also Zürcher 1980: 127, and Bokenkamp 1997a: 383; 399, n. 34; 424–27.

20. This list is derived from the Vedic pantheon, on which see S. Lévi 1915. The Jains also recognized eight classes of supernatural beings (*vyantara*) living in the crevices of mountains and forests, but their list is slightly different: piśācas, bhūtas, yakṣas, rākṣasas, kiṃnaras, kiṃpuruṣas, mahoragas, and gandharvas. For a complete list (in Sanskrit and Chinese) of the Tantric deities represented in the two great maṇḍalas of Shingon Tantrism, see Tajima 1959: 132–41, 190–97.

21. On the nāgas/dragons in India, China, and Japan, see, for instance, de Visser 1913; Combasz 1939–45; Vogel 1926; Banerjea 1956: 344–51; Bloss 1973; Rawlinson 1986. For a recent discussion of nāga lore in Japan, see Tanaka 1992.

22. The classical model, predating Buddhism in China, is Tung Chung-shu's (ca. 179–104 B.C.E.) rain ritual for the state, which recommends the use of clay dragons in the colors of the five directions (see *Ch'un-ch'iu fan-lu*). See also de Visser 1935; and des Rotours 1966.

23. On this ritual, see the famous study by Chavannes 1919.

24. See Lalou 1938.

25. See Renou and Filliozat 1985: 331.

26. See Coomaraswamy 1928–31; Lévi and Chavannes 1915; Banerjea 1956: 335–44, 354–61 (on Gaṇeśa), 361 (on Skanda).

27. See Renou and Filliozat 1985: 528; and La Vallée Poussin 1923–31, English trans. 1988–91, 2: 393–95.

28. On the asuras, *see Hōbōgirin*, vol. 1, 1929; Lin Li-kouang 1949; Mus 1939: 155–83.

29. On the Japanese *tengu*, see de Visser 1908; Rotermund 1991b; Chigiri 1973 and 1975.

30. Chinese transformations of garuḍas may be, for example, behind the "Horse *ch'ie-lo*" and the "Tiger *ch'ieh-lo*" mentioned by the Taoist master Pai Yü-ch'an (1194–1227?) as playing a part in twelfth- and thirteenth-century esoteric Buddhist rituals; see HY 1296, 1: 11b.

31. Banerjea 1956: 351–53. The association of the god or goddess of sericulture with the horse goes back to a legend first recorded in the fourth-century *Sou-shen chi*. According to the story, a girl promised to marry her pet horse if it could bring her father home from an extended journey. The horse succeeded in that task, but the girl's father killed it after he learned about the promise and spread its skin in the courtyard to dry. All of a sudden the skin moved, wrapped itself around the girl, and disappeared with her. A little later people discovered the horseskin in a tree, but the girl had already been transformed into a silkworm. See *Shou-shen chi* 14: 172–73. The horse is associated in this legend with a constellation, but has originally no connection with Buddhism or the kiṃnaras. Later, the legend seems to have mixed with various Buddhist traditions about horse-demons or horse-divinities, such as that about Hayagrīva, the horse-headed Kuan-yin, on whom see van Gulik 1935 and Stein 1986. This symbolic association may also explain why the Indian patriarch Aśvaghoṣa (Ch. Ma-ming) came to be perceived as a god of sericulture in China. On Aśvaghoṣa as Lord of Silk, see Birnbaum 1983: 111–14.

32. See de Mallmann 1975: 122.

33. See *Cheng-fa nien-ch'u ching*, T. 721, vol. 27, ch. 16–17, summarized in Lin Li-kouang, who offers a long and comprehensive treatment of who becomes what kind of preta and how, and what they do then. See Lin Li-kouang 1949: 16–20. See also Mus 1939: 254–57.

34. As already mentioned, the term "preta" is a Buddhist phonetic variation on the "fathers" (*pitara*) of pan-Indian belief. The pretas are the spirits of the dead, but (for Buddhists) the unhappy dead—needful and deserving of offerings but also capable of doing harm, in particular to children (especially those pretas who died a violent death). On Japanese pretas (*gaki*), see LaFleur 1989.

35. On the piśācas, see de Mallmann 1975: 302; on the rākṣasas, see ibid., 315.

36. On the vetālas (cetālas), see de Mallmann 1975: 445–46; on the kumbhāṇḍas, see Mochizuki Shinkō 1958–63, vol. 4: 3386b–87a. The vetālas, a sort of vampire lodging inside corpses, were well-known in India through the *Vetālapañcaviṃśatikā* (Twenty-Five Vampire Stories), a collection of tales translated into French by Louis Renou (*Contes du vampire*, Paris: Gallimard, 1963).

37. On the ḍākiṇīs, see pp. 261–63 and 270–71; on the pūtanas, see de Mallmann 1975: 314, and Filliozat 1937.

38. On these "little mothers," see Iyanaga 1999: 47–50.

39. See Peri 1917, Murray 1981–82.

40. On Skanda, see Filliozat 1937, and pp. 218–24 and 255–56.

41. For a good survey of Chinese demonology, see De Groot 1892–1910, vol. 5; and Kiang 1937. On this, Strickmann noted: Chinese demons are designated by the terms *kuei-shen*, or *shen-ming*: These terms reveal an ambiguity that is parallel to that of the Greek *daimon* itself. These demons are spirits of the dead and something more. The importation of a vast body of diverse Indian demonology to China and Japan, and the different stages of its acceptance and acculturation, are documented all through the Chinese and Japanese literature. Other comparable demonological *Völkerwanderungen* of demonological personnel across Eurasia have been suggested, though they are less fully attested to in conventional sources. In an early work, Dumézil marshaled the evidence for an equivalence between Indian gandharvas and Greco-Roman centaurs (Dumézil 1929). Like their Greek counterparts, the gandharvas were famous for their science, their musical talents, and their sexual vigor. More daring comparative hypotheses have been put forward by Jurgis Baltrušaitis (1981), who views the efflorescence of demoniform gargoyles in the Gothic art of the thirteenth century as being ultimately due to East Asian influences; the relevant chapter of his book on the fantastic elements in Gothic art is entitled "Far Eastern Prodigies" (*Prodiges extrême-orientaux*). Evidence for the perpetual interest even vague rumors of such phenomena evoked in medieval Europe is provided by Rudolph Wittkower (1977).

42. Strickmann refers here to Liu Hsin's (d. 23 C.E.) *Ch'i-lüeh* (completed in 6 B.C.E.), which was based on the bibliographical work of his father, Liu Hsiang (79–8 B.C.E.). The *Ch'i-lüeh* itself was lost during the T'ang dynasty, but it formed the basis for Pan Ku's (32–92 C.E.) bibliography included in the *Han-shu* (Pan-ku, in fact, lists all the titles of the *Ch'i-lüeh*). The "demonologies" mentioned by Strickmann are listed in the subdivision "Various Divinations" (*tsa-chan*), in the "Five Agents" (*wu-hsing*) category. The *Shan-hai ching* (see note 43 below) is an exception, in that it occurs under the subdivision "Methods [Based on] Shape" (*hsing-fa*). See *Han-shu* 30.

43. For a study and complete translation of the *Shan-hai ching*, see Mathieu 1983; see also Campany 1996: 34–36, 133–37. Note that this work was also used as a talisman and is described as the scriptural equivalent of the "nine caldrons" on which Yü the Great represented all the demons of China. See D. Harper 1985: 479.

44. See Eliasberg 1984; Bodde 1975. On demons and graves, see Cedzich 1994.

45. See D. Harper 1985 and 1998; see also Kalinowski 1986; and Poo Mu-chou 1993. The "spell-binding" manuscript is translated in Harper 1996.

46. These manuscripts have been studied by D. Harper 1982 and 1998. See also Murakami 1985; Ma Chi-hsing and Li Hsüeh-ch'in, "Wo kuo hsien i fa-hsien te tsui ku i-fang: po-shu *Wu-shih-erh ping-fang*," in *Ma-wang-tui Han mu yen-chiu*

(Hunan: Hu-nan Jen-min ch'u-pan-she, 1981), 226–34. On Ma-wang-tui, see also Akahori 1978b; and *Ma-wang-tui Han-mu yen-chiu*, op. cit.

47. On this point Strickmann also explained: The terrestrial and subterranean nature of demons and the malevolent dead is self-evident; peril emanating from the earth was associated especially with the earth's wilder recesses, the mountains. But terror also dropped from the skies, for many demons prove to have astral associations. Like the "seizers" or "snatchers" of Indian demonology, a number of Chinese demons are actually members of ill-disposed constellations—including sky-going beasts like the White Tiger and Dog of Heaven. These malevolent stars of course operated according to patterns recorded in the almanacs: Today, as in the third century B.C.E., consulting the almanac permits the anxious parent or the therapeutic specialist to identify the agency responsible for an affliction that has been noted as beginning at a particular time, or to foretell the possible sources of danger on a given day and take suitable prophylactic measures (Hou 1979a).

48. For travelers' accounts of the Other World, see Demiéville 1976; Teiser 1988; and Campany 1990. In the Taoist tradition, there is the well-known story (see *Sou-shen chi*, or *T'ai-p'ing kuang-chi*) of Hu Mu-pan's discovery of the world of the dead after entering T'ai Shan. In *Chen-kao* 15.2a, the story is mentioned disparagingly amid a general reference to tales of those returned from the dead. We are told that Hu "entered the 'heavenly grotto' (*tung-t'ien*) without knowing it," most likely because spirits deliberately confused him, not wishing him to know "the facts"—namely, that he had obtained a much sought-after privilege in Taoist eyes. On the Taoist notion of hell, see Robinet 1984, 1: 137–38. On Chinese hells in general, see Sawada 1969; Teiser 1993.

49. Strickmann 1979.

50. This is still the case today among Japanese Buddhist scholars, who persist in labeling the Tachikawa-ryū of Shingon Buddhism as *jakyō* (the Japanese reading for *hsieh-chiao*, "perverse teaching"). See, for instance, Mizuhara 1931 and Moriyama 1965.

51. The exact referents of the Chinese physiological terms *ch'i* and *ching*, or of the related term *shen* (usually translated as "spirit"), have not yet been established with absolute certainty. It appears that they must be imagined as a continuum rather than as essentially different substances or agents. In early sources *ching* is described as the essential extract of *ch'i*, which in turn is the basis for the formation of *shen*. Within human physiology, although *ching* seems closely related to the sexual fluids (semen and menstrual blood), D. Harper (1998: 119–25) points out that the two are not by themselves equivalent. For *ching* in the sense of "essential spirits" or demonic manifestations of animals, plants, and trees, see the rich material gathered in De Groot 1892–1910, vol. 5, chaps. 5–7.

52. Although this interpretation is indeed rather common and at least implicitly expressed in ancient texts such as the *Tso-chuan* (Duke Chao, seventh year), it should be mentioned that many sources explain *kuei* ("ghost" or "demon") not as the spirit of a dead person returning to the living but as that which, after a per-

son's death, reintegrates with nature—that is, bones and flesh with the earth, and breath (*ch'i*) with the ether (*t'ien*); see, for instance, *Li-chi*, "Chiao T'e-sheng," 26: 15b, "Chi-i," 47: 10a–11a; *Lun-heng*, "Lun-ssu," 20: 315.

53. *Yen-shih chia hsün* 6, by Yen Chih-t'ui (531-ca. 590). See the translation by Teng Ssu-yü, 1968.

54. See, for example, the sources collected in De Groot 1892–1910, vol. 5, chap. 12, esp. p. 773. The "killer ghosts" also play a role in early Taoist texts; see, in particular, HY 1208 (a compilation of early Celestial Master materials possibly dating to the second or third century C.E.), 1: 2a, 13b, 21b; HY 421 (compiled by T'ao Hung-ching), 3: 14b, 20b.

55. *T'ai-p'ing kuang-chi* 363: 2882.

56. See D. Harper 1996: 242 and entries no. 9, 27, 44, 52.

57. *Cho-ying t'ing pi-chi*, by Tai Kuan (*Shou-fu hsü*).

58. On this topic, Strickmann noted: In astrology and the almanac, as well as in Taoist scriptures, "the killers" also figure as a large, organized group of dangerous star-demons. They are listed in Hou 1979a: 197, no. 10. Like all star-demons, they have their regular periodicities when special precautions must be taken to avoid encountering them. Confusion or conflation with the familial vampires was all too easy, and no doubt occurred quite early on. The beliefs surrounding the domestic killers recall the complex of South Slavic vampirism. There, too, a newly buried family member might return to kill his or her closest kin. Only after the vampire had exterminated its own family would it broaden its activities to include all co-villagers living within the sound of the village church-bell (Bachtold-Staübli 1927, vol. 6: 812–23, s.v. "Nachzehrer"). In fairness to the Chinese ancestors whose traditional reputation for benignity is under assault, it must be pointed out that the nuances of terminology both transcend and transect the traditional boundaries of the idealized spirit world, and vault over the barrier that officially separates the demons from the gods. *Kuei* ("ghost," "demon," "demon-soul") and *shen* ("spirit," "god") are often found closely linked in compound form such as *kuei-shen*, which most commonly means "gods" or "godlings." The *kuei*, with all their own harmful protean qualities, are here bound together with the *shen*, whose associations are normally more beneficial. For example, when it is determined that a person has one or more *kuei* lodged in his body, the implications of this diagnosis are almost invariably pathological, whereas many medieval Taoists and Buddhists devoted much thought and effort to incorporating and animating as many *shen* within their bodies as they could, stuffing themselves with an entire luminous pantheon. Yet unwanted or outraged *shen* can also wreak havoc when they take possession of someone against his or her will. Needless to say, the optimal outcome of proper burial rites and offerings is to turn your own ancestors into gods—respectable members of the otherworldly administrative hierarchy.

Strickmann concludes by arguing that the business of distinguishing between Chinese gods, ghosts, and ancestors has occupied anthropologists in recent years (Jordan 1972, Wolf 1974). However, the point of several essays in Wolf 1974 is that they are not different beings. For instance, one person's ancestors can be someone else's ghosts. Concerning the Western belief in ghosts, see Schmitt 1994. On Chinese demonology and westward influences, see Baltrušaitis 1981: 143, passim.

59. See *Lun-heng*, "Ting-kuei," 344.

60. *Chou-hou pei-chi fang* (HY 1295, 1: 14b–15a).

61. Ibid., 1: 15a.

62. See HY 639 (one of the original Shang-ch'ing scriptures revealed to Yang Hsi): 9a; cf. Bokenkamp 1997a: 287 and 322–23; also Strickmann 1981: 160.

63. HY 639: 10a; Bokenkamp 1997a: 287–88, 324–25.

64. See Maspero 1981: 331–37. For an early fourth-century account of the three corpse-demons, who are already said to spy on their hosts and report their moral transgressions to the heavenly authorities, see *Pao-p'u-tzu nei-p'ien chiao-shih* 6: 125.

65. See HY 1026, 83: 8a–b.

66. See Strickmann 1988: 29–36.

67. On these tomb-contracts and related documents, dating from the Eastern Han dynasty and later, see Kleeman 1984; Seidel 1985 and 1987b; Hansen 1995a, chaps. 6–7. The texts served to identify, legitimize, and transfer deceased persons to the registers of an amazingly elaborate subterranean bureaucracy. Donald Harper has traced antecedents of this legalistic funerary tradition to the fourth century B.C.E. (Harper 1994), and Huang Sheng-chang (Huang 1996) has recently discussed a number of Ch'in and early Han examples of what he calls "Announcements to the Earth [Spirits]" (*kao-ti tz'u*, Kleeman's "grave-quelling texts" and Seidel's "celestial ordinances"). This legislative ordering of religious life in visible and invisible worlds takes several forms: *hsien-chieh* (precepts for immortals, i.e., living adepts), *kuei-lü* (statutes for the shades, canons of retributions that will be visited on the dead for their attacks on the living), and *k'e-p'in* (a complementary genre of lists that stipulate offerings in rites for the salvation of demons).

68. See Kleeman 1984: 19–20; Seidel 1987b: 43.

69. See, for example, the following translation of a document dating to 175 C.E. in Seidel 1987b: 31.

Heaven above is blue,
Limitless is the underworld.
The dead belong to the realm of Yin,
The living belong to the realm of Yang.
[The living have] their village home,
The dead have their hamlets.
The living are under the jurisdiction of Ch'ang-an in the West,
The dead are under the jurisdiction of Mount T'ai in the East.
In joy they do not [remember] each other,
[In grief] they do not think of each other.

70. See also Cedzich 1993.

71. See Seidel 1987a: 39–42.

72. The phrase is, for instance, very frequent in the *kirigami* (esoteric slips of paper transmitted at the time of initiation) of the Sōtō Zen tradition in Japan.

See Sugimoto Shunryū, ed., *Zōtei Tōjō shitsunai kirigami narabini sanwa no kenkyū* (Tokyo: Sōtōshū shūmucho, 1982 [1938]).

73. These law codes have been studied by Hulsewé 1985. D. Harper 1994 sees a connection not only between the Ch'in law codes and the "Spellbinding" manuscript: Discussing an official document that reports the amazing resurrection of a man from death, he argues for close links between legal administration and funerary practice from the fourth century B.C.E. on as well. The report, rediscovered in a tomb of the late Warring States or early Ch'in period in Fang-ma-t'an (Kansu) in 1986, is dated 269 B.C.E. It was addressed by a local administrator to the royal court of the state of Ch'in. According to the account, the resurrection was the result of a legal negotiation between a famous late Warring States general and functionaries of the netherworld administration on behalf of the deceased, a protégé of the general who had committed suicide after stabbing another man. Though it is unclear why the report was placed in the tomb and who the occupant of the tomb was, Harper points out that the report itself and the story it tells share the same bureaucratic context. Harper also draws a parallel between the description of the negotiation in this document and the memoranda addressed by officials of the early Han administration directly to the underworld authorities. In his words, "no later than the fourth century B.C. the underworld already resembled a bureaucratic state; and dealings with the underworld bureaucracy conformed to the norms of the Warring States bureaucracy."

74. See Okanishi 1972, 5: 79b–80a.

75. Nickerson 1996: 272, n. 8, informs us that "Nü-ch'ing" is referred to in the *Demon-Statutes of Nü-ch'ing* itself as a revealer of statutes (probably the text itself) and as the star T'ai-i (HY 789, 5: 4a6 and 2: 5b8). In the Ling-pao scriptures (e.g., HY 456, passim), Nü-ch'ing appears as the supervisor of the recordkeeping of the good and evil behavior in the offices of the Three Primes (San-yüan), and somewhat later the name designates one of the twenty-four prisons for sinners (e.g., HY 184). For the latter interpretation, see also the interesting quotation from Yen Chih-t'ui's *Yüan-hun chih* in De Groot 1892–1910, vol. 4: 442–43; here the Nü-ch'ing Pavilion is the third "hell" beneath the Yellow Springs, which is reserved only for women.

76. HY 789, 1: 1a–b.

77. Ibid., 1: 1b.

78. Ibid., 1: 1b–2a.

79. Ibid., 1: 2a.

80. On this, Strickmann noted: Descriptions of monsters and odd theriomorphic beings are also found in the occult prophetic literature that began to be written from the first century C.E. on. These texts included lists of demons' names, to be used in controlling them, and Anna Seidel has noted that Taoist authors would have discovered the control of demons through naming, and the model of the demon-list itself, in this literature originally designed for use by the monarch. A curious example is the work called *Pictures [Drawn in Accordance with the Instruction of the Legendary Beast] Po-tse*, said to have been an album of paintings of weird spirits. A medieval manuscript in this tradition was found at Tun-huang; it

contains nineteen pictures of animals and human figures (Seidel 1983–85: 320–23; Kiang 1937: 71–79).

81. HY 789, 2: 6a.

82. Despite its being entirely in Chinese, and seeming like quite a colloquial enumeration, this list actually has Indian cognates. For example, such lists were a well-established Buddhist scriptural genre in Indian literature. The *Saddharma-smṛtyupasthāna-sūtra* gives a long accounting of the various sorts of pretas, or ghosts/demons: thirty-six varieties are listed, according to form, habitat, characteristic action, and eating-habits—cauldron-bodied demons, demons with needle-mouths, demons who eat vomit, etc. (Lin Li-kouang 1949: 16–18).

83. Ibid., 2: 2b.

84. Ibid., 2: 2b.

85. Ibid., 2: 2b-3a.

86. Ibid., 2: 3a–b.

87. Ibid., 2: 3b–4a.

88. Ibid., 3: 2a–b. Despite these warnings, male homosexuality seems to have been widespread in Taoism, as the paintings on the walls of one famous Taoist center in Szechwan, Mount Ch'ing-ch'eng, clearly indicate. On Taoist homosexuality, see Vitiello 1992.

89. On the three calamities (*san-tsai*, i.e., the three apocalyptical agents of Indian cosmology, water, wind, fire) at the end of a kalpa, see *Chen-kao* 2 and 3.9a–b. The changes that marked the year Jen-chen of T'ai-p'ing were an indication that this was the time. See *Chen-kao* 6.7a (in section 42c): "It is hard enough . . . to be born human, then a man, then intact, then in China . . . then [at this time] . . . [implication: but you have been so favored]." See also ibid., 6.8a.

90. HY 789, 1: 8a–b.

91. This is the form of the famous *Book of the Yellow Court* (*Huang-t'ing ching*), recitation of which guarantees one's bodily integrity; see Strickmann 1981: 35–36 and Schipper 1975: 1–11.

92. HY 789, 5: 1a.

93. For an interesting discussion of the songs of such child-mediums by the first-century critic Wang Ch'ung, see *Lun-heng*, "Ting-kuei." Wang argues that the "prophetic" utterances of both mediums and children have no referent; they are merely spontaneous symptoms of a surplus of yang breath (*ch'i*).

94. HY 789, 5: 1a.

95. See ibid., 5.16; 2a; 5.3b; also 1.8b.

96. Ibid., 5: 1b–2a.

97. HY 789, 5: 2a.

98. Ibid., 5: 3a. On Li Hung, see Seidel 1970, 1978a; Strickmann 1981; and Mollier 1990.

99. HY 789, 5: 4b.

100. See HY 184, *chüan* 2–5, which comprises a full-scale pantheon under the rubric of "Statutes of Nü-ch'ing."

101. See HY 1419, 2: 8a.

102. HY 1194: 2b mentions the "Golden House" (Chin-shih), which during the fifth century was a common, prophetic code for the Liu-Sung dynasty. See Mollier 1990, Introduction and chap. 2.

103. This work (HY 461) was a text of the ritual tradition of the Celestial Heart (T'ien-hsin), which originated in the tenth century in South China. See Strickmann 1975 and Boltz 1987: 35.

Chapter 3: The Literature of Spells

1. On this text, see Mollier 1990.
2. HY 335: 1.2a–2b.
3. On the Ling-pao tradition, see Bokenkamp 1983–85, and Bell 1988.
4. HY 335: 1.2a–3b.
5. Ibid., 1.4a–b.
6. Ibid., 1.6a–b.
7. Ibid., 1.6b–7b.
8. Ibid., 1.7b.
9. See Bokenkamp 1983–85.
10. On the rise of the Buddhist cult of the book, see Schopen 1975. Nevertheless, Strickmann here somewhat overemphasizes the influence of Buddhism on the Chinese cult of the book. In a culture where writing (as *wen*) has always been regarded as an emanation of the ultimate principle, scriptures were naturally held in high esteem. In early Taoism, the *ching* was believed to have a celestial nature. On this point, see Robinet 1984, 1: 112–22.
11. The same is true in the case of Japan; see Rotermund 1991a.
12. On this question, see Robinet 1993: 19–24; Strickmann 1981: 118–21.
13. Strickmann 1981: 220, quoting the *Annals of the Sage of Latter Time*, HY 442.
14. The ambivalence of the demons is taken advantage of: from enemies, they become allies or, rather, servants. Note that the text, despite its title, contains no spell—unless it was itself used as one, like the *Hṛdaya-sūtra* in Buddhism. On the latter, see Lopez 1990.
15. T. 2897, 85: 1425a13–20. On this text, cf. Overmyer 1989–90.
16. HY 335: 1.5b.
17. Ibid., 2.8b.
18. "Master of the Law" (*fa-shih*) renders *Dharma-bhāṇaka* ("preacher of the Law"); see Shizutani 1974: 286–88. It was a standard term for a ritual practicant in both medieval Buddhism and Taoism; in Fukien and Taiwan, the same term now designates vernacular exorcists, or "magicians" (as opposed to "literary" Taoists, who use classical Chinese in their rituals). See Schipper 1993.
19. See Shizutani 1974.
20. HY 369: 2a, 15b.
21. *Annals of the Sage of Latter Time*; see Robinet 1993: 19–24; Strickmann 1981: 220.
22. Another tradition maintains that the Abyss is actually the third of the

Three Caverns, situated beneath heaven and earth, but this seems to be an isolated view (HY 1303, Robinet 1983–85: 423, n. 116).

23. *Chen-kao*, HY 1010: 10.10b4–11a3. This exorcistic star-spirit, T'ien-p'eng, served under the Supreme Emperor of the Dark Heavens. On the T'ien-p'eng spell, see also the *T'ai-shang t'ung-yüan Pei-ti t'ien-p'eng hu-ming hsiao-tsai shen-chou miao-ching* (HY 53) and the *Tao-fa hui-yüan* (HY 1210), 157.18, 159.3–11, 19–23 (quoted in Katz 1995: 85). This deity seems identical with T'ien-feng, the first of the "nine spirits" of the occulted *chia*, enumerated in the *Wu-hsing ta-i* of Hsiao Chi (ca. 530–614) and associated with the nine stars of the esoteric Dipper. See Nakamura 1973: 172–74; Kalinowski 1991. On Taoist astrology, see Schafer 1977. On Tantric astrology, the classic work remains Morita 1941; see also Birnbaum 1980.

24. See James A. Matisoff, *Blessing, Curses, Hopes, and Fears: Psycho-ostensive Expressions in Yiddish* (1979; reprint, Stanford: Stanford University Press, 2000).

25. On these Five Monarchs (or "Five Emperors," Wu-ti), sometimes confused with the "Five Commissioners of Epidemics" (Wu-wen shih-che) or other similar groups of five deities, see Katz 1995: 49–59.

26. Doolittle 1966 (1865), 2: 273–75.

27. *Chin-lou tzu* 14, p. 268 (by Hsiao I, 508–55).

28. Ibid., 12, p. 226.

29. Among the various works on dhāraṇīs, see Burnouf 1844: 51, 68, 121, 515, 540 ff.; Burnouf 1973 (1852): 238–41, 278; Winternitz 1933, vol. 2: 380–87; Waddell 1912; La Vallée Poussin 1898: 119–13; and Lamotte 1949–76: 1854–69. In Japanese, see: Ōmura 1972 (1818); Maruyama Tatsuo 1899; *Darani jiten* (Tokyo; reprinted 1974); Takubo Shūyo, *Shingon darani-zō no kaisetsu* (1950; Tokyo, 2nd revised ed., 1967); Yoshida Ekō, *Kondai ryōbu shingon kaigi* (Nara, 1970); and Yoritomi Motohiro, "Jōyō shingon no kaisetsu," in *Gendai mikkyō kōza* 4 (Tokyo 1975), 315–412. The study of dhāraṇī in Japan is closely connected with that of the Siddhaṃ syllabary, a form of the Brahmī script. The traditional literature on these two related subjects is enormous and represents an unexploited mine of information on linguistic study. See van Gulik 1956. The standard manual on bījas was compiled in Japan by Chōzen (?–1680) and first printed in 1937 at Kōyasan. See also Tambiah 1980; R. Vira and Shodo Taki, eds., *Dakṣiṇāmūrti Uddhārakośa: A Dictionary of the Secret Tantric Syllabic Code* (Lahore, 1938); Reis-Habito 1993.

30. See Gonda 1963; Alper 1989; Bharati 1965b: 101–63; and Padoux 1975 (1963).

31. Dhāraṇīs are quintessential résumés of important points of doctrine or mnemonic devices suggesting or symbolizing points, or whole classes, of doctrine. The use of the term "dhāraṇī" in the old, mnemonic sense is still attested to in Buddhabhadra's translation of the *Avataṃsaka-sūtra* (in 60 *chüan*, made in 425): *chüan* 26, 48. See Ōmura 1972 (1918): 81, for a list of different types of dhāraṇīs; see also Bernhard 1967. Those interested in the mnemonic aspects of dhāraṇīs should also consult Frances Yates, *The Art of Memory* (1966), which describes the elaborate mnemonic systems in use in Europe from classical antiquity through

the Renaissance, including internal visualizations that strikingly recall Taoist and Tantric practice.

32. The most comprehensive analysis of dhāraṇīs is probably Lamotte 1976 (1962): 1854–69. A text clearly linking dhāraṇīs and memory can be found in T. 1336 (*T'o-lo-ni tsa-chi*, translated during the Liang dynasty). On dhāraṇīs and the *gumonji* ritual associated with the Bodhisattva Ākāśagarbha, see Waterhouse 1979; Yamasaki 1988.

33. Unfortunately, a recent work on mantras (Alper 1989) fails to clearly contrast mantras and dhāraṇīs.

34. Sometimes the two terms can be used in apposition, as in the title of *Ta-lun chin-kang tsung-ch'ih t'o-lo-ni ching* (T. 1230, 21: 161b).

35. Strickmann 1990.

36. The efflorescence of dhāraṇī sūtras and practice that occurred during this period was a very imposing phenomenon that later chroniclers could not deny, even though they turned a cold eye on it. Yüan Buddhists in general held mantra-based demonifuge ritual in contempt and hence omitted it from their writings. In the *Fo-tsu li-tai t'ung-tsai* (1344), the fourth-century monk Śrīmitra is described as the first transmitter and originator of the fashion, which the fourteenth-century author Mei-wu Nien-ch'ang sees as simply a way of making offerings to the gods so that they will expell disease-demons. We are told that many Indian charlatans arrived during Śrīmitra's time claiming to be bhikṣus (monks) and practiced lowly, vile acts like the Taoists' thunder-rites. Thunder-rites (*lei-fa*) were exorcistic rituals that became very popular during the twelfth and thirteenth centuries. Taoist priests employed in them the powers of thunder and lightning, which they generated through the same meditative processes that were also the basis of "Inner Alchemy" (*nei-tan*). In addition, the general symbolism and the divinities invoked in these rites show heavy Tantric Buddhist influences. Because of their dramatic appeal, the thunder-rites were often appropriated by self-acclaimed ritual specialists who presumably performed them without the necessary, highly sophisticated meditations. The same can be said of the Tantric and proto-Tantric rituals brought to China from the fifth century on, or perhaps even earlier, by practitioners like the fourth-century Śrīmitra. This explains the fourteenth-century author's association of early Buddhist exorcisms with the much later Taoist thunder rites. Śrīmitra is credited in particular with the translation of the *Peacock-King Scripture* (although his translation is no longer extant). This tradition goes back to the *Kao-seng chuan* (T. 2059, 50: 328a), which nevertheless mentions earlier cases, like that of Ho-lo-chieh, a third-century monk who, during an epidemic, "treated illnesses with spells, curing eight or nine out of ten" (ibid., 386c); or a contemporary of Śrīmitra's, Fo-t'u-teng, who is said to have brought a prince back to life through a ritual involving a willow branch and a spell (ibid., 384b). On these cases, and the use of spells in Chinese Buddhism, see Kieschnick 1997; and Naomi Gentetsu, "*Kōsōden* no ju," *Tōyō shien* 33 (1989): 32–48.

37. T. 1378A, 21: 901c; see also the *A-cha-p'o-chü kuei-shen ta-chiang shang fo t'o-lo-ni ching* T. 1237, 21: 178a, and T. 1238, 21: 179c (quoted in Duquenne 1983b:

624); another version of this text is found in the *T'o-lo-ni tsa-chi* (T. 1336, 21: 628c–629a). See also Katz 1995.

38. Sometimes, however, the figure who proffers a protective spell is a bodhisattva, such as Samantabhadra in Dharmarakṣa's translation of the *Lotus Sūtra*, on which see Burnouf 1973 (1852): 278.

39. T. 1336: 627a. This *Dhāraṇī Miscellany* was, with the *Consecration Sūtra* (T. 1331) and the *Spirit-Spells Spoken by the Seven Buddhas and Eight Bodhisattvas* (*Ch'i-fo pa-p'u-sa so-shuo ta t'o-lo-ni shen-chou ching*, T. 1332), one of the three great collections of dhāraṇīs compiled during the Six Dynasties period.

40. There are remarkable accounts of live toads being used to treat cancer of the breast in eighteenth-century England. They would be applied in succession, one after the other, each toad allegedly sucking, swelling up, and dying. For toads sucking out venom, see Kennedy 1982.

41. See *T'ai-shang ch'ih-wen tung-shen san-lu* (preface dated 632); HY 589: 14a.

42. T. 2904, p. 1446b.

43. HY 632, 761.

44. See Lévi and Chavannes 1915; Hoernle 1893–1912. In the Bower manuscript, for instance, after the monk Svāti has been bitten by a cobra, the Buddha tells Ānanda: "Go thou, O Ānanda, and with the word of the Tathāgata save the mendicant Svāti with that great Māyūri spell, the queen of the magic art! Grant him safety, security, defence, salvation, protection, relief and recovery, preservation from danger, counteraction of the poison, destruction of the poison, and apply a ligature to the wound, a ligature to the vein! Deliver him from seizure by a Dêva, from seizure by a Nāga, from seizure by an Asura, from seizure by a Maruta, from seizure by a Garuḍa, from seizure by a Gandharva, from seizure by a Kinnara, from seizure by a Mahōraga, from seizure by a Yaksha, from seizure by a Bhûta, from seizure by a Kumbhāṇḍa, from seizure by a Pūtana, from seizure by a Kaṭapūtana, from seizure by Skanda, from seizure by mania, from seizure by unnatural change in appearance, from seizure by epilepsy, from seizure by the evil eye, from the exercise of witchcraft, from destruction by *kaṅkhōrda* [black magic], from injury by Vetālas that attend at burning-places, from [various kinds of fevers]" (Hoernle, 1893–1912, 226–27). This passage is followed by a list of ordinary diseases. The manuscript gives a list of twenty-one *grahas*, or "seizures," that is nearly the same list as that found in the *Mahāvyutpatti*. The term *graha* came to be applied to the nine planets (the *nava-graha*) held responsible for demonic influences; see Markel 1995; Frank 1991: 236–39. On nāgas and other supernatural beings, see Frank 1991, 231–33. In Tantric astrology, Svāti later became K'ang-hsiu, one of the twenty-eight celestial mansions (see *Hsiu-yao ching*, T. 1299, 21: 839b–c, 396a).

45. T. 1393, 21: 910b.

46. Ibid., 910c5–15.

47. On this demon, Strickmann noted: Deep Sands appears in a number of Chinese Buddhist spell-books and demon-lists from the fourth century on. See, for instance: T. 620, 15: 341c7–8; T. 852, 18: 139b-c. He successfully entered the mature Tantric system of the eighth century (cf. T. 1291, 21: 376b–377a) and found

a place in one of its two great maṇḍalas; he was also sometimes identified with the Lord of T'ai Shan, the mountain of the dead. He also appears in Po Yü-ch'an's analysis of the Tantric ["yoga"] practice of his time (HY 1296, 1.11b ff.). Having thus grown in complexity, the cult of Deep Sands was taken to Japan early in the ninth century and further developed there. He is depicted on a pillar within the tenth-century pagoda at the Daigo ji, south of Kyoto, and appears fairly prominently in Japanese Tantric ritual and iconographic manuscripts from the eleventh century on (see, for instance, *Asaba-shō*, T. Zuzō, vol. 6: 2254). Meanwhile, in China, his cult apparently continued undiminished, though leaving few traces in the surviving written record before the thirteenth century. It is then that Deep Sands suddenly resurfaces in an early version of the tale of the seventh-century monk Hsüan-chuang's journey to India in quest of Buddhist scriptures; Deep Sands is one of the demons encountered and converted along the way. See also *Kakuzen shō* [T. Zuzō, vol. 5: 560c–562b, plates 389–90], where it is said that: (a) he appeared to Hsüan-chuang in the desert; (b) he appeared to Tao-hsüan on Chung-nan shan; (c) he is a transformation of Vaiśravaṇa, guardian of the northern direction; (d) he is identified with T'ai-shan Fu-chün; (e) he is also identified with the brigand/murderer Aṅgulīmāla (whose tale offers many similarities with the legend of Āṭavaka, on which see Duquenne 1983b). We see at work here a common pattern for assimilation of military divinities, especially members of the Chinese popular religious pantheon. In the sixteenth century, the demon at last comes into his full powers as "Sandy," one of Hsüan-chuang's droll companions in the *Journey to the West* (*Hsi-yu chi*), one of China's greatest novels and among the most popular (see Dudbridge 1970: 18–21). In the form conferred on him by the novel, Deep Sands is still very much alive in popular drama and storytelling—all in all, a career that can probably be matched by very few demons worldwide.

A few words on Deep Sands's acolyte, the god Floating Hill (Fu-ch'iu), on whom see *Asaba-shō*, T. Zuzō, vol. 9: 522c–524a, plate 104. According to the *Ta-chi ching*, he is one of these deities converted by Avalokiteśvara. The text gives a full account of Hsüan-chuang's experience, from which it appears that the god was earlier connected with Shu province's Fu-ch'iu ssu [Floating Hill Temple], and that he appeared to a monk in his yakṣa form, bestowing upon him dhāraṇīs and mantras. An image was made, and he was enshrined as protector of the temple. On these two figures, see also Murayama 1981: 212–15.

48. T. 1393, 21: 911a6–12.

49. On Hui-chien's authorship, see Strickmann 1990: 90–93. Kuo Li-ying (1994: 154, n. 25), however, offers some reservations.

50. See T. 1331, 21: 517c–521a.

51. There is a large literature on *abhiṣeka* (Ch. *kuan-ting*, J. *kanjō*), a ritual based on the analogy between the consecration of a crown prince and the bodhisattva's attainment of the tenth *bhūmi*, by which he becomes a "Dharma king"; see, for instance, the description in *Ch'an pi-yao ching* (T. 613). For a discussion of the royal symbolism, see Snellgrove 1959b. Per Kvaerne (1975) has also studied the sexual symbolism inherent in such consecration rituals. See also Eichinger

1981. The consecration ritual became particularly important in medieval Japan, and in turn legitimized the development of imperial ideology. On this question, see Rousselle 1935; Abe Yasurō 1984; and Yamamoto Hiroko 1993.

52. On the *gter-ma* tradition, see, for instance, Gyatso 1993, 1996, and n.d.; Michael Aris 1989; and Cabezón and Jackson 1996. In Chinese Taoism, too, there was a tradition of discovery of texts and talismans; see Kaltenmark 1960.

53. On this question, see Teiser 1988 and Cole 1998.

54. On the Healing Buddha (Bhaiṣajyaguru), see Birnbaum 1979.

55. On the *Book of Consecration* generally, see Strickmann 1990; and Strickmann 1982a: 57–58.

56. Cf. T. 1331, 21: 518c5–14 and ibid., 21: 910b16–19.

57. Ibid., 519b–c.

58. See ibid., 519c–520a.

59. Ibid., 520b8.

60. Ibid., 520c15–17.

61. Ibid., 520c19–28.

62. Ibid., 535c–536a.

63. According to its colophon, this text in twelve chapters was translated in 455 from an original of Indian provenance via Khotan; see T. 620, 15: 342b. "Meditation sickness" is also treated at length by Chih-i, the founder of the T'ien-t'ai school, in his *Mo-ho-chih-kuan* (T. 1911, 46: 106a–107c) and his *Hsiao chih-kuan* (T. 1915); on the latter, see Luk 1964: 147–51. See also Demiéville 1985 (1937): 80–82; Ando Shun'yū 1970; Yamano 1984 and 1985.

64. T. 620, 15: 341a–b.

65. On this question, see Faure 1998: 84–86.

66. See "'Mara kō' ni tsuite," in Minakata 1971–75, vol. 5: 73–97.

Chapter 4: Ensigillation

1. Pelliot 1953: 17. See also *Sui shu* 35: 1093.

2. Pelliot 1953: 17.

3. See Takakusu 1896: 150.

4. Pelliot 1953: 18. The ritual manufacture of multiple images thus appears to have an Indian origin—yet another example of a Buddhist ritual activity in which Indian and Chinese ideas and practices coalesce. But, as Hou Chin-lang (1984) has shown, the Chinese verb "to stamp" or "make a seal-impression" (*yin*) was also used to designate the process of casting an image with a mold pressed into sand or clay. At Tun-huang in the tenth century, monks and laypersons ritualistically gathered on the morning of the fifteenth day of the first month on the banks of a nearby river. In the course of their ritual they manufactured ex-votos representing stūpas or Buddhist deities, using the clay or sand of the river bank. The purpose of the ceremony (*yin sha fo*, "stamping buddhas in sand") was to invoke the favor of the Buddhist pantheon during the coming New Year. Hou points out the larger context of Buddhist practice: The procedures described by the pilgrim I-ching in 692 were still being carried out in twentieth-century Thailand, Laos, Burma, and

Tibet, and were at one time also known in Japan. He also finds evidence linking the printed scrolls of multiple, identical buddha-images with the metamorphosis of the Buddha into multiple forms by means of visualization in the course of meditation. Hou has shown that the production of these scrolls was one of the activities prescribed for the six monthly days of fasting, and thus essentially an individual occupation, in contrast to the communal production of images in clay or sand; see Hou 1984. The *Questions of Subāhu* (*Subāhu-paripṛcchā*, T. 895, 18: 720b) recommends stamping ten myriad miniature stūpas in clay or sand as a means of annihilating past transgressions. See also Giuseppe Tucci, *Indo-Tibetica* (Rome: Reale Accademia Italia, 1932), 1: 53–60; trans. as *Stūpa, Art, Architecture and Symbolism*, New Delhi: Aditya Prakashan, 1988.

5. This view underlies the entire chapter on Taoism in Needham 1970 (1956), vol. 2: 33–164.

6. This interpretation was in fact given by Ware 1933: 246: "They make seals of wood on which they carve the stars, the signs of the zodiac, the sun, and the moon. Breathing deeply as they grasp it, they make an imprint on the sick person. Many are [thus] cured."

7. See Demiéville 1985 (1937): 65–69, 73–76; and Duquenne 1983a.

8. HY 1260: 12a–13a. On the use of dreams as diagnostic indicators in the Chinese tradition, see Strickmann 1988; Drège 1981a and 1981b.

9. On this subject, Strickmann wrote: The *Book of the Inner Effulgences of the Yellow Court* (*Huang-t'ing nei-ching yü-ching chu*) named and described the body's inner spirit-personnel. Its recitation guaranteed their watchfulness and thus made the reciter impregnable against demonic assailants. Based on an older extant prototype, it was one of the original scriptures of the Mao Shan corpus. See Strickmann 1981: 198–202.

10. HY 1260: 13b. On diagnosis according to facial color, see Hou 1979b.

11. On Fan Li, a transcendent being of antiquity, see Kaltenmark 1987 (1953): 103–4. The theme of geophysical change and cosmic resonance is associated with magic seals in what follows.

12. Here Strickmann noted: I have found no other reference to Li Tao-hua; my rendering is conjectural.

13. On this, Strickmann wrote: According to the "Book of Spellbinding" ("Chin-ching") appended to Sun Ssu-mo's seventh-century *Supplementary Prescriptions Worth a Thousand* [*Cash*] (*Ch'ien-chin i-fang*), pressure applied to this spot on the healer's hand will instantly summon spirits to furnish him with information; see *Ch'ien-chin i-fang* 29: 346a–b.

14. The Eight Trigrams have long been the organizing spatial principle of Chinese ritual; see Kalinowski 1983–85.

15. Strickmann explained: The dance called the Step of Yü supposedly mimics the limping gait of the legendary demiurge Yü the Great. Linked with the seven (or nine) stars of Ursa Major, it is a mode of ritual motion shared by Taoist masters with ancient Chinese sorcerers. See Schipper 1993: 173–74 and Granet 1953a: 243–49.

16. Here Strickmann wrote: Elsewhere, the text specifies that sounding the bells of heaven designates a tooth-grinding from left to right and is used for summoning spirits; striking heaven's stone-chimes involves grinding from right to left and is used for subjugating spirits (HY 1260: 18a).

17. T'ai-shang Lao-chün, the deified Lao-tzu, is said to have founded Taoism with a revelation to Chang Tao-ling in 142 C.E., and he remained one of the system's chief deities during most of the medieval period. On the divinization of Lao-tzu, see Seidel 1969.

18. On this, Strickmann noted: Though the text here makes no mention of paper or ink, it is at least possible that the talismans were to be manufactured by means of the seal itself, as we will shortly find out, from sixth- and seventh-century Buddhist scriptures.

19. HY 1260: 15b–20a. Strickmann translates *hsieh* as "wraiths," or "wraith-breaths"; they are "bent" or "twisted" pathogens, contrasted with the "straight" or "right" influences, emanations, or other representatives of the Tao. See Strickmann 1980: 225.

20. The Five Ways of Rebirth (*gati*) are as god (*deva*), human (*manuṣya*), animal (*tiryag-yoni*), ghost (*preta*), and hell-being (*naraka*). A sixth category, sometimes added, is reserved for the *asuras*. Good descriptions can be found in Lin Li-kouang 1949 and Mus 1939.

21. Here Strickmann commented: *Mudrā*, or "seal," is here given exceptionally, pretentiously, in a cumbersome three-syllable Chinese transcription (modern pronunciation *wen-t'ou-lou*), rather than the usual Chinese equivalent, *yin*, "seal." "Ninety-five rites" or "ninety-five teachings" is a conventional designation for all the non-Buddhist communions and practices with which ancient India teemed. As this passage clearly shows, Buddhists were supposed to take over the best of these and gain all their attendant benefits, a technique that Tantric Buddhist ritualists adopted with a will.

22. *Mahārṣi* (Great Immortal) is an epithet of the Buddha himself; see Mochizuki Shinkō 1958–63 (1936), s.v. *daisen*, vol. 4: 2398b–c.

23. The thirty-two primary and eighty secondary marks are standard for buddhas and enlightened beings, and distinguish them from the commonality. The solar radiance is a halo, or aureole. Buddhas are, canonically, twice as tall as ordinary men. Note the identification, characteristic of Tantric ritual, of the adept with the Buddha—on which more later.

24. On these gods or spirit-kings of the five directions, Strickmann noted: Despite their ostensibly Sanskrit names (in Chinese transcription), this pentad does not appear to correspond to any Indian set of guardians. Significantly, the coordination of colors and directions given here is not Indian, but purely Chinese.

25. The "spirit-kings" (*shen-wang*) are rulers over vast spirit-armies and belong to the populous class of demons who have been subdued, converted to Buddhism, and enrolled as protectors of the faithful. Images of them have survived in early medieval Chinese Buddhist art; see Bunker 1964; and Ho-nan sheng wen-hua-chü wen-wu kung-tso tui, ed., *Kung-hsien shih-k'u ssu* (Peking: Wen-wu ch'u-pan she, 1963), plates 223–28. The term *shen-wang* was also used in Taoism, and

passed into Japanese religion with the awesome figure of Gozu Tennō, the "Ox-head Heavenly Monarch," also called *shinnō* (= *shen-wang*), a plague deity who became identified with the Japanese god Susanoo no mikoto, the unruly brother of the sun-goddess Amaterasu. On this god and his demonic hordes, see Yamamoto 1998: 503–646. As Paul Katz remarks, the title "king" (*wang*) and other similar official titles awarded by the state to local deities usually denote attempts "to conceal the original demonic attributes of many such deities" (Katz 1995: 29). On Asian plague gods and demons, see also Nicholas 1981, Benedict 1996, Katz 1987, Gould-Martin 1978, Rotermund 1991b (1981), and Ōshima 1985.

26. The text itself notes that *mudrā* in the language of westerners (i.e., residents of the Indian subcontinent) means "spirit-seal" in the language of China.

27. Here Strickmann wrote: *Dharmācārya*, or "Master of the Law," is more usually found in Chinese as *fa-shih* (which renders *Dharma-bhāṇaka*, "preacher of the Law"). The Chinese author of our text has evidently attempted a re-Sanskritization.

28. This is evidently the Step of Yü once again, mentioned in note 15 above.

29. The text has "the 404 diseases." This traditional number is usually explained as the basic number of diseases (101) multiplied by the "three poisons" (or passions, *tridoṣa*) to which are added 101 diseases of various kinds. See, for instance, Saṅgharakṣa's *Yogācārabhūmi*, T. 607 (trans. An Shih-kao), and T. 606 (trans. Dharmarakṣa), 15: 235a, 188c, 209b, 185a; and the *Sūtra on Medicine* (*Fo-i ching*), T. 793, 17: 737. See also Lamotte 1949–76: 36; Demiéville 1985 (1937): 77.

30. Here Strickmann noted: I have not found Sanskrit sources, if any, for these Sanskrit-seeming names.

31. T. 1331, 21: 515a4–516a15.

32. Ibid., 516c29–517b27. On Hārītī, see Peri 1917; Foucher 1905–51, vol. 2 (1918): 103–55; Kobayashi Taichirō 1938; and, more recently, Murray 1981–82; Frank 1991: 218–25. Rolf Stein has also shown how the imagery of fecundity—Hārītī surrounded by children—influenced the representation of the Chinese "Laughing Buddha," Pu-tai (J. Hotei); see Stein 1991 (1981): 131–32.

33. See also T. 1331, 21: 516b–c, where the author distinguishes between mudrās with and without attributes.

34. On the fly-whisk, see Mujaku Dōchū 1963: 791–92.

35. For a more detailed discussion of this point, see Strickmann 1996: 24–27.

36. See Dubs 1938, vol. 3: 537–43, esp. 542–43: "Use peachwood seals, six inches long and three inches square, vari-colored, on which are written characters according to the regular procedure, and display them on gates and doors." Often the terminology used in conjunction with these sealing rituals referred to numerico-calendar associations of the type used in the Han-era systems of *I-ching* astrology—"firm *mao*" and "gentle *mao*" days, odd and even numbers, and "five" as the directionally central one of the odd numbers (ibid., pp. 539–40).

37. *Pao-p'u-tzu nei-p'ien*, 17.2a, ed. Wang Ming, *Pao-p'u-tzu nei-p'ien chiao-shih*, 1980: 274.

38. Ibid., 17.13a, ed. Wang Ming 1980: 285.

39. On this Strickmann wrote: The "Yellow God's Emblem of Transcendence"

was one of the terms applied by our sixth-century Taoist text to its own seal, which was also to be used against aquatic monsters and in the tracks of dangerous beasts.

40. *Pao-p'u-tzu nei-p'ien*, ed. Wang Ming 1980: 287; see Ware 1966: 299.

41. *Shodō zenshū* (Tokyo: Heibonsha, 1968), Supplement 1: 30, 53.

42. See Kleeman 1984.

43. Here Strickmann noted: See Wu Jung-ts'eng, "Chen-mu-wen chung so chien-tao-te Tung Han Tao-wu kuan-hsi," *Wen-wu* 298 (1981): 61. Wu points out that fifth- and sixth-century Buddhist authors of anti-Taoist diatribes criticized Taoist priests for "irresponsibly serving the forces of evil and manufacturing the Yellow God's Emblem of Transcendence, with which they kill demons." This pre-Taoist artifact thus appears to have been adopted by Taoists at an early date, and it long continued in use among them. I owe this reference to Donald Harper's concise account of the Yellow God's role at this early period as chief representative of the Monarch of Heaven and as recordkeeper of the dead; see Harper 1982: 473–76. Some authorities take the two characters that I have translated as "emblem of transcendence" (*yüeh-chang*) to be the personal name of the deity Huang Yüeh-chang. Sun Ssu-mo's "Book of Spellbinding" gives a demon-dispelling incantation that makes the "Yellow God" (Huang-shen, here written with the homophonous character *huang*, "august") and Yüeh Chang (a proper noun, or "seal of transcendence"?) into two complementary personages or entities: "Before me, the August God/ Behind me, Yüeh Chang,"; see *Ch'ien-chin i-fang* 29: 247a.

44. For a comprehensive account of Chinese seals, see van Gulik 1958: 415–57.

45. See Robert Duquenne's essential essay, "Daigensui" (1983b); and Miyasaka 1965. On the relations between the Chinese god Marshall Wen and Āṭavaka, Paul Katz notes: "I can only hypothesize that Marshall Wen's similarities to Āṭavaka may represent one form of Tantric Buddhism's influence on Taoism (and local cults) described by scholars such as Michel Strickmann and Rolf Stein" (Katz 1995: 80).

46. T. 1238, 21: 183c–184a.

47. On later Taoist "summoning for interrogation," see Boltz 1985.

48. See Hou 1979a: 219–25.

49. See Blacker 1975: 181–85.

50. For the crow in the sun, see Loewe 1979: 127–31.

51. T. 1238, 21: 185b17–23.

52. Ibid., 186b–187b.

53. On Jāṅgulī (Jungle-Woman) Strickmann also wrote: The Buddha rather spoils this splendid image of independent womanhood (the sort of image that buddhas regularly spoiled) by clarifying—quite unnecessarily, to our minds—that even though Jāṅgulī chooses to appear in the form of a woman, she is not really a woman at all, but is in fact a man, since thanks to their miraculous powers buddhas and bodhisattvas are able to take any form they choose in order to conquer the various poisons. This sort of rationale is typical of Buddhist scripture; given the association of the goddess (now supposedly a god in disguise) with snakes, we may recall the statement, attributed to the Buddha, that it would be better for a

monk to put his penis into the mouth of a poisonous serpent than into a woman's vagina. Some people who think to find feminist ideals in Buddhism will be sorely disabused.

54. On *ku* poisoning, see Feng and Shryock 1935; De Groot 1892–1910, vol. 5: 826–79; and Paul Unschuld 1985: 46–50.

55. An image of Jāṅgulī appears in the long handscroll painted by Chang Shen-wen (completed 1173–76) kept in the National Palace Museum in Taipei. A color reproduction is in Li Lin-ts'an, *Nan-chao Ta-li-kuo hsin tzu-liao te tsung-ho yen-chiu* (Taipei: Kuo-li ku-kung po-wu-yüan, 1982), 110, image no. 99 (Li misnumbers the images on this page; it should be image no. 97). For a Japanese representation, see Frank 1991: 216–17. For the goddess as a form of Kuan-yin, see Stein 1986; and de Mallmann 1975: 198–99.

56. See de Mallmann 1975: 198–99.

57. The system is described in the *Book of Spellbinding* (*Chin ching*) comprising chapters 29 and 30 of Sun Ssu-mo's early seventh-century medical collection, the *Ch'ien-chin i-fang*.

58. This fivefold symbolism, based on the cross-cultural physiological datum of the five fingers, is perhaps the single most important factor that made possible the synthesis between the Yin-Yang, Taoist, and Buddhist cosmological systems. It found its expression in the five-degree stūpa of esoteric Buddhism as it developed in medieval Japan. For a description of the five places of the body/mudrā (*yin-shen wu-ch'u*), see the *Chu-fo ching-chieh she chen-shih ching*, a Tattvasaṃgraha work translated by Prajñā: crown of the head, right shoulder, left shoulder, top of the heart, and top of the throat (T. 868, 18: 272c). An alternative list is found in the *Ta-sheng miao chi-hsiang p'u-sa shuo ch'u-tsai chiao ling fa-lun*, translated by Śīla-bhadra (T. 966, 19: 345a): forehead, right and left shoulders, heart, and throat; and in the *I-tzu ting-lun-wang nien-sung i-kuei* (T. 954B, 19: 311a): the two eyes, the two eyebrows, and the space between the eyebrows. For the "five places of the lower body" (*hsia-t'i wu-ch'u*), see the *Ting lun-wang ta man-t'u-lo kuan-ting i-kuei*, a short *abhiṣeka* ritual (T. 959, 19: 329b). One also finds other lists mentioning four, seven, ten, thirteen, or sixteen places. The ritual generation of Mahāvairocana's cosmic body according to T. 959 goes as follows:

earth	bīja *a* (J. *a*)	lower body (i.e., the sexual organ)
water	bīja *vi* (J. *bi*)	navel
fire	bīja *ra* (J. *ra*)	heart
wind	bīja *hūṃ* (J. *un*)	white tuft between eyebrows
space:	bīja *khaṃ* (J. *ken*)	crown of head

These five bījas are also associated with the five viscera of Chinese medicine: liver, heart, lungs, kidneys, and spleen. For a numerological classification of the five fingers in Taoism, see Saso 1978: 220–21. For a similar Buddhist schema of the two hands, see the *Dhāraṇī Book of Āṭavaka*, T. 1265, 21: 295b; also Arlington 1927 and Saunders 1960.

59. On HY 589: 14b–15b. On the placement or imposition of mantras on the

human body or other objects to be sanctified (and by the same token protected), a procedure known as *nyāsa*, see Padoux 1980.

60. On this god (or "king of science," *vidyārāja*, Ch. *ming-wang*, J. *myōō*), see Iyanaga 1983–85: 694–98; Frank 1991: 158–59; Hayakawa Junzaburō 1915: 411; and Minakata 1971–75, vol. 10: 73. On the *vidyārāja* class, see Przyluski 1923; Soymié 1987.

61. See Bischoff 1956; and Iyanaga 1983–85.

62. T. 1227, 21: 150b.

63. Ibid.

64. T. 1229, 21: 160a.

65. For a description of similar seals and talismans, see Ono Seishū, *Kaji kitō himitsu taizen* (Tokyo: Daibunkan, 1971), 253–59 and 433–53. For an explication of charms and spells, see Doré 1914–31, vols. 1–3; and Ch'en Hsiang-ch'un 1942.

66. See Hayakawa 1915: 411. A conflation of two basic Ucchuṣma scriptures, T. 1228 and 1229, was printed in Nanking in 1882, and reprinted in the miscellany *Mi-chiao t'ung-kuan* (Taipei: Tzu-yu ch'u-pan, 1976), 319–44.

67. Stein 2438; printed in the Taishō edition of the Buddhist canon as T. 2906 (*San-wan fo t'ung ken-pen shen-pi chih yin ping fa-lung chung-shang tsun-wang fo-fa*). See also P. 3874, which is a series of seals accompanied by instructional text. The latter was studied by Michel Soymié in his 1987–88 seminar at the École Pratique des Hautes Études, fourth section.

68. Nāgārjuna appears as a master of magic in a Koutchean manuscript (between ca. 500–1000) studied by Filliozat 1948: 10–11. In medieval Japan, Nāgārjuna was also worshipped as the founder of the craft of fortune-telling; see Waley 1936: 552. An exorcistic painting seen by John Lagerwey in Fukien a few years ago, in which Nāgārjuna appeared alongside Lao-tzu, seems to indicate that his fame as a magician has withstood all cultural revolutions (Lagerwey, private communication).

69. T. 2906, 85: 1451c. Here Strickmann wrote: In a cosmological epic current in the last century among the Altai Turks, from the blood of the Future Buddha Maitreya, shed as he and the Bodhisattva Mañjuśrī battle with two warriors sent up out of the earth by Erlik Khan, the earth will catch fire, bringing about the destined end of the world; see Wilhelm Radloff, *Aus Siberien* (Leipzig, 1893; reprint Oosterhout, 1868), 2: 13–14; and Nora K. Chadwick and Victor Zhirmunsky, *Oral Epics of Central Asia* (Cambridge: Cambridge University Press, 1969), 168–69.

70. Here Strickmann noted: This fragment, Peking Tun-huang Collection (Peking, National Library), no. 8738, was kindly brought to my attention by Kenneth Dean.

71. On this dhāraṇī, see *Kakuzen shō*, s.v. "Nyoirin," DNBZ, vol. 47: 196–97.

72. On mudrās as finger-seals, see Saunders 1960; Yamasaki 1988.

73. See Michel Strickmann, "Heralds of Maitreya," unpublished paper given at the Princeton University Maitreya Conference, May 1983. The most famous "historical" example is that of Kūkai (Kōbō daishi, 774–835), founder of the Shingon sect of Japanese Tantrism, who is said to await for Maitreya's coming at the sect's headquarters on Mount Kōya, south of Osaka. See Miyata 1970: 132–39.

74. On Chinese mummies, see Pokora 1985. Much has been written in particular on the mummification of Buddhist monks; see, for instance, Andō Kōsei 1961 and 1968; Hori 1962; Naitō 1974; Nihon miira kenkyū gurūpu 1969; Sano and Naitō 1969; Togawa 1974; Demiéville 1965; Cockburn and Cockburn 1983; Faure 1991: 148–69; and Sharf 1992.

75. See Lamotte 1949–76, vol. 1: x–xiv. There were even Jain biographies of Nāgārjuna, on which see Granoff 1988.

76. On the *Lung-shu wu-ming lun* (T. 1420), which Strickmann refers to elsewhere as "a wild array of extravagant magic," see Osabe 1982: 234–47. See also *Higashiyama Ōrai*, in Waley 1936: 552. Nāgārjuna's Five Gates, based on the Five Phases of Chinese cosmology, is also widely used by the Japanese priest Eisai in his *Shutten taikō* (Essentials of Coming Out of Entanglement); see *Nihon daizōkyō, Tendaishū mikkyō*, vol. 48: 648–55.

77. T. 1420, 21: 963a. The jujube was a fruit associated with Taoist immortals.

78. Ibid., 963b4–16.

79. In East Asian magic mirrors, the inscription on the back of the mirror is reflected from its face onto a wall or other remote surface.

80. On this point, Strickmann noted: In a private communication, Glen Dudbridge writes: "'Life-preserving silks' (*hsü-ming lü*) were worn on the fifth of the fifth lunar month already in ancient times, and the ritual protection conferred by their blend of five cardinal colours is explained in fragmentary passages of the Han work *Feng-su t'ung-i* (see *Feng-su t'ung-i chiao-shih*, ed. Tientsin 1980, *i-wen*, pp. 414–415, with text-critical notes on the fragments and their sources; compare Bodde 1975: 306–308). No less than three stories in the eighth-century *Kuang-i chi*, ed. Peking [Chung-hua shu-chü] 1961, 298.2373–4, 451.3684, 451.3689), echoes of which lingered even in the last years of traditional society (*Sung shih*, ed. Peking [Chung-hua shu-chü] 1977, 112.2681; Tun Li-ch'en, *Yen-ching sui-shih chi*, ed. Peking [Chung-hua shu-chü] 1961, pp. 62–63; see Bodde 1965: 44). In all three stories it is the duty of a young wife to offer seasonal 'life-preserving' gifts to her in-laws on the Double Fifth and on certain other annual festivals. The gifts were apparently worth keeping: to lose or destroy them removed their ritual protection."

81. T. 1420, 21: 968b–c.

82. HY 1211, 27: 8b–22a. From this source we also learn that seals could be functionally specialized, as in the case of a "Mao Shan" seal wielded by the living to achieve transcendence. With its inscription slightly altered, the same seal accompanied the bodies of the dead, being destined for their own use in summoning back their departed ethereal souls, a *sine qua non* for immortality (ibid., 10b–11a).

83. See pp. 140–43.

84. HY 854: 1.10a–b. Does the apparent anomaly (rare indeed were left-handed swordsmen in China) represent an intentional inversion of Buddhist practice, or a scribal error?

85. HY 854: 1.28b–29a.

86. See *I-chien chih* (Peking: Chung-hua shu-chü, 1981); also E. Davis 1994.

87. *I-chien chih* 3: 996.

88. Ibid., 2: 574.
89. Ibid., 3: 1458.
90. Mackay 1895: 312.
91. De Groot 1892–1910, vol. 6: 1050.
92. See Strickmann 1982b; Lemoine 1978.
93. Lemoine 1982: 28.
94. Ibid., p. 135, and pl. 255.
95. Graham 1954: 41. Here Strickmann noted: One observer of Singapore has noticed that householders there bring a variety of objects to be consecrated by exorcists and mediums at the temple, including images, domestic articles, and mirrors: "A frequent practice is for clean shirts and blouses to be brought for stamping at the back of the neck. In such cases the *dang-ki* (*t'ung-chi*, "medium") normally uses a seal about two inches square bearing an insignia [*sic*] which shows the name of the *shan* and the temple. He licks the seal and stamps it on the object. . . . The stamp marks remain visible on the backs of many worshippers and are a means of identifying devotees of spirit mediumship in everyday life." Instead of the Taoist's (and official's) vermilion, the *dang-ki*'s seal is inked with blood from his cut tongue; see Elliott 1955: 58.
96. On the ritual use of this seal, see Yamamoto 1993: 47–51, 163–75. See also T. 951, 19: 238b23.
97. Werner 1932: 331–32.
98. *Pen-ts'ao ching chi-chu*, by T'ao Hung-ching; see Mori Risshi, annotator, *Honzōkyō shūchū* (Osaka: Maeda shoten, 1972), 97, s.v. *niu-huang*. See also Daniel Léger, "Les Bezoards: 'Pierres animales' rituelles," in *L'Homme et l'animal* (1975): 194–204. Among old Central Asian Turks and all Altaic people, bezoar was also manipulated to produce rain, snow, wind. See Roux 1966a: 218.
99. On the use of bezoar in Aizen (Skt. rāgarāja) rituals, see Yamamoto 1993 and Tanaka 1992. Mochizuki 1958–63 (i.e., the *Mochizuki bukkyō daijiten*) describes the *goō kaji* as a ritual based on the *Caṇḍīdevīdhāraṇī* (T. 1075, translated by Vajrabodhi): "When a woman has no boy or girl, if she writes this mantra on the birchbark (from a kind of birch found in Manchuria) with 'ox-yellow' (bezoar), in no time she will get a boy or a girl." It also says: "If one desires a child, one writes this dhāraṇī on a leaf and on the bark of a birch tree, and one also draws a young boy, one wraps this with purple color, one recites 1,080 times, and if it fixes in the hair, one will get pregnant."
100. Mochizuki 1958–63, vol. 2: 1115a, s.v. *goō kaji*; see also *Keiran shūyō shū*, T. 2410, 76: 778c.
101. See Fuad Köprülü, "Une institution magique chez les anciens Turcs: yat," *Actes du IIe congrès international d'histoire des religions* (Paris, 1925): 440–51; Roux 1966b: 159–63; and idem, 1984: 95–98.
102. On the power of seals over the natural elements, Strickmann noted: A medieval Taoist work of uncertain date, *The Most High's Book of Transcendent Seals for Communicating with the Invisible World* (*T'ai-shang t'ung-hsüan ling-pao yin ching*, HY 858), specifies that if rubbed with ox bezoar and powdered cin-

nabar, one of its seals will not only summon all manner of spirits but will work large-scale geological, hydraulic, and cosmological changes as well. These include shifting mountains, draining seas, causing lightning and thunder, causing darkness in the heavens and over the earth, making the sun and moon fall from the sky, and bringing clouds and rains—powers also attributed to Turco-Mongol bezoar-stones (HY 858: 4b). The same mixture of bezoar and cinnabar can be smeared on the seal, which is then held facing the East, and the great demon-commander A-t'o-k'o will arrive with his spirit-troops to "shrink the veins of the earth" over a distance of a thousand leagues or ten thousand leagues, 'like swallowing a mouthful of rice," enabling you to reach the farthest destination with a minimum of effort (ibid., p. 5b). A-t'o-k'o apparently derives from Āṭavaka, a Tantric Buddhist patron of sealing, as we have seen. On this deity, see Miyasaka 1965.

103. Roux 1966b: 164.

104. Weinreich 1909: 1–75.

105. See Marc Bloch 1973, and Bächtold-Stäubli 1927, vol. 3: 1938.

106. See Otto Weinreich, "Zum Wundertypus der synanacrōsis," *Archiv für Religionswissenschaft* 32 (1935): 246–64; *synanachrōsis* is "the mingling (or contact) of bodies."

107. See Herbert Fischer, "Heigebarden," *Antaios Jahrbuch* 2 (1961): 318–47; reprinted in Elfriede Grabner, ed., *Volksmedizin: Probleme und Forschungsgeschichte* (Darmstadt: Wissenschaftliche Buchgesellschaft, 1967), 413–43; and idem, "The Use of Gesture in Preparing Medicaments and in Healing," *History of Religions* 5, 1 (1965): 18–53.

108. On this point, Strickmann wrote: Recent biochemical research has revealed that ox-bile is the best source of the amino-acid taurine, which has only recently been recognized as essential in a number of biochemical pathways. Foremost among the properties to which it contributes is acuity of vision, and it is found highly concentrated in the retinas of kittens, whose visual tissue is still developing. The full range of its biological activity is not yet known, but ox-bile may well have figured in alexipharmic preparations from the earliest time. Its use in making the *tilaka*-mark (in proximity to the pineal-gland, the "third eye") may well have referred to its enhancing visual perception in terms of inner vision.

109. See *T'o-lo-ni chi ching*, T. 901, 18: 876b.

110. HY 1010, 10.21b.

111. Ibid., 10.3a–b.

112. Dennys 1876: 70.

113. Minakata and Dickens 1973 (1905). Francis L. K. Hsu (1952: 44) describes the use of hand prints as apotropaic signs during a cholera epidemic in the western Chinese province of Yunnan in 1942. The hand was first pressed in decomposed limestone, then on the object destined for protection—notably, the gates and walls of the family home. For the use of the hand and the fingers in East Asia as imprints or seals on official documents, see Minakata Kumagusu, "The Antiquity of the Finger-Print Method," in idem 1971–75, vol. 10: 40–43, 47–48 (reprinted from *Nature* [1894–96]).

114. De Groot 1892–1910, vol. 6: 1051, 1056.

115. In the words of a turn-of-the-century observer, "Gegen geringes Entgelt lässt man sich Stöcke, Pilgerkleid, Handtücher oder irgend etwas abstempeln, als Wahrzeichen, dass man an dem betreffenden Ort gewesen. Dergleichen Stücke werden dann zu Hause sorgfältig aufbewahrt. Die Japaner kleiden sich auf die Pilgerfahrt in leichten, weissen Baumwohlstoff und bringen mitunter diese Kleider über und über mit Stempeln bedeckt zurück" (For a small amount, one gets one's staff, pilgrim's outfit, towel, or just anything stamped as a proof that one has been at that place. Later, such items are stored carefully away at home. On these pilgrimages the Japanese dress in gowns of light, white cotton, which they sometimes bring back covered all over with stamps; Spörry 1901: 24).

116. See Bizot 1981. The term for the Country of the Crossed Legs (or Feet) is "Chiao-chih," and the natives were often said to cut their hair and tattoo their bodies to resemble the type of dragon known as *chiao*; see Stein 1947: 298, Kaltenmark 1948: 2.

117. See Galavaris 1970.

118. See des Rotours 1952. See also Kaltenmark 1960; Robinet 1993: 24–37; Faure 1996: 225–28.

119. De Groot 1892–1910, vol. 6: 1052. Compare the *Schluckbilde* of Bavaria and Austria; also, perhaps, the ABC cakes used to promote the learning of the alphabet by children; Bächtold-Staübli 1927, vol. 1: 14–15, s.v. *Abc*.

120. See Bächtold-Stäubli 1927, vol. 7: 1706, s.v. *Siegelerde*.

121. Strickmann added on this: The extensive body of material on sealing in the ancient and modern Middle East can only be mentioned in passing. The Muslim tradition preserves ritual practices going back to ancient Mesopotamia, suitably reworked (even as Buddhism retains aspects of ancient Vedic tradition in new vestments). But Islamic occultism also includes numerous elements that were most likely imported into the region from abroad. These included the art of catoptromancy from ancient Greece (Delatte 1932), and magic mirrors, divining-cards, and geomancy (*Punktierkunst*), all probably from China. Seals represent an aspect of culture shared by East Asia with the most ancient Middle East, and it may be that Islamic culture preserved traces of their encounter. H. A. Winkler (1930) furnishes abundant material and close analyses. Much of this is of great relevance for comparison with East Asian data. See in particular ibid., p. 112. One is also reminded of the special development of the concept of seals and sealing in early Christianity, particularly in connection with the "seal of the spirit" conveyed in the rite of baptism. Drawing on the broad range of seals in secular Greco-Roman use (official and private seal-rings, seal-stones, and seals for branding animals, slaves, soldiers, and clothing), as well as the more specifically religious use of seals and marks in pagan rituals and Judaism (branding or tattooing slaves of the gods; circumcision as the "seal of the covenant"), Christians as well as Gnostics applied this rich range of metaphor to their own rites of initiation and dedication. See Dölger 1911; and Lampe 1951.

122. See Chapin 1940.

Chapter 5: The Genealogy of Spirit Possession

1. A number of reasons have been advanced to explain this fact. A sociological explanation is given by I. M. Lewis (1986 and 1989 [1971]), who sees in possession an "oblique aggressive strategy," i.e., a way for oppressed women to voice their grievances. Along the same line, see Padel 1983 and Bargen 1997. Another explanation, emphasizing the political context and questions of lineage, is given by Tanaka Takako, who argues that influential women tended to fall prey to malevolent spirits bent on revenge because they were perceived as the most vulnerable link in a family lineage. A case in point is that of the Somedono imperial consort, who became possessed in 865 by the "vengeful spirit" (*onryō*) of the priest Shinzei (a.k.a. "the holy man of Katsuragi") at a time when two factions were vying for legitimacy. See Tanaka 1992: 83–152, and Faure 1998: 135–36, 162–63. Of course, these two types of explanations are not incompatible.

2. See, for instance, the cases recorded in the *Eiga monogatari* (ca. 1092), a work attributed to Akazome Emon (fl. 976–1041), in Matsumura Hiroshi and Yamanaka Yutaka, eds.; *Nihon koten bungaku taikei* 75: 41–46 (Tokyo: Iwanami shoten, 1964–65), translated by William and Helen McCullough, 1980: 84–88.

3. This is the theme of various Nō plays, like *Aoi no ue*. See Bargen 1997: 76–108; Barnes 1989; and Hosokawa 1993: 13–55.

4. For an enlightening analysis of witchcraft in contemporary France, see Favret-Saada 1980.

5. Morris 1964: 149–50.

6. Ibid., 152.

7. Alexander Macdonald 1975: 117.

8. One of the reasons Japanese scholars have tried to demarcate their "pure" brand of "esoteric Buddhism" from Indo-Tibetan "Tantric Buddhism" has to do with the negative connotation of the latter, which is well known for its "degenerate" sexual practices. However, as Alex Wayman points out, "To be practical, it is passing strange that anyone would bother with the Tantra to justify his 'degenerate' practice, for who so bent among worldly persons would divert his energies by muttering a mantra a thousand times at dawn, noon, sunset, and midnight, with fasting and other inhibitions, to engage in a 'degenerate' practice, when, as we know so well, people at large engage in degenerate practices without bothering to mortify themselves at dawn, noon, sunset, and midnight!" (Wayman 1995 [1973]: 6). Furthermore, as Rolf Stein (1975: 483–84) has shown, despite the poor translations of sexual elements, late Japanese oral traditions of the end of the thirteenth century show sexual elements known otherwise only in the *Caṇḍamahāroṣaṇa*, an Indian Tantra translated into Tibetan in the twelfth century. On Japanese notions of "esotericism" (*mikkyō*), see Matsunaga 1965; Tsuda 1978.

9. On Chinese Tantrism, see Osabe 1971 and 1982; as well as Orzech 1989.

10. For an analysis of the traditional Indian ritual structure, see Henri Hubert's and Marcel Mauss's classic work on *Sacrifice* (Hubert and Mauss 1981 [1898]), a sociological elaboration of Sylvain Lévi's description of Brahmanical ritual (Lévi 1966 [1896]).

11. On Vedic Homa, see Staal 1983; Hooykas 1983–85. On the Buddhist fire ritual, see Strickmann 1983 and 1996: 337–68.

12. See Strickmann 1983.

13. Hooykaas 1966b.

14. See Stablein 1975.

15. Among the large body of literature on possession in India and Indianized Asia, see Kapferer 1983; Heinze 1988; Tambiah 1970; Obeyesekere 1984; Belo 1960; Miller 1979; Hitchcock and Jones 1976; Alexander Macdonald 1987; Hiltebeitel 1989; and Freed and Freed 1993.

16. On the East Asian developments of the figure of Avalokiteśvara, the best work remains Stein 1986.

17. On this incantation, see Meisezahl 1962 and 1965. Amoghapāśa ("the Slipknot That Never Misses Its Target") is the name given to the twelve-armed form of Avalokiteśvara.

18. T. 1097, 20: 426a–427a.

19. Divination was forbidden in early Buddhism. For instance, the Vinaya lists (to reject them) a series of Brahmanic techniques, including a method to "get oracles through the use of a magic mirror." See Buddhaghosa's commentary in Rhys-Davids and Rhys-Davids 1899–1921, Part 1: 24. See also Esnoul 1968, Orofino 1994. On other forms of Buddhist divination, see Kuo Li-ying 1994b, and Strickmann, *Chinese Poetry and Prophecy* (forthcoming).

20. In Chapter 4 we examined an exorcistic text of comparable tone, though not including child-mediums—namely, the section of the Āṭavaka scripture called "The Great General's Rites of Exorcism for Driving Away Demons" (see p. 144).

21. See Osabe 1963.

22. On Acala (J. Fudō), see Takai Kankai, *Fudō-son to goma hihō* (Tokyo: Fudō zenshū kōkankai, 1941); see also the *Fudō-son gushō*, a Tachikawa text, in Hirotani Yūtarō 1925: 222–34; Nakano Genzō, *Fudō Myōō-zō* (Tokyo, 1986); Frank 1991: 148–53; Brinker 1990.

23. T. 1202, 12: 24b.

24. On catoptromancy, see Delatte 1932; Baltrušaitis 1979; Kaltenmark 1974: 151–61. On the use of this technique to invoke Marshall Wen, a Taoist deity reminiscent of Āṭavaka, see Katz 1995: 84; on mirror technology in East Asia, see Needham 1962 (1954): 87–97.

25. See Lalou 1938.

26. On Kulika, see *Fudō-son gushō*, in Hirotani 1925: 227b–228a; Frank 1991: 153. A text translated by Vajrabodhi, T. 1202, 21: 246, explains how to obtain your own *kulika* as an otherworldly servant (immediately after directions for *āveśa*, using young children: the two are doubtless related). See also T. 1246, 21: 220–21; T. Zuzō 3090, vol. 6.

27. T. 867, 18: 269b. See also: T. 1199, 21: 6c (in five-syllable verses): "Or again, take un-sick/virgin boys or girls/and perform the *āveśa* rite/to ask on matters of the three times:/all will be determined." And T. 1202, 21: 23, 24b: "Hold a mirror against your chest, have a little boy or girl look into it and tell you what they see; you should call the dragon-spirit and ask its name; bespell boys

or girls; spirit will enter their hearts, tell you all you want to ask about the three times." On this question, see also Yoritomi 1979: 185.

28. On *āveśa*, see *Hōbōgirin*, vol. 1, s.v. "abesha"; and Mikkyō jiten hensankai, ed., *Mikkyō daijiten* 1: 33a.

29. See *Susiddhi-mahātantra*, T. 893, 18: 625b.

30. Taoists use a child as a "medium," but it is to send orders to spirits. Compare this with the role of the young possessed boy, serving as a "messenger of the gods" in the *paritta* ceremony in Sri Lanka, as described in Waldschmidt 1967: 474–76. The child-mediums (in Hokkien, *tang-ki*, or "oracle-youth"; in Mandarin, *t'ung-chi*) used by vernacular exorcists cut their tongues, pierce their cheeks, and flail their backs to impregnate talismans with their blood. See Elliott 1955: 56–58; Schipper 1993: 44–48; and B. Berthier 1987.

31. Chou 1944–45: 278–79.

32. HY 589, 6b.

33. T. 923, 19: 28c.

34. See Lalou 1955; Orofino 1994.

35. On the animation of icons, see Strickmann 1996: 165–211. Strickmann describes striking parallels between procedures used to evoke a spirit into a child-medium and the animation of icons, as well as between their oracular functions. See also Gombrich 1966: 23–27; Henderson and Hurvitz 1956; Frank 1986; Faure 1996: 237–61; and Brinker 1997–98.

36. Strickmann interprets the Chinese term *k'ung-tsang hsiang* as "hollow statue" rather than as a reference to Hsü-k'ung-tsang (Ākāśagarbha, "Space-Womb"), a bodhisattva commonly associated, since Kūkai, with the morning star and the *gumonji* practice (lit., "seeking, hearing, and retaining," a kind of mnemotechnical method based on the morning star meditation). This practice was first introduced into Chinese Tantrism through the *Hsü-k'ung-tsang ch'iu-wen-ch'i fa* (T. 1145), translated in 717 by Śubhakarasiṃha; see also *Kakuzen shō*, DNBZ 48: 1312–39; Yamasaki 1988; Hakeda 1972: 19–22. Ākāśagarbha also played an important role in Buddhist repentance rituals; see Kuo Li-ying 1994a: 69–70, 136–38. On this figure, see also *Kakuzen shō*, DNBZ 48: 1262–1311; De Visser 1931; Frank 1991: 132–33.

37. The obscure term that is rendered literally here "purple ore water" perhaps refers to water in which amethyst has been steeped.

38. A variant states that it is the tips of the fingers that are to be rubbed.

39. Concerning a similar practice performed by the Central Asian monk Fo-t'u-teng (d. 348), see Wright 1948: 337–38, 344–45, 353.

40. T. 895, 18: 728a–c.

41. See *Taishō shinshū daizōkyō sakuin, Mikkyō-bu*, vol. 1: 356b.

42. Lokesh Chandra, *A Tibetan-Sanskrit Dictionary*, vol. 2: 1454.

43. On this Strickmann noted: The word *senā* means "army," but *prasena* is glossed in those few Sanskrit dictionaries that list it as a term for a game of chess. In my perplexity, I turned to colleagues in Berkeley's Department of South and South Asian Studies. Frits Staal's immediate response was that Prasena is one of the many names of Skanda, a major South Indian god supposed to be the son of

Śiva and also known as Mahāsena, "the General." Yet Professor Staal was unable to find confirmation of his statement in written sources, and thus concluded that his information must derive from the oral tradition to which he had been exposed during long years of fieldwork in South India. George Hart, an authority on Tamil and South Indian traditions, knew of no such identification and expressed doubts about the accuracy of the reconstruction *prasena* itself; it seemed to him an improbable word. Yet on further inquiry, he agreed that *prasena* did occur in male proper names; indeed, his wife had a nephew named Prasena. Still, he knew of no tradition identifying this name with Skanda (or Murugan, as this god of war is known in Tamil). Finally, P. S. Jaini shared Professor Hart's doubts about the likelihood of *prasena* as the Sanskrit word behind the Chinese transcription. He suggested, rather, *prasanna*, "bright" or "clear," and believed that this might most probably be the name of a gandharva—an airborne spirit of a sort very frequently linked with spirit possession.

In summary, if the true word is *prasena*, its real meaning may be uncertain, but it does occur with some frequency in male names even today. This may be due to its having figured in the names of a number of famous ancient and medieval rulers, such as Prasenajit. And in their names, its presence may or may not be due to its association with a particular god; evidence appears to be lacking. If we assume that the Japanese scholars and the Tibetan translators are mistaken, and the original term was *prasanna*, then we must direct our inquiries toward another region of the Indian pantheon: the realm of the gandharvas.

I describe these perplexities here because they obviously affect the direction of our studies and also because they seem to have a wider significance. Although our purpose is not primarily philological, philology nonetheless provides us with the basic elements for an analysis on which all the rest depends. Nowhere is its importance greater than in the complex, cross-cultural field of Buddhist Studies. Linguistic or philological uncertainty therefore puts all more highly synthetic studies at risk. But such uncertainty may in itself be a highly useful indicator, pointing to basic problem areas in cultural history. In undertaking a systematic study of spirit possession in medieval Buddhism, we have entered a region of history and philology that is especially poorly charted, and where even doctors disagree. To some extent, the same is true for the study of Buddhist ritual as a whole. We are dealing with phenomena that at one time or another were diffused over almost all Asia, that interacted in different ways with various local traditions, and that have survived only sporadically, in various degrees of assimilation. Features which once formed a part of a single ritual complex may now be found widely scattered in one or another of the participant cultures. It may therefore prove necessary to deviate from a strict chronological sequence and overleap the confines of a single culture. Whether or not such acrobatics bring us closer to a more adequate reconstruction of medieval rituals, the reader must judge. We may also have to follow up tenuous hints and take risks. It is in this spirit that I attempt to advance our understanding of Buddhist spirit-possession techniques by examining aspects of the cult of Skanda—a possible if not certain *prasena*-figure.

44. Nebesky-Wojkowitz 1956: 462–64.

45. Chime Radha 1981: 8–12.

46. See Alexander Macdonald 1975: 126–27. Contrary to Macdonald, who does not think that *pra*-ceremonies reflect an Indian influence on Tibet, Strickmann argues that we are in presence of a type of phenomena found in all societies where Tantric culture spread—although voluntary possession clearly predates Tantrism. But again, Asian "shamanism," as we know it, is not a "primitive" technique of ecstasis (as Eliade and Blacker would have us believe): It is always a "secondary" shamanism, influenced by Indian and Chinese practices.

47. See Peri 1916.

48. See R. A. Stein 1991 (1981).

49. Usually, the terms *kalala* and *arbuda*, borrowed from Indian medicine, refer to the first two stages of embryonic gestation. On this question, see Sanford 1997.

50. T. 1028A, 19: 741c. An expanded version is attributed to Śubhakarasiṃha (T. 1028B). This work was not included in the versions of the *Kumāratantra* studied by Filliozat (1937). The latter was translated at the end of the tenth century by Dharmabhadra as the *Book of Rāvaṇa's Explanations of How to Cure the Ailments of Children* (T. 1330)—on which see the discussion later in this chapter. Another important scripture is the *Mahāsahasrapramardinī*, translated about the same time into Chinese by Dānapāla (T. 999). This text, in which Skanda or Rāvaṇa has been replaced by a gandharva named Candana, was the source of an iconographical and liturgical tradition that can be found throughout Asia. (I owe this information to Robert Duquenne, who is presently working on this tradition). See, for instance, the *Dōjikyō-hō*, included by Kakuzen (1143–ca. 1218) in his *Kakuzen shō*, T. Zuzō, vol. 4: 366b–375b; and the work of the same title in *Asabā-shō*, T. Zuzō, vol. 9: 471a–477a.

51. T. 999, 19: 591a–b.

52. Hoernle 1893–1912: 227. This Peacock Spell was elaborated from elements found in the *Jātaka* and the *Dīghanikāya*. The most elaborated Chinese translation is that realized by I-ching (T. 985). The *Book of the Peacock Spell* also influenced Taoism, as can be seen in the *T'ai-shang yüan-shih t'ien-tsun shuo K'ung-ch'üeh ching pai-wen* (HY 1423, on which see Boltz 1987: 249).

53. T. 985, 19: 472c.

54. On the peacock as a vehicle of Skanda, see Kramrisch 1981.

55. T. 1330, 21: 492c–494b.

56. Ibid., 491c–492a. On Mātṛnandā, the "cat-demon," see Mochizuki Shinkō 1958–63, vol. 4: 3386b.

57. See Filliozat 1937, and Bagchi 1940.

58. Filliozat 1937: 43–45.

59. Ibid., 53.

60. On this "religion," see Filliozat 1973, Introduction, vii–xliii.

61. Gombrich 1971: 172–76; Wirz 1966 (1953).

62. Another reflection of Skanda within a Tantric Buddhist context is found in a form of the Bodhisattva Mañjuśrī called Kārttikeya Mañjuśrī ("Mañjuśrī of the Pleiades"); on the Tantric Mañjuśrī, see Birnbaum 1983. Images of this figure

share with Skanda the attribute of youth but also, more specifically, a particular infantine coiffure consisting of three locks of hair (the *tricāra*) and a necklace of animal claws worn by children for protection against demons; see de Mallmann 1964, and idem 1975: 33–35, 45–46; P. Agrawala 1967. Among the devotees of Viṣṇu, Skanda is found as the Bālarāma aspect of the young Viṣṇu, Kṛṣṇa. There is even a veiled hint of Skanda's presence in certain Chinese exorcistic texts of the later Middle Ages. His association with the six stars of the Pleiades may have had Chinese repercussions, possibly bringing him into relation with the exorcistic cult of the Southern Dipper constellation (which counterbalanced the Northern Dipper, Ursa Major, and its Tantric goddess, Mārīcī, on whom see Frank 1991: 230–33; Hall 1990). At the beginning of the thirteenth century, Skanda's name figures in a remarkable syncretic genealogy of the pagan gods, patrons of Chinese sorcerers, put forward by the Taoist master Pai Yü-ch'an. The list of reprehensible deities opens with the name of "Satan"; Pai was familiar with Manichaeism as it then survived along the southeastern Chinese seaboard (HY 1296, 8b–9a).

63. On the *gōhō*, see Blacker 1963; on the "thunder-child," see Yanagita Kunio 1990, vol. 11: 92–117; and Ouwehand 1964: 141–54.

64. On the "holy fool" in Chinese and Japanese traditions, see Strickmann 1994; Schipper 1966; Faure 1991: 115–25; Shahar 1998: 30–44.

65. See Schipper 1993: 44–48.

66. See Alexander Macdonald 1975: 126–27; Allen 1975.

67. For an analysis of the symbolic, social, and sexual roles of children (*chigo*) in medieval Buddhism, see Faure 1998; and Hosokawa 1993: 57–84.

Chapter 6: Tantrists, Foxes, and Shamans

1. On Amoghavajra, see Chou 1944–45; Orlando 1980 and 1981.

2. On the integration of Śiva into the Buddhist pantheon and his role in Tantric Buddhism, see Iyanaga 1983 and 1983–85.

3. Whereas the first three modes are self-explanatory, the fourth, *vaśīkaraṇa* (Ch. *ching-ai*, J. *keiai*) refers to taming through sexual union, and its aims vary: for instance, obtaining a desired woman, children, or easy childbirth. Sometimes a fifth mode (actually a variant of *vaśīkaraṇa*) is distinguished: *ākarṣaṇa* ("catching" or "capture," also called *vaśya* or *priyāṅkara*).The first classification of Tantric rituals may be that of two texts translated by Bodhiruci ca. 709, describing *pauṣṭika* and *śāntika* rituals. See T. 951, 19: 261c and T. 952, 19: 272c; also Strickmann 1983: 434–35. For a study of rites of subjugation and pacification, see Hayami 1975: 83 ff. For alternate English translations of the names of these rituals, see Payne 1991, 61.

4. See Lalou 1932 and 1936; Ariane MacDonald 1962; Matsunaga 1983–85.

5. Waddell 1895: 102.

6. On Hārītī, see *Kakuzen shō*, s.v. "Kariteimo," DNBZ 50: 2098–2118; *Haritizō* (coll. Daigo-ji), in T. Zuzō 3145; *Karitei-zō* (Coll. Daigo-ji), in ibid., 3146. See also Peri 1917; Murray 1981–82; Frank 1991: 218–25. On Ucchuṣma, see *Kakuzen shō*, s.v. "Ususama," DNBZ 49; *Asaba-shō*, T. Zuzō 3190, vol. 9: 404b–413c; *Usu-*

sama myōō shusen reiyō roku, in Hayakawa 1915: 392–431. See also Frank 1991: 158–59; Iyanaga 1983–85: 693–98; Nicolas-Vandier 1974–76 (vol. 1: 11–14, 187; vol. 2: pls. 5, 63).

7. T. 1199, 19: 6b–7a.

8. T. 1200, 19: 12a5–8.

9. Ibid., 12a20–23.

10. Ibid., 12a24–12b3.

11. On this, Strickmann also wrote: There is an allusion to the special function of Acala and his boy-servant Ceṭaka in dealing with cases of malignant spirit-possession in the *Susiddhi-mahātantra*, an important encyclopedic compendium of ritual translated by Śubhakarasiṃha sometime during the first third of the eighth century: "If you wish to obtain the subjugation of all remaining demons and *āveśa* [presumably meaning here evil, involuntary possession by demons], always employ the mantra expounded by the Messenger, Ceṭaka, and the others, and you will speedily achieve success" (T. 893, 18: 604c).

12. For stories about obtaining an otherworldly servant, see: T. 1202, 21: 246; and T. 1246, 21: 220–21; both texts are related to *āveśa*. See also Sanford 1991a. Incidentally, references to *āveśa* ("aweisha") can be found in the writings of Gustav Meyrinck, author of a novel entitled *The Golem* (1915, New York: Ungar, 1964). On the theme of the golem, see Idel 1990.

13. T. 953: 289b. On these mudrās or "seals," see Saunders 1960.

14. See T. 865: 218b.

15. On Vaiśravaṇa, see *Kakuzen shō*, s.v. "Bishamon," in DNBZ 50: 2236–51. See also Granoff 1970; Frank 1991: 194–97.

16. T. 1248, 21: 226b–226c.

17. On this figure, see Lamotte 1966.

18. T. 997: 569b.

19. On this, Strickmann added: For the sake of completeness, we should record two further translations of Tantric texts that include instructions for performing *āveśa*. Both were made at the end of the tenth century; one is a new version of the *Questions of Subāhu* (*Miao-pi p'u-sa so-wen ching*, T. 896). The other is dedicated to the Tantric deity Yamāntaka ("Slayer of Yama," Yama being the god of death). It follows the usual procedure with a child-medium; the child's possessed state is called "awakening" (in the sense of enlightenment, or clairvoyance). The trance is broken when the priest recites the Buddha-Samādhi Spell; when the child hears it he will suddenly fall to the ground. The priest then calls out the child's real name, raises him up, bathes him, gives him a meal, and sends him home with all sorts of presents (T. 1217, 21: 92a).

20. *Chou-hou pei-chi fang*, HY 1295, 1: 9–11.

21. Ibid., 3: 62.

22. A definition of madness, from a Buddhist standpoint, can be found in T. 901 (*Collected Dhāraṇī Sūtras*), 18: 858a. For a discussion of conceptions of madness in the context of medieval Japan, see Hosokawa 1993: 15–47.

23. A case in point is that of a representative of "wild Ch'an" (*k'uang-ch'an*)

during the Sung period, the popular saint Tao-chi, also known as Chi-kung ("Mr. Chi") or Chi-tien ("Crazy Chi"). In modern popular religion, Chi-tien is also known to possess his devotees. See Shahar 1998; and DeBernardi 1987.

24. *Chou-hou pei-chi fang*, HY 1295, 3: 61–62.

25. Ibid., 62.

26. Ibid., 64.

27. Ibid.

28. Ibid., 64–65.

29. *Chu-ping yüan-hou lun* 2: 12–13.

30. Ibid.

31. See van Gulik 1961. For a partial translation, see Hsia, Veith, and Geertsma 1986; and Wile 1991. See also Sakade 1986 and 1989a: 3–9; Macé 1985.

32. See Wile 1991.

33. See Wang T'ao's *Wai-t'ai pi-yao* 13: 368a.

34. T. 946, 19: 178c–179a.

35. Perry 1980: 215.

36. See D. Harper 1982, recipes 146–49, 154.

37. Here Strickmann noted: Fumigation was also used in Chinese courts for interrogating suspects. The longtime Peking resident Lewis C. Arlington chose to illustrate his memoirs with gruesome color plates showing various forms of judicial torture. Facing p. 78 is a depiction of the method for extorting a confession by fumigating the prisoner with red-pepper fumes. Arlington comments, "This is said to have been a most horrible punishment. During the process, which sometimes lasted for an hour, the victim would turn all colours of the rainbow, and some more" (Arlington 1931). On Chinese supplices, see also Doolittle 1966 (1865).

38. *Wai-t'ai pi-yao* 13: 368.

39. Ibid., 369.

40. From Vāgbhaṭa's *Aṣṭāṅgahṛdaya*, in Filliozat 1937: 58–59.

41. *Nü-k'o pai-wen* (A Hundred Questions on Gynecology), 1: 47a.

42. Sometimes there is a fine line between game-playing and possession. For an account of the civet-cat possession-game in Malaysia, see J. O'May, "Playing the Were-Beast: A Malay Game," *Folklore* 21 (1910): 371–74. O'May describes a game of Malay boys, played on moonlight nights, during which a boy turns into a civet-cat: "White cloth wraps head, patted on back or swung backward and forward, spells are sung; he falls asleep, and wakes as a civet-cat. If one calls his own name, he wakes as himself." On cat-demons, see, for instance, T. 901, passim. On the Japanese folklore of possession, see Orikuchi Shinobu hakushi kinen kodai kenkyūjo, ed., *Orikuchi Shinobu zenshū* (Tokyo: Chūōkōronsha, 1971), vol. 7: 32, 42; vol. 6: 242; vol. 5: 202; and vol. 8: 200.

43. Wadley 1976. A case of snake-woman is also described in Blacker 1978.

44. Belo 1960: 201–25.

45. These *graha* were sometimes assimilated with the twelve cyclical animals (rat, ox, tiger, hare, dragon, snake, horse, goat, monkey, rooster, dog, boar), represented with a human body and an animal head (see, for instance, the set dis-

played at the Metropolitan Museum in New York). On Taoist representations—also found in Tantric Buddhism—of the viscera as animal-spirits, see Robinet 1993: 68–69.

46. On Mārīcī, a deity who became the protector of warriors, see *Kakuzen shō*, DNBZ 50: 2210–18; see also Hall 1990; Frank 1991: 230–33.

47. On the Tantric rites centered on Garuḍa, see *Kakuzen shō*, DNBZ 50: 2129–52.

48. Elliott 1955, pl. 6. The monkey-god incarnates at his annual festival, on the sixteenth of the eighth lunar month: see Joan Law and Barbara E. Ward, *Chinese Festivals* (Hong Kong, 1982): 73–76. In a festival held in Kowloon, the monkey manifests himself regularly on the first and fifteenth days of every lunar month. He does so by entering into the body of a medium—a man in his early forties—and speaking through him. The medium acts like a monkey. See also O'May's description of another Malay game, the "monkey-dance," in which a monkey-spirit is caused to enter a girl of about ten years old; see O'May, "Playing the Were-Beast," 465 (note 42 above). On the monkey-god Sun Wu-k'ung, see Meir Shahar, "The Lingyin Si Monkey Disciples and the Origins of Sun Wukong," *Harvard Journal of Asiatic Studies* 53, 1 (1992): 193–224.

49. The theriomorphic pantheon of Tantric Buddhism derives in part from the notion of *teng-liu shen* (J. *tōrujin*), a term referring to the body of a buddha who takes the same form as the evil being to tame. Buddhist borrowings from the Hindu pantheon were thus justified by the desire to extend salvation to all beings (not only demons but also outcasts like the *caṇḍāla* or the *mātaṅga*).

50. On this popular deity, see Getty 1936; Banerjea 1956: 354–61; Bühnemann 1988 and 1989; Courtright 1985; R. Brown 1991; Sanford 1991b; Kabanoff 1994; and Strickmann 1996, chap. 5 ("L'amour chez les éléphants").

51. Bhandarkar 1913: 147, quoting the *Mānava-gṛhyasūtra*.

52. For more details on these beings, see Strickmann 1996: 310–22. In Japan, the *vināyakas* were often assimilated to the *kōjin* ("raging deities") category, on which, see, for instance, Yamamoto 1998; and Kelsey 1981.

53. See Courtright 1985.

54. T. 1270, 21: 303b–c; see also Stein 1986: 38; Sanford 1991b; Kabanoff 1994; and Frank 1991: 226–27. This text and the following (the *Ta-shih chou-fa ching*, T. 1268) are described in Tokiwa Daijō, ed., *Bussho kaisetsu daijiten*, 7: 271b–273. For a representation of this dual-bodied deity (J. *sōshin* Kangiten), see, for instance, Frank 1991: 228–29.

55. T. 1268, 21: 300c12–15; cf. T. 1271, 21: 306a13–18.

56. For a detailed analysis of these two figures, see Strickmann 1996: 266–72.

57. See Nicolas-Vandier 1974–76, vol. 1: 212; vol. 2: pl. 103.

58. T. 1272, 21: 307b.

59. Ibid., 311b.

60. Ibid., 313a.

61. Ibid., 318a–321b.

62. See Strickmann 1996, chap. 5; R. Brown 1991; Kabanoff 1994.

63. This point is elaborated on in Strickmann 1996: 272–76.

64. See, for instance, the role of symbolic animal metamorphoses in medieval Japanese Buddhism, in Yamamoto 1993: 290–380.

65. Dudbridge 1970: 115–16.

66. See van Gulik 1967.

67. See Von der Goltz 1883: 22.

68. On the Chinese anticlerical critique against Buddhism, see André Lévy 1971: 97–113.

69. Hou 1979a: 210.

70. *Shuo wen chieh-tzu* 10A: 36a.

71. D. Harper 1982: 373. See also idem, 1988: 265.

72. MacIntyre 1886: 53. On this question, see also J. Lévi 1984. Lévi's article is one of the contributions to a special issue of *Études mongoles et sibériennes* dedicated to the image of the fox in European and Asian cultures.

73. On the use of fox-parts to cure maladies, Strickmann also wrote: Just as the homeopathic principle of *similia similibus curantur* governs the choice of remedy, so it may shed fresh light on the origins and rationale behind certain animal drugs from China's intriguing repertory. It is also said that foxes store various sorts of medicine in their burrows, and sometimes offer it to their human intimates (MacIntyre 1886: 55). To all this we may compare Moroccan tradition: "The fox contains 366 medicines. If a person is in love with somebody and wants to cure himself of it, he burns the dung of a fox and fumigates himself with the smoke. If a little child cries at night the eye-tooth of a fox is hung round its neck. . . . A deaf person pours the melted fat of a fox into his ear to get rid of his deafness. . . . The melted brain of a fox is put on syphilitic sores and kept there four or five days. . . . Another remedy for syphilis is to roast a fox with head and hair and entrails until it is charred, and to give the powder made of it, mixed with honey, to the patient to eat. . . . Men who have been made impotent by witchcraft burn the penis of a fox and fumigate their own with smoke. The gall of a fox is used by women for practising witchcraft, for example, with a view to inducing a man to divorce a rival wife" (Westermarck 1926, vol. 2: 321–22).

74. *Chinese-English Glossary of Common Terms in Traditional Chinese Medicine* (Hong Kong, 1982): 133.

75. For a synopsis of these stories, see J. Lévi 1984; Bouchy 1984.

76. T. 945, 19: 135b.

77. On the Tibetan ḍākiṇīs, see Herrmann-Pfandt 1992–93. On the Japanese deity Dakini-ten and its Indian antecedents, see Iyanaga 1999.

78. Stein 1959.

79. Stein 1972: 76.

80. Despite the fact that these idealized images of ḍākiṇīs as "sky-walkers" have recently become convenient feminist symbols (see, for instance, Shaw 1994), Hermann-Pfandt's more nuanced analysis (1992–93) reminds us of the ambivalent nature (and the dark side) of such symbols. See also Gyatso 1998: 243–64.

81. Banerjea 1956: 494.

82. See de Mallmann 1963: 234, 297.

83. Banerjea 1956: 34.

84. On this question, see the rich essay by Iyanaga (1999); see also Sasama 1988.

85. Read 1941: 178.

86. *Chou-hou pei-chi fang*, HY 1295, p. 234.

87. T. 901, 18: 792b.

88. On Japanese fox lore, see Gorai 1985; Bouchy 1984 and 1992; Hiruta 1985.

89. This ritual is described in *Kakuzen shō*, s.v. "Rokuji-kyō," DNBZ 46: 802–37.

90. Does this triad comprise a sorceress with her two fox-acolytes, as Strickmann indicates, or is it a representation of the three "divine foxes" (the celestial, the human, and the terrestrial)? On these three types of foxes, see Yamamoto 1993: 338–70. Yamamoto argues in particular that the apparition of these three "foxes" (which no longer have any relation with the real animal) is due to a play of words on (or a misreading of) the term "*miketsu* [*no kami*]"—a term referring to the god Inari—as *mi-kitsu*[*ne*], "three foxes." See ibid., 354. Actually, in the representation given in *Kakuzen shō*, DNBZ 46: 330, the woman is shown along with a large bird and a fox. These three figures, often represented in medieval Japan, were called "heavenly fox" (*tenko*), "earthly fox" (*chiko*), and "human form [fox"] (*ningyō*). For similar representations, see T. 2484, 78: 297, T. 2485: 340, T. 2486: 406, T. 2489: 518, and T. 2495: 628. On Dakini rituals in the Tendai school, see *Keiran shūyō shū*, T. 2410, 76: 631b–633c. On the cult of Inari, see, among others, Bouchy 1984 and 1992; Kondō 1978; Gorai 1985; Matsumae 1988.

91. Blacker 1975: 56–61; see also Bouchy 1984. A similar stigma attaches in China to families bearing the name Hu, which is homophonous with the word for fox.

92. Blacker 1975: 67. See also the recent work of Tanaka Takako (1993), *Gehō to aihō no chūsei* (Love Rites and Heretical Rites in the Medieval Age). On Izuna, see Frank 1991: 293–94.

93. On the Tantric elements in Nichiren doctrine, see Frank 1981–82.

94. Percival Lowell 1894: 157. Admittedly, Lowell (1855–1916) was more perspicacious as an astronomer, and he is remembered for his prediction of Pluto's discovery.

95. On the cult of the *Lotus Sūtra* in Japanese Buddhism, see the various essays in Tanabe and Tanabe 1989; on the relations between Tendai *hongaku* ideology and the Nichiren tradition, see Stone 1995.

96. The assimilation of the dākiṇī with the jackal appears in the "apocryphal" (that is, Chinese) *Śūraṃgama-sūtra* (*Shou-leng-yen ching*): see T. 945, 19: 135b.

97. See Buchanan 1935; Bouchy 1984 and 1992; Gorai 1985; and Yamamoto 1993.

98. De Visser 1908: 105–29.

99. Ibid., p. 118.

100. On the Tengu, see De Visser 1908; Chigiri 1973 and 1975; Rotermund 1991b.

101. On the animation of puppets, see J. M. Law 1995, and 1997: 30–48.

102. On "love rituals" (J. *aihō*), see Tanaka 1993.

103. D. Harper 1985.

104. *Ta-T'ang Ch'ing-lung ssu san-ch'ao kung-feng ta-te hsing-chuang*, T. 2057, 50: 295a.

105. On this question, see Strickmann 1996: 235–38; and Boltz 1985: 130–32. Among early occurrences of the term "summoning for interrogation" (*k'ao-chao*), we may mention one in a set of instructions for the ritual of transmitting Taoist scriptures, written by Lu Hsiu-ching (406–77). The Taoist master is authorized to summon for interrogation (*k'ao-chao*) the spirits of all the regions—and a list of types of spirits follows that is reminiscent of the demon-inventories in the *Maṇiratna Book* and the *Spirit-Spells of the Abyss* (HY 528, p. 6a). The same term was used in the exorcistic instructions presented by the demon-commander Āṭavaka, in a Buddhist scripture from the first half of the sixth century, the *Dhāraṇī Book of Āṭavaka*, full of information on the use of demonifugic seals (see pp. 143–51).

106. On the differences between these groups of specialists and the distinctions between classical and vernacular rituals, see Schipper 1985b.

107. Jordan and Overmyer 1986.

108. Waley 1936: 550.

109. Delatte 1932: 122–31.

110. In fact, Buddhist scripture had recorded catoptromancy as being current in India long before this. The *Brahmajāla-sūtra* of the *Dīghanikāya* (from around the beginning of the Christian era) provides the classic inventory of mantic techniques in use among the brahmans—and therefore condemned by Buddhist monks. Among the methods listed is "obtaining oracular answers by means of the magic mirror." On this technique, the fifth-century commentator Buddhaghoṣa explains that it was customary to make a god appear in a mirror and answer questions put to him. Next the sūtra mentions "obtaining oracular answers from a god." The latter technique is also said to have required a female medium; but a temple prostitute (*devadāsī*, "slave of the god") was the appropriate vehicle, in contrast to the girl of good family supposed to have been used in the preceding method (Rhys-Davids and Rhys-Davids 1899–1921, vol. 1: 24). A primary function of Tantric Buddhist revelation was to create an acceptable Buddhist version of such practices. The Indologist Theodor Zachariae believed that the mirror that a widow about to immolate herself carried with her onto the pyre was originally meant to facilitate her prophetic vision as she stood on the threshold of the other world.

111. If of Greek origin, the technique of catoptromancy is likely to have passed to India during the Hellenistic period, as did Greek medicine, mathematics, and genethliac astrology (see Pingree 1978). Specialists would then have to determine whether Islamic practice derived directly from the ancient Mediterranean legacy, its Byzantine elaborations, or an Indian source—or, indeed, from a mixture of all of these. For the technology of Chinese mirrors, see Needham 1962 (1954): 87–97; on magic mirrors generally, see Baltrušaitis 1979 and Hartlaub 1951. Elling Eide cogently observes that the mirror's function of foreshadowing the future is

implied, and sometimes explicitly stated, in works of traditional Chinese and Japanese historiography that have the word "mirror" or "speculum" in their titles. From the past events which they record, the wise may discern the future (Eide 1973: 384, no. 11).

112. Burkert 1979.

113. Yet some scholars persist: Rémi Mathieu, for instance, argues that the term "shamanism" remains perfectly justified in the case of ancient China; see Mathieu 1987.

114. See Mironov and Shirokogoroff 1924; Shirokogoroff 1935.

115. This is a view endorsed by Eliade, who stresses, however, that shamanism is not the creation of Buddhism; see Eliade 1964: 432–33.

116. Filliozat 1935b; see also Bartlett 1973.

117. See Strickmann 1982b.

118. Van der Loon 1977.

BIBLIOGRAPHY

Primary Sources

Abhidharmakośa, by Vasubandhu. Trans. Hsüan-tsang. T. 1558, vol. 29. See also the French translation by Louis de la Vallée Poussin, *L'Abhidharmakośa de Vasubandhu*. Brussels: Institut Belge des Hautes Études Chinoises, 1971. 6 vols. Mélanges Chinois et Bouddhiques, vol. 16.

Abridged Code of Master Lu. See *Lu hsien-sheng tao-men k'o-lüeh*.

A-cha-p'o-chü kuei-shen ta-chiang shang fo t'o-lo-ni shen-chou ching (Book of Spells of Āṭavaka, King of Demons). T. 1238, vol. 21.

A-cha-p'o-chü kuei-shen ta-chiang shang fo t'o-lo-ni shen-chou ching (Book of Spells of Āṭavaka, King of Demons). T. 1237, vol. 21.

A-cha-p'o-chü yüan-shuai ta-chiang shang fo t'o-lo-ni ching hsiu-hsing yi-kuei. T. 1239, vol. 21.

Agni-purāṇa. (1) *Collection of Hindu Mythology and Traditions*. Ed. Rajendralala Mitra. Biblioteca Indica. 3 vols. Calcutta: Ganesha Press, 1873–79. (2) Ed. Pandita Ananda Asrama. Published by Hai Natayana Apte. Ananda Asrama Sanskrit Series. Poona, 1900.

Agrapradīpa-dhāraṇī. See *Fo-shuo t'o-lo-ni po ching*.

Amoghapāśa-sūtra. See *Pu-k'ung chüan-so t'o-lo-ni tzu-tsai-wang chou ching*.

Annals of the Sage of Latter Time, Lord of the Golden Gateway of Supreme Purity. See *Shang-ch'ing hou-sheng tao-chün lieh-chi*.

Asaba-shō, by Shōchō (1205–82). T. Zuzō, vols. 6–9.

Aṣṭāṅga Hṛdaya of Vāgbhaṭa, eighth century, with commentary by Kavirāja Atrideva Gupta. Ed. Śrī Yadunandana Upādhyāya. Kashi Sanskrit Series, 150. Varanasi: Chowkhamba Sanskrit Series Office, 1970.

Besson zakki, by Shinkaku (1117–80). T. Zuzō 3007, vol. 3.

Book of Consecration. See *Kuan-ting ching*.

Book of Exorcistic Healing. See *Chin ching*.

Book of Rāvaṇa's Explanations of How to Cure the Ailments of Children. See *Lo-fo-nu shuo chiu-liao hsiao-erh chi-ping ching*.

Book of the Demon-Dispellers. See *Tung-chen t'ai-shang shuo chih-hui hsiao-mo chen-ching*.
Book of the Dhāraṇī for Protecting Children. See *Hu chu t'ung-tzu t'o-lo-ni ching*.
Book of the Dhāraṇī of Golden Gaṇapati. See *Chin-se chia-na-po-ti t'o-lo-ni ching*.
Book of the Great Peace. See *T'ai-p'ing ching*.
Book of the Incantations and Dhāraṇī of the Jāṅgulī Woman. See *Ch'ang-ch'ü-li tu-nü t'o-lo-ni chou ching*.
Book of the Lotus of the True Law. See *Miao-fa lien-hua ching*.
Book of the Peacock Spell. See *Fo-mu ta k'ung-ch'üeh ming-wang ching*.
Book of the Spirit-Spells of the Eightfold Yang of Heaven and Earth. See *T'ien-ti pa-yang shen-chou ching*.
Book of the Very Auspicious Spells of the Spirits. See *Ta-chi-i shen-chou ching*.
Book of the Yellow Court. See *Huang-t'ing nei-ching yü-ching ching-chu*.
Book on Discerning the Rewards of Good and Evil. See *Chan ch'a shan-e yeh-pao ching*.
Brahmajāla-sūtra. See *Dīghanikāya*.
Byaku shō, by Chōen (1218–78). T. Zuzō 3191, vol. 10.
Byakuhō kushō, by Ryōson, based on the teaching of Ryōzen (1258–1341). T. Zuzō 3119, vols. 6–7.
Catuḥsatya-śāstra (Śāstra of the Four Truths), by Vasuvarman. Trans. Paramārtha. T. 1647, vol. 32.
Chan ch'a shan-e yeh-pao ching (Book on Discerning the Rewards of Good and Evil). T. 839, vol. 17.
Ch'an chen i-shih, by Fang Ju-hao (Ming). (1) Harbin: Hei-lung chiang jen-min, 1986. (2) Chiang Chü-jong, Li Ping, eds., Chung-kuo ku-tien hsiao-shuo yen-chiu tzu-liao ts'ung-shu, Shanghai: Ku-chi ch'u-pan she, 1990.
Ch'an pi-yao ching. Trans. Kumārajīva. T. 613, vol. 15.
Ch'ang-ch'ü-li tu-nü t'o-lo-ni chou ching (Book of the Incantations and Dhāraṇī of the Jāṅgulī Woman), by Gupta (fl. ca. 650). T. 1265, vol. 21.
Chen-kao (Declarations of the Perfect Ones), by T'ao Hung-ching (456–536). HY 1010 (CT 1016, TT 637–40).
Chen-shu San-kuo chih, with P'ei Tsung-chih commentary. Peking: Chung-hua shu-chü, 1959.
Cheng-fa nien-ch'u ching (*Saddharmasmṛtyupasthāna-sūtra*), by Gautama Prajñāruci (fl. ca. 516–43). T. 721, vol. 17, chaps. 16–17.
Cheng-ho sheng chi tsung lu (A Sagely Benefaction of the Regnant Harmony Era). Ed. Shen Fu et al., by imperial order, issued 1122. Reprint, 2 vols., Peking, 1952, 1982.
Cheng-i fa-wen ching chang-kuan p'in (Chapter on Petitions and Officials of the Cheng-i Canon). HY 1208.
Cheng-i fa-wen hsiu-chen yao-chih (Essentials of the Practice of Perfection). 1 *chüan*. Six Dynasties. HY 1260 (CT 1270, TT 1003).
Ch'i-ch'ien fo shen-fu ching (Divine Talismans of the Seven Thousand Buddhas). Anonymous. T. 2904, vol. 85.
Ch'i-fo pa-p'u-sa so-shuo ta t'o-lo-ni shen-chou ching (Spirit Spells Spoken by the

Seven Buddhas and Eight Bodhisattvas). Anonymous (317–420). T. 1332, vol. 21.
Ch'ien-chin i-fang (Supplementary Prescriptions Worth a Thousand [Cash]), 682, by Sun Ssu-mo (581–682). Peking: Jen-min wei-sheng ch'u-pan she, 1982.
Ch'ien-chin yao-fang (Important Prescriptions Worth a Thousand [Cash]), 650–59, by Sun Ssu-mo (581–682). Peking: Jen-min wei-sheng ch'u-pan she, 1955. See also *Pei-chi ch'ien-chin yao-fang*.
Chih ch'an-ping pi-yao fa (Secret Essentials for Treating Dhyāna Ailments), 682. T. 620, vol. 15.
Ch'ih-sung-tzu chang-li (Master Red Pine's Petition Almanac). HY 615 (TT 333–35).
Ch'ih-sung-tzu chou hou yao-chüeh (Handy Medicinal Formulas of Master Red Pine). HY 880 (CT 881, TT 582–83).
Chin ching (Book of Spellbinding). Chapters 29 and 30 of Sun Ssu-mo's *Ch'ien-chin i-fang* (facsimile of 1878 printed edition, Taipei: Kuo-li Chung-kuo i-yao yen-chiu-so, 1965).
Chin-kang-feng lou-ko i-ch'ieh yü-chih ching (Yogin's Book of All the Yogas of the Diamond-Pinnacle Pavilion). Trans. Vajrabodhi. T. 867, vol. 18; or T. 2228, vol. 61: *Chin-kang-feng lou-ko i-ch'ieh yu-chih ching hsiu-hsing fa*.
Chin-kang-sa-to shuo p'in-na-yeh-chia-t'ien ch'eng-ch'iu i-kuei ching, by Dharmabhadra (fl. 980–1000). T. 1272, vol. 21.
Chin-kang san-mei ching. Apocryphon. T. 273, vol. 9.
Chin-kang-ting ching ta yü-ch'ieh pi-mi hsin-ti fa-men i-chüeh, written (not simply translated) by Amoghavajra. T. 1798, vol. 39.
Chin-kang-ting i-ch'ieh ju-lai chen-shih she ta-ch'eng hsien cheng ta-chiao wang-ching (*Sarvatathāgatatattva-saṃgraha*, Compendium of Truth of All the Tathāgatas). T. 865, vol. 18.
Chin-kuei yao lueh fang lun. Ming edition, Tokyo, 1968, 1973, 1977.
Chin-se chia-na-po-ti t'o-lo-ni ching, attributed to Vajrabodhi. T. 1269, vol. 21.
Chin-so liu-chu yin (Guide of the Moving Pearls of the Golden Lock), annotated by Li Ch'un-feng (fl. 632). HY 1009 (CT 1015, TT 631–36).
Ch'ing-se ta chin-kang yao-cha p'i-kuei-mo fa (Ritual of the Blue-Faced Vajrayakṣa for Driving off Demons and Devils). T. 1221, vol. 21.
Ching-shih cheng-lei Ta-kuan pen-ts'ao (Materia Medica of the Great Prospect Era Classified and Verified from the Classics and Histories), 1108. Ed. Ai Sheng. Reprint of 1302 edition, Tokyo, 1970.
Ching-yüeh ch'üan-shu (Collected Treatises), by Cheng Chieh-pin, 1624. Reprint of Yüeh-ssu lou edition, Taipei, 1972.
Chiu T'ang shu (completed 945), attributed to Liu Hsü. 16 vols. Peking: Chung-hua shu-chü, 1975.
Chou-hou fang. See *Chou-hou pei-chi fang*.
Chou-hou pei-chi fang (Prescriptions Within Arm's Reach for Use in Emergencies), by Ko Hung (283–343). Annotated and edited by T'ao Hung-ching (456–536). HY 1295 (TT 1013–15). Peking: Jen-min wei-sheng ch'u-pan she, 1963.

Chu-fo ching-chieh she chen-shih ching. Trans. Prajña. T. 868, vol. 18.
Ch'u-hsüeh chi, by Hsü Chien (659–729) et al. Reprint, Peking: Chung-hua shu-chü, 1962, 1980.
Chu-ping yüan-hou lun (On the Origins and Symptoms of Diseases), 610. Comp. Ch'ao Yüan-fang. Peking: Jen-min wei-sheng ch'u-pan she, 1955, 1982 (reprint of 1891 edition). See also Southern Sung edition, Osaka: Tōyō igaku kenkyūkai, 1981.
Ch'üan T'ang shih (1705–6). Ed. Sheng Tsu. 2 vols. Taipei: Hung-yeh shu-chü, 1977.
Ch'üan T'ang wen (ca. 1814), by Tung Kao et al. Taipei: Hua-wen shu-chü, 1965.
Chūgoku iseki kō (1826), by Tanba (Taki) Mototane (1789–1827). Reprint, Peking: Jen-min wei-sheng ch'u-pan she, 1956, 1983.
Ch'un-ch'iu fan-lu (Abundant Dew of Springs and Autumns). Annotated and edited by Su Yü, *Ch'un-ch'iu fan-lu i-cheng*, 1914. Reprint, Taipei: Ho-lo, 1974.
Collected Dhāraṇī Sūtras. See *T'o-lo-ni chi ching*.
Compendium of Truth of All the Tathāgatas. See *Chin-kang-ting i-ch'ieh ju-lai chen-shih she ta-ch'eng hsien cheng ta-chiao wang-ching*.
Declarations of the Perfect Ones. See *Chen-kao*.
Demon-Statutes in Transcendent Script. See *Shan-ch'ing ku-sui ling-wen kuei-lü*.
Demon-Statutes of Nü-ch'ing. See *Nü-ch'ing kuei-lü*.
Denjutsu isshinkai mon, by Kōjō (779–858). T. 2379, vol. 74.
Denshibyō kuden (Oral Tradition on Corpse-Vector Disease). T. 2507, vol. 79.
Dhāraṇī Book of Āṭavaka, General of the Demons. See *A-cha-p'o-chü kuei-shen ta-chiang shang fo t'o-lo-ni shen-chou ching*.
Dhāraṇī Miscellany. See *T'o-lo-ni tsa-chi*.
Dharma-samuccaya. Ed. and trans. Lin Li-Kouang, *Compendium de la Vraie Loi*. 3 vols. Paris: Adrien Maisonneuve, 1946, 1969, 1973.
Dīghanikāya. Trans. T. W. Rhys-Davids and C. A. F. Rhys-Davids, *Dialogues of the Buddha*. 3 vols. London: Pāli Text Society, 1899, 1910, 1921. Reprint 1956, 1965, 1966.
Divine Talismans of the Seven Thousand Buddhas. See *Ch'i-ch'ien fo shen-fu ching*.
Dōkyō hiketsu shūsei [*Tao-chiao pi-chüeh chi-ch'eng*]. Ed. Michael R. Saso. Tokyo: Ryūkei shosha, 1978.
Essential Secrets of the Yogasiddhi of Vināyaka-Gaṇapati. See *P'i-na-yeh-chia E-na-po-ti yü-ch'ieh hsi-ti-p'in pi-yao*. T. 1273.
Essentials of the Practice of Perfection. See *Cheng-i fa-wen hsiu-chen yao-chih*.
Fa-mieh ching (Book on the Extinction of the Law). Anonymous (420–79). See also: *Fo-shuo fa mieh-chin ching*. T. 396, vol. 12, and T. 2874, vol. 85; *Shih-chia p'u*, T. 2040, vol. 50: 83–84.
Fa-yüan chu-lin, 668, by Tao-shih. T. 2122, vol. 53.
Fan-i-ming-i chi [*Mahāvyutpatti*], by Fa-yün (1088–1158). T. 2131, vol. 54.
Fan-wang ching. T. 1484, vol. 24.
Feng-fa-yao, by Hsi Ch'ao. In *Hung-ming chi*. T. 2102, vol. 52: 86–89.

Fifty-Two Medical Prescriptions. See *Wu-shih-erh ping-fang*.
Fo-i ching (Sūtra on Medicine). T. 793, vol. 17.
Fo mieh-tu hou kuan-lien tsang-sung ching. T. 392, vol. 12.
Fo-mu ta k'ung-ch'üeh ming-wang ching [*Mahāmāyūri(vidyārājñi)-sūtra*] (Book of the Peacock Spell). Trans. Amoghavajra. T. 982, vol. 21.
Fo-shuo hsüan-shih Pa-t'o so-shuo shen-chou ching (Spirit-Spell Spoken by the Sorcerer Bhadra). Trans. Dharmarakṣa. T. 1378A, vol. 21.
Fo-shuo kuan-wu-liang-shou fo ching. T. 365, vol. 12.
Fo-shuo miao-chi-hsiang ts'ui-sheng ken-pen ta-chiao ching (*Krodhavijayakalpa-guhya-tantra*). Trans. Fa-hsien. T. 1217, vol. 21.
Fo-shuo Mo-ni-lo-t'an ching [*Maṇiratna-sūtra*] (Wishing-Jewel Book), end of fourth century. T. 1393, vol. 21.
Fo-shuo p'i-na-yeh ching. Anonymous. T. 898, vol. 18.
Fo-shuo t'o-lo-ni po ching [*Agrapradīpa-dhāraṇī*]. T. 1352, vol. 21.
Fo-tsu li-tai t'ung-tsai (1344), by Mei-wu Nien-ch'ang (1282–?). T. 2036, vol. 49.
Fo-tsu t'ung-chi (ca. 1258–69), by Zhipan. T. 2035, vol. 49.
Fudō gushō (Humble Extracts on Fudō). In Hirotani Yutarō, ed., *Kinsei bukkyō shūsetsu*, 222–34. Tokyo: Hirotani kokusho kankōkai, 1925.
Genkō shakusho (1322), by Kokan Shiren (1278–1346). DNBZ, vol. 62: 66–230.
Great Rites of Shang-ch'ing and ling-pao. See *Shang-ch'ing ling-pao ta-fa*.
Great Rites of the Jade Hall. See *Wu-shang hsüan-yüan san-t'ien yü-t'ang ta-fa*.
Guhya-tantra. Trans. Amoghavajra. T. 897, vol. 18.
Hai-ch'iung Pai chen-jen yü-lu (Recorded Sayings of the Perfected Pai Hai-ch'iung [Yü-ch'an]). 4 *chüan*. Pai Yü-ch'an (1194–?). HY 1296 (CT 1307, TT 1016).
Hai-tung kao-seng chuan [*Haedong kosung chŏn*], by Kakhun (dates unknown). T. 2065, vol. 50.
Han-shu, by Pan Ku (32–92 C.E.). Comm. Yen Shih-ku. Peking: Chung-hua shu-chü, 1962.
Hevajra-tantra. English trans. D. L. Snellgrove, *The Hevajra-Tantra: A Critical Study*. 2 vols. London: Oxford University Press, 1959.
Honchō kōsōden, by Shiban (1626–1710). DNBZ, vol. 63: 1–407.
Hsiang-erh [*Lao-tzu hsiang-erh chu*], attributed to Chang-Lu (d. ca. 220). Ed. Jao Tsung-i, *Lao-tzu hsiang-erh chu chiao-chien*. Hong Kong, 1956.
Hsiao chih-kuan (full title *Hsiu-hsi chih-kuan tso-ch'an fa-yao*), by Chih-i (538–97). T. 1915, vol. 46.
Hsiao-mo chih-hui ching (full title: *Tung-chen t'ai-shang shuo chih-hui hsiao-mo chen ching*; Book of the Devil-Destroyers of Wisdom). HY 1333 (TT 1032).
Hsien-ch'uan wai-k'o pi-fang (1378), by Chao I-chen. HY 1157 (TT 823–24).
Hsin T'ang shu (1043–60), by Ou-yang Hsiu (1007–72), Song Ch'i (998–1061) et al. 20 vols. Peking: Chung-hua shu-chü, 1975.
Hsiu-yao ching. Trans. Amoghavajra. T. 1299, vol. 21.
Hsü kao-seng chuan, by Tao-hsüan (596–667). T. 2060, vol. 50.
Hsü-k'ung-tsang ch'iu-wen-ch'i fa (Ākāśagarbha's Ritual for Seeking, Hearing, and Retaining). Trans. Śubhakarasiṃha. T. 445, vol. 20.

Hsüan-tu lü wen (Writings and Precepts of the Capital of Darkness). HY 188 (TT 78).

Hu chu-t'ung t'ung-tzu t'o-lo-ni ching (Book of the Dhāraṇī for Protecting Children). Trans. Bodhiruci. T. 1028A, vol. 19.

Huai-nan hung-lieh chi-chieh. Ed. Liu Wen-tien. Shanghai: Commercial Press, 1923.

Huang-ti chiu ting shen-tan ching chüeh (Explanations to the Yellow Emperor's Canon of the Nine-Vessel Spiritual Elixir). Comp. ca. tenth century. HY 884 (CT 885, TT 584–85).

Huang-ti nei-ching ling-shu shing. Ed. Wang Ping (762). Typeset reprint of Ming edition, Peking: Jen-min wei-sheng ch'u-pan she, 1979.

Huang-ti nei-ching su-wen. Shanghai: Shang-hai k'o-hsüeh chi-shu ch'u-pan-she, 1959.

Huang-ti nei-ching su-wen ling-shu ho-pien. Reprint, Peking: Society for Research in Chinese and Western Medicine, 1922.

Huang-ti pa-shih-i nan-ching tsuan-t'u chü-chieh (Illustrated Explanations of the Yellow Emperor's Book of Eighty-One Difficulties), by Li Ch'iung (Sung). HY 1018 (CT 1024, TT 668–70).

Huang-t'ing ching (Book of the Yellow Court). HY 332. Critical edition in K. M. Schipper, *Concordance du Hiuang-t'ing king*, Paris: École Française d'Extrême-Orient, 1975.

Huang-t'ing nei-ching yü-ching ching-chu (Book of the Inner Effulgences of the Yellow Court). Commentary by Liang-ch'iu tzu (T'ang). HY 402 (TT 190).

Hui-chi chin-kang chin pai-pien-fa ching (Rites of the Vajra-Being of Impure Traces for Exorcising the Hundred Weirds), by Ajitasena (A-chih-ta-hsien, eighth century). T. 1229, vol. 21.

Hung-ming chi, by Seng-yu. T. 2102, vol. 52.

I-ch'ieh ching yin-i (Sounds and Meanings of All the Scriptures), by Hui-lin. T. 2128, vol. 54.

I-ch'ieh ju-lai chen-shih she ta-ch'eng hsien-cheng san-mei ta-chiao-wang ching [*Sarvatathāgatha-tattvasamgraha sūtra*]. T. 882, vol. 21.

I-chien chih (Record of the Listener), by Hung Mai (1123–1202). Revised by Ho Chuo. 4 vols. Peking: Chung-hua shu-chü, 1981.

I-tzu ch'i-te fo-ting ching [*Uṣṇīṣacakravarti-tantra*], by Amoghavajra. T. 953, vol. 19.

I-wen lei-chü, by Ou-yang Hsün (557–641). Peking: Chung-hua shu-chü, 1965. (Taipei: Hsing-hsing shu-chü, 1960.)

Instantly Efficacious Āveśa Ritual Explained by Maheśvara. See *Su-chi li-yen Mo-hsi-shou-lo-t'ien shuo a-wei-she fa*.

Ishinpō (Prescriptions from [or Methods Forming] the Heart of Medicine), 984, by Tanba no Yasuyori. Peking: Jen-min wei-sheng ch'u-pan she, ed., 1955. (See also facsimile edition of Nakarai's family edition, Osaka: Oriento shuppan, 1991.)

Jang-yü-li t'ung-nü ching (Book of the Jāṅgulī Girl). Trans. Amoghavajra (eighth century). T. 1264B, vol. 21.

Jang-yü-li tu-nü t'o-lo-ni ching. T. 1265, vol. 21.
Jih chih lu chi-shih, by Huang Ju-ch'eng. Reprint, Taipei: Shih-chieh shu-chü, 1962. (Also: Ed. Lo Pao-chün and Lü Tsung-li. Shih-chia-chuang: Hua-shan i-wen ch'u-pan she, 1990.)
Kakuzen shō, by Kakuzen (1143–1213). T. Zuzō, vols. 4–5, 3022. DNBZ, vols. 45–51.
Kao-seng chuan (Biographies of Eminent Monks), by Hui-chiao (497–554). T. 2059, vol. 50.
Kāśyapa Saṃhitā. In. P. V. Tewari, ed. *Kāśyapa Saṃhitā or Vṛddhajīvakīya Tantra*. Varanasi: Chaukhambha Visvabharati, 1996.
Keiran shūyō shū (Collection of Leaves from Mountain Streams), by Kōshō (1276–1350). T. 2410, vol. 76.
Kuan-hsin lun (Treatise on Mind-Contemplation), by Chih-i. T. 1920, vol. 46.
Kuan-ting ching (Book of Consecration), by Śrīmitra (fl. 317–27) or Hui-chien (ca. 457). T. 1331, vol. 21.
Kuan wu-liang-shou ching. See *Fo-shuo kuan-wu-liang-shou fo ching*.
Kuang-chih san-tsang ho-shang piao-chih chi. See *Tai-tsung chao tseng Ssu-k'ung ta-pien cheng Kuang-chih san-tsang ho-shang piao-chih chi*.
Lao-tzu. Ed. Ssu-pu ts'ung-k'an. Shanghai: Shang-wu yin-shu-kuan, 1937–38.
Li chi. Sinological Index Series. Trans. James Legge, *The Sacred Books of China: The Texts of Confucianism*, Part III (Sacred Books of the East, 27; Oxford 1885; reprint, Delhi 1968).
Li-chi, Shih-san ching chu shu. Photographic reproduction, Peking: Chung-hua shu-chü, 1983.
Ling-pao wu-liang tu-jen shang-p'in miao-ching. See *Tu-jen ching*.
Ling-shu ching. Anonymous. Taipei: Chung-hua shu-chü.
Lo-fo-nu shuo chiu-liao hsiao-erh chi-ping ching (Book of Rāvaṇa's Explanations of How to Cure the Ailments of Children), by Dharmabhadra (fl. 980–1000). T. 1330, vol. 21.
The Lotus Sūtra. See *Miao-fa lien-hua ching*.
Lu hsien-sheng tao-men k'o-lüeh (Abridged Code of Master Lu for the Taoist Community), by Lu Hsiu-ching (406–77). HY 1119 (CT 1127, TT 671).
Lun-heng, by Wang Ch'ung (27–97). Shanghai: Jen-min ch'u-pan she, 1974.
Lun-heng chao-shih. Ed. Huang Hui. Reprint, Taipei: Commercial Press, 1964; Peking: Chung-hua shu-chü, 1990.
Lun-yü, by K'ung-tzu (Confucius). In *Harvard-Yenching Institute Sinological Series*, Supplement No. 16: *A Concordance to the Analects of Confucius*. Reprint, Taipei: Chinese Materials and Research Aids Service Center, 1972 (1966).
Lung-shu wu-ming lun (Nāgārjuna's Treatise on the Five Sciences). T. 1420, vol. 21.
Ma-wang-tui Han-mu po-shu (Silk Manuscripts from Han Tombs of Ma-wang-tui). Peking: Wen-wu ch'u-pan she, 1985.
Mahābhārata. 21 vols. Ed. Visnu S. Sukthankar et al. Poona: Bhandarkar Oriental Research Institute, 1933–60.

Mahāmāyūri. See *Fo-mu ta k'ung-ch'üeh ming-wang ching*.
Mahāparinirvāṇa-sūtra. See *Ta-pan nieh-p'an ching* and *Ta-pan ni-yüan ching*.
Mahāsahasrapramardinī. See *Shou-hu ta-ch'ien-kuo-t'u ching*.
Mahāvairocana-sūtra. See *Ta pi-lu-che-na ch'eng-fo shen-pien chia-chih ching*.
Mai-ching (Canon of the Pulse), by Wang Shu-ho (ca. 280 C.E.). *Tōyō igaku zenpon sōsho*. Osaka: Oriento shuppan, 1981.
Maṇiratna Book. See *Fo-shuo Mo-ni-lo-t'an ching*.
Mañjūśrīmūlakalpa. See *Ta-fang-kuang p'u-sa ts'ang wen-shu-shih-li ken-pen i-kuei ching*.
Mao shan chih (Chronicles of Mao Shan). HY 304 (TT 153–58).
Marvelous Book of the Celestial Youth, Protector of Life. See *T'ai-shang t'ai-ch'ing t'ien-t'ung hu-ming miao-ching*.
Matsya-purāṇa. Ananda Aśram Sanskrit Series. Poona, 1907.
The Medicine Buddha's Contemplation Ritual. See *Yao-shih ju-lai kuan-hsing i-kuei fa*.
Miao-fa lien-hua ching [*Saddharmapuṇḍarīka*] (The Lotus Sūtra). Trans. Kumārajīva. T. 269, vol. 9; trans. Dharmarakṣa, T. 263, vol. 9.
Miao-pi-p'u-sa so-wen ching [*Subāhu-paripṛcchā*] (Questions of Subāhu). Trans. Fa-t'ien (fl. ca. 973–1001). T. 896, vol. 18.
Ming-pao chi (Record of the Responses of the Beyond), by T'ang Lin. T. 2082, vol. 51.
Mo-ho-chih-kuan, by Chih-i (538–97). T. 1911, vol. 46.
The Most High's Book of Transcendent Seals for Communicating with the Invisible World. See *T'ai-shang t'ung-hsüan ling-pao yin ching*.
The Most High's Secrets of the Perfected for Aiding the State and Succoring the People. See *T'ai-shang chu-kuo ch'iu-min ts'ung-chen pi-yao*.
Nāgārjuna's Treatise on the Five Sciences. See *Lung-shu wu-ming lun*.
Nan-ching chi-chu (Classic of Difficult Issues, Collected Annotations), by Lü Kuang et al. Ed. Wang Chiu-ssu et al. (1505). Edition of 1789/1815, with added collation notes, reprint, Peking, 1956. See also Shanghai: Commercial Press, 1955.
Nan-ching ching shih (Classic of Difficult Issues, Explained Through the Inner Canon), by Hsü Ta-ch'un (ca. 1727), in *Hsü Ling-t'ai i shu ch'üan chi*.
Nan-ching pen i (Classic of Difficult Issues, Original Meanings), by Hua Shou (ca. 1361, printed in 1366). Taipei, 1976.
Nittō guhō junrei kōki, by Ennin (793–866). DNBZ, vol. 72: 84–133.
Nü-ch'ing kuei-lü (Demon-Statutes of Nü-ch'ing). HY 789 (TT 563).
Nü-k'o pai-wen (A Hundred Questions on Gynecology), by Ch'i Chung-fu (Sung). Peking: Chung-kuo shu-tien ying-yin, 1986 (facsimile of the Shih-chieh shu-chü edition).
Oral Tradition on Corpse-Vector Disease. See *Denshibyō kuden*.
Pan-chou san-mei ching [*Pratyutpanna-samādhi-sūtra; Bhadrapāla-sūtra*], by Lokakṣema. T. 417, vol. 13.
Pao-p'u-tzu nei-p'ien (Inner Chapters of the Book of the Master Who Embraces

Simplicity), ca. 320, by Ko Hung (283–343). Ed. Wang Ming, *Pao-p'u-tzu nei-p'ien chiao-shih*. Peking: Chung-hua shu-chü, 1980.

Pei-chi ch'ien-chin yao-fang (Important Prescriptions Worth a Thousand [Cash] for Urgent Need), after 652, by Sun Ssu-mo (581–682). Ed. Edo igakukan, 1849. Reprint, Taipei, 1965; Peking: Jen-min wei-sheng ch'u-pan-she, 1955, 1987. (See also Sung edition, in *Tōyō igaku zenpon sōsho*. Osaka: Oriento shuppan, 1989.)

Pei-fang P'i-sha-men t'ien-wang sui-chün hu-fa chen-yen (Mantra of the Heavenly King of the Northern Direction, Vaiśravaṇa, and His Dharma-Protecting Retinue). Trans. Amoghavajra. T. 1248, vol. 21.

Pei-t'ang shu-ch'ao. 160 *chüan*. Comp. Yü Shih-nan (558–638). Collated and annotated by K'ung Kuang-t'ao (1888). Facsimile of 1888 edition, Taipei: Wen-hai ch'u-pan-she.

Pen-ts'ao ching chi-chu (Writings and Commentaries on Materia Medica), by T'ao Hung-ching (456–536). Facsimile edition, Shanghai, 1955.

Pen-ts'ao kang-mu (Summa on Materia Medica), 1596, by Li Shih-chen (1518–93). Shanghai: Commercial Press, 1933; Taipei: Wen-kuang t'u-shu ching-ssu, 1966; Peking: Jen-min wei-sheng ch'u-pan she, 1977, 1987.

P'en-ts'ao p'in-hui ching-yao, 1505, by Ch'iu Chün et al. Shanghai: Commercial Press, 1936.

Pen-ts'ao yen-i (Dilatations on the Materia Medica), by K'ou Tsung-shih (1116, printed in 1119). Revised ed. by Yen Cheng-hua, Ch'ang Chang-fu, Huang Yu-ch'ün. Peking: Jen-min wei-sheng ch'u-p'an-she, 1959, 1990.

P'i-na-yeh-chia E-na-po-ti yü-ch'ieh hsi-ti-p'in pi-yao (Essential Secrets of the Yogasiddhi of Vināyaka-Gaṇapati). T. 1273, vol. 21.

Pratyutpanna-samādhi. See *Pan-chou san-mei ching*.

Prescriptions Within Arm's Reach for Use in Emergencies. See *Chou-hou pei-chi fang*.

Prolegomena to the Five Talismans of Ling-pao. See *T'ai-shang ling-pao wu-fu hsü*.

Protocols for the Rite of the Yellow Script. See *Shang-ch'ing huang-shu kuo-tu i*.

Pu-k'ung chüan-so t'o-lo-ni tzu-tsai-wang chou ching [*Amoghapāśa-sūtra*] by Pao-ssu-wei (Ratnacinta). T. 1097, vol. 20.

Pu-ting shih-che t'o-lo-ni pi-mi-fa (Secret Rites of the Spells of the Divine Emissary, the Immovable One). Trans. Vajrabodhi. T. 1202, vol. 21.

Questions of Subāhu. See *Su-po-hu t'ung-tzu ch'ing-wen ching* and *Miao-pi p'u-sa so-wen ching*.

Rāvaṇa's Kumāra-tantra. See *Lo-fo-nu shuo chiu-liao hsiao-erh chi-ping ching*.

Red Script of the Three Registers of Divinity. See *T'ai-shang ch'ih-wen tung-shen san-lu*.

Rites of the Vajra-Being of Impure Traces for Exorcising the Hundred Weirds. See *Hui-chi chin-kang chin pai-pien-fa ching*.

Ritual of the Blue-Faced Vajrayakṣa for Driving off Demons and Devils. See *Ch'ing-se ta chin-kang yao-cha p'i-kuei-mo fa*.

Rituals of the God Vināyaka Explained by Vajrasattva. See *Chin-kang-sa-to shuo p'in-na-yeh-chia-t'ien ch'eng-ch'iu i-kuei ching*.

Saddharmapuṇḍarīka-sūtra. See *Miao-fa lien-hua ching* (The Lotus Sūtra).
Saddharmasmṛtyupasthāna-sāsra. Trans. Gautama Prajñāruci. T. 721, vol. 17.
Samguk yusa (Chronicles of the Three [Korean] Kingdoms), by Ilyŏn (1206–89). T. 2039, vol. 49.
Saṃyuktāgama. Trans. Guṇabhadra. T. 99, vol. 2.
San-huang nei-pi wen (Script of the Inner Secrets of the Three High Lords). HY 854.
San-t'ien nei-chieh ching (Inner Explanation of the Three Heavens), by "Master Hsü." HY 1196.
San-tung chu-nang. Comp. Wang Hsüan-ho (fl. 664–84). HY 1131 (TT 780–82).
San-wan fo t'ung ken-pen shen-pi chih yin ping fa-lung chung-shang tsun-wang fo-fa. T. 2906, vol. 85 (Stein 2438).
San-yin chi-i ping-yüan lun-ts'ui (The Three Causes Epitomized and Unified: The Quintessence of Doctrine on the Origin of Medical Disorders), by Ch'en Yen (ca. 1174). Published under the title *San-yin chi-i ping-cheng fang-lun*, Peking, 1957.
Sarvatathāgata tattvasaṃgraha sūtra. See *I-ch'ieh ju-lai chen-shih she ta-ch'eng hsien-cheng san-mei ta-chiao-wang ching*.
Secret Essentials for Treating Dhyāna Ailments. See *Chih ch'an-ping pi-yao fa*.
Secret Rites of the Spells of the Divine Emissary, the Immovable One. See *Pu-ting shih-che t'o-lo-ni pi-mi-fa*.
Shan-hai ching (Book of Mountains and Seas). Ed. Che-chiang shu-chü.
Shan-hai ching chieh-chu (Commentary on the *Shan-hai ching*). Ed. Shih I-hsing. Taipei: I-wen yin-shu-kuan, 1974.
Shang-ch'ing hou-sheng tao-chün lieh-chi (Annals of the Sage of Latter Time, Lord of the Golden Gateway of Supreme Purity), by W. Yüan-yu. HY 442 (TT 198).
Shang-ch'ing huang-shu kuo-tu i (Protocols for the Rite of the Yellow Script). HY 1284 (TT 1009).
Shang-ch'ing ku-sui ling-wen kuei-lü (Demon-Statutes in Transcendent Script, the Marrow of the Shang-ch'ing Heaven). HY 461 (TT 461, HY 203).
Shang-ch'ing ling-pao ta-fa (Great Rites of Shang-ch'ing and Ling-pao). HY 1211 (TT 942–62).
Shang-ch'ing t'ien-hsin cheng-fa (True Rites of the Heart of Heaven According to the Shang-ch'ing). HY 566 (CT 566, TT 318–19).
Shang-hai ching chiao-chu, by Yüan K'o. Shanghai: Shang-hai ku-chi ch'u-pan she, 1980.
Shang han lun (Treatise on Cold Damages Disorders). Reprint of the Chao K'ai-mei version (Ming), Tokyo: Ryōgen, 1968, 1973, 1977.
Shen-nung pen-ts'ao ching (Shen-nung Pharmacopoeia). Anonymous (late first century or second century C.E.). Ed. Ssu-pu pei-yao. Peking: Jen-min wei-sheng ch'u-pan-she, 1963, 1982.
Shen-seng chuan (Biographies of Divine Monks). T. 2064, vol. 50.
Shih-chi, by Ssu-ma Chien (ca. 135–93 B.C.E.). Trans. Burton Watson, *Records of the Grand Historian of China*, New York: Columbia University Press, 1961.
Shih-chia-p'u. Trans. Seng-yu. T. 2040, vol. 50.

Shih-san ching chu shu. Photographic reproduction of the 1816 woodblock edition. Taipei: I-wen ch'u-pan-she.
Shou-hu kuo-chieh chu t'o-lo-ni ching (Book of the Dhāraṇī of the Lord Who Protects the Realm), ca. 800–806. Trans. Prajña and Muniśrī. T. 997, vol. 19.
Shou-hu ta-ch'ien-kuo-t'u ching (Mahāsahasrapramardinī). Trans. Dānapāla. T. 999, vol. 19.
Shou-leng-yen ching. See *Ta fo-ting ju-lai mi-yin hsiu-cheng liao-i chu p'u-sa wan-hsing shou-leng-yen ching.*
Shou-leng-yen san-mei ching [*Śūraṃgama-samādhi-sūtra*]. Trans. Kumārajīva. T. 642. Vol. 15.
Shou-wen chieh-tzu, by Hsü Shen (d. ca. 120). Peking: Chung-hua shu-chü, 1963.
Sou-shen chi (In Search of the Supernatural), by Kan Pao (fl. 317–350). Peking: Chung-hua shu-chü, 1979. Partial French translation by Rémi Mathieu, *À la recherche des esprits,* Paris: Gallimard, 1992.
Spirit-Spells of the Abyss. See *Tung-yüan shen-chou ching* and *T'ai-shang tung-yüan san-mei shen-chou chai shih-fang ch'an-i.*
Spirit-Spell Spoken by the Sorcerer Bhadra. See *Fo-shuo hsüan-shih Pa-t'o so-shuo shen-chou ching.*
Su-chi li-yen Mo-hsi-shou-lo t'ien shuo a-wei-she fa (Instantly Efficacious Āveśa Ritual Explained by Maheśvara). Trans. Amoghavajra (705–74). T. 1277, vol. 21.
Su-hsi-ti-chieh-lo ching [*Susiddhi-mahātantra*]. Trans. Śubhakarasiṃha (fl. 716–35). T. 893, vol. 18.
Su-po-hu t'ung-tzu ch'ing-wen ching [*Subāhu-paripṛcchā*] (Questions of Subāhu). Trans. Śubhakarasiṃha (fl. 716–35). T. 895, vol. 18.
Subāhu-paripṛcchā. See *Su-po-hu t'ung-tzu ch'ing-wen ching* and *Miao-pi p'u-sa so-wen ching.*
Sui shu (History of the Sui Dynasty), 636, by Wei Cheng (580–643) et al. Peking: Chung-hua shu-chü, 1973; Taipei: Hung-yeh shu-chü, 1974.
Sung kao-seng chuan (Sung Biographies of Eminent Monks), by Tsan-ning. T. 2061, vol. 50.
Śūraṃgama-samādhi. See *Shou-leng-yen san-mei ching.*
Susiddhi-mahātantra. See *Su-hsi-ti-chieh-lo ching.*
Suśruta Saṃhitā, with the commentary of Atrideva, second or third century. Ed. Bhaskara Govinda Ghanekar. Trans. A. F. R. Hoernle, *The Suśruta-Saṃhitā or the Hindu System of Medicine According to Suśruta.* Fascicle 1 (Sūtrasthāna 1–14). Calcutta: Asiatic Society of Bengal, 1897.
Ta-chi ching. Trans. Seng-chiu. T. 397, vol. 13.
Ta-chi-i shen-chou ching. T. 1335, vol. 21.
Ta chih-tu lun, attributed to Nāgārjuna. Trans. Kumārajīva. T. 1509, vol. 25.
Ta fang-kuang p'u-sa ts'ang wen-shu-shih-li ken-pen i-kuei ching [*Mañjuśrīmūla-kalpa*]. T. 1191, vol. 20.
Ta fang-teng t'o-lo-ni ching. Trans. Fa-chung. T. 1339, vol. 21.
Ta fo-ting ju-lai mi-yin hsiu-cheng liao-i chu p'u-sa wan-hsing shou-leng-yen ching [*Śúraṃgama-sūtra*], 705. T. 945, vol. 19.

Ta-jih ching. See *Ta Pi-lu-che-na ch'eng-fo shen-pien chia-ch'ih ching*.
Ta-jih ching i-hsi yen-mi ch'ao, by Chüeh-yüan (ca. 1075). ZZ vol. 37.
Ta-kuan pen-ts'ao. See *Ching-shih cheng-lei Ta-kuan pen-ts'ao*.
Ta-lun chin-kang tsung-ch'ih t'o-lo-ni chin. T. 1230, vol. 21.
Ta-pan ni-yüan ching [*Mahāparinirvāṇa-sūtra*]. Trans. Fa-hsien et al. T. 376, vol. 12.
Ta-pan nieh-p'an ching [*Mahāparinirvāṇa-sūtra*]. Trans. Hui-yen and Hsieh Ling-yün. T. 375, vol. 12.
Ta Pi-lu-che-na ch'eng-fo shen-pien chia-ch'ih ching [*Mahāvairocana-sūtra*]. Trans. Śubhakarasiṃha and I-hsing. T. 848, vol. 18.
Ta-sheng huan-hsi shuang-shen ta-tzu-tsai-t'ien p'i-na-yeh-chia-wang kuei-i nien-sung kung-yang fa (Rite of Vināyaka). Trans. Śubhakarasiṃha. T. 1270, vol. 21.
Ta-sheng huan-hsi-t'ien p'u-sa hsiu-hsing pi-mi-fa i-kuei (Rite of Vināyaka). Trans. Amoghavajra. T. 1271, vol. 21.
Ta-shih chou-fa ching (Greater Book of Rites and Mantras of the Messenger). Trans. Bodhiruci. T. 1268, vol. 21.
Ta-T'ang Ch'ing-lung ssu san-ch'ao kung-feng ta-te hsing-chuang. T. 2057, vol. 50.
Ta-wei-li Wu-ch'u-se-mo ming-wang ching (Book of the Majestic Wisdom-King Ucchuṣma). Trans. Ajitasena (fl. ca. 732). T. 1227, vol. 21.
T'ai-p'ing ching. HY 1093 (CT 746–55). Ed. Wang Ming, *T'ai-p'ing ching ho-chiao*. Peking: Chung-hua shu-chü, 1979.
T'ai-p'ing kuang-chi (978). Comp. Li Fang (925–66) et al. Peking: Jen-min wen-hsüeh ch'u-pan-she, 1959; Chung-hua shu-chü, 1981. Taipei: Ku-hsin shu-chü, 1980.
T'ai-p'ing yü-lan (983). Comp. Li Fang et al. Peking: Chung-hua shu-chü, 1960, 1992.
T'ai-shang ch'ih-wen tung-shen san-lu (Red Script of the Three Registers of Divinity), main text attributed to T'ao Hung-ching (456–536), commentary attributed to Li Ch'un-feng (602–70), preface dated 632. HY 589 (CT 589, TT 324).
T'ai-shang chu-kuo chiu-min ts'ung-chen pi-yao (The Most High's Secrets of the Perfected for Aiding the State and Succoring the People), by Yüan Miao-tsung (fl. 1086–1116). HY 1217 (TT 986–87).
T'ai-shang Lao-chün chung-ching (Middle Book of the Most High Lord Lao). Anonymous. HY 1160 (CT 1160, TT 839).
T'ai-shang ling-pao wu-fu hsü (Prolegomena to the Five Talismans of Ling-pao). HY 388 (CT 388, TT 183).
T'ai-shang shuo hsüan-t'ien ta-sheng chen-wu pen-chuan miao-ching. HY 753 (TT 530–31).
T'ai-shang t'ai-ch'ing t'ien-t'ung hu-ming miao-ching (Marvelous Book of the Celestial Youth, Protector of Life). HY 632 (TT 341).
T'ai-shang t'ung-hsüan ling-pao pen-hsing yin-yüan ching (Scripture on the Causation from Past Deeds). HY 1106 (TT 758).
T'ai-shang t'ung-hsüan ling-pao yin ching (The Most High's Book of Transcen-

dent Seals for Communicating with the Invisible World). HY 858 (CT 859, TT 576).
T'ai-shang t'ung-yüan pei-ti t'ien-p'eng hu-ming hsiao-tsai shen-chou miao-ching. HY 53 (TT 29).
T'ai-shang tung-yüan san-mei shen-chou chai shih-fang ch'an-i (Spirit-Spells of the Abyss). Revised by Tu Kuang-t'ing (850–933). HY 527 (CT 527, TT 294).
T'ai-shang yüan-shih t'ien-tsun shuo K'ung-ch'üeh ching pai-wen. HY 1423 (CT 1435).
Tai-tsung chao tseng Ssu-k'ung ta-pien cheng Kuang-chih san-tsang ho-shang piao-chih chi, written by Amoghavajra. T. 2120, vol. 52.
T'ang-yeh pen-ts'ao (Materia Medica), by Wang Hao-ku (ca. 1246). Facsimile reprint of the 1601 Ming edition, Peking: Jen-min wei-sheng ch'u-pan she, 1956.
Tao-fa hui-yüan. HY 1210 (TT 884–941).
Tao-hsüan lü-shih kan-t'ung lu (Record of the Numinous Responses), by Tao-hsüan (596–667). T. 2107, vol. 52.
Tao-men ting-chih. HY 1214 (TT 973–75).
Teng-chen yin chüeh (Secret Instructions for the Ascent to Perfection), by T'ao Hung-ching (456–536). HY 421 (TT 193). See also *T'ai-p'ing yü-lan* 665.
Ti-li san-mei-ye pu-t'ung tsun wei-nu-wang shih-che nien-sung fa [*Trisamayarāja*]. Trans. Amoghavajra. T. 1200, vol. 21.
T'ien-hsin cheng-fa. See *Shang-ch'ing t'ien-hsin cheng-fa.*
T'ien-ti pa-yang shen-chou ching (Book of Spirit-Spells of the Eightfold Yang of Heaven and Earth). T. 2897, vol. 85.
T'o-lo-ni chi ching (Collected Dhāraṇī Sūtras), Comp. Atikūṭa, 653–54. T. 901, vol. 18.
T'o-lo-ni tsa-chi (Dhāraṇī Miscellany). Anonymous. Comp. first half of sixth century. T. 1336, vol. 21.
Tongui pogam (Precious Mirror of Eastern Medicine), 1613. Reprint, Taipei, 1972.
Tso-chuan, Shih-san ching chu-shu. Photographic reproduction, Peking: Chung-hua shu-chü, 1983.
Tsu-pi shih-i mai chiu ching (Moxabustion Canon for the Eleven Foot and Arm Vessels). Anonymous (before 168 B.C.E.), in *Han-mu po-shu*, 1985.
Tu-jen ching (Book of Salvation). Full title: *Ling-pao wu-liang tu-jen shang-p'in miao-ching.* HY 1 (TT 1–13).
Tung-chen huang-shu (Yellow Script of the Cave of Perfection). HY 1332 (TT 1031).
Tung-chen t'ai-shang shuo chih-hui hsiao-mo chen-ching (Book of the Demon-Dispellers Spoken by the Supreme Lord of Tung-chen). HY 1333 (CT 1344, TT 1032).
Tung-yüan shen-chou ching (Spirit-Spells of the Abyss). HY 335 (TT 170–73).
Vimalakīrtinirdeśa. T. 475, vol. 14. Trans. Kumārajīva. French translation by Etienne Lamotte, *L'enseignement de Vimalakīrti.* Louvain: Institut Orientaliste, 1962.

Wai-t'ai pi-yao (Secret Essentials from the Outer Tribunal), by Wang T'ao (ca. 670–755), preface dated 752. Peking: Jen-min wei-sheng ch'u-pan-she, 1955, 1982. (See also the Sung edition, *Tōyō igaku zenpon sōsho*, first period, Osaka: Oriento shuppan, 1981.)

Wakan sanzai zu'e, by Terashima Ryōan. 2 vols. Tokyo: Tōkyō bijutsu, 1970.

Wen-i lun (Treatise on Warm Factor Epidemic Disorders), by Wu Yu-hsing (ca. 1642). Reprint of 1897 edition, Peking, 1955.

Wu-hsing ta-i (Compendium of the Fives Phases), by Hsiao Chi (ca. 530–614). Ed. *Chih pu-tsu chai ts'ung-shu* (1813). Japanese translation by Nakamura Shōhachi, 1973; French translation by Marc Kalinowski, 1991.

Wu-shang hsüan-yüan san-t'ien yü-t'ang ta-fa (Great Rites of the Jade Hall), ca. 1158. Comp. Lu Shih-chung. HY 220 (TT 100–104).

Wu-shang pi-yao (ca. 577). HY 1130 (TT 768–79). (See synopsis in Lagerwey 1981.)

Wu-shih-erh ping-fang (Fifty-Two Medical Prescriptions). Anonymous (second century B.C.E.). Peking: Wen-wu ch'u-pan she, 1979.

Yao-shih ju-lai kuan-hsing i-kuei fa (The Medicine Buddha's Contemplation Ritual). Trans. Vajrabodhi. T. 923, vol. 19.

Yao-shih liu-li-kuang ju-lai pen-yüan kung-te ching (Sūtra on the Merits of the Fundamental Vows of the Master of Healing, the Lapis Lazuli Radiance Tathāgata). Trans. Hsüan-tsang (ca. 650). T. 450, vol. 14.

Yen-shih chia-hsün (Family Instructions of Master Yen), by Yen Chih-t'ui (531–ca. 590). Chou Fa-kao, ed., *Yen-shih chia-hsün hui-chu*. Taipei, 1960.

Yogācārabhūmi, by Saṅgharakṣa. Trans. An Shih-kao. T. 607, vol. 15; trans. Dharmarakṣa, T. 606, vol. 15.

Yogin's Book of All the Yogas of the Diamond-Pinnacle Pavilion. See *Chin-kang-feng lou-ko i-ch'ieh yü-chih ching*.

Yu-p'o-se chieh ching (Treatise on Upāsaka Precepts). Trans. Dharmakṣema, ca. 414–21. T. 1488, vol. 24.

Yü-t'ang ta-fa. See *Wu-shang hsüan-yüan san-t'ien yü-t'ang ta fa*.

Yün-chi ch'i-ch'ien (ca. 1022), by Chang Chün-fang (fl. 1008–29). HY 1026 (CT 1032, TT 677–702).

Yün-meng Shui-hu-ti Ch'in mu. Peking: Wen-wu ch'u-pan she, 1981.

Zenrin shōkisen, by Mujaku Dōchū (1653–1744). Tokyo: Seishin shobō, 1963.

Secondary Sources

Abe Yasurō. 1984. "Jidō setsuwa no keisei." *Kokugo kokubun* 600–601, 1–29, 30–56.

———. 1993. "Jidō setsuwa to chigo." In Kamata Tōji, ed., *Ōdō shinkō*, 283–312. Minshū shūkyōshi sōsho 27. Tokyo: Yūzankaku shuppan.

Ackerknecht, Erwin. 1971. *Medicine and Ethnology: Selected Essays*. Ed. H. H. Walser and H. M. Koelbing. Bern: Hans Huber.

Agrawala, Prithivi Kumar. 1967. *Skanda-Kārttikeya: A Study in the Origin and Development*. Varanasi: Benares Hindu University.

Agrawala, Vasudeva Kumar. 1970. *Ancient Indian Folk Cults*. Varanasi: Prithivi Prakashan.

Ahern, Emily M. 1975. "The Power and Pollution of Chinese Women." In Margery Wolf and Roxane Witke, eds., *Women in Chinese Society*, 193–214. Stanford, Calif.: Stanford University Press.

———. 1978. "Sacred and Secular Medicine in a Taiwanese Village." In Arthur Kleinman, P. Kunstadter, E. Russel Alexander and J. L. Gates, eds., *Culture and Healing in Chinese Society*, 37–60. Cambridge, Mass.: Schenkman Publishing.

Akahori Akira. 1978a. "Bu'i kandai ikan ni tsuite" (On the Han Medical Texts of Wooden Strips from Wuwei, Gansu). *Tōhō gakuhō* 50: 75–107.

———. 1978b. "Medical Manuscripts Found in Han Tomb no. 3 at Ma-wang-tui." *Sudhoffs Archiv* 63: 297–301.

———. 1979. "*In yō jūichi myaku kyū kyō* to Somon: Somon no seiritsu ni tsuite no ichi kōsatsu." *Nihon ishigaku zasshi* 25, 3: 277–90.

———. 1981. "*In yō jūichi myaku kyū kyō* no kenkyū." *Tōhō gakuhō* 53: 299–339.

———. 1989. "Drug Taking and Immortality." In Livia Kohn and Sakade Yoshinobu, eds., *Taoist Meditation and Longevity Techniques*, 73–98. Michigan Monographs on Chinese Studies 61. Ann Arbor: Center for Chinese Studies, The University of Michigan.

Akatsuka Tadashi. 1985–86. *Akatsuka Tadashi chosaku shū*. Tokyo: Kenbunsha.

Akizuki Kan'ei. 1985. *Dōkyō kenkyū no susume: Sono genjō to mondaiten o kangaeru*. Tokyo: Hirakawa shuppansha.

Allan, Sarah, and Alvin P. Cohen, eds. 1979. *Legend, Lore, and Religion in China: Essays in Honor of Wolfram Eberhard on His Seventieth Birthday*. Reprint, San Francisco: Chinese Materials Center.

Allen, Michael. 1975. *The Cult of Kumārī: Virgin Worship in Nepal*. Delhi: Motilal Banarsidass.

Alper, Harvey P., ed. 1989. *Mantra*. Albany: State University of New York Press.

Anderson, Poul. 1980. *The Method of Holding the Three Ones: A Taoist Manual of the Fourth Century A.D.* Studies on Asian Topics, 1. London: Curzon Press.

———. 1989–90. "The Practice of *Bugang*: Historical Introduction." *Cahiers d'Extrême-Asie* 5: 15–53.

———. 1994. "Talking to the Gods: Visionary Divination in Early Taoism (The Sanhuang Tradition)." *Taoist Resources* 5, 1: 1–24.

———. 1995. "The Transformation of the Body in Taoist Ritual." In Jane Marie Law, ed., *Religious Reflections on the Human Body*, 186–208. Bloomington: Indiana University Press.

Andō Kōsei. 1961. *Nihon no miira*. Tokyo: Mainichi shinbunsha.

———. 1968. "Des momies au Japon et de leur culte." *L'Homme* 8, 2: 5–18.

Andō Shun'yū. 1970. "Shibyōhō to shite no Tendai shikan." *Ōtani daigaku kenkyū nenpō* 23: 1–58.

Ang, Isabelle, and Pierre-Étienne Will, eds. 1994. *Nombres, astres, plantes et viscères: Sept essais sur l'histoire des sciences et des techniques en Asie orientale*. Paris: Collège de France, Institut des Hautes Études Chinoises.

Aris, Michael. 1989. *Hidden Treasures and Secret Lives*. London: Kegan Paul.

Arlington, Lewis Charles. 1927. "Chinese Versus Western Chiromancy." *China Journal of Science and Arts* 7: 170–75, 228–35.

———. 1931. *Through the Dragon's Eyes*. London: Constable.

Aubert, Jean-Jacques. 1989. "Threatened Wombs: Aspects of Ancient Uterine Magic." *Greek, Roman, and Byzantine Studies* 30, 3: 421–49.

Augé, Marc. 1986. "L'anthropologie de la maladie." *L'Homme* 26: 81–90.

Augé, Marc, and Claudine Herzlich, eds. 1984. *Le Sens du mal: anthropologie, histoire, sociologie de la maladie*. Paris: Éditions des Archives contemporaines.

Bächtold-Stäubli, Hanns. 1927–42. *Handwörterbuch des deutschen Aberglaubens*. Berlin: Walter de Gruyter.

Bagchi, P. C. 1940. "New Materials for the Study of the *Kumāra-tantra* of Rāvaṇa." *Indian Culture* 7: 269–86.

Baldrian-Hussein, Farzeen. 1984. *Procédés secrets du joyau magique: Traité d'alchimie taoïste du XIe siècle*. Paris: Les Deux Océans.

———. 1989–90. "Inner Alchemy: Notes on the Origin and Use of the Term *Neidan*." *Cahiers d'Extrême-Asie* 5: 163–90.

Baltruśaitis, Jurgis. 1979. *Réveils et prodiges dans l'art gothique*. Paris: Armand Colin.

———. 1981 (1955). *Le Moyen Age fantastique: Antiquités et exotismes dans l'art gothique*. Paris: Flammarion.

Banerjea, Jitendra Nath. 1938. "Some Folk Goddesses of Ancient and Mediaeval India." *Indian Historical Quarterly* 14: 101–9.

———. 1956. *The Development of Hindu Iconography*. Calcutta. Revised ed., New Delhi, 1974.

Bapat, P. V., and Hirakawa Akira. 1970. *'Shan-Chien-P'i-P'o-Sha': A Chinese Version of Samantapāsādikā by Saṅghabhadra*. Poona: Bhandarkar Oriental Research Institute.

Baptandier (Berthier), Brigitte. 1987. "Enfants de divination, voyageuers du destin." *L'Homme* 27, 101: 86–100.

———. 1988. *La Dame-du-bord-de-l'eau*. Nanterre: Société d'Ethnologie.

———. 1996. "Le rituel d'ouverture des passes: Un concept de l'enfance." *L'Homme* 137: 119–42.

Bargen, Doris G. 1997. *A Woman's Weapon: Spirit Possession in* "The Tale of Genji." Honolulu: University of Hawai'i Press.

Barkan, Leonard. 1975. *Nature's Work of Art: The Human Body as Image of the World*. New Haven, Conn.: Yale University Press.

Barnes, Nancy J. 1989. "Lady Rokujō's Ghost: Spirit Possession, Buddhism, and Healing in Japanese Literature." *Literature and Medicine* 8: 106–21.

Barrett, Timothy H. 1982. "Taoist and Buddhist Mysteries in the Interpretation of the Tao-te-ching." *Journal of the Royal Asiatic Society* 2: 35–43.

———. 1996. *Taoism Under the T'ang: Religion and Empire During the Golden Age of Chinese History*. London: Wellsweep Press.

Bartlett, Harley Harris. 1973. *The Labors of the Datoe and Other Essays on the*

Bataks of Asahan, North Sumatra. Ann Arbor: Center for South and Southeast Asian Studies, University of Michigan.
Basham, A. L. 1976. "The Practice of Medicine in Ancient and Medieval India." In Charles Leslie, ed., *Asian Medical Systems: A Comparative Study*, 18–43. Berkeley: University of California Press.
Beckwith, Christopher. 1979. "The Introduction of Greek Medicine into Tibet in the Seventh and Eighth Centuries." *Journal of the American Oriental Society* 99, 2: 297–313.
Bell, Catherine. 1988. "Ritualization of Texts and Textualization of Ritual in the Codification of Taoist Liturgy." *History of Religions* 27, 4: 366–92.
Belo, Jane. 1960. *Trance in Bali*. New York: Columbia University Press.
Benedict, Carol. 1988. "Bubonic Plague in Nineteenth-Century China." *Modern China* 14, 2: 107–55.
———. 1993. "Policing the Sick: Plague and the Origins of State Medicine in Late Imperial China." *Late Imperial China* 14, 2: 60–77.
———. 1996. *Bubonic Plague in Nineteenth-Century China*. Stanford, Calif.: Stanford University Press.
Benveniste, Emile. 1969. *Le voaculaire des institutions indo-européennes*. 2 vols. Paris: Éditions de Minuit.
Bernhard, F. 1967. "Zur Entstehung einer Dhāraṇī." *Zeitschrift der Deutschen Morgenlandischen Gessellschaft* 117: 148–68.
Berthier(-Caillet), Laurence. 1980. "Vers une réhabilitation des démons japonais: À propos de la survivance du caractère propitiatoire des *oni* dans le folklore japonais." In *Mélanges offerts à M. Charles Haguenauer en l'honneur de son quatre-vingtième anniversaire: Études japonaises*, 443–57. Paris: L'Asiathèque.
———. 1981. *Syncrétisme au Japon. Omizutori: Le rituel de l'eau de Jouvence*. Cahiers d'Études et de Documents sur les Religions du Japon, vol. 6. Paris: École Pratiques des Hautes Études, Ve section.
Bertuccioli, Giuliano. 1974. "Reminiscences of Mao-shan." *East and West*, n.s., 24, 3–4: 3–16.
Beyer, Stephan. 1978. *The Cult of Tārā: Magic and Ritual in Tibet*. Berkeley: University of California Press.
Bhandarkar, R. G. 1913. *Vaiṣṇavism, Śaivism and Minor Religious Systems*. Reprint, Varanasi: Indological Book House, 1965.
Bharati, Agehananda. 1965a. "Śākta and Vajrayāna: Their Place in Indian Thought." Kōyasan daigaku, ed., *Mikkyōgaku mikkyōshi ronbunshū*, 73–99. Kyoto: Naigai Press.
———. 1965b. *The Tantric Tradition*. London. Reprint, New York: Doubleday, 1970.
Bhattacharya, N. N. 1992 (1982). *History of the Tantric Religion: A Historical, Ritualistic and Philosophical Study*. New Delhi: Manohar.
Biardeau, Madeleine. 1991 (1981). "Skanda, a Great Sovereign God of South India." In Yves Bonnefoy, ed., *Asian Mythologies*, 92–95. Trans. Wendy Doniger. Chicago: University of Chicago Press.

Birnbaum, Raoul. 1979. *The Healing Buddha*. Boulder, Colo.: Shambhala.

———. 1980. "Introduction to the Study of T'ang Buddhist Astrology: Research Notes on Primary Sources and Basic Principles." *Bulletin of the Society for the Study of Chinese Religions* 8: 5–19.

———. 1983. *Studies on the Mysteries of Mañjuśrī: A Group of East Asian Maṇḍalas and Their Traditional Symbolism*. Society for the Study of Chinese Religions Monograph No. 2. Boulder, Colo.: Society for the Study of Chinese Religions.

———. 1985–86. "Seeking Longevity in Chinese Buddhism: Long Life Deities and Their Symbolism." *Journal of Chinese Religions* 13–14: 143–76.

Bischoff, F. A. 1950. *Contribution à l'étude des divinités mineures du bouddhisme tantrique: Āryamahābalanāma-mahāyanasūtra*, Buddhica, 1st series, 10. Paris: Geuthner.

Bizot, François. 1976. *Recherches sur le bouddhisme khmer: I. Le Figuier à cinq branches*. Paris: École Française d'Extrême-Orient.

———. 1980. "La grotte de la naissance." *Bulletin de l'École Française d'Extrême-Orient* 67: 221–73.

———. 1981. *Le Don de soi-même*. Publications de l'EFEO, 130. Paris: École Française d'Extrême-Orient.

———. 1983–85. "Notes sur les *yantra* bouddhiques d'Indochine." In Michel Strickmann, ed., *Tantric and Taoist Studies in Honour of R. A. Stein*, vol. 1: 155–91. Brussels: Institut Belge des Hautes Études Chinoises.

Black, William George. 1883. *Folk-Medicine: A Chapter in the History of Culture*. London: The Folklore Society.

Blacker, Carmen. 1963. "The Divine Boy in Japanese Buddhism." *Asian Folklore Studies* 22: 77–88.

———. 1967. "Supernatural Abductions in Japanese Folklore." *Asian Folklore Studies* 26, 2: 111–48.

———. 1973. "Animal Witchcraft in Japan." In Venetia Newall, ed., *The Witch Figure: Folklore Essays by a Group of Scholars in England Honouring the Seventy-fifth Birthday of Katherine M. Briggs*. London.

———. 1975. *The Catalpa Bow: A Study of Shamanistic Practices in Japan*. London: Allen and Unwin. Revised ed., 1986.

———. 1978. "The Snake-Woman." In Porter and Russell, eds., *Animals in Folklore*, 113–25. London.

Blacker, Carmen, and Michael Loewe, eds. 1981. *Oracles and Divination*. Boulder, Colo.: Shambhala.

Bloch, Marc. 1973 (1924). *The Royal Touch*. Trans. J. E. Anderson. London: Routledge and Kegan Paul.

Bloch, Maurice, and Jonathan Parry, eds. 1982. *Death and the Regeneration of Life*. Cambridge: Cambridge University Press.

Blondeau, Anne-Marie, and Kristofer Schipper, eds. 1988. *Essais sur le rituel*. 2 vols. Louvain: Peeters.

Bloss, Lowell W. 1973. "The Buddha and the Nāga: A Study in Buddhist Folk Religiosity." *History of Religions* 13, 1: 36–53.

Bock, Felicia G. 1985. *Classical Learning and Taoist Practices in Early Japan, with a Translation of Books XVI and XX of the Engi-shiki*. Center for Asian Studies, Occasional Paper no. 17. Tempe: Arizona State University.

Bodde, Derk, trans. 1965. *Annual Customs and Festivals in Peking, as Recorded in the Yen-ching Sui-shih-chi by Tun Li-ch'en*. Taipei: Orient Cultural Service, 1984; 2nd ed., Hong Kong.

———. 1975. *Festivals in Classical China: New Year and Other Annual Observances During the Han Dynasty, 206 B.C.–A.D. 220*. Princeton, N.J.: Princeton University Press.

———. 1985. "Sex in Chinese Civilization." *Proceedings of the American Philosophical Society* 129, 2: 161–71.

Boddy, Janice. 1989. *Wombs and Alien Spirits: Women, Men, and the Zār Cult in Northern Sudan*. Madison: University of Wisconsin Press.

Bokenkamp, Stephen R. 1983. "The Entheogenic Herb Calamus in Taoist Literature." *Phi Theta Papers* 15: 6–22.

———. 1983–85. "Sources of the Ling-pao Scriptures." In Michel Strickmann, ed., *Tantric and Taoist Studies in Honour of R. A. Stein*, vol. 2: 434–86. Brussels: Institut Belge des Hautes Études Chinoises.

———. 1986. "The Peach Flower Font and the Grotto Passage." *Journal of the American Oriental Society* 106, 1: 65–77.

———. 1996a. "Answering a Summons." In Donald S. Lopez, Jr., ed., *Religions of China in Practice*, 188–202. Princeton, N.J.: Princeton University Press.

———. 1996b. "The Purification Ritual of the Luminous Perfected." In Donald S. Lopez, Jr., ed., *Religions of China in Practice*, 268–77. Princeton, N.J.: Princeton University Press.

———. 1996–97. "The Yao Boduo Stele as Evidence for the 'Dao-Buddhism' of the Early Lingbao Scriptures." *Cahiers d'Extrême-Asie* 9: 55–67.

———. 1997a. *Early Daoist Scriptures*. Berkeley: University of California Press.

———. 1997b. "Time After Time: Taoist Apocalyptic History and the Founding of the T'ang Dynasty." *Asia Major*, third series, 7, 1: 59–88.

Boltz, Judith M. 1983–85. "Opening the Gates of Purgatory: A Twelfth-Century Taoist Technique for the Salvation of Lost Souls." In Michel Strickmann, ed., *Tantric and Taoist Studies in Honour of R. A. Stein*, vol. 2: 487–511. Brussels: Institut Belge des Hautes Études Chinoises.

———. 1985. "Taoist Rites of Exorcism." Ph.D. dissertation, University of California, Berkeley.

———. 1986. "In Homage to T'ien-fei." *Journal of the American Oriental Society* 106: 211–32.

———. 1987. *A Survey of Taoist Literature, Tenth to Seventeenth Centuries*. Berkeley: Institute of East Asian Studies, University of California.

———. 1993. "Not by the Seal of Office Alone: New Weapons in the Battle with the Supernatural." In Patricia Ebrey and Peter N. Gregory, eds., *Religion and Society in T'ang and Sung China*, 241–305. Honolulu: University of Hawai'i Press.

Bouchy, Anne-Marie [Anne]. 1984. "Le renard: Élément de la conception du monde dans la tradition japonaise." *Études mongoles et sibériennes* 15, *Le renard: Tours, détours et retours*, 17–70.

———. 1992. *Les oracles de Shirataka: Ou la sibylle d'Osaka*. Paris: Éditions Philippe Picquier.

Bourke, John Gregory. 1891. *Scatologic Rites of all Nations*. Washington, D.C.: W. H. Lowdermilk.

Bridgman, Robert F. 1981. "Les fonctions physiologiques chez l'homme dans la Chine antique." *History and Philosophy of the Life Sciences* 3, 1: 3–30.

Brinker, Helmut. 1990. "Gemalt aus Vertrauen auf Fudō Myōō." *Asiatische Studien/Études Asiatiques* 44, 2: 267–347.

———. 1997–98. "Facing the Unseen: On the Interior Adornment of Eizon's Iconic Body." *Archives of Asian Art* 50: 42–61.

Brown, Carolyn T., ed. 1988. *Psycho-Sinology: The Universe of Dreams in Chinese Culture*. Lanham, Md.: University Press of America.

Brown, Peter. 1981. *The Cult of the Saints: Its Rise and Function in Latin Christianity*. Chicago: University of Chicago Press.

Brown, Robert L., ed. 1991. *Ganesh: Studies of an Asian God*. Albany, N.Y.: State University of New York Press.

Brun, Viggo, and Trond Schumacher. 1987. *Traditional Herbal Medicine in Northern Thailand*. Berkeley: University of California Press.

Brunner, Hélène. 1986a. "Maṇḍala et yantra dans le śivaïsme āgamique." In André Padoux, ed., *Mantras et diagrammes rituels dans l'hindouisme*, 11–35. Paris: Éditions du CNRS.

———. 1986b. "Les membres de Śiva." *Asiatische Studien/Études Asiatiques* 40: 89–132.

Buchanan, Daniel C. 1935. *Inari: Its Origin, Development, and Nature*. Transactions of the Royal Asiatic Society of Japan. Tokyo: Royal Asiatic Society of Japan.

Buddhagosa. 1975. *The Path of Purification (Visuddhimagga)*. Trans. Bhikku Ñānamoli. Kandy: Buddhist Publication Society.

Bühnemann, Gudrun. 1988. *The Worship of Mahāgaṇapati According to the Nityotsava*. Wichtrach (Switzerland).

———. 1989. "The Heavenly Bodies (*Navagraha*) in Hindu Ritual." *Saṃbhāsa* 11: 1–9.

Bunker, Emma. 1964. "The Spirit Kings in Sixth-Century Chinese Buddhist Sculpture." *Archives of the Chinese Art Society of America* 18: 26–37.

Burang, Theodore. 1974. *The Tibetan Art of Healing*. London: Watkins.

Burgess, James. 1904. "The *Navagraha* or Nine Planets and Their Names." *Indian Antiquary* 33: 61–66.

Burkert, Walter. 1979. *Structure and History in Greek Mythology and Ritual*. Berkeley: University of California Press.

Burnouf, Eugène. 1844. *Introduction à l'histoire du bouddhisme indien*. Paris: Imprimerie Royale.

———. 1973 (1852). *Le Lotus de la Bonne Loi*. Paris: Adrien Maisonneuve.

Bush, Susan. 1974. "Thunder Monsters and Wind Spirits in Early Sixth-Century

China and the Epitaph Tablet of Lady Yüan." *Boston Museum Bulletin* 72, 367: 24–54.
Buswell, Robert E., Jr., ed. 1990. *Chinese Buddhist Apocrypha*. Honolulu: University of Hawai'i Press.
Cabezón, José, and Roger Jackson, eds. 1996. *Tibetan Literature: Studies in Genre*. Ithaca, N.Y.: Snow Lion.
Cadière, Léopold. 1992 (1944–56). *Croyances et pratiques religieuses des Viêtnamiens*. 3 vols. Paris: École Française d'Extrême-Orient.
Campany, Robert F. 1990. "Return from Death Narratives in Early Medieval China." *Journal of Chinese Religions* 18: 91–125.
———. 1991. "Notes on the Devotional Uses and Symbolic Functions of Sūtra Texts as Depicted in Early Chinese Buddhist Miracle Tales and Hagiographies." *Journal of the International Association of Buddhist Studies* 14, 1: 28–72.
———. 1996. *Strange Writing: Anomaly Accounts in Early Medieval China*. Albany: State University of New York Press.
Camporesi, Piero. 1995. *Juice of Life: The Symbolic and Magic Significance of Blood*. Trans. Robert R. Barr. New York: Continuum.
Cannadine, David, and Simon Price, eds. 1987. *Rituals of Royalty: Power and Ceremonial in Traditional Societies*. Cambridge: Cambridge University Press.
Caquot, André, and Marcel Leibovici, eds. 1968. *La divination*. 2 vols. Paris.
Casal, U. A. 1959. "The Goblin Fox and Badger and Other Witch Animals of Japan." *Folklore Studies* 18: 1–94.
Cass, Victoria B. 1986. "Female Healers in the Ming and the Lodge of Ritual and Ceremony." *Journal of the American Oriental Society* 106, 1: 233–240.
Cedzich, Ursula-Angelika. 1985. "Wu-t'ung: Zur bewegten Geschichte eines Kultes." In Gert Neundorf, Karl-Heinz Pohl, and Hans-Hermann Schmidt, eds., *Religion und Philosophie in Ostasien, Festschrift für Hans Steininger*, 33–60. Würzburg: Königshausen und Neumann.
———. 1987. "Das Ritual der Himmelmeister im Spiegel früher Quellen: Übersetzung und Untersuchung des liturgischen Materials im dritten *chüan* des *Teng-chen yin-chüeh*." Ph.D. dissertation, University of Würzburg.
———. 1993. "Ghosts and Demons, Law and Order: Grave Quelling Texts and Early Taoist Liturgy." *Taoist Resources* 4, 2: 23–35.
Cham, Hok-lam. 1990. "A Mongolian Legend of the Building of Peking." *Asia Major*, third series, 3, 2: 63–93.
Chandra, Lokesh. 1976. *Tibetan-Sanskrit Dictionary Based on a Close Comparative Study of Sanskrit Originals and Tibetan Translations of Several Texts*. Śata-Piṭaka Series, vol. 3. Kyoto: Rinser Book Co.
———. 1978. *Mudrās in Japan: Symbolic Hand-gestures in Japanese Mantrayāna*. Śata-Piṭaka Series, vol. 243. New Delhi: Sharada Rani.
Chao P'u-shan. 1983. *Chung-kuo ku-tai i-hsüeh*. Peking.
Chao Wei-pang. 1946. "The Chinese Science of Fate-Calculation." *Folklore Studies* 5: 279–315.

Chapin, Helen M. 1940. "Toward the Study of the Sword as Dynastic Talisman." Ph.D. dissertation, University of California, Berkeley.

———. 1972. *A Long Roll of Buddhist Images*. Ed. Alexander Soper. Ascona: Artibus Asiae.

Chappell, David W. 1980. "Early Forebodings of the Death of Buddhism." *Numen* 17: 122–54.

Chatterjee, Asim Kumar. 1970. *The Cult of Skanda-Kārttikeya in Ancient India*. Calcutta: Punthi Pustak.

Chavannes, Édouard. 1910. *Le T'ai Chan: Essai de monographie d'un culte chinois*.

———. 1919. "Le jet des dragons." *Mémoires concernant l'Asie Orientale publiés par l'Académie des Inscriptions et Belles-Lettres*, vol. 3: 53–220. Paris: Ernest Leroux.

———. 1910–34. *Cinq cents contes et apologues extraits du Tripiṭaka chinois*. 4 vols. Paris. Revised ed., 3 vols., Paris: Adrien Maisonneuve, 1962.

Chen, K. K. 1925. "Chinese Drug Stores." *Annals of Medical History* 7, 2: 103–9.

Ch'en Hsiang-ch'un. 1942. "Examples of Charms Against Epidemics, with Short Explanations." *Folklore Studies* 1: 37–54.

Ch'en, Kenneth. 1964. *Buddhism in China: A Historical Survey*. Princeton, N.J.: Princeton University Press.

———. 1973. *The Chinese Transformation of Buddhism*. Princeton, N.J.: Princeton University Press.

Ch'en Pang-hsien. 1937. *Chung-kuo i-hsüeh shih*. Revised ed., Shanghai: Commercial Press, 1954. (Taipei, 1965.)

Ch'en Sheng-k'un. 1981. *Chung-kuo chi-ping shih*. Taipei: Tzu-jan k'o-hsüeh ch'u-pan-she.

Ch'en Shih-hsiang, trans. 1953. *The Biography of Ku K'ai-chih*. Berkeley: University of California Press.

Ch'en Yao-hung et al. 1991. *Chung-kuo No wen-hua*. Peking: Hsin-hua ch'u-pan-she.

Chigiri Mitsutoshi. 1973. *Tengu kō*. Tokyo: Tōshobō.

———. 1975. *Tengu no kenkyū*. Tokyo: Tairiki shobō.

Chime Radha, Lama. 1981. "Tibet." In Carmen Blacker and Michael Loewe, eds., *Oracles and Divination*, 3–37. London: Random House.

Chou Yi-liang. 1944–45. "Tantrism in China." *Harvard Journal of Asiatic Studies* 8: 241–332.

Chow Tse-tsung. 1978. "The Childbirth Myth and Ancient Chinese Medicine: A Study of Aspects of the *Wu* Tradition." In David T. Roy and Tsuen-hsuin Tsieh, eds., *Ancient China: Studies in Early Civilization*, 43–89. Hong Kong: Chinese University Press.

Chu Kun-liang. 1987. *Les aspects rituels du théâtre chinois*. Paris: Institut des Hautes Études Chinoises.

Clarke, John Henry. 1925. *A Dictionary of Practical Materia Medica*. 3 vols. London: Homoeopathic Publishing.

Cockburn, Aidan, and Eve Cockburn, eds. 1983. *Mummies, Disease, and Ancient Cultures*. Cambridge: Cambridge University Press.

Cole, Alan. 1998. *Mothers and Sons in Chinese Buddhism*. Stanford, Calif.: Stanford University Press.

Combaz, Gilbert. 1939–45. “Masques et dragons en Asie.” *Mélanges Chinois et Bouddhiques* 7: 1–328.

Conner, Linda, Petty Asch, and Timothy Asch. 1986. *Jero Tapakan, Balinese Healer: An Ethnographic Film Monograph*. Cambridge: Cambridge University Press.

Coomaraswamy, Ananda K. 1928. *Yakṣas: Essays in the Water Cosmology*. Revised ed. by Paul Schroeder. Oxford: Oxford University Press, 1993.

———. 1928–29. “A Chinese Buddhist Water Vessel and Its Indian Prototype.” *Artibus Asiae*, 122–41.

Coomaraswamy, Ananda K., and Duggirāla Gōpālakrishnāyya, trans. 1936. *The Mirror of Gesture: Being the Abhinaya darpaṇa of Nandikeśvara*. New York: E. Weyhe.

Cooper, William C., and Nathan Sivin. 1972. “Man as a Medicine: Pharmacological and Ritual Aspects of Drugs Derived from the Human Body.” In Nathan Sivin and Shigeru Nakayama, eds., *Chinese Science: Explorations of an Ancient Tradition*, 203–72. MIT East Asian Science Series, 2. Cambridge, Mass.: MIT Press.

Courtright, Paul B. 1985. *Gaṇeśa, Lord of Obstacles, Lord of Beginnings*. New York and Oxford: Oxford University Press.

Cowdry, E. V. 1921. “Taoist Ideas of Human Anatomy.” *Annals of Medical History* 3, 4: 301–9.

Croissant, Doris. 1990. “Der Unsterbliche Leib: Ahneneffigies und Reliquienporträt in der Porträtplastik Chinas und Japans.” In Martin Kraatz et al., eds., *Das Bildnis in der Kunst des Orients*, 235–68. Stuttgart: Steiner Verlag.

Croizier, Ralph C. 1968. *Traditional Medicine in Modern China: Science, Nationalism and the Tensions of Cultural Change*. Harvard East Asian Series. Cambridge, Mass.: Harvard University Press.

———. 1973. “Traditional Medicine in Modern China: Social, Political and Cultural Aspects.” In Guenter B. Risse, ed., *Modern China and Traditional Chinese Medicine: A Symposium Held at the University of Wisconsin, Madison*, 30–46. Springfield, Ill.: Thomas.

Cutler, Norman, and Joanna Punzo Waghorne, eds. 1985. *Gods of Flesh, Gods of Stone*. Chambersburg, Pa.: Anima.

Czaja, Michael. 1974. *Gods of Myth and Stone: Phallicism in Japanese Folk Religion*. New York: Weatherhill.

Das Gupta, Shashibusan. 1976 (1946). *Obscure Religious Cults as a Background to Bengali Literature*. Calcutta: Firma KLM.

Davis, Edward L. 1994. “The Words of Hung Mai.” Ph.D. dissertation, University of California, Berkeley.

Davis, Natalie Z. 1987. *Fiction in the Archives: Pardon Tales and Their Tellers in Sixteenth-Century France*. Stanford, Calif.: Stanford University Press.

Davis, Tenney, and Chao Yün-ts'ung. 1940. “A Fifteenth-Century Chinese En-

cyclopedia of Alchemy." *Proceedings of the American Academy of Arts and Sciences* 73: 391–99.
Davis, Winston. 1980. *Dōjo: Magic and Exorcism in Modern Japan*. Stanford, Calif.: Stanford University Press.
Dean, Kenneth. 1988. "Funerals in Fujian." *Cahiers d'Extrême-Asie* 4: 19–78.
———. 1990. "Mu-lien and Lei Yu-sheng ('Thunder Is Noisy') in the Theatrical and Funerary Traditions of Fukien." In David Johnson, ed., *Ritual Opera, Operatic Ritual: Mu-lien Rescues His Mother in Chinese Popular Culture*, 46–104. Berkeley: University of California Institute of East Asian Studies.
———. 1995. *Taoist Ritual and Popular Cults of Southeast China*. Princeton, N.J.: Princeton University Press.
DeBernardi, Jean. 1987. "The God of War and the Vagabond Buddha." *Modern China* 13, 3: 310–32.
Decaux, Jacques. 1989. *Les quatre livres de l'empereur jaune: Le canon taoïque retrouvé*. Taipei: European Languages Publications.
De Groot, J. J. M. 1892–1910. *The Religious System of China: Its Ancient Forms, Evolution, History and Present Aspects—Manners, Customs, and Social Institutions Connected Therewith*. 6 vols. Revised ed., Taipei: Southern Materials Center, 1964.
———. 1893. *Le Code du Mahāyāna en Chine, son influence sur la vie monacale et sur le monde laïc*. Amsterdam.
———. 1977 (1886). *Les Fêtes annuellement célébrées à Emoui (Amoy)*. 2 vols. Amsterdam: Johannes Müller. Reprint, Taipei: Ch'eng-wen, 1971.
Delahaye, Hubert. 1983. "Les antécédents magiques des statues chinoises." *Revue d'esthétique*, n.s. 5, "Autour de la Chine," 45–53.
Delatte, Armand. 1932. *La catoptromancie grecque et ses dérivés*. Liège: Bibliothèque de la Faculté de Philosophie et Lettres de l'Université de Liège.
———. 1938. *Herbarius: Recherches sur le cérémonial usité chez les anciens pour la cueillette des simples et des plantes magiques*.
de Mallmann, Marie-Thérèse. 1948. *Introduction à l'étude d'Avalokiteçvara*. Paris: Presses Universitaires de France.
———. 1963. *Les enseignements iconographiques de l'Agni-purāṇa*. Annales du Musée Guimet, Bibliothèques d'études, vol. 67. Paris: Presses Universitaires de France.
———. 1964a. "Divinités hindoues dans le tantrisme bouddhique." *Arts asiatiques* 10: 67–86.
———. 1964b. *Étude iconographique sur Mañjuśrī*. Paris: École Française d'Extrême-Orient.
———. 1975. *Introduction à l'iconographie du tantrisme bouddhique*. Bibliothèque du Centre de Recherches sur l'Asie et la Haute Asie, vol. 1. Paris: Adrien Maisonneuve.
Demiéville, Paul. 1937. "Butsuzō." In *Hōbōgirin* 3: 210–15. Paris: Adrien Maisonneuve.
———. 1965. "Momies d'Extrême-Orient." *Journal des savants* (troisième

centenaire), 144–70. Reprinted in idem, *Choix d'études sinologiques*, Leiden, 1973: 407–32.
———. 1973a. *Choix d'études bouddhiques*, 1929–70. Leiden.
———. 1973b. *Choix d'études sinologiques*, 1929–70. Leiden.
———. 1976. "Une descente aux enfers sous les T'ang: La biographie de Houang Che-k'iang," in *Études d'histoire et de littérature chinoises offertes au professeur Jaroslav Průšek*, 71–84. Paris: Presses Universitaires de France.
———. 1985 (1937). *Buddhism and Healing: Demiéville's Article "Byō" from Hōbōgirin*. Trans. Mark Tatz. Lanham, Md.: University Press of America.
Dennys, N. B. 1876. *The Folk-Lore of China*. London and Hong Kong: Trübner.
Despeux, Catherine. 1976. *T'ai ki k'iuan: Technique de longue vie, technique de combat*. Mémoires de l'Institut des Hautes Études Chinoises, vol. 3. Paris: Collège de France, Institut des Hautes Études Chinoises.
———, trans. 1979. *Traité d'alchimie et de physiologie taoïste* (Weisheng Sheng lixue mingzhi), by Zhao Bichen. Paris: Les Deux Océans.
———. 1985. *'Shanghanlun': Le Traité des "coups de froid" de Zhang Zhongjing*. Paris: Éditions de la Tisserande.
———. 1987. *Zhenjiu jing: Prescriptions d'acuponcture valant mille onces d'or*. Paris: Guy Trédaniel.
———. 1989. "Gymnastics: The Ancient Tradition." In Livia Kohn and Sakade Yoshinobu, eds. 1989. *Taoist Meditation and Longevity Techniques*, 225–61. Michigan Monographs on Chinese Studies, 61. Ann Arbor: Center for Chinese Studies, The University of Michigan.
———. 1990. *Immortelles de la Chine ancienne: Taoïsme et alchimie féminine*. Puiseaux: Pardès.
———. 1995. *Le Taoïsme et le corps humain: Le 'Xiuzhen tu.'* Paris: Guy Trédaniel.
des Rotours, Robert. 1952. "Les insignes en deux parties (*fou*) sous la dynastie des T'ang (618–907)." *T'oung Pao* 41: 1–148.
———. 1966. "Le culte des cinq dragons sous la dynastie des T'ang (618–907)." In *Mélanges de sinologie offerts à Paul Demiéville*, vol. 1: 261–80. Paris: Presses Universitaires de France.
Devereux, Georges. 1983. *Baubô, la vulve mythique*. Paris: J.-C. Godefroy.
De Visser, Marinus Willem. 1908. "The Tengu." *Transactions of the Asiatic Society of Japan* 36, 2: 25–89.
———. 1913. *The Dragon in China and Japan*. Amsterdam: Johannes Müller.
———. 1915. *The Bodhisattva Ti-tsang (Jizō) in China and Japan*. Berlin: Oesterheld.
———. 1923. *The Arhats in China and Japan*. Berlin: Oesterheld.
———. 1931. *The Bodhisattva Ākāśagarbha (Kokūzō) in China and Japan*. Amsterdam: Koninklijke Akademie van Wetenschappen.
———. 1929. *Ancient Buddhism in Japan: Sūtras and Ceremonies*. Paris: Paul Geuthner.
DeWoskin, Kenneth J. 1983. *Doctors, Diviners, and Magicians of Ancient China: Biographies of "Fang-chih."* New York: Columbia University Press.

Diehl, Carl Gustav. 1956. *Instrument and Purpose: Studies on Rites and Rituals in South India*. Lund: C. W. K. Gleerup.

Diény, Jean-Pierre. 1987. *Le symbolisme du dragon dans la Chine antique*. Paris: Institut des Hautes Études du Collège de France.

Dimock, Edward C., Jr. 1966. *The Place of the Hidden Moon: Erotic Mysticism in the Vaiṣṇava-Sahajiyā Cult of Bengal*. Chicago: University of Chicago Press. Reprint, Delhi: Motilal Banarsidass, 1991.

Dölger, Franz Josef. 1911. Sphragis: *Eine altchristliche Taufbezeichnung in ihren Beziehungen zur profanen and religiösen Kultur des Altertums*. Paderhorn: Ferdinand Schoningh.

Doolittle, Rev. Justus. 1966 (1865). *Social Life of the Chinese: With Some Account of Their Religious, Governmental, Educational, and Business Customs and Opinions*. 2 vols. Reprint, Taipei: Ch'eng-wen.

Doré, Henry, S. J. 1914–31. *Researches into Chinese Superstitions*. Trans. M. Kennely. Shanghai: T'usewei Printing Press. 10 vols. Reprint, Taipei, 1966.

Douglas, Mary. 1966. *Purity and Danger: An Analysis of Concepts of Pollution and Taboo*. London: Routledge and Kegan Paul.

———. 1970. *Natural Symbols: Explorations in Cosmology*. New York: Pantheon Books.

Drège, Jean-Pierre. 1981a. "Clefs des songes de Touen-houang." In Michel Soymié, ed., *Nouvelles contributions aux études de Touen-houang*, 205–49. Geneva: Librairie Droz.

———. 1981b. "Notes d'onirologie chinoise." *Bulletin de l'École Française d'Extrême-Orient* 70: 271–89.

———, ed. 1996. *De Dunhuang au Japon: Études chinoises et bouddhiques offertes à Michel Soymié*. Geneva: Librairie Droz.

Duara, Prasenjit. 1988. "Superscribing Symbols: The Myth of Guandi, Chinese God of War." *Journal of Asian Studies* 47, 4: 778–95.

Dubs, Homer H., trans. 1938. *The History of the Former Han Dynasty by Pan Ku*. 3 vols. Baltimore, Md.: Waverly Press.

Dudbridge, Glen. 1970. *The Hsi-yu chi: A Study of Antecedents to the Sixteenth-Century Chinese Novel*. Cambridge: Cambridge University Press.

———. 1978. *The Legend of Miao-shan*. Oxford Oriental Monographs no. 1. London: Ithaca Press.

———. 1995. *Religious Experience and Lay Society in T'ang China: A Reading of Tai Fu's Kuang-i Chi*. Cambridge: Cambridge University Press.

———. 1996–97. "The General of the Five Paths in Tang and Pre-Tang China." *Cahiers d'Extrême-Asie* 9: 85–98.

Dumézil, Georges. 1924. *Le festin d'immortalité: Étude de mythologie comparée indo-européenne*. Paris: Annales du Musée Guimet.

———. 1929. *Le problème des Centaures: Étude de mythologie comparée indo-européenne*. Paris: Annales du Musée Guimet.

———. 1995 (1968–73). *Mythe et épopée*. Quarto. Paris: Gallimard.

Dunstan, Helen. 1975. "The Late Ming Epidemics: A Preliminary Survey." *Ch'ing-shih wen-t'i* 3, 3: 1–59.

Duquenne, Robert. 1979. "Chūtai." In *Hōbōgirin* 5: 527–51. Paris: Adrien Maisonneuve.

———. 1983a. "Dai." In *Hōbōgirin* 6: 585–92. Paris: Adrien Maisonneuve.

———. 1983b. "Daigensui." In *Hōbōgirin* 6: 610–40. Paris: Adrien Maisonneuve.

———. 1994. "Pérégrinations entre l'Inde et le Japon: Du 'Mont en Tête d'Éléphant' et d'autres montagnes sacrées." In Fukui Fumimasa and Gérard Fussman, eds., *Bouddhisme et cultures locales: Quelques cas de réciproques adaptations*, 199–223. Paris: École Française d'Extrême-Orient.

Durand, Maurice. 1959. *Technique et panthéon des médiums vietnamiens*. Paris: École Française d'Extrême-Orient.

Durt, Hubert. 1983. "Daigenshuri." In *Hōbōgirin* 6: 599–609. Paris: Adrien Maisonneuve.

———. 1987. "The Meaning of Archeology in Ancient Buddhism: Notes on the Stūpas of Aśoka and the Worship of the 'Buddhas of the Past' According to Three Stories in the *Samguk Yusa*." In *Buddhism and Science: Commemorative Volume for the Eightieth Anniversary of the Founding of Tongguk University*, 1223–41. Seoul: Tongguk University.

Dzo Ching-chuan. 1984. "La composition du *Dongyuan Shenzhou jing*." In *Les peintures murales et les manuscrits de Dunhuang*, 79–87. Paris: Éditions de la Fondation Singer-Polignac.

Eberhard, Wolfram. 1967. *Sin and Guilt in Traditional China*. Berkeley: University of California Press.

———. 1968. *The Local Cultures of South and East China*. Trans. Alide Eberhard. Leiden: E. J. Brill.

———. 1970. *Sternkunde und Weltbild im alten China*. Taipei: Ch'eng-wen.

Eck, Diana. 1985. *Darśan: Seeing the Divine Image in India*. Chambersburg, Pa.: Anima Books.

Edsman, Carl-Martin, ed. 1967. *Studies in Shamanism*. Stockholm: Almquist and Wiksell.

Eichinger Ferro-Luzzi, G. 1981. "Abhiṣeka, the Indian Rite That Defies Definition." *Anthropos* 76: 707–42.

Eider, Matthias. 1943. "Eiserne Degen und Schwerter aus der Han-Zeit." *Monumenta Serica* 8: 394–400.

Eliade, Mircea. 1958. *Yoga: Immortality and Freedom*. New York: Pantheon Books.

———. 1974 (1964). *Shamanism: Archaic Techniques of Ecstasy*. Trans. Willard R. Trask. Princeton, N.J.: Princeton University Press.

Eliasberg, Danielle. 1984. "Quelques aspects du grand exorcisme no à Touen-houang." In Michel Soymié, ed., *Contributions aux études sur Touen-houang*, vol. 3: 237–53. Paris: École Française d'Extrême-Orient.

Elliott, Alan J. A. 1955. *Chinese Spirit Medium Cults in Singapore*. London: University of London Press.

Engelhardt, Ute. 1987. *Die klassische Tradition der Qi-Übungen: Eine Darstellung anhand des Tang-zeitlichen Textes 'Fuqi jingyi lun' von Sima Chengzhen*.

Münchener Ostasiatische Studien, 44. Wiesbaden: Franz Steiner Verlag.
———. 1989. "*Qi* for Life: Longevity in the Tang." In Livia Kohn and Sakade Yoshinobu, eds., *Taoist Meditation and Longevity Techniques*, 263–96. Michigan Monographs on Chinese Studies, 61. Ann Arbor: Center for Chinese Studies, The University of Michigan.
Epler, Dean C., Jr. 1980. "Blood-Letting in Early Chinese Medicine and Its Relation to the Origin of Acupuncture." *Bulletin of the History of Medicine* 54: 337–67.
Eskildsen, Stephen. 1998. *Asceticism in Early Taoist Religion*. Albany: State University of New York Press.
Esnoul, Anne-Marie. 1968. "La divination dans l'Inde." In André Caquot and Marcel Leibovici, eds., *La divination*, 1: 119–21. Paris, 1968.
Fairchild, William D. 1952. "Shamanism in Japan." *Folklore Studies* 21: 1–122.
Fan Hsing-chün. 1986. *Chung-kuo i-hsüeh shih-lüeh*. Peking: Chung-i ku-chi ch'u-pan-she.
Farquhar, Judith. 1986. "Knowledge and Practice in Chinese Medicine." Ph.D. dissertation, Department of Anthropology, University of Chicago.
Faure, Bernard. 1987. "Space and Place in Chinese Religious Traditions." *History of Religions* 26, 4: 337–56.
———. 1988. *La volonté d'orthodoxie dans le bouddhisme chinois*. Paris: Éditions du CNRS.
———. 1991. *The Rhetoric of Immediacy: A Cultural Critique of Chan/Zen Buddhism*. Princeton, N.J.: Princeton University Press.
———. 1996. *Visions of Power: Imagining Medieval Japanese Buddhism*. Princeton, N.J.: Princeton University Press.
———. 1998. *The Red Thread: Buddhist Approaches to Sexuality*. Princeton, N.J.: Princeton University Press.
Favret-Saada, Jeanne. 1980. *Deadly Words: Witchcraft in the Bocage*. Cambridge: Cambridge University Press.
Fazzioli, Edoardo, and Eileen Fazzioli, trans. 1989. *'Ben cao,' rimedi naturali dell'antica Cina nella raccolta dell'imperatore Xiao Zong*. Milan: Arnoldo Mondadori Editore S.P.A.
Feher, Michel, ed. 1989. *Fragments for a History of the Human Body*. 3 vols. New York: Urzone.
Feifel, E. 1944–46. "Pao-p'u Tzu." *Monumenta Serica* 6 (1941): 113–211; 9 (1944): 1–33; 11 (1946): 1–32.
Feldhaus, Anne. 1995. *Water and Womanhood: Religious Meanings of Rivers in Maharashtra*. New York: Oxford University Press.
Feng Han-yi and John K. Shryock. 1935. "The Black Magic in China Known as *Ku*." *Journal of the American Oriental Society* 55: 1–30.
Filliozat, Jean. 1934. "La médecine indienne et l'expansion bouddhique en Extrême-Orient." *Journal Asiatique* 224: 301–11.
———. 1935a. "Le Kumāratantra de Rāvaṇa." *Journal Asiatique* 226: 1–66.
———. 1935b. "La médecine indienne et la magie des Santals." *Journal Asiatique* 226: 277–84.

———. 1937. *Étude de démonologie indienne: Le Kumāratantra de Rāvaṇa et les textes parallèles indiens, tibétains, chinois, cambodgien et arabe*. Paris: Imprimerie Nationale.

———. 1948. *Fragments de textes koutchéens de médecine et de magie: Textes parallèles sanskrits et tibétains, traduction et glossaire*. Paris: Adrien Maisonneuve.

———. 1949. *La doctrine classique de la médecine indienne: Ses origines et ses parallèles grecs*. Paris: École Française d'Extrême-Orient. English trans. by Dev Raj Chanana, *The Classical Doctrine of Indian Medicine*. Delhi: Munshiram Manoharlal, 1964.

———. 1960. "Les encyclopédies de l'Inde." *Cahiers d'Histoire mondiale* 9, 3: 659–64.

———. 1963. "La mort volontaire par le feu et la tradition bouddhique indienne." *Journal Asiatique* 251: 21–51.

———. 1969. "Taoïsme et Yoga." *Journal Asiatique* 257: 41–87.

———, ed. and trans. 1973. *Un texte de la religion Kaumāra: Le Tirumurukārruppatai*. Pondichery.

———. 1991. *Religion, Philosophy, Yoga*. Delhi: Motilal Banarsidass.

Filliozat, Jean, and Louis Renou. 1985 (1947–53). *L'Inde classique: Manuel des études indiennes*. 2 vols. Paris: École Française d'Extrême-Orient.

Finckh, Elisabeth. 1978. *Foundations of Tibetan Medicine, Vol. 1*. London: Watkins.

———. 1982. "Tibetan Medicine: Theory and Practice." *American Journal of Chinese Medicine* 9, 4: 259–67.

Firth, Raymond. 1966. "Ritual Drama in Malay Spirit Mediumship." *Comparative Studies in Society and History* 9: 190–217.

Fischer, Herbert. 1961. "Heigebärden." *Antaios* 2: 318–47. Reprinted in E. Grabner, ed., *Volksmedizin: Probleme und Forschungsgeschichte*, 413–43. Darmstadt.

———. 1967. "The Use of Gesture in Preparing Medicaments and in Healing." *History of Religions* 5, 1: 18–53.

Fischer, Klaus. 1979. *Erotik und Askese in Kult und Kunst der Inder*. Köln.

Fischer, Stephen R. 1982. *The Complete Medieval Dreambook: A Multilingual, Alphabetical Somnium Danielis Collation*. Bern: Peter Lang.

Flint, Valerie I. J. 1991. *The Rise of Magic in Early Medieval Europe*. Oxford: Clarendon Press.

Flückiger, Friedrich A., and Daniel Hanbury. 1879. *Pharmacographia: A History of the Principal Drugs of Vegetable Origin Met With in Great Britain and British India*. London: Macmillan.

Fontein, Jan. 1967. *The Pilgrimage of Sudhana: A Study of the Gaṇḍavyūha Illustrations in China, Japan and Java*. The Hague and Paris: Mouton.

Forke, Alfred. 1925. *The World-Conception of the Chinese*. London: A. Probsthain.

———, trans. 1962 (1907). *Lun Heng*. Reprint, New York: Paragon Book Gallery.

Forte, Antonino. 1988. *Mingtang and Buddhist Utopias in the History of the Astronomical Clock: The Tower, Statue and Armillary Sphere Constructed by Empress Wu*. Rome/Paris: Istituto Italiano per il medio ed estremo Oriente/École Française d'Extrême-Orient.

Foucault, Michel. 1973. *The Birth of the Clinic*. New York: Vintage Books.

Foucher, Alfred. 1900–1905. *Étude sur l'iconographie bouddhique de l'Inde*. 2 vols. Paris.

———. 1905–51. *L'Art gréco-bouddhique du Gandhāra*. 4 vols. Paris: Imprimerie Nationale.

Frank, Bernard. 1958. "*Kata-imi* et *kata-tagae*: Étude sur les interdits de direction à l'époque Heian." *Bulletin de la Maison Franco-Japonaise* 5, 2–4: 1–246.

———. 1981–82. "Résumé de cours et travaux: Civilisation Japonaise." In *Annuaire du Collège de France*, 587–611. Paris: Collège de France.

———. 1986. "Vacuité et 'corps actualisé': Le problème de la présence des 'Personnages Vénérés' dans leurs images selon la tradition du bouddhisme japonais." In *Le Temps de la réflexion: Corps des dieux*, 7: 141–70. Reprinted in *Journal of the International Association of Buddhist Studies* 11, 2 (1988): 53–86.

———. 1990. "Les *deva* de la tradition bouddhique et la société japonaise: L'exemple d'Indra/Taishakuten." In Alain Forrest, Eiichi Katō, and Léon Vandermeersch, eds., *Bouddhisme et sociétés asiatiques: Clergés, sociétés et pouvoirs*, 61–74. Paris: Éditions L'Harmattan.

———. 1991. *Le panthéon bouddhique au Japon: Collections d'Emile Guimet*. Paris: Réunion des Musées Nationaux.

Franke, Herbert. 1990. "The Taoist Elements in the Buddhist Great Bear Sūtra (Pei-tou ching)." *Asia Major*, third series, 3: 58–87.

Frédéric, Louis. 1995. *Buddhism*, trans. Nissim Marshall. Paris and New York: Flammarion.

Freed, Ruth S., and Stanley A. Freed. 1993. *Ghosts: Life and Death in North India*. American Museum of Natural History, Anthropological Papers, 72. New York: American Museum of Natural History.

Frey, Emil F. "Saints in Medical History." *Clio Medica* 14, 1: 35–70.

Fu Daiwie. 1993–94. "A Contextual and Taxonomic Study of the 'Divine Marvels' and 'Strange Occurrences' in the *Mengxi bitan*." *Chinese Science* 11: 1–35.

Fujii Masao. 1977. *Bukkyō girei jiten*. Tokyo: Tōkyōdō shuppan.

Fujiki Toshirō. 1976. *Somon igaku no sekai*. Tokyo: Sekibundō.

———. 1979. *Shinkyū igaku genryū kō*. Tokyo: Sekibundō.

Fukui Kōjun. 1957. *Dōkyō no kisōteki kenkyū*. Tokyo: Tōkyōdō shuppan.

Fukunaga Katsumi. 1990. *Bukkyō igaku jiten*. Tokyo: Yūzankaku.

Furth, Charlotte. 1986. "Blood, Body and Gender: Medical Images of the Female Condition in China, 1600–1850." *Chinese Science* 7: 43–66.

———. 1987. "Concepts of Pregnancy, Childbirth, and Infancy in Ch'ing Dynasty China." *Journal of Asian Studies* 46, 1: 7–35.

———. 1988. "Androgynous Males and Deficient Females: Biology and Gender Boundaries in Sixteenth- and Seventeenth-Century China." *Late Imperial China* 9, 2: 1–31.

———. 1994. "Rethinking Van Gulik: Sexuality and Reproduction in Traditional Chinese Medicine." In Christina K. Gilmartin, Gail Herstatter, Lisa Rofel, and Tyrene White, eds., *Engendering China: Women, Culture, and the State*, 121–46. Cambridge, Mass.: Harvard University Press.

Fushimi Inari taisha, ed. 1953. *Inari taisha yuishoki shūsei*. Kyoto: Fushimi Inari taisha.

Gadon, Elinor W. 1997. "The Hindu Goddess Shasthi: Protector of Women and Children." In Joan Marfer, ed., *From the Realm of the Ancestors: An Anthology in Honor of Marija Gimbutas*, 293–308. San Diego: Paradigm Publishing.

Galavaris, George. 1970. *Bread and the Liturgy: The Symbolism of Early Christian and Byzantine Bread Stamps*. Madison: University of Wisconsin Press.

Galdston, Iago. 1963. *Man's Image in Medicine and Anthropology*. New York: Institute of Social and Historical Medicine, New York Academy of Medicine.

Gehman, Henri S. 1942 (1938). *The John Scheide Biblical Papyri: Ezekiel*. Princeton, N.J.: Princeton University Press.

George, Christopher S., ed. and trans. 1974. *The Caṇḍamahāroṣaṇa Tantra: Chapters I–VIII*. American Oriental Series, vol. 56. New Haven, Conn.: American Oriental Society.

Gernet, Jacques. 1956. *Les aspects économiques du bouddhisme dans la société chinoise du Ve au Xe siècle*. Paris: École Française d'Extrême-Orient. English translation by Franciscus Verellen, *Buddhism in Chinese Society: An Economic History from the Fifth to the Tenth Centuries*. New York: Columbia University Press, 1995.

———. 1959. "Écrit et histoire en Chine." *Journal de psychologie normale et pathologique* 56: 31–40.

———. 1960. "Les suicides par le feu chez les bouddhistes chinois du Ve au Xe siècle." In *Mélanges publiés par l'Institut des Hautes Études Chinoises*, vol. 2: 527–58. Paris: Presses Universitaires de France.

———. 1970 (1962). *Everyday Life in China on the Eve of the Mongol Invasion*. Reprint, Stanford, Calif.: Stanford University Press.

———. 1973. "Chūgoku no kagaku to uranai no jutsu." *Tōhōgaku* 45: 1–11.

———. 1994. *L'intelligence de la Chine: Le social et le mental*. Paris: Gallimard.

Getty, Alice. 1936. *Gaṇeśa: A Monograph on the Elephant-Faced God*. Oxford: Clarendon Press.

Giles, Herbert A. 1923. *The Travels of Fa-hsien*. Cambridge: Cambridge University Press.

Girardot, Norman. 1983. "Let's Get Physical: The Way of Liturgical Taoism." *History of Religions* 23, 2: 169–80.

Goepper, Roger. 1979. "Some Thoughts on the Icon in Esoteric Buddhism of East Asia." In Wolfgang Bauer, ed., *Studia Sino-Mongolica: Festschrift für Herbert Franke, Münchener Ostasiatische Studien* 25: 245–54. Wiesbaden.
———. 1983a. "An Early Work by Kōen in Cologne." *Asiatische Studien/Etudes asiatiques* 37, 2: 67–103.
———. 1983b. *Das Kultbild im Ritus des esoterischen Buddhismus in Japan.* Opladen.
Gombrich, Richard. 1966. "The Consecration of a Buddhist Image." *Journal of Asian Studies* 26: 23–36.
———. 1971. *Precept and Practice: Traditional Buddhism in the Rural Highlands of Ceylon.* Oxford: Clarendon Press.
Gonda, Jan. 1963. "The Indian Mantra." *Oriens* 16: 244–97. Reprinted in idem, *Selected Studies*, Leiden: E. J. Brill, 1975, vol. 4: 248–301.
———. 1969. *Eye and Gaze in the Veda.* Amsterdam and London: North-Holland Publishing Company.
———. 1970. *Viṣṇuism and Śivaism: A Comparison.* London: Athlone Press.
———. 1975. *Selected Studies.* 5 vols. Leiden: E. J. Brill.
Goodrich, Anne S. 1964. *The Peking Temple of the Eastern Peak: The Tung-yüeh Miao in Peking and Its Lore.* Nagoya: Monumenta Serica.
———. 1991. *Peking Paper Gods: A Look at Home Worship.* Monumenta Serica Monograph Series, 23. Nettetal: Steyler Verlag.
Gorai Shigeru, ed. 1985. *Inari shinkō no kenkyū.* Kyoto: Sanyō shinbun-sha.
Goudriaan, Teun, ed. and trans. 1965. *Kāśyapa's Book of Wisdom: A Ritual Handbook of the Vaikhānasas.* The Hague.
Goudriaan, Teun, and Sanjukta Gupta. 1981. *Hindu Tantric and Śākta Literature.* Wiesbaden: Otto Harrassowitz.
Gould-Martin, Katherine. 1978. "Ong-ia-kong: The Plague God as Modern Physician." In A. Kleiman, P. Kunstadter, E. Russel Alexander, and J. L. Gates, eds., *Culture and Healing in Chinese Society.* Cambridge, Mass.: Schenkman Publishing.
Graham, David C. 1945. "Incantations and the Exorcism of Demons Among the Ch'iang." *Journal of the West China Border Research Society*, Series A, 16: 52–56.
———. 1954. *Songs and Stories of the Ch'uan Miao.* Washington, D.C.: Smithsonian Institute.
———. 1961. *Folk Religion in Southwest China.* Washington, D.C.: Smithsonian Press.
Granet, Marcel. 1959 (1926). *Danses et légendes de la Chine ancienne.* 2 vols. Paris: Presses Universitaires de France.
———. 1953a. "Remarques sur le taoïsme ancien." In idem, *Études sociologiques sur la Chine*, 243–49. Paris: Presses Universitaires de France.
———. 1953b. "La droite et la gauche en Chine." In idem, *Études sociologiques sur la Chine*, 267–78. Paris: Presses Universitaires de France.
———. 1968 (1934). *La pensée chinoise.* Paris: Albin Michel.
Granoff, Phyllis. 1970. "Tobatsu Bishamon: Three Japanese Statues in the U.S.

and an Outline of the Rise of This Cult in East Asia." *East and West* 20: 144–68.
———. 1988. "Jain Biographies of Nāgārjuna: Notes on the Composing of a Biography in Medieval India." In Phyllis Granoff and Koichi Shinohara, eds., *Monks and Magicians: Religious Biographies in Asia*, 45–66. Oakville, Ont.: Mosaic Press.
Gupta, Sanjukta, Dirk Jan Hoens, and Teun Goudriaan. 1979. *Hindu Tantrism.* Leiden: E. J. Brill.
Gyatso, Janet. 1986. "Signs, Memory and History: A Tantric Buddhist Theory of Scriptural Transmission." *Journal of the International Association of Buddhist Studies* 9, 2: 7–35.
———, ed. 1992. *In the Mirror of Memory: Reflections on Mindfulness and Remembrance in Indian and Tibetan Buddhism.* Albany: State University of New York Press.
———. 1993. "The Logic of Legitimation in the Tibetan Treasure Tradition." *History of Religions* 33, 1: 97–134.
———. 1996. "Drawn from the Tibetan Treasury: The *gTer ma* Literature." In José Cabezón and Roger Jackson, eds., *Tibetan Literature: Studies in Genre*, 147–69. Ithaca, N.Y.: Snow Lion.
———. 1998. *Apparitions of the Self: The Secret Autobiographies of a Tibetan Visionary.* Princeton, N.J.: Princeton University Press.
———. n.d. "The Relic Text as Prophecy: The Semantic Drift of *Byang-bu* and Its Appropriation in the Treasure Tradition." Unpublished paper.
Gyss-Vermande, Caroline. 1988. "Démons et merveilles: Vision de la nature dans une peinture liturgique du XVe siècle." *Arts asiatiques* 43: 106–22.
———. 1991. "Les messagers divins et leur iconographie." *Arts asiatiques* 46: 17, 96–110.
Hakeda Yoshito S. 1972. *Kūkai: Major Works, Translated with an Account of His Life and a Study of His Thought.* New York: Columbia University Press.
Haldar, J. R. 1977. *Early Buddhist Mythology.* New Delhi: Manohar.
Hall, David G. 1990. "Marishiten: Buddhism and the Warrior Goddess." Ph.D. dissertation, University of California, Berkeley.
Hand, Wayland D. 1980. *Magical Medicine: The Folkloric Component of Medicine in the Folk Belief, Custom, and Ritual of the Peoples of Europe and America.* Berkeley: University of California Press.
Hansen, Valerie. 1990. *Changing Gods in Medieval China, 1127–1276.* Princeton, N.J.: Princeton University Press.
———. 1995a. *Negotiating Daily Life in Traditional China: How Ordinary People Used Contracts, 600–1400.* New Haven and London: Yale University Press.
———. 1995b. "Why Bury Contracts in Tombs?" *Cahiers d'Extrême-Asie* 8: 59–66.
Harper, Donald. 1982. "The *Wu Shih Erh Ping Fan*: Translation and Prolegomena." Ph.D. dissertation, University of California, Berkeley.
———. 1985. "A Chinese Demonography of the Third Century B.C." *Harvard Journal of Asiatic Studies* 45, 2: 459–98.

———. 1986. "The *Analects* Jade Candle: A Classic of T'ang Drinking Custom." *T'ang Studies* 4: 74–75.

———. 1987. "The Sexual Arts of Ancient China as Described in a Manuscript of the Second Century B.C." *Harvard Journal of Asiatic Studies* 47: 539–93.

———. 1988. "A Note on Nightmare Magic in Ancient and Medieval China." *T'ang Studies* 6: 69–76.

———. 1994. "Resurrection in Warring States Popular Religion." *Taoist Resources* 5, 2: 13–29.

———. 1996. "Spellbinding." In Donald S. Lopez, Jr., ed., *Religions of China in Practice*, 241–50. Princeton, N.J.: Princeton University Press.

———. 1998. *Early Chinese Medical Literature: The Mawangdui Medical Manuscripts*. London: Kegan Paul International.

Harper, Katherine Anne. 1989. *The Iconography of the Saptamatrikas: Seven Hindu Goddesses of Spiritual Transformation*. Lewiston, N.Y.: Edwin Mellen Press.

Harrell, Stevan. 1979. "The Concept of Soul in Chinese Folk Religion." *Journal of Asian Studies* 38, 3: 519–28.

Hartlaub, Gustav F. 1951. *Zauber des Spiegels: Geschichte und Bedeutung des Spiegels in der Kunst*. Munich: R. Piper.

Harvey, Youngsook Kim. 1980. "Possession Sickness and Women Shamans in Korea." In Nancy A. Falk and Rita M. Gross, eds., *Unspoken Worlds*, 41–52. San Francisco: Harper and Row.

Hattori Toshirō. 1975. *Ochō kizoku no byōjō shindan*. Tokyo: Yoshikawa kōbunkan.

———. 1982. *Shaka no igaku*. Reimei bukkyō sōsho. Nagoya: Reimei shobō.

Hayakawa Junzaburō, ed. 1915. *Shinkō sōsho*. Tokyo: Kokusho kankōkai.

Hayami Takusu. 1975. *Heian kizoku shakai to bukkyō*. Tokyo.

Hayashiyama Masao. 1979. *Tōyō igaku tsūshi: Kanpō, shinkyū, dōin igaku no shiteki kōsatsu*. Tokyo: Shizensha.

He P'eng-yoke. 1967. *The Astronomical Chapters of the Chin Shu*. Paris: Mouton.

Heinze, Ruth-Inge. 1988. *Trance and Healing in Southeast Asia Today*. Bangkok: White Lotus.

Henderson, Gregory, and Leon Hurvitz. 1956. "The Buddha of Seiryōji: New Finds and New Theory." *Artibus Asiae* 19: 5–55.

Henderson, John B. 1984. *The Development and Decline of Chinese Cosmology*. New York: Columbia University Press.

Herrmann-Pfandt, Adelheid. 1992–93. "Ḍākiṇīs in Indo-Tibetan Tantric Buddhism: Some Results of Recent Research." *Studies in Central and East Asian Religions* 5–6: 45–63.

Hertz, Robert. 1960 (1907). *Death and the Right Hand*. Trans. Rodney Needham. Glencoe, Ill.: The Free Press.

———. 1973 (1909). "The Preeminence of the Right Hand: A Study in Religious Poetry." In Rodney Needham, ed., *Right and Left: Essays on Dual Symbolic Classification*, 3–31. Chicago: University of Chicago Press.

Hiltebeitel, Alf, ed. 1989. *Criminal Gods and Demon Devotees: Essays on the Guardians of Popular Hinduism*. Albany: State University of New York Press.
Hirotani Yutarō, ed. 1925. *Kinsei bukkyō shūsetsu*. Tokyo: Hirotani kokusho kankōkai.
Hiruta Genshirō. 1985. *Hayariyamai to kitsune-tsuki: Kinsei shomin no iryō jijō*. Tokyo: Misuzu shobō.
Hitchcock, John T., and Rex L. Jones, eds. 1976. *Spirit Possession in the Nepal Himalayas*. New Delhi.
Ho Ping-yü, and Joseph Needham. 1959. "Elixir Poisoning in Mediaeval China." *Janus* 48: 233–51.
Hōbōgirin: Dictionnaire encyclopédique du bouddhisme d'après les sources chinoises et japonaises. vols. 1–. Paris: Adrien Maisonneuve, 1927–.
Hoeppli, R. 1954–56. "Malaria in Chinese Medicine." *Sinologica* 4: 91–101.
Hoernle, F. Rudolph, ed. and trans. 1893–1912. *The Bower Manuscript*. Calcutta: Superintendant Government Printing.
———. 1907. *Studies in the Medicine of Ancient India. Part I: Osteology, or the Bones of the Human Body*. Oxford: Clarendon Press.
———. 1916. *Manuscript Remains of Buddhist Literature Found in Eastern Turkestan*. Oxford: Clarendon Press. Reprint, Amsterdam: St. Leonard, 1970.
Hooykaas, C. 1966a. *Āgama-Tīrtha: Five Studies on Hindu-Balinese Religion*. Verhandelingen der Koninklijke Nederlandse Akademie van Wetenschappen, afd. Letterkunde, vol. 70, 4. Amsterdam and London: North-Holland Publishing Company.
———. 1966b. *Surya-sevana: The Way to God of a Balinese Siva Priest*. Verhandelingen der koninklijke Nederlandse Akademie van Wetenschappen, afd. Letterkunde, vol. 72, 3. Amsterdam and London: North-Holland Publishing Company.
———. 1983–85. "Homa in India and Bali." In Michel Strickmann, ed., *Tantric and Taoist Studies in Honour of R. A. Stein*, vol. 2: 512–91. Brussels: Institut Belge des Hautes Études Chinoises.
Hori, Ichirō. 1955. *Wagakuni minkan shinkō shi no kenkyū*. Tokyo: Sōgensha.
———. 1962. "Self-Mummified Buddhas in Japan: An Aspect of the Shugendō ('Mountain Asceticism') Sect." *History of Religions* 1: 222–42.
———. 1971. *Nihon no shāmanisumu*. Kōdansha gendai shinsho. Tokyo: Kōdansha.
Hosokawa Ryōichi. 1993. *Itsudatsu no Nihon chūsei: Kyōki, tōsaku, ma no sekai*. Tokyo: JICC shuppankyoku.
Hou Chin-lang. 1975. *Monnaies d'offrande et la notion de trésorerie dans la religion chinoise*. Mémoires de l'Institut des Hautes Études Chinoises, vol. 1. Paris: Collège de France, Institut des Hautes Études Chinoises.
———. 1979a. "The Baleful Stars in Chinese Belief." In Holmes Welch and Anna K. Seidel, eds., *Facets of Taoism*. New Haven, Conn.: Yale University Press.

———. 1979b. "Physiognomonie d'après le teint sous la dynastie des T'ang (une étude sur le manuscrit P. 3390)." In Michel Soymié, ed., *Contributions aux études de Touen-houang*, 55–71. Geneva and Paris: Librairie Droz.

———. 1984. "La cérémonie du Yin-sha-fo d'après les manuscrits de Touen-houang." In Michel Soymié, ed., *Contributions aux études sur Touen-houang*. Paris: École Française d'Extrême-Orient.

Howard, Angela. 1983. "Planet Worship: Some Evidence, Mainly Textual, in Chinese Esoteric Buddhism." *Asiatische Studien/Études asiatiques* 32: 104–19.

Hsia, Emil C. H., Ilza Veith, and Robert H. Geertsma, trans. 1986. *The Essentials of Medicine in Ancient China and Japan: Yasuyori Tamba's 'Ishimpo,' Books 1, 2, 26, 27, and 28*. Leiden: E. J. Brill.

Hsu, Francis L. K. 1952. *Religion, Science and Human Crises*. London: Routledge and Kegan Paul.

Hu Shiu-ying. 1980. *An Enumeration of Chinese Materia Medica*. Hong Kong: Chinese University of Hong Kong.

Huang Sheng-chang. 1996. "Chieh-k'ai kao-ti tz'e chu mi." *Ku-kung wen-wu yüeh-k'an* 11: 124–34.

Huard, Pierre, and Ming Wong. 1968. *Chinese Medicine*. New York: McGraw-Hill.

———. 1971. *Soins et techniques du corps en Chine, au Japon, et en Inde*. Paris: Berg International.

Hubert, Henri, and Marcel Mauss. 1981 (1898). *Sacrifice: Its Nature and Function*. Midway Reprint, Chicago: University of Chicago Press.

Huc, Evariste-Régis. 1928. *Travels in Tartary, Thibet and China, 1844–1849*. 2 vols. London: Routledge and Kegan Paul.

Hulsewé, A. F. P. 1955. *Remnants of Han Law, Vol. 1*. Leiden: E. J. Brill.

———. 1965. "Texts in Tombs." *Asiatische Studien* 18–19: 78–89.

———. 1978. "The Chin Documents Discovered in Hupei in 1975." *T'oung Pao* 64: 175–217, 338.

———. 1985. *Remnants of Ch'in Law: An Annotated Translation of the Ch'in Legal and Administrative Rules of the Third Century B.C. Discovered in the Yün-meng Prefecture, Hu-pei Province, in 1975*. Leiden: E. J. Brill.

Hume, Edward H. 1940. *The Chinese Way in Medicine*. Baltimore, Md.: Johns Hopkins Press.

Hume, Robert Ernest. 1921. *The Thirteen Principal Upanishads*. Oxford: Oxford University Press.

Huntington, Richard, and Peter Metcalf. 1979. *Celebrations of Death: The Anthropology of Mortuary Ritual*. Cambridge: Cambridge University Press.

Hymes, Robert P. 1987. "Not Quite Gentlemen? Doctors in Sung and Yuan." *Chinese Science* 8: 9–76.

Idel, Moshe. 1990. *Golem: Jewish Magical and Mystical Traditions on the Artificial Anthropoid*. Albany, N.Y.: State University of New York Press.

Ilyŏn. 1972. *Samguk Yusa: Legends and History of the Three Kingdoms of Ancient Korea*. Trans. Ha Tae-Hung and Grafton K. Mintz. Seoul: Yonsei University Press.

Imamura Michio. 1983. *Nihon no minkan iryō*. Nihon minzokugaku kenkyū sōsho. Tokyo: Kōbundō.
Imamura Yoshio, ed. 1980–81. *Yuyō zasso* [*Yu-yang tsa-tsu*]. 5 vols. Tokyo: Heibonsha.
Ishida Hidemi. 1989a. "Body and Mind: The Chinese Perspective." In Livia Kohn and Sakade Yoshinobu, eds. 1989. *Taoist Meditation and Longevity Techniques*, 41–71. Michigan Monographs on Chinese Studies, 61. Ann Arbor: Center for Chinese Studies, The University of Michigan.
———. 1989b. "Son Shibaku no seishin shippei kan." In *Senkin hō kenkyū shiryō shū*, 68–87. *Tōyō igaku zenpon sōsho* 15. Osaka: Oriento shuppan.
Ishida Hisatoyo. 1987. *Esoteric Buddhist Painting*. Trans. Dale Saunders. New York and Tokyo: Kōdansha.
Ishidoya Tsutomu. 1933. *Chinesische Drogen*. Tokyo: Keijo University.
Ishiguro Takatoshi. 1959. *Nihon no tsukimono*. Tokyo: Miraisha.
Ishihara Akira and Howard S. Levy. 1968. *The Tao of Sex*. New York: Harper.
Iyanaga Nobumi. 1983. "Daijizaiten (Maheśvara)." In *Hōbōgirin* 6: 713–65. Paris: Adrien Maisonneuve.
———. 1983–85. "Récits de la soumission de Maheśvara par Trailokyavijaya—d'après les sources chinoises et japonaises." In Michel Strickmann, ed., *Tantric and Taoist Studies in Honour of R. A. Stein*, vol. 3: 633–745. Brussels: Institut Belge des Hautes Études Chinoises.
———. 1994. "Daikoku-ten." In *Hōbōgirin* 7: 839–920. Paris: Adrien Maisonneuve.
———. 1996–97. "Le Roi Māra du Sixième Ciel et le mythe médiéval de la création du Japon." *Cahiers d'Extrême-Asie* 9: 323–96.
———. 1999. "Ḍākiṇī et l'Empereur: Mystique bouddhique de la royauté dans le Japon médiéval." *Versus* 83/84: 40–111.
Jaggi, O. P. 1973. *Yogic and Tantric Medicine*. History of Science and Technology in India, vol. 5. Delhi: Atma Ram and Sons.
Jan Yün-hua. 1977. "The Power of Recitation: An Unstudied Aspect of Chinese Buddhism." *Studi Storico Religiosi* 1–2: 289–99.
Jannett, Ann Bowman. 1987. *Epidemics and Mortality in Early Modern Japan*. Princeton, N.J.: Princeton University Press.
Jao Tsung-i. 1982. *Yün-meng Shui-hu-ti Ch'in chien*. Hong Kong.
Jao Tsung-i and Tseng Hsien-t'ung. 1962. *Yün-meng Ch'in chien jih shu yen-chiu*. Hong Kong: Chinese University Press.
Johnson, David. 1985. "The City God Cults of T'ang and Sung China." *Harvard Journal of Asiatic Studies* 45: 363–457.
Johnson, David, Andrew J. Nathan, and Evelyn S. Rawski, eds. 1985. *Popular Culture in Late Imperial China*. Berkeley: University of California Press.
Jordan, David K. 1972. *Gods, Ghosts, and Ancestors*. Berkeley: University of California Press.
Jordan, David K., and Daniel L. Overmyer. 1986. *The Flying Phoenix: Aspects of Chinese Sectarianism in Taiwan*. Princeton, N.J.: Princeton University Press.
Kabanoff, Alexander. 1994. "The Kangi-ten (Gaṇapati) Cult in Medieval Japa-

nese Mikkyō." In Ian Astley, ed., *Esoteric Buddhism in Japan*, 99–126. SBS Monographs, 1. Copenhagen and Aarhus: The Seminar for Buddhist Studies.

Kakar, Sudhir. 1982. *Shamans, Mystics and Doctors: A Psychological Inquiry into India and Its Healing Traditions*. New York: Alfred A. Knopf.

Kalinowski, Marc. 1983–85. "La transmission du dispositif des neuf palais sous les Six Dynasties." In Michel Strickmann, ed., *Tantric and Taoist Studies in Honour of R. A. Stein*, vol. 3: 773–811. Brussels: Institut Belge des Hautes Études Chinoises.

———. 1986. "Les traités de Shuihudi et l'hémérologie chinoise à la fin des Royaumes Combattants." *T'oung Pao* 72: 175–228.

———. 1989–90. "La littérature divinatoire dans le *Daozang*." *Cahiers d'Extrême-Asie* 5: 85–114.

———. 1991. *Cosmologie et divination dans la Chine ancienne: Le Compendium des Cinq Agents (Wuxing dayi, VIe siècle)*. Paris: École Française d'Extrême-Orient.

———. 1996. "Mythe, cosmogonie et théogonie dans la Chine ancienne." *L'Homme* 137, 1: 41–60.

Kaltenmark, Max. 1948. "Le dompteur des flots." *Han-hiue* 3, 1–2: 1–112.

———. 1960. "*Ling-pao*: Note sur un terme du taoïsme religieux." In *Mélanges publiés par l'Institut des Hautes Études Chinoises*, vol. 2: 559–88. Paris: Presses Universitaires de France.

———. 1974. "Miroirs magiques." In *Mélanges de sinologie offerts à M. Paul Demiéville*, vol. 2: 151–66. Paris: Institut des Hautes Études Chinoises.

———. 1982. "Quelques remarques sur le T'ai-chang ling-pao wou-fou siu." *Zinbun, Memoirs of the Research Institute for Humanistic Studies* 18: 1–10.

———. 1985. "La légende de la ville immergée en Chine." *Cahiers d'Extrême-Asie* 1: 1–10.

———, trans. 1987 (1953). *Le 'Lie Sien Tchouan': Biographies légendaires des Immortels taoïstes de l'antiquité*. Paris: Collège de France, Institut des Hautes Études Chinoises.

Kamata Shigeo. 1986. *Chūgoku bukkyō girei*. Tokyo: Daizō shuppan.

Kamens, Edward. *The Three Jewels: A Study and Translation of Minamoto Tamenori's Sanbōe*. Ann Arbor: Center for Japanese Studies, The University of Michigan.

Kanō Yoshimitsu. 1987. *Chūgoku igaku no tanjō*. Tokyo: Tōkyō daigaku.

Kapferer, Bruce. 1983. *A Celebration of Demons: Exorcism and the Aesthetics of Healing in Sri Lanka*. Bloomington: Indiana University Press.

Karlgren, Bernard, trans. 1950. *The Book of Odes*. Stockholm: The Museum of Far Eastern Antiquities.

Katz, Paul R. 1987. "Demons or Deities? The *Wangye* of Taiwan." *Asian Folklore Studies* 46, 2: 197–215.

———. 1995. *Demon Hordes and Burning Boats: The Cult of Marshal Wen in Late Imperial Chekiang*. Albany: State University of New York Press.

Keegan, Paul. 1988. "The *Huang-ti nei-ching*: The Structure of the Compilation, the Significance of the Structure." Ph.D. dissertation. Ann Arbor, Michigan.

Kelsey, Michael. 1981. "The Raging Deity in Japanese Mythology." *Asian Folklore Studies* 40, 2: 213–36.

Kennedy, Alison. 1982. "Ecce Bufo: The Toad in Nature and in Olmec Iconography." *Current Anthropology* 23, 3: 273–90.

Keupers, John. 1977. "A Description of the Fa-ch'ang Ritual as Practiced by the Lü-Shan Taoists of Northern Taiwan." In Michael Saso and David W. Chappell, eds., *Buddhist and Taoist Studies, I*. Honolulu: University of Hawai'i Press.

Kiang Chao-yuan. 1937. *Le voyage dans la Chine ancienne, considéré principalement sous son aspect magique et religieux*. Translation by Fan Jen. Shanghai. Reprint, Vientiane: Editions Vithagna, 1975.

Kieschnick, John. 1997. *The Eminent Monk: Buddhist Ideals in Medieval Chinese Hagiography*. Kuroda Institute Series in East Asian Buddhism, 10. Honolulu: University of Hawai'i Press.

Kirfel, Willibald. 1920. *Die Kosmographie der Inder nach den Quellen dargestellt*. Bonn and Leipzig: C. Schroeder.

———. 1949. *Der Rosenkrantz, Ursprung und Ausbreitung*. Walldorf-Hessen: Verlag für Orientkunde.

———. 1951. *Die Fünf Elemente, inbesondere Wasser und Feuer*. Walldorf-Hessen: Verlag für Orientkunde.

Kita Teikichi. 1975. *Tsukimono*. Ed. Yamada Norio. Tokyo: Hōbunkan.

———. 1976. *Fukujin*. Ed. Yamada Norio. Tokyo: Hōbunkan.

Kleeman, Terry F. 1984. "Land Contracts and Related Documents." In *Chūgoku no shūkyō: shisō to kagaku*, 1–34. Tokyo: Kokusho kankōkai.

———, trans. 1994. *A God's Own Tale: 'The Book of Transformations' of Wenchang, the Divine Lord of Zitong*. Albany: State University of New York Press.

———. 1996. "The Lives and Teachings of the Divine Lord of Zitong." In Donald S. Lopez, Jr., ed., *Religions of China in Practice*, 64–73. Princeton, N.J.: Princeton University Press.

Kleinman, Arthur. 1980. *Patients and Healers in the Context of Culture: An Exploration of the Borderlands Between Anthropology, Medicine and Psychiatry*. Berkeley: University of California Press.

———. 1986. *Social Origins of Distress and Disease: Depression, Neurasthenia and Pain in Modern China*. New Haven, Conn.: Yale University Press.

Kleinmann, Arthur, P. Kunstadter, E. Russel Alexander, and J. L. Gates, eds. 1978. *Culture and Healing in Chinese Society: Anthropological, Psychiatric, and Public Health Studies*. Cambridge, Mass.: Schenkman Publishing.

Kleinman, Arthur, and Lin Tsung-yi, eds. 1981. *Normal and Abnormal Behavior in Chinese Culture*. Boston: Kluwer.

Knipe, David M. 1972. "One Fire, Three Fires, Five Fires: Vedic Symbols in Transformation." *History of Religions* 12: 28–41.

Knox, Ronald A. 1950. *Enthusiasm*. New York: Oxford University Press.

Kobayashi Taichirō. 1938. "Shina ni okeru Karitei: Sono shinkō to sono zuzō ni tsuite." *Shina bukkyō shigaku* 2, 3: 1–48.

———. 1940. "Tanabata to Makora." *Shina bukkyō shigaku* 4, 3: 1–34; 4, 4: 30–53.
———. 1974. *Kobayashi Taichirō chosakushū*, vol. 7: *Shūkyō geijutsu-ron hen*, I. Tokyo: Tankōsha.
Kohn, Livia. 1988. "Medicine and Immortality in T'ang China." *Journal of the American Oriental Society* 108, 3: 465–69.
———. 1989a. "Guarding the One: Concentrative Meditation in Taoism." In Livia Kohn and Sakade Yoshinobu, eds., *Taoist Meditation and Longevity Techniques*, 125–58. Michigan Monographs on Chinese Studies, 61. Ann Arbor: Center for Chinese Studies, The University of Michigan.
———. 1989b. "Taoist Insight Meditation: The Tang Practice of *Neiguan*." In Livia Kohn and Sakade Yoshinobu, eds., *Taoist Meditation and Longevity Techniques*, 193–224. Michigan Monographs on Chinese Studies, 61. Ann Arbor: Center for Chinese Studies, The University of Michigan.
Kohn, Livia, and Sakade Yoshinobu, eds. 1989. *Taoist Meditation and Longevity Techniques*. Michigan Monographs on Chinese Studies, 61. Ann Arbor: Center for Chinese Studies, The University of Michigan.
Komatsu Kazuhiko. 1982. *Hyōrei shinkō ron*. Tokyo: Dentō to gendaisha.
Kondō Yoshihiro. 1978. *Inari shinkō*. Hanawa shinsho 52. Tokyo: Hanawa shobō.
Kovacks, Jürgen, and Paul U. Unschuld, trans. 1999. *Essential Subtleties on the Silver Sea: The 'Yin-hai jing-wei': A Chinese Classic on Opthalmology*. Berkeley: University of California.
Kramrisch, Stella. 1981. *Manifestations of Shiva*. Philadelphia: Philadelphia Museum of Art.
Kroll, Paul W. 1996. "Body Gods and Inner Vision: The Scripture of the Yellow Court." In Donald S. Lopez, Jr., ed., *Religions of China in Practice*, 149–55. Princeton, N.J.: Princeton University Press.
Kubo Noritada. 1961. *Kōshin shinkō no kenkyū*. Tokyo: Nihon gakujutsu shinkōkai.
Kuhn, Philip A. 1991. *Soul-Stealers: The Chinese Sorcery Scare of 1768*. Cambridge, Mass.: Harvard University Press.
Kuo Li-ch'eng. 1967. *Hang-shen yen-chiu*. Taipei: Kuo-li pien-i-kuan Chung-huan ts'ung-shu wei-yüan-hui.
Kuo Li-ying. 1994a. *Confession et contrition dans le bouddhisme chinois du Ve au Xe siècle*. Paris: École Française d'Extrême-Orient.
———. 1994b. "Divination, jeux de hasard et purification dans le bouddhisme chinois: Autour d'un *sūtra* apocryphe chinois, le *Zhanchajing*." In Fukui Fumimasa and Gérard Fussman, eds., *Bouddhisme et cultures locales: Quelques cas de réciproques adaptations*, 145–63. Paris: École Française d'Extrême-Orient.
———. Forthcoming. "Dakini." In *Hōbōgirin*, vol. 8. Paris: Adrien Maisonneuve.
Kuriyama Shigehisa. 1986. "Varieties of Haptic Experience: A Comparative

Study of Greek and Chinese Pulse Diagnosis." Ph.D. dissertation. Harvard University.
———. 1994. "The Imagination of Winds and the Development of the Chinese Conception of the Body." In Angela Zito and Tani E. Barlow, eds., *Body, Subject and Power in China*, 23–41. Chicago: University of Chicago Press.
Kuroda Toshio. 1980. "Shintō in the History of Japanese Religion." Trans. James C. Dobbins and Suzanne Gay. *Journal of Japanese Studies* 7, 1: 1–21.
———. 1989. "Historical Consciousness and *Hon-jaku* Philosophy in the Medieval Period on Mount Hiei." Trans. Allan Grapard. In George Tanabe and Willa Tanabe, eds., *The Lotus Sūtra in Japanese Culture*, 143–58. Honolulu: University of Hawai'i Press.
———. 1996. "The World of Spirit Pacification: Issues of State and Religion." Trans. Allan Grapard. *Japanese Journal of Religious Studies* 23, 3–4: 321–51.
Kushida Ryōkō. 1973 (1964). *Shingon mikkyō seiritsu katei no kenkyū*. Tokyo: Sankibō.
Kvaerne, Per. 1975. "On the Concept of *Sahaja* in Indian Buddhist Tantric Literature." *Temenos* 11: 88–135.
LaFleur, William. 1989. "Hungry Ghosts and Hungry People: Somaticity and Rationality in Medieval Japan." In Michel Feher, ed., *Fragments for a History of the Human Body*, Part 1: 270–303. New York: Urzone.
Lagerwey, John. 1981. *Wu-shang pi-yao, somme taoïste du Ve siècle*. Paris: École Française d'Extrême-Orient.
———. 1987. "Les têtes des démons tombent par milliers: Le Fachang, rituel exorciste du nord de Taiwan." *L'Homme* 27, 101: 101–16.
———. 1988. *Taoist Ritual in Chinese Society and History*. New York: Macmillan.
———. 1992. "La ritualité chinoise." *Bulletin de l'École Française d'Extrême-Orient* 79, 2: 359–73.
Lai, Whalen W. 1987. "The Earliest Folk Buddhist Religion in China: *T'i-wei Po-li Ching* and Its Historical Significance." In David W. Chappell, ed., *Buddhist and Taoist Practice in Medieval Chinese Society: Buddhist and Taoist Studies II*, 11–35. Honolulu: University of Hawai'i Press.
———. 1990. "The *Chan-ch'a ching*: Religion and Magic in Medieval China." In Robert E. Buswell, Jr., ed., *Chinese Buddhist Apocrypha*, 175–206. Honolulu: University of Hawai'i Press.
Lalou, Marcelle. 1930. *Iconographie des étoffes peintes (paṭa) dans le Mañjuçrîmûlakalpa*. Paris: Paul Geuthner.
———. 1932. "Un traité de magie bouddhique." In *Études d'Orientalisme publiées par le Musée Guimet à la mémoire de Raymonde Linossier*, 303–22. Paris: Librairie Ernest Leroux.
———. 1936. "*Mañjuśrīmūlakalpa* et *Tārāmūlakalpa*." *Harvard Journal of Asiatic Studies* 1: 327–59.
———. 1938. "Le culte des Nāga et la thérapeutique." *Journal Asiatique* 226: 1–19.

———. 1946. *Mythologie indienne et peintures de Haute-Asie*. Ascona: Artibus Asiae.

———. 1955. "A la recherche du Vidhyādharapiṭaka: Le cycle du *Subāhupari-pṛcchā-tantra*." In *Mélanges Yamaguchi Susumu: Indogaku bukkyōgaku ronsō*, 68–72. Kyoto.

———. 1965. "Préliminaires d'une étude des Gaṇacakra." In Kōyasan daigaku, ed., *Mikkyōgaku mikkyōshi ronbunshū*, 41–46. Kyoto: Naigai Press.

Lamotte, Étienne, trans. 1949–76. *Le Traité de la grande vertu de sagesse de Nāgārjuna*. 4 vols. Louvain: Institut Orientaliste.

———. 1958. *Histoire du bouddhisme indien des origines à l'ère Śaka*. Louvain: Institut Orientaliste.

———. 1966. "Vajrapāṇi en Inde." In *Mélanges de sinologie offerts à M. Paul Demiéville*, vol. 1: 113–59. Paris: Presses Universitaires de France.

———, trans. 1976 (1962). *L'enseignement de Vimalakīrti (Vimalakīrti-nirdeśa)*. English translation by Sara Boin, *The Teaching of Vimalakīrti*. London: Pali Text Society.

Lampe, W. H. 1951. *The Seal Spirit: A Study in the Doctrine of Baptism and Confirmation in the New Testament and the Fathers*. London: Society for Promoting Christian Knowledge.

Laqueur, Thomas. 1990. *Making Sex: Body and Gender from the Greeks to Freud*. Cambridge, Mass.: Harvard University Press.

Laufer, Berthold. 1978. *Sino-Iranica: Chinese Contributions to the History of Civilization in Ancient Iran*. Chicago: Field Museum of National History. Reprint, Taipei: Ch'eng-wen Publishing.

La Vallée Poussin, Louis de. 1898. *Bouddhisme: Études et matériaux*. London: E. van Goethem.

———, trans. 1923–31. *L'Abhidharmakośa de Vasubandhu*. 6 vols. Paris: Paul Geuthner. English translation by Leo Pruden, *Abhidharmakośabhāṣyam*. 4 vols. Berkeley: Asian Humanities Press, 1988–91.

Law, Bimala Chun. 1936. *The Buddhist Conception of Spirits*. London: Luzac.

———. 1973. *Heaven and Hell in Buddhist Perspective*. Varanasi: Bhartiya Publishing.

Law, Jane Marie. 1993. "Of Plagues and Puppets: On the Significance of the Name Hyakudayū in Japanese Religions." *Transactions of the Asiatic Society of Japan*, fourth series, 8: 108–32.

———. 1995. "The Puppet as Body Substitute: *Ningyō* in the Japanese *Shiki Sanbasō* Performance." In Jane Marie Law, ed., *Religious Reflections on the Human Body*. Bloomington: Indiana University Press.

———. 1997. *Puppets of Nostalgia*. Princeton, N.J.: Princeton University Press.

Lawson, H. D. 1935. *Social Pathology in China*. Ch'eng Wen Reprint Series, No. 295. Taipei: Ch'eng Wen Publishing, 1974.

Le Blanc, Charles. 1985. *Huai Nan Tzu: Philosophical Synthesis in Early Han Thought*. Hong Kong: Hong Kong University Press.

Le Blanc, Charles, and Rémy Mathieu, eds. 1992. *Mythes et philosophies à*

l'aube de la Chine impériale: Études sur le 'Huainan zi.' Montreal: Presses de l'Université de Montréal.
Ledderose, Lothar. 1984. "Some Taoist Elements in the Calligraphy of the Six Dynasties." *T'oung Pao* 70, 4–5: 246–78.
Lee, T'ao. 1943. "Medical Ethics in Ancient China." *Bulletin of History of Medicine* 13: 268–77.
———. 1953. "Achievements of Chinese Medicine in the Sui (589–617 A.D.) and T'ang (618–907 A.D.) Dynasties." *Chinese Medical Journal* 71: 301–20.
Legge, James. 1886. *A Record of Buddhist Kingdoms: An Account by the Chinese Monk Fa-Hsien of His Travels in India and Ceylon (399 A.D. to 414 A.D.) in Search of the Buddhist Books of Discipline.* Reprint, Oxford: Clarendon Press, 1965.
Leiris, Michel. 1989 (1958). *La possession et ses aspects théâtraux chez les Ethiopiens de Gondar.* Paris: Fata Morgana.
Lemoine, Jacques. 1978. "Asie orientale." In *Ethnologie régionale,* 2: 808–14. Encyclopédie de la Pléiade. Paris: Gallimard.
———. 1982. *Yao Ceremonial Paintings.* Bangkok: White Lotus.
———. 1992. "Techniques de l'action directe: Variations miao-yao dans l'intervention chamanique." *Bulletin de l'École Française d'Extrême-Orient* 79, 2: 149–82.
Leslie, Charles, ed. 1976. *Asian Medical Systems: A Comparative Study.* Berkeley: University of California Press.
Lessing, Ferdinand D. 1976. *Ritual and Symbol: Collected Essays on Lamaism and Chinese Symbolism.* Taipei.
Leung, Angela K. "Organized Medicine in Ming-Qing China: State and Private Medical Institutions in the Lower Yangze Region." *Late Imperial China* 8, 1: 134–66.
Lévi, Jean. 1983. "L'abstinence des cérérales chez les taoïstes." *Études Chinoises* 1: 3–47.
———. 1984. "Le renard, la morte et la courtisane dans la Chine classique." *Études mongoles et sibériennes* 15, *Le renard: Tours, détours et retours,* 111–39.
———. 1986a. "Les fonctionnaires et le divin." *Cahiers d'Extrême-Asie* 2: 81–110.
———. 1986b. "Vers des céréales et dieux du corps dans le taoïsme." *Le temps de la réflexion* 7: 99–119.
———. 1987. "Les fonctions religieuses de la bureaucratie céleste." *L'Homme* 101: 35–57.
———. 1989. *Les fonctionnaires divins: Politique, despotisme et mystique en Chine ancienne.* Paris: Seuil.
Lévi, Sylvain. 1915. "Le catalogue géographique des Yakṣa dans la Mahāmāyūrī." *Journal Asiatique* 4: 19–138.
———. 1966 (1896). *La doctrine du sacrifice dans les Brāhmaṇas.* Paris: Presses Universitaires de France.
Lévi, Sylvain, and Édouard Chavannes. 1915. "Quelques titres énigmatiques

dans la hiérarchie ecclésiastique du bouddhisme indien." *Journal Asiatique* 5: 193–223; 6: 307–10.
———. 1916. "Les seize Arhat protecteurs de la Loi." *Journal Asiatique* 8: 5–48, 189–304.
Lévy, André. 1971. *Études sur le conte et le roman chinois*. Paris: Institut des Hautes Études Chinoises.
———. 1980. "Le moine et la courtisane: Formation et évolution d'un thème littéraire d'origine song." *Études Song*, série II: *Civilisation*, 2: 139–58. Paris: École des Hautes Études en Sciences Sociales.
Levy, Howard S. 1956. "Yellow Turban Religion and Rebellion at the End of the Han." *Journal of the American Oriental Society* 76: 214–27.
Lévy, Paul. 1957. *Buddhism, a "Mystery Religion"?* London. Reprint, New York: Schocken Books, 1968.
Lewis, I. M. 1986. *Religion in Context: Cults and Charisma*. Cambridge: Cambridge University Press.
———. 1989 (1971). *Ecstatic Religion: An Anthropological Study of Spirit Possession and Shamanism*. London and New York: Routledge.
Li Hui-lin. 1978. "Hallucinogenic Plants in Chinese Herbals." *Journal of Psychedelic Drugs* 10, 1: 17–26.
———, trans. 1979. *Nan-fang ts'ao-mu chuang: A Fourth-Century Flora of Southeast Asia*. Hong Kong: Chinese University of Hong Kong.
Li Shih-chen, comp. 1973. *Chinese Medicinal Herbs*. Trans. F. Porter Smith and G. A. Stuart. San Francisco: Georgetown Press.
Li Wei-tsu. 1948. "On the Cult of the Four Sacred Animals in the Neighbourhood of Peking." *Folklore Studies* 7: 1–94.
Lin Fu-shih. 1995. "Religious Taoism and Dreams: An Analysis of the Dream-Data Collected in the *Yün-chi ch'i-ch'ien*." *Cahiers d'Extrême-Asie* 8: 95–112.
Lin Li-kouang. 1949. *L'Aide-mémoire de la Vraie Loi (Saddharma-smṛtyupasthāna-sūtra): Recherches sur un sūtra développé du Petit Véhicule*. Musée Guimet, Bibliothèque d'Études, vol. 54. Paris: Adrien Maisonneuve.
Liu Chih-wan. 1974. *Essays on Chinese Folk Beliefs and Folk Cults*. Monograph Series, 22. Taipei: Institute of Sinology, Academia Sinica.
———. 1984. *Chūgoku dōkyō no matsuri to shinkō*. 2 vols. Tokyo: Eifusha.
Liu Ts'un-yan. 1971. "The Taoists' Knowledge of Tuberculosis in the Twelfth Century." *T'oung Pao* 57, 5: 285–301.
Lock, Margaret. 1980. *East Asian Medicine in Urban Japan*. Berkeley: University of California Press.
Loewe, Michael. 1979. *Ways to Paradise: The Chinese Quest for Immortality*. London: Allen and Unwin.
Loomis, C. Grant. 1940. "Hagiological Healing." *Bulletin of the History of Medicine* 8, 1: 636–42.
Lopez, Donald S., Jr. 1990. "Inscribing the Bodhisattva's Speech: On the *Heart Sūtra*'s Mantra." *History of Religions* 29, 4: 351–72.
———, ed. 1996. *Religions of China in Practice*. Princeton, N.J.: Princeton University Press.

Lowell, Percival. 1894. *Occult Japan, or the Way of the Gods: An Esoteric Study of Japanese Personality and Possession*. Boston.

Luk, Charles (Lu K'uan-yü). 1964. *The Secrets of Chinese Meditation: Self-Cultivation by Mind Control as Taught in the Ch'an, Mahāyāna and Taoist Schools in China*. London: Rider.

Ma Chi-hsing. 1990. *Chung i wen-hsien hsüeh*. Shanghai: Shang-hai k'e-hsüeh chi-shu ch'u-pan-she.

Macdonald, Alexander W. 1967. *Matériaux pour l'étude de la littérature populaire tibétaine*. Paris: Presses Universitaires de France.

———. 1975. *Essays on the Ethnography of Nepal and South Asia*. Kathmandu: Ratna Pustak Bhandar.

———, ed. 1987. "Rituels himalayens." Special issue of *L'Ethnographie* 83: 100–121.

Macdonald, Ariane, ed. and trans. 1962. *Le Maṇḍala du Mañjuśrīmūlakalpa*. Paris: Adrien Maisonneuve.

Macé, François. 1994. "La maladie, les kami et les bouddhas au VIIe siècle à travers la dernière maladie de l'empereur Tenmu." In G. Siary and H. Benyamou, eds., *Médecine et société au Japon*, 45–56. Paris: L'Harmattan.

———. 1997. "Le cortège fantôme: Les funerailles et la déification de Toyotomi Hideyoshi." *Cahiers d'Extrême-Asie* 9: 441–62.

Macé, Mieko. 1985. "La médecine à l'époque de Heian: Son organisation, son contenu théorique et ses rapports avec les courants de pensée contemporains." Ph.D. dissertation, Université de Paris–VII.

———. 1992. "Évolution de la médecine japonaise face au modèle chinois des origines jusqu'au milieu du XVIIIe siècle: Autonomie par la synthèse." *Cipango* 1: 111–60.

———. 1994. "La médecine dans la civilisation de l'époque de Heian." In G. Siary and H. Benyamou, eds., *Médecine et société au Japon*, 57–83, Paris: L'Harmattan.

MacIntyre, John. 1886. "Roadside Religion in Manchuria." *Journal of the North China Branch of the Royal Asiatic Society* 21, 1: 43–66.

Mackay, George. 1895. *From Far Formosa: The Island, Its People and Missions*. New York: Fleming Revell.

Mair, Victor. 1983. *Tun-huang Popular Narratives*. Cambridge: Cambridge University Press.

———. 1988. *Painting and Performance: Chinese Picture Recitation and Its Indian Genesis*. Honolulu: University of Hawai'i Press.

———. 1989. *T'ang Transformation Texts*. Cambridge, Mass.: Harvard University Press.

Makita Tairyō. 1976. *Gikyō kenkyū*. Kyoto: Jinbun kagaku kenkyūjo.

———. 1981–84. *Chūgoku bukkyō-shi kenkyū*. 2 vols. Tokyo: Daitō shuppansha.

Makita Tairyō and Fukui Fumimasa, eds. 1984. *Tonkō to chūgoku bukkyō*. Kōza Tonkō 7. Tokyo: Daitō shuppansha.

Malamoud, Charles. 1989. *Cuire le monde: Rite et pensée dans l'Inde ancienne*. Paris: Éditions La Découverte.

Malet, Christian. 1982. "Les relations thérapeute-malade dans la société chinoise de Taiwan." *Bulletin de l'Ethnomédecine* 17: 3–38.

Mark, Lindy Li. 1979. "Orthography Riddles, Divination, and Word Magic: An Exploration in Folklore and Culture." In Sarah Allan and Alvin P. Cohen, eds., *Legend, Lore, and Religion in China: Essays in Honor of Wolfram Eberhard on His Seventieth Birthday*, 43–69. Reprint, San Francisco: Chinese Materials Center.

Markel, Stephen. 1995. *Origins of the Indian Planetary Deities*. Lewiston, N.Y.: Edwin Mellen Press.

Maruyama Masao. 1977. *Shinkyū igaku to koten no kenkyū: Maruyama Masao Tōyō igaku ronshū*. Osaka: Sōgensha.

Maspero, Henri. 1933. "Le mot *ming*." *Journal Asiatique* 223: 249–96.

———. 1950. *Les religions chinoises: Mélanges posthumes sur les religions et l'histoire de la Chine*. 2 vols. Paris: Presses Universitaires de France.

———. 1978. *China in Antiquity*. Translation by Frank A. Kierman, Jr. Amherst, Mass.: University of Massachusetts Press.

———. 1981. *Taoism and Chinese Religion*. Amherst, Mass.: University of Massachusetts Press.

Massin, Christophe. 1982. *La médecine tibétaine*. Paris: Guy Trédaniel–Éditions de la Maisnie.

Mathieu, Rémi. 1983. *Étude sur la mythologie et l'ethnographie de la Chine ancienne*. Mémoires de l'Institut des Hautes Études Chinoises. Paris: Collège de France.

———. 1987. "Chamanes et chamanisme en Chine ancienne." *L'Homme* 101: 10–34.

Matignon, J. J. 1936 (1902). *Superstition, crime et misère en Chine*. Lyon: Stock.

Matsumae Takeshi, ed. 1988. *Inari Myōjin*. Tokyo: Chikuma shobō.

Matsunaga Yūkei. 1965. "Indian Esoteric Buddhism as Studied in Japan." In Kōyasan daigaku, ed., *Mikkyōgaku mikkyōshi ronbunshū*, 229–42. Kyoto: Naigai Press.

———. 1983–85. "On the Date of the *Mañjuśrīmūlakalpa*." In Michel Strickmann, ed., *Tantric and Taoist Studies in Honour of R. A. Stein*, vol. 3: 882–94. Brussels: Institut Belge des Hautes Études Chinoises.

Mauss, Marcel. 1975 (1903). *A General Theory of Magic*. New York: Norton Paperbacks.

Mayer, Fanny Hagin, ed. 1986. *The Yanagita Kunio Guide to the Japanese Folk Tale*. Bloomington: Indiana University Press.

McCullough, Helen Craig, trans. 1988. *The Tale of the Heike*. Stanford, Calif.: Stanford University Press.

McCullough, William H. 1973. "Spirit Possession in the Heian Period." In Ōta Saburō and Fukuda Rikutarō, eds., *Studies in Japanese Culture*, vol. 1: 91–98. Tokyo: Japan PEN Club.

McCullough, William H., and Helen Craig McCullough, trans. 1980. *A Tale of Flowering Fortunes: Annals of Japanese Aristocratic Life in the Heian Period*. 2 vols. Stanford, Calif.: Stanford University Press.

McNeill, William H. 1976. *Plagues and Peoples*. New York: Anchor Books.
Meisezahl, R. O. 1962. "*The Amoghapāśahṛdayadhāraṇī*." *Monumenta Nipponica* 17: 267–328.
———. 1965. "The Amoghapāśahṛdaya Manuscript Formerly Kept in the Reiunji Temple and Its Collateral Texts in Tibetan Transliteration." Kōyasan daigaku, ed., *Mikkyōgaku mikkyōshi ronbunshū*, 179–216. Kyoto: Naigai Press.
Métailié, Georges. 1988. "Des mots et des plantes dans le *Bencao gangmu* de Li Shizhen." *Extrême-Orient, Extrême-Occident* 10: 27–43.
Meyer, Fernand. 1988. *Gso-ba Rig-pa: Le système médical tibétain*. Paris: Presses du CNRS.
———. 1990. "Étude d'une série de peintures médicales créée à Lhasa au XVIIe siècle." In *Tibet: Civilisation et société*, 29–58. Paris: Éditions de la Fondation Singer-Polignac.
Michihata Ryōshū. 1957. *Tōdai bukkyōshi no kenkyū*. Kyoto: Hōzōkan.
———. 1979. *Chūgoku bukkyō shisō no kenkyū*. Kyoto: Heirakuji shoten.
———. 1980. *Chūgoku bukkyō to shakai to no kōshō*. Kyoto: Heirakuji shoten.
Miki Sakae. 1973 (1956). *Chōsen isho shi*. Tokyo: Gakujutsu tosho kankōkai.
———. 1985. *Chōsen iji nenpyō*. Kyoto: Shibunkaku shuppan.
———, ed. 1961. *Chōsen igaku oyobi shippei shi*. Osaka.
Mikkyō jiten hensankai, ed. 1979. *Mikkyō daijiten*. 6 vols. Reprint, Taipei: Hsin-wen-feng.
Miller, Caspar J., S.J. 1979. *Faith-Healers in the Himalayas*. Kathmandu.
Minakata Kumagusu. 1971–75. *Minakata Kumagusu zenshū*. 12 vols. Tokyo: Heibonsha.
Minakata Kumagusu and F. Victor Dickins. 1973 (1905). *Hōjōki: A Japanese Thoreau of the Twelfth Century*. Reprinted in Minakata Kumagusu, *Minakata Kumagusu zenshū*, vol. 10: 1–25. Tokyo: Heibonsha.
Mironov, N. D., and Shirokogoroff, S. M. 1924. "Śramaṇa-Shaman: Etymology of the Word 'Shaman.'" *Journal of the Royal Asiatic Society*, North-China Branch, vol. 55.
Miyakawa Hisayuki. 1973 (1964). *Rikuchō shi kenkyū: shūkyō hen*. Kyoto: Heirakuji shoten.
———. 1974 (1948). *Rikuchō shūkyō shi*. 2nd ed. Tokyo.
———. 1979. "Local Cults Around Mount Lu at the Time of Sun En's Rebellion." In Holmes Welch and Anna Seidel, eds., *Facets of Taoism: Essays in Chinese Religion*, 83–102. New Haven, Conn.: Yale University Press.
Miyasaka Yūshō. 1965. "Āṭavaka ni tsuite." In Kōyasan daigaku, ed., *Mikkyōgaku mikkyōshi ronbunshū*, 357–82. Kyoto: Naigai Press.
Miyashita Saburō. 1963. "Zui Tō jidai no iryō." In *Chūgoku chūsei kagaku gijutsu shi no kenkyū*, 260–88. Tokyo: Kadokawa shoten.
———. 1967. "Sōgen no iryō." In *Sōgen jidai no kagaku gijutsu shi*, 123–70. Kyoto: Kyōto Daigaku, Jinbun kagaku kenkyūjo.
———. 1977. "A Historical Analysis of Chinese Formularies and Prescriptions: Three Examples." *Nihon ishigaku zasshi* 23, 2: 283–300.

———. 1979. "Malaria (*Yao*) in Chinese Medicine During the Chin and Yüan Periods." *Acta Asiatica* 36: 90–112.

Miyata Noboru. 1970. *Miroku shinkō no kenkyū: Nihon ni okeru dentōteki meshiakan*. Tokyo: Miraisha.

———. 1988. "Types of Maitreya Belief in Japan." In Alan Sponberg and Helen Hardacre, eds., *Maitreya, the Future Buddha*, 175–90. Cambridge: Cambridge University Press.

Mizayaki Eishū. 1985. *Kishimojin shinkō*. Minshū shūkyō sōsho 9. Tokyo: Yūzankaku shuppan.

Mizuhara Gyōhei. 1931. *Jakyō Tachikawa-ryū no kenkyū*. Kyoto.

Mochizuki Shinkō, ed. 1958–63 (1936). *Mochizuki bukkyō daijiten*. 10 vols. Tokyo: Sekai seiten kankō kyōkai. Reprint, Taipei: Horizon Publishing Company, 1977.

Mollier, Christine. 1990. *Une apocalypse taoïste du Ve siècle: Le livre des incantations divines des grottes abyssales*. Institut des Hautes Études Chinoises. Paris: Collège de France.

Morgan, Carole. 1990–91. "T'ang Geomancy: The *Wu-hsing* ('Five Names') Theory and Its Legacy." *T'ang Studies* 8–9: 45–76.

Mori Mikisaburō. 1943. "Shina no kamigami no kanryōteki seikaku." *Shinagaku* 11, 1: 49–81.

Morita Den'ichirō. 1985. *Chūgoku kodai igaku shisō no kenkyū*. Tokyo: Yūzankaku shuppan.

Morita Ryūsen. 1941. *Mikkyō sensei hō*. 2 vols. Kōyasan daigaku shuppanbu. Revised ed., Kyoto: Rinsen shoten, 1974.

Moriyama Shōshin. 1965. *Tachikawa jakyō to sono shakaiteki haikei no kenkyū*. Tokyo: Kokusho kankōkai.

Morrell, Robert, trans. 1985. *Sand and Pebbles (Shasekishū): The Tales of Mujū Ichien—A Voice for Pluralism in Kamakura Buddhism*. Albany: State University of New York Press.

Morris, Ivan, trans. 1991 (1964). *The Pillow Book of Sei Shōnagon*. New York: Columbia University Press.

Mortier, F. 1936. "Les animaux dans la divination et la médecine populaire chinoise." *Bulletin de la Société Royale Belge d'Anthropologie* 51: 268–75.

Mujaku Dōchū. 1963. *Zenrin shōkisen*. Tokyo: Seishin shobō.

Müller, Reinhold F. G. 1925. "Über Skelett-Darstellungen in Asia Major." In Bruno Schindler and Friedrich Weller, eds., *Asia Major* 2, 3–4: 530–63.

Murakami Kajitsu. 1985. "Gojūni byōhō no jinbuyaku." In Yamada Keiji, ed., *Shin hakken Chūgoku kagakushi shiryō no kenkyū: Ronkō hen*, 167–223. Kyoto: Kyoto Daigaku, Jinbun kagaku kenkyūjo.

Murayama Shūichi. 1981. *Nihon onmyōdō-shi sōsetsu*. Tokyo: Hanawa shobō.

Murayama Shūichi et al., eds. 1993. *Onmyōdō sōsho*. 4 vols. Tokyo: Meicho shuppan.

Murray, Julia K. 1981–82. "Representations of Hārītī, the Mother of Demons, and the Theme of 'Raising the Alms-Bowl' in Chinese Paintings." *Artibus Asiae* 43: 253–68.

Mus, Paul. 1928. "Le Bouddha paré." *Bulletin de l'École Française d'Extrême-Orient* 28, 1–2: 153–280.
———. 1935. *Barabuḍur: Esquisse d'une histoire du bouddhisme fondée sur la critique archéologique des textes.* 2 vols. Hanoi: Imprimerie d'Extrême-Orient. Reprint, New York: Arno Press, 1978. English translation by Alexander W. Macdonald, *Barabuḍur: Sketch of a History of Buddhism Based on Archaeological Criticism of the Texts.* New Delhi: Indira Gandhi National Centre for the Arts, 1998.
———. 1939. *La Lumière sur les Six Voies: Tableau de la transmigration bouddhique.* Paris: Institut d'Ethnologie.
Naitō Masatoshi. 1974. *Miira shinkō no kenkyū.* Tokyo: Yamato shobō.
Nakamura Hajime. 1980. *Indian Buddhism: A Survey with Bibliographic Notes.* Hirakata, Osaka: Kansai University of Foreign Studies Publications.
Nakamura Shōhachi. 1973. *Gogyō taigi* [*Wu-hsing ta-i*]. Chūgoku koten shinsho. Tokyo: Meitoku.
———. 1984. *Gogyō taigi kōchū.* Tokyo: Meitoku.
Nakayama Shigeru. 1966. "Characteristics of Chinese Astrology." *Isis* 54: 442–54.
Naquin, Susan. 1976. *Millenarian Rebellion in China: The Eight Trigrams Uprising of 1813.* New Haven, Conn.: Yale University Press.
Nathan, Tobie. 1983. "La possession: Définition ethnopsychanalytique et illustrations cliniques." *Nouvelle Revue d'Ethnopsychiatrie* 1: 109–23.
———. 1988. *Le sperme du diable: Éléments d'ethnopsychothérapie.* Paris: Presses Universitaires de France.
Nattier, Jan. 1991. *Once Upon a Future Time: Studies in a Buddhist Prophecy of Decline.* Berkeley, Calif.: Asian Humanities Press.
Nebesky-Wojkowitz, René de. 1956. *Oracles and Demons of Tibet: The Cult and Iconography of the Tibetan Protective Deities.* The Hague: Mouton. Reprint, Taipei: SMC Publishing, 1990.
Needham, Joseph. 1962 (1954). *Science and Civilization in China, Vol. I: Introductory Orientations.* Cambridge: Cambridge University Press.
———. 1969. *The Grand Titration: Science and Society in East and West.* London.
———. 1970 (1956). *Science and Civilization in China, Vol. II: History of Scientific Thought.* Cambridge: Cambridge University Press.
———. 1976 (1959). *Science and Civilization in China, Vol. III: Mathematics and the Sciences of the Heavens and the Earth.* Cambridge: Cambridge University Press.
———. 1980. *Science and Civilization in China, Vol. V, Part 1: Chemistry and Chemical Technology.* Cambridge: Cambridge University Press.
———. 1983 (1974). *Science and Civilization in China, Vol. V, Part 2: Spagyrical Discovery and Invention: Magisteries of Gold and Immortality.* Cambridge: Cambridge University Press.
Needham, Joseph, and Ho Peng Yoke (Ho Ping-yu). 1959. "Elixir Poisoning in Medieval China." *Janus* 48: 221–51.

Needham, Joseph, and Lu Gwei-djen. 1970. "Hygiene and Preventive Medicine in Ancient China." In Joseph Needham, ed., *Clerks and Craftsmen in China and the West*, 340–78. Cambridge: Cambridge University Press.

———. 1980. *Celestial Lancets*. Cambridge: Cambridge University Press.

Nevius, Rev. John Livingstone. 1869. *China and the Chinese: A General Description*. New York: Harper's.

———. 1894. *Demon Possession and Allied Themes: Being an Inductive Study of Phenomena of Our Own Times*. 3rd ed. Chicago: F. H. Revell Company.

Ngo Van Xuyet. 1976. *Divination, magie et politique dans la Chine ancienne*. Paris: Presses Universitaires de France.

Nicholas, Ralph W. 1981. "The Goddess Śītalā and Epidemic Smallpox in Bengal." *Journal Asiatique* 41, 1: 21–44.

Nickerson, Peter. 1994. "Taoism, Death, and Bureaucracy in Early Medieval China." Ph.D. dissertation, University of California, Berkeley.

———. 1996. "Abridged Codes of Master Lu for the Daoist Community." In Donald S. Lopez, Jr., ed., *Religions of China in Practice*, 347–59. Princeton, N.J.: Princeton University Press.

———. 1997. "The Great Petition for Sepulchral Plaints." In Stephen Bokenkamp, ed., *Early Daoist Scriptures*, 230–74. Berkeley: University of California Press.

Nicolas-Vandier, Nicole, et al. 1974–76. *Bannières et peintures de Touen-houang conservées au Musée Guimet: Catalogue descriptif*. Mission Paul Pelliot, Documents archéologiques, 14. 2 vols. Paris: Centre National de la Recherche Scientifique.

Nihon Daizōkyō. Edited by Naka Takkei et al. Tokyo: Nihon Daizōkyō Hensankai, 1914–19.

Nihon miira kenkyū gurūpu, ed. 1969. *Nihon miira no kenkyū*. Tokyo: Heibonsha.

Niida Noboru. 1960. *Chūgoku hōseishi kenkyū: Tochihō, torihikihō*. Tokyo: Tokyo Daigaku shuppansha.

Obeyesekere, Gananath. 1970. "The Idiom of Demonic Possession: A Case Study." *Social Sciences and Medicine* 4: 97–112.

———. 1981. *Medusa's Hair: An Essay on Personal Symbols and Religious Experience*. Chicago: University of Chicago Press.

———. 1984. *The Goddess Pattini*. Chicago: University of Chicago Press.

Obringer, Frédéric. 1995. "Poisoning and Toxicomany in Medieval China: Physiological Reality or Political Accusation?" In K. Hashimoto, C. Jami, and L. Skar, eds., *East Asian Science: Tradition and Beyond*, 215–20. Osaka: Kansai University Press.

Oda Susumu. 1980. *Nihon no kyōki-shi*. Tokyo: Shisakusha.

O'Flaherty, Wendy Doniger. 1973. *Śiva: The Erotic Ascetic*. New York: Oxford University Press.

———, ed. 1980. *Karma and Rebirth in Classical Indian Traditions*. Berkeley: University of California Press.

———. 1984. *Dreams, Illusions, and Other Realities*. Chicago: University of Chicago Press.

Ōfuchi Ninji. 1974. "On *Ku Ling-pao-ching*." *Acta Asiatica* 27: 33–56.

———. 1979. "The Formation of the Taoist Canon." In Holmes Welch and Anna Seidel, eds., *Facets of Taoism*, 253–67. New Haven, Conn.: Yale University Press.

———. 1983. *Chūgokujin no shūkyō girei: Bukkyō, dōkyō, minkan shinkō*. Tokyo: Fukutake shoten.

———. 1991. *Shoki no dōkyō*. Tokyo: Sōbunsha.

Ogawa Takuji. 1935. *Shina rekishi chiri kenkyū*. 3rd ed. Tokyo and Kyoto.

Ogawa Teizō, ed. 1983. *History of Pathology: Proceedings of the Eighth International Symposium on the Comparative History of Medicine, East and West*. Osaka: Division of Medical History, The Taniguchi Foundation.

Ohnuki-Tierney, Emiko. 1984. *Illness and Culture in Contemporary Japan*. Cambridge: Cambridge University Press.

———. 1987. *The Monkey as Mirror: Symbolic Transformations in Japanese History and Ritual*. Princeton, N.J.: Princeton University Press.

Okada Shigekiyo. 1982. *Kodai no imi: Nihonjin no kiso shinkō*. Tokyo: Kokusho kankōkai.

Okanishi Tameto. 1958. *Sung i-ch'ien i-chi k'ao*. 4 vols. Peking. Reprint, Taipei, 1969.

———, ed. 1964. *Ch'ung-chi Hsin-hsiu pen-ts'ao*. Taipei: National Research Institute for Chinese Medicine.

———, ed. 1972. *Honzōkyō shūchū* [*Pen-ts'ao ching chi-chu*]. Compiled by Mori Risshi. Osaka: Shionogi Research Laboratory.

———. 1974. *Chūgoku isho honzō kō*. Osaka: Minami Ōsaka insatsu sentā.

Ōmura Seigai. 1972 (1918). *Mikkyō hattatsu-shi*. Tokyo: Kokusho kankōkai.

O'Neill, Ynez Violé, and Gerald L. Chan. 1976. "A Chinese Coroner's Manual and the Evolution of Anatomy." *Journal of the History of Medicine* 31: 3–16.

Onishi Yoshinori. 1997. *Feminine Multiplicity: A Study of Groups of Multiple Goddesses in India*. Delhi: Sri Satguru Publications.

Ono Genmyō, ed. 1933–36. *Bussho kaisetsu daijiten*. 12 vols. Reprinted in 14 vols., Tokyo: Bunreisha, 1974–78.

Ono Shihei. 1963. "Taizan kara Hoto e." *Bunka* 27: 80–111.

Onozawa Seiichi et al. 1981 (1978). *Ki no shisō: Chūgoku ni okeru shizen kan to ningen kan no tenkai*. Tokyo: Tōkyō daigaku shuppankai.

Orlando, Raffaello. 1980. "The Last Will of Amoghavajra." Istituto Orientale di Napoli, *Annali* 40 (n.s. 30): 89–113.

———. 1981. "A Study of Chinese Documents Concerning the Life of the Tantric Buddhist Patriarch Amoghavajra." Ph.D. dissertation, Princeton University.

Orofino, Giacomella. 1994. "Divination with Mirrors: Observations on a Simile Found in the Kālacakra Literature." In Per Kvaerne, ed., *Tibetan Studies*, vol. 2: 612–28. Oslo.

Ortner, Sherry B. 1978. *Sherpas Through Their Rituals*. Cambridge: Cambridge University Press.

Orzech, Charles D. 1989. "Seeing Chen-yen Buddhism: Traditional Scholarship and the Vajrayāna in China." *History of Religions* 29, 2: 87–114.

———. 1995. "A Buddhist Image of (Im)Perfect Rule in Fifth-Century China." *Cahiers d'Extrême-Asie* 8: 139–53.

Osabe Kazuo. 1963. *Ichigyō zenji no kenkyū*. Kobe: Shōka daigaku gakujutsu kenkyūkai.

———. 1971. *Tōdai mikkyōshi zakkō*. Kobe: Shōka daigaku gakujutsu kenkyūkai.

———. 1982. *Tō Sō mikkyōshi ronkō*. Kyoto: Nagata bunshōdō.

Ōshima Tatehiko. 1985. *Ekijin to sono shūhen*. Tokyo: Iwazaki bijutsukansha.

Ōtsuka Keisetsu. 1966. *Rinshō ōyō Shōkan ron gaisetsu*. Osaka: Sōgensha.

Ōtsuka Yasuo. 1976. "Chinese Traditional Medicine in Japan." In Charles Leslie, ed., *Asian Medical Systems: A Comparative Study*, 322–40. Berkeley: University of California Press.

———. 1996. *Tōyō igaku*. Iwanami shinsho. Tokyo: Iwanami shoten.

Ouwehand, Cornelius. 1964. *Namazu-e and Their Themes: An Interpretive Approach to Some Aspects of Japanese Folk Religion*. Leiden: E. J. Brill.

Overmyer, Daniel L. 1976. *Folk Buddhist Religion: Dissenting Sects in Late Imperial China*. Cambridge, Mass.: Harvard University Press.

———. 1989–90. "Attitudes Toward Popular Religion in Ritual Texts of the Chinese State: *The Collected Statutes of the Great Ming*." *Cahiers d'Extrême-Asie* 5: 191–211.

Padel, Ruth. 1983. "Women: Model for Possession by Greek Daemons." In Averil Cameron and Amélie Kuhrt, eds. *Images of Women in Antiquity*, 3–19. London and Camberra: Croom Helm.

Padoux, André. 1975 (1963). *Recherches sur la symbolique et l'énergie de la parole dans certains textes tantriques*. Paris: Éditions E. de Boccard.

———. 1980. "Contributions à l'étude du Mantraśāstra, II." *Bulletin de l'École Française d'Extrême-Orient* 67: 59–102.

———, ed. 1986. *Mantras et diagrammes rituels dans l'hindouisme*. Paris: Éditions du CNRS.

———. 1988. *L'énergie de la parole: Cosmogonies de la parole tantrique*. Paris: Soleil Noir.

———, ed. 1990. *L'image divine: Culte et méditation dans l'hindouisme*. Paris: Éditions du CNRS.

Parker, Robert. 1981. *Miasma: Pollution and Purification in Early Greek Religion*. Oxford: Clarendon Press.

Payne, Richard K. 1991. *The Tantric Ritual of Japan—Feeding the Gods: The Shingon Fire Ritual*. Delhi: Aditya Prakshan.

Pelliot, Paul. 1953. *Les débuts de l'imprimerie en Chine*. Paris: Adrien Maisonneuve.

Peri, Noël. 1916. "Le dieu Wei-t'ouo." *Bulletin de l'École Française d'Extrême-Orient* 16, 3: 41–56.

———. 1917. "Hārītī la Mère-de-démons." *Bulletin de l'École Française d'Extrême-Orient* 17: 1–102.

Perry, Lily M. 1980. *Medicinal Plants of East and Southeast Asia: Attributed Properties and Uses*. Cambridge, Mass.: MIT Press.

Pingree, David. 1978. *The Yavanajātaka of Sphujidhvaya*. Harvard Oriental Series, 48. Cambridge, Mass.: Harvard University Press.

Plutschow, Herbert E. 1990. *Chaos and Cosmos: Ritual in Early and Medieval Japanese Literature*. Leiden: E. J. Brill.

Pohlman, A. G. 1907. "*The Purple Island* by Phineas Fletcher: A Seventeenth-Century Layman's Poetical Conception of the Human Body." *Johns Hopkins Hospital Bulletin* 27: 1–12.

Pokora, Timoteus. 1985. "'Living Corpses' in Early Medieval China: Sources and Opinions." In Gert Neundorf, Karl-Heinz Pohl, and Hans-Hermann Schmidt, eds., *Religion und Philosophie in Ostasien: Festschrift für Hans Steininger*, 344–57. Würzburg: Königshausen and Neumann.

Poo Mu-chou. 1993. "Popular Religion in Pre-Imperial China: Observations on the Almanacs of Shui-hu-ti." *T'oung Pao* 79: 225–48.

Porkert, Manfred. 1960–61. "Untersuchungen einiger philosophisch-wissenschaftlicher Grundbegriffe und Beziehungen in Chinesischen." *Zeitschrift der Deutschen Morgenländischen Gesellschaft* 110: 422–52.

———. 1974. *The Theoretical Foundations of Chinese Medicine: Systems of Correspondence*. MIT East Asian Science Series, 3. Cambridge, Mass.: MIT Press.

Potter, Jack M. 1970. "Wind, Water, Bones and Souls: The Religious World of the Cantonese Peasant." *Journal of Oriental Studies* 8, 1: 139–53.

Prebish, Charles S. 1975. *Buddhist Monastic Discipline: The Sanskrit Prātimokṣa Sūtras of the Mahāsāṃghikas and Mūlasarvāstivādins*. University Park and London: Pennsylvania State University Press.

Pregadio, Fabrizio. 1990. "The Medical Texts of Ma-wang-tui." *Cahiers d'Extrême-Asie* 5: 381–86.

———. 1996. *Zhouyi Cantong qi: Dal 'Libro dei Mutamenti' all'Elisir d'Oro*. Venice: Cafoscarina.

Przyluski, Jean. 1923. "Les Vidyārāja: Contribution à l'histoire de la magie dans les sectes mahāyānistes." *Bulletin de l'École Française d'Extrême-Orient* 23: 301–18.

———. 1927. "La place de Māra dans la mythologie bouddhique." *Journal Asiatique* 210, 1: 115–23.

Rambelli, Fabio. 1994. "True Words, Silence, and the Adamantine Dance: On Mikkyō and the Formation of Shingon Discourse." *Japanese Journal of Religious Studies* 21, 4: 373–405.

Rana, S. S. 1995. *A Study of the Skanda Cult*. Delhi: Nag Publishers.

Ranger, Terence, and Paul Slack, eds. 1992. *Epidemics and Ideas: Essays on the Historical Perception of Pestilence*. Cambridge: Cambridge University Press.

Ratchnevsky, Paul. 1985 (1937). *Un code des Yüan*. Paris: Institut des Hautes Études Chinoises.

Rawlinson, Andrew. 1986. "Nāgas and the Magical Cosmology of Buddhism." *History of Religions* 16, 2: 135–53.

Read, Bernard E. 1936. *Chinese Medical Plants from the Pen Ts'ao Kang Mu*. Peking: The French Bookstore.

———. 1941. *Chinese Materia Medica: Insects and Drugs*, part 10, "Insects." Peking: the French Bookstore.

———. 1987. *Chinese Herbal Medicine*. Boston: Shambhala.

Reischauer, Edwin O. 1955a. *Ennin's Diary: The Record of a Pilgrimage to China in Search of the Law*. New York: Reginald Press.

———. 1955b. *Ennin's Travels in T'ang China*. New York: Reginald Press.

Reiter, Florian C. 1988. "The Visible Divinity: The Sacred Icon in Religious Taoism." *Nachrichte der Gesellschaft für Natur- und Völkerkunde Ostasiens* 144: 51–70.

———. 1992. "Conditions, Ways and Means of Healing in the Perspective of the Chinese Taoist." *Oriens* 33: 348–62.

———. 1998. *The Aspirations and Standards of Taoist Priests in the Early Tang Period*. Asien- und Afrika-Studien 1 der Humboldt-Universität zu Berlin. Wiesbaden: Harrassowitz Verlag.

Renondeau, Georges. 1965. "Le Shugendō—Histoire, doctrine et rites des anachorètes dits *yamabushi*." *Cahiers de la Société Asiatique* 18: 1–150.

Renou, Louis. 1978. *L'Inde fondamentale*. Ed. Charles Malamoud. Collection Savoir. Paris: Hermann.

Renou, Louis, and Jean Filliozat, eds. 1985 (1947). *L'Inde classique: Manuel des études indiennes*. 2 vols. Paris: Librairie d'Amérique et d'Orient.

Rhys-Davids, T. W., and C. A. F. Rhys-Davids, trans. 1899–1921. *Dialogues of the Buddha*. 3 vols. London: Pāli Text Society.

Riegel, Jeffrey K. 1982. "Early Chinese Target Magic." *Journal of Chinese Religion* 10: 1–18.

Robinet, Isabelle. 1976. "Randonnées extatiques des taoïstes dans les astres." *Monumenta Serica* 32: 159–273.

———. 1977. *Les commentaires du Tao tö king jusqu'au VIIe siècle*. Paris: Institut des Hautes Études Chinoises.

———. 1979. "Metamorphosis and Deliverance from the Corpse in Taoism." *History of Religions* 19, 1: 37–70.

———. 1983–85. "Le *Ta-tung cheng-ching*." In Michel Strickmann, ed., *Tantric and Taoist Studies in Honour of R. A. Stein*, vol. 2: 744–82. Brussels: Institut Belge des Hautes Études Chinoises.

———. 1984. *La révélation du Shangqing dans l'histoire du taoïsme*. 2 vols. Publications de l'École Française d'Extrême-Orient, 137. Paris: École Française d'Extrême-Orient.

———. 1986. "L'alchimie interne dans le taoïsme." *Cahiers d'Extrême-Asie* 2: 241–52.

———. 1989a. "Visualization and Ecstatic Flight in Shangqing Taoism." In Livia Kohn and Sakade Yoshinobu, eds., *Taoist Meditation and Longevity*

Techniques, 159–91. Michigan Monographs on Chinese Studies, 61. Ann Arbor: Center for Chinese Studies, The University of Michigan.

———. 1989b. "Original Contributions of *Neidan* to Taoism and Chinese Thought." In Livia Kohn and Sakade Yoshinobu, eds., *Taoist Meditation and Longevity Techniques*, 297–330. Michigan Monographs on Chinese Studies, 61. Ann Arbor: Center for Chinese Studies, The University of Michigan.

———. 1989–90. "Recherches sur l'alchimie intérieure (*neidan*): L'École Zhenyuan." *Cahiers d'Extrême-Asie* 5: 141–62.

———. 1993. *Taoist Meditation: The Mao-shan Tradition of Great Purity*. Trans. Julian F. Pas and Norman J. Girardot. Albany: State University of New York Press.

———. 1995. *Introduction à l'alchimie intérieure taoïste: De l'unité et de la multiplicité*. Paris: Éditions du Cerf.

———. 1996. *Taoism: Growth of a Religion*. Trans. Phyllis Brooks. Stanford, Calif.: Stanford University Press.

Roșu, Arion. 1978. *Les conceptions psychologiques dans les textes médicaux indiens*. Paris: Éditions E. de Boccard.

———. 1986. "*Mantra* and *yantra* dans la médecine et l'alchimie indiennes." *Journal Asiatique* 274: 203–68.

Rotermund, Hartmund O. 1980. "Quelques aspects de la magie verbale dans les croyances populaires du Japon." In *Mélanges offerts à M. Charles Haguenauer en l'honneur de son quatre-vingtième anniversaire: Études japonaises*, 425–42. Paris: L'Asiathèque.

———. 1991a. *Hôsôgami ou la petite vérole aisément*. Paris: Maisonneuve et Larose.

———. 1991b (1981). "The Tengu Demons of Japan." In Yves Bonnefoy, ed., *Asian Mythologies*, 285–87. Chicago: University of Chicago Press.

———. 1995. "L'offrande de fleurs en mémoire du Bouddha, ou l'art de disséquer les insectes." In Anne-Marie Blondeau and Kristofer Schipper, eds., *Essais sur le rituel*, vol. 2: 139–52. Louvain and Paris: Peeters.

Rouget, Gilbert. 1985. *Music and Trance: A Theory of the Relations Between Music and Possession*. Trans. Derek Coltman. Chicago: University of Chicago Press.

Rousselle, E. 1935. "Ein Abhiṣekha-Ritus in Mantra-Buddhismus" (Shingon Sekte in Japan). *Sinica* 1935: 58–90; 193.

Roux, Jean-Paul. 1966a. "Le Chaman." In *Le Monde du sorcier*, 206–31. Sources Orientales. Paris: Seuil.

———. 1966b. *Faune et flore sacrées dans les sociétés altaïques*. Paris: Adrien Maisonneuve.

———. 1984. *La religion des Turcs et des Mongols*. Paris: Payot.

Ruegg, David Seyfort. 1964. "Sur les rapports entre le bouddhisme et le 'substrat religieux' indien et tibétain." *Journal Asiatique* 252: 77–95.

Saigō Nobutsuna. 1972. *Kodaijin to yume*. Tokyo: Heibonsha.

Sailey, Jay. 1978. *The Master Who Embraces Simplicity: A Study of the Philosopher Ko Hung, A.D. 283–343*. San Francisco: Chinese Materials Center.

Sakade Yoshinobu. 1986. "The Taoist Character of the 'Chapter on Nourishing Life' of the *Ishinpō*." *Kansai daigaku [bungaku ronshū] sōritsu hyakunen kinengō*: 775–98.
———, ed. 1988. *Chūgoku kodai yōsei shisō no sōgōteki kenkyū*. Tokyo: Hirakawa shuppansha.
———. 1989a. "Longevity Techniques in Japan: Ancient Sources and Contemporary Studies." In Livia Kohn and Sakade Yoshinobu, eds., *Taoist Meditation and Longevity Techniques*, 1–40. Michigan Monographs on Chinese Studies, 61. Ann Arbor: Center for Chinese Studies, The University of Michigan.
———. 1989b. "Son Shibaku ni okeru iryō to dōkyō." In *Senkin hō kenkyū shiryō shū*, 52–67. In Tōyō igaku zenpon sōsho 15. Osaka: Oriento shuppan.
———. 1991. *Chūgoku kodai no senpō: gijutsu to jujutsu no shūhen*. Tokyo: Kenbun shuppan.
Sakai Tadao. 1960. *Chūgoku zensho no kenkyū*. Tokyo: Kōbundō.
———. 1977. *Dōkyō no sōgōteki kenkyū*. Tokyo: Kokusho kankōkai.
Sāṃkṛtyāyana, R. 1934. "Recherches bouddhiques: L'origine du Vajrayāna et les quatre-vingt siddhas." *Journal Asiatique* 225, 2: 209–30.
Sanford, James H. 1980. "Maṇḍalas of the Heart: Two Prose Works by Ikkyū Sōjun." *Monumenta Nipponica* 36, 3: 273–98.
———. 1991a. "The Abominable Tachikawa Skull Ritual." *Monumenta Nipponica* 46: 1–20.
———. 1991b. "Literary Aspects of Japan's Dual-Gaṇeśa Cult." In Robert L. Brown, ed., *Ganesh: Studies of an Asian God*, 287–335. Albany: State University of New York Press.
———. 1994. "Breath of Life: The Esoteric Nenbutsu." In Ian Astley, ed., *Esoteric Buddhism in Japan*, 65–98. Seminar for Buddhist Studies Monographs, 1. Copenhagen and Aarhus: The Seminar for Buddhist Studies.
———. 1997. "Wind, Water, Stūpas, Maṇḍalas: Fetal Buddhahood in Shingon." *Japanese Journal of Religious Studies* 24, 1–2: 1–38.
Sano Bunkichi and Naitō Masatoshi. 1969. *Nihon no sokushinbutsu*. Tokyo: Kōfusha shoten.
Sano Kenji. 1994. *Hoshi no shinkō: Myōken, Kokūzō*. Tokyo: Hokushindō.
Sasama Yoshihiko. 1988. *Dakini shinkō to sono zō*. Tokyo: Daiichi shobō.
———. 1989. *Kangiten (Shōden) shinkō to zokushin*. Tokyo: Yūzankaku.
Saso, Michael R. 1974. "Orthodoxy and Heterodoxy in Taoist Ritual." In Arthur P. Wolf, ed., *Religion and Ritual in Chinese Society*, 235–336. Stanford, Calif.: Stanford University Press.
———. 1978. *The Teachings of Taoist Master Chuang*. New Haven, Conn.: Yale University Press.
Saunders, E. Dale. 1960. *Mudrā: A Study of Symbolic Gestures in Japanese Buddhist Sculpture*. Princeton, N.J.: Princeton University Press.
Sawada Mizuho. 1969. *Jigoku-hen: Chūgoku no meikai-setsu*. Kyoto: Hōzōkan.
———. 1975. *Zōho Hōkan no kenkyū*. Tokyo: Kokusho kankōkai.
———. 1976. *Kishu dangi*. Tokyo: Kokusho kankōkai.
———. 1982. *Chūgoku no minkan shinkō*. Tokyo: Kōsakusha.

Schafer, Edward H. 1963. *The Golden Peaches of Samarkand: A Study of T'ang Exotics*. Berkeley: University of California Press.

———. 1967. *The Vermilion Bird*. Berkeley: University of California Press.

———. 1975. "The Stove God and the Alchemists." In L. G. Thompson, ed., *Studia Asiatica: Essays in Felicitation of the Seventy-fifth Anniversary of Professor Ch'en Shou-yi*, 261–66. San Francisco: Chinese Materials Center.

———. 1977. *Pacing the Void: T'ang Approaches to the Stars*. Berkeley: University of California Press.

Schiffeler, John Wm. 1980. "Chinese Folk Medicine: A Study of the *Shan-hai ching*." *Asian Folklore Studies* 39, 2: 41–83.

Schipper, Kristofer M. 1965. *L'Empereur Wou des Han dans la légende taoïste: Han Wou-ti nei-tchouan*. Paris: École Française d'Extrême-Orient.

———. 1966. "The Divine Jester: Some Remarks on the Gods of the Chinese Marionnette Theater." *Academia Sinica, Bulletin of the Institute of Ethnology* 21: 81–94.

———. 1974. "The Written Memorial in Taoist Ceremonies." In Arthur Wolf, ed., *Religion and Ritual in Chinese Society*, 309–24. Stanford, Calif.: Stanford University Press.

———. 1975. *Le Fen-teng: Rituel taoïste*. Paris: École Française d'Extrême-Orient.

———. 1978. "The Taoist Body." *History of Religions* 17, 3–4: 355–86.

———. 1983–85. "Taoist Ritual and Local Cults of the T'ang Dynasty." In Michel Strickmann, ed., *Tantric and Taoist Studies in Honour of R. A. Stein*, vol. 3: 812–34. Mélanges Chinois et Bouddhiques, 22. Brussels: Institut Belge des Hautes Études Chinoises.

———. 1985a. "Seigneurs royaux, dieux des épidémies." *Archives de sciences sociales des religions* 59: 31–40.

———. 1985b. "Vernacular and Classical Ritual in Taoism." *Journal of Asian Studies* 45, 1: 21–57.

———. 1990a. "Mu-lien Plays in Taoist Liturgical Context." In David Johnson, ed., *Ritual Opera, Operatic Ritual*, 127–54. Berkeley, Calif.: Chinese Popular Culture Project.

———. 1990b. "Purifier l'autel, tracer les limites à travers les rituels taoïstes." In Marcel Détienne, ed., *Tracés et fondations*, 31–47. Louvain and Paris: Peeters.

———. 1993. *The Taoist Body*. Trans. Karen Duval. Berkeley: University of California Press.

Schipper, Kristofer M., and Wang Hsiu-huei. 1986. "Progressive and Regressive Time Cycles in Taoist Ritual." In J. T. Frazer et al., eds., *Time, Science, and Society in China and the West*, 185–205. Amherst: University of Massachusetts Press.

Schmitt, Jean-Claude. 1994. *Les revenants: Les vivants et les morts dans la société médiévale*. Paris: Gallimard. English translation by Teresa Lavender Fagan, *Ghosts in the Middle Ages: The Living and the Dead in Medieval Society*. Chicago: University of Chicago Press, 1998.

Schopen, Gregory. 1975. "The Phrase '*sa pṛthivīpradeśaś caityabhūto bhavet*' in the *Vajracchedikā*: Notes on the Cult of the Book in Mahāyāna." *Indo-Iranian Journal* 17, 3–4: 147–81.

———. 1987. "Burial 'Ad Sanctos' and the Physical Presence of the Buddha in Early Indian Buddhism: A Study in the Archeology of Religions." *Religion* 17: 193–225.

———. 1991. "Archeology and Protestant Presuppositions in the Study of Indian Buddhism." *History of Religions* 31, 1: 1–23.

Seaman, Gary. 1981a. "In the Presence of Authority: Hierarchical Roles in Chinese Spirit Medium Cults." In Arthur Kleinman and Lin Tsung-yi, eds., *Normal and Abnormal Behavior in Chinese Culture*, 61–74. Dordrecht. The Netherlands.

———. 1981b. "The Sexual Politics of Karmic Retribution." In Emily Martin Ahern and Hill Gates, eds., *The Anthropology of Taiwanese Society*, 381–96. Stanford, Calif.: Stanford University Press.

Seidel, Anna K. 1969. *La Divinisation de Lao-tseu dans le taoïsme des Han*. Paris: École Française d'Extrême-Orient.

———. 1970. "The Image of the Perfect Ruler in Early Taoist Messianism." *History of Religions* 9: 216–47.

———. 1975. "Buying One's Way to Heaven: The Celestial Treasury in Chinese Religion." *History of Religions* 17, 3: 419–31.

———. 1978a. "Der Kaiser und sein Ratgeber: Lao-tzu und der Taoismus der Han-Zeit." *Saeculum* 29: 18–50.

———. 1978b. "Das neue Testament des Tao: Lao-tzu und die Entstehung der taoistischen Religion am Ender der Han-Zeit." *Saeculum* 29: 147–72.

———. 1981. "*Kokuhō*, note à propos du terme "trésor national" en Chine et au Japon." *Bulletin de l'École Française d'Extrême-Orient* 69: 229–61.

———. 1982. "Tokens of Immortality in Han Graves." *Numen* 29: 79–122.

———. 1983. "Dabi." In *Hōbōgirin* 6: 573–85. Paris: Adrien Maisonneuve.

———. 1983–85. "Imperial Treasures and Taoist Sacraments: Taoist Roots in the Apocrypha." In Michel Strickmann, ed., *Tantric and Taoist Studies in Honour of R. A. Stein*, vol. 2: 291–371. Mélanges Chinois et Bouddhiques, 21. Brussels: Institut Belge des Hautes Études Chinoises.

———. 1985. "Geleitbrief an die Unterwelt—Jenseitsvorstellungen in der Graburkunden der späteren Han-Zeit." In G. Naundorf, K. H. Pohl, and H. H. Schmidt, eds., *Religion und Philosophie in Ostasien: Festschrift für Hans Steininger*, 161–83.

———. 1987a. "Post-Mortem Immortality, or the Taoist Resurrection of the Body." In *Gilgul: Essays on Transformation, Revolution and Permanence in the History of Religions, Dedicated to R. J. Zwi Verblowsky*. Leiden: E. J. Brill, 223–37.

———. 1987b. "Traces of Han Religion in Funeral Texts Found in Tombs." In Akizuki Kan'ei, ed., *Dōkyō to shūkyō bunka*, 21–57. Tokyo: Hirakawa shuppansha.

———. 1989–90. "Chronicle of Taoist Studies in the West, 1950–1990." *Cahiers d'Extrême-Asie* 5: 223–347.

Sen, Sukumar. 1945. "Two Medical Texts in Chinese Translation." *Vishvabharati Annals* 1: 70–95.

———. 1965. "On Dhāraṇī and Pratisarā." Kōyasan daigaku, ed., *Mikkyōgaku mikkyōshi ronbunshū*, 67–72. Kyoto: Naigai Press.

Sendrail, Marcel. 1980. *Histoire culturelle de la maladie*. Paris: Privat.

Shahar, Meir. 1998. *Crazy Ji: Chinese Religion and Popular Literature*. Cambridge, Mass.: Harvard University Press.

Shahar, Meir, and Robert P. Weller, eds. 1996. *Unruly Gods: Divinity and Society in China*. Honolulu: University of Hawai'i Press.

Sharf, Robert. 1992. "The Idolization of Enlightenment: On the Mummification of Ch'an Masters in Medieval China." *History of Religions* 32, 1: 1–31.

Shaw, Miranda. 1994. *Passionate Enlightenment: Women in Tantric Buddhism*. Princeton, N.J.: Princeton University Press.

Shigematsu Akihisa. 1985. *Kodai kokka to dōkyō*. Tokyo: Yoshikawa kōbunkan.

Shimode, Sekiyo. 1968. *Shinsen shisō*. Tokyo: Yoshikawa kōbunkan.

———. 1972. *Nihon kodai no jingi to dōkyō*. Tokyo: Yoshikawa kōbunkan.

Shinmura Taku. 1985. *Nihon iryō shakai shi no kenkyū*. Tokyo: Hōsei daigaku shuppankyoku.

Shirokogoroff, S. M. 1935. *Psychomental Complex of the Tungus*. London: K. Paul, Trench, Trübner. Reprint, New York: AMS Press, 1980.

Shizutani Masao. 1974. *Shoki daijō bukkyō no seiritsu katei*. Kyoto: Hyakkaen.

Shōwa butten kankōkai, ed. 1977. *Inari o tazunete*. Osaka: Bunshindō.

Sivin, Nathan. 1967. "A Seventh-Century Chinese Medical Case History." *Bulletin of the History of Medicine* 41: 267–73.

———. 1968. *Chinese Alchemy: Preliminary Studies*. Harvard Monographs in the History of Science, 1. Cambridge, Mass.: Harvard University Press.

———. 1973. "*T'ien lao shen kuang ching*: The Celestial Elder's Canon of the Spirit Lights (An Ancient Chinese Book of Interior Astrology)." *Io* 1973, 4: 232–38.

———, ed. 1977a. *Science and Technology in East Asia: Articles from Isis, 1913–1975*. New York: Science History Publications.

———. 1977b. "Social Relations of Curing in Traditional China: Preliminary Considerations." *Nihon ishigaku zasshi* 23: 505–32.

———. 1978. "On the Word 'Taoism' as a Source of Perplexity: With Special Reference to the Relations of Science and Religion in Traditional China." *History of Religions* 17: 303–30.

———. 1987. *Traditional Medicine in Contemporary China*. Ann Arbor: Center for Chinese Studies, The University of Michigan.

———. 1988. "Science and Medicine in Imperial China: The State of the Field." *Journal of Asian Studies* 47, 1: 41–90.

———. 1995. *Medicine, Philosophy and Religion in Ancient China: Researches and Reflections*. Aldershot, Eng.: Variorum.

Sivin, Nathan, and Nakayama Shigeru. 1972. *Chinese Science: Explorations of an Ancient Tradition*. MIT East Asian Science Series, 2. Cambridge, Mass.: MIT Press.

Skar, Lowell. 1996–97. "Administering Thunder: A Thirteenth-Century Memorial Deliberating the Thunder Rites." *Cahiers d'Extrême-Asie* 9: 159–202.

Sleeman, William H. 1971 (1915). *Sleeman in Oudh: An Abridgment of W. H. Sleeman's 'A Journey Through the Kingdom of Oude, 1849–1850.'* Cambridge: Cambridge University Press.

Smith, Richard J. 1991. *Fortune-Tellers and Philosophers: Divination in Traditional Chinese Society*. Boulder, Colo., and San Francisco: Westview Press.

Snellgrove, David L., ed. and trans. 1959a. *The Hevajra Tantra: A Critical Study*. 2 vols. London Oriental Series, 6. London: Oxford University Press.

———. 1959b. "The Notion of Divine Kingship in Tantric Buddhism." In *The Sacral Kingship: Studies in the History of Religions*, vol. 4: 204–18. Leiden: E. J. Brill.

———. 1987. *Indo-Tibetan Buddhism: Indian Buddhists and Their Tibetan Successors*. 2 vols. Boston: Shambhala.

Soper, Alexander C. 1959. *Literary Evidence for Early Buddhist Art in China*. Ascona: Artibus Asiae.

Soymié, Michel. 1956. "Le Lo-feou chan: Étude de géographie religieuse." *Bulletin de l'École Française d'Extrême-Orient* 48: 1–139.

———. 1961. "Sources et sourciers en Chine." *Bulletin de la Maison Franco-Japonaise*, n.s., 7, 1: 1–56.

———. 1977. "Les dix jours de jeûne du taoïsme." In *Dōkyō kenkyū ronshū* (Yoshioka Yoshitoyo Festschrift), 1–21. Tokyo: Kokusho kankōkai.

———, ed. 1979. *Contributions aux études de Touen-houang*. Hautes Études Orientales, 2. Geneva and Paris: Librairie Droz.

———. 1981. *Nouvelles contributions aux études de Touen-houang*. Hautes Études Orientales, 10. Geneva and Paris: Librairie Droz.

———. 1984. *Contributions aux études de Touen-houang*, vol. 3. Publications de l'École Française d'Extrême-Orient, 135. Paris: École Française d'Extrême-Orient.

———. 1987. "Notes d'iconographie bouddhique: Des Vidyārāja et Vajradhara de Touen-houang." *Cahiers d'Extrême-Asie* 3: 9–26.

Spiro, Melford E. 1976. "Supernaturally Caused Illness in Traditional Burmese Medicine." In Charles Leslie, ed., *Asian Medical Systems: A Comparative Study*, 385–99. Berkeley: University of California Press.

Sponberg, Alan, and Helen Hardacre, eds. 1988. *Maitreya, the Future Buddha*. Cambridge: Cambridge University Press.

Spörry, Hans. 1901. *Das Stempelwesen in Japan*. Zurich: F. Lohbauer.

Staal, Frits, ed. 1983. *Agni: The Vedic Ritual of the Fire Altar*. 2 vols. Berkeley, Calif.: Asian Humanities Press.

———. 1985. "Substitutions de paradigmes et religions d'Asie." *Cahiers d'Extrême-Asie* 1: 21–59.

———. 1990. *Jouer avec le feu*. Paris: Collège de France.

Stablein, William George. 1975. "Mahākāla Neo-Shaman: Master of the Ritual." In John Hitchcock and Rex Jones, eds., *Spirit Possession in the Nepal Himalayas*. London: Aris and Phillips.

———. 1976a. "The *Mahākālatantra*: A Theory of Ritual Blessings and Tantric Buddhism." Ph.D. dissertation, Columbia University.
———. 1976b. "Tibetan Mantra Medical System." *Tibetan Review* 2: 6–7.
———. 1978. "A Descriptive Analysis of the Content of Nepalese Buddhist *Pūjās* as a Medical-Cultural System with References to Tibetan Parallels." In James Fisher, ed., *Himalayan Anthropology*, 529–37. The Hague: Mouton.
Stein, Rolf A. 1947. "Le Lin-yi, sa contribution à la formation du Champa et ses liens avec la Chine." *Han-hiue* 2, 1–3: 1–335.
———. 1957. "Le Liṅga des danses masquées lamaïques et la théorie des âmes." *Sino-Indian Studies* 5, 3–4: 200–36.
———. 1959. *Recherches sur l'épopée et le barde au Tibet*. Bibliothèque de l'Institut des Hautes Études Chinoises, 13. Paris: Presses Universitaires de France.
———. 1963. "Remarques sur les mouvements du taoïsme politico-religieux au IIe siècle ap. J.C." *T'oung Pao* 50: 1–78.
———. 1972. *Tibetan Civilization*. Stanford, Calif.: Stanford University Press.
———. 1975. "Étude du monde chinois: Institutions et concepts." *Annuaire du Collège de France*, 481–95. Paris: Collège de France.
———. 1979. "Religious Taoism and Popular Religion from the Second to Seventh Centuries." In Anna K. Seidel and Holmes H. Welch, eds., *Facets of Taoism: Essays on Chinese Religion*, 53–81. New Haven, Conn.: Yale University Press.
———. 1981. "Saint et divin." *Journal Asiatique* 269: 231–75.
———. 1986. "Avalokiteśvara/Kouan-yin, un exemple de transformation d'un dieu en déesse." *Cahiers d'Extrême-Asie* 2: 17–80.
———. 1988. *Grottes-matrices et lieux saints de la déesse en Asie Orientale*. Publications de l'EFEO, 151. Paris: École Française d'Extrême-Orient.
———. 1990. *The World in Miniature: Container Gardens and Dwellings in Far Eastern Religious Thought*. Trans. Phyllis Brooks. Stanford, Calif.: Stanford University Press.
———. 1991 (1981). "The Guardian of the Gate: An Example of Buddhist Mythology, from India to Japan." In Yves Bonnefoy, ed., *Asian Mythologies*, 122–36. Trans. Wendy Doniger. Chicago: University of Chicago Press.
Stewart, Tony K. 1995a. "Encountering the Smallpox Goddess: The Auspicious Song of Śītalā." In Donald S. Lopez, Jr., ed., *Religions of India in Practice*, 389–98. Princeton, N.J.: Princeton University Press.
———. 1995b. "The Goddess of Saṣṭhī Protects Children." In Donald S. Lopez, Jr., ed., *Religions of India in Practice*, 352–66. Princeton, N.J.: Princeton University Press.
Stone, Jacqueline. 1995. "Medieval Tendai Hongaku Thought and the New Kamakura Buddhism: A Reconsideration." *Japanese Journal of Religious Studies* 22, 2: 17–48.
Strickmann, Michel. 1975. "Sōdai no raigi: Shinsō undō to Dōka nanshū ni tsuite no ryakusetsu." *Tōhō shūkyō* 46: 15–28.

———. 1977. "The Mao Shan Revelations: Taoism and the Aristocracy." *T'oung Pao* 64: 1–64.
———. 1978a. "The Longest Taoist Scripture." *History of Religions* 17: 331–54.
———. 1978b. "A Taoist Confirmation of Liang Wu Ti's Suppression of Taoism." *Journal of the American Oriental Society* 98: 467–75.
———. 1979. "On the Alchemy of T'ao Hung-ching." In Anna K. Seidel and Holmes H. Welch, eds., *Facets of Taoism: Essays on Chinese Religion*, 123–92. New Haven, Conn.: Yale University Press.
———. 1980. "History, Anthropology, and Chinese Religion." *Harvard Journal of Asiatic Studies*, 40, 1: 203–48.
———. 1981. *Le taoïsme du Mao Chan: Chronique d'une révélation*. Paris.
———. 1982a. "India in the Chinese Looking-Glass." In D. Klimburg-Salter, ed., *The Silk Route and the Diamond Path: Esoteric Buddhist Art on the Trans-Himalayan Trade Routes*, 52–63. Los Angeles: UCLA Art Council.
———. 1982b. "The Tao Among the Yao: Taoism and the Sinification of South China." In Sakai Tadao sensei koki shukuga kinen no kai, ed., *Rekishi ni okeru minshū to bunka*, 23–30. Tokyo: Kokusho kankōkai.
———. 1983. "Homa in East Asia." In Frits Staal, ed., *Agni: The Vedic Ritual of the Fire Altar*, vol. 2: 418–55. Berkeley, Calif.: Asian Humanities Press.
———, ed. 1983–85. *Tantric and Taoist Studies in Honour of R. A. Stein*, 3 vols. Brussels: Institut Belge des Hautes Études Chinoises.
———. 1985. "Therapeutische Rituale und das Problem des Bösen in frühen Taoismus." In Gert Naundorf, Karl-Heinz Pohl, and Hans-Hermann Schmidt, eds., *Religion und Philosophie in Ostasien: Festschrift für Hans Steininger zum 65. Geburtstag*, 185–200. Würzburg: Königshausen und Neumann.
———. 1988. "Dreamwork of Psycho-Sinologists: Doctors, Taoists, Monks." In Carolyn T. Brown, ed., *Psycho-Sinology: The Universe of Dreams in Chinese Culture*, 25–46. Lanham, Md.: University Press of America.
———. 1990. "The Consecration Sūtra: A Buddhist Book of Spells." In Robert E. Buswell, Jr., ed., *Chinese Buddhist Apocrypha*, 75–118. Honolulu: University of Hawai'i Press.
———. 1990–91. "Buddhas In and Out of Bodies." *Discours social/Social Discourse* 3, 3–4: 107–20.
———. 1993. "The Seal of the Law: A Ritual Implement and the Origins of Printing." *Asia Major*, third series, 6, 2: 1–83.
———. 1994. "Saintly Fools and Chinese Masters (Holy Fools)." *Asia Major*, third series, 7, 1: 35–57.
———. 1995. "The Seal of the Jungle Woman." *Asia Major*, third series, 8, 2: 147–53.
———. 1996. *Mantras et Mandarins: Le bouddhisme tantrique en Chine*. Paris: Gallimard.
———. Forthcoming. *Chinese Poetry and Prophecy*. Stanford, Calif.: Stanford University Press.
Stuart, G. A. 1924 (1911). *Chinese Materia Medica: Vegetable Kingdom*. Re-

printed as *Chinese Medicinal Herbs*, San Francisco: Georgetown Press, 1973.

Sweet, Michael J., and Zwilling, Leonard. 1993. "The First Medicalization: The Taxonomy and Etiology of Queerness in Classical Indian Medicine." *Journal of the History of Sexuality* 3: 590–607.

Szasz, Thomas S. 1978. *The Myth of Psychotherapy*. Garden City, N.Y.: Anchor Press/Doubleday.

Taishō shinshū daizōkyō kankōkai, ed. 1964–71. *Taishō shinshū daizōkyō sakuin, Mikkyō-bu*, 2 vols. Tokyo.

Tajima Ryūjun. 1959. *Les deux grands maṇḍalas et la doctrine de l'ésotérisme Shingon*. Tokyo: Nakayama shobō busshorin.

———. 1992. *Étude sur le Mahāvairocana-sūtra (Dainichikyō) avec la traduction commentée du premier chapitre*. Revised ed., Paris: Adrien Maisonneuve. English translation in Alex Wayman and Tajima Ryūjun, *The Enlightenment of Vairocana*. Delhi: Motilal Banarsidass, 1992.

Takakusu Junjirō, trans. 1896. *A Record of the Buddhist Religion as Practised in India and the Malay Archipelago*. Oxford: Clarendon Press.

———. 1928. "Le voyage de Kanshin en Orient (742–754)." *Bulletin de l'École Française d'Extrême-Orient* 28: 1–62.

Tambiah, Stanley J. 1970. *Buddhism and the Spirit Cults in North-East Thailand*. Cambridge: Cambridge University Press.

———. 1973. "Form and Meaning of Magical Acts: A Point of View." In R. Horton and R. Finnegan, eds., *Modes of Thought*, 199–229. London: Faber.

———. 1977. "The Cosmological and Performative Significance of a Thai Cult of Healing Through Meditation." *Culture, Medicine and Psychiatry* 1: 97–132.

———. 1980. "The Magical Power of Words." *Man* 3: 175–208.

———. 1984. *The Buddhist Saints of the Forest and the Cult of Amulets: A Study in Charisma, Hagiography, Sectarianism and Millennial Buddhism*. Cambridge: Cambridge University Press.

Tanabe, George J., Jr. 1992. *Myōe the Dreamkeeper: Fantasy and Knowledge in Early Kamakura Buddhism*. Cambridge, Mass.: Harvard University Press.

Tanabe, George J., Jr., and Willa Tanabe, eds. 1989. *The Lotus Sūtra in Japanese Culture*. Honolulu: University of Hawai'i Press.

Tanaka Takako. 1992. *"Akujo" ron*. Tokyo: Kinokuniya shoten.

———. 1993. *Gehō to aihō no chūsei*. Tokyo: Sunakoya shobō.

T'ang Yung-t'ung. 1975. *Han Wei liang Chin Nan-pei ch'ao fo-chiao shih*. Reprint, Taipei: Ting-wen shu-chü.

Tatsukawa Shōji. 1971. *Byōki no shakai shi*. Tokyo: NHK Books.

———. 1976. *Nihonjin no byōreki*. Chūkō shinsho. Tokyo: Chūō kōronsha.

Teiser, Stephen. 1988. *The Ghost Festival in Medieval China*. Princeton, N.J.: Princeton University Press.

———. 1993. "The Growth of the Purgatory." In Peter N. Gregory and Patricia Ebrey, eds., *Religion and Society in T'ang and Sung China*, 114–57. Honolulu: University of Hawai'i Press.

———. 1994. *The Scripture of the Ten Kings*. Honolulu: University of Hawai'i Press.

Teng Ssu-yü, trans. 1968. *Family Instructions for the Yen Clan*. Leiden: E. J. Brill.

Ter Haar, Barend. 1992. *The White Lotus Teachings in Chinese Religious History*. Leiden: E. J. Brill.

Thierry, François. 1987. *Amulettes de Chine et du Viet-nam: Rites magiques et symboliques de la Chine ancienne*. Paris: Le Léopard d'or.

Thompson, Laurence G. 1990. "Medicine and Religion in Late Ming China." *Journal of Chinese Religions* 18: 45–59.

———. 1991. "Consecration Magic in Chinese Religion." *Journal of Chinese Religions* 19: 1–12.

Togawa Anshō. 1974. *Dewa sanzan no miira-butsu*. Tokyo: Chūō shoin.

Topley, Marjorie. 1970. "Chinese Traditional Ideas and the Treatment of Disease." *Man* 5: 421–37.

———. 1976. "Chinese Traditional Etiology and Methods of Cure in Hong Kong." In Charles Leslie, ed., *Asian Medical Systems: A Comparative Study*, 243–71. Berkeley: University of California Press.

Tseng Wen-shing. 1973. "The Development of Psychiatric Concepts in Traditional Chinese Medicine." *Archives of General Psychiatry* 29: 569–75.

Tsuda Shin'ichi. 1978. "A Critical Tantrism." *Memoirs of the Research Department, Tōyō Bunko* 36: 167–231.

Tubielewicz, Jolanta. 1980. *Superstitions, Magic and Mantic Practices in the Heian Period*. Warsaw: Wydaw-a VW.

Twitchett, Denis. 1979. "Population and Pestilence in T'ang China." In Wolfgang Bauer, ed., *Studia Sino-Mongolica: Festschrift für Herbert Franke*, 35–68. Wiesbaden.

Unschuld, Paul U. 1973. *Pen-ts'ao: 2000 Jahre Traditionelle Pharmazeutische Literatur Chinas*. Munich: H. Moos Verlag.

———. 1977. "Arzeinmittelmissbrauch und heterodoxe Heiltätigkeit im China der Keiserzeit: Ausgewählte Materialen zu Gesetzgebung und Rechsprechung." *Sudhoffs Archiv* 61, 4: 353–89.

———. 1979a. "The Chinese Reception of Indian Medicine in the First Millennium A.D." *Bulletin of the History of Medicine* 53, 3: 329–45.

———. 1979b. *Medical Ethics in Imperial China: A Study in Historical Anthropology*. Berkeley: University of California Press.

———. 1980. "Concepts of Illness in Ancient China: The Case of Demonological Medicine." *Journal of Medicine and Philosophy* 5, 2: 117–32.

———. 1982. "Der Wind als Ursache des Krankseins: Einige Gedanken zu Yamada Keijis Analyse der *Shao-shih* Texte des *Huang-ti nei-ching*." *T'oung Pao* 68, 1–3: 91–131.

———. 1985. *Medicine in China: A History of Ideas*. Berkeley: University of California Press.

———. 1986a. *Medicine in China: A History of Pharmaceutics*. Berkeley: University of California Press.

———, trans. 1986b. *Nan-ching: The Classic of Difficult Issues*. Berkeley: University of California Press.

Unschuld, Ulrike. 1977. "Chinese Pharmacology: Its Development in the Thirteenth Century." *Isis* 68, 242: 224–48.

Van der Loon, Piet. 1977. "Les origines rituelles du théâtre chinois." *Journal Asiatique* 265: 141–68.

van Gulik, Robert H. 1935. *Hayagrīva: The Mantrayānic Aspect of the Horse Cult in China and Japan*. Leiden: E. J. Brill.

———. 1956. *Siddhaṃ: An Essay on the History of Sanskrit Studies in China and Japan*. Nagpur: International Academy of Indian Culture.

———. 1958. *Chinese Pictorial Art as Viewed by the Connoisseur*. Rome: Istituto per il Medio ed Estremo Oriente.

———. 1961. *Sexual Life in Ancient China: A Preliminary Survey of Chinese Sex and Society from ca. 1500 B.C. till 1644 A.D.* Leiden: E. J. Brill.

———. 1967. *The Gibbon in China: An Essay in Chinese Animal Lore*. Leiden: E. J. Brill.

Vandermeersch, Léon. 1980. *Wangdao ou la voie royale: Recherche sur l'esprit des institutions de la Chine archaïque*. 2 vols. Paris: École Française d'Extrême-Orient.

Varenne, Jean. 1976. *Yoga and the Hindu Tradition*. Trans. Derek Coltman. Chicago: University of Chicago Press.

Veith, Ilza. 1963. "The Supernatural in Far Eastern Concepts of Mental Disease." *Bulletin of the History of Medicine* 37: 139–58.

———. 1965. *Hysteria: The History of a Disease*. Chicago: University of Chicago Press.

———, trans. 1966. *The Yellow Emperor's Classic of Internal Medicine*. Berkeley: University of California Press.

Verellen, Franciscus. 1989. *Du Guangting (850–933), taoïste de cour à la fin de la Chine médiévale*. Mémoires de l'Institut des Hautes Études Chinoises. Paris: Collège de France.

———. 1995. "The Beyond Within: Grotto-Heavens (*dongtian*) in Taoist Ritual and Cosmology." *Cahiers d'Extrême-Asie* 8: 265–90.

Vitiello, Giovanni. 1992. "Taoist Themes in Chinese Homoerotic Themes." In Michael L. Stemmeler and José Ignacio Cabezón, eds., *Religion, Homosexuality, and Literature*, 95–103. Las Colinas, Tex.: Monument Press.

Vogel, Jean Philippe. 1926. *Indian Serpent Lore: Or, The Nagas in Hindu Legend and Art*. London: A Probsthain. Reprint, Varanasi: Prithivi Prakashan, 1972.

Von Glahn, Richard. 1991. "The Enchantment of Wealth: The God Wutong in the Social History of Jiangnan." *Harvard Journal of Asiatic Studies* 51, 2: 651–714.

Von Verschuer, Charlotte. 1995. "Le Japon, contrée du Penglai?—Note sur le mercure." *Cahiers d'Extrême-Asie* 8: 439–52.

Wada Tetsujō. 1918. *Inshi to jashin*. Tokyo: Hakubunkan.

Waddell, L. Austine. 1895. *The Buddhism of Tibet, or Lamaism*. London. Revised ed., *Tibetan Buddhism with Its Mystic Cults, Symbolism and Mythology*. New York: Dover Publications, 1972.

———. 1912. "The 'Dhāraṇī' Cult in Buddhism: Its Origin, Deified Literature and Images." *Ostasiatische Zeitschrift* 1, 2: 155–95.

Wadley, Susan Snow. 1976. *Shakti: Power in the Conceptual Structure of the Karimpur Region*. Chicago: Department of Anthropology, University of Chicago.

Wagner, Rudolph G. 1973. "Lebenstil und Drogen in chinesischen Mittelalter." *T'oung Pao* 59: 79–178.

Waldschmidt, Ernst. 1967. "Das Paritta, eine magische Zeremonie der buddhistischen Priester auf Ceylon." *Baessler-Archiv* 17 (1934): 139–50. Reprinted in idem, *Von Ceylon bis Turfan: Schrifte zur Geschichte, Literatur, Religion und Kunst des indischen Kulturraumes*, 465–78 and pl. 35–38. Göttingen: Vandenhoeck und Ruprecht, 1967.

Waley, Arthur. 1931–32. "New Light on Buddhism in Medieval India." *Mélanges Chinois et Bouddhiques* 1: 355–76.

———. 1936. "An Eleventh-Century Correspondence." In *Études d'Orientalisme publiées par le Musée Guimet à la mémoire de Raymonde Linossier*, 531–62. Paris: Librairie Ernest Leroux.

———. 1963. "The Poetry of Chinese Mirrors." In idem, *The Secret History of the Mongols and Other Pieces*, 75–81. London: Allen and Unwin.

Wallace, Anthony F. 1965. *Religion, an Anthropological View*. New York: Random House.

Wallace, Vesna A. 1995. "Buddhist Tantric Medicine in the *Kālacakratantra*." *Pacific World*, n.s., 11: 155–74.

Wang Chi-min. 1926. "China's Contribution to Medicine in the Past." *Annals of Medical History* 8, 3: 192–201.

Wang Ch'iu-kuei et al., eds. 1989. *Chung-kuo min-chien hsin-yang tzu-liao hui-pien*. Taipei: Hsüeh-sheng shu-chü.

Wang Ming. 1979 (1960). *T'ai-p'ing ching ho-chiao*. Peking: Chung-hua shu-chü.

Wang-Toutain, Françoise. 1988. *Le Bodhisattva Kṣitigarbha en Chine du Ve au XIIIe siècle*. Paris: École Française d'Extrême-Orient.

Ward, Barbara E. 1982. *Chinese Festivals*. Hong Kong: South China Morning Post, Ltd.

Ware, James R. 1933. "The *Wei Shu* and the *Sui Shu* on Taoism." *Journal of the American Oriental Society* 53, 3: 215–50.

———, trans. 1966. *Alchemy, Medicine and Religion in the China of A.D. 320: The Nei P'ien of Ko Hung (Pao-p'u tzu)*. New York: Dover Publications.

Waterhouse, David. 1979. "Notes on the *Kuji*." *Journal of Japanese Studies* 5, 2: 1–37.

Watson, Burton, trans. 1961. *Records of the Grand Historian of China*. New York: Columbia University Press.

Watson, James L. 1982. "Of Flesh and Bones: The Management of Death Pollution in Cantonese Society." In Maurice Bloch and Jonathan Parry, eds., *Death and the Regeneration of Life*. Cambridge: Cambridge University Press.

Watson, James L., and Evelyn Rawski, eds. 1988. *Death Rituals in Late Imperial and Modern China*. Berkeley: University of California Press.
Wayman, Alex. 1965. "The Fivefold Ritual Symbolism of Passion." In Kōyasan daigaku, ed., *Mikkyōgaku mikkyōshi ronbunshū*, 117–44. Kyoto: Naigai Press.
———. 1974. "The Mirror as a Pan-Buddhist Metaphor-Simile." *History of Religions* 13: 251–69.
———. 1982. "The Human Body as Microcosm in India, Greek Cosmology, and Sixteenth-Century Europe." *History of Religions* 22, 2: 172–90.
———. 1995 (1973). *The Buddhist Tantras: Light on Indo-Tibetan Esotericism*. London and New York: Kegan Paul International.
Weinreich, Otto. 1909. *Heilungswunder*. Giessen: Alfred Töppelmann.
Weinstein, Stanley. 1974. "The Beginnings of Esoteric Buddhism in Japan: The Neglected Tendai Tradition." *Journal of Asian Studies* 34, 1: 177–91.
Welch, Holmes H. 1967. *The Practice of Chinese Buddhism, 1900–1950*. Cambridge, Mass.: Harvard University Press.
———. 1969–70. "The Bellagio Conference on Taoist Studies." *History of Religions* 9, 2–3: 107–36.
Welch, Holmes, and Anna K. Seidel. 1979. *Facets of Taoism*. New Haven, Conn.: Yale University Press.
Weller, Robert P. 1987. *Unities and Diversities in Chinese Religions*. Seattle: University of Washington Press.
Werner, E. T. C. 1932. *A Dictionary of Chinese Mythology*. Shanghai: Kelly and Walsh.
Westermarck, E. 1926. *Ritual and Belief in Morocco*. London: Macmillan. Reprint, New Hyde Park, N.Y.: University Books, 1968.
White, David G. 1984. "Why Gurus Are Heavy." *Numen* 31, 1: 40–73.
———. 1987. "*Dakkhina* and *agnicayana*: An Extended Application of Paul Mus's Typology." *History of Religions* 26, 2: 188–213.
———. 1996. *The Alchemical Body: Siddha Traditions in Medieval India*. Chicago: University of Chicago Press.
Wile, Douglas. 1991. *Art of the Bedchamber: The Chinese Sexology Classics*. Albany: State University of New York Press.
Winkler, H. A. 1930. *Siegel und Charaktere in der muhammedanischen Zauberei*. Berlin: W. de Gruyter.
Winkler, John J. 1990. *The Constraints of Desire: The Anthropology of Sex and Gender in Ancient Greece*. New York and London: Routledge.
Winternitz, Maurice. 1933. *A History of Indian Literature, Vol. 2: Buddhist Literature and Jaina Literature*. Trans. S. Ketkar and H. Kohn. Calcutta: University of Calcutta.
Wirz, Paul. 1954. *Exorcism and the Art of Healing in Ceylon*. Leiden: E. J. Brill.
———. 1972. *Kataragama: The Holiest Place in Ceylon*. 2nd ed. Colombo: Lake House Investments.
Wittkower, Rudolf. 1963. *Born Under Saturn*. New York: Random House.
———. 1977. *Allegory and the Migration of Symbols*. Boulder, Colo.: Westview Press.

Wolf, Arthur P., ed. 1974. *Religion and Ritual in Chinese Society*. Stanford, Calif.: Stanford University Press.
Wong, Chi-min K., and Wu Lien-teh. 1936. *A History of Chinese Medicine*. Shanghai. Reprint, Taipei: Southern Materials Center, 1977.
Wright, Arthur F. 1948. "Fo-t'u-têng: A Biography." *Harvard Journal of Asiatic Studies* 11: 321–71.
Wu Pei-yi. 1978. "Self-Examination and Confession in Traditional China." *Harvard Journal of Asiatic Studies* 39, 1: 5–38.
Wujastyk, Dominik. 1999. "Miscarriages of Justice: Demonic Vengeance in Classical Indian Medicine." In Roy Porter and Hohn Hinnells, eds., *Religion, Health and Suffering*, 1–20. London: Kegan Paul International.
Yabudaka Ichirō. 1975. *Hōkyōin-tō no kigen; zoku: Gorin-tō no kigen*. Kyoto: Sōgeisha.
Yamada Keiji. 1979. "The Formation of the *Huang-ti Nei-ching*." *Acta Asiatica* 36: 67–89.
———. 1985. *Shin hakken chūgoku kagakushi shiryō no kenkyū*. Kyoto: Kyōto daigaku jinbun kagaku kenkyūjo.
Yamada Toshiaki. 1989. "Longevity Techniques and the Compilation of the *Lingbao Wufuxu*." In Livia Kohn and Sakade Yoshinobu, eds., *Taoist Meditation and Longevity Techniques*, 99–124. Michigan Monographs on Chinese Studies, 61. Ann Arbor: Center for Chinese Studies, The University of Michigan.
Yamamoto Hiroko. 1993. *Henjō fu: Chūsei shinbutsu shūgo no sekai*. Tokyo: Shunjūsha.
———. 1998. *Ijin: Chūsei Nihon no hikyō-teki sekai*. Tokyo: Heibonsha.
Yamano Toshio. 1984. "Makashikan byōkankyō no kenkyū." *Ōtani daigaku daigakuin kenkyū kiyō* 1: 105–24.
———. 1985. "Tendai Chigi no igaku shisō josetsu." *Shinshū sōgō kenkyūjo kiyō* 3: 115–42.
Yamasaki Taikō. 1988. *Shingon: Japanese Esoteric Buddhism*. Boston: Shambhala.
Yamazaki Tasuku. 1931. *Nihon ekishi oyobi bōeki shi*. Tokyo: Kasseisha.
Yanagita Kunio. 1990. *Imōto no chikara*. In Yanagita Tamemasa et al., eds., *Yanagita Kunio zenshū*, vol. 11: 7–304. Tokyo: Chikuma shobō.
Yang, C. K. 1961. *Religion in Chinese Society*. Berkeley: University of California Press.
Yang Lien-sheng. 1961. *Studies in Chinese Institutional History*. Cambridge, Mass.: Harvard University Press.
Yano Michio. 1986. *Mikkyō senseijutsu: Sukuyōdō to Indo senseijutsu*. Tokyo: Tōkyō bijutsu.
Yap, P. M. 1974. *Comparative Psychiatry: A Theoretical Framework*. Ed. M. P. Lau and A. B. Stokes. Monograph Series, 3. Toronto: Clarke Institute of Psychiatry.
Yates, Frances. 1966. *The Art of Memory*. Chicago: University of Chicago Press.
Yi Nŭng-hwa. 1955 (1918). *Chosŏn pulgyo t'ongsa*. Tokyo: Kokusho kankōkai.
———. 1959. *Han'guk Togyosa*. Seoul: Ton'guk Taehakkyo.

Yoshida Teigo. 1972. *Nihon no tsukimono*. Chūkō shinsho. Tokyo: Chūō kōronsha.

Yoshikawa Tadao. 1992. "Nitchū muei: Shikaisen-kō." In Yoshikawa Tadao, ed., *Chūgoku kodōkyōshi kenkyū*, 175–216. Kyoto: Dōbōsha.

———, ed. 1997. "An Annotated Japanese Translation of the *Zhengao*, II." *Tōhō gakuhō* 69: 603–828.

Yoshimoto Shōji. 1983. "Dōkyō to Chūgoku igaku." In Fukui Kōjun et al., eds. *Dōkyō, Vol. 2: Dōkyō no tenkai*, 255–310. Tokyo: Hiragawa shuppansha.

———. 1989. *Furō chōju no igaku*. Tokyo: Hirakawa shuppansha.

Yoshioka Yoshitoyo. 1959–76. *Dōkyō to bukkyō*. 3 vols. Tokyo: Toshima shobō.

Yu, Anthony C., trans. 1977–83. *The Journey to the West*. 4 vols. Chicago: University of Chicago Press.

Yü Chün-fang. 1981. *The Renewal of Buddhism in China: Chu-hung and the Late Ming Synthesis*. New York: Columbia University Press.

Yü Ying-shih. 1965. "Life and Immortality in the Mind of Han China." *Harvard Journal of Asiatic Studies* 25: 89–122.

Yüan K'o, comp. 1982. *Chung-kuo shen-hua ch'uan-shuo tz'u-tien*. Shanghai.

Zago, Marcel. 1972. *Rites et cérémonies en milieu bouddhiste lao*. Rome: Universita Gregoriana.

Zimmerman, Francis. 1989. *Le discours des remèdes au pays des épices: Enquête sur la médecine hindoue*. Paris: Payot.

Zürcher, Erik. 1959. *The Buddhist Conquest of China: The Spread and Adaptation of Buddhism in Early Medieval China*. 2 vols. Leiden: E. J. Brill. Reprint, 1972.

———. 1980. "Buddhist Influence on Early Taoism: A Survey of Scriptural Evidence." *T'oung Pao* 66, 1–3: 84–147.

———. 1982a. "Eschatology and Messianism in Early Chinese Buddhism." In W. L. Idema, ed., *Leiden Studies in Sinology*, 34–56. Sinica Leidensia, 15. Leiden: E. J. Brill.

———. 1982b. "Prince Moonlight: Messianism and Eschatology in Early Medieval Chinese Buddhism." *T'oung Pao* 68: 1–75.

———. 1985. "The Lord of Heaven and the Demons: Strange Stories from a Late Ming Christian Manuscript." In Gert Neundorf, Karl-Heinz Pohl, and Hans-Hermann Schmidt, eds., *Religion und Philosophie in Ostasien: Festschrift für Hans Steininger*, 359–75. Würzburg: Königshausen und Neumann.

Zysk, Kenneth G. 1989. "*Mantra* in *Āyurveda*: A Study of the Use of Magico-Religious Speech in Ancient Indian Medicine." In Harvey Alper, ed., *Mantra*, 123–43. Albany: State University of New York Press.

———. 1991. *Asceticism and Healing in Ancient India: Medicine in the Buddhist Monastery*. New York: Oxford University Press.

———. 1993. *Religious Medicine: The History and Evolution of Indian Medicine*. New Brunswick, N.J., and London: Transaction Publishers.

———. 1996. *Medicine in the Veda: Religious Healing in the Veda*. Delhi: Motilal Banarsidass.

INDEX

Acala (Immovable One), 206–7, 209–10, 233–35, 274
Acupuncture, 29, 32, 49, 150, 241, 242–43
Ajitasena, 156
Ambiguity, terminological and textual, 24–25, 72, 73–74, 194–98, 241, 254–55, 309n18, 316n18, 321n84
Amoghapāśa-sūtra, 204–6
Amoghavajra, 154, 206, 228–38, 255, 273, 274
Amoy, 183
Ānanda, 109
Ancestors, cult of, 4; curses of, 94; deeds of, 42; deified, 112; ghosts of, 74; merit of, 91; spirits of, 66; tablet of, 96. *See also* Filial piety; Heredity
Animals, demonic, 63–67, 69, 251–56, 256–58, 260. *See also* Bezoar; Carnivores, Dietary codes; Fox-demons; Garuḍa; Ox King; Sacrifices; Snake
Annals of the Sage of Latter Time, 52–57
Anthelmintics, 25, 37. *See also* Herbals; Worms
Apocalypse, visions of, 50–57, 60–61, 85–88, 92–95, 100, 104, 150, 198
Ascetic, practice of, 78, 141, 151, 169
Aśoka, King, 170
Astrology, 16, 140–41
Asuras, 63, 65
Aśvaghoṣa, 177, 302n31
Āṭavaka, Demon-General, 143–51, 295n136
Atikūṭa, 264
Auto-possession, *see* Possession, induced or voluntary
Avalokiteśvara (Kuan-yin), 65, 150, 166–67, 169, 186, 104–6, 253, 254, 265, 319n55
Āveśa, 204–18, 228–38, 269–70, 273–75, 279

Bali, 251
Beating, exorcistic, 144–45, 150, 236–38, 264
Behavior, codes of, 54–57, 87–88, 177
Bewitchment, demonic (*kuei-mei*), 245, 247, 248–49
Bezoar, 146–47, 170–71, 185–86, 188. *See also* Fumigation
Blacker, Carmen, 197, 268, 271–72, 278
Bodde, Derk, 69
Bodhiruci, 254–55, 330n3
Bodhisattva, *see* Aśvaghoṣa; Avalokiteśvara; Kṣitigarbha; Nāgārjuna
Body, apply seals to, 125, 128–30, 148–49, 151, 152–56, 157, 159–61, 165, 167, 172, 174–76, 180, 181–82, 184, 188, 193, 230–31; host to deities, 3, 6, 133,

100; child-mediums and, 86, 206–18, 226, 229–31; seals and, 167, 176; Shang-ch'ing, 91, 100; spells and, 211–12, 236
Proto-Tantric texts, 103–9, 138, 151, 198. *See also* Tantric Buddhism
Pseudo-Sanskrit, 106
"Psycho-sinology," 22
Psychoses, 26, 27. See also *K'uang*; Mania; *Tien-k'uang*
Psychosomatic ailments, 72–73
Psychotherapy, Taoist healing as, 23
Pulses, diagnostic, 181, 244
Puppet(eer), 226, 272, 276
Purgatory, 81. *See also* Feng-tu
Purification, 6, 62. *See also* Dietary codes

Questions of Subāhu, 210–14, 215, 217, 237, 277, 315n4, 331n19

Rain, ritual for, 35, 64, 102, 186
Rākṣasas, 63, 64, 66, 92, 149, 219–20
Rebirth, cycle of, 43–44, 66, 99, 119, 175, 265
Recitation, *see* Book; *Dhāraṇī*; *Mantra*; Names; Spells; Thread
Red Script, 155–56, 209–10, 274
Register: Black, 47; of Death, 79, 82; of Life, 79; of spirits, 95. *See also* Names
Repentance, 1–2
Retribution, 39–40
Ritual, *see* Child-medium; Exorcism; Possession; Seals; Spells; Sword, ritual use of; Talisman; Yü, Step of

Sacrament, *see* Consecration
Sacrifices, blood, 3–4, 6, 13, 15, 51–52, 61. *See also* Carnivores
Śākyamuni, 113, 119, 201. *See also* Buddha
Samādhi, 148, 167–69, 208, 236, 331n19
Schipper, Kristofer M., 285n4
Scripture, "apocryphal," 58–59
Seals, Buddhist, 132–40, 143–51, 152–56, 157–61, 163–70, 170–78; official, 142–43, 156, 179; Taoist canon, 123–31. *See also* Wood, seals made of
Secrecy, 15, 82, 98, 159, 175, 232, 261
Secret Rites of the Spells of the Divine Emissary, 206–7, 274
Sei Shonagon (968–1025), *Pillow Book* of, 195–97
"Sepulchral infestation" (*chu-lien*), 74–75
Sepulchral lawsuit, see *Chung-sung*
Serpent-demons, 81. *See also* Mahoragas; Nāgas; Snake
Sexagesimal cycle, 16, 70, 83, 140–41, 188, 295n136
Sexuality, demons and, 122, 245–46, 257–58, 260
Shaman(ism), 2–4, 6, 203, 271–72, 278–91
Shan-hai ching, see *Book of Mountains and Seas*
Shang-ch'ing (Supreme Purity), 19, 57, 80–81, 88, 90, 96, 97, 99, 100, 244. *See also* Mao Shan, textual legacy of
Shen-nung pen-ts'ao ching, 80–81
Shih (corpse), *see* Corpse; Corpse-demons; Corpse-vector; Worms
Shingon Buddhism, *see* Tantric Buddhism, Shingon
Shintō, 184, 265, 270, 271
Śiva, 229–33, 235, 253, 256
Sivin, Nathan, 26–27
Six Syllables, Ritual of, 265–67, 273
Skanda, 67, 218–23, 256, 328n43
Sleep, demon-possession, 238–39. *See also* Dream
Snake, 64, 65, 90, 104, 108–9, 151–54, 207, 234, 258, 260. *See also* Animals; Mahoragas; Nāgas; Serpent-demons
Sorcerers, 248, 250, 265, 267, 271, 325n15
Sorcery, 104, 109, 110, 112, 163–64, 180–81. See also *Ku* magic, or poison
Southern Dipper, 150